SINCE THE CIVIL WAR

BY

CHARLES RAMSDELL LINGLEY

PROFESSOR OF HISTORY, DARTMOUTH COLLEGE

Revised Edition

NEW YORK
THE CENTURY CO.

PRINTED IN U. S. A.

239

TO

MY WIFE

CONTENTS

MAPS AND DIAGRAMS

The maps showing the railroads are from Johnson and Van Metre, *Principles of Railroad Transportation*, by courtesy of the publishers, D. Appleton & Co. Harper & Bros. allowed me to use a map appearing in Ogg, *National Progress*. A. J. Nystrom & Co. and the McKinley Publishing Co. have allowed me to draw new maps on outlines copyrighted by them.

C. R. L.

SINCE THE CIVIL WAR

SINCE THE CIVIL WAR

CHAPTER I

RECONSTRUCTION AND ITS AFTERMATH

With malice toward none; with charity for all; with firmness in the right, . . . let us strive . . . to do all which may achieve and cherish a just and lasting peace.

ABRAHAM LINCOLN.

The Military Reconstruction Act of March 2, 1867, "was written with a steel pen made out of a bayonet."

JAMES A. GARFIELD.

The negro-Republican régime in the South was "a grotesque parody of government, a hideous orgy of anarchy, violence, unrestrained corruption, undisguised, ostentatious, insulting robbery."

W. E. H. LECKY.

ABRAHAM LINCOLN in the presidential chair was regarded by many of the politicians of his party as an "unutterable calamity"; and although the news of Lincoln's assassination was received with expressions of genuine grief, the accession of Vice-President Andrew Johnson was, nevertheless, looked upon as a "Godsend to the country." As the Civil War came to a close, Lincoln opposed severe punishments for the leaders of the Confederacy; he urged respect for the rights of the southern people; he desired to recognize the existence of a Union element in the South, to restore the states to their usual relations with as little ill-feeling as possible, and in the restoration process to interfere but little with the normal powers of the states. Johnson, on the contrary, "breathed fire and hemp." "Treason," he asserted again and again, "should be made odious, and traitors must be

3

punished and impoverished. Their great plantations must be seized, and divided into small farms and sold to honest, industrious men.'' For a time it seemed that the curtain would go down on the tragedy of Civil War only to rise immediately on the execution of the Confederate leaders and the confiscation of their property. A large and active group of Washington politicians believed in the necessity of a stern accounting with the ''rebels.'' Lincoln's gentleness seemed to these bitter northerners like a calamity; Johnson's vindictiveness like a Godsend to the country. In the conflict between the policy of clemency and the policy of severity is to be found the beginning of the period of reconstruction.

Andrew Johnson was a compact, sturdy figure, his eyes black, his complexion swarthy. In politics he had always been a Democrat. So diverse were his characteristics that one is tempted to ascribe two personalities to him. He was a tenacious man, possessed of a rude intellectual force, a rough-and-ready stump speaker, intensely loyal, industrious, sincere, self-reliant. His courage was put to the test again and again, and nobody ever said that it failed. His loyalty held him in the Union in 1861, although he was a senator from Tennessee and his state as well as his southern colleagues were withdrawing. His public and private integrity withstood a hostile investigation that included the testimony of all strata of society, from cabinet officers to felons in prison. Later, at the most critical moment of his whole career, when he had hardly a friend on whom to lean, he was unflurried, dignified, undismayed.

Although Johnson was born in North Carolina, the greater part of his life was spent in eastern Tennessee. His education was of the slightest. His wife taught him to write, and while he plied his tailor's trade she read books to him that appealed to his eager intellect. When scarcely of voting age he became mayor of the town in which he lived and by sheer force of character made his way up into the state legislature, the federal House of Representatives and the Senate. President Lincoln made him military governor of Tennessee in 1862. In 1864 many Democrats and most Republicans joined to form a Union party, and in order to emphasize its non-sectional and non-partisan character they nominated Andrew Johnson as Lincoln's running mate. And now this unschooled, poor-white, slave-holding, Jeffersonian, states-right Democrat had become President of the United States.

It was scarcely to be expected that a man who had fought his way to the fore in eastern Tennessee during those controversial years would possess the characteristics of a diplomat. Even his friends found him uncommunicative, too often defiant and violent in controversy, irritating in manners, indiscreet, and lacking flexibility in the management of men. The messages which he wrote as President were dignified and judicious, and his addresses were not lacking in power, but he was prone to indulge in unseemly repartee with his hearers when speaking on the stump.[1] He exchanged epithets with bystanders who were all too ready to spur him on with their "Give it to 'em, Andy!" and "Bully for you, Andy!" giving the presidency the "ill-savor of a corner grocery" and filling his supporters with amazement and chagrin. The North soon looked upon him as a vulgar boor and remembered that he had been intoxicated when inaugurated as Vice-President. Unhappily, too, he was distrustful by nature, giving his confidence reluctantly and with reserve, so that he was almost without friends or spokesmen in either house of Congress. His policies have commended themselves, on the whole, even after the scrutiny of more than half a century. The extent to which he was able to put them into effect is part of the history of reconstruction.

[1] Johnson did not, to be sure, compose all his state papers himself,— nor do other presidents. A well-known instance of his reliance upon other men is the message to Congress of December, 1865, which was written in part, if not entirely, by the eminent historian George Bancroft. The ideas, however, were Johnson's.

The close of the Civil War found the nation as well as the several sections of the country facing a variety of complicated and pressing social, economic and political problems. Vast armies had to be demobilized and re-absorbed into the economic life of the nation. Production of the material of war had to give way to the production of machinery, the building of railroads and the tilling of the soil. The South faced economic demoralization. The federal government had to determine the basis on which the lately rebellious states should again become normal units in the nation, and the civil, social and economic status of the negro had to be readjusted in the light of the outcome of the war. Most of these problems, moreover, had to be solved through political agencies, such as party conventions and legislatures, with all the limitations of partisanship that these terms convey. And they had obviously to be solved through human beings possessed of all the prejudices and passions that the war had aroused: through Andrew Johnson with his force and tactlessness; through able, domineering and vindictive Thaddeus Stevens; through narrow and idealistic Charles Sumner and demagogic Benjamin F. Butler; as well as through finer spirits like William Pitt Fessenden and Lyman Trumbull.

In their attitude toward the South, the people of the North, as well as the politicians, fell into two groups. The smaller or radical party desired a stern reckoning with all "rebels" and the imprisonment and execution of the leaders.[2] They hoped, also, to effect an immediate extension to the negroes of the right to vote. It was this faction that welcomed the accession of Johnson to the Presidency. The other group was much the larger and was inclined toward gentler measures and toward leaving the question of suffrage largely for the

[2] Jefferson Davis, the President of the Confederate States, was held in prison until 1867 and then released. He died in 1889. Suggestions that General Lee, the most prominent military leader, be arrested and tried met with such opposition from General Grant that the project was dropped. Lee died in 1870.

future. Lincoln and his Secretary of State, Seward, were representative of this party. The attitude of the South toward the North was more difficult to determine. To be sure the rebellious states were beaten, and recognized the fact. There was general admission that slavery was at an end. But careful observers differed as to whether the South accepted its defeat in good faith and would treat the blacks justly, or whether it was sullen, unrepentant and ready to adopt any measures short of actual slavery to repress the negro.[3]

In theory, the union of the states was still intact. The South had attempted to secede and had failed. Practically, however, the southern states were out of connection with the remainder of the nation and some method must be found of reconstructing the broken federation. President Lincoln had already outlined a plan in his proclamation of December 8, 1863. Excluding the leaders of the Confederacy, he offered pardon to all others who had participated in the rebellion, if they would take an oath of loyalty to the Union and agree to accept the laws and proclamations concerning slavery. As soon as the number of citizens thus pardoned in each state reached ten per cent. of the number of votes cast in that state at the election of 1860, they might establish a government which he would recognize. It was his expectation that a loyal body of reconstructed voters would collect around this nucleus, so that in no great while the entire South would be restored to normal relations. At the same time he called attention to the fact that under the Constitution the admission into Congress of senators and representatives sent by these governments must rest exclusively with the houses of Congress themselves. In pursuance of his policy he had already appointed military governors in states where the federal army

[3] The Thirteenth Amendment to the Constitution, abolishing slavery, was adopted by Congress early in 1865, but was not ratified by a sufficient number of states and proclaimed in force until December 18 of that year.

had secured a foothold, and they directed the re-establishment of civil government. The radicals opposed the plan because it left much power, including the question of negro suffrage, in the hands of the states. A contest between Congress and the executive was clearly imminent when the assassin's bullet removed the patient and conciliatory Lincoln.

Lincoln's determination to leave control over their restoration as far as possible in the hands of the states was in line with Johnson's Democratic, states-rights theories. Moreover, the new executive retained his predecessor's cabinet, including Seward, whose influence was promptly thrown on the side of moderation. To the consternation of the radicals the President issued a proclamation announcing a reconstruction policy which substantially followed that of Lincoln. Like his predecessor he intended to confine the voting power to the whites, leaving to the states themselves the question whether the ballot should be extended to any of the blacks. Wherever Lincoln had not already acted, he appointed military governors who directed the establishment of state governments, the revival of the functions of county and municipal officials, the repeal of the acts of secession, the repudiation of the war debts, and the election of new state legislatures, governors, senators and representatives.

During the last half of 1865 the President's policy met with wide approval among the people of the North, where both Republicans and Democrats expressed satisfaction with his conciliatory attitude. The South was not unpleased, as was indicated by the speed with which men presented themselves for pardon and assisted in setting up new state governments. Nevertheless there were disquieting possibilities of dissension. Northern radicals could be counted upon to oppose so moderate a policy. Ex-Confederates began to be elected to federal office by the President's newly reconstructed state governments,—even Alexander H. Stephens, former Vice-President of the Confederacy, as senator from Georgia—and many a northerner shook his head in doubt, and wondered whether there might be some truth in the assertion that the South was trying to vault into the saddle once more. There was a reaction, too, against the great power which the executive arm of the government had exercised in war time. Congress felt that it had been thrust aside, its functions reduced and its prestige diminished. It could be looked to for an assertion of its desire to dominate reconstruction.

Before the opening of Congress in December, 1865, the Republican members of the House held a caucus at which they decided to refuse admission to the newly chosen southern representatives, even those from the President's own state— Tennessee. When the session began, the clerk, as was customary, read the names of the members,—omitting the names of all from southern states, in accord with instructions given him by the caucus. The northern members, to be sure, held a wide variety of opinions in regard to the best method of restoring the confederate states to the Union, but on one point there was agreement—that Congress ought to withhold approval of executive reconstruction until it could decide upon a program of its own.

The leader, not to say the dictator, of the House, was Thaddeus Stevens, a vindictive old man who asserted that the South had no rights except those given her by her conqueror. Under the spur of his energetic will, a joint congressional committee of fifteen was chosen to report whether any of the southern states were entitled to representation in Congress. The appointment of the committee was the call to battle between the executive and the legislature, between the Lincoln-Johnson policy of a clement reconstruction, and the Stevens theory that the South should be punished and humiliated. With so tenacious a man as Andrew Johnson in the presidential chair, and with so determined a fighter as Thaddeus Stevens in control of the joint committee, a battle was inevitable, in which quarter would be neither asked nor given.

Unhappily for themselves, the southern states played un-
wittingly into the hands of Stevens and his radical colleagues.
The outcome of the war had placed upon the freedmen responsibilities which they could not be expected to carry. To
many of them emancipation meant merely cessation from
work. Vagabondage was common. Rumor was widespread
that the government was going to give each negro forty acres
of land and a mule, and the blacks loafed about, awaiting the
division. The strict regulations which had surrounded the
former slave were discarded and it was necessary to accustom
him to a new régime. ''The race was free, but without status,
without leaders, without property, and without education.''
Fully alive to the dangers of giving unrestricted freedom
to so large a body of ignorant negroes, the southern whites
passed the ''black codes,'' which placed numerous limitations
on the civil liberty of ''persons of color.'' In some cases they
were forbidden to carry arms, to act as witnesses in court
except in cases involving their own race, and to serve on
juries or in the militia. Vagrancy laws enabled the magis-
trates to set unemployed blacks at work under arrangements
that amounted almost to peonage. It is now evident that the
South was actuated by what it considered the necessities of
its situation and not merely by a spirit of defiance. Yet the
fear on the part of the North that slavery was being restored
under a disguise was not unnatural. Radical northern newspapers and leading extremists in Congress exaggerated the
importance of the codes until they seemed like a systematic attempt to evade the results of the war.

As Republican leaders in Congress saw the satisfaction
created in the South by the President's policy, and discovered
that northern Democrats were rallying to his support, the
jealousies of partisanship caused them still further to increase their grip on the process of reconstruction. A disquieting by-product of the Thirteenth Amendment, abolishing
slavery, also began to appear. Hitherto only three-fifths of

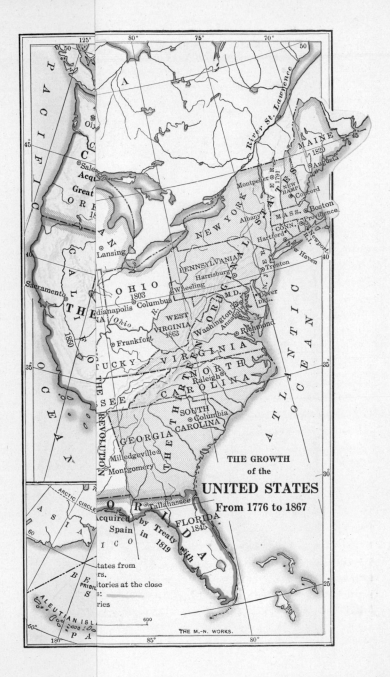

THE GROWTH
of the
UNITED STATES
From 1776 to 1867

THE M.-N. WORKS.

the negroes had been counted in apportioning representation in the House of Representatives. As soon as the slaves became free, however, they were counted as if they were whites, and thereby the strength of the South in Congress would be increased. The results therefore of the lenient policy toward the South seemed to be the repression of the negro and the political alliance of the late Confederacy with the Democrats of the North. These considerations, together with the increased representation of the South constituted a political danger which the North could hardly be expected to view with satisfaction. Thorough-going partisans began to declare that the party which had saved the Union ought to govern it.

The first action of the leaders in Congress was the introduction of a bill to continue and extend the powers of the Freedmen's Bureau. This was a Federal organization which had been founded in March, 1865, and was to continue one year after the close of the war. The bill presented to Johnson in 1866 extended its functions for two years longer. The Bureau was intended to exert a sort of guardianship over the negro race in making the transition from slavery to freedom: it performed relief work for the poor; it took over land which had been abandoned by Confederates or confiscated by the Union, and managed it for the benefit of the freedmen; it directed education among the negroes, supervised the making of labor contracts and even established courts of its own or surveyed the action of state courts involving the rights of the former slaves. The Bureau achieved considerable unpopularity in the South for several reasons,—among them the fact that many of its officials used their positions to direct the colored race into the Republican party. President Johnson's veto of the Freedmen's Bureau bill on February 19, 1866, widened the breach between him and Congress, and thereby postponed still further the admission of the representatives of the southern state governments. Three days later Johnson addressed a crowd which collected before the White House. In the course of his speech he lost control of himself to such an extent as to indulge in undignified remarks and personalities, and even to charge leaders in Congress with seeking to destroy the fundamental principles of American government. Thoughtful men everywhere were dismayed.

In the meantime a Civil Rights bill was pending in Congress, the purpose of which was to declare negroes to be citizens of the United States and to give them rights equal to those accorded other citizens, notwithstanding local or state laws and ordinances. The President objected to the bill as an unconstitutional invasion of the rights of the states, but it was promptly passed over the veto. Scarcely any members of Congress now supported him except the Democrats. The conservative or conciliatory Republicans were lost to him for good. Throughout the North it was felt that protection must be accorded the freedmen against the black codes, and when the President opposed it he lost ground outside of Congress as well as in it. "From that time Johnson was beaten."

Stevens in the House, and Sumner and others in the Senate were now in a position to press successfully a stern, congressional reconstruction policy to replace that of the executive. The first item in the radical program was the Fourteenth Amendment, which passed Congress in June, 1866, although it did not become of force until 1868. It contained four sections: (1) making citizens of all persons born or naturalized in the United States and forbidding states to abridge their rights; (2) providing for the reduction of the representation in Congress of any state that denied the vote to any male citizens of voting age except those guilty of crimes; (3) disabling confederate leaders from holding political office except with the permission of Congress; and (4) prohibiting the payment of confederate debts. The first section was, of course, designed to put the civil rights of the negro into the Constitution where they would be safe from hostile legislation. The second sought to get negro suffrage into the South by indirection at a time when a positive suffrage amendment could not be passed. The third was to take the pardoning power out of executive hands.

At this point there came a halt in the controversy until the country could be heard from in the congressional elections of 1866. Both sides made unusual efforts to organize political sentiment. Both attempted to demonstrate their thoroughly national character by holding conventions attended by southern as well as northern delegates. Each angled for the soldier vote by encouraging conferences of veterans. Late in July occurred an incident which the radicals were able to use to advantage. A crowd of negroes attending a convention in New Orleans in behalf of suffrage for their race became engaged in a fight with white anti-suffragists and many of the blacks were killed. The riot was commonly referred to in the North as a "massacre," the moral of which was that the negroes must be protected against the "unrepentant rebels." But it was Johnson himself who furnished greatest aid to his adversaries. Having been invited to speak in Chicago, he determined upon an electioneering trip, "swinging around the circle," he called it. Again he was guilty of gross indiscretions. He made personal allusions, held angry colloquies with the crowd and at one place met such opposition that he had to retire unheard. It mattered little that the greater part of his speeches was sound and substantial. His lapses were held up to public scorn and he returned to Washington amid the hoots of his enemies. It was commonly believed that he had been intoxicated. Probably no orator, *The Nation* sarcastically remarked, ever accomplished so much by a fortnight's speaking. There could be little doubt as to the outcome of the elections. The Republicans carried almost every northern state and obtained a two-thirds majority in each house of Congress, with which to override vetoes.

As if impelled by some perverse fate the southern whites

during the fall and winter of 1866–67 did the thing for which the bitterest enemy of the South might have wished. Except in Tennessee, the legislature of every confederate state refused with almost complete unanimity to ratify the Fourteenth Amendment. Natural as the act was, it gave the North apparently overwhelming proof that the former "rebels" were still defiant. Encouraged by the results of the election and aroused by the attitude of the South toward the Amendment, Congress proceeded to encroach upon prerogatives that had hitherto been considered purely executive, and also to pass a most extreme plan of reconstruction.

The first of these measures, the Tenure of Office Act, was passed over a veto on March 2, 1867. It forbade the president to remove civil officers except with the consent of the Senate. Members of the Cabinet, even, could not be dismissed without the permission of the upper house. In addition, any infractions of the law were declared to be "high misdemeanors." The purposes of so extraordinary an act were quite apparent. The first provision was intended to force the chief executive to share his power over removals with the Senate,—in direct reversal of previous practice since Washington's presidency. The inclusion of Cabinet officers was for the purpose of protecting Edwin M. Stanton, the Secretary of War. Stanton was in sympathy with the radicals, and it was essential to keep him in a post of advantage from which he could inform Johnson's enemies about what was taking place in the President's official family. The infraction of the law was declared to be a high misdemeanor because of the constitutional provision that the president may be removed for "high Crimes and Misdemeanors." Along with the Tenure of Office act was passed a measure which had been secretly drafted by Secretary Stanton himself. It made General Grant, who had charge of the military establishment, almost independent of the President.

On the same day, and over a veto also, was passed the Reconstruction Act, the most important piece of legislation during the decade after the war. It represented the desires of Thaddeus Stevens and was passed mainly because of his masterful leadership. At the outset the new Act declared the existing southern state governments to be illegal and inadequate, and divided the South into five military districts. Over each was to be a commanding general who should preserve order, and continue civil officers and civil courts, or replace them with military tribunals as he wished. Under his direction each state was to frame and adopt a new constitution which must provide for negro suffrage. When Congress should approve the constitution and when a legislature elected under its provisions should adopt the Fourteenth Amendment, the state might be readmitted to the Union.

The Reconstruction Act was remarkable in several features. The provision imposing negro suffrage was carried through the Senate with difficulty and only as the result of the tireless activity of Charles Sumner. Sumner and other radicals were determined that the blacks should be enfranchised in order that they might protect themselves from hostile local legislation and also in order that they might form part of a southern Republican party. Even more noteworthy was the military character of the Act. The President had already exercised his prerogative of declaring the country at peace on August 20, 1866, more than six months before the Act was passed. In the decision in the Milligan case, which preceded the Act by nearly three months, the Supreme Court had decided that military tribunals were unconstitutional except where war made the operation of civil courts impossible. Congress, however, was more interested in a method that promised the speedy accomplishment of its purposes than it was in the opinions of the executive and judicial departments.[4]

---

[4] The radical leaders in Congress were at first minded to discipline the Court for so inopportune a decision as that in the Milligan case. There was talk of impeaching the judges, and a bill was introduced in

Despite his dissent from its provisions, the President at once set military reconstruction in operation. When he mitigated its harshness, however, where latitude was allowed him, Congress passed additional acts, over the veto, of course, extending and defining the powers of the commanding generals. Armed with complete authority, the generals proceeded to remove many of the ordinary civil officers and to replace them with their own appointees, to compel order by means of the soldiery, to set aside court decrees and even to close the courts and to enact legislation. In the meanwhile a total of 703,000 black and 627,000 white voters were registered, delegates to constitutional conventions were elected, constitutions were drawn up and adopted which permitted negro suffrage, and state officers and legislators elected. In conformity with the provisions of the Act, the newly chosen legislatures ratified the Fourteenth Amendment to the Constitution, sent representatives and senators to Washington, where they were admitted to Congress, and by 1871 the last confederate state was reconstructed.

The commanding generals were honest and efficient, in the main, even if their stern rule was distasteful to the South, but the régime of the newly elected state officers and legislators was a period of dishonesty and incapacity. Most of the experienced and influential whites had been excluded from participation in politics through the operation of the presidential proclamations and the reconstruction acts. In all the legislatures there were large numbers of blacks—sometimes, indeed, they were in the majority. Two parties appeared. The radical or Republican group included the negroes, a few southern whites, commonly called "scalawags," and various northerners known as "carpet-baggers." These last were in some cases mere adventurers and in others men of ability who were attracted to the South for one reason or another, and

the House, but not passed, requiring a unanimous decision of the Court in cases involving the constitutionality of acts of Congress.

took a prominent part in political affairs. The old-time whites held both kinds in equal detestation. The other party was called conservative or Democratic, and was composed of the great mass of the whites. Many of them had been Whigs before the war, but in the face of negro-Republican domination, nearly all threw in their lot with the conservatives.

Not all the activities of the legislatures were bad. Provisions were made for education, for example, that were in line with the needs of the states. Nevertheless, their conduct in the main was such as to drive the South to despair, and almost into revolt. In the South Carolina legislature only twenty-two members out of 155 could read and write. The negroes were in the majority and although they paid only $143 in taxes altogether, they helped add $20,000,000 to the state debt in four years. In Arkansas the running expenses of the state increased 1500 per cent.; in Louisiana the public debt mounted from $14,000,000 to $48,000,000 between 1868 and 1871. Only ignorance and dishonesty could explain such extravagance and waste. Submission, however, was not merely advisable; it presented the only prospect of peace. Open resentment was largely suppressed, but it was inevitable that the whites should become hostile to the blacks, and that they should loathe the Republican party for its ruthless imposition of a system which governed them without their consent and which placed them at the mercy of the incompetent and unscrupulous. A system which made a negro [5] the successor of Jefferson Davis in the United States Senate could scarcely fail to throw the majority of southern whites into the ranks of the enemies of the Republican organization.[6]

One step remained to ensure the continuance of negro suffrage—the adoption of a constitutional provision. In 1869 Congress referred to the states the Fifteenth Amendment, which was declared in force a year later. By its terms the

[5] The colored senator was Rev. Hiram R. Revels.
[6] A number of these states later repudiated their debts.

United States and the states are forbidden to abridge the right of citizens to vote on account of race, color or previous condition of servitude.

While radical reconstruction was being forced to its bitter conclusion, the opponents of the President were maturing plans for his impeachment and removal from office. By the terms of the Constitution, the chief executive may be impeached for "Treason, Bribery, or other high Crimes and Misdemeanors." Early in the struggle between President Johnson and Congress a few members of the House of Representatives urged an attempt to impeach him. Such extremists as James M. Ashley of Ohio, and Benjamin F. Butler of Massachusetts, believed that he had even been implicated in the plot to assassinate Lincoln. A thorough-going search through his private as well as his public career failed to produce any evidence that could be interpreted as sufficient to meet constitutional demands, and a motion to impeach was voted down in the House by a large majority. So indiscreet a man as the President, however, was likely at some time to furnish a reason for further effort. The occasion came in the removal of the Secretary of War, Edwin M. Stanton.

Stanton, although of a domineering and brusque personality, had ably administered the War Department under Lincoln and Johnson. During the controversy between the President and Congress, Stanton had remained in the Cabinet but was closely in touch with his chief's opponents and had even drafted one of the reconstruction acts. Johnson had tolerated the questionable conduct of his Secretary, despite the advice of many of his supporters, until August 5, 1867, when he requested Stanton's resignation. The latter took refuge behind the Tenure of Office Act, denying the right of the President to remove him, but yielding his office at Johnson's insistence. This episode had occurred during a recess of Congress and, in accord with the law, the removal of Stanton was reported when it convened in December. The Senate at once refused to concur and Stanton returned to his office. The President now found himself forced, by what he regarded as an unconstitutional law, into the unbearable position of including one of his enemies within his official family, and once more he ordered the Secretary to retire. But meanwhile the House of Representatives had been active and had on February 24, 1868, impeached the President for "high crimes and misdemeanors."

The trial was conducted before the Senate, as the Constitution provides, the Chief Justice of the Supreme Court acting as the presiding officer. The House chose a board of seven managers to conduct the prosecution, of whom Thaddeus Stevens and Benjamin F. Butler were best known. The President was defended by able counsel, including former Attorney-General Stanbery, Benjamin R. Curtis, who had earlier sat upon the Supreme Court, and William M. Evarts, an eminent lawyer and leader of the bar in New York. The charges, although eleven in number, centered about four accusations: (1) that the dismissal of Secretary Stanton was contrary to the Tenure of Office Act; (2) that the President had declared that part of a certain act of Congress was unconstitutional; (3) that he had attempted to bring Congress into disgrace in his speeches; and (4) that in general he had opposed the execution of several acts of Congress. The President's counsel asked for forty days in which to prepare their case. They were given ten, although members of the House had been preparing for more than a year to resort to impeachment. The trial lasted from early March to late May.

As the trial wore on, it became increasingly evident that the House had but little substance on which to base an impeachment, and that the force back of it was intense hatred of the President. It was made clear to senators who were inclined to waver towards the side of acquittal that their political careers were at an end if they failed to vote guilty. The general conference of the Methodist Episcopal Church even appointed an hour of prayer that the Senate might be moved to convict. The lawyers for the defense so far out-generaled the prosecutors that one who reads the records at the present day finds difficulty in thinking of them as more than the account of a pitiful farce. At length on May 16 the Senate was prepared to make its decision. The last charge was voted upon first. It was a very general accusation, drawn up by Stevens, and seemed most likely to secure the necessary two-thirds for conviction. Fifty-four members would vote. Twelve of them were Democrats and were known to be for acquittal. The majority of the Republicans were for conviction. A small group had given no indication of their position, and their votes would be the decisive ones. As the roll was called each senator replied "Guilty" or "Not guilty," while floor and galleries counted off the vote as the knitting women clicked off the day's toll of heads during the days when the guillotine made a reign of terror in France. The result was thirty-five votes for conviction and nineteen for acquittal. As thirty-six were necessary, Johnson had escaped. A recess of ten days was taken during which the prosecution sought some shred of evidence which might prove that some one of the nineteen had accepted a bribe for his vote, but to no avail. When the Senate convened again there was no change in the vote on the second and third articles, and the attempt to convict was abandoned.

For the first time in many months Johnson enjoyed a respite from the attacks of his foes. Stanton relinquished his office, and the integrity of the executive power was preserved. The race of the dictator of the House had been run, for Stevens lived less than three months after the trial.

The continuous controversies of the Johnson administration almost completely pressed into the background two diplomatic accomplishments of no little importance. The more dramatic of these related to the French invasion of

Mexico. During 1861, naval vessels of England, France and Spain had entered Mexican ports in order to compel the payment of debts said to be due those countries, but England and Spain had soon withdrawn and had left France to proceed alone. French troops thereupon had invaded the country, captured Mexico City and established an empire with Archduke Maximilian of Austria as its head, despite the protests and opposition of the Mexicans under their leader Juarez. The United States had expressed dissent and alarm, meanwhile, but because of the war was in no position to take action.

As soon as civil strife was finished, however, Johnson and Seward took vigorous steps. An army under General Sheridan was sent to the border, and diplomatic pressure was exerted to convince France of the desirability of withdrawal. The occupation of Mexico was, apparently, not popular in France, and in the face of American opposition the French government sought a means of dropping the project. Accordingly the invading forces were withdrawn early in 1867, leaving the hapless Maximilian to the Mexicans, by whom he was subsequently seized and shot.

While the Mexican difficulty was being brought to a successful outcome, the government of Russia offered to sell to the United States her immense Alaskan possessions west and northwest of Canada. Secretary Seward, was enthusiastically disposed to accept the offer and a treaty was accordingly drawn up on March 30, 1867, providing for the acquisition of the territory for $7,200,000. The Senate, however, was far less inclined to seize the opportunity. Little was known about Alaska, and the cost seemed almost prohibitive in view of the financial strain caused by the war. Nevertheless the inclination to acquire territory was strong and there was a widespread desire to accede to the wishes of Russia who was understood to have been well-disposed toward the United States during the war. Under the operation of these forces the Senate changed its attitude and ratified the treaty on April 9, 1867. By this act the United States came into possession of an area measuring nearly 600,-000 square miles, and stores of fish, furs, timber, coal and precious metals whose size is even yet little understood.

It was not long before it became apparent that radical reconstruction had been founded too little upon the hard facts of social and political conditions in the South, and too much upon benevolent but mistaken theories, and upon prejudices, partisanship and emotion. It was inevitable that there should be an aftermath.

At the close of reconstruction in 1871, the southern negro was a citizen of civil and political importance. As a voter, he was on an equality with the whites; he belonged to the Republican party and his party was a powerful factor in the politics of the South; his position was secured, or at least seemed to be secured, by amendments to the federal Constitution. Legally and constitutionally his position appeared to be impregnable. In the mind of the southern white, however, the amendments vied with military reconstruction in their injustice and unwisdom. To his mind they constituted an attempt to abolish the belief of the white man in the essential inferiority of the black, to make the pyramid of government stand on its apex, and to place the very issues of existence within the power of the congenitally unfit. To the discontent aroused by war were added political and racial antagonism, which blazed at times into fury. The southern whites began to invent methods for overcoming the power of the freedmen in politics and for insuring themselves against possible danger of violence at the hands of the blacks.

The most famous device was the Ku Klux Klan or the Invisible Empire, a somewhat loosely organized secret society which originated in Tennessee during the turmoil immediately after the close of the war. In theory and practice its operations were simple and effective. Its chief officials were the Grand Wizard, the Grand Dragon, the Grand Titan. Local branches were Dens, each headed by a Grand Cyclops. The Den worked usually at night, when the members assembled clad in long white robes and white masks or hoods, discussed cases which needed attention, and then rode forth on horses whose bodies were covered and whose feet were muffled. The exploits of the Klan expanded, in the exaggerated stories common among the negroes, into the most amazing achievements. The members were said to take themselves to pieces, drink entire pailfuls of water, and devour "fried nigger meat." Usually the person about to be "visited" received a notice that the dreaded Klan was upon him. He was warned to cease his political activities or perhaps to leave the neighborhood. If the threat proved ineffective, whipping or some worse punishment was likely to follow.

In 1872 Congress unintentionally aided in the process of overcoming negro domination by the passage of the Amnesty Act. It will be remembered that a part of the Fourteenth Amendment, passed in 1868, had prohibited former Confederate leaders from holding political office except with the permission of Congress. Bills had been immediately presented and passed—hundreds of them in a single month—which removed the disabilities from individuals named in the bills. In 1871 the President had urged Congress to pass a general act which would take off the restrictions from all southerners except possibly a few prominent leaders, thus doing away with the congestion of private bills which consumed so much time. At length Congress acted—in 1872—and removed the disabilities from all except a few hundred important officials.[7] On the restoration of this right such men as Alexander H. Stephens, former Vice-President of the Confederate States,

[7] These last disabilities were removed by Congress on June 6, 1898.

and Gen. Wade Hampton, one of the most influential South Carolinians, could again take an active part in politics. With their return, the cause of white supremacy received a powerful impetus.

In taking this step, however, Congress did not intend to allow the legal and constitutional rights of the blacks to be waived without a contest. Reports reached the North concerning the activities of the southern whites—reports which in no way minimized the amount of intimidation and violence involved—and in response to this information Congress passed the enforcement laws of 1870–1871, generally known as the "Force Acts." [8] These laws laid heavy penalties upon individuals who should prevent citizens from exercising their constitutional political powers—primarily the right to vote. As offenses under these acts were within the jurisdiction of the federal courts and as the federal officials manifested an inclination to carry out the law, the number of indictments was considerable. Convictions, however, were infrequent. The famous Ku Klux Act of 1871 amplified the law of 1870 and was aimed at combinations or conspiracies of persons who resorted to intimidation. It authorized the president to suspend the privilege of the writ of *habeas corpus* and made it his duty to employ armed force to suppress opposition.

Additional sting was given the enforcement laws by provision for the superintendence of federal elections, under specified conditions, by federal officials called "supervisors of election." The supervisors were given large powers over the registration of voters and the casting and counting of ballots, so as to ensure a fair vote and an honest count. Since

---

[8] The threats used to keep the negroes away from the polls are typified in the following, which was published in Mississippi:

"The Terry Terribles will be here Monday to see there is a fair election.

"The Byram Bulldozers will be here Monday to see there is a fair election.

here, again, federal troops stood behind the law, it was manifest that the central government would show some degree of determination in its handling of the southern situation. Nevertheless, the result was merely to delay the gradual elimination of the blacks from political activity, not to prevent it. In practice the Republican state governments in the South were continued in the seats of authority only through the presence of the federal soldiery. In one way or another the whites gained the upper hand, so that by 1877 only South Carolina and Louisiana had failed to achieve self-government unhampered by federal force.

In the meantime the enforcement acts were being slowly weakened by the Supreme Court in several decisions bearing upon the Fourteenth Amendment. The significant portion of Section I of the amendment is as follows:

No State shall make or enforce any law which shall abridge the privileges or immunities of citizens of the United States; nor shall any State deprive any person of life, liberty, or property, without due process of law; nor deny to any person within its jurisdiction the equal protection of the laws.

In several cases involving the enforcement acts, the Court found portions of the laws in conflict with the Constitution and finally, in 1883, the decision in United States *v.* Harris completed their destruction. Here the court met a complaint that a group of white men had taken some negroes away from the officers of the law and ill-treated them. Such conduct seemed to be contrary to that part of the Ku Klux Act which forbade combinations designed to deprive citizens of their legal rights. The Court, however, called attention to the important words, ''No *State* shall make or enforce,'' and was of

"The Edwards Dragoons will be here Monday to see there is a fair election.
"Who cares if the McGill men don't like it.
"The whole State of Mississippi is interested in the election.
"It *shall* be a Democratic victory."

opinion that the constitutional power of Congress extends only to cases where *States* have acted in such a manner as to deprive citizens of their rights. If *individuals,* on the contrary, conspire to take away these rights, relief must be sought at the hands of the state government. As the great purpose of the Ku Klux Act had been to combat precisely such individual combinations, it appeared that the Court had, at a blow, demolished the law. Not long afterwards the Court declared unconstitutional the Civil Rights Act of 1875, which had been designed to insure equal rights to negroes in hotels, conveyances and theatres. Here again the Court was of opinion that the Fourteenth Amendment grants no power to the United States but forbids certain activities by the states.[9]

Stuffing the ballot box was common in South Carolina and other states. In one election in this state the number of votes cast were almost double the number of names on the polling list. In some places the imposition of a poll tax peacefully eliminated the impecunious freedman. In Mississippi the state legislature laid out the "shoestring" election district, 300 miles long and about 20 miles wide, which included many of the sections where the negroes were most numerous, in order that their votes might have as little effect as possible. By hook or by crook, then, in simple and devious ways, the dangers of negro domination were averted. Nevertheless the provisions of the law for federal supervision of elections remained, becoming a bone of contention during a later administration.

About 1890 there began a new era in the elimination of the negro from politics in the South. The people of that section disliked the methods which they felt the necessity of using, and searched about for a less crude device. Furthermore

[9] In regard to segregation of the races in railroad coaches, the Court decided, 1910, that constitutional rights are not interfered with when separate accommodations are provided, if the accommodations be equally good. Chiles *v.* Chesapeake and Ohio Railroad Co., **218** U. S., 71.

the rise of a new political movement in some parts of the South in the late eighties and early nineties was making divisions among the Democrats and was encouraging attempts by the two factions to control the negro vote. Suddenly, a relatively small number of negro voters became a powerful and purchasable make-weight. Both sides, perhaps, were a bit disturbed at this development. At any rate, additional impetus was given to the movement for the suppression of the negro. Eventually plans were originated, some of which were clearly constitutional and all of which carried a certain appearance of legality.

The first steps were taken by Mississippi in 1890. The new state constitution of that year required as prerequisite to the voting privilege, the payment of all taxes which were legally demanded of the citizen during the two preceding years—a provision to which no constitutional exception could be taken, and which effectively debarred large numbers of colored voters. Further, it provided that after January 1, 1892, every voter must be able to read any section of the state constitution or be able to give an interpretation of it *when read to him*. As the election officials who would judge the ability of the applicant properly to interpret the constitution would certainly be whites, it was clear that the ignorant black would have scant chance of passing the educational test. Several other states followed in the wake of Mississippi, until in 1898 Louisiana discovered a new barrier through which only whites might make their way to the voting lists. This was the famous "grandfather clause." In brief, it allowed citizens to vote who had that right before January 1, 1867, together with the descendants of such citizens, regardless of their educational and property qualifications. As no negroes had voted in the state before that date, they were effectively debarred. Under the influence of such pressure, the negro vote promptly dwindled away to negligible proportions. In Louisiana, to cite one case, there were 127,263 registered colored voters in

1896, and 5,354 in 1900. Between these two years the new state constitution had been passed. In 1915 the Supreme Court finally declared a grandfather clause unconstitutional on the ground that its only possible intention was to evade that provision of the Fifteenth Amendment which forbids the states to abridge, on account of color, the rights of citizens of the United States to vote.

The history of the effects of the war and of reconstruction on the political status of the negro has been concisely summarized as falling into three periods. Soon after the close of the war: (1) the negroes were more powerful in politics than their numbers, intelligence and property seemed to justify; (2) the Republican party was a power in the South; and (3) the negroes enjoyed political rights on a legal and constitutional equality with the whites. By 1877 the first of these generalizations was no longer a fact; by 1890 the Republican party had ceased to be of importance in the South; and by the opening of the twentieth century, the negro as a possible voter was not on a legal and constitutional equality with the white.

In the sphere of government the war and reconstruction were of lasting importance. Preeminently it was definitely established that the federal government is supreme over the states. Although the Constitution had seemed to many to establish that supremacy in no uncertain terms, it can not be doubted that only as a result of the war and reconstruction did the theory receive a degree of popular assent that approached unanimity. Temporarily, at least, reconstruction added greatly to the prestige and self-confidence of Congress. During the war the powers of the President had necessarily expanded. The reaction, although hastened by the character and disposition of President Johnson, was inevitable. The depression of the executive elevated the legislature and not until the beginning of the twentieth century did the scales swing back again toward their former position.

BIBLIOGRAPHICAL NOTE

General. The best general account of the period 1865–1917 is
to be found in the following volumes of *The American Nation: A
History:* W. A. Dunning, *Reconstruction Political and Economic,
1865–1877* (1907); E. E. Sparks, *National Development, 1877–
1885* (1907); D. R. Dewey, *National Problems, 1885–1897* (1907);
J. H. Latané, *America as a World Power, 1897–1907* (1907); F. A.
Ogg, *National Progress 1907–1917* (1918). The volumes vary in
excellence and interest, but set a high standard, especially in their
recognition of the importance of economic facts, and contain excellent bibliographical material. The following single volumes are
useful: E. B. Andrews, *United States in Our Own Time, 1870–1903*
(1903); C. A. Beard, *Contemporary American History* (1914); P.
L. Haworth, *Reconstruction and Union, 1865–1912* (1912); P. L.
Haworth, *United States in Our Own Time, 1865–1920;* E. P. Oberholtzer, *History of the United States since the Civil War* (to be in
several volumes, of which three have appeared, covering 1865–1878);
F. L. Paxson, *The New Nation* (1915); F. L. Paxson, *Recent History of United States* (1921); H. T. Peck, *Twenty Years of the
Republic, 1885–1905* (1907), readable and especially valuable in
its interpretation of the period which it covers; J. F. Rhodes, *History of the United States from Hayes to McKinley, 1877–1896*
(1919), and *McKinley and Roosevelt Administrations* (1922);
Muzzey, *The United States of America,* vol. II, *From the Civil War*
(1924); Shippee, *Recent American History* (1924); J. S. Bassett,
Short History of the United States (1913); Harlow, *The Growth
of the United States* (1925); and Schlesinger, *Political and Social
History of the United States 1829–1925* have excellent chapters;
F. J. Turner in the *Encyclopaedia Britannica* (11th ed.), article
"United States History 1865–1910," is brief but inclusive; the
later chapters of Max Farrand, *Development of the United States*
(1918), present a new point of view. *The Chronicles of America
Series* (1919 and later), edited by Allen Johnson, contains valuable
volumes on especial topics. For party platforms and election
statistics consult Edward Stanwood, *A History of the Presidency*
(2 vols., 2nd ed., 1916). On economic tendencies, Faulkner,
American Economic History (1924); Lippincott, *Economic De-*

velopment of the United States (1921); Bogart, *Economic History of the United States* (rev. ed. 1918).

Reconstruction. The most valuable single volume on the reconstruction period is the volume by Dunning already referred to; W. L. Fleming, *Sequel of Appomattox* (1919), is also excellent; J. F. Rhodes, *History of the United States since the Compromise of 1850,* vols. VI, VII (1906), is the best detailed account; James Schouler, *History of the United States,* vol. VII (1913), presents a new view of President Johnson. Valuable biographies are J. A. Woodburn, *The Life of Thaddeus Stevens* (1913); G. H. Haynes, *Charles Sumner* (1909); Horace White, *The Life of Lyman Trumbull* (1913). On impeachment, D. W. Dewitt, *The Impeachment and Trial of Andrew Johnson* (1903), is best. W. A. Dunning, *Essays on Civil War and Reconstruction* (ed. 1910), is strong on the constitutional changes. Studies on reconstruction in the several states have been published by W. W. Davis (Florida), (1913); W. L. Fleming (Alabama), (1905); J. W. Garner (Mississippi) (1901); J. G. deR. Hamilton (North Carolina), (1914); C. W. Ramsdell (Texas), (1910); and others. For documentary material, W. L. Fleming, *Documentary History of Reconstruction* (2 vols., 1906–7), is essential. Edward Channing, A. B. Hart and F. J. Turner, *Guide to the Study and Reading of American History* (1912), provides full references to a wide variety of works covering 1865–1911. Consult also Appleton's *Annual Cyclopaedia, 1861–1902.* On foreign relations, J. B. Moore, *Digest of International Law,* 8 vols., (1906).

On Alaska, J. P. Nichols, *Alaska* (1924).

Periodical literature. The most useful periodicals are: *American Economic Review* (1911—); *American Historical Review* (1895—); *American Political Science Review* (1907—); *Atlantic Monthly* (1857—); *Century Magazine* (1870—); *Harper's Weekly* (1857–1916); *Harvard Law Review; History Teachers' Magazine,* continued as *Historical Outlook* (1909—); *Journal of Political Economy* (1892—); *Nation* (1865—); *North American Review* (1815—); *Political Science Quarterly* (1886—); *Quarterly Journal of Economics* (1886—); *Scribner's Magazine* (1887—); *Yale Review* (1892–1911, *new series,* 1912—).

CHAPTER II

IN PRESIDENT GRANT'S TIME

Well, what are you going to do about it?

WILLIAM M. ("Boss") TWEED.

It was my fortune, or misfortune, to be called to the office of Chief
Executive without any previous political training. From the age of
17 I had never even witnessed the excitement attending a Presidential
campaign but twice antecedent to my own candidacy, and at but one
of them was I eligible as a voter. . . . Failures have been errors of
judgment, not of intent.

PRESIDENT GRANT, Dec. 5, 1876.

ASIDE from President Lincoln, the most prominent personality on the northern side during the latter part
of the Civil War was General Ulysses S. Grant. His
successes in the Mississippi Valley in the early days of the
war, when success was none too common, his capture of Vicks-
burg at the turning point of the conflict, and his dogged drive
toward Richmond had established his military reputation.
When the drive toward Richmond resulted at last in the capture of Lee's army and its surrender at Appomattox, the victorious North turned with gratitude to Grant and made him
a popular idol, while the politicians began to question whether
his popularity might not be put to account in the field of
politics.

Grant himself had never paid any attention to matters
of government. In only one presidential election had he so
much as voted for a candidate, and then it was for a Democrat, James Buchanan. In 1860 he was prevented from voting for Senator Stephen A. Douglas and against Abraham
Lincoln only by the fact that he had not fulfilled the residence
requirement for suffrage in the town where he was living.
Nevertheless in his capacity as general of the army his head-

31

quarters after the war were in Washington and his duties brought him into contact with the politicians and eventually entangled him in the controversy between the President and Congress. Circumstances at first threw him into close association with Johnson, but at the time of the Stanton episode late in 1867 a misunderstanding arose between them which developed into a question of veracity, and then into open hostility. As Grant was almost sure to be nominated by one party or the other, the opponents of Johnson took up the General's quarrel with alacrity. Only one question troubled them,—the question whether Grant would support the radical congressional plan of reconstruction—and when discreet inquiry seemed to indicate that no danger was to be feared on this score, all doubt vanished. From then on the popular hero was the inevitable choice for the next Republican nomination.

The convention of the National Union Republican Party, as it was called at that time, was held in Chicago, May 20, 1868, during the interval between the votes on the eleventh and second charges of the impeachment of President Johnson. General Grant was unanimously nominated for the presidency and Schuyler Colfax, Speaker of the House of Representatives, for the second place on the ticket. The platform asserted that the public debt ought to be paid in full, that pensions for the veterans were an obligation and that immigration ought to be encouraged. The administration of President Johnson was denounced and the thirty-five senators who voted for his conviction in the impeachment trial were commended. The most significant planks, however, were those about reconstruction and negro suffrage. Hitherto the congressional plan of reconstruction had been the plan of a group in the Republican party,—a group, to be sure, that was fast increasing in size, but a group nevertheless. The plan was now made definitely and officially a party principle, to be upheld by all who wished to maintain their standing in the organization. In drafting the negro suffrage plank, the convention faced a dilemma. It desired to force the South to allow the negro to vote; but at the same time it had to recognize the fact that northern states commonly denied the freedmen the ballot,— the Fifteenth Amendment having not yet been ratified. Accordingly it asserted that "every consideration of public safety, of gratitude, and of justice" demanded equal suffrage in the South, but that "in the loyal states" the question "properly" belonged to the states themselves.

The Democrats met at Tammany Hall in New York on July 4. Their platform approved the pension laws, advocated the sale of public land to actual occupants, praised the administration of President Johnson, arraigned the radicals and declared the reconstruction acts "unconstitutional, revolutionary, and void." If the radical party should win in the election, the Democrats asserted, the result would be "a subjected and conquered people, amid the ruins of liberty and the scattered fragments of the Constitution." The regulation of the suffrage, one plank declared, had always been in the hands of the individual states. The most prominent place in the platform, however, was given to the question of the public debt. Part of the bonds issued during the war had, by acts of Congress, been made payable in "dollars," a word which might mean either paper dollars or gold dollars. Paper, however, was much less valuable than gold, times were hard, and many people held the opinion that the debt could properly be paid in paper. Such was the "Ohio idea," which was made part of the Democratic platform.

The choice of a candidate required twenty-two ballots. Early trials indicated the strength of George H. Pendleton, popularly known as "Gentleman George" and the chief exponent of the "Ohio idea." Johnson also had support. Chief Justice Salmon P. Chase, having failed to obtain the Republican nomination, allowed it to be known that he was willing to become the Democratic candidate. At length, on

the twenty-second ballot, a few votes were cast for Governor
Horatio Seymour of New York, the chairman of the convention. The move met with enthusiastic approval, despite Seymour's insistence that he would not be a candidate, and he
was unanimously chosen.

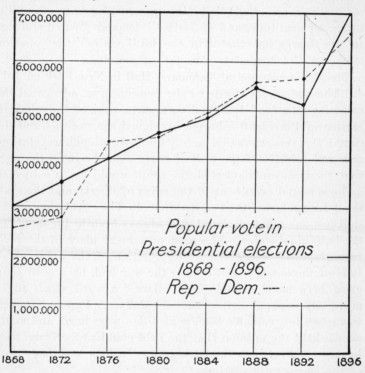

Popular vote in
Presidential elections
1868 - 1896.
Rep — Dem ---

The developments of the campaign depended largely upon
occurrences in the South. Military reconstruction had not
been wholly completed in Virginia, Mississippi, Texas and
Georgia. The last of these states had once been readmitted to
the Union, but had immediately expelled the negro members
of its legislature, and was thereupon placed again under military rule. The Ku Klux Klan was meanwhile in general op-

eration throughout the South and its activities, both real and imaginary, received wide advertisement in the North. Public interest, therefore, in the underlying issues of the campaign centered upon the attitude of the candidates toward the southern question. General Grant was understood to be with the radicals and Seymour with the conservatives. The result of the election was the choice of the Republican leader by an apparently large majority. He carried twenty-six out of thirty-four states, with 214 out of 294 electoral votes, but he received a popular majority of only 300,000. Examination of the returns indicated a strong conservative minority in many of the solid Republican states. The strength of the radicals in the South, moreover, was due, in the main, to negro-carpetbag domination, and when these states should become conservative, as they were sure to do, the political parties would be almost evenly divided.[1]

The man who was now entering upon his first experience as the holder of an elective office had risen from obscurity to public favor in the space of a few years. Although a graduate of West Point, with eleven years of military experience afterward, his career before 1861 had been hardly more than a failure. He had left the army in 1854 rather than stand trial on a charge of drunkenness; had grubbed a scanty living out of "Hard Scrabble," a farm in Missouri; had tried his hand at real estate, acted as clerk in a custom-house and worked in a leather store at $800 a year. Then came the war, and in less than three years Grant had received the title of Lieutenant-General, which only Washington and Winfield Scott had borne before him, and had become General-in-Chief of all the armies of the United States. Always an uncom-

---

[1] The closing months of Johnson's administration found him almost in a state of isolation. The incoming President refused to have any social relations with him, or even to ride with him from the White House to the Capitol on inauguration day. After the installation of his successor, Johnson returned to Tennessee but was later chosen to the Senate, where he served but a short time before his death.

municative man, he kept his own counsel during the interval between his election and his inauguration. He saw few politicians, asked no advice about his cabinet, sought no assistance in preparing his inaugural address and made no suggestions to the leaders of his party concerning legislation that he would like to see passed. His first act, the appointment of his cabinet, caused a gasp of surprise and dismay. Most of the men named were but little known and some of them were not aware that they were being chosen until the list was made public. The Secretary of State, Elihu Washburne, was a close personal friend, and was appointed merely that he might hold the position long enough to enjoy the title and then retire. He was succeeded by Hamilton Fish, of New York, who proved to be a wise choice. The Secretary of the Treasury was A. T. Stewart, a rich merchant of New York, but he had to withdraw immediately on account of a law forbidding any person "interested in carrying on the business of trade or commerce" to hold the office. The Secretary of the Navy, A. E. Borie, was a rich invalid of Philadelphia, who had almost no qualifications for his office and resigned at once. Better appointments were former Governor J. D. Cox, of Ohio, as Secretary of the Interior, and Judge E. R. Hoar, of Massachusetts, as Attorney-General.

When the Congress elected with Grant assembled in 1869 its first act was a measure providing for the payment of the public debt in coin. On the southern question General Grant had earlier inclined toward moderation, but radical counsels and the logic of events led him to join Congress in the passage of the enforcement act and the Ku Klux Act, both of which have already been mentioned. Two diverse currents of opinion compelled Congress to revise the Tenure of Office Act. The President and the House wished to repeal the law forthwith and completely; the Senate was determined to cling to the power over removals which had been wrested from Johnson. In the end, a modified and weakened law was enacted in 1869, which, as *The Nation* remarked, put Grant "on a tether." [2]

It was during this, the first year of Grant's administration, that there occurred the famous gold conspiracy of 1869. Jay Gould and James Fisk, Jr., two of the most unscrupulous stock gamblers of the time, determined to corner the supply of gold and then run its market price up to a high level, in order to further certain interests which they had recently purchased. The likelihood that the conspirators could carry out the plan depended largely on the Secretary of the Treasury, George S. Boutwell, who was accustomed to sell several millions of dollars' worth of gold each month. If the sales could be stopped Gould and Fisk might be successful. Accordingly, they got on friendly terms with the President through cultivating the acquaintance of his brother-in-law, were seen publicly with him at the theatre and other places, and subsequently he wrote to the Secretary expressing his opinion that the sales had better stop. Gould apparently was informed of this decision by the brother-in-law, even before the message reached the Secretary, and immediately bought up so much gold as to run the price to an unparalleled figure. This was on "Black Friday," September 24. The Secretary became alarmed, rumors were abroad that the administration was implicated in the conspiracy, and at noon, after consultation with the President, he decided to place four millions in gold on the market. At once the price dropped, brokers went bankrupt, and Gould and Fisk had to take refuge behind armed guards to save their lives. The President had not been a party to the plans of the speculators, but his blindness to their real purposes and his association with them during the period when their scheme was being

[2] The new law compelled the president to obtain the consent of the Senate for appointments to vacancies occurring during a recess of the Senate. If the president failed to obtain such consent, the office remained vacant. It retained the clauses making infractions of the law "high misdemeanors," *Cf.* p. 14.

perfected made him a target for all manner of accusations.

Further astonishment was caused by the attitude of the President toward two of the three really able men in his cabinet. In June, 1870, he suddenly called for the resignation of Judge Hoar. It appeared that he was seeking votes in the Senate for a treaty in which he was interested and that some of the southern members demanded the post of attorney-general for a southern man in return for their support. Secretary Cox's resignation came soon afterward. He had taken his department out of politics, had furthered the cause of civil service reform and had protected his employees from political party assessments. These acts brought him into collision with the politicians, who had the ear of the President, and Cox had to retire. Both Hoar and Cox were succeeded by mediocre men.

The treaty which caused the removal of Secretary Hoar was one that the President had arranged providing for the annexation of Santo Domingo.[3] The Senate was opposed to ratification, but General Grant was accustomed to overcoming difficulties and he urged his case with all the power at his command. One result was an unseemly wrangle between the President and Senator Charles Sumner over the latter's refusal to support ratification. General Grant, in resentment, procured the withdrawal of the Senator's friend, John Lothrop Motley from England, whither he had been sent as minister, and later the exclusion of Sumner from the chairmanship of the Committee on Foreign Relations, a post in which he had displayed great ability for ten years. Eventually the President had to give way on Santo Domingo, as the Senate did not agree with him in his estimate of its probable value.

---

[3] When the project was placed before the cabinet, it met with awkward and chilling silence. The Secretary of State, even, had not given his authority and consent to the arrangement of a treaty, and offered to resign. After an embarrassing few minutes, Grant turned to other matters, and did not again consult his cabinet advisors on the subject. Cf. *Atlantic Monthly*, Aug. 1895, pp. 162–173.

In its conduct of our relations with England, on the other hand, the administration met with success and received popular approval. Ever since the war the people of the North had desired an opportunity to make Great Britain suffer for her attitude during that struggle. Senator Sumner struck a popular chord when he suggested that England should pay heavy damages on the ground that her encouragement of the South had prolonged the war. Specifically, however, the United States demanded reparation for destruction committed by the *Alabama* and other vessels that had been built in English ports. In 1870 Europe was in a state of apprehension on account of the Franco-Prussian War, and Secretary Fish seized the opportunity to press our claims upon England. The latter, meanwhile, had abated somewhat her earlier attitude of unwillingness to arbitrate, and Fish placed little emphasis on Senator Sumner's suggestions of a claim for indirect damages. The Treaty of Washington signed and ratified in May, 1871, provided for the arbitration of the *Alabama* claims under such rules that a decision favorable to the American side of the case was made exceedingly probable. Each of five governments appointed a representative— the United States, Great Britain, Italy, Switzerland and Brazil. The meeting took place in Geneva and resulted favorably to the American demands. England was declared to have failed to preserve the proper attitude for a neutral during the war and was ordered in 1872 to make compensation in the amount of $15,500,000.

The United States had need of any feeling of national pride that might come as the result of the Geneva award, to offset the shame of domestic revelations, for one of the characteristics of the decade after the war was the wide-spread corruption in political and commercial life. One of the most flagrant examples was the Tweed Ring in New York. The government of that city was in the hands of a band of highwaymen, of whom William M. Tweed, the leader of Tammany

Hall, was chief. Through the purchase of votes and the skil-ful distribution of the proceeds of their control, they managed to keep in power despite a growing suspicion that something was wrong. A favorite method of defrauding the city was to raise an account. One who had a bill against the city for $5,000 would be asked to present one for $55,000. When he did so, he would receive his $5,000 and the remainder would be divided among the members of the Ring. The plasterer, for example, who worked on the County Court House pre-sented bills for nearly $3,000,000 in nine months. The New York *Times* and the cartoons of Thomas Nast in *Harper's Weekly* were the chief agents in arousing the people of the city to their situation. The former obtained and published proofs of the rascality of the Ring, mass meetings were held and an election in November, 1871, overturned Tweed and his associates. Some of them fled from the country, while Tweed himself died in jail.

More important both because of its effect on national poli-tics and because of its influence on railway legislation for many years afterward was the Credit Mobilier scandal. The Credit Mobilier was a construction company composed of a selected group of stockholders of the Union Pacific Railroad, the transcontinental line which was being built between 1865 and 1869. In their capacity as railroad stockholders they awarded themselves as stockholders of the construction company the contract to build and equip a large part of the railway. The terms which they gave themselves were so gen-erous as to insure a handsome profit. Chief among the mem-bers of the Credit Mobilier was Oakes Ames, a member of Congress from Massachusetts. Late in 1867 Ames became fearful of railroad legislation that was being introduced in Washington and he therefore decided to take steps to protect the enterprise. He was given 343 shares of Credit Mobilier stock, which he placed among members of Congress where, as he said, they would "do most good." Rumors concerning

the nature of the transaction resulted finally in accusations
in the New York *Sun* during 1872, which involved the names
of many prominent politicians. Congressional committees
were at once appointed to investigate the charges, and their
reports caused genuine sensations. Ames was found guilty
of selling stock at lower than face value in order to influence
votes in Congress and was censured by the House of Representatives. The Vice-President, Schuyler Colfax, and several
others were so entangled in the affair as to lose their reputa-
tions and retire from public life for good. Still others such
as James A. Garfield were suspected of complicity and were
placed for many years on the defensive.[4]

Fear was wide-spread that political life in Washington was
riddled with corruption. Corporations which were large
and wealthy for that day were already getting a controlling
grip on the legislatures of the states, and if the Credit Mobilier scandal were typical, had begun to reach out to Congress. Had the charges been made a little earlier they might
have influenced the election of 1872, which turned largely on
certain omissions and failings of the administraton, and espe-
cally of General Grant himself.

There is something intensely pathetic in General Grant as
President of the United States—this short, slouchy, taciturn,
unostentatious man who was more at ease with men who
talked horses than with men who talked government or literature; this President who was unacquainted with either the
theory or the practice of politics, who consulted nobody in
choosing his cabinet or writing his inaugural address, who had
scarcely visited a state capital except to capture it and had
been elected to the executive chair in times that were to try
men's souls. An indolent man, he called himself, but the
world knew that he was tireless and irresistible on the field

---

[4] The most recent and scholarly life of Garfield, by Professor T. C.
Smith, takes the position that Garfield was completely innocent. *Cf.*
vol. I, chap xv, *Life and Letters of J. A. Garfield.*

when necessity demanded, persistent, imperturbable, simple
and direct in his language, and upright in his character.
The tragedy of President Grant's career was his choice of
friends and advisors. In Congress he followed the counsels
of second-rate men who gave him second-rate advice; outside he associated too frequently with questionable characters
who cleverly used him as a mask for schemes that were an insult to his integrity, but which his lack of experience and his
utter inability to judge character kept hidden from his view.
Honorable himself and loyal to a fault to his friends, he believed in the honesty of men who betrayed him, long after the
rest of the world had discovered what they were. He could
accept costly gifts from admirers and appoint these same men
to offices, without dreaming that their generosity had sprung
from any motive except gratitude for his services during the
war.[5]

In view of these facts, an anti-Grant movement was almost
inevitable in the presidential campaign of 1872. Indeed a
local revolt against some of the principles of the Republican
party had already started before the General's first election.
In 1865 a constitutional convention in Missouri had deprived
southern sympathizers of the right to vote and hold office.
A wing of the Republican party, led by Colonel B. Gratz
Brown, had begun a counter-movement, intended to remove
the restrictions on the southerners, and also to reform other
abuses in the state. Colonel Brown had early received the assistance of General Carl Schurz, a man of ability with the
temperament of a reformer. The Brown-Schurz faction had
quickly increased in numbers, had become known as the Liberal Republican party and had attracted such interest

---

[5] In 1884, a year before his death, the dishonesty of a trusted friend
left him bankrupt, while a painful and malignant disease began slowly
to eat away his life. Nevertheless, with characteristic courage he set
himself to the task of dictating his *Memoirs*, or more often penciling
sentences when he was unable to speak, in order that he might repay
his debts with the proceeds.

throughout the country that a national conference was called for May, 1872, at Cincinnati. In adopting a conciliatory southern policy, the Liberal Republicans became opposed to the President, who had by this time become thoroughly committed to the radical program. Other critics of the administration, mainly Republicans, became interested in the Liberal revolt—those who deprecated the President's choice of associates and advisors, the civil service reformers who were aroused by the dismissal of Secretaries Hoar and Cox, and the tariff reformers who had vainly attempted to arouse enthusiasm for their plans. The deficiencies of Grant, then, enlivened and made formidable an insurrection which might otherwise have remained local and harmless.

On account of the varied character of the elements which composed it and the independent spirit of its members, the Cincinnati assembly resembled a mass meeting rather than a well-organized political conference. It numbered among its members, nevertheless, many men of influence and repute. Some of the most powerful newspaper editors of the country, also, were friendly to its purpose, so that it seemed likely to be a decisive factor in the coming campaign. In most respects the platform reflected the anti-Grant character of the convention. It condemned the administration for keeping unworthy men in power, favored the removal of all disabilities imposed on southerners because of the rebellion, objected to interference by the federal government in local affairs—a reference to the use of troops to enforce the radical reconstruction policy—and advocated civil service reform. The convention found difficulty in stating its attitude toward the tariff question. It was deemed necessary to get the support of Horace Greeley, the editor of the New York *Tribune,* the most powerful northern newspaper of Civil War times, but Greeley was an avowed protectionist. The platform, therefore, evaded the issue by referring it to the people in their congressional districts, and to Congress. But the rock on which the movement met shipwreck was the nomination of a candidate. Many able men were available—Charles Francis Adams, who had been minister to England, Senator Lyman Trumbull, B. Gratz Brown and Judge David Davis of the Supreme Court. Any one of them would have made a strong candidate. The convention, however, passed over all of them and nominated Greeley, long known as being against tariff reform, against civil service reform and hostile to the Democrats, whose support must be obtained in order to achieve success. Although a journalist of great influence and capacity, Greeley was an erratic individual, whose appearance and manner were the joy of the cartoonist.

The Republican convention met on June 5, and unanimously re-nominated Grant. The platform recited the achievements of the party since 1861, urged the reform of the civil service, advocated import duties and approved of the enforcement acts and amnesty.

To the Democrats the greatest likelihood of success seemed to lie in the adoption of the Liberal Republican nominee and platform. Such a course, to be sure, would commit them to a candidate who had excoriated their party for years in his newspaper, and to the three war amendments to the Constitution, which the Liberal Republicans had accepted. Yet it promised the South relief from military enforcement of obnoxious laws, and that was worth much. Both Greeley and his platform were accordingly accepted.

The enthusiasm for the Liberal movement which was observable at the opening of the campaign rapidly dwindled as the significance of the nomination became more clear. Greeley was open to attack from too many quarters. The cartoons of Nast in *Harper's Weekly,* especially, held him up to merciless ridicule. In the end he was defeated by 750,-000 votes in a total of six and a half million, a disaster which, together with the death of his wife and the overwork of the campaign, resulted in his death shortly after the election. As for the Republicans they elected not only their candidate but also a sufficient majority in Congress to carry out any program that the party might desire. *The radical reconstruction program, which had been first made a plank in the party platform in 1868, had now been successfully defended against internal schism.*

On March 3, 1873, as Grant's first term was drawing to a close, Congress passed a measure increasing the salary of public officials from the president to the members of the House of Representatives. The increase for Congressmen was made retroactive, so that each of them would receive $5,000 for the two years just past. To a country whose fears and suspicions had been aroused by the Credit Mobilier scandal, such a questionable act as the "salary grab" and the "back pay steal" was a fresh indication that corruption was entrenched in Washington. Senators and Representatives began at once to hear from their constituencies. Many of them returned the increase to the treasury and when the next session opened, the law was repealed except so far as it applied to the president and the justices of the Supreme Court.

The congressional elections of 1874 indicated the extent of the popular distrust of the administration. In New York, where Samuel J. Tilden was chosen governor, and in such Republican strongholds as Massachusetts and Pennsylvania the Democrats were successful. In the House of Representatives the Republican two-thirds majority was wiped out and the Democrats given complete control. Even the redoubtable Benjamin F. Butler lost his seat.

Further apprehensions were aroused by rumors concerning the operations of a "Whiskey Ring." For some years it had been suspected that a ring of revenue officials with accomplices in Washington were in collusion with the distillers to defraud the government of the lawful tax on whiskey. Part of the illegal gains were said to have gone into the campaign fund for Grant's re-election, although he was ignorant of the source of the revenue. Benjamin H. Bristow, who became Secretary of the Treasury in 1874, began the attempt to stop the frauds and capture the guilty parties. This was no simple task, because information of impending action was surreptitiously sent out by officials in Washington. Finally Secretary Bristow got the information which he sought, and then moved to capture the criminals. One of the most prominent members of the Ring was an internal revenue official in St. Louis who, it was recollected, had entertained President Grant, had presented him with a pair of horses and a wagon, and had given the General's private secretary a diamond shirt-stud valued at $2,400. Public opinion was yet further shocked, however, when the trail of indictments led to the President's private secretary, General Babcock. On first receiving news of Bristow's discoveries, Grant had written "Let no guilty man escape"; but later he became secretly and then openly hostile to the investigation. During the trial of Babcock, the President asked to be a witness in his behalf. A verdict of acquittal was given, but afterwards the two men had a private conference, and when "Grant came out, his face was set in silence." Babcock never returned to the White House as Secretary, but was given the post of Superintendent of Public Buildings and Grounds. Several of the members of the Ring were imprisoned but were later pardoned by the President. In the meanwhile Grant seems to have been brought to believe that Bristow was persecuting Babcock with a view to getting the favor of the reform element in the party and eventually the presidential nomination. Relations between the two became strained and Bristow resigned.

The last year of Grant's second administration was blackened by the case of W. W. Belknap, who was then Secretary of War. Investigation by a House committee uncovered the fact that since 1870 an employee in the Indian service had paid $12,000 and later $6,000 a year for the privilege of retaining his office. The money had been paid at first to Mrs. Belknap, who had made the arrangement, and after her death to the Secretary himself. The House unanimously voted to impeach him, but on the day when the vote was taken he resigned and the President accepted his resignation. Only the fact that he was out of office prevented the Senate from declaring him guilty, and critics of the administration noted that the President had saved another friend from deserved punishment.

It would be easy to over-estimate the responsibility of General Grant for the political corruption of his administrations. For the most part the wrong-doing of the time began before his first election. Democrats as well as Republicans participated in many of the scandals. Politicians in the cities, the states and the nation seemed to be determined to have a share in the enormous wealth that was being created in America, and they got it by means that varied from the merely unethical and indiscreet, to the openly corrupt. As for the President, his own defense, given in his last message to Congress, may be taken as the best one: "Failures have been errors of judgment, not of intent."

Under the circumstances, however, it was natural that the presidential campaign of 1876 should turn upon the failings of the administration. Popular interest in the southern issue was on the wane. Early in the election year, nevertheless, James G. Blaine, Republican leader in the House, made a forceful attack on Jefferson Davis, as the wilful author of the "gigantic murders and crimes at Andersonville," a southern prison in which federal captives had been held. Instantly the sectional hatred flared up and Blaine, already a well-known leader, became a prominent candidate for the nomination. Republican reformers generally favored Bristow. A third-term boom for Grant was effectively crushed by an adverse resolution in the House.

The Republican nominating convention met on June 14,

The virtues of Blaine were set forth in a famous speech by Robert G. Ingersoll in which he referred to the attack on Davis: "Like an armed warrior, like a plumed knight James G. Blaine marched down the halls of the American Congress and threw his shining lance full and fair against the brazen forehead of every traitor to his country." The "plumed knight," however, was open to attack concerning a scandal during the Grant régime, and the convention turned to Governor Rutherford B. Hayes, of Ohio, a man of quiet ability who had been unconnected with Washington politics, was relatively unknown and, therefore, not handicapped by the antagonisms of previous opponents. The platform emphasized the services of the party during the war, touched lightly on the events of the preceding eight years, advocated payment of the public debt, and favored import duties and the reform of the civil service.

The Democrats met on June 27. There was little opposition to the nomination of Governor Samuel J. Tilden, of New York, a wealthy lawyer who had made a record as a reformer in opposition to "Boss" Tweed and a corrupt canal ring. The platform was distinctly a reform document. It demanded reform in the governments of states and nation, in the currency system, the tariff, the scale of public expense, and the civil service. An eloquent paragraph exhibited those corruptions of the administration which had caused such general dismay.

There was little in the campaign that was distinctive, and on November 8, the morning after the election, it seemed clear that Tilden had been successful. He had carried the doubtful states of Connecticut, New York, New Jersey and Indiana. When the figures were all gathered, it was found that his popular vote exceeded that of his rival by more than 250,000. But there were disputes in three states, Florida, Louisiana and South Carolina. Hayes would be elected only if the electoral votes of all these states could be obtained for him. If, however, Tilden received even one electoral vote from any of the states, the victory would be his. Hayes was conceded 166 electoral votes; Tilden 184. Nineteen were in dispute. The Republican leaders at once claimed the nineteen disputed votes, and asserted that their candidate was elected. The Democrats had no doubt of the victory of Tilden.[6] The capitals of the three doubtful states now became the centers of observation. Troops had long been stationed in South Carolina and Louisiana, and others were promptly sent to Florida. Prominent politicians from both parties also flocked thither, in order to uphold the party interests.

In South Carolina it became evident that a majority of the popular vote was for Hayes, although both the Democratic and the Republican electors sent in returns to Washington. In Florida there was a board of canvassers which had power to exclude false or fraudulent votes. It was composed of two Republicans and one Democrat. When all the ballots had been sent in, the Democrats claimed a majority of ninety; the Republicans a majority of forty-five. The board went over the returns and by a partisan vote threw out enough to make the Republican majority 924. Thereupon they sent Republican electoral votes to Washington; but the Governor of the State certified that the Democratic electors had been chosen, and sent Democratic returns to the capital. The situation in Louisiana was still more complicated. Political corruption and intimidation had been commonplaces in that state. On the face of the returns, Tilden's electors had received majorities varying from 6,000 to 9,000. As in Florida there was a board of canvassers which was here composed of four Republicans, three of whom were men of low character. The vote of the state was offered to the Democrats, once for $1,000,000 and once for $200,000, but the offer was not taken. The board then threw out enough ballots to choose all the Hayes

6 There was also a technical question concerning one elector in Oregon, which was easily settled.

electors. As in the other cases, Democratic electors also sent ballots to Washington.[7]

There was no federal agency with power to determine which set of electors were to be counted, and the fact that the federal Senate was Republican and the House Democratic seemed to preclude the possibility of legislation on the subject. No such critical situation had ever resulted from an election, and a means of settlement must quickly be discovered, for only three months would elapse after the electoral votes were sent to Washington, before the term of General Grant would expire. The means devised was the Electoral Commission. This body was to be composed of five senators, five representatives, and five justices of the Supreme Court. The Senate and the House were each to choose their five members, and four members of the Court were designated by the Act which established the Commission, with power to choose a fifth. It was understood that seven would be Republicans, seven Democrats and that the fifteenth member would be Justice David Davis, an Independent, who would be selected by his four colleagues. On him in all probability, the burden of the decision would fall. On the day when the Senate agreed to the plan, however, the Democrats and Independents in the Illinois legislature chose Justice Davis as United States Senator and under these circumstances he refused to serve on the Commission. It was too late to withdraw, and since all the remaining justices from whom a commissioner must be chosen were Republicans, the Democrats were compelled to accept a body on which they were outnumbered eight to seven.

The Electoral Commission sat all through the month of February, 1877. Its decisions were uniformly in favor of Hayes electors by a vote of eight to seven, always along party lines, and on March 2, it was formally announced that Hayes had been elected. The disappointment of the Democrats was

[7] See Lonn, *Reconstruction in Louisiana*, pp. 201, 443 *ff.*, for accounts of the performances of the returning boards.

bitter and lasting, for their candidate had received over a quarter of a million popular votes more than his opponent, and yet had been declared defeated. For a time there was some fear of civil war. Tilden, however, accepted the decision of the Commission in good faith, and forbade his friends and his party to resist. Moreover, close friends of the Republican candidate assured southern Democratic politicians that Hayes if elected would adopt a conciliatory policy toward the South, and would allow the southern states to govern themselves unhampered by federal interference. Peaceful counsels prevailed, therefore, and the closing days of President Grant's administration were undisturbed by threats of strife.

The question whether Hayes was fairly elected is a fascinating one. There is no doubt that there was fraud and intimidation on both sides, in the disputed states. In Louisiana, for example, the Democrats prevented many negroes from voting by outrageous intimidation, while the Republicans had many negroes fraudulently registered. Little is known, also, of the activities of the "visiting statesmen," as those politicians were called who went to the South to care for their party interests. It is known that they were well provided with money and that the boards of canvassers contained many unscrupulous men. Nor is it likely that politicians who lived in the days of the Credit Mobilier and the Whiskey Ring would falter at a bargain which would affect the election of a president. Republicans looked upon the Democrats as being so wicked that they were justified in "fighting the devil with fire." [8] Democrats looked upon the election as so clearly theirs that no objection ought to be made to their taking what belonged to them. It seems certain, however, that Hayes had

[8] Stanley Matthews, counsel for Hayes, before the Electoral Commission, wrote to Hayes immediately after the election when it seemed that the Republicans had lost: "I felt as if a great conspiracy of ignorance, superstition, and brutality had succeeded in overthrowing the hopes of a Christian civilization as represented and embodied in the Republican party." Williams, *R. B. Hayes*, I, 493 n.

no hand in any bargains made by his supporters. As for Tilden, his wealth was such that he could have purchased votes if he had desired to do so, and the fact that all the votes went to his rival indicates that he did not yield to the temptation. Moreover, one of his closest associates, Henry Watterson, the journalist, tells of one occasion when the presidency was offered to Tilden and refused by him. Perhaps a definitive statement of the rights and wrongs of this famous election will never be made; for one after another the men most intimately associated with it have died leaving some account of their activities, but none of them has told much more than was already known.

The importance of the result, however, should not be overlooked. Whatever its virtues or defects, the radical reconstruction program, which had been written into the party platform in 1868 and defended against a party schism in 1872, was, by the *election of 1876, successfully upheld against the united onslaught of the Democrats.*

BIBLIOGRAPHICAL NOTE

Dunning, Rhodes, Oberholtzer and Schouler, together with most of the works referred to at the close of Chapter I, continue to be useful. L. A. Coolidge, *Ulysses S. Grant* (1917), is not as partisan as most of the biographies of the time and is valuable despite a lack of a thorough understanding of the period. The following are valuable for especial topics: H. Adams, *Historical Essays* (1891); C. F. Adams, Jr. and H. Adams, *Chapters of Erie* (1886), (gold conspiracy); C. F. Adams, Jr., *Charles Francis Adams* (Treaty of Washington); C. F. Adams, Jr., "The Treaty of Washington" in *Lee at Appomattox, and Other Papers* (1902); James Bryce, *American Commonwealth* (vol. II, various editions since 1888, contains famous chapter on the Tammany Tweed ring); A. B. Paine, *Thomas Nast, His Period and His Pictures* (1904), (Tweed ring); E. D. Ross, *The Liberal Republican Movement* (1919). P. L. Haworth, *Hayes-Tilden Disputed Presidential Election of 1876* (1906), is a thorough study; on this election, see also John Bigelow,

The Life of S. J. Tilden (2 vols., 1895); C. R. Williams, *Life of Rutherford B. Hayes* (2 vols., 1914); T. C. Smith, *The Life and Letters of James A. Garfield* (2 vols., 1925); E. Lonn, *Reconstruction in Louisiana* (1918).

CHAPTER III

ECONOMIC FOUNDATIONS OF THE NEW ERA

Industrial America is a product of the decades succeeding the Civil War; yet even in 1865 we were a large manufacturing nation.

B. J. HENDRICK.

During the years from 1870 to 1895 the occupation of a large majority of persons employed in the production, the transportation, the marketing of almost every article in common use, was more or less modified.

E. STANWOOD.

There is no denying that the government of cities is the one conspicuous failure in the United States.

JAMES BRYCE.

WITH the close of Grant's administration, the main immediate problems connected with political reconstruction came to an end. During the war, however, important economic and social developments had been taking place throughout the United States which were destined to take on greater and greater significance. The reconstruction problem looked backward to the war; the new developments looked forward to a new America. Reconstruction affected fewer and fewer people as time went on; the later changes ultimately transformed the daily life of every individual in the nation. Not only did they determine the means by which he earned his livelihood, but the comforts which he enjoyed, the conditions of rural or urban life which surrounded him, the ease with which he visited other portions of the country or obtained information concerning them, the number and variety of the foreign products that could be brought to him, the political problems upon which he thought and voted, and the attitude of the government toward his class in society. Most of these changes were distinguishable during the twenty-five years following the war and could be stated in brief and definite terms.

54

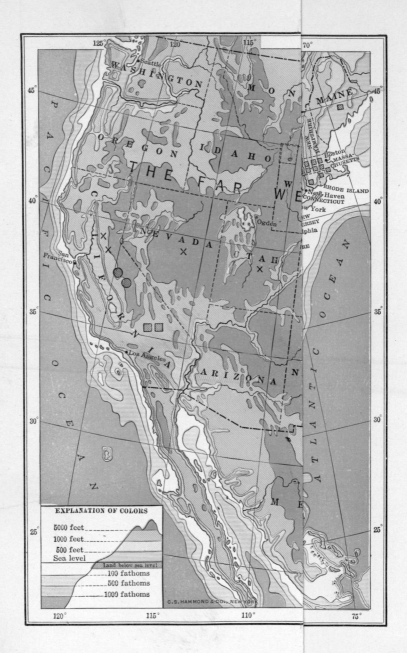

EXPLANATION OF COLORS

5000 feet

1000 feet

500 feet

Sea level

land below sea level

100 fathoms

500 fathoms

1000 fathoms

C. S. HAMMOND & CO., NEW YORK

From the standpoint of population, the growth of the country before 1890, although not so rapid as it had been before the war, was both constant and important. Between 1870 and 1890 the numbers of people increased from nearly thirty-nine millions to nearly sixty-three millions, the rate each decade being not far from twenty-five per cent. Six states added more than a million each to their population— New York and Pennsylania in the Northeast; Ohio, Illinois and Kansas in the Middle West; and Texas in the South. No fewer than seventeen others expanded by half a million or more—ten of the seventeen being in the valley drained by the Mississippi River system.

Detailed study of particular sections of the country discloses a continuous shifting of population which indicates changes in the economic life of the people. In northern New England, the numbers increased slowly. Both Maine and New Hampshire lost from 1860 to 1870; nearly half of Maine's counties and nearly two-thirds of Vermont's lost population between 1880 and 1890; the people were abandoning the rural districts to flock to the cities or migrate to the West. Shipbuilding fell off in Maine; the dairy interests languished in Vermont, less wheat was being planted and the farmers, no longer growing woo', were selling their flocks. Most of the growth was to be found in the industrial counties. The traditional New England thrift, however, was not lost with the migration of the people, for savings bank deposits were increasing, and the state of Vermont was free from debt in 1880, and all its counties in 1890. The South, between 1870 and 1890, increased in numbers a little less rapidly than the country as a whole. On the Atlantic Coast the greatest relative expansion was in Florida; in the western South, in Texas. The increase was almost wholly native, as immigration did not flow into that section.

The great expansion of the Middle West, from Ohio to Kansas, was based upon the public land policy of the federal government. Substantially all this region had once been in the possession of the United States, which had early adopted a system of laying out townships six miles on a side, with subdivisions one mile square (containing 640 acres), called sections. An important feature of the policy had been the encouragement of education and of transportation through the gift of large grants of the public land. Moreover, settlement had been stimulated by the disposal of land to purchasers at extremely liberal figures. In 1862 the famous Homestead Act had inaugurated a still more generous policy. Under this law the citizen might settle upon a quarter-section and receive a title after five years of actual occupation, with no charge other than a slight fee. More and more the eastern farmer "resented the stumps and ridges which interrupted his plow."

. . . here I must labor each day in the field
And the winter consumes all the summer doth yield.

Illinois, Iowa and Kansas were "the place of the rainbow, and the pot of gold." "When we 've wood and prairie land," as one of the songs of the day alluringly promised,

Won by our toil,
We 'll reign like kings in fairy land,
Lords of the soil!

Millions of acres were taken up under the Homestead Act both by natives and by immigrants, 1,300,000 people poured into Illinois between 1870 and 1890; over 1,000,000 into Kansas, and nearly that number into Nebraska; in the Dakotas a young man of college age in 1890 might have remembered almost the entire significant portion of the history of his state and have been one of the oldest inhabitants. The frontier of settlement advanced from the western edge of Missouri into mid-Kansas, and almost met the growing population of the Far West, whose economic possibilities had already attracted attention.

The discovery of gold-dust in a mill-race in California had drawn the "Forty-niners" to

> . . . lands of gold
> That lay toward the sun.

For a few years fabulous sums of the precious metal had been extracted from the ground by the hordes of treasure-seekers who had come from all over the world by boat, pack-animal or "prairie schooner," around Cape Horn, across the Isthmus of Panama or over the western mountains. When the yield of the mines had slackened, some of the population had filtered off to newer fields, but more had settled down to exploit the agricultural and lumber resources of California. In Nevada a rich vein of silver called the "Comstock Lode" had been discovered; in 1873 a group operating the "Virginia Consolidated" mine struck the great "bonanza," and the output reached unheard-of proportions. The success of the mines, however, was essential to Nevada, which had few other resources to develop, and when the yield slowed down the population growth of the state noticeably slackened. In Colorado during the late fifties some prospectors had struck gold, and another rush had made "Pike's Peak or Bust" its slogan. Some had returned, "Busted by Thunder," but others had better fortune, discovered gold, silver or lead, and helped lay the foundations of Denver and Leadville. In Idaho and Montana, in Wyoming and South Dakota and other states, prospectors found gold, silver, copper and lead, and thus attracted much of the population that later settled down to occupations which were less feverish and more reliable than mining. In general, the advance of population into the Middle West was more or less regular, as wave on wave made its way into the Mississippi Basin; in the Far West, however, population extended in long arms up the fertile valleys of Washington, Oregon and California, or was found in scattered islands where mineral wealth had been discovered in the Rocky Mountain region.

From the standpoint of absolute growth, the expansion of most of the far western states was not imposing, but the relative increase was suggestive of the future. Colorado nearly quadrupled in a decade (1870–1880), and Washington equalled the record in the following ten years. California grew faster from 1870 to 1890 than it had done in the gold days, indicating that its development was based on something more lasting than a fickle vein of ore. Meanwhile politicians were fanning the desire of the growing territories to become states, and in 1889 North Dakota, South Dakota, Montana and Washington were admitted, and in the following year Idaho and Wyoming. Of these, only Washington and the Dakotas had populations equivalent to the federal ratio for representation in the House.[1] Utah was kept outside for a few years longer, until 1896, when the Mormon Church gave satisfactory indication that anti-polygamy laws were being enforced.

The migration westward, which has been a constant factor in American development since early times, continued unabated after the Civil War; indeed the restless spirit aroused by the four years of conflict undoubtedly tended to increase this steady shift toward the West. By 1890 approximately a fifth of the native Americans were to be found in states other than those in which they had been born. 95,000 natives of Maine, for example, were to be found in Massachusetts; 17,000 were in California; and considerable numbers in every state between the two. The North Carolinians were equally well distributed. 43,000 were in South Carolina, 18,000 in

[1] The ratio was 151,912, but, by a provision of the Constitution, states are given a representative even if they do not contain the requisite number.

Texas, and 5,500 in Washington. Every state had contributed to populate every other, although in general the migration tended to take place on east and west lines, and predominantly westward.

Immigration, another constant factor in American development, underwent important changes during the twenty-
five years from 1865 to 1890. Although the inward tide was
smaller in periods of economic depression, it was correspondingly larger in times of prosperity. During the twenty
years after 1870 it amounted to more than 8,000,000, and in
the single year 1882 reached the unprecedented total of 789,-
000. A combination of circumstances tended to thrust emi-
grants out of European countries and attract them to America. Hard times, overpopulation, compulsory military service and anti-Jewish persecution created a desire to leave; improved steamship facilities, cheap land and plenty of opportunity for unskilled manual labor constituted a magnet in
America.[2]

That peak year, 1882, was a turning point in several respects in the history of immigration into the United States.
It was in this year that the Chinese were excluded; that immigration from Italy, Austria-Hungary and Russia became
of sufficient size to be impressive; and that the first inclusive
federal immigration act was passed. The law of 1882 defined, in general, the policy which the nation has pursued
ever since. It placed a tax of fifty cents on all incomers,
to be paid by the ship companies; it forbade the landing of
objectionable persons, such as convicts and lunatics; and it
placed on the owners of vessels the expense of returning immigrants not permitted to land. All these provisions were

[2] *Cf.* Hamlin Garland's recollection of the attraction of western land
for the immigrant of the eighties: "Trains swarming with immigrants
from every country of the world were haltingly creeping out upon the
level lands. Norwegians, Swedes, Danes, Scotchmen, Englishmen, and
Russians all mingled in this flood of land-seekers rolling toward the
sundown plain." *Son of the Middle Border*, 301.

amended or developed in later laws, like that of 1885 for-bidding persons or corporations to prepay the transportation of laborers or to encourage immigration under contract to perform work.

More important than the legislation controlling the flow of immigrants were several slow but decisive changes in the characteristics of the new-comers. Whereas the earlier Irish, Germans and English had frequently taken up western land and become farmers, the growing numbers of Italians, Austrians and Russians tended to settle in manufacturing and urban centers where the demand for manual laborers was greatest.[3] In the main they were less intelligent than the earlier immigrants, and were destined to provide fewer public leaders, and more hewers of wood and drawers of water. Alien colonies grew in the cities,—areas in which the language, the customs and the newspapers were those of Naples, Vienna or Kiev. The social effects of the new immigration were difficult to estimate. To be sure, the foreign elements increased the problems of municipal government, but they also performed essential manual work on the fast-growing railroads, in the factories, and on the highways. They were content to work for a wage that meant a lowered standard for the American laborer, but they forced him out of the ranks of the unskilled, and up into the ranks of the foreman; and the Irish maid-servant and the French-Canadian factory operative drove the New England girl of the older stock out of domestic service and the cotton-mill into school-teaching and office work.[4]

[3] Put into simplest terms, the census of 1890 showed that of every hundred aliens who had come to the United States between 1870 and 1890, thirty-seven were to be found in the states from Maine to Pennsylvania, four from Delaware to Texas, forty-seven from Ohio to Kansas, and twelve in the Far West (for the most part Chinese).

[4] A striking exhibit of the contribution to American life made by aliens is that given in Husband, *Americans by Adoption* (Boston, 1920). To mention only those who achieved renown after the Civil War: *Carl Schurz* came from Germany in 1852, became an anti-slavery leader, minister to Spain, brigadier-general during the Civil War, member of

The growing size of the cities and their increasing racial complexity hastened—if they did not bring about—a remarkable series of changes. In a word, the overgrown villages of the first half of the nineteenth century began their transformation into modern municipalities.

The police force, for example, had in earlier times consisted of mere night-watchmen—men who worked at a trade during the day, and performed an inexpert and somewhat haphazard police service during the night hours. They were not in uniform, were not trained and not dependable. The cities presented a sharp challenge to such a situation. Unruly natives and lawless immigrants formed gangs that infested the streets,—such as the "Rats" and the "Blood Cubs" in Philadelphia. In Boston in 1837, a single street fight between the fire companies and the Irish population of the city involved about 15,000 persons. People and property alike called for protection. Hence arose, about the middle of the century, the professional uniformed police departments of New York, Philadelphia and other cities. The professionalization of the fire departments occurred about the same time. Earlier fire protection had been in the hands of volunteer companies composed too frequently of rowdies from various sections of the city. Frequently their main interest in a fire was the opportunity for plunder. Commonly the rivalry of the companies with one another was more keen than their desire to serve

the United States Senate, Secretary of the Interior under President Hayes, and editor of the New York *Evening Post; Theodore Thomas* immigrated from Germany in 1845, and did a pioneer work in the development of symphony orchestras; *Andrew Carnegie* was born in Scotland in 1835, was brought as a lad to Pennsylvania, where he accumulated a princely fortune as a steel manufacturer; *J. J. Hill,* a Canadian, crossed the border just before the Civil War, settled in St. Paul, developed the economic resources of the Northwest, and became the greatest railroad builder of that section of the county; *Augustus St. Gaudens,* a native of Dublin, was brought by his parents in 1848 when he was a few months old. Famine in Ireland forced his parents to seek a land where food was more plentiful. St. Gaudens became America's greatest sculptor.

None of these men, it will be noticed, were of the later south and east European stock.

the public interest. Sometimes they fell upon one another on the way to fires, and forgot the conflagration in the zest of combat with fists, knives or axes. At times they were even accused of levying tribute on property owners, whose refusal to pay might result in a blaze on the property of the recalcitrant.[5] So undesirable a situation called for a complete change. In New York, at the close of the Civil War, 163 volunteer companies were disbanded, and a professional system established. In Chicago the great fire of 1871, and in Boston the disastrous conflagration of 1872 compelled radical reorganizations.

In numerous other ways the metamorphosis of the American city was made evident. Adequate water supplies were procured,—a notable illustration of which was the Croton reservoir in New York, built as early as 1842. Sewers and pavements were laid,—the new immigrants providing much of the manual labor. Horse-car tracks were laid in the streets,— only to be pulled up and replaced with heavier ones when electric power began to be used about 1890. City parks were planned. Public buildings were constructed, as well as a huge number of dwellings.

Crudity and corruption characterized the change. The architecture of even the best private and public buildings aroused the amusement and scorn of a later and better trained generation. Streets frequently were laid out too narrow for the traffic demands of busier days. Buildings crowded together and flimsily constructed of wood invited devastating fires. Lack of proper sanitary precautions, and ignorance of the methods of disease prevention encouraged epidemics of smallpox, typhus and other diseases which scourged the

5 *Cf. Reminiscences of Augustus St. Gaudens*, I, 20: "The street fights began with the enemies of West Broadway, who ran with Fire-Engine Company Number Sixteen, the 'Gotham,' and with those of Greene Street and other distant territories, who ran with other engines. Showers of stones, isolated personal struggles, and one solitary encounter with a negro boy, stand out conspicuously. . . . "

cities. The construction of public buildings, the paving of the streets, and the granting of franchises to street car companies provided a golden age for favoritism and "graft." [6] These and other similar considerations led James Bryce in 1888 to make a charge which many students of public affairs have thought severe but well-deserved: "There is no denying that the government of cities is the one conspicuous failure in the United States."

A peculiar accompaniment of the increased population of the country and the congestion in the cities was the rise of athletic games and contests on an extensively organized scale. In earlier times the vast majority of men and boys had manual labor to do on farms and in the small workshops. Long hours and hard work left neither time nor energy for exertion beyond an occasional horse-race, wrestling match, or fist fight. The rapid growth of the cities brought about a change. More men lived a sedentary life in offices, banks and stores. The development of schools and colleges brought together large numbers of young men who required an outlet for their superabundant physical energy.

The result was that the generation from 1865 to 1895 was the period of organization in American sporting life. Immediately after the Civil War such famous horse races began as those for the Travers Stakes, the Saratoga Cup and the Belmont Stakes. In 1876 the Intercollegiate Association of Amateur Athletes of America and the National Base Ball Association were organized; in 1881 the first national tennis championship was held; city athletic clubs like those in Boston and New York, and the increasingly popular country clubs were products of the eighties; golf began to claim its

---

[6] In 1884 the New York city government granted a charter to the Broadway Surface Railway Company. It was later discovered that twenty of the twenty-two aldermen had been implicated in frauds connected with the grant. Several were sentenced to prison and six fled from the country. *Cf.* Carman, *Street Surface Railway Franchises of New York.*

devotees in the early nineties; and the League of American Wheelmen counted over 100,000 members in 1898.[7]

Of the great economic interests of the United States, the most widespread was agriculture. In the Northeast, to be sure, the amount of improved farm land was growing smaller. In New England the tendency was visible after 1850, and became pronounced after 1880. The Middle States, likewise, fell back distinctly after the latter year. These portions of the country were rapidly becoming urban and industrialized. The opening of the prairie lands of the West, combined with the extension and improvement of the railroads were producing a competition with which the poorer farms of the Northeast could not cope. Wheat, flour, corn, meats and other food supplies were being laid down in the eastern cities at such low prices that the younger generation was forced to abandon the rural communities and seek a livelihood in the industrial towns.

In the South, agriculture had always been the main economic resource before the war, and must continue to be so afterward. The twenty-five years following 1865 were spent,

[7] A notable article on the rise of sport is that of Professor F. L. Paxson in the *Mississippi Valley Historical Review* for Sept., 1917.

The height reached during the first generation in the field of track athletics is indicated by the records made in the meet between the London Athletic Club and the New York Athletic Club on Sept. 21, 1895. In that year, England and America were searched for the best performers in their several events. The American team won all the first places,—but the names of the victors suggest one of the effects of immigration. The events, with their winners and records follow:

100 yard dash—Wefers—9 $\frac{4}{5}$ secs. Equalling world's record.
220 yard dash—Wefers—21 $\frac{3}{5}$ secs. New world's record.
440 yard dash—Burke—49 secs.
880 yard run—Kilpatrick—1 min. 53 $\frac{2}{5}$ secs. New world's record.
1 mile run—Conneff—4 mins. 18 $\frac{1}{5}$ secs.
3 mile run—Conneff—15 mins. 36 $\frac{1}{5}$ secs.
120 yard hurdle—Chase—15 $\frac{2}{5}$ secs.
Hammer throw—Mitchell 137 ft. 5 $\frac{1}{2}$ in.
High jump—Sweeney—6 ft., 5$\frac{5}{8}$ in., new world's record.
Broad jump—Bloss—22 ft., 6 in.
Shot put—Gray—43 ft., 5 in.

in fact, in recovery from the devastation and decay which the armies and the general cessation from regular work had brought about on the farms of the South. Although conditions varied from place to place, the situation in many states was little short of pitiable. Factories, public buildings, houses and barns, household furniture and farm tools were burned, wrecked or fallen into ruins.[8] Good land was in the market at ruinously low prices; poor land was deserted, or begged in vain for purchasers. Rapid communication was out of the question. For some months after Lee's surrender, the post office ceased to function. Highways had fallen into disrepair or were impassable; two-thirds of the railroads were bankrupt; and rolling stock was worn out or destroyed. Capital and credit, of course, were largely gone, and the banks in distress. Bands of thieves infested many districts; federal officers stationed in the South were frequently dishonest and defrauded the people; and the lawlessness which war encourages was observable on all sides.[9]

The greatest difficulty, however, was the scarcity of tools and seeds, and the demoralization of the labor system. The man-power of the South had been lost in the war, or had emerged crippled, discouraged or worn out. The negroes had not been ideal workmen under the slavery régime; now, as freedmen, they found difficulty in adjusting themselves to the economic obligations of their new status, and evinced a tendency to rove restlessly about, instead of settling down to the stern task of helping to rebuild the shattered South.

[8] Compare the statement of General Boynton quoted by Fleming, *Sequel of Appomattox*, 5: "Window-glass has given way to thin boards, in railway coaches and in the cities. Furniture is marred and broken, and none has been replaced for four years. . . . A complete set of crockery is never seen, and in very few families is there enough to set a table. . . . A set of forks with whole tines is a curiosity. Clocks and watches have nearly all stopped. . . . Hair brushes and tooth brushes have all worn out."

[9] The federal secretary of the treasury, Hugh McCulloch, once declared: "I am sure I sent some honest cotton agents South; but it sometimes seems doubtful whether any of them remained honest very long."

"The swiftness with which they were led to make their flight from slavery into freedom left no time for the collection of any property on the way."

It was manifest that the first problem was to revive the agricultural activities of the old days, and that the main resource must be cotton, the demand for which in the markets of the North and of Europe was such as to make it the best "money crop." A labor system was introduced known as share-farming or cropping. Under this system the plantation owner who had more property than he could cultivate under the new conditions let parts of his land to tenants, supplying them with buildings, tools, seed and perhaps credit at the village store for the supplies necessary for the year. The tenant, who had neither money nor credit with which to buy land, furnished the labor, and at the harvest each received a specified share of the product, commonly a half. The system had its disadvantages: it kept the farmer always in debt; it discouraged extra activity on the part of either farmer or landlord, because half of the resulting product went to the other party to the contract; and since the only valuable security which the plantation owner had was the crop—the land being almost unsalable—he insisted on the cultivation of cotton, which was a safe crop, and avoided experimentation and diversification. On the other hand, the system enabled the landowner to take advantage of the labor supply and to supervise the untutored negro,—and most important of all *it kept the South alive.* In addition to the large plantations, cultivated by several tenant farmers, the number of small farms tilled by independent owners or renters increased. Due to this tendency and to the opening of many small holdings in the Southwest, the size of the average farm diminished. *The great plantations were replaced by small farms;* the traditional plantation owner gave way to the farmer of moderate means. For good or for ill, southern society was revolutionized as much at the top as at the bottom.

Owing to the insistence of land owners upon cotton culture, the South first caught up with its *ante-bellum* production in the cultivation of this staple, for shortly before 1880 the crop exceeded that of 1860. Leadership in the production of tobacco, the second great southern crop, sharply shifted after the war from Virginia to Kentucky. The Atlantic coast states, except North Carolina, fell back distinctly. Maryland, indeed, never again produced much more than half as great a crop as she did in 1860, while Virginia did not equal her former record until the opening of the twentieth century, although the South as a whole recovered in the late eighties. Rice culture, likewise, did not recover readily for South Carolina alone produced almost as much in 1860 as the entire South in 1890, and not until the development of production in Louisiana after 1890 did the crop assume its former importance.[10] The production of sugar in Louisiana in 1890 was but little greater than it had been in 1860, and in the production of cereals the South did not keep pace with the upper Mississippi Valley before 1890. On the other hand the rapid growth of Texas was one of the outstanding features of southern development during the period, for that state improved an amount of farm land between 1870 and 1890, roughly equivalent to the combined areas of New Hampshire, Vermont and Massachusetts. There was observable, moreover, a certain hopefulness, a certain resiliency of purpose, a pride in the achievements of the past and in the possibilities of the future. In these respects the South was a new South by 1890.

Greater than the South as a food-producing area, was the belt of states from Ohio and Michigan to Kansas and the Dakotas:

[10] "The rice planters were driven from the Carolina and Georgia shores during the war, labor was in a disorganized and chaotic state, production had almost ceased, and at its close, dams, flood-gates, canals, mills and houses were either dilapidated or destroyed." Quoted in Banks, *Land Tenure in Ga.*, 66.

Where there's more of reaping and less of sowing,
That's where the West begins.

The unparalleled growth of agriculture in this section was
founded upon four recent developments: the growth of the
population through large native and immigrant increases
created a pressure for more land; the opening of the prairies
by the Homestead Act and other legislation provided almost
limitless space for agricultural expansion; improvements in
railway and steamship transportation made possible the rapid
and cheap marketing of western products in eastern cities
and in Europe; and finally the invention of agricultural
machinery, which could be used to advantage on the large
and relatively level prairie farms, completed the revolution
of American agriculture. Such devices as the reaper had been
in use long before the Civil War, but the reduction of the
labor supply from 1861 to 1865 had hastened the replacement
of men by machines. A reaper which merely cut the grain
and tossed it aside, gave way to a binder which both cut the
grain and bound it into sheaves; and this in turn was followed
by a combined reaper and thresher with which it was "necessary only to drive across the wheat field in order to obtain the
grain ready for transportation to the elevator or elsewhere."
"The world learned how to shift the labor of binding wheat,
mowing hay, husking corn, and threshing grain from the
human muscle to the animal."

When Cyrus McCormick moved his reaper works to Chicago in 1848, the manufacture of agricultural machinery concentrated in Illinois, which rapidly became the center of the
most productive agricultural area in the United States. In
that state, for example, production increased fifteen-fold between 1840 and 1890, although the number of agricultural
workers increased only four-fold. The change was due in the
main to the use of machinery, which as William H. Seward
declared, "pushed the frontier westward at the rate of
thirty miles a year."

The number of mid-western farms increased nearly a million from 1870 to 1890, and the acreage in improved land grew by an amount equivalent to the combined areas of the British Isles, Belgium, the Netherlands, and Denmark, with a generous margin to spare. Corn, wheat, oats and other cereals demanded improved outlets to world markets. Elevators for the storage of grain were constructed with a capacity of 300,000 to 1,000,000 bushels, and revolutionary improvements were made in methods of loading and unloading the product.[11]

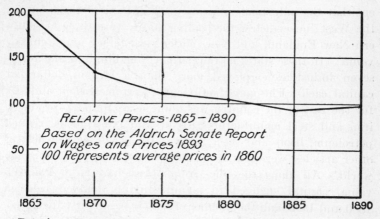

RELATIVE PRICES-1865 – 1890
Based on the Aldrich Senate Report
on Wages and Prices 1893
100 Represents average prices in 1860

Despite the growth of the agricultural interests of the Middle West, however, the farmer did not reach prosperity. For twenty years after 1873 prices fell steadily both in the United States and in other countries of the world, and the agricultural classes found themselves receiving a smaller and smaller return for their products. Unrest grew to distress,

[11] An outstanding illustration of the prairie farm was that of Dalrymple in Dakota. It consisted of 75,000 acres. All the planting was done by machinery, the motive power being supplied by 400 horses and mules. 115 binders and harvesters, and 21 threshers were used in reaping the crop. Each thresher required 25 men and 20 horses. Sometimes as many as 50 cars were loaded with wheat in a day. The workmen were mainly Swedes, Danes and Germans. *Cf. Annual Cyclopaedia*, 1881, p. 204.

and distress to acute depression, while the demands of the farmers for relief frequently determined the trend of midwestern politics.[12]

Less general than agriculture, but more characteristic of the period after the war, was the development of manufacturing. The census of 1870 was faulty and inadequate, but it was sufficiently accurate to indicate that the manufacturing region was preëminently that north of the Potomac-Ohio river line and east of the Mississippi. By 1890 it was apparent that the industrial interests were shifting slightly toward the West; nevertheless the leading states were those of southern New England, and New York, New Jersey and Pennsylvania. In these states no fewer than four hundred and fortyseven industries employed more than a million dollars of capital each. The manufacturing of cotton, woolen and silk for the rest of the country was done here; foundry products, iron and steel manufactures, silver and brass goods, refined petroleum, boots and shoes, paper and books, with a host of other articles, were sent from this section to every part of the world. All along the line, from Massachusetts to Pennsylvania, capital engaged in manufacturing doubled between 1880 and 1890, and the number of employees greatly increased.

Although the industrial life of the South belongs, for the most part, to the years since 1890, the coal and iron deposits of Alabama were known and utilized before that year, the number of cotton mill spindles in North Carolina tripled between 1880 and 1890, and cotton expositions were held in Atlanta in 1881 and New Orleans in 1884. It was in the eighties, also, that the Chesapeake and Ohio Railroad and the Norfolk and Western led to the exploitation of the coal deposits of Virginia and West Virginia, especially the famous Pocahontas field.

[12] Hamlin Garland, *Main Travelled Roads*, portrays the hardships of western farm life.

Some aspects of the growth of manufacturing in the North are well illustrated in the development of the mineral resources around Lake Superior. The presence of iron ore, in this region had been known since 1844, but its utilization had been greatly restricted by insufficient transportation facilities. The opening of the St. Mary's Ship Canal at Sault Ste. Marie in 1855 had given part of the needed relief by permitting the passage of shipping from Lake Superior to Lake Huron. The extension of railroads to the more important mining centers gave access to ample supplies of the raw material needed for an age of steel. The Marquette iron range in northern Michigan, the Gogebic in Michigan and Wisconsin, the Menominee near Marquette, the Vermilion Lake and Mesabec ore beds near Duluth,—all these combined to yield millions of tons of ore, caused the development of numerous mining towns and laid the foundations of a gigantic expansion in the production of steel. As the iron and steel industry with its furnaces, machinery and skilled labor was already established at points in Illinois, Ohio and western Pennsylvania, it was cheaper to transport the ore to these places than to transfer the industry to the mines. Ore vessels were constructed capable of carrying mammoth cargoes; docks, railroads and canals were built; and the products of the mines taken to lake and inland cities. Improvements, meanwhile, were being continually made in the steel industry, such as the Bessemer process, by which the impurities were burned out of the iron ore, and exactly enough carbon introduced into the molten metal to transform it into steel.

Although the steel industry was established in many places, its most dramatic growth occurred in those parts of eastern Ohio and western Pennsylvania that center about the city of Pittsburgh. Placed strategically at the point where the Alleghany and Monongahela rivers join to form the Ohio, in the midst of an area rich in coal and natural gas, near the point where Edward L. Drake first drilled for petroleum in 1859, Pittsburgh rapidly became the center of a region in which the development of manufacturing and the construction of railroads dwarfed other interests. A large portion of the ore mined in the Lake Superior fields was carried to the Pittsburgh district to be transformed into steel products of all kinds. Moreover, the fortunes made by private individuals in the region, and the inflow of alien laborers to work in the factories and on the railroads raised weighty social and industrial problems.[13]

Manifestly the extension of agriculture and industry in so large a country as the United States was dependent upon the corresponding growth of the means of transportation, both by water and by rail. A detailed account of the expansion of the railway net, with the accompanying implications in the fields of finance and politics, is a matter for later consideration.[14] Certain of its general features may be mentioned, however, because they are intimately interwoven with the economic developments which have just been explained.

The concentration of the population in the cities, of which New York and Chicago were outstanding examples, was one of these features. From the time of the first census, the city of New York continued to maintain its position as the most populous city of the nation. Between 1850 and 1890 it added a round million to its numbers, containing 1,515,000 persons at the later date. Moreover it was the center of a thriving and thickly settled region extending from New Haven on the one side to Philadelphia on the other—the most densely populated area in America. The uninterrupted expansion of the city indicated that the reasons for its growth were constant in their operation. And, in fact, the reasons were not diffi-

---

[13] For an illuminating account of the growth of Cleveland as a transfer point in the coal and iron industry, see Croly, *M. A. Hanna*, chaps. vii, viii.

[14] See chap. IX.

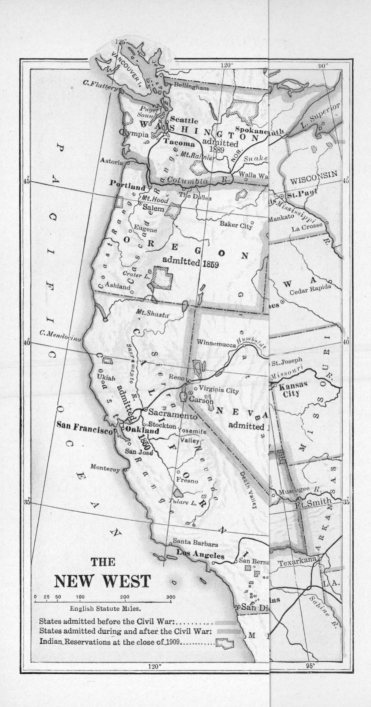

THE
NEW WEST

0 25 50   100   200   300

English Statute Miles.

States admitted before the Civil War:..........
States admitted during and after the Civil War:
Indian Reservations at the close of 1909...........

cult to find. It was blessed with one of the world's finest harbors and had access to the interior of the state by way of the Hudson and Mohawk rivers. These natural advantages had long since been recognized and had been increased by the construction of the Erie Canal in 1825 which, with the Great Lakes and the several canals connecting the Lakes with the Ohio Valley, had given New York an early hold and almost a monopoly on the trade between the upper Mississippi, the Lakes and the coast. The city, therefore, became an importing and exporting center; its shipping interests grew, immigration flowed in, and its manufacturing establishments soon outstripped those of any other industrial center; the great printing and publishing, banking and commercial firms were drawn irresistibly to the most populous city, and Wall Street became the synonym for the financial center of the nation.

In 1840 Chicago had been an unimportant settlement of 4,500 persons, but by the opening of the war it had grown to twenty-five times that size, and added 800,000 between 1870 and 1890. It had early become evident that the city was the natural outlet toward the East for the grain trade and the slaughtering and meat-packing industry of the upper Mississippi Valley. Before the late sixties, however, railway connection was defective, being composed of many short lines rather than of one continuous road, so that freight had to be loaded and unloaded many times during its passage to the seaboard. This situation, which had been merely inconvenient before the war, had become little short of intolerable during the struggle, because the closing of the Mississippi had cut off from the Middle West its water outlet toward the South and had diverted more freight to the railroads. After the war, Cornelius Vanderbilt, president of the Hudson River Railroad, combined a number of the shorter roads so as to give uninterrupted communication between Chicago and New York, to tap the trade of the Mississippi Valley, and to compete with water traffic by way of the Great Lakes and the Erie Canal. Other railroads saw the possibilities in the western trade, and the Baltimore and Ohio, the Grand Trunk, and the Erie followed the lead of Vanderbilt. A similar development, although on a smaller scale, accompanied the growth of other northern cities. The retroactive effects of the roads on the distribution of the population are too detailed for discussion, but a single example may typify many. In 1870 the Maine farmer supplied much of the meat consumed in Boston; by 1895, he was getting his own meat from the West. He must, therefore, adapt himself to the new conditions if he could, move to the manufacturing cities as so many of his neighbors did, or migrate to the West.

Like the growth of New York and Chicago, the development of California had an important effect on the history of American railway transportation. Although it had been agitated for many years, the project for a railroad from the Mississippi to the Pacific Coast had not reached the construction stage until the congressional acts of 1862 and 1864 provided for a line to be built from Omaha to San Francisco. The Union Pacific Railroad had been incorporated to build the eastern end, while the western end was to be constructed by the Central Pacific Railroad Company, a California corporation. The latter act, that of 1864, had given the roads substantial financial assistance and half the public land on a strip forty miles wide along the line of the track. Many difficulties had stood in the way—lack of funds, problems of construction and inadequate labor supply. Eventually they had all been overcome by the energy and skill of such men as Stanford, Crocker and Huntington. Imported Chinese coolies had met the labor demand and construction was speeded up. Actual building had begun in 1863 and six years later the two roads met at Promontory Point near Ogden in Utah, where the last spike was driven, the engines

Facing on the single track,
Half a world behind each back.

During the four years following the completion of the transcontinental line, 24,000 miles of new railroad were constructed, much of which was built into the wilderness ahead of settlement. So great an expansion, coming at a time when immense stretches of new land were being opened and industry being developed on a large scale, could hardly fail to result in over-speculation. The results appeared in 1873. Jay Cooke & Company, the most important financial concern in the country, had been back of the Northern Pacific Railroad, marketing large quantities of its bonds and so providing capital for construction, the purchase of equipment, the payment of wages and so on. Obviously a large amount of money was thus being put into an enterprise from which returns would come only after a considerable period; and yet construction had to be continued, or what was already invested would be lost. What Cooke was doing for the Northern Pacific was being done for the Chesapeake and Ohio by Fisk and Hatch, and by other firms for speculative enterprises in every corner of the land.

The process of putting capital into fixed form could hardly go on forever, and several events led to a final crash. In 1871 and 1872 great fires in Chicago and Boston destroyed millions of dollars' worth of property. Early in 1873 the government investigation of the Credit Mobilier Company led to widespread distrust of the roads and made investors conservative about buying bonds. On September 18, 1873, Jay Cooke & Company found itself unable to continue business and closed its doors. The failure was a thunderbolt to the financial world. Indeed, so unbelievable was the news that an energetic policeman arrested a small newsboy who shouted his "Extra—All about the failure of Jay Cooke."

If Jay Cooke & Company fell, the sky might fall. People rushed to withdraw their funds from the banks. Fisk and Hatch opened their doors for fifteen minutes and received calls for $1,500,000. They closed at once. The smaller financial institutions followed the bigger ones. Stocks fell, the Exchange was closed, there was a money famine. Industrial concerns, dependent on the banks, failed by scores. Industrial paralysis, with railroad receiverships, laborers out of employment, riots and their accompaniments, showed how deepseated had been the trouble. Not until late in the decade did business recover its former prosperity.

With the return of more stable conditions the construction of railroads continued unabated. The Northern Pacific ran near the Canadian line and connected the upper Mississippi Valley with the coast, carrying in its trail the manners and customs of the East. Two lines in the South were extended to the Pacific, so that by the middle eighties four great main avenues gave passage through a region over which, so recently, the miner and the trapper had forced a dangerous path.

The fact that it was often necessary, in building the railroads across the plains, to detail half the working force to protect the remainder against the Indians, calls attention to one unmistakable result of the conquest of the Far West. The construction of the railroads spelled the doom of the wild Indian. Far back in 1834 the government had adopted the policy of setting aside large tracts of land west of the Mississippi for the use of the Indian tribes. Most of the savages had been stationed in an immense area between southern Minnesota and Texas, while other smaller reservations had been scattered over most of the states west of the river. On the whole, the government had dealt with the Indians in tribes, not as individuals. The rapid inflow of population to the fertile lands, together with the rush of prospectors to newly discovered supplies of gold and silver, caused increasing demands from the Indians for protection, and from the whites for the extinguishment of Indian land titles.

The classical illustration of this tendency is found in the case of the Sioux Indians in South Dakota. The discovery of gold in the region of the Black Hills, on the Sioux reservation, aroused agitation for the removal of the tribe to make way for settlers and miners. But the execution of the scheme was not so simple as its conception. The removal of the Sioux necessitated the transfer of the Poncas, a peaceful tribe which lay immediately east. The latter, not unnaturally, objected, quarrels arose and eventually the Poncas were practically broken to pieces. The Sioux, not satisfied, attempted to regain the Black Hills, fought the famous Sioux War of 1876, led by Sitting Bull, but were crushed and forced to give up the unequal contest.

It would not be worth while to enter into the details of the numerous Indian conflicts after the Civil War. It is enough to notice that stirring accounts of them may be read in the memoirs of such soldiers as Custer, Sheridan and Miles, and that they cost millions of dollars and hundreds of lives. Finally it became evident that the attempt to deal with the Indians in tribes was a failure and it was determined to break up the tribal holdings of land so as to give each individual a small piece for his private property, and to open the remainder to settlement by the whites. In pursuance of such a policy, the Dawes Act of 1887 provided for the allotment of a quarter-section to each head of a family, with the proviso that the owner should not sell the land within twenty-five years. This was intended to protect the Indian from shrewd "land-sharks." Citizenship was given with the ownership of the land, in the hope that a sort of assimilation might gradually take place, and earnest attempts were made to provide education for the red-man. Not all these hopes were realized, however, and the later Burke Act, 1906, attempted further protection.

While the Indian was being restricted to a small part of the great region west of the Mississippi, there was being enacted on the plains one of the most picturesque of all American dramas. Beyond the settled parts of the states just west of the "Father of Waters," bounded north and south by Canada and the Rio Grande, and extending west into the valleys of the Rocky Mountains, lay an endless empire of rolling land. Parts of it were well watered. Here the soil was fertile, the grass luxuriant, and dotted with the yellow of the wild sunflower, the white of the Indian basket grass and the blue of the larkspur. A larger part of the plains lacked rainfall and had little vegetation except for the dusty, gray sage-brush. Even in 1865, no small part of the prairies were still looked upon as the "Great American Desert." In the winter, the northern prairies were swept by bitter winds from Hudson Bay; in the summer,

> The sun is as the sun was before God thought of shade.[15]

The chief inhabitants of the region were bands of Indians, here and there a gang of desperadoes—often rough refugees from the East— wild animals, and unbelievably huge herds of buffalo. Overhead, flocks of passenger pigeons that fairly darkened the sky; or a lone hawk floating lazily in the blue. Such was the stage on which the drama was enacted.

The chief actors were the steer and the cowboy—both of Mexican, and earlier of Spanish origin. Cattle turned loose long before by Spanish ranchers in Mexico had multiplied, spread out across the Rio Grande, and had run wild—wild as Texas steers. An accident disclosed the fact that these could winter safely and even advantageously on the northern

---

[15] *Cf.* the following recollections of Hamlin Garland: "Meanwhile an ominous change had crept over the plain. The winds were hot and dry and the grass, baked on the stem, had become as inflammable as hay. . . . The sky, absolutely cloudless, began to scare us with its light. The sun rose through the dusty air, sinister with flare of horizontal heat." "Winter! No one knows what winter means until he has lived through one in a pine-board shanty on a Dakota plain with only buffalo bones for fuel." *Son of the Middle Border,* pp. 308, 309.

plains. The city dwellers of the East constituted a market, or more accurately would constitute a market if the cattle could be economically transported from the plains to the slaughter houses of the mid-western cities,—Omaha, Kansas City, St. Louis and Chicago.

The railroads which were built out across the plains in the late sixties and during the seventies provided the needed transportation link. As the Union Pacific, the Kansas Pacific, and the Atchison, Topeka and Santa Fé reached likely spots, villages began to appear, like Ogallala (Neb.), and Abilene, Caldwell and Dodge City (Kan.). Cattle that cost four or five dollars to raise were worth twenty-five to forty-five at the railroad. Out of these circumstances arose the "round-up" and the "long drive."

Twice each year, in the spring and in the fall, the wild Texas cattle were rounded-up and corraled by cowboys. 2000–4000 head were then started on the long trail under the leadership of a boss, six or eight cowboys and a cook with his cook-wagon. The route lay toward the nearest railroad cowtown, and was determined by the supply of good grass and water. At the railroad they were purchased by dealers and shipped to the slaughter houses, or were driven on to ranches in Kansas and Nebraska or even Dakota and Montana for further fattening and later sale.[16] It was in the cattle town that the tourist and the eastern buyer became acquainted with the cowboy.

It is obvious that the long drive was dependent on great stretches of open country, free grass, and free access to water, —in a word, "the unfenced blue." But the railroad, which had so suddenly originated the cattle industry, brought it to a close with almost equal abruptness. Farmers followed the railways out into the plains and took up "homesteads,"—the increase of population in Kansas alone from 1860–1890 being

[16] An investigation conducted by the government in 1885 indicated that 5,201,132 head were driven north from Texas between 1866 and 1884. *Cf.* Nimmo, *Range and Ranch Cattle Traffic*, p. 31.

1,200,000. The homesteaders picked up the best grazing lands and the water supplies, fenced them in with wire, and closed the trail from Texas to the ranches. There ensued an infinite variety of small quarrels between the cattlemen and the farmers. But the farmer had received his land from the government. The government had to protect him; and the cattlemen had perforce to watch the free grass and free water disappear. The Indians were driven into reservations; the buffalo were slaughtered by hunters; and the desperadoes were dispersed or driven by government troops into the mountains. By 1890 the long drive was a tale that is told; the cattle were bred on ranches and transported by the ubiquitous railroad; a few buffalo were preserved as relics in Yellowstone Park; the cowboy was exploited by Buffalo Bill in his Wild West Show as an interesting historical character; and a few words like "sombrero," "corral" and "chaps," together with a mass of cowboy poetry (written for the most part since 1890 and not by cowboys), recall a unique stage of western development.[17]

In addition to the expansion of the several economic interests of the various sections of the country, inventions and improvements were taking place which affected the general problems of production and distribution. Improvements in machinery saved forty to eighty per cent. of the time and labor demanded in the production of important manufactured goods. Cheapened steel affected all kinds of industry. The development of steam-power and the beginnings of the practical use of electricity for power and light multiplied the effectiveness of human hands or added to human comfort. Cheaper and quicker transportation almost revolutionized the distribution of economic goods. The increased use of the tele-

---

[17] The extinction of the buffalo, which was the main source of meat supply for the Indian, doubtless helped starve the red-man into submission, and therefore into the acceptance of the government's policy of putting the tribes on reservations.

graph and cable shortened distances and brought together producers and consumers that had in earlier times been weeks of travel apart.

The necessarily statistical character of an account of economic development should not obscure the meaning of its details. Increased population, with its horde of incoming aliens, created a demand for standing room, necessitated westward expansion, and made the West more than ever a new country with new problems. The growth of agriculture enlarged a class that had not hitherto been as influential as it was destined to be, and brought into politics the economic needs of the farmer. Manufacturing brought great wealth into the hands of a few, created an increasing demand for protective tariffs and gave rise to strikes and other industrial problems. The concentration of especial interests in especial sections made likely the emergence of sectional antagonisms. Back of tariff and finance, therefore, back of transportation and labor, of new political parties and revolts in the old ones, of the great strikes and the increasing importance of some of the sections, lay the economic foundations of the new era.

BIBLIOGRAPHICAL NOTE

No thorough study of the economic history of the United States after the Civil War has yet been made. A general account is H. U. Faulkner, *American Economic History* (1924); E. L. Bogart, *Economic History of the United States* (1907), and various later editions, is useful, as well as E. E. Sparks, *National Development* (1907). On the South, consult articles by St. G. L. Sioussat, in *History Teachers' Magazine* (Sept., Oct., 1916); P. A. Bruce, *Rise of the New South* (1905); J. C. Ballagh (ed.), *South in the Building of the Nation* (1909), vol. VI; M. B. Hammond, *Cotton Industry* (1897). R. P. Porter, *West from the Census of 1880* (1882), is a useful compendium. A remarkable volume on a single state is *The Industrial State 1870–1893*, by Bogart and Thompson, vol. IV of the Centennial History of Illinois (1922); similar volumes for other portions of the country would be invaluable. L. A. Chase, *Rural Michigan* (1922).

The best account of the cattle country is that in Nimmo, *Range and Ranch Cattle Traffic,* in House of Representatives Executive Document No. 267, 2nd session, 48th. Congress, vol. 29 (Serial No. 2304); see also E. Hough, *Story of the Cowboy* (1898), *Passing of the Frontier* (1918) and *North of 36* (1923); F. L. Paxson, *Last American Frontier* (1910), "The Cow Country" in *American Historical Review* (Oct. 1916), and *History of the American Frontier 1763–1893* (1924), chap. LVI; R. A. Clemen, *The American Livestock and Meat Industry* (1923); Hagedorn, *Roosevelt in the Bad Lands* (1921); P. A. Rollins, *The Cowboy* (1922); J. H. Lomax, *Cowboy Songs* (1910); N. Thorp, *Songs of the Cowboy* (1921); J. H. Cook, *Fifty Years on the Old Frontier* (1923); T. Roosevelt, *Hunting Trips of a Ranchman* (1885). An interesting minor point may be studied in Smithsonian Report, U. S. National Museum, 1897 pt. II, 373–534, W. T. Hornaday, "The Extermination of the American Bison." N. A. Miles, *Serving the Republic* (1911), contains reminiscences of Indian conflicts.

On the Far West, in addition to Porter, Hough and Paxson, Katharine Coman, *Economic Beginnings of the Far West* (2 vols., 1912); H. K. White, *Union Pacific Railway* (1898); L. H. Haney, *Congressional History of Railways* (2 vols., 1908–1910); S. E. White, *The Forty-Niners* (1918).

There is also an abundance of useful illustrative fiction, such as: Bret Harte, *Luck of Roaring Camp,* and other stories (Far West); Edward Eggleston, *Hoosier Schoolmaster* (Indiana); W. D. Howells, *Rise of Silas Lapham* (New England); G. W. Cable, *Old Creole Days* (New Orleans); C. E. Craddock, *In the Tennessee Mountains;* F. H. Smith, *Colonel Carter* (Virginia); Hamlin Garland, *Main Travelled Roads* and *Son of the Middle Border* (Middle West); P. L. Ford, *Hon. Peter Sterling* (New York); S. E. White, *Gold* (California); and *Riverman* (Lake Superior lumber); John Hay, *Breadwinners* (industrial); H. Quick, *Vandermarck's Folly,* and *Hawkeye* (Iowa); B. Tarkington, *Conquest of Canaan, Midlander, Magnificent Ambersons* (Middle West).

On the history of agriculture: Schmidt and Ross, *Readings in the Economic History of American Agriculture* (1925); E. M. Banks, *Economics of Land Tenure in Georgia* (1905); H. Thompson, *The*

New South (1921), with a useful bibliography. Some of the articles on individual states in the *Annual Cyclopaedia* are helpful.

On the rise and problems of the city: R. Fosdick, *American Police Systems* (1920); J. Bryce, *American Commonwealth*, I, 637 (1888 and later eds.); H. J. Carman, *Street Surface Railway Franchises of New York City* (1919); J. A. Riis, *Battle with the Slums* (1902); H. G. James, *Municipal Functions* (1917); Weber, *Growth of Cities in the Nineteenth Century* (1899); D. F. Wilcox, *The American City* (1904); C. A. Beard, *American City Government* (1912). On immigration, consult bibliography of chap. XIX.

For other references to economic aspects of the period, see chapters, IX, XI, XIV.

CHAPTER IV

POLITICAL AND INTELLECTUAL BACKGROUND OF THE NEW ISSUES

Since the first success of The Republican Party, no Republican Convention has afforded a valid reason for the adoption of an opposition platform or the nomination of opposition candidates.

FRANK HENDRICK.

Nothing ever done by Tammany or by the Southern Democrats in the way of fraudulent management of primaries and of stuffing and padding the district associations, has surpassed what Platt has been doing recently.

THEODORE ROOSEVELT (1895).

No man can acquire a million without helping a million men to increase their little fortunes all the way down through all the social grades.

WILLIAM G. SUMNER.

The Journalists are now the Kings and Clergy: henceforth Historians . . . must write . . . according as this or the other Able Editor, or Combination of Able Editors, gains the world's ear

THOMAS CARLYLE.

POWERFUL as economic forces were from 1865 to 1900, they did not alone determine the direction of American progress during those years. Different individuals and different sections of the country reacted differently to the same economic facts; a formula that explained a phenomenon satisfactorily to one group, carried no conviction to another; political parties built up their platforms on economic self-interest, and yet they sometimes had their ideals; theories that seemed to explain economic development were found to be inadequate and were replaced by others; and practices that had earlier been regarded with indifference began to offend the public sense of good taste or morals or justice, and gave way to more enlightened standards. Some understand-

84

ing is necessary, therefore, of the more common theories, ideals, creeds and practices, because they supplemented the economic foundations that underlay American progress for a quarter century after the war.

THE POLITICAL BACKGROUND

Since the Republican party was almost continuously in power during this period, its composition, spirit and ideals were fundamental in political history. Throughout the North, especially in the Northeast, the intellectual and prosperous classes, the capitalists and manufacturers, were more likely to be found among the Republicans than among the Democrats. In fact such party leaders as Senator George F. Hoar went so far as to assert that the organization comprised the manufacturers and skilled laborers of the East, the soldiers, the church members, the clergymen, the school-teachers, the reformers and the men who were doing the great work of temperance, education and philanthropy. The history of the party, also, was no small factor in its successes. Many northerners had cast their first ballot in the fifties, with all the zeal of crusaders; they looked back upon the beginnings of Republicanism as they might have remembered the origin of a sacred faith; they thought of their party as the body which had abolished slavery and restored the Union; and they treasured the names of its Lincoln, its Seward, its Sumner and Grant and Sherman. The Republican party, wrote Edward MacPherson in 1888, in a history of the organization, is

both in the purity of its doctrines, the beneficent sweep of its measures, in its courage, its steadfastness, its fidelity, in its achievements and in its example, the most resplendent political organization the world has ever seen.

Senator Hoar declared that no party in history, not even that which inaugurated the Constitution, had ever accomplished so much in so short a time. It had been formed, he said, to prevent the extension of slavery into the territories, but the "providence of God imposed upon it far larger duties." The Republican party gave "honest, wise, safe, liberal, progressive American counsel" and the Democrats "unwise, unsafe, illiberal, obstructive, un-American counsel." He remembered the Republican nominating convention of 1880 as a scene of "indescribable sublimity," comparable in "grandeur and impressiveness to the mighty torrent of Niagara."

During the generation after the war the recollection of the struggle was fresh in men's minds and its influence was a force in party councils. The Democrats were looked upon as having sympathized with the "rebellion" and having been the party of disunion. In campaign after campaign the people were warned not to admit to power the party which had been "traitor" to the Union. Roscoe Conkling, the most influential politician in New York, declared in 1877 that the Democrats wished to regain power in order to use the funds in the United States Treasury to repay Confederate war debts and to provide pensions for southern soldiers. As late even as 1888 the nation was urged to recollect that the Democratic party had been the "mainstay and support of the Rebellion," while the Republicans were the "party that served the Nation."

At a later time it was pointed out that the party had not been founded solely on idealism; that the adherence of Pennsylvania to the party, for example, was due at least in a measure to Republican advocacy of a protective tariff; that Salmon P. Chase and Edwin M. Stanton, two of the leading members of Lincoln's cabinet, had been Democrats; and that Lincoln's second election and the successful outcome of the war had been due partly to the support of his political opponents. As time went on, also, some of the leaders of the Republican party declared that its original ideals had become obscured in more practical considerations. They felt that abuses had grown up which had been little noticed because of the necessity of keeping in power that party which they regarded as the only patriotic one. They asserted that many of the managers had become arrogant and corrupt. All this helped to explain the strength of such revolts as that of the Liberal Republican movement of 1872. Nevertheless, during the greater part of the twenty-five years after the war, hosts of Republicans cherished such a picture as that drawn by Senator Hoar and Edward MacPherson, and it was that picture which held them within the party and made patriotism and Republicanism synonymous terms.

Those Republicans, however, who took the more critical attitude toward their party formed the core of the "Mugwump" or Independent movement. Their philosophy was simple. They believed that there ought to be a political element which was not rigidly controlled by the discipline of party organization, which would act upon its own judgment for the public interest, and which should be a reminder to both parties that neither could venture upon mischievous policies without endangering its control over the machinery of government. Theoretically, at least, the Independent believed that it was more important that government be well administered than that it be administered by one set of men or another. The weakness of this group, aside from its small size, was its impatience and impracticability. By nature the Independent was an individualist, forming his own opinion and holding it with tenacity. In such a body there could not be long-continued cooperation or singleness of purpose; each new problem caused new decisions resulting in the break-up of the group and the formation of new alignments. The Independent group, therefore, varied in strength from campaign to campaign. To the typical party worker, who looked upon politics as a warfare for the spoils of office, the Independent was variously denounced as a deserter, a traitor, an apostate and a guerilla deploying between the lines and foraging now on one side and now on the other. To the party wheel-horse, independent voting seemed impracticable, and the atmosphere of reform too "highly scented."

The Democrats, laboring under the disadvantage of a reputation for disloyalty during the war, and kept out of power for most of the time during the period, were forced into a defensive position where they could complain or criticize, but not present a program of constructive achievement. They denounced the election of 1876 as a great "fraud"; they looked upon the Republicans as the organ of those who demanded class advantages; they condemned the party as wasteful, corrupt and extravagant in administration, careless of the distress of the masses, and desirous of increasing the authority of the federal government at the expense of the powers of the states. Their own mission they felt to be the constant assertion of the opposite principles of government and administration. They felt that they in particular represented government by the people for the equal good of all classes. In conformity to what they believed to be the principles of Jefferson and Jackson they professed faith in the capacity of the plain people. They advocated frugality and economy in government expenditure and looked with alarm on any extension of federal power that invaded the traditional domain of local activity.

The intensification of party spirit and party loyalty, which was so typical of the times, "delivered the citizen more effectually, bound hand and foot, into the power of the party embodied in its Organization." The organization, meanwhile, was being improved and strengthened. Its permanent National Committee which had existed from *ante-bellum* days, was supplemented in both parties immediately after the war by the congressional committee, whose mission it was to carry the elections for the House of Representatives. Increased attention was paid to state and local organizations. Party regularity became almost military in its character. Veterans of the war were at a premium as candidates for political office; old soldiers were commonly given the preference for positions in the post offices, custom houses and the like; and a traitor to the party was only less despicable than a traitor to the country. Party conventions in states and counties chose delegates to national conventions and nominated candidates for office. State, county and town committees raised money, employed speakers, distributed literature, formed torch-light companies to march in party processions and, most important of all, got out the voters on election day. By such means the National Committee was enabled to keep in close touch with the rank and file of the party, and so complete did the organization become that it deserved and won the name, "the machine."

The master-spirit of the machine was usually the "Boss," a professional politician who generally did not himself hold elective office or show concern in constructive programs of legislation or in the public welfare. Instead, his interests lay in winning elections; dividing the offices among the party workers; distributing profitable contracts for public work; procuring the passage of legislation desired by industrial or railroad companies, or blocking measures objected to by them. A vivid picture of the activites of the boss in New York, drawn by Elihu Root, will serve to portray conditions in many states and cities from 1865 to 1890:

From the days of Fenton, and Conkling, and Arthur, and Cornell, and Platt, from the days of David B. Hill, down to the present time, the government of the state ·has presented two different lines of activity, one of the constitutional and statutory officers of the state, and the other of the party leaders,— they call them party bosses. They call the system—I do not coin the phrase, I adopt it because it carries its own meaning—the system they call "invisible government." For I do not remember how many years, Mr. Conkling was the supreme ruler in this state; the governor did not count, the legislatures did not count;

comptrollers and secretaries of state and what not, did not count. It was what Mr. Conkling said; and in a great outburst of public rage he was pulled down.

Then Mr. Platt ruled the state; for nigh upon twenty years he ruled it. It was not the governor; it was not the legislature; it was not any elected officers; it was Mr. Platt. And the capitol was not here (in Albany); it was at 49 Broadway; with Mr. Platt and his lieutenants. It makes no difference what name you give, whether you call it Fenton or Conkling or Cornell or Arthur or Platt, or by the names of men now living. The ruler of the state during the greater part of the forty years of my acquaintance with the state government has not been any man authorized by the constitution or by the law.[1]

Under such conditions, corruption was naturally a commonplace in politics. In the campaigns, the party managers were too often men to whom "nothing was dreadful but defeat." At every presidential election, immense sums of money were poured into the most important doubtful states—Connecticut, New York, New Jersey and Indiana. Twenty to seventy-five dollars was said to have been the price of a vote in Indiana in 1880; and ten to fifteen per cent. of the vote in Connecticut was thought to be purchasable. In New York ballot-box stuffing and repeating were the rule in sections of the city. Employers exerted a less crude but equally efficacious pressure upon their employees to vote "right." Municipal government also was often characterized by that extreme of corruption which called out the scorn of writers on public affairs. The New York *Times* complained in 1877 that the government of the city was no more a popular government than Turkish rule in Bulgaria, and that if the Tammany leaders did not collect revenue with the horse-whip and sabre, it was because the forms of law afforded a means that was pleasanter, easier and quite as effective.

Federal officials, it must be admitted, did not set a high

---

[1] *Addresses on Government and Citizenship*, p. 202.

standard for local officers to follow. During Grant's administration five judges of a United States Court were driven from
office by threats of impeachment; members of the Committee
on Military Affairs in the House of Representatives sold their
privilege of selecting young men to be educated at West
Point; and candidates for even the highest offices in the gift
of the nation were sometimes men whose political past would
not bear the light of day. More difficult to overcome was
the lack of a decent sense of propriety among many public
officers. Members of the Senate practiced before the Supreme
Court, the justices of which they had an important share in
appointing; senators and representatives traded in the securities of railroads which were seeking favors at the hands of
Congress; and even in the most critical circles, corrupt practices were condoned on the ground that all the most reputable
people were more or less engaged in similar activities. Most
difficult of all to understand was the unfaltering support accorded by men of the utmost integrity to party leaders whose
evil character was known on all sides. Men who would not
themselves be guilty of dishonest acts and who vehemently
condemned such deeds among their political opponents, failed
to make any energetic protest within their own ranks for fear
that they might bring about a party split and thus give the
"enemy" a victory.

The political practices which prevailed for at least a quarter
of a century after 1865 were notoriously bad. Yet the student of the period must be sensitive to higher aspirations
and better practices among many of the politicians, and
among the rank and file of the people. George F. Hoar,
John Sherman, Rutherford B. Hayes, Grover Cleveland and
many others were incorruptible. The exposure of scandalous
actions on the part of certain high officials blasted their
careers, indicating that the body of the people would not
condone dishonesty, and the parties found it advisable to accept the resignations of some of their more notorious cam-

paign managers. Moreover, the American people of all classes were a political people, with a capacity for political organization and activity, and with a passion for change. The cruder forms of corruption were successfully combated, and the popular, as well as the official sense of good taste and propriety gradually reached higher levels.

Another fundamental political consideration after the Civil War was the gradual reduction of the power of the executive department. During the war the authority exercised by President Lincoln had risen to great heights, partly because of his personal characteristics and partly because the exigencies of the times demanded quick executive action. After the conflict was past, however, the legislative body naturally reasserted itself. Moreover, the quarrel between President Johnson and Congress, as has been shown, took the form of a contest for control over appointments to office and especially over appointments to the cabinet. The resulting impeachment, although it did not result in conviction, brought about a distinct shrinkage in executive prestige. Grant was so inexperienced in politics and so naïve in his judgments of his associates that he fell completely into the power of the machine and failed to revive the former importance and independence of his office.

The ascendancy which thus slipped out of the hands of the executive was seized by the Senate, where it remained for a long period, despite efforts on the part of the president and the House of Representatives to prevent it. So remarkable and continuous a domination is not to be explained by a single formula. The long term of the members of the Senate, the traditional high reputation of the body and the undoubted ability of many of its members assisted in upholding its prestige. Its small size as compared with the House of Representatives gave it greater flexibility. Furthermore, certain Senate practices were instrumental in giving that body its primacy. Under the provisions of the Constitution the

Senate has power to ratify or reject the nominations of the executive to many important positions within his gift, and by the close of reconstruction it had acquired a firm control over such appointments. "Senatorial courtesy" bade every member, regardless of party, to concur with the decision of the senators from any state with regard to the appointments in which they were interested. When, therefore, the executive wished to change conditions in a given office he must have the acquiescence of the senators from the state in which the change was to occur. If he did not, the entire body would rally to the support of their colleagues and refuse to confirm the objectionable nominations. With such a weapon the Senate was usually able to force the executive into submission, or at least to make reforms extremely difficult. In Senator Hoar's suggestive words, senators went to the White House to give advice, not to receive it.

In connection with revenue legislation the Senate seized the leadership by means of an evasion of the Constitution. According to the terms of that document, all bills for raising revenue must originate in the House of Representatives, but the Senate may propose amendments. Relying upon this power the Senate constantly revised measures to the extent of changing their character completely and even of grafting part or all of one proposal upon the title of another. In one case, early in the period, the Senate "amended" a House bill of four lines which repealed the tariff on tea and coffee; the "amendment" consisted of twenty pages, containing a general revision of customs duties and internal revenue taxes. At a later time the Senate Finance Committee drew up a tariff bill even before Congress had assembled.

The primacy of the Senate quickly led to recognition of the value of seats in it. Influential state politicians sought election in order to control the patronage. Competent judges in the early nineties declared, for example, that the senators from New York, Pennsylvania and Maryland were all of this type. Another considerable fraction was composed of powerful business men, directors in large corporations, who found it to their advantage to be in this most influential law-making body and who were known as oil or silver or lumber senators. So was laid the foundation of the complaint that the Senate was a millionaires' club. And so, too, it came about that much of state politics revolved about the choice of members for the upper house, for senators were elected by the state legislatures until long after 1890. The power of the House of Representatives, in contrast with the Senate, was relatively small except during the single session 1889–1891, when Thomas B. Reed was in control, although individual members sometimes wielded considerable influence.

The Interpretation of the War Amendments

Somewhat comparable to the shift in the center of power from one federal authority to another, was the change which took place in the relative strength of the state and national governments. This transfer was most clearly seen in the decisions of the Supreme Court in cases involving the Fourteenth Amendment.

Previous to 1868, when the Amendment became part of the Constitution, comparatively little state legislation relating to private property had been reviewed by the Court. Ever since the establishment of the federal government, cases involving the constitutionality of state legislation had been appealed to United States Courts when they had been objected to as running counter to the clauses of the Constitution forbidding states to enact bills of attainder, *ex post facto* laws, or laws impairing the obligation of contracts. Their number, however, had been relatively small, and normally the acts of state legislatures had not been reviewed by federal courts; or in other words the tendency had been to preserve the individuality and strength of the several states. After the war, the Fourteenth and Fifteenth Amendments placed additional prohibitions on the states, and the decisions of the Supreme Court determined the meaning and extent of the added pro-' visions. The interpretation of the Fourteenth Amendment was especially important. Most significant was the interpretation of Section I, which reads as follows:

All persons born or naturalized in the United States, and subject to the jurisdiction thereof, are citizens of the United States and of the State wherein they reside. No State shall make or enforce any law which shall abridge the privileges and immunities of citizens of the United States; nor shall any State deprive any person of life, liberty, or property, without due process of law; nor deny to any person within its jurisdiction the equal protection of the laws.

So vague and inclusive were these phases that many important questions immediately sprang from them. What were the privileges and immunities of the citizen? Did those of the citizen of the United States differ from those of the citizen of a state? Was a corporation a person? What was liberty? What was due process of law? Hitherto the protection of life, liberty and property had rested, in the main, upon the individual states, and cases involving these subjects had been decided by state courts. Were the state courts to be superseded, in relation to these vital subjects, by the United States Supreme Court?

It has already been shown that the purpose of the Fourteenth Amendment was the protection of the recently freed negro. The Thirteenth Amendment had forbidden slavery, but the southern states had passed apprentice and vagrancy laws which reduced the negro to a condition closely resembling slavery in certain of its aspects. The Fourteenth Amendment was designed to remedy such a condition by forbidding the states to abridge the privileges of citizens, or to deprive persons of life, liberty or property. Were the very vague phrases of the Amendment merely in keeping with the vagueness of many of the other grants of power in the Constitution, or were they designedly expressed in such a way as to accomplish something more than the protection of the freedman?

The first decision of the Supreme Court involving the Amendment was that given in the Slaughter House Cases in 1873, which did not concern the negro in any way. In 1869 the legislature of Louisiana had given a corporation in that state the exclusive right to slaughter cattle within a large area, and had forbidden other persons to construct slaughter-houses within the limits of this region; but the corporation had to allow any other persons to use its buildings and equipment, charging fixed fees for the privilege. Cases were brought before the courts to determine whether the statute violated that part of the Fourteenth Amendment which forbids a state to pass any act abridging the privileges of citizens and taking away their property without due process of law. By a vote of five to four the Supreme Court upheld the constitutionality of the statute.

In the first place the majority held that the purpose of the Amendment was primarily the protection of the negro. This purpose, the Court thought, lay at the foundation of all three of the war amendments and without it no one of them would ever have been suggested. The majority did not believe that the Congress which passed the amendments or the state legislatures which ratified them intended to transfer the protection of the great body of civil rights from the states to the federal government.

The Court then proceeded to draw a distinction between the rights of citizens of the United States, and the rights of citizens of a state. The individual, according to the decision, has one body of rights as a citizen of the nation—such as the right of petition, the right to use the navigable rivers, and to be protected by the federal government on the high seas and in foreign lands. He has another series of rights as a citizen of a state—such as the right to acquire and possess property and to pursue and obtain happiness and safety, subject to such restraints as the government may prescribe for the general good. Now the language of the amendment in regard to these latter privileges is significant: No State shall make or enforce any law which shall abridge the privileges or immunites *of citizens of the United States.* In other words, the Court declared, the states are forbidden to trespass upon those rights which the individual possesses *as a federal citizen.* It was not the intention of the amendment to "constitute this court a perpetual censor upon all legislation of the States, on the civil rights of their own citizens."

Neither did the Court believe that "due process of law" had been interfered with by the Louisiana legislation. In reply to the objection that the slaughter-house law violated the clause, "nor shall any State deny to any person within its jurisdiction the equal protection of the laws," the majority declared:

We doubt very much whether any action of a State not directed by way of discrimination against the negroes as a class, or on account of their race, will ever be held to come within the purview of this provision.

In brief, then, the majority was inclined to preserve the balance between the states and the national government very much as it had been. It believed that the amendments should be applied mainly if not wholly to the fortunes of the freedman and that judicial review of such legislation as that in Louisiana concerning the slaughter of cattle should end in the state courts.

For a time the interpretation of the Court remained that given by the majority in this decision. When western state legislatures passed laws regulating the rates which railroads and some other corporations might legally charge for their services, the Court at first showed an inclination to allow the states a free hand. Regulation of this sort, it was held, did not deprive the citizen or the corporation of property without due process of law. It is doubtless safe to say that hundreds of important statutes in all the states were saved by this decision from being declared unconstitutional and invalid. The theory of local control over the great body of human activities was firmly woven into American judicial practice, leaving to the federal courts the protection of the smaller body of distinctly federal privileges and immunities.

The Slaughter House cases, however, were decided by the narrow margin of five to four, and as time elapsed it became apparent that the opinion might undergo a transformation. An interesting prelude to the change was an argument by Roscoe Conkling in San Mateo County v. Southern Pacific Railroad Company in 1882. Conkling was acting as attorney for the railroad and was attempting to show that the roads were protected, by the Fourteenth Amendment, from state laws which taxed their property unduly. Conkling argued that the Amendment had not been designed merely for the protection of the freedman, and in order to substantiate his contention, he produced a manuscript copy of the journal of the Congressional committee that had drawn up the proposals which later became the Fourteenth Amendment. He had himself been a member of the committee. The journal, it should be noticed, had never hitherto been utilized in public.

Conkling stated that at the time when the Amendment was being drafted, individuals and companies were appealing for congressional protection against state taxation laws, and that it had been the purpose of the committee to frame an amendment which should protect whites as well as blacks and operate in behalf of corporations as well as individuals. In other words, Conkling was making the interesting contention that his committee had had a far wider and deeper purpose in mind in phrasing the Amendment than had been commonly understood and that the demand for the protection of the negro from harsh southern legislation had been utilized to answer the request of business for federal assistance. The safety of the negro was put to the fore; the purpose of the committee to strengthen the legal position of the corporations was kept behind the doors of the committee-room; and the phrases of the Amendment had been designedly made general in order to accomplish both purposes. The sequel appeared four years later, in 1886, when the case Santa Clara County v. Southern Pacific Railroad brought the question before the Court. At this time Mr. Chief Justice Waite announced the opinion of himself and his colleagues that a corporation was a "person" within the meaning of the Amendment and thus entitled to its protection.

Later decisions, such as that of 1889 in Chicago, Milwaukee and St. Paul Railway Company v. Minnesota, left no doubt of the fact that the Court had come to look upon the Fourteenth Amendment as much more than a protective device for the negro. The full meaning of the change, however, did not appear until after 1890, and is a matter for later consideration. In brief, then, before 1890, the Supreme Court was content in the main to avoid the review of state legislation concerning the ownership and control of private property, a practice which lodged great powers in the state courts and legislatures. By that year, however, it was manifest that the Court had undergone a complete change and that it had adopted a theory which would greatly enlarge the functions of the federal courts, at the expense of the states. The medium through which the change had come was the Fourteenth Amendment.

THE PREVAILING ECONOMIC THEORIES

The demand on the part of business men for protection from state legislation, which Rosco Conkling described in the

San Mateo case, arose from their belief in the economic doctrine of *laissez faire*. Believers in this theory looked upon legislation which regulated business as a species of meddling or interference. The individual, they thought, should be allowed to do very much as he pleased, entering into whatever business he wished, and buying and selling where and how and at what prices suited his interests, stimulated and controlled by competition, but without direction or restriction by the government. It was believed that the amazing success of the American business pioneer was proof of the wisdom of the *laissez faire* philosophy. The economic giant and hero was the self-made man.

Economic abuses, according to the *laissez faire* philosophy, would normally be corrected by economic law, chiefly through competition. If, for illustration, any industry demanded greater returns for its products than proved to be just in the long run, unattached capital would be attracted into that line of production, competition would ensue, prices would be again lowered and justice would result. Every business man would exert himself to discover that employment which would bring greatest return for the capital which he had at his command. He would therefore choose such an industry and so direct it as to make his product of the greatest value possible. Hence although he sought his own interests, he would in fact promote the interest of the public.

Indeed the philosopher of *laissez faire* was sincerely convinced that his system ultimately benefited society as a whole. Andrew Carnegie, an iron and steel manufacturer, presented this thesis in an article in the *North American Review* in 1889. The reign of individualism, he held, was the order of the day, was inevitable and desirable. Under it the poorer classes were better off than they had ever been in the world's history. "We start then," he said, "with a condition of affairs under which the best interests of the race are promoted, but which inevitably gives wealth to the few. Thus far, accepting conditions as they exist, the situation can be surveyed and pronounced good.'' Let the man of ability, he advised, accumulate a large fortune and then discharge his duty to the public through philanthropic enterprises, such as the foundation of libraries. Society would be more highly benefited in this way than by allowing the millions to circulate in small sums through the hands of the masses. Statistical studies of the distribution of wealth seemed to justify Carnegie's judgment that the existing tendency was for wealth to settle into the hands of the few. In 1893 it was estimated that three one-hundredths of one per cent. of the people owned twenty per cent. of the nation's wealth.

Although the *laissez faire* theory was dominant later even than 1890, it was apparent before that time that its sway was being challenged. The adherents of *laissez faire* themselves did not desire to have the doctrine applied fully and evenly. They demanded government protection for their enterprises through the medium of high protective import tariffs, and they sought subsidies and grants of public land for the railroads. Naturally it was not long before the classes whose desires conflicted with the manufacturing and railroad interests began in their turn to seek aid from the government. The people of the Middle West, for example, were not content to allow the railroad companies to control their affairs and establish their rates without let or hindrance from the state legislatures. The factory system in the Northeast, likewise, raised questions which were directed toward the foundations of *laissez faire*. Under the factory régime employers found it advantageous to open their doors to women and children and to keep them at machines for long, hard days which unfitted the women for domestic duties and for raising families, and which stunted the children in body and mind. Out of these circumstances arose a demand for restrictions on the freedom of employers to fix the conditions under which their employees worked.

Opposition to an industrial system based upon *laissez faire* would have been even greater during the seventies and eighties if it had not been for two sources of national wealth— the public lands and the supplies of lumber, ore, coal and similar gifts of nature. When the supply of land in the West was substantially unlimited, a sufficient part of the population could relieve its economic distresses by migrating, as multitudes did. Such huge stores of natural wealth were being discovered that there seemed to be no end to them. But in the late eighties when the best public lands were nearly exhausted and the need of more careful husbanding of the national resources became apparent to far-sighted men, advanced thinkers began to question the validity of an economic theory which allowed quite so much freedom to individuals. For the time, however, such questions did not arise in the minds of the masses.

As the *laissez faire* doctrine underlay the problem of the relation between government and industry, so the quantity theory of money was fundamental in the monetary question. According to the quantity theory, money is like any other commodity in that its value rises and falls with variations in the supply and demand for it. Suppose, for example, that a given community is entirely isolated from the rest of the world. It possesses precisely enough pieces of money to satisfy the needs of its people. Suddenly the number of pieces is doubled. The supply is twice as great as business requires. If no new elements enter into the situation, the value of each piece becomes half as great as before "its purchasing power is cut in two" and prices double.[2] A bushel of potatoes that formerly sold for a dollar now sells at two dollars. A farmer who has mortgaged his farm for $1,000 and who relies upon his sales of potatoes to pay off his debt is highly benefited by the change, while the creditor is cor-

[2] In practice, new elements do enter into the situation so that the theory requires much qualification. *Cf.* Taussig, *Principles of Economics* (1915), I, ch. 18.

respondingly harmed. The debtor is obliged to raise only half as many potatoes; the creditor receives money that buys half the commodities that could have been purchased with his money at the time of the loan.

On the other hand, suppose the number of pieces of money is instantly halved, and all other factors continue unchanged. There is now twice as great a demand for each piece, it becomes more desirable and will purchase more goods. Prices, that is to say, go down. Dollar potatoes now sell for fifty cents. The debtor farmer must grow twice as many potatoes as he had contemplated; the creditor finds that he receives money that has doubled in purchasing power.

It has already been said that the quarter century after the war was, in the main, a period of falling prices. The farmer found the size of his mortgage, as measured in bushels of wheat and potatoes, growing steadily and relentlessly greater. The creditor received a return which purchased larger and larger quantities of commodities. The debtor class was mainly in the West; the creditors, mainly in the East. The westerners desired a larger quantity of money which would, as they believed, send prices upward; the East, depending upon similar reasoning, desired a contraction in supply. The former were called inflationists; the latter, contractionists. Much of the monetary history of the country after the Civil War was concerned with the attempt of the inflationists to expand the supply of currency, and the contractionists to prevent inflation.

The Intellectual and Cultural Background

The intellectual and cultural background of the thirty-five years after the war, so far as it can be considered at this point, was to be found mainly in the development of the school, the church and the newspaper.

The Civil War undoubtedly checked the expansion of the

American school system, both in the North and in the South, —more seriously in the latter. Upon the cessation of hostilities, the former Confederate states made immediate plans for the reconstruction of their shattered educational organization. Schools were to be repaired and rebuilt, money raised, and in general the ante-bellum standards reestablished or surpassed. Unhappily, however, the plans remained merely —plans. The needed funds were not forthcoming. In North Carolina, in 1870, to cite a single but typical case, only $40,-000 appear to have been expended in behalf of education. In the same year and in the same state, only one child in eleven of school age was actually enrolled. The school buildings were all too frequently pitiable shacks, unsanitary and in disrepair. It is the considered opinion of Professor E. W. Knight of the University of North Carolina, after long study of the situation, that public school facilities in the South did not recover their earlier standards until 1900, and even at that time conditions in some places suffered by comparison with 1860. The average value of southern public school buildings in 1900 was estimated at the astonishingly low figure of $100.

"Most of the perplexing problems which confront public education in the South today," says Professor Knight, "grew out of the mistakes of reconstruction." The war, of course, had left the South impoverished, lacking leaders, discouraged and insecure. Well-meant efforts were made by the Freedmen's Bureau and by northern individuals and associations to extend the benefits of education to the late slaves. It is not agreed, however, on all sides that these missionary efforts were successful. Too often founded on the idea that the negro could be intellectually emancipated by precisely the same sort of book-learning that the white youth of the North received, the educational crusade failed to commend itself to the more conservative element of the South. Then came political reconstruction with its appalling accompaniment of

ignorance, prejudice and corruption. Insecure in their political institutions, the southern states dreaded to add to the
already intolerable tax burden by making appropriations for
schools, feeling all too sure that such funds if they were
raised would only go to fill the pockets of the despoilers. In
the mid-seventies, moreover, Charles Sumner's proposed civil
rights bill was being discussed in Congress. Among its provisions was one compelling the South to give the negro equal
rights with the whites in schools. Although this clause was
omitted from the act as passed in 1875, the southern states
feared that mixed schools might be forced upon them, and in
many cases they would have preferred no schools whatever to
schools in which white and negro children sat side by side.
To the poverty and discouragement of the war, therefore,
were added the extortion and disheartenment of the reconstruction era,—and education in the South was set back a
full generation.

The most helpful effort made by the North in aid of public
education in the South was the Peabody Educational Fund of
$2,000,000 established by George Peabody in 1867. Under
the able leadership of Dr. Barnas Sears, former president of
Brown University, the income of the Fund was wisely expended in states and communities which were ready to supplement the benefaction by funds of their own. During the
first ten years, nearly one million dollars were distributed,
and proved a great stimulus to the revival of the public school
system.[3]

The effect of the war on education in the North was
naturally far less severe, and the recovery more quickly
brought about. Not only did the rapidly increasing wealth
of the North make the expansion of the public school system
possible, but several other powerful forces worked toward the
same end. Such a force was the rapid urbanization of the

[3] On this subject, see two excellent volumes by Professor E. W.
Knight: *Public Education in North Carolina* (1916); and *Public
Education in the South* (1922).

Northeast,—a condition favorable to the demand for good schools. The demand for women operatives in the factories and for women typists, clerks, accountants and school teachers called them away from the traditional household service, and out into the more rapid currents of life. A natural next step was the demand for education for girls on a par with boys. Moreover, one of the demands of the growing labor unions was a public, tax-supported school system where the children of the poorer classes might be given an opportunity somewhat comparable to that which their more fortunate fellows received.[4] The immigrant stream, growing continually larger, and increasingly composed of the illiterate and less easily assimilable southern and eastern Europeans seemed to call for the free public school if only as a measure of public safety.

The major changes in American education between 1865 and 1900 are easily distinguishable. A comparison of the census of 1900 with that of 1870 indicates that the number of pupils in the public schools more than doubled (from 6,900,-000 to 15,500,000), and that expenditures more than tripled (from $63,000,000 to $215,000,000). In the former year, fifty-seven per cent. of the children of school age were actually enrolled, while in the latter year seventy-two per cent. were on the books. The American youth, then, was at least being exposed to the elementary educational process. Along with the increasing army of pupils went the demand for better trained teachers. The first state normal school, that at Lexington, Massachusetts, was followed by twelve others in nine states before the Civil War. Afterwards the growth was more rapid, particularly between 1870 and 1900. A byproduct was the replacement of men teachers in the elementary schools by women.

---

[4] Perhaps it would be more accurate to say that the working classes had fought this good fight before the Civil War, and were now harvesting the results.

The public high school, supported by taxation and supplied in many places with free text-books was likewise a characteristic feature of the thirty-five years following the war. Although established in some states a generation before the war, the high school did not come to its maturity until the last quarter of the century. Between 1890 and 1900 the number of students increased from 203,000 to 519,000. The curriculum of the schools reflected the new generation with its manual training, domestic arts, book-keeping, typewriting and other supplements to the older subjects of study.

In the higher ranges, the modifications were equally noticeable. The demand for education for women had shown itself in the founding of the Emma Willard Seminary at Troy in 1821 and the Mt. Holyoke Seminary in 1837. It continued to be felt as other colleges strictly for women were founded, and some of the older colleges for men opened to them, or new ones established on the co-educational basis. The colleges of the colonial type had been entirely for men, and mainly under the direction of sectarian organizations. The newer states met the new situation by the development of the state university,—supported by the public regardless of religious affiliations and open to all properly qualified students, men and women alike. The most important legislative factor in this process was the Morrill Act of July 2, 1862, which provided for a grant to each state of 30,000 acres of public land for every senator and representative in Congress to which the state was entitled. The land was to be used to promote education in the agricultural and mechanic arts, and in the natural sciences. The advantages of the law were quickly seen, and between 1865 and 1890, seventeen state universities were founded, most of them in the Middle and Far West. Many of these underwent a phenomenal growth and had a great influence on the states in which they were established. More colleges, indeed, were founded between 1865 and 1900 than in all the previous years in the country's history.

It is highly difficult, if not impossible, to estimate the power and effect of organized religion—the American church—on the history of the United States during the thirty-five years from 1865 to 1900. Too many of the studies made of this subject have been narrowly sectarian, or concerned chiefly with proving that one creed or another was the correct and popular one. It is possible, nevertheless, to indicate in a very general way a few of the major forces which were at work on American religious life.

The tendency of religious groups to divide and subdivide is no new fact in the religious history either of the world as a whole or of the United States in particular. Just previous to the Civil War there were about 100 separate church groups; in 1900 there were approximately 150. Sometimes the divisions represented genuine differences in creed, as between Quakers and Episcopalians; sometimes, merely color as in the case of the negro and the white Methodist churches, or geography as in the case of the northern and southern branches of the Baptist church; sometimes the establishment of a new type of thought like Christian Science. Immigration distinctly affected the religious situation, either enlarging an establishment already in America, as the Irish and Germans strengthened the Catholic church, or founding new ones like the Russian, Austrian, Danish, Welsh and other sects. A very slight compensating tendency is observable in the attempts of churches which divided into northern and southern branches over the slavery question to unite their forces. In general, however, the attempts seem not to have amounted to much. As regards the number of communicants in the American churches between 1865 and 1900, the information is none too clear or reliable. On the whole, it is certainly true that the absolute number greatly increased, and in all probability increased, in proportion, more rapidly than the population.

More characteristic of the generation after the Civil War was the clash between the traditional American creeds and practices on the one hand, and modern economic and scientific life on the other. So far-reaching was this impact that it deserves more attention in general and in detail than it has ever experienced at the hands of American students. If it were possible to fix an exact date and a single event as the beginning of the conflict, the date would doubtless be 1859 and the event the publication of Charles Darwin's *Origin of Species*. The concept of an evolutionary process had long been in the air, and yet the theories of Darwin came into the American theological world "like a plough into an ant-hill." Man, it appeared, was not an instantaneous creation in the hands of an All Powerful, but the outcome of an infinitely slow and orderly process of development, a process which extended back for countless ages, was still operating, and seemed likely to continue to operate for indefinite ages to come. "If this hypothesis be true," asserted an American clergyman, "then is the Bible an unbearable fiction, . . . then have we Christians for nearly two thousand years been duped by a monstrous lie."

Then the geologists. Their evidence, they said, indicated that the formation of the universe had likewise consumed countless ages, that vast periods of time had elapsed while the crust of the earth was cooling, its mountain ranges being thrust upwards, and its valleys being engraved by the erosion of numberless rains and spring freshets. Not different were the conclusions of many astronomers, archæologists, anthropologists and geographers in their individual scientific fields. Modern scholarship seemed to marshal a devastating attack on those early pages of the book of Genesis which describe the earth and mankind as originating within the space of a week at a divine fiat.

It was about the mid-century likewise that the higher critics began their quiet assault on what seemed to be the citadel

of organized religion in America,—nam
validity of the Bible. On the basis of histo
scientific discoveries, and internal evidence
Bible itself, the critics undertook the car
study of the Old Testament. Did Moses wri
erally ascribed to him? Did any single
Pentateuch? Were the pages of the Old Te
to be a veracious historical record dictated b
were they an account of the religious theorie
of the Hebrew people? Their conclusions
pact of the new scientific hypotheses. Mos
did not write all that was accorded to him ; t
was not an historical chronicle but a hym
were collected the expression of religious th
of centuries of Jewish life; Job was a fable
to illustrate and teach religious truth, rathe
exactly the words and deeds of historical char

The hypotheses of the scientists and hig
perhaps, popularized more fully in the U
Robert G. Ingersoll than by any other person
a powerful orator, and an able lawyer, lectur
speaker. Shrewd, witty and a born iconoc
the theories of the doctors to the level of
street. "Some Mistakes of Moses," for
popular lecture which attempted ruthlessly to
books of the Bible to the touch of recent s
"How many beasts, fowls and creeping thi
Ingersoll, "did Noah take into the ark ? . .
get there? Did the polar bear leave his
journey toward the tropics? How did he
ark was? . . . What had these animals to e
journey? What did they eat while in the
on, applying to every detail of the Biblical st
of its reasonableness.

The response to the scientists and the pop

More characteristic of the generation after the Civil War was the clash between the traditional American creeds and practices on the one hand, and modern economic and scientific life on the other. So far-reaching was this impact that it deserves more attention in general and in detail than it has ever experienced at the hands of American students. If it were possible to fix an exact date and a single event as the beginning of the conflict, the date would doubtless be 1859 and the event the publication of Charles Darwin's *Origin of Species*. The concept of an evolutionary process had long been in the air, and yet the theories of Darwin came into the American theological world "like a plough into an ant-hill." Man, it appeared, was not an instantaneous creation in the hands of an All Powerful, but the outcome of an infinitely slow and orderly process of development, a process which extended back for countless ages, was still operating, and seemed likely to continue to operate for indefinite ages to come. "If this hypothesis be true," asserted an American clergyman, "then is the Bible an unbearable fiction, . . . then have we Christians for nearly two thousand years been duped by a monstrous lie."

Then the geologists. Their evidence, they said, indicated that the formation of the universe had likewise consumed countless ages, that vast periods of time had elapsed while the crust of the earth was cooling, its mountain ranges being thrust upwards, and its valleys being engraved by the erosion of numberless rains and spring freshets. Not different were the conclusions of many astronomers, archæologists, anthropologists and geographers in their individual scientific fields. Modern scholarship seemed to marshal a devastating attack on those early pages of the book of Genesis which describe the earth and mankind as originating within the space of a week at a divine fiat.

It was about the mid-century likewise that the higher critics began their quiet assault on what seemed to be the citadel

of organized religion in America,—namely the textual
validity of the Bible. On the basis of historical records, new
scientific discoveries, and internal evidence supplied by the
Bible itself, the critics undertook the careful and critical
study of the Old Testament. Did Moses write the books generally ascribed to him? Did any single hand write the
Pentateuch? Were the pages of the Old Testament intended
to be a veracious historical record dictated by Omniscence, or
were they an account of the religious theories and aspirations
of the Hebrew people? Their conclusions added to the impact of the new scientific hypotheses. Moses, they believed,
did not write all that was accorded to him; the book of David
was not an historical chronicle but a hymn-book in which
were collected the expression of religious thought and faith
of centuries of Jewish life; Job was a fable or story designed
to illustrate and teach religious truth, rather than to record
exactly the words and deeds of historical characters.

The hypotheses of the scientists and higher critics were,
perhaps, popularized more fully in the United States by
Robert G. Ingersoll than by any other person. Ingersoll was
a powerful orator, and an able lawyer, lecturer and campaign
speaker. Shrewd, witty and a born iconoclast, he brought
the theories of the doctors to the level of the man on the
street. "Some Mistakes of Moses," for example, was a
popular lecture which attempted ruthlessly to bring the early
books of the Bible to the touch of recent scientific theory.
"How many beasts, fowls and creeping things," demanded
Ingersoll, "did Noah take into the ark? . . . How did they
get there? Did the polar bear leave his field of ice and
journey toward the tropics? How did he know where the
ark was? . . . What had these animals to eat while on the
journey? What did they eat while in the ark?" And so
on, applying to every detail of the Biblical story the question
of its reasonableness.

The response to the scientists and the popularizers was a

religious controversy which lasted for decades, and indeed is far from ended yet. Proponents of the two sides combatted one another in the columns of the periodicals. Clergymen who adopted the newer theories were tried for heresy.[5] Faith in the Bible, in the creeds, in the organization of the church, in religion itself was shaken to the heart.

Nor was this the entire assault of modern civilization on organized religion. The shift of the population from the rural districts to the cities depleted the country churches, the bulwarks of substantial conservatism. In the city, the "meeting-house" was less the center of all life than it had been in the town and village. European immigrants, with their un-American idea of Sunday observance, and the growth of athletic sports tended to make the seventh day less a Sabbath and more a holiday. Economic prosperity decreased the privations of people, and made less necessary a refuge in a loving and protecting Omnipotence. The hordes of native and immigrant laborers, finding the church not alive to their distress and ambitions gradually fell away from its ministrations.

Organized religion, therefore, faced no less momentous a task than the re-definition of religion itself; the separation of the basic and essential beliefs from the accidental and trivial; a new evaluation of the Bible; and a revision of the duties and possibilities of the church as an institution.[6]

The answers of the numerous sects and the several parts of the country were, of course, as diverse as, in the nature of the case, they could well be. One experiment was the frank renewal of the interest in the religion of the fathers by means of camp and revival meetings of the old-fashioned type. Dwight L. Moody as the preacher and Ira D. Sankey as the musical director made an extremely effective pair of evan-

---

[5] See for example the Andover trial in Tucker, *My Generation*, chap. vii; *cf.* Rainsford, *Story of a Varied Life*, pp. 176–177.
[6] *Cf.* Tucker, *My Generation*, chap. 1.

gelists who were heard and heeded by thousands, if not hundreds of thousands.

The most characteristic note, however, was struck by several organizations whose aim was less the saving of souls for a coming eternity, and more the alleviation of distress during the present. One of the earliest of these was the United States Christian Commission which was formed during the Civil War. Its main purpose was the unification of the Christian people of the country in behalf of the men of every state who had gone into the war, not merely by conducting religious services, but by helping to care for the wounded, and taking comforts to the soldiers everywhere.

The Young Men's Christian Association, which gave the impetus to the Christian Commission, had been founded previous to the Civil War, but its great growth and importance came afterwards. In 1870 its membership was 51,000, but growth during the eighties was extraordinary and by 1900 it had 255,000 names on its rolls. At first it acted as an adjunct to the church, being designed to stimulate a religious life among men and boys. In the main it was inter-denominational, including in its ranks men of most Protestant sects. Under the stimulus of the new era, it began to take on new functions. It gave courses of lectures and entertainments; it held classes in which industrial and other instruction was given; it developed indoor games, like basketball; and it built gymnasiums and conducted classes in physical exercise. By 1900, indeed, more men were enrolled in the "gym" classes than in the educational and Bible classes combined.

A score of organizations for young people followed the lead of the Y. M. C. A. Perhaps the most extraordinary of these was the Young People's Society of Christian Endeavor —the "Y. P. S. C. E."—which had a combined social and religious purpose. Although not founded until 1881 (by the Rev. F. E. Clark, in Portland, Maine), it had 253 societies in 1885; 15,500 in 1890; and 42,221 in 1900, with an estimated membership of 2,111,050.

The new note then was the socialization of the church—harnessing its power to all the needs of society. The settlement house carried the new note into a new field.[7] Like the settlement house in its general purpose was the "institutional church." Here the social, educational or relief work definitely centered about the church building. It attempted to demonstrate the interest of the church in the physical and intellectual needs of people, as well as in their spiritual welfare. Accordingly church buildings or new buildings constructed for the purpose were utilized for kindergartens, educational classes for adults, gymnasiums and the like, and employees or members of the church were sent out into the neighborhood to find and relieve need wherever found, and regardless of creed or nationality. The socialization of the church, then, was an important part of its response to the challenge of the new order.

The newspaper press was also undergoing a transformation in the quarter century after the war. The great expansion of the numbers and influence of American newspapers before and during that struggle had been due to the ability of individuals. James Gordon Bennett had founded the New York *Herald*, for example, in 1835, and from then on the *Herald* had been "Bennett's paper." Similarly the *Tribune* had represented Horace Greeley and the *Times*, Henry J. Raymond. The war affected the newspapers, as it did so many other American institutions. Metropolitan papers, in order to keep pace with their competitors, had to maintain representatives at the front. The amount of telegraphic news increased from two or three columns to as many pages. Sunday editions were demanded. Circulation figures increased rapidly. Technical resources for the gathering of news had to be expanded and

[7] *Cf.* p. 433.

systematized, expenditures were greater, and more men cooperated in the publication of a single issue.

Raymond died in 1869, Greeley and Bennett in 1872; and
although the *Sun* was the embodiment of Charles A. Dana
until his death in 1897, the *Nation* and the *Evening
Post* of Edwin L. Godkin until 1899, nevertheless the tendency was away from the newspaper which reflected an individual and toward that which represented a group; away
from the editorial which expressed the views of a well-known
writer, to the editorial page which combined the labors of
many anonymous contributors. The financial basis of the
newspaper also underwent a transition. As advertising became more and more general, the revenues of newspapers
tended to depend more on the favor of the advertiser than
upon the subscriber, giving the former a powerful although
indirect influence on editorial policies.

The influence of the press in politics was rapidly growing.
A larger number of newspapers became sufficiently independent to attack abuses in both parties. The New York *Times*
and Thomas Nast's cartoons in *Harper's Weekly* were most
important factors in the overthrow of the Tweed Ring in New
York City, and in the elections of 1884 and later, newspapers
exerted an unusual power. Press associations in New York
and the West led the way to the Associated Press, with its
wide-spread cooperative resources for gathering news.

As important as the character of the press, was the amount
and distribution of its circulation. Between 1870 and 1890
the number of newspapers published and the aggregate circulation increased almost exactly threefold—about five times
as fast as the population was growing. In the latter year
the entire circulation for the country was over four and a
half billion copies, of which about sixty per cent. were dailies.
So great had been the growth of the press during the seventies
that the census authorities in 1880 made a careful study of
the statistical aspects of the subject. It appeared from this

search that newspapers were published in 2,073 of the 2,605 counties in the Union. Without some such means of spreading information, it would have been impossible to conduct the great presidential campaigns, in which the entire country was educated in the tariff and other important issues.

The expansion of the press is well exemplified by the use of the telegraph in the spread of information. When Lincoln was nominated for the presidency in 1860, a single telegraph operator was able to send out all the press matter supplied to him. In 1892, at the Democratic convention, the Western Union Telegraph Company had one hundred operators in the hall. Mechanical invention, meanwhile, was able to keep pace with the demand for news. The first Hoe press of 1847 had been so improved by 1871 that it printed ten to twelve thousand eight-page papers in an hour, and twenty-five years later the capacity had been increased between six and sevenfold.

BIBLIOGRAPHICAL NOTE

Nearly all material on party history is so partisan that it should be read with critical skepticism: Francis Curtis, *The Republican Party*, 1854–1904 (2 vols., 1904); J. D. Long, *Republican Party* (1888); for the Independent attitude, consult *Harper's Weekly* during the campaign of 1884. As the Republicans were in power most of the time from 1865–1913, there is more biographical and autobiographical material about Republicans than about Democratic leaders. Local studies of political conditions and the social structure of the parties are almost entirely lacking. On the personal side, the following are essential: G. F. Parker, *Writings and Speeches of Grover Cleveland* (1892); T. E. Burton, *John Sherman* (1906); J. B. Foraker, *Notes of a Busy Life* (2 vols., 1916), throws light on the ideals and practices of a politician; G. F. Hoar, *Autobiography of Seventy Years* (2 vols., 1903), gives the New England Republican point of view; Rollo Ogden, *Life and Letters of E. L. Godkin* (2 vols., 1907); G. F. Parker, *Recollections of Grover Cleveland* (1909), is useful, but sketchy; R. M. McElroy, *Grover Cleveland, the Man and the Statesman*

(2 vols., 1923); T. C. Platt, *Autobiography* (1910), interestingly portrays the philosophy of a machine politician, but should be read with care; John Sherman, *Recollections of Forty Years in House, Senate and Cabinet* (2 vols., 1895); Edward Stanwood, *James G. Blaine* (1905), is highly favorable to Blaine; W. M. Stewart, *Reminiscences* (1908), is interesting, partisan, and unreliable. For a general estimate of the autobiographical material of the period, consult *History Teachers' Magazine* (later the *Historical Outlook*), "Recent American History Through the Actors' Eyes," March, 1916.

Jesse Macy, *Party Organization and Machinery* (1904); M. G. Ostrogorski, *Democracy and Political Parties* (2 vols., 1902), gives a keen and pessimistic account of American political practices in vol. II; J. A. Woodburn, *Political Parties and Party Problems in the United States* (1903, and later editions) gives a succinct account in good temper.

For the Fourteenth Amendment: C. G. Haines, *American Doctrine of Judicial Supremacy* (1914); C. W. Collins, *The Fourteenth Amendment and the States* (1912 is a careful study, which is critical of the prevailing later interpretation of the Amendment. The Slaughter House case, giving the earlier interpretation is in J. W. Wallace, *Cases argued and adjudged in the Supreme Court* (Supreme Court Reports), XVI, 36.

L. H. Haney, *History of Economic Thought* (1911), on *laissez faire*. J. L. Laughlin, *Principles of Money* (1903); and Irving Fisher, *Why is the Dollar Shrinking?* (1914), present two sides of the quantity theory of money.

An outstanding interpretation of the religious history of the thirty years following 1865 is W. J. Tucker, *My Generation* (1919); see also J. Hastings, Ed., *Encyclopedia of Religion and Ethics* (12 vols., 1922); A. D. White, *Warfare of Science with Theology in Christendom* (2 vols., 1896); W. S. Rainsford, *Story of a Varied Life* (1922); H. K. Carroll, *Religious Forces of the United States* (1912); R. G. Ingersoll, *Works* (Dresden ed., 12 vols., 1902); L. W. Bacon, *History of American Christianity* (1916); H. K. Rowe, *History of Religion in the United States* (1924); F. E. Clark, *Memories of Many Men in Many Lands* (1922). The periodicals of the seventies and eighties contain numerous articles on the evolution controversy. *The Annual Cyclopædia* is a mine of information about the activities of the several sects.

The growth of newspapers is described in *The Bookman*, XIV, 567–584, XV, 26–44; see also Rollo Ogden, *Life and Letters of Godkin*, already mentioned; G. H. Payne, *History of Journalism in the United States* (1920); J. M. Lee, *History of American Journalism* (1917); G. Pollak, *Fifty Years of American Idealism: the New York Nation, 1865–1915* (1915); E. Davis, *History of the New York Times 1851–1921* (1921); A. Nevins, *The Evening Post, A Century of Journalism* (1922); R. Hooker, *The Story of an Independent Newspaper* (the Springfield *Republican*) (1924); O. G. Villard, *Some Newspapers and Newspaper Men* (1923).

On education: F. P. Graves, *A History of Education in Modern Times* (1913); E. G. Dexter, *History of Education in the United States* (1904); E. P. Cubberley, *Public Education in the United States* (1919); E. W. Knight, *Public Education in the South* (1922). In recent years many of the colleges have published more or less elaborate histories. These naturally are concerned mainly with accounts of buildings and local celebrities, but give ample data on general collegiate tendencies. See, for example: T. W. Goodspeed, *A History of the University of Chicago* (1916); J. K. Lord, *History of Dartmouth College* (vol. II, 1913); B. E. Powell, *University of Illinois* (vol. I, 1918); G. F. Smythe, *Kenyon College* (1924); K. P. Battle, *University of North Carolina* (vol. I, 1907); *Ohio State University*, T. C. Mendenhall, ed. (vol. I, 1920); W. H. S. Demarest, *Rutgers College* (1924); E. L. Green, *University of South Carolina* (1916); P. A. Bruce, *University of Virginia* (5 vols., 1920–1922).

CHAPTER V

THE NEW ISSUES

The extreme protective system, which had been at the first a temporary expedient for aiding in the struggle for the Union, adopted hastily and without any thought of deliberation, gradually became accepted as a permanent institution.

F. W. TAUSSIG.

We demand the immediate and unconditional repeal of the specie-resumption act of January 14, 1875, . . . and we call upon all patriotic men to organize . . . and stop the present suicidal and destructive policy of contraction.

GREENBACK PARTY PLATFORM, 1876.

There is no duty which so much embarrasses the Executive and heads of Departments as that of appointments, nor is there any such arduous and thankless labor imposed on Senators and Representatives as that of finding places for constituents.

PRESIDENT U. S. GRANT, 1870.

OUT of the economic and political circumstances which have just been described, there was emerging between 1865 and 1875 a wide variety of national problems. Such questions were those concerning the proper relation between the government and the railroads and industrial enterprises; the welfare of the agricultural and wage-earning classes; the assimilation of the hordes of immigrants; the conservation of the resources of the nation in lumber, minerals and oil; the tariff, the financial obligations of the government, the reform of the civil service, and a host of lesser matters. The animosities aroused by the war, however, and the insistent nature of the reconstruction question almost completely distracted attention from most of these problems. Only upon the tariff, finance and the civil service did the public interest focus long enough to effect results.

118

The tariff problem has periodically been settled and unsettled since the establishment of the federal government. Just previous to the war a low protective tariff had been adopted, but the outbreak of the conflict had necessitated a larger income; and, aside from loans, the passage of an internal revenue act, together with a higher protective tarff, had been the chief means adopted to meet the demand. By 1864 the country had found itself in need of still greater revenues, and again the internal and tariff taxes had been increased. These acts were in force at the close of the war. The internal revenue act levied taxes upon products, trades, and professions, upon liquors and tobacco, upon manufactures, auctions, slaughtered cattle, railroads, advertisements and a large number of smaller sources of income.

The circumstances that had surrounded the framing and passage of the tariff act of 1864 had been somewhat peculiar. The need of the nation for revenue had been supreme and there had been no desire to stint the administration if funds could bring the struggle to a successful conclusion. Congress had been willing to levy almost any rates that anybody desired. The combination of a willingness among the legislators to raise rates to any height necessary for obtaining revenue, and a conviction on their part that high rates were for the good of the country brought about a situation eminently satisfactory to the protectionist element. There had been no time to spend in long discussions of the wisdom of the act and no desire to do so; and moreover the act had been looked upon as merely a temporary expedient. It is not possible to describe accurately the personal influences which surrounded the passage of the law. It is possible, however, to note that many industries had highly prospered under the war revenue legislation. Sugar refining had increased; whiskey distilling had fared well under the operation of the internal revenue laws; the demands of the army had given stimulus to the woolen mills, which had worked to capacity night and day; and the manufacture and use of sewing machines, agricultural implements and the like had been part of the industrial expansion of the times. Large fortunes had been made in the production of rifles, woolen clothing, cotton cloth and other commodities, especially when government contracts could be obtained. Naturally the tax-levying activities of Congress had tended to draw the business interests together to oppose or influence particular rates. The brewers, the cap and hat manufacturers, and others had objected to the taxes on their products; the National Association of Wool Manufacturers and the American Iron and Steel Association had been formed partly with the idea of influencing congressional tariff action.

After the close of the war, the tariff, among other things, seemed to many to require an overhauling. Justin S. Morrill, a member of the House Committee on Ways and Means, and one of the framers of the act of 1864, argued in favor of the protective system although he warned his colleagues:

At the same time it is a mistake of the friends of a sound tariff to insist upon the extreme rates imposed during the war, if less will raise the necessary revenue. . . . Whatever percentage of duties were imposed upon foreign goods to cover internal taxes upon home manufacturers, should not now be claimed as the lawful prize of protection where such taxes have been repealed. . . . The small increase of the tariff for this reason on iron, salt, woolen, and cottons can not be maintained except on the principle of obtaining a proper amount of revenue.

Sentiment was strong against the tariff in the agricultural parts of the West and especially in those sections not committed to wool-growing. Great personal influence was exerted on the side of "tariff-reform" by David A. Wells, a painstaking and able student of economic conditions who was appointed special commissioner of the revenue in 1866. As a result of his investigations he became converted from a believer in protection to the leader of the opposition, and his reports had a considerable influence in the formation of opinion in favor of revision. The American Free Trade League was formed and included such influential figures as Carl Schurz, Jacob D. Cox, Horace White, Edward Atkinson, E. L. Godkin, editor of *The Nation*, and many others. William B. Allison and James A. Garfield, both prominent Republican members of the House, were in favor of downward revision.

In 1867 a bill providing for many reductions passed the Senate as an amendment to a House bill which proposed to raise rates. Far more than a majority in the House were ready to accept the Senate measure, but according to the rules it was necessary to obtain a two-thirds vote in order to get the amended bill before the House for action. This it was impossible to do. Nevertheless, the wool growers and manufacturers were able "through their large influence, persistent pressure and adroit management" to procure an act in the same session which increased the duties on wool and woolens far above the war rate. In 1869 the duties on copper were raised, as were those on steel rails, marble, flax and some other commodities in 1870.

The growth of the Liberal Republican movement in 1872, with its advocacy of downward revision, frightened somewhat the protectionist leaders of the Republican organization. It was believed that a slight concession might prevent a more radical action, and just before the campaign a ten per cent. reduction was brought about. In 1873 the industrial depression so lowered the revenues as to present a plausible opportunity for restoring duties to their former level in 1875, where they remained for nearly a decade.

The lack of effective action on the part of the tariff reformers of both parties was due to a variety of causes. In the years immediately following the war, the Republicans in Congress were more interested in their quarrel with President Johnson than in tariff reform. Furthermore, the unpopular internal revenues were being quickly reduced between 1867 and 1872, and it was argued that a simultaneous reduction of import taxes would decrease the revenue too greatly. Moreover there was no solidarity among the Democrats, the South was discredited, and at first not fully represented. Wells was driven out of office in 1870, the Liberal Republican movement was a failure, the protected manufacturers knew precisely what they wanted, they knew how to achieve results and some of them were willing to employ methods that the reformers were above using. As time went on and the country was, in the main, rather prosperous, many people and especially the business men made up their minds that the war tariffs were a positive benefit to the country. For these reasons a war policy which had generally been considered a temporary expedient became a permanent political issue and a national problem.

The positions of the two political parties on the tariff were not sharply defined during the ten years immediately following the war. The Democrats seemed naturally destined for the rôle of revisionists because of their party traditions, their support in the South—ordinarily a strong, low-tariff section —and because they were out of power when high tariffs were enacted. Yet the party was far from united on the subject. Some prominent leaders were frankly protectionists, such as Samuel J. Randall of Pennsylvania, who was Speaker of the House for two terms and part of another. The party platform ordinarily was silent or non-committal. In 1868, for example, the Democratic tariff plank was wide and generous enough for a complete platform. The party stood for

a tariff for revenue upon foreign imports, and such equal taxation under the internal revenue laws as will afford incidental protection to domestic manufacturers, and as will, without impairing the revenue, impose the least burden upon, and best promote and encourage, the great industrial interests of the country.

In 1872 the "straight" Democrats, that is, those who refused to support Greeley, were for a "judicious" revenue tariff; but in 1876 the party denounced the existing system as "a masterpiece of injustice, inequality and false pretence." Democratic state platforms were even less firm; in fact, the eastern states seemed committed to protection. In Congress, however, most of the opposition to the passage of tariff acts was supplied by the Democrats.

The attitude of the Republicans was more important, because theirs was the party in power. There was, as has been shown, a strong tariff-reform element, and in some of the conventions care seems to have been taken to avoid any definite statement of principles—doubtless on account of the well-known differences in the party—and for many years there was no clearly defined statement of the attitude of the organization. Yet it must be emphasized that Republicans were usually protectionists in the practical business of voting in Congress. Skilful Republican leaders gave way a little in the face of opposition but regained the lost ground and a little more, after the opposition retreated. Since the war-tariffs had been passed under Republican rule, it was easy to clothe them with the sanctity of party accomplishments.

Fully as technical as the tariff problem, and presenting a wider range for the legislative activities of Congress, was the financial situation in which the country found itself in 1865. The total expenditures from June 30, 1861, to June 30, 1865, had been somewhat more than three and one-third billions of dollars, an amount almost double the aggregate disbursements from 1789 to 1861. Officers accustomed to a modest budget and used to working with machinery and precedents which were adapted to the day of small things, had been suddenly called upon to work under revolutionized conditions. From the point of view of expense, merely, one year's operations during the war had been equivalent to thirty-six times the average outlay of the years hitherto. As has been shown, the major part of the income necessary for meeting the increased expenses had been obtained by means of the tariff and internal revenue taxes.

The tariff worked to the advantage of many people, and its retention was insistently demanded by them; the internal revenue taxes were disliked, and few things were more popular after the war than their reduction. In 1866 an act was passed which lowered the internal revenue by an amount estimated at forty-five to sixty millions of dollars. In succeeding years further reductions were made, so that by 1870 the scale was low enough to withstand attacks until 1883.

The national debt was the source of more complicated questions. It was composed, on June 30, 1866, of a variety of loans carrying five different rates of interest and maturing in nineteen different periods of time. Parts of it had been borrowed in times of distress at high rates; but after the struggle was successfully ended, the credit of the government was good, and enough money could be obtained at low interest charges to cancel the old debt and establish a new one with the interest account correspondingly reduced. Hugh McCulloch and John Sherman as secretaries of the treasury were most influential in accomplishing this transition, and by 1879 the process was completed and a yearly saving of fourteen million dollars effected.

Differences of opinion concerning the kind of money with which the principal of the debt should be paid brought this matter into the field of politics. When the earliest loans had been contracted, no stipulation had been made in regard to the medium of payment. Later loans had been made redeemable in ''coin,'' without specifying either gold or silver; while still later bonds had been sold under condition that the interest be paid in coin, although nothing had been said about the principal. There was considerable demand for redemption of the bonds in paper money, except where there was agreement to the contrary, although the previous custom of the government had been to pay in coin. The proposal to repay the debt in paper currency, the "Ohio idea," gained considerable ground in the Middle West, as has already been explained. In the campaign of 1868 the Democratic platform advocated the Ohio plan. Some of the Republicans, like Thaddeus Stevens, agreed with this policy; some of the Democrats opposed it—Horatio Seymour, the presidential candidate, among them. Nevertheless the Democratic platform committed the party to payments in greenbacks unless express contract prevented, while the Republicans denounced this policy as "repudiation" and promised the payment in "good faith" according to the "spirit" and "letter" of the laws. The credit of the government was highly benefited by the payment of the debt in gold, yet the bonds had been purchased during the war with depreciated paper, and gold redemption greatly enriched the purchasers at the expense of the remainder of the population. It is hardly surprising that the debtor classes were not enthusiastic over this outcome. The Republicans on being successful in the election and coming into power, carried out their campaign promises and pledged the faith of the country to the payment of the debt in coin or its equivalent.

The income tax was a method of raising revenue which did not produce any considerable returns until after the war was over. Acts passed during the war had levied a tax on all incomes over six hundred dollars and had introduced progressively increasing rates on higher amounts. Incomes above $5,000, for example, were taxed ten per cent. The greatest number of people were reached and the largest returns obtained in 1866 when nearly half a million persons paid an aggregate of about seventy-three million dollars. The entire system was abolished in 1872.

Aside from the tariff, the "legal-tender" notes gave rise to the greatest number of political and constitutional tangles. By acts of February 25, 1862, and later, Congress had provided for the issue of four hundred and fifty million dollars of United States paper notes, which were commonly known as greenbacks or legal-tenders. The latter name came from the fact that, under the law, the United States notes were legal tender for all debts, public or private, except customs duties and interest on the public debt. In other words, the law compelled creditors to receive the greenbacks in payment of all debts, with the two exceptions mentioned. Three main questions arose in connection with these issues of paper: whether Congress had power under the Constitution to make them legal tender; whether their volume should be allowed to remain at war magnitude, be somewhat contracted or entirely done away with; and whether the government should resume specie payments—that is, exchange gold for paper on the demand of holders of the latter.

The first of these questions was twice decided in the Supreme Court. In 1870, in Hepburn v. Griswold, the point at issue was whether the greenbacks could lawfully be offered to satisfy a debt contracted before the legal-tender act had been passed. As it happened, Salmon P. Chase, who had been Secretary of the Treasury during the war, was now Chief Justice of the Supreme Court and delivered the majority opinion. By a vote of four to three it decided that the greenbacks were not legal tender for contracts made previous to the passage of the law. At the time when the case was decided, however, there were two vacancies on the bench which were immediately filled, and shortly thereafter two new cases involving the legal-tender act were brought before the Court (Knox v. Lee, and Parker v. Davis). The decision, which was announced in 1871, over-ruled the judgment in Hepburn v. Griswold and held by a vote of five to four that the legal-tender act was constitutional as applied to contracts made either before or after its passage.

The second question relating to the greenbacks was that in regard to their volume. At first Congress adopted the policy of contraction and when greenbacks came into the treasury they were destroyed. As continued contraction tended to make the volume of currency smaller and to make money harder to get, and therefore, to raise its value, the debtor classes began to object. As early as 1865 there was strong sentiment against contraction and in favor of paying the public debt in paper. Economic distress in the West furthered the movement and some of the Republican leaders were doubtful of the wisdom of reducing the outstanding stock of paper. Contraction was stopped, therefore, in 1868, and only President Grant's veto in 1874 prevented an increase in the amount. Eventually, in 1878, the amount then in circulation —$346,681,000—was fixed by a law forbidding further contraction.[1]

The western farmers, meanwhile, were feeling the pinch of falling prices. Believing that their ills were due to the scarcity of money, they opposed the policy of contraction and even launched the Greenback party to carry out their principles. In 1876 it polled 80,000 votes, and in 1878 at the time of the congressional elections over 1,000,000, but thereafter its strength rapidly declined. Neither the East nor the West understood the motives of the other in this controversy. Eastern congressmen considered western insistence upon a large volume of currency as a dishonest movement to reduce bond values by legislation. Such an action, they asserted, would do away with the national integrity. The people of the West thought of the eastern bondholders as "fat bullionists" who dined at costly restaurants on terrapin and Burgundy and paid for their luxuries with bonds whose values were raised by a contracted currency.

The third question relating to the greenbacks was that of the resumption of specie payments. At the close of the war practically all the money in circulation was paper, which passed at a depreciated value because it was not redeemable

---

[1] This is the amount still outstanding.

in coin. The obvious thing was to resume the exchange of specie for paper and thus restore the latter to par value, but serious obstacles stood in the way. A money crisis in 1873 aroused a clamor for larger supplies of paper; gold was hard to procure, as France and Germany were both accumulating a redemption fund and specie was actually flowing out of the country. Outside of the treasury there was little gold in the United States, the amount being less than one hundred million dollars as late as 1877. The friends of resumption could not be sure of the feasibility of their project, and the opponents were aggressive and numerous.

In the elections of 1874 the Republicans were severely defeated, and it was seen that the Democrats would have a clear majority in the next House of Representatives. Hence the Republicans hurried through a resumption bill on January 14, 1875—a sort of deathbed act. It authorized the secretary of the treasury to raise gold for redemption purposes, and set January 1, 1879, as the date when resumption should take place. As in the case of the tariff, the political parties found difficulty in determining which side of the resumption question they desired to take. Although the Democratic platform of 1868 contained a greenback plank, yet some of its leaders opposed, and the state platforms of 1875 and 1876 demanded resumption. The national platform of the latter year both denounced the Republicans for not making progress toward resumption and demanded the repeal of the act of 1875, without disclosing whether the party was prepared to offer any improvements. In November, 1877, a bill practically repealing the resumption act passed the House—the western and southern Democrats furnishing most of the affirmative votes, assisted by twenty-seven Republicans,—but it did not come to a vote in the senate. A resolution declaring it to be the opinion of Congress that United States bonds were payable in silver was introduced and advocated by many Republicans. On the other hand, eastern state Democratic and

Republican platforms were much alike. Apparently, therefore, differences of opinion in regard to the greenbacks and resumption were caused as much by sectional as by party considerations.[2]

More lasting than finance as a political issue but less enduring than the tariff, was the reform of the civil service. In its widest sense, the term civil service included all non-military government officers from cabinet officials and supreme court judges to the humblest employee in the postal or naval service. The reform, however, was directed mainly toward the appointment and tenure of the lower officers. Before the Civil War the "spoils system" had been in full swing; appointments to positions had been frankly used as rewards for party activity; office-holders had been openly assessed a fraction of their salaries in order to fill the treasure chest at campaign times; rotation in office had been the rule. During the war, President Lincoln had found his ante-room filled with wrangling, importunate office-seekers who consumed time which he needed for the problems of the conflict. As he himself had expressed the situation, he was like a man who was letting offices in one end of his house while the other end was burning down. During the war, also, the patronage at the disposal of the government had vastly increased. Not only had the number of laborers, clerks and officials become greater, but numerous contracts had been let for the production of war materials, and manufacturers and merchants intrigued for a share of federal business. "Influence," and position had been more powerful than merit in procuring the favor of government officers.

After the war many abuses that had earlier been overlooked began to attract the attention of a few thoughtful men. It was estimated that not more than one-half to three-fourths of the legitimate internal revenue was collected during John-

2 For later stages of resumption, *cf.* pp. 153–154.

son's presidency, so corrupt and inefficient were the revenue collectors. Endless Indian troubles and countless losses of money resulted from the corruption of the federal Indian agents. Conditions were even worse during the Grant régime. The President's appointments were wretched; he placed his relatives in official positions; revenue frauds amounting to $75,000,000 were discovered during his second administration. In certain departments, it was customary, when vacancies occurred, to allow the salaries to "lapse"—that is, accumulate —so as to provide a fund to satisfy patronage seekers. In one case, thirty-five persons were put on the "lapse fund" for eight days at the end of a fiscal year, in order to "sop up" a little surplus which was in danger of being saved and returned to the treasury. One customs collector at the port of New York removed employees at an average rate of one every three days; another, three every four days; and another, three every five days, in order to provide places for party workers. One secretary in an important department of the government had seventeen clerks for whom he had no employment. The party assessments on office-holders became little short of outrageous. Two or three per cent. of the salary of the lower officers was called for, while the more important officials were expected to contribute much larger sums. In New York—for the system held in the states and cities—candidates for the mayoralty were reputed to pay $25,000 to $30,-000; judges, $10,000 to $15,000; and representatives in Congress, $10,000. While these conditions were by no means wholly due to the spoils system, the method of appointment in the civil service made a bad matter worse.

Conditions such as these could hardly fail to produce a reform movement. In fact, as far back as 1853 some elementary and ineffective legislation had attempted a partial remedy. The war gave added impetus to the movement, and attention turned to the reform systems of Great Britain and other countries, where problems similar to ours had already been met and solved. The first American who really grasped civil service reform was Thomas A. Jenckes, a member of Congress from Rhode Island. He introduced reform bills in 1865 and later, based on studies of English practice and on correspondence with the leaders of reform there; but no legislation resulted. In brief, his plan provided for the appointment of employees in the public service on the basis of ability, determined by competitive examinations. After a time Jenckes and his associates achieved considerable success and finally interested President Grant in their project. In 1871 they got a rider attached to an appropriation bill which authorized the chief executive to prescribe rules for the admission of persons into the civil service and allowed him to appoint a commission to put the act into effect. George William Curtis, a well-known reformer, was made chairman, and rules were formulated which were applied to the departments at Washington and to federal offices in New York. Grant, although favorable to the reform, was not enthusiastic about it, and soon made an appointment which was so offensive that Curtis resigned. Congress, nothing loath, refused to continue the necessary appropriations and the reform project continued in a state of suspended animation until the inauguration of President Hayes.

The human elements in the struggle for civil service reform, both during the decade after the war and for many years later, are necessary for an understanding of the course of the controversy and its outcome. These elements included the advocates of the patronage system, the reformers and the president.

Sometimes the advocates of the patronage system viewed the reform with contempt. Roscoe Conkling, for example, expressed his sentiments in the remark, "When Dr. Johnson said that patriotism was the last refuge of the scoundrel he ignored the enormous possibilities of the word reform!" Sometimes they attempted to discredit the project by an exaggeration of its effects, as when John A. Logan declared that he saw in it a life-tenure and an aristocratic caste. "It will not be apparent how great is its enormity," he declared in Congress, "how vicious are its practices and how poisonous are its influences until we are too far encircled by its coils to shake them off." The strength of the exponents of the patronage system, however, lay not in their capacity for contempt and ridicule, but in a theory of government that was founded upon certain very definite human characteristics. The theory may be clearly seen in the *Autobiography* of Thomas C. Platt, a colleague of Conkling in the Senate and for many years the boss of New York state. It may be expressed somewhat as follows.

In the field of actual politics, parties are a necessity and organization is essential. It is the duty of the citizen, therefore, to support the party that stands for right policies and to adhere closely to its official organization. Loyalty should be rewarded by appointment to positions within the gift of the party; and disloyalty should be looked upon as political treason. One who votes for anybody except the organization candidate feels himself superior to his party, is faithless to the great ideal and is only a little less despicable than he who, having been elected to an office through the energy and devotion of the party workers, is then so ungrateful as to refuse to appoint the workers to positions within his gift. Positions constitute the cohesive force that holds the organization intact.

The second of the human elements, the reform group, was led by such men as George William Curtis, Dorman B. Eaton and Carl Schurz, with the support of periodicals like *Harper's Weekly* and *The Nation*. The career and character of Curtis is typical at once of the strength and the weakness of the group. As a young man Curtis had intended to enter a business career, but finding it unsuited to his tastes he had abandoned his ambition, spent some years in European travel and then devoted himself to literary work, first on *Harper's Magazine* and afterwards, for many years, as editor of *Harper's Weekly*. He had early interested himself in politics, had been in the convention which nominated Lincoln, had taken part in numerous state and national political conferences and conventions, was president of the Metropolitan Museum of Art in New York and chancellor of the University of the State of New York. For many years, during the period when civil service reform was making its fight for recognition, Curtis was the president and one of the moving spirits of the National Civil Service Reform League. In politics he was an independent Republican. Although of the intellectual class, like the other prominent leaders of the reform movement, he was a man of practical political ability, not a mere observer of politics, so that he and his associates made up in capacity and influence what they lacked in breadth of appeal. Some of the leaders were patient men who expected that results would come slowly and who were ready to accept half a loaf of reform rather than no loaf at all, but there were also such impatient critics as E. L. Godkin who put so much emphasis on the failures of the reformers as to overshadow their positive achievements. Moreover, there were the well-meaning but impracticable people who constituted what Theodore Roosevelt once called the "lunatic fringe" of reform movements.

The attitude of the exponents of the patronage system toward the reformers was one of undisguised contempt. In a famous speech delivered at a New York state convention in Rochester in September, 1877, Conkling poured his scorn on the reform element in general and on Curtis in particular, as "man-milliners," "carpet-knights of politics," "grasshoppers in the corner of a fence," and disciples of ladies' magazines with their "rancid, canting self-righteousness."

The third personal element in the reform controversy was the chief executive. Beginning with Grant, if not with Lincoln, the presidents were favorable to the progress of reform, but they were surrounded by circumstances that made vigorous action a difficult matter. The task of distributing the patronage was a burden from which they would have been glad to be relieved, yet the demands of the party organization were insistent, and to turn a constantly deaf ear to them would have been to court political disaster. The executive was always in the position of desiring to further an ideal and being obliged to face the hard facts of politics. The progress which he made, therefore, depended on how resolutely he could press forward his ideal in the face of continued opposition. A great difficulty lay in getting subordinates—in the cabinet, for example—who were in sympathy with progress, and sometimes even the vice-presidential nomination was given to the patronage element in the party in order to placate that faction, while the presidential nominee was disposed to reform.

Public opinion was slow in forming and was lacking in the means of definite expression. For many years after the war there was widespread fear that the installation of a Democratic president would result in the wholesale debauch of the offices, and sober northerners believed, or thought they believed, that "rebels" would again be in power if a Democrat were elected. Under such conditions and because the offices were already filled with Republicans, the Republican North was willing to leave things as they were.

The party pronouncements on civil service reform were as evasive as they were on finance and the tariff. To be sure the Liberal Republicans in 1872 sincerely desired reform and made it the subject of a definite plank in their platform, but the wing of the Democratic party that refused to ally with them was silent on the civil service, and the "straight" Republicans advocated reform in doubtful and unconvincing terms. In 1876 both party platforms were even more vague, although Hayes himself was openly committed to the improvement of the service.

BIBLIOGRAPHICAL NOTE

The best work on the tariff is F. W. Taussig, *Tariff History of the United States*, a scholarly and nonpartisan account, although giving slight attention to legislative history; Ida M. Tarbell, *Tariff in Our Times* (1911), emphasizes the personal and social sides of tariff history and is hostile to protection; Edward Stanwood, *American Tariff Controversies* (2 vols., 1903), devotes considerable attention to the historical setting and legislative history of tariff acts, and is distinctly friendly to protection.

The most useful single volume of financial history is D. R. Dewey, *Financial History of the United States* (5th ed., 1915), which is concise, accurate and equipped with full bibliographies; A. B. Hepburn, *History of Currency in the United States* (1915), is by an expert; A. D. Noyes, *Forty Years of American Finance* (1909), continues the same author's *Thirty Years* and is reliable; T. E. Burton, *John Sherman* (1906), is useful here. The legal-tender decisions are in J. W. Wallace, *Cases argued and adjudged in the Supreme Court*, VIII, 603, and XII, 457.

The standard work on the civil service is C. R. Fish, *The Civil Service and the Patronage* (1905); the reports of the Civil Service Commission, especially the Fourth Report, are essential; the articles by D. B. Eaton in J. J. Lalor, *Cyclopaedia of Political Science* (3 vols., 1893), are justly well known; G. W. Curtis, *Orations and Addresses* (2 vols., 1894), and Edward Cary, *George William Curtis* (1894), are excellent. The politician's side may be found in A. R. Conkling, *Life and Letters of Roscoe Conkling* (1889); T. C. Platt, *Autobiography* (1910); and H. F. Gosnell, *Boss Platt and His New York Machine* (1924).

CHAPTER VI

THE ADMINISTRATION OF RUTHERFORD B. HAYES

The great fraud of 1876–77, by which . . . the candidate defeated at the polls was declared to be President, and . . . the will of the people was set aside under a threat of military violence, struck a deadly blow at our system of representative government.

DEMOCRATIC PLATFORM, 1880.

The great service of President Hayes to reform is to have shown that it is perfectly practicable.

GEORGE W. CURTIS.

I am in favor of issuing paper money enough to stuff down the bond-holders until they are sick.

RICHARD P. BLAND.

THE conditions which confronted President Hayes when the final decision of the Electoral Commission placed him in the executive chair did not make it probable that he could carry out a program of positive achievement. The withdrawal of troops from the South had been almost completed, but the process of reconstruction had been so dominated by suspicion, ignorance and vindictiveness that sectional hostility was still acute. As has been seen, the economic problems which faced the country were for the most part unsolved; on the subjects of tariff, finance and the civil service, neither party was prepared to present a united front; and the lack of foresight and statesmanlike leadership in the parties had given selfish interests an opportunity to seize control. Nor did the circumstances surrounding the election of Hayes tend to simplify his task, for the disappointment of the Democrats was extreme, and they found a natural difficulty in adjusting themselves to the decision against Tilden. Democratic newspapers dubbed Hayes "His Fraudulency" and "The

Boss Thief,'' printed his picture with ''Fraud'' printed across his brow and referred to his election as the ''steal'' and a ''political crime.''

The man who was to essay leadership under such conditions had back of him a useful even if not brilliant career. He had been born in Ohio in 1822, had graduated from Kenyon College as valedictorian of his class, attended Harvard Law School and served on the Union side during the war, retiring with the rank of a brevet Major General. He had been twice elected to Congress, but had resigned after his second election to become governor of his native state, a position which he had filled for three terms.

Hayes was a man of the substantial, conscientious and hardworking type. He was not brilliant or magnetic, he originated no innovations, burst into no flights of imaginative oratory. His state papers were planned with painstaking care —first, frequently, jotted down in his diary and then elaborated, revised, recopied and revised again. The vivid imagination and high-strung emotions that made Clay and Blaine great campaigners were lacking in Hayes. He was gentle, dignified, simple, systematic, thoughtful, serene, correct. In making his judgments on public questions he was sensitive to moral forces. The emancipation of the slaves was not merely wise and just to him—it was ''Providential.'' He favored a single six-year term for the president because it would safeguard him from selfish scheming for another period of power. Partly because of the lack of dash and compelling force in Hayes, but more because of the low standards of political action which were common at the time, his scruples seemed puritanical and were held up to ridicule as the milk-and-water and ''old-Woman'' policies of ''Granny Hayes.'' His public, as well as his private life, was unimpeached in a time when lofty principles were not common and when scandal attached itself to public officers of every grade. To his probity and the ''safe'' character of his views, as well as to his record as governor of an important state, was due his elevation to the presidency.[1] In his habit of self-analysis, Hayes was reminiscent of John Quincy Adams. Like Adams he kept a diary from his early youth, the serious and mature entries in which cause the reader to wonder whether Hayes ever had a childhood. When he had just passed his twentieth birthday he confided to his diary that he found himself unsatisfied with his progress in Blackstone, that he must curb his "propensity" to read newspapers to the exclusion of more substantial matter, and in general that he was "greatly deficient in many particulars." Then and in later years he noted hostile criticisms of himself and combated them, recorded remarks that he had heard, propounded questions for future thought, expressed a modest ambition or admitted a curbed elation over success.

In the field of politics Hayes was looked upon as a reliable party man, a reputation which was justified by his rigid adherence to his party and by his attitude toward the opposition. In both these respects he was the ordinary partisan. Nevertheless he thought out his views with unusual care, made them a matter of conscience and measured policies by ethical standards that were more exacting than the usual politician of the time was accustomed to exercise. The only remark of his that gained wide circulation reflects his type of partisanship: "he serves his party best who serves his country best." In these latter respects—his thoughtfulness, conscientiousness, exacting standards of conduct and less narrowly partisan spirit —he formed a contrast to the most influential leaders of his

[1] For a time public interest was absorbed by the determination of President and Mrs. Hayes to serve no wines of any kind in the White House. Finally a delicious frozen punch was served at about the middle of the state dinners, known to the thirsty as "the Life-saving Station." It was popularly understood to be liberally strengthened with old Santa Croix rum, but the President later asserted that he had caused the punch to be sharpened with the flavor of Jamaica rum and that no drop of spirits was inserted. What the *chef* really did, perhaps nobody knows. At any rate, both sides were satisfied. Williams, *R. B. Hayes*, II, p. 312 note.

party organization. Altogether it seemed likely at the start that Hayes might have friction with the Republican chiefs.

The opening of the administration found public interest centered on the inaugural address and the Cabinet.[2] The inaugural set forth with clearness and dignity the problems which the administration desired to solve: the removal of the barriers between the sections on the basis of the acceptance of the war amendments, southern self-government and the material development of the South; reform in the civil service, thorough, radical and complete; and the resumption of specie payments. To the choice of a cabinet, Hayes devoted much painstaking care. For Secretary of State, he nominated William M. Evarts of New York, an eminent lawyer who had aided Charles Francis Adams in his diplomatic battle with England during the Civil War and later in the Geneva Arbitration, had shown wit and finesse in the defence of Andrew Johnson in the impeachment trial, and had valiantly assisted the Republican cause before the Electoral Commission. In addition, Evarts was a man of the world who knew how to make the most of social occasions and was an orator of reputation. The Secretary of the Treasury was John Sherman of Ohio, who had been for years chairman of the finance committee of the Senate, and was an example of the more statesmanlike type of senator of war and reconstruction times.

The nomination of Carl Schurz, as Secretary of the Interior, and David M. Key, as Postmaster-General, caused an uproar among the party leaders. Schurz was a cosmopolitan, a German-American, a scholar, orator, veteran of the Civil War, friend of Lincoln, and independent thinker. His devotion to the cause of civil service reform recommended him to the friendship of the President and to the enmity of the political leaders. The politicians scored Schurz as not a trustworthy Republican—he was independent by nature and had been a

2 Because March 4 fell on Sunday, the oath of office was privately administered to Hayes on Saturday evening, March 3. Williams, *Hayes*, II, p. 5.

leader in the Liberal Republican movement; and they denounced him as an impractical man, whose head was full of transcendental theories—which was a method of saying that he was a civil service reformer. No little excitement was occasioned by the appointment of Key. The President had desired to appoint to the cabinet a southerner of influence, and had thought of Joseph E. Johnston as Secretary of War. The choice of General Johnston would have been an act of great magnanimity, but since General Sherman, to whom Johnston had surrendered only twelve years before, was commander of the army, it would have placed Sherman in a singular position of taking military orders from a former leading "rebel." When Hayes consulted his party associates, however, he found their feelings expressed in the exclamation of one of them: "Great God! Governor, I hope you are not thinking of doing anything of that kind!" He thereupon reluctantly gave way and turned to Key for the position of Postmaster General. The latter was less prominent than Johnston, but had been a Confederate leader, was a Democrat and a man of moderate counsels. The remaining members of the cabinet were men of much less moment, but altogether it is clear that few presidents have been surrounded by so able a group of advisors.[3]

Seldom, also, has a president's announcement of his cabinet caused so much dissent among his own supporters. Senator Cameron, of Pennsylvania, had urged a cabinet appointment for his son, and on being refused became hostile to Hayes. Senator Blaine, of Maine, was piqued because Hayes refused to offer a place to a Maine man; the friends of General John A. Logan, of Illinois, were dissatisfied at the failure of Hayes to understand the qualifications of their favorite; Conkling disliked Evarts and besides desired a place for his associate Thomas C. Platt; and the latter considered the nomination

[3] George W. McCrary was Secretary of War; Richard W. Thompson, Secretary of the Navy; Charles Devens, Attorney-General.

of Evarts a "straight-arm" blow at the Republican organization. Departing, therefore, from the custom in such cases, the Senate withheld confirmation of the nominations for several days, during which it became apparent that the rest of the country had received the announcement of the cabinet with favor, and then the opposition disappeared. During the remainder of his presidency, however, Hayes fared badly in making his nominations to office, for fifty-one of them were rejected outright, a larger number than had ever before been disagreed to when the president and the Senate were of the same party. The frequency with which the nominations were rejected and the combative manner in which the contests were carried on by the Senate indicated that it was determined to regain and hold fast the influence in federal counsels that it had relinquished to the executive during the war.

Aside from the nomination of members of the cabinet, the first important executive action that tested the attitude of the Senate toward the President was in relation to the southern problem. By March, 1877, all the former Confederate states except Louisiana and South Carolina had freed themselves from Republican rule by the methods already mentioned, and in these states the Republicans were kept in power only by the presence of troops. In Louisiana, both Packard, a Republican carpet-bagger, and Nicholls, a Louisiana Democrat, claimed to be the rightful governor. In South Carolina, the Republican contestant was Chamberlain, a native of Massachusetts; the Democrat was Wade Hampton, a typical old-time southerner. Hayes could withdraw the troops, in pursuance of his conciliatory policy, but if he did the Republican governments would certainly collapse because they were unsupported by public opinion. Furthermore, the returning board which had declared Hayes the choice of Louisiana in the presidential election had asserted that the Republican Packard was elected. Blaine, in the Senate, championed the doctrine that Hayes could not forsake the southern Republicans without invalidating his own title. Speaking in a confident and aggressive manner, he held that the honor, faith and credit of the party bound it to uphold the Republican claimants. Nevertheless, the President investigated conditions in both states, satisfied himself that public opinion was back of the Democratic governments and then recalled the troops, hardly more than a month after his inauguration. The Republican governments in the two states promptly gave way to the Democrats, and the storm was on in the Senate.[4]

The Republican politicians believed that no good thing could come from the "rebels," that the President was abandoning the negro, and that he was surrendering the principles for which the party had contended. "Stalwarts," was the name applied by Blaine to these uncompromising party men who would not relinquish the grip of the organization on the southern states. Hayes was freely charged with having promised the removal of the military forces in return for the electoral votes of the two states concerned, and some color seems to be lent to this accusation when he proceeded to reward the Louisiana and Florida returning boards with appointments to office. Even the New York *Times,* which usually supported Hayes with vigor, characterized the Louisiana settlement as "a surrender." William E. Chandler who had assisted Hayes as counsel in the disputed election attacked him in a pamphlet, "Can such Things be and overcome us like a Summer Cloud without our Special Wonder?" Most of the influential leaders in both houses of Congress scarcely disguised their hostility. Indeed the discontent went back into the states where, as in New Hampshire, a contest over the endorsement of Hayes was so bitter that the newspaper

---

[4] Chamberlain, the Republican claimant in South Carolina, wrote in 1901 that he was "quite ready now to say that he feels sure that there was no possibility of securing permanent good government in South Carolina through Republican influences." *Atlantic Monthly,* LXXXVII, p. 482.

reporters had to be excluded from the state convention to prevent public reports of schism in the party. The Democrats could not come to his support since they were unable to forget the election of 1876 even in their satisfaction over the treatment accorded the South. In six weeks the President was without the backing of most of his party leaders. On the other hand, a few men of the type represented by Hoar and Sherman commended the President's policy. Independent publications such as *Harper's Weekly* did likewise, and when the Republican convention of 1880 drew up the party platform the leaders made a virtue of necessity and adopted a plank enthusiastically supporting the Hayes administration, without urging his renomination.

After he had finished with the southern problem, Hayes confided to his diary, "Now for civil service reform!" And for appointments in general he recorded several principles: no sweeping changes; recommendations by congressmen to be investigated—not merely accepted; and no relatives of himself or his wife to be appointed, however good their qualifications might be. In the meanwhile Secretary Schurz set to work to put the Department of the Interior on a merit basis. The principles that Hayes set up for himself and the steps that Schurz took were in conformity with the party platform of 1876 and with the President's inaugural address; nevertheless the party leaders were displeased, if not surprised, for platform promises were lightly regarded and inaugural addresses were sometimes not to be taken very seriously.

The earliest acts of Hayes were not such as to facilitate the further progress of reform. The appointment of the members of the Louisiana Returning Board to federal offices gave color to charges that they were receiving their reward for assisting the President into his position. Furthermore, on June 22, 1877, he issued an executive order forbidding any United States officials to take part in the management of political organizations and declaring that political assessments

on federal officers would not be allowed. So drastic an order
brought amazement to the party leaders, who had not dreamed
of anything so radical. Perhaps the order was too sudden
and sweeping, considering the practices of the time. At any
rate it was not enforced and the President seemed to have set
a standard to which he had not the courage to adhere.
Nevertheless, reform principles were successfullly tested in
the New York Post Office by Thomas L. James, a vigorous
exponent of the merit system who had been appointed by
President Grant and was now re-appointed and upheld by
President Hayes.

But the great battle for the new idea came in connection
with the New York Custom House. Through the port of
New York came two-thirds to three-fourths of the goods
which were imported into this country, and the necessity for
a businesslike conduct of the custom house seemed obvious.
Yet there had for some time been complaints concerning the
service, and Sherman appointed commissions, with the approval of the President, to investigate conditions in New
York and elsewhere. The commission which studied the situation in New York reported that one-fifth of the persons
employed there were superfluous, that inefficiency and neglect
of duty were common, and that the positions at the disposal
of the collector had for years been used for the reward
of party activity. The commission recommended sweeping
changes which Secretary Sherman and President Hayes approved. It then appeared that the New York officials were
not favorable to the President's reform plans. Furthermore,
Chester A. Arthur, the collector of the port, was a close
friend of Roscoe Conkling, the head of the state machine; and
A. B. Cornell, the naval officer, was chairman of the state and
national Republican committees. It was evident that an
attempt to change conditions in New York would precipitate
a test of strength between the administration and the New
York organization.

As Arthur and Cornell would not further the desired reforms and would not resign, the President suspended them. When he nominated their successors, however, the Senate, led by Conkling, bitterly opposed. Eventually the President's nominations were confirmed, an outcome which seems to have been brought about in part at least by letters from Secretary Sherman to personal friends in the Senate in which he urgently pressed the case of the administration. The President's victory emphasized the disagreement of the powerful state organization with the reform idea, and while the reformers rejoiced that the warfare had been carried into the enemy's country, newspaper opinion varied between the view that the President was playing politics and that he was actuated by the highest motives only. Agitation for reform, meanwhile, continued to increase. The literary men among the reformers, aided by scores of lesser lights, conducted a campaign of education; the New York Civil Service Reform Association, founded in 1877, and the National Civil Service Reform League, in 1881, gave evidence of an effort towards the organization of reform sentiment.

While the attention of the President and the politicians was directed toward the reform of the civil service, there occurred an event for which none of them was prepared. Early in the summer of 1877 train hands on the Baltimore and Ohio Railroad struck because of the reduction in wages, the fourth cut that they had suffered in seven years. The strike spread with the speed of a prairie fire over most of the northern roads between New England and the Mississippi. At the height of the controversy at least 100,000 strikers and six or seven thousand miles of railway were involved, while at several points especially Martinsburg, West Virginia, and Pittsburgh, rioting and destruction took place. A considerable number of people were killed or wounded, and the loss of property in Pittsburgh alone was estimated at five to ten millions of dollars. Eventually, when the state militia failed to check the disorder, the President was called upon for federal troops and these proved effectual. That even so thoughtful and conscientious a man as Hayes was far from understanding the meaning of the strike was indicated in his message to Congress in which he merely expressed his gratification that the troops had been able to repress the disorder. Repression, that is to say, was the one resource that occurred to the mind of the chief executive and to the majority of the men of his day. That repression alone could not remedy evils permanently, that salutary force ought to be immediately supplemented by a study of the rights and wrongs of the two sides and by a dispassionate correction of abuses,—all this did not even remotely occur to the thoughts of the political leaders of the time.

The breach in the ranks of the Republicans which was made by the events of the early days of the Hayes administration was closed in the face of an attack by the common enemy—the Democrats. The latter, being in control of the House, appointed the ''Potter Committee'' to investigate the title of Hayes to the presidency, hoping to discredit him and thereby turn the tables in the election of 1880.[5] The committee examined witnesses and reported, the Democrats asserting that Tilden had been elected and the Republicans that Hayes had been. The Republican Senate, meanwhile, had prepared a counterblast. By legal proceedings a committee had obtained from the Western Union Telegraph Company over thirty thousand of the telegrams sent by both parties during the campaign. The Republicans declared that the

[5] The succession of Republican presidents since the Civil War has obscured the fact that the House of Representatives after 1874 was more often Democratic than Republican.

Hayes had a Democratic House during his entire term and a Democratic Senate during the last two years. Between 1875 and 1897— eleven Congresses—eight were Democratic in the House.

It would be an interesting study to discover when and why, in any particular state, the ante-bellum Democrats who supported the war returned to their earlier allegiance. In Illinois, apparently, radical reconstruction and interest in Tilden brought about the shift.

"cipher despatches" among these messages showed that the Democrats had offered a substantial bribe for the vote of an Oregon Republican elector. Before the despatches were returned to the telegraph company, somebody took the precaution to destroy those that concerned Republican compaign methods and to retain those relating to the Democrats. The latter were published by the New York *Tribune* and revealed attempts to bribe the Florida and South Carolina Returning Boards. Most of them had been sent by Tilden's nephew or received by him, so that the corrupt trail seemed to lead straight to the candidate himself, but the evidence was inconclusive. The Potter Committee then investigated the telegrams, together with a great number of witnesses, and another partisan report resulted. It thus appeared that both pot and kettle were black and there the matter rested. The Democrats had done themselves no good and had done the Republicans no harm.[6]

The Democrats also attacked the election laws, under which federal officials supervised elections, and federal judges and marshals had jurisdiction over cases concerning the suffrage. Under these laws, also, troops could be used to enforce the judgments of the Courts. There is no doubt that intimidation, unfair practices and bribery were all too common in the North as well as in the South. The lack of official ballots and secret voting made abuses inevitable. In New York, Cincinnati and other northern cities, and on a smaller scale

[6] Many of the despatches were in a complicated cipher which resisted all attempts at solution. The *Tribune* published samples from time to time, keeping interest alive in the hope that somebody might solve the riddle. Finally two members of the *Tribune* staff were successful in discovering the key to the cipher in a way that recalls the paper-covered detective story. The newspaper aroused and excited public interest by publishing specimens and eventually achieved a sensation by putting the most damaging material into print on October 16, 1878. One of the telegrams, with its translation, ran as follows:
"Absolutely Petersburg can procured by Copenhagen may Thomas prompt Edinburgh must if river take be you less London Thames will."
Translation: If Returning Board can be procured absolutely, will you deposit 30,000 dollars? May take less. Must be prompt. Thomas.

in the rural districts, abuses of one sort or another were normal accompaniments of elections. Intimidation in the South was notorious and not denied. The existing election laws gave the dominant party an opportunity to appoint large numbers of deputy-marshals—largely party workers, of course—paying them from the national treasury and so solidifying the party organization. In the election of 1876 about $275,000 had been spent in this way. Some of the federal supervisors had been extremely energetic—so much so that in one case in Louisiana their registration lists showed 8,000 more colored voters in 1876 than were discovered by the census enumerators four years later.

If the Republicans saw involved in the laws both a principle and a party weapon, the Democrats saw both a principle and an opportunity. They attached a "rider" to an army appropriation bill, which made it unlawful to use any part of the army for any other than the purpose expressly authorized by the Constitution or by act of Congress. Since the Constitution allowed the use of troops only to "execute the laws of the Union, to suppress Insurrections and repel Invasions," the new law would prevent the employment of armed forces for civil purposes at the polling places. The President was compelled to yield to save the appropriation bill.

In the next Congress the Democrats controlled both House and Senate and they advanced to the attack on the remainder of the election laws. Attempts were made to prevent the appointment of special deputy-marshals by forbidding the payment of any compensation to them or to the regular marshals when used in elections. Each time that Congress passed such a law the President vetoed it, even though special sessions had to be called to make up for lost time. He saw in the use of the rider a dangerous assertion of coercive power on the part of Congress. By means of it, Congress was withholding funds essential for military and civil purposes until the President should assent to legislation totally unconnected with the appropriations. He felt himself being threatened and driven by a hostile legislature. For the President to give way before such constraint would be to lose the veto power and to destroy the independence of the executive as a branch of the government. The Democrats were unable to muster force enough to overrule the veto, and here the matter rested while other forces, which have already been described, were sapping the strength of the election laws.[7] On the whole, the result was probably to bring the Republican factions together and so to strengthen the party for the election of 1880. The Democrats, on the other hand, probably lost ground.

In the meanwhile a difficult and technical problem—the monetary question—was forcing itself upon the attention of Congress and of the country. The rapid development of the economic life of the United States was demanding an increased volume of currency with which to perform the multitude of exchanges which constantly take place in the life of an industrial people. Unless the volume of the currency expanded proportionately with the increase of business, or there was a corresponding increase in the use of bank checks, the demand for money would cause its value to go up—that is, prices to go down. If the volume expanded more rapidly than was necessitated by business, the value of money would fall and prices would go up. A change in the price level in either direction, as has been seen, would harm important groups of people. The exact amount, however, by which the volume should be increased was not easy to determine. Furthermore, assuming that both gold and silver should be coined, what amount of each would constitute the most desirable combination? What ought to be the weight of the coins? If paper currency was to supplement the precious metals, what amount of it should be in circulation? These are difficult questions under any circumstances. They did not become less so when

[7] *Cf.* above, p. 25.

answered by a bulky and uninformed Congress acting under the influence of definite personal, sectional and property interests.

Several facts tended to restrict the kind of money whose volume could be greatly increased. It was not advisable to expand the greenbacks because legislation had already limited their amount and because such action would unfavorably affect the approaching resumption of specie payments. The quantity of national bank notes, another common form of paper money, was somewhat rigidly determined by the amount of federal bonds outstanding, for the national bank notes were issued upon the federal bonds as security. Moreover, the bonds were being rapidly paid off during the seventies and it was, therefore, impossible to expect any increase of the currency from this source. Normally the supply of gold available for coinage did not vary greatly from year to year and certainly did not respond with exactness to the demand of industry for a greater or smaller volume of circulating medium. It seemed to remain for silver to supply any needed increase.

But silver was not in common use except as a subsidiary coin. For many years the value of the bullion necessary for coining a silver dollar had been greater than the value of the coin. Nobody therefore brought his silver to the mint but sold it instead in the commercial markets. Indeed so insignificant was the amount of silver usually coined into dollars that an act of 1873 systematizing the coinage laws had omitted the silver dollar completely from the list of coins. The omission was later referred to by the friends of silver currency as the "Crime of 1873." At the same time a remarkable coincidence was providing the motive power for the demand that silver be more largely used as currency. Early in the seventies Germany and the Latin Monetary Union (France, Switzerland, Belgium, Italy and Greece), had reduced the amount of their silver coinage, thus throwing a large supply

of bullion on the market.   Simultaneously, enlarged supplies
of silver were being found in western United States.   A
Nevada mine, for example, which had produced six hundred
and forty-five thousand dollars' worth of ore in 1873 had
turned out nearly twenty-five times that amount two years
later.   Naturally the market price of silver fell and the mine
owners began to seek an outlet for their product.   Thus the
people who were convinced that the volume of the currency
was insufficient for the industrial demands of the nation received a new and powerful reenforcement from the producers
of silver ore.   There arose what the New York *Tribune*
referred to as ''The Cloud in the West.''

Inevitably the cloud in the West threw its shadow into
Congress where the demand was insistent that the government ''do something for silver.''   A commission had been
appointed in 1876 to study the currency problem and make
recommendations.   When the report was made it appeared
that the opinions of the members were so divergent that little
was gained from the investigation.   While the commission
was deliberating, Richard P. Bland of Missouri introduced a
bill providing for the free and unlimited coinage of silver.
Under its provisions the owner of silver bullion could present
any quantity of his commodity to the government to be coined
under the conditions which controlled the coinage of gold.
The House responded readily to Bland's proposal.   In the
Senate, under the leadership of William B. Allison, the free
and unlimited feature of the bill was dropped and a provision
adopted limiting the purchase of bullion to an amount not
greater than four million dollars' worth per month and not
less than two million dollars' worth.   The bullion so obtained
was to be coined into silver dollars, which were to be legal tender for all debts public and private.   Bland was ready to accept the compromise because he hoped to be able to increase the
use of silver by subsequent legislation.   ''If we cannot do
that,'' he said, ''I am in favor of issuing paper money enough

to stuff down the bond-holders until they are sick." The remark was typical of the sectional and class hatreds and misunderstandings which this debate aroused, and of the maze of ignorance in which both sides were groping. To the silver faction, their opponents were "mendacious hirelings" and "Gilded Shylocks." God, in His infinite wisdom had imbedded silver in the western mountains for a beneficent purpose. "The country," said one speaker, "is in an agony of business distress and looks for some relief by a gradual increase of the currency." On the other hand, the opponents of silver scorned the "delusion" of a "clipped" coin and the dishonest proposition to make ninety cents' worth of silver pass as a dollar. The "storm-driven, buffeted, and scarred" ship of industrial peace, an easterner declared, "deeply laden with all precious and golden treasure is sighted in the offing! . . . shall we put out the lights? . . . Dare we remove the ship's helm, leaving her crippled and helpless?"

Sherman believed that this limited amount of silver could be taken into the currency system without difficulty, but President Hayes thought that harm would result from making the silver dollar a legal tender when the market value of the bullion in the coin was not equal in value to that of the gold dollar. He therefore vetoed the bill on February 28, 1878. He could not carry Congress with him, however, and the measure was passed over the veto on the same day.

Party lines had disappeared during the debates over the passage of the act. Eastern members of both houses and of both parties had been opposed, with few exceptions, to the increased use of silver; the westerners had been equally united in its favor. The East, the creditor section and the holder of most of the Civil War bonds, had no desire to try an experiment with the currency which would, in their opinion, reduce the purchasing power of their income. The debtor West looked with disfavor upon an increase in the real amount of their debts which was brought about by an inadequate supply of currency. Since prices continued to decline they believed that the remedy was a greater quantity of money. Evidently the greenback controversy was reviving in a new garb.

The approach of the resumption of specie payments which had been set, it will be remembered, for January 1, 1879, increased the burden under which the westerners and the debtor classes in general were working. Favorable commercial conditions and Sherman's foresight, tact and intelligence made it possible to overcome the various difficulties in the way of accumulating a sufficient reserve of gold, and on December 31, 1878, the Treasury had on hand about $140,000,000 of the precious metal, an amount nearly equal to forty per cent. of the paper in circulation. Despite the desirability of resumption, the first effects of preparations for it were harmful to considerable bodies of people. As January 1 approached, the greenbacks, which had been circulating at a depreciated value, rose nearer and nearer to par. Debts which had been incurred when paper dollars were worth sixty cents in gold, had to be paid in dollars worth eighty, ninety or a hundred cents, according to the date when the debt fell due. Business men who were heavily in debt and farmers whose property was mortgaged found their burden daily growing in size.

Notwithstanding the steady advance of paper toward par value, Sherman nervously awaited business hours on January 2, 1879 (since the first fell on Sunday), to see whether there would be such a rush of holders of paper who would wish gold that his slender stock would be wiped out. New York, the financial center, was watched with especial anxiety. To Sherman's surprise, only $135,000 of paper was presented for redemption in gold; to his amazement and relief, $400,000 in gold was presented in exchange for paper. Evidently, now that paper and metal were interchangeable, people preferred the lighter and more convenient medium. Favorable business conditions enabled the government to continue specie payments; a huge grain crop in 1879, coupled with crop failures in England, caused unprecedented exports of wheat, corn and other products, and a corresponding importation of gold. The damage resulting from the appreciation of paper was temporary in character; the public credit was vastly benefited; and the greater amount of stability in the value of paper proved invaluable to industry.

Happily Hayes's stormy political relations were balanced by comparative quiet in foreign affairs. Only Mexico caused trouble, and that was of negligible importance. A few raiders made sporadic excursions into Texas, which necessitated an expedition for the punishment of the marauders. General Ord was directed to cross the border if necessary, but General Diaz, at the head of the Mexican government, concluded an agreement for cooperation with the United States in the protection of the boundary. The agreement was only partly successful, however, and on several occasions troops crossed the Rio Grande and fought with bandits.

On the Pacific Coast, meanwhile, the Chinese question was becoming a political issue. In earlier times the immigration of the Chinese had been encouraged because of the need of a cheap labor supply when the transcontinental railroads were being built. As the coast filled up, however, with native population, and the demand for laborers fell off, there arose numerous objections to the oriental. It was seen that since he was willing to work for extremely low wages he could drive American laborers out of their places. Labor leaders such as Dennis Kearney held meetings on the "sand lots" in San Francisco and aroused anti-Chinese feeling. Riots and violence, even, were not unknown.

Just before the inauguration of President Hayes a commission of inquiry had visited the coast and examined many witnesses. The commission reported that the resources of the Pacific states had been more rapidly developed wth coolie labor than they would otherwise have been, but that the Chinese lived under filthy conditions, formed an inferior foreign element and were, on the whole, undesirable. It recommended that the executive take steps in the direction of a modification of the existing treaty with China, for fear that the problem might spread eastward with increasing immigration. The electioneering possibilities of the subject had appealed to both parties and they had earnestly demanded action in their platforms of 1876. Opinion was forming throughout the country, aided by Bret Harte's famous lines:

> Which I wish to remark
> And my language is plain,
> That for ways that are dark
> And tricks that are vain,
> The heathen Chinee is peculiar—
> Which the same I would rise to explain.

Action by Congress was hindered by the Burlingame treaty of 1868 with China, which covered the subject of immigration in unmistakable language. By its provisions citizens of China were to have the same rights of travel and residence in America as the subjects of the most favored nation. Reciprocally, China was to grant equal privileges to citizens of the United States. The process of modifying a treaty through the ordinary diplomatic channels was so slow that Congress sought to avoid delay by passing a law forbidding shipmasters to bring in more than fifteen Chinese at one time, and calling upon the President to notify China that the terms of the Burlingame treaty, in so far as they related to immigration, would not hold after July 1, 1879, when the proposed legislation would take effect. President Hayes sympathized with the purpose of the bill but felt obliged to veto it because of the Burlingame treaty. The veto message recalled that the treaty had been of American seeking and that its ratification had been applauded all over the country. The abrogation of part of the agreement would be equivalent to abrogation of

the whole, leaving American citizens in China without adequate treaty protection. Furthermore Hayes felt that treaties could not rightfully be violated by legislation, but
advocated other measures for the relief of the people of the
Pacific Coast. He thereupon sent to China a commission,
headed by James B. Angell of Michigan, which succeeded in
liberally modifying the existing treaty. Under the new arrangement the United States might "regulate, limit, or suspend" the immigration of Chinese laborers; and as the treaty
was promptly ratified, it redounded somewhat to the credit of
the Republicans in the election of 1880.

The administration of Hayes was, on the whole, an admirable one. The problems which he faced were varied and
difficult, but most of them were met wisely and with success.
To be sure, he did not grasp the social and economic forces
behind the monetary agitation; nor did he have the insight
and originality necessary for attacking the problem of industrial unrest as it appeared in the strike of 1877. But
neither did his associates, nor his successors in the presidency
for many years to come. On the other hand, the ethical
standards of the administration were high and the atmosphere
of the White House sane and wholesome. The home life of
the President was exceptionally attractive, for Mrs. Hayes
was a woman of unusual charm and social capacity. The attitude of Hayes on the southern question and on civil service
reform was courageous and progressive. And most of all, his
ideas on public questions were stated with unmistakable clearness in a day when old issues were sinking into the background
and both parties were reluctant to define their position on the
new ones.

BIBLIOGRAPHICAL NOTE

A great contribution to the understanding of Hayes's administration was made by the publication of C. R. Williams, *Life of
Rutherford B. Hayes* (2 vols., 1914). It is complete and contains

copious extracts from Hayes's diary, but is written with less of the critical spirit than is desirable; J. F. Rhodes has a valuable chapter in his *Historical Essays* (1909); J. W. Burgess, *Administration of R. B. Hayes* (1916), is a eulogy; V. L. Shores, *Hayes-Conkling Controversy* (1919), describes the civil service quarrel; J. R. Commons and others, *History of Labor in the United States* (2 vols., 1918), describes the strike of 1877; so also does J. F. Rhodes, *History of the United States from Hayes to McKinley* (1919) with full references. On the Chinese affair, consult Mrs. M. E. B. S. Coolidge, *Chinese Immigration* (1909). Most of the general histories already mentioned dwell at length on the Hayes administration.

For the official messages of this and succeeding adminstrations, the most convenient source is J. D. Richardson, *Messages and Papers of the Presidents* (10 vols., 1903).

CHAPTER VII

THE POLITICS OF THE EARLY EIGHTIES

After we have won the race, . . . we will give those who are entitled to positions office. What are we up here for?
WEBSTER FLANAGAN.

I concur in the Secretary's recommendation that the provision for coinage of a fixed amount (of silver) each month be repealed. . . .
    I . . . concur with the Secretary in recommending the abolition of . . . internal-revenue taxes. . . .
    The tariff laws also need revision. . . .
    If Congress should deem it advisable . . . to establish competitive tests for admission to the service, no doubts such as have been suggested shall deter me from giving the measure my earnest support.
CHESTER A. ARTHUR, first message to Congress, 1881.

THE Hayes administration was scarcely half over when the politicians began to look forward to the election of 1880. At the outset of his campaign, Hayes had advocated a single term for the executive and there was no widespread movement among the politicians to influence him to change his attitude. His enemies, indeed, had already turned to General Grant. There had been a third-term boom for the General during his second administration and he had indicated that he was not formidably opposed to further continuance in office. Suddenly, however, the anti-third-term feeling had risen to impressive proportions, whereupon the House of Representatives had adopted a resolution which characterized any departure from the two-term precedent as "unwise, unpatriotic, and fraught with peril to our free institutions." As the resolution passed by an overwhelming vote—233–18—nothing further was heard of a third-term boom.

The Hayes administration put a different complexion on

the matter. The wheel-horses of the party were not enthusiastic over the President or his policies, and in their extremity they looked to Grant. The New York State Republican Convention, under control of Roscoe Conkling and his forces, instructed delegates to support the General as a candidate for the nomination and endeavored to forestall opposition to a third term. It declared that the objection to a third presidential term applied only to a third consecutive term and hence was inapplicable to the re-election of Grant. Grant, meanwhile, presented a spectacle that was at once humorous and pathetic. He had not expected, on leaving the presidency, to return to power again, had dropped consideration of the political future and had given himself up to the enjoyment of foreign travel. The royal reception accorded him wherever he went suggested to his political supporters that they utilize his popularity. It was foreseen that when he returned to America he would receive a tremendous ovation, on the wave of which he might be carried into office. He was flooded with advice and entreaties that he act in accordance with this plan. His family was eager to return to the position of social eminence which they had occupied, and pressure from them was incessant. At first he did nothing either to aid or to hinder the boom, then gave way to the pressure and at last became extremely anxious to obtain the coveted prize.

If the politicians did, in truth, desire a relaxation from the patronage standards of the Hayes régime, they did not make that the ostensible purpose of their campaign. They argued that the times demanded a strong man; that foreign travel had greatly broadened the General and given him a knowledge of other forms of government; that he had been great as a commander of armies, greater as a President, and that as a citizen of the Republic he "shone with a luster that challenged the admiration of the world." Behind him were Conkling and Platt, with the New York state organization under their control, Don Cameron who held Pennsylvania in his hand, General Logan, strong in Illinois, and lesser leaders who wielded much power in smaller states. Many business men were ready to lend their aid; the powerful Methodist Church, to which he belonged, was favorable to him; and, of course, his popularity as a military leader was unbounded. His return to the United States while the enthusiasm was at its height was the signal for an unprecedented ovation. The opponents of a third term painted in high colors the danger of a revival of the scandals of Grant's days in the presidential chair, formed "No Third Term" leagues, called an "Anti-Third-Term" convention and decried the danger of continuing a military man in civil office. *The Nation* scoffed at the educational effect of foreign travel on a man who was fifty-seven years of age and could understand the language in only one of the countries in which he travelled. A large fraction of the Republican press, in fact, was in opposition. "Anything to beat Grant" and "No third term" were their war-cries. Nor was there any lack of Republican candidates to oppose the Grant movement and to give promise of a lively nominating convention. Blaine's popularity was as widespread as ever. Those who feared the nomination of either Grant or Blaine favored Senator George F. Edmunds of Vermont or Secretary Sherman. Both of these men were of statesmanlike proportions, but Edmunds was never widely popular and Sherman was lacking in the arts of the politician —"the human icicle," T. C. Platt called him.

The Republican nominating convention of 1880 met in Chicago in a building described as "one of the most splendid barns" ever built. This convention is unusually worthy of study because it involved most of the elements which entered into American politics in the early eighties. It was long memorable as making a record for that form of enthusiasm which bursts into demonstrations. "Great applause," "loud laughter," "cheers" and "hisses long and furious" dot the newspaper accounts of its deliberations. The members "acted like so many Bedlamites," one of the delegates said. On one day the opening prayer was so unexpectedly short that there was applause and laughter. The keen contest for the nomination resulted in galleries packed with supporters of the several candidates, who cheered furiously as their favorite delegates appeared. As the galleries came down nearly to the level of the floor, the spectators were almost as much members of the convention as the delegates themselves. It was under such conditions, then, that the convention proceeded to the serious business of adopting principles and choosing a leader.

Three hundred and six of the 757 delegates were sworn supporters of Grant—pledged to die, if they died at all, "with their boots on," one of their leaders boasted. In each of the big delegations—those from New York, Pennsylvania and Illinois—a minority was unfavorable to Grant. This minority could be counted in the General's column if the convention could be forced to adopt the so-called "unit-rule," under which the delegation from a state casts all its votes for the candidate favored by the majority. In this particular case, the minorities in New York, Pennsylvania and Illinois numbered more than sixty delegates, so that the adoption of the rule was a stake worth playing for. The plan formulated by the Grant leaders was worthy of the time.

Donald Cameron of Pennsylvania was chairman of the National Republican Committee. Following the usual custom, Cameron was to call the convention to order and present the temporary chairman who had been chosen by the Committee. As the Grant supporters were in a minority even on the Committee, provision was made to meet the emergency in case the majority insisted on the appointment of an anti-Grant chairman. Cameron was to announce the name, a Grant delegate was to move to substitute a Grant man instead, and Cameron would enforce the unit-rule in the resulting ballot. This would ensure control of the organization of the convention and, doubtless, of the nomination of the candidate.

Unhappily for this well-laid plan, rumor of it leaked out, and the majority of the National Committee—opposed to Grant—conveyed information to Cameron that he must agree to give up such a scheme or be ousted from his position. Cameron, convinced that his enemies were determined, gave up his project, and Senator George F. Hoar, who favored neither Grant nor Blaine, was made temporary and later permanent chairman.

Although defeated in the first skirmish, the Grant forces pressed forward for renewed conflict. Conkling presented a resolution that every member of the convention be bound in honor to support the eventual candidate, whoever he might be. The resolution passed 716 to three; and he then moved that the three who had voted in the negative had thereby forfeited their votes in the convention. James A. Garfield of Ohio led the opposition to such rough-shod action and Conkling angrily withdrew his resolution amid hisses. When Garfield reported from the Committee on Rules in regard to the regulations under which the convention should deliberate, he moved that the unit rule be not adopted and the convention upheld him. It was manifest that the delegates were not in a mood to surrender to a junto of powerful machine politicians.

The way having now been cleared for action, the convention adopted a platform. This was composed largely of a summary of the achievements of the party and denunciation of the opposition. Most of the planks were abstract or perfunctory, or expressed in such a way as not to commit the party seriously. *Harper's Weekly*, a Republican periodical, regretted the character of the platform and remarked that such documents are expected to say

> An undisputed thing
> In such a solemn way.

Judged by this criterion, the platform was ideal.   The obligations of the country to the veterans were emphasized and the restriction of Chinese immigration called for.   On the tariff, the only utterance was an avowal that duties levied for the purposes of revenue should discriminate in favor of labor. After this declaration of faith had been unanimously adopted, a Massachusetts delegate presented an additional plank advocating civil service reform.

The convention was now badly put to it.   To reject a plank which had been accepted both in 1872 and in 1876 would discredit the party, particularly as the platform just adopted had accused the opposition of sacrificing patriotism "to a supreme and insatiable lust for office."   Nevertheless the opposition to its adoption was formidable, and it had already been twice rejected in the Committee on Resolutions, which drew up the platform.   There seemed no way of avoiding the issue, however, and the plank was thereupon adopted, though not before Webster Flanagan of Texas had blurted out, "After we have won the race, . . . we will give those who are entitled to positions office.   What are we up here for?"

With the speeches presenting candidates to the convention, the real business of the week began.   Senator Conkling aroused a tempest of enthusiasm for General Grant in a famous speech which began with the lines,

> When asked what state he hails from,
> Our sole reply shall be,
> He comes from Appomattox
> And its famous apple tree.

Garfield presented Sherman's name.   At the outset General Grant led, Blaine was a close second and Sherman third. This order continued for thirty-five ballots.   By that time Blaine and Grant had fought each other to a standstill.   The General's three hundred and six held together without a break, and Blaine's forces were equally determined.[1]   There was little chance of compromise, as Grant and Blaine were not on speaking terms, and Conkling and Blaine looked upon each other with unconcealed hatred. Since Sherman was handicapped by lack of united support from his own state, the natural solution of the problem seemed to be the choice of some other leader who might harmonize the contending factions. On the thirty-fourth ballot, seventeen votes were given to Garfield; on the next, fifty; then a stampede began, in spite of a protest by Garfield, and on the thirty-sixth ballot a union of the Blaine and Sherman forces made him the choice of the convention. The nominee for the vice-presidency was Chester A. Arthur, who was one of the leading supporters of Grant and a member of the Conkling group.

The choice of Garfield was well received by the country, perhaps the more so as a relief from the danger of a third term. The nominee was a man of great industry, possessed of a store of information, tactful, modest, popular, an effective orator, and a veteran of the war. His rise from canal boy to candidate for the presidency exemplified the possibilities before industrious youth and gave rise to many a homily on democratic America. Yet his friends had to defend his relation to a paving scandal in the District of Columbia and an unwise connection with the Credit Mobilier of 1873. In neither of these cases does Garfield seem to have been corrupt, but in neither does he appear in a highly favorable light.[2]

As the Republicans were dispersing, the Greenback convention was assembling. Their strength in the campaign was almost negligible but their platform presaged the future.

---

[1] For Platt's account of the annual reunion and banquet of the three hundred and six—"The Old Guard"—see *Autobiography*, p. 115.

[2] Garfield's early career as a canal boy led to such campaign songs as the following:

He early learned to paddle well his own forlorn canoe,
Upon Ohio's grand canal he held the hellum true.
And now the people shout to him: "Lo! 't is for you we wait.
We want to see Jim Garfield guide our glorious ship of state."

Money to be issued only by the government, the volume of money increased, ameliorative labor legislation, restriction of Chinese immigration, regulation of interstate commerce, an income tax, government for the people rather than for classes, wider suffrage,—all these were advocated in concise and unmistakable terms. James B. Weaver was the presidential candidate.

Among the Democrats, the all important question was whether Tilden would be a candidate again. He naturally wished for a renomination and an opportunity to prove by an election that he had been "fraudulently" deprived of the presidency in 1876. The party, likewise, seemed to need his services, as no other leader of equal prominence had appeared. On the other hand, his health had rapidly failed since 1876 and it was apparent that he was unequal to the exacting labors of the presidency. Not until just before the meeting of the convention, however, did he make known his wishes and then he declared that he desired nothing so much as an honorable discharge from public service and that he "renounced" the renomination. The party took him at his word and turned to the adoption of a platform and the choice of another leader.

The platform reflected the bitterness of the party over the "great fraud" of 1876–1877 and advocated tariff for revenue only, civil service reform and the restriction of Chinese immigration. In other words, except for the usual self-congratulation and the denunciation of the opposition, the Democratic platform closely resembled that of the Republicans. The convention then nominated for the presidency General Winfield S. Hancock, a modest, brave Union soldier, of whom Grant once said, "his name was never mentioned as having committed in battle a blunder for which he was responsible." He was not an experienced politician, but was popular even in the South.

On the whole the Democratic convention was much less interesting than its Republican predecessor. There were no fierce factional quarrels to arouse the emotions to concert pitch. The applause spurted out here and there like the "jets from a splitting hose" in the "Ki yi yi yi" which characterized the cheers of the lower wards of New York, in contrast to the rolling billows of applause which formed so memorable an element in the opposition gathering. The New York *Tribune,* although hostile to everything Democratic, perhaps stated the fact when it commented on the lack of enthusiasm. The convention, the *Tribune* noted, was well-behaved, but a mob without leaders; there were no Conklings or Garfields or Logans, only John Kelleys and Wade Hamptons.

The campaign of 1880 reflected the lack of definite utterances in the party platforms. Since each side was loath to press forward to the solution of any real problem facing the nation, the campaign was confined, for the most part, to petty or even corrupt partisanship. The career of General Garfield was carefully overhauled for evidences of scandal. Arthur's failings as a public officer were duly paraded. General Hancock was ridiculed as "a good man weighing two hundred and forty pounds." Some attempt was made by the Republicans to make an issue of the tariff, and a remark of Hancock to the effect that the tariff was a "local issue" was jeered at as proving an ignorance of public questions. There was little response to the "bloody shirt" and little interest in "the great fraud." A modicum of enthusiasm was injected into the canvass by the participation of Conkling and General Grant. The former was not happily disposed toward the Republican candidate and Grant had always refused to make campaign speeches, but as the autumn came on and defeat seemed imminent, these two leaders were prevailed upon to lend their assistance. Near the end of the campaign a letter was circulated in the Pacific states, purporting to have been written by Garfield to a Mr. Morey, and expressing opposition to the restriction of Chinese immigration. The signature was a forgery, but complete exposure in the short time before election day was impossible and the letter perhaps injured Garfield on the coast. Nevertheless Garfield and Arthur won, although their popular plurality was only 9,500 in a total of about nine millions. The electoral vote was 214 to 155 and showed that the division among the states was sectional, for in the North Hancock carried only New Jersey, together with Nevada and five electoral votes in California, the result probably of the Morey letter.

Two aspects of the campaign had especial significance. The attempt by Conkling and his associates to choose the Republican nominee through the shrewd manipulation of political machinery, and against the wishes of the rank and file of the party, was a move on the part of the greater state bosses to get control of the national organization, so that they might manage it as they managed their local committees and conventions. The second notable circumstance concerned the collection and expenditure of the campaign funds.

Even before the convention met, the Republican Congressional Committee, pursuing the common practice of the time, addressed a letter to all federal employees, except heads of departments, in which the suggestion was made that the office holders would doubtless consider it a "privilege and a pleasure" to contribute to the campaign funds an amount equal to two per cent. of their salaries. The Republican National Committee also made its demands on office holders— usually five per cent. of a year's salary. The Democrats, having no hold on the federal offices, had to content themselves with the cultivation of the possibilities in states which they controlled. In New York, Senator Platt was chairman of the executive committee and he sent a similar communication to federal employees in the state. Even the office boy in a rural post office was not overlooked, and when contributions were not forthcoming, the names of delinquents were sent to their superiors. Other developments appeared after the election was over. In February, 1881, a dinner was given in honor of Senator S. W. Dorsey, secretary of the Republican National Committee, to whom credit was given for carrying the state of Indiana. General Grant presided and grace was asked by Reverend Henry Ward Beecher. Dorsey was an Arkansas carpet-bagger, who had been connected with a railroad swindle and was soon, as it turned out, to be indicted for complication in other frauds. The substance of the speeches was that the prospect of success in the campaign seemed waning, that Indiana was essential to success and that Dorsey was the agent who accomplished the task. Arthur, who was one of the speakers, explained the *modus operandi:* "Indiana was really, I suppose, a Democratic State. It had been put down on the books always as a State that might be carried by close and perfect organization and a great deal of—(laughter). I see the reporters are present, therefore I will simply say that everybody showed a great deal of interest in the occasion and distributed tracts and political documents all through the State."

With the victory accomplished, the politicians turned from the contest with the common enemy to the question of the division of the spoils; from the ostensible issue of platforms, to the real issue that Flanagan had personified. Although the Republicans had presented a united front to their opponents, there were factional troubles within the party that all but dwarfed the larger contest. The "Stalwarts" were composed of the thorough "organization men" like Conkling, Platt and Arthur; the "Half-breeds" were anti-organization men and more sympathetic with the administration. The commander of the Stalwarts and one of the most influential leaders in the country was Roscoe Conkling, Senator from New York. In person Conkling was a tall, handsome, imperious man, with something of the theatrical in his appearance and manner. As a politician he was aggressive, fearless, scornful, shrewd and adroit when he chose to be, and masterful, always. As an orator he knew how to play on the feelings of the crowd; his vocabulary, when he turned upon one whom he disliked, was memorable for its wealth of invective and ridicule, and especially he uncorked the vials of his wrath on any who were not strictly organization men. Although an able man and a successful lawyer, Conkling seems to have had less interest in the public welfare than in conventions, elections and patronage.

The announcement of Garfield's choice of a Cabinet was the signal for a fierce patronage fight. James G. Blaine, the choice for Secretary of State, was distasteful in the extreme to Conkling. Many years before (in 1866), during a debate in the House, Blaine had compared Conkling to Henry Winter Davis as

Hyperion to a satyr, Thersites to Hercules, mud to marble, dung-hill to diamond, a singed cat to a Bengal tiger, a whining puppy to a roaring lion.

He had contemptuously referred to Conkling's "haughty disdain, his grandiloquent swell, his majestic, supereminent, overpowering, turkey-gobbler strut." Accordingly when Garfield disregarded Conkling's wishes in regard to the representation which New York should have in the cabinet, Conkling laid the blame upon his old enemy.[3]

As soon as the administration was in office, the Senate met in executive session to act on appointments, and it appeared that the parties were evenly divided, the balance of power lying in the hands of two Independents. President Garfield sent in his list of nominees for office without consulting Conkling in regard to New York appointments. Among them was William H. Robertson for the coveted position of collector

---

[3] William Windom, of Minn., was Secretary of the Treasury; R. T. Lincoln, of Ill., Secretary of War; Wayne MacVeagh, of Pa., Attorney-General; T. L. James, of N. Y., Postmaster-General; W. H. Hunt, of La., Secretary of the Navy; S. J. Kirkwood, of Ia., Secretary of the Interior.

for the port of New York. As Robertson had been opposed
to Grant and to the unit rule in the Republican convention,
Conkling's rage reached a fever pitch. In an attempt to
discredit the President before the country, he made public
a letter from Garfield giving countenance to the practice of
levying campaign assessments on federal employees. Conkling's point of view is not difficult to understand. Consultation with the senators from a state with regard to nominations to offices within its boundaries was the common custom;
Conkling had sunk his dislike of Garfield during the campaign in order to assist in a party victory; moreover, he and
Platt, the other New York senator, understood that Garfield
had agreed to dispense New York patronage in conformity to
the wishes of the Stalwarts, in case Conkling took the stump.
He had carried out his part of the bargain and now desired
his *quid pro quo*.

Meanwhile the Senate was trying to organize and having
failed because of the even division of the parties, stopped the
attempt long enough to act on the nominations. The President then withdrew all except that of Robertson, thus indicating that offices in which other senators were concerned
would not be filled until the New York case was settled.
Foreseeing that the members would wish to clear the way for
their own interests and that Robertson's nomination was
likely to be agreed to, Conkling and Platt resigned their posts
and appealed to the New York legislature for a re-election as
a vindication of the stand they had taken. As the legislature was Republican and as Vice-President Arthur went to
Albany to urge their case, they seemed likely to succeed; but
to their mortification they were both defeated after an extended contest, and Conkling retired permanently to private
life. Platt, who was promptly dubbed "Me Too," also relinquished public office, but only for a time. In the meanwhile,
as soon as Conkling and Platt had left the Senate, the nomi-

nation of Robertson had been approved, and Garfield was triumphant.

Further light was thrown upon political conditions by the investigations of the "star routes." These were routes in the South and West where mails had to be carried by stage lines, and were under the control of the Second Assistant Postmaster-General, Thomas J. Brady. Rumors had been common for some years that they were a source of corruption. Garfield's Postmaster-General, Thomas L. James, had already made a reputation as the reform postmaster of New York, and he set himself to investigate the reports. Among other things it was discovered that a combination of public men and contractors had succeeded in raising the compensation on 134 star routes from $143,169 to $622,808, dividing the extra profits among themselves. Brady and Senator Dorsey, the active agent in the campaign in Indiana, were accused of being in the "ring" and were indicted on the ground of conspiracy to defraud the government. Brady attempted to block the investigation by threatening Garfield with an exposure of the campaign methods, and when the threat failed he made public a letter from the President to "My dear Hubbell," chairman of the Congressional Committee, similar to that which Conkling had earlier published. The trials of the conspirators dragged on until 1883 and resulted in the acquittal of all the accused except one of the least important. Yet some good was accomplished, for the ring was broken up. Dorsey retired from public life, and renewed attention was drawn to the need of better federal officials.

During the course of the trials, the country was shocked by the assassination of the President on July 2, 1881, at the hands of a disappointed office seeker named Guiteau. Despite a strong constitution Garfield grew slowly weaker and died on September 19. The catastrophe affected the country the more profoundly because of its connection with the factional quarrel in the Republican party and because, following the recent murder of the Russian Czar, it seemed to show that democratic government was no guarantee against violence.[4]

The consternation with which the elevation of Chester A. Arthur to the presidency was received was not confined to the Democrats. An oft-repeated remark made at the time was expressive of the opinion of those best acquainted with the new executive: " 'Chet' Arthur President of the United States! Good God!'' In truth Arthur's previous career hardly justified anything except consternation. He had been identified always with machine politics and particularly with the Conkling group; he had been a prominent figure in the opposition to Hayes when the latter attempted to improve conditions in the New York Customs House; and had taken an active and undignified share in the quarrel between Garfield and Conkling. Chester A. Arthur, however, was a combination of characteristics such as enlist the interest of the student of human nature. Of Vermont birth, educated at Union College where he had taken high rank, he had taught school for a time, had entered the practice of law in New York, had made a good war record, and had been a member of the Republican party from its beginning. In many ways Arthur was made for politics. He was the "man of the world" in appearance, polished, refined, well-groomed, scrupulously careful about his attire, a *bon-vivant*. Yet he was equally at home in the atmosphere of politics in the early eighties; a leader of the " 'Johnnies'' and "Jakes,'' the "Barneys'' and "Mikes'' of New York City. Dignity char-

---

[4] The death of the President emphasized the need of a presidential succession law. Under an act of 1792, the president and vice-president were succeeded by the president of the Senate and the speaker of the House. When Garfield died, the Senate had not yet elected a presiding officer and the House had not met. The death of Arthur would have left the country without a legal head. The Presidential Succession Act of 1886 remedied the fault by providing for the succession of the cabinet in order, beginning with the Secretary of State. The presiding officers of the Senate and House were omitted, because they might not be of the dominant party.

acterized him, whether in the "knock-down" and "drag-out" caucus or at an exclusive White House reception. He possessed a social refinement that is not usually associated with ward politics but which forms an element of the "gentleman" in the best sense of that abused word.

Yet they who feared that President Arthur would be like Chester A. Arthur, the collector of the port, were treated to a revelation. The suddenness with which the elevation to the responsibility of the executive's position broadened the view of the President proved that he possessed qualities which had been merely hidden in the pursuit of ordinary partisan politics. Platt, expectant of the dismissal of Robertson, now that a Stalwart was in power, fell back in disgust and disowned his former associate, for it appeared that Arthur intended to further the principles of reform. His first annual message to Congress contained a sane discussion of the civil service and the needed remedies, which committed him whole-heartedly to the competitive system. Although he did not go as far as some reformers would have had him, he went so much farther than was expected that commendation was enthusiastic, even on the part of the most prominent leaders in the reform element. In the same message he urged the repeal of the Bland-Allison silver-coinage act, the reduction of the internal revenue, revision of the tariff, a better navy, post-office savings banks, and enlightened Indian legislation. Altogether it was clear that he had laid aside much of the partisan in succeeding to his high office.[5]

The Chinese problem soon provided him with an opportunity to show an independence of judgment, together with an indifference to mere popularity, which were in keeping with the new Arthur, but which were a surprise to his former as-

[5] The cabinet was composed of F. T. Frelinghuysen, N. J., Secretary of State; C. J. Folger, N. Y., Secretary of the Treasury; R. T. Lincoln, Ill., Secretary of War; B. H. Brewster, Pa., Attorney-General; T. O. Howe, Wis., Postmaster-General; W. E. Chandler, N. H., Secretary of the Navy; H. M. Teller, Colo., Secretary of the Interior.

sociates. As a result of the changes in the Burlingame treaty, which gave the United States authority to suspend the immigration of Chinese laborers, Congress passed a bill in 1882 to prohibit the incoming of laborers for twenty years, western Republicans joining with the Democrats in its passage.[6] Arthur vetoed the measure on the ground that a stoppage for so great a period as twenty years violated those provisions of the treaty which allowed us merely to suspend immigration, not to prohibit it. An attempt to overcome the veto failed for lack of the necessary two-thirds majority. Congress did, however, pass legislation suspending the immigration of laborers for ten years, and this bill the President signed. Later acts have merely extended this law or made it more effective.

Arthur also exercised the veto upon a rivers and harbors bill. It had, of course, long been the custom for the federal government to aid in the improvement of the harbors and internal water-ways of the country. But the modest sums of *ante-bellum* days grew rapidly after the war, stimulated by immense federal revenues, until the suggested legislation of 1882 appropriated nearly nineteen million dollars. It provided not merely for the dredging of great rivers like the Mississippi and Ohio, but also for the Lamprey River in New Hampshire, the Waccemaw in North Carolina, together with Goose Rapids and Cheesequake Creek. Some of these, the opposition declared, might better be paved than dredged.[7] It might seem that a bill against which such obvious objections could be raised would be doomed to failure. But the argument of Ransom of North Carolina, who had charge of the bill in its later stages in the Senate, seems to have been a decisive one. Somebody had objected that the members of the committee had cared for the interests of their own states

6 Above, p. 155.
7 Some thoroughly unselfish members of Congress like Senator Hoar, however, believed the bill a justifiable one and voted for it. See Hoar, *Autobiography*, II, chapter VIII.

merely. Ransom repelled the charge. He showed that the New England states had been looked out for; "Look next to New York, that great grand, magnificent State . . . that empire in itself. . . . Go to Delaware, little, glorious Delaware." The committee had retained $20,000 for Delaware. "Go next . . . to great, grand old Virginia." Virginia had received something. "Go to Missouri, the young beautiful, growing, powerful State of my friend over the way." And so on—all had been treated with thoughtful care. Ransom was wise in his day and generation. Although Arthur objected to the bill on the grounds of extravagance and of the official demoralization which accompanied it, nevertheless Republicans and Democrats alike joined in passing over the veto an act which would get money into their home states.

The congressional elections in the fall of 1882 indicated that the factional disputes among the Republicans, and their failure to reform conditions in the civil service had presented the opposition with an opportunity. In the House of Representatives, Republican control was replaced by a Democratic majority of sixty-nine; the state legislatures chosen were Democratic in such numbers as to make sure the even division of the Senate when new members were elected; in Pennsylvania, a Democratic reformer, Robert E. Pattison, was elected governor, and in New York another, Grover Cleveland, was successful by the unprecedented majority of 190,000.

The results of the campaign added interest to a civil service reform bill which had been drafted by some reformers led by Dorman B. Eaton, and which had been presented to the Senate by George H. Pendleton, of Ohio. The debate elicited several points of view. Pendleton set forth the evils of the existing system of appointments, and emphasized the superior advantages of appointment after competitive examination. The Democrats were in distress. Although Pendleton was himself a Democrat and the party platforms had been advocating reform, nevertheless the election of 1884 was not far ahead, Democratic success seemed likely, and the party leaders desired an unrestrained opportunity to fill the offices with their followers. Senator Williams expressed a conviction that the Republican party was a party of corruption and continued:

> The only way to reform is to put a good honest Democratic president in in 1884; then turn on the hose and give him a good hickory broom and tell him to sweep the dirt away.

The Republicans, on their side, were fearful of the same clean sweep that Williams hoped for, and they therefore looked with greater equanimity upon a bill which might retain in office the existing office-holders, most of whom belonged to their party. This aspect of the situation was not lost upon such Democrats as Senator Brown who moved that the measure be entitled "a bill to perpetuate in office the Republicans who now hold the patronage of the government." In the Senate only five members voted against its passage, but thirty-three absented themselves; and in the House forty-seven opposed, while eighty-seven were absent. A little study of the debate makes it clear that the passage of the act was due to conviction in favor of reform on the part of a few and to fear of public opinion on the part of many others. Undoubtedly many of the absentees were members who would not vote for the measure and were fearful of the results of voting against it. The President signed the bill January 16, 1883.

The Pendleton act left large discretion in the hands of the president. It authorized the appointment of a commission of three who should prepare and put into effect suitable rules for carrying out the law. The act also provided that government offices should be arranged in classes and that entrance to any class should be obtained by competitive examination; that no person should be removed from the service for refusing to contribute to political funds; and that examinations should be held in one or more places in each state and territory where candidates appeared. The system was to be inaugurated in customs districts and post offices where the number of employees was as many as fifty, but could be extended later under direction of the president. The soliciting or receiving of contributions by federal officials of all grades, for political purposes, was forbidden. With the exceptions just mentioned, officers could be removed from office as before, but the purpose of removal was now gone. Since the appointee to the vacancy must be the successful competitor in an examination, the chief who removed an officer could not replace him with a personal friend or party worker.

The first commission was headed by Dorman B. Eaton. The work of grading officials and placing them within the protection of the law began at once, and by the close of President Arthur's term nearly 16,000 were classified. Fortunately, the work of the commission was carried on sensibly and slowly, and no backward steps had to be taken.

The attitude of Congress toward tariff revision illustrates many of the characteristics of congressional action during the early eighties. In his first message to Congress, Arthur said that the surplus for the year was $100,000,000, and therefore urged the reduction of the internal revenue taxes and the revision of the tariff. In May, 1882, Congress authorized a tariff commission to investigate and report, and in conformity with the law Arthur appointed its nine members. All of them were protectionists and the chairman, John L. Hayes, was secretary of the Wool Manufacturers' Association. After holding hearings in more than a score of cities and examining some hundreds of witnesses, the commission recommended reductions varying from nothing in some cases to forty or fifty per cent. in others. The average reduction was twenty to twenty-five per cent.

Using the report as a foundation, the Senate drew up a tariff measure, added it to a House bill which provided for a reduction of the internal revenues, and passed the combination. Meanwhile, lobbyists poured into Washington to guard the interests of the producers of lumber, pig-iron, sugar and other materials upon which the tariff might be reduced. When the Senate bill reached the House it contained lower duties than the protectionist members desired. The latter, although in possession of the organization of the House, were not strong enough to restore higher rates, but under the shrewd management of Thomas B. Reed, one of their number, they were able to refer the bill to a conference committee of the two houses which contained seven strong protectionists out of ten members.[8] Reed admitted that the proceedings were "unusual in their nature and very forcible in their character" but he felt that a change in the tariff had been promised and that the only way to bring it about in the face of Democratic opposition was to settle the details "in the quiet of a conference committee." A "great emergency" having arisen, he would take extraordinary measures. The bill produced under these circumstances reduced the internal revenue taxes, lowered some of the tariff duties and raised others, but left the general level at the point where it had been at the close of the war. *The Nation*, favorable to reform, scornfully characterized the act as "taking a shaving off the duty on iron wire, and adding it to the duty on glue!" Senator Sherman, a protectionist member of the conference committee, wrote an account of the whole procedure many years afterward. After commending the spirit and proposals of the tariff commission and mentioning the successful efforts of many persons to have their individual interests looked out for, he expressed a regret that he did not defeat the bill, as he could have done in view of the evenly balanced party situation in the Senate at that time.

[8] An account of this peculiar manœuvre may be found in Taussig, *Tariff History*, 6th ed., p. 232 n.

BIBLIOGRAPHICAL NOTE

The election of 1880 is well treated by Sparks, Stanwood, Andrews, and Rhodes. Senator G. F. Hoar, the chairman of the Republican nominating convention, has a valuable chapter in his *Autobiography of Seventy Years*. Such newspapers as the New York *Times* and *Tribune* are invaluable for a discussion of the conventions. An invaluable service is the publication of T. C. Smith, *The Life and Letters of James A. Garfield* (2 vols., 1925).

The events of the administration, such as the tariff debates, the passage of the civil service law and others are discussed in the special works mentioned in Chapter V. Consult also: Edward Stanwood, *J. G. Blaine;* T. C. Platt, *Autobiography;* and A. R. Conkling, *Life and Letters of Roscoe Conkling*. The *Annual Cyclopaedia* contains several excellent articles on the tariff (1882, 1883), civil service reform (1883), star route trials (1882, 1883). H. C. Thomas, *The Return of the Democratic Party to Power in 1884* (1919), contains useful chapters on Garfield and Arthur.

CHAPTER VIII

THE OVERTURN OF 1884

We love him [Cleveland] most of all for the enemies he has made.

GENERAL E. S. BRAGG.

I have a hungry party behind me . . . Sometimes the pressure is almost overwhelming, and a President cannot always get at the exact truth, but I want . . . all my friends to know, that I am trying to do what is right.

GROVER CLEVELAND.

THE election of 1880 was memorable only for the type of politics with which that contest was so inextricably involved. The party leaders were second-rate men; the platforms, except for that of the Greenback party, were as lacking in definiteness as the most timid office-seeker could desire; in brief, it was a cross-section of American professional politics at its worst. The election of 1884 was a distinct, although not a complete contrast. It was not a campaign of platforms, but like the election of 1824 it was a battle of men. Two genuine leaders, each representing a distinct type of politics, contended for an opportunity to try out a philosophy of government in the executive chair. In 1880 the conventions were the chief interest—the campaign was dull. The campaign of 1884, on the other hand, was one of the most remarkable in our history.

It will be remembered that the year 1882 had been characterized by political upheavals. In Pennsylvania the Greenbackers had demanded that currency be issued only by the central government—not by the national banks—and that measures be taken to curb monopolies; the independent Republicans had revolted against Cameron, and demanded civil service reform and the overthrow of bossism; and the Democrats had elected a governor of the reformer type, Robert E. Pattison. Massachusetts Republicans had gasped the day after the election to find that "Ben" Butler, who bore a questionable reputation as a politician, as a soldier and as a man, had been elected by a combination of Greenbackers and Democrats on a reform program. In New York the Democrats had taken advantage of a factional quarrel among their opponents to elect as governor a man who had achieved a reputation as a reformer—Grover Cleveland. That some of the states which had been Democratic in 1882, had become Republican again in 1883 illustrates the unstable character of the politics of the time.

The beginning of the convention season of 1884 gave hint of the vigorous campaign ahead. An Anti-Monopoly party nominated Benjamin F. Butler, who was also supported by the Greenbackers. The Prohibitionists presented a ticket headed by John P. St. John. The action of the Republican convention, which met in Chicago on June 3, proved to be the turning point in the campaign. President Arthur was frankly a candidate for another term, but he did not have the united support of the professional politicians and was distrusted by most of the reform element. Nor had his veto of the Chinese immigration bill and the rivers and harbors act tended to increase his popularity. Most enthusiastic, confident and vociferous were the supporters of James G. Blaine, of Maine. The independent element hoped to nominate Senator Edmunds, of Vermont, and was particularly disturbed at the character of the workers for the "Man from Maine." His campaign manager, Stephen B. Elkins, had been charged with a discreditable connection with the star-route scandals; men of the Platt type were urging that it was now Blaine's "turn"; and Powell Clayton, an Arkansas carpet-bagger of ill-repute, was the Blaine candidate for the position of temporary chairman of the convention.

Before a candidate was chosen the delega
adoption of the platform. This was of the u
an advance over that of 1880 in several r
mitted the party to a protective tariff and
terstate commerce law and the extension
reform.

The balloting for candidates proved that
the choice of the convention. The mere me
threw the delegates into storms of applause
first ballot he received votes from every state
five. On the fourth ballot he received an
jority and became the nominee. John A.
a prominent politician and soldier, was n
vice-presidency—a tail to the ticket, in t
Democrats, which was designed to "Wag
Soldier Vote.'' The choice of Blaine was
by the different factions in the convention.
delegates, in a special train, went from Ch
Maine, before starting for home, in order pe
their support to the candidate. On the oth
Roosevelt disgustedly remarked that he was
ranch in the West to stay he knew not h
William Curtis sadly declared that he had b
birth of the Republican party and feared t
witness of its death. Other reformers were

The outspoken Republican opposition to
nite aid and comfort to the Democrats whos
ing a month later, could take advantage of t
in the opposition. During the interval bet
ventions the growing sentiment in favor
of Grover Cleveland received the additiona
pendent Republican support. The Democr
an object of suspicion to them, but they wer
risks of even a Democratic administratio
proved integrity should be nominated, and

service reform and the overthrow of bossism; and the Democrats had elected a governor of the reformer type, Robert E. Pattison. Massachusetts Republicans had gasped the day after the election to find that "Ben" Butler, who bore a questionable reputation as a politician, as a soldier and as a man, had been elected by a combination of Greenbackers and Democrats on a reform program. In New York the Democrats had taken advantage of a factional quarrel among their opponents to elect as governor a man who had achieved a reputation as a reformer—Grover Cleveland. That some of the states which had been Democratic in 1882, had become Republican again in 1883 illustrates the unstable character of the politics of the time.

The beginning of the convention season of 1884 gave hint of the vigorous campaign ahead. An Anti-Monopoly party nominated Benjamin F. Butler, who was also supported by the Greenbackers. The Prohibitionists presented a ticket headed by John P. St. John. The action of the Republican convention, which met in Chicago on June 3, proved to be the turning point in the campaign. President Arthur was frankly a candidate for another term, but he did not have the united support of the professional politicians and was distrusted by most of the reform element. Nor had his veto of the Chinese immigration bill and the rivers and harbors act tended to increase his popularity. Most enthusiastic, confident and vociferous were the supporters of James G. Blaine, of Maine. The independent element hoped to nominate Senator Edmunds, of Vermont, and was particularly disturbed at the character of the workers for the "Man from Maine." His campaign manager, Stephen B. Elkins, had been charged with a discreditable connection with the star-route scandals; men of the Platt type were urging that it was now Blaine's "turn"; and Powell Clayton, an Arkansas carpet-bagger of ill-repute, was the Blaine candidate for the position of temporary chairman of the convention.

Before a candidate was chosen the delegates turned to the adoption of the platform. This was of the usual type but was an advance over that of 1880 in several respects. It committed the party to a protective tariff and advocated an interstate commerce law and the extension of civil service reform.

The balloting for candidates proved that Blaine was clearly the choice of the convention. The mere mention of his name threw the delegates into storms of applause and even on the first ballot he received votes from every state in the union save five. On the fourth ballot he received an overwhelming majority and became the nominee. John A. Logan of Illinois, a prominent politician and soldier, was nominated for the vice-presidency—a tail to the ticket, in the opinion of the Democrats, which was designed to "Wag Invitation to the Soldier Vote." The choice of Blaine was variously received by the different factions in the convention. The Pacific coast delegates, in a special train, went from Chicago to Augusta, Maine, before starting for home, in order personally to pledge their support to the candidate. On the other hand, Theodore Roosevelt disgustedly remarked that he was going to a cattle-ranch in the West to stay he knew not how long. George William Curtis sadly declared that he had been present at the birth of the Republican party and feared that he was to be a witness of its death. Other reformers were no less disaffected.

The outspoken Republican opposition to Blaine gave infinite aid and comfort to the Democrats whose convention, coming a month later, could take advantage of the growing schism in the opposition. During the interval between the two conventions the growing sentiment in favor of the nomination of Grover Cleveland received the additional impetus of independent Republican support. The Democratic party was still an object of suspicion to them, but they were ready to run the risks of even a Democratic administration, if a leader of proved integrity should be nominated, and Cleveland seemed to them to meet the demands of the times. The first work of the convention, which met in Chicago on July 8, was the adoption of a reform platform. Characterizing the opposition party as a "reminiscence," it condemned Republican misrule, and promised reform; it proposed a revision of the tariff that would be fair to all interests, and reductions which would promote industry, do no harm to labor and raise sufficient revenue; and it briefly advocated "honest" civil service reform.

The enthusiasm which the independent Republicans were manifesting for Cleveland was balanced by the hostility of elements within his party. As Governor he had exercised his veto power with complete disregard for the effect on his own political future. He had vetoed a popular measure reducing fares on the New York City elevated railroad, basing his objections on the ground that the bill violated the provisions of the fundamental railroad law of the state. He was opposed by Tammany Hall, led by John Kelley, who declared that the labor element disliked him. Kelley's reputation, however, was such that his hostility seemed like a compliment and gave force to General Bragg's assertion, in seconding the nomination of Cleveland, that his friends "love him most for the enemies he has made." The first ballot proved that the Governor was stronger than his competitors, Senator Bayard, Allen G. Thurman, Samuel J. Randall and several men of lesser importance, and on the second ballot he received the nomination.

The choice of Cleveland gave the independent movement more than the expected impetus. The New York *Times* at once crossed the line into the Cleveland camp and *Harper's Weekly,* long a supporter of the Republicans, the Boston *Herald,* Springfield *Republican,* New York *Evening Post, The Nation,* the Chicago *Times* and a host of less important ones followed. A conference of Independents in New York City, which was composed of five hundred delegates and which enlisted the support of such men as Carl Schurz, George William Curtis, Henry C. Lea, Charles J. Bonaparte, Moorfield Storey and President Seelye of Amherst College, gave striking evidence of the revolt which Blaine's nomination had aroused. Curtis said in the conference, that the chief issue of the campaign was moral rather than political. The New York *Times* declared that the issue was a personal one. Some of the better element, however, like Senator Hoar, earnestly urged the election of Blaine, while Senator Edmunds refused either to aid or oppose his party. Others, like Roosevelt, were unable to give ungrudging support, but felt that reform would be better promoted by working within the party than by withdrawing. It is obvious that Blaine and Cleveland, not the platforms of the parties, had become the issue of the campaign.

James G. Blaine was born in Pennsylvania in 1830, was educated at Washington College in his native state, later moved to Augusta, Maine, and purchased an interest in the Kennebec *Journal*. On assuming his journalistic duties he familiarized himself with the politics of the state and became powerful in local, and later in federal affairs. He was a member of the first Republican convention and was chairman of the state Republican committee for more than twenty years, from which point of vantage he had a prevailing influence in Maine politics. He served in the state and federal legislatures as well as in Garfield's cabinet and was a prominent candidate for the presidential nomination in 1876 and in 1880.

Grover Cleveland, although only seven years younger than Blaine, was relatively inexperienced on the stage of national affairs. He was born in New Jersey, the son of a Presbyterian minister, grew up with little education, moved to New York, was salesman in a village store and later clerk in a law office, at the age of eighteen. Although he had been sheriff of Erie county, it was not until 1881, when he became mayor of Buf-

falo, that he took an important part in politics, and here
his record as the business-like "veto mayor" was such as to
carry him into the governor's chair a year later. The huge
majority which he received in the gubernatorial contest was
not wholly due to his own strength—doubtless factional quarrels among the Republicans assisted him—but the prominence
which this election gave him and his conduct as Governor
made inevitable his candidacy for higher office.

Few men could have been nominated who would have presented a more complete contrast than Blaine and Cleveland.
In personality Blaine was magnetic, approachable, high-
strung, possessed of a vivid imagination and of a marvelous
memory for facts, names and faces. Over him men went "insane in pairs," either devotedly admiring or completely dis-
trusting him. Cleveland was almost devoid of personal charm
except to his most intimate associates. He was brusque and
tactless, unimaginative, plodding, commonplace in his tastes
and in the elements of his character. Men threw their hats
in the air and cheered themselves hoarse at the name of
Blaine; to Cleveland's courage, earnestness and honesty, they
gave a tribute of admiration. When the campaign was at
fever heat, Blaine was lifting crowds of eager listeners to the
mountain peaks of enthusiasm; Cleveland was in the governor's room in Albany, phlegmatically plodding away at the
business of his office. He was too heavy, unimaginative, direct, to indulge in flights of oratory. Yet scarcely anything
that Blaine said still lives, while some of Cleveland's phrases
have passed into the language of everyday.

No less a contrast existed between Blaine and Cleveland as
political characters. The former's experience in the machinery of politics, in the disposal of its loaves and fishes
has already been mentioned. Of that part of politics, Cleveland had had no experience. It is said that he never was in
Washington, except for a single day, until he went there to become President. Both were bold and active fighters, but

Blaine was a strategist, a manager and a diplomat, while Cleveland could merely state the policy which he desired to see put into effect, and then crash ahead. Blaine had the instinct for the popular thing, was never ahead of his party, was surrounded by his followers; Cleveland saw the thing which he felt a moral imperative to accomplish and was far in advance of his fellows. The Republican was popular among the professional political element in his party and was supported by it; the Democrat never was. Cleveland openly declared his attitude on controverted issues, in words that admitted of no ambiguity and at times when only silence or soft words would save him from defeat. Blaine lacked something—perhaps it was moral courage and the indifference to immediate results which were necessary for so exalted an action. Cleveland had more of the reformer in his nature, and had so keen a sense of responsibility and duty that his political career was a succession of battles against things that seemed wrong to him. Blaine accepted the party standards as they were; he belonged to the past, to the policies and political morality of war and reconstruction; Cleveland belonged to the transition from reconstruction to the twentieth century.

The particular thing, however, that came out of Blaine's past to dog his foot-steps, give him the enmity of the Independents—better known as the ''Mugwumps''—and threaten him with defeat, was a series of transactions exposed in the Mulligan letters. In order to understand these, it is necessary to inquire into events that occurred fifteen years before the overturn of 1884. In April, 1869, a bill favorable to the Little Rock and Fort Smith Railroad—an Arkansas land-grant enterprise—was before the House of Representatives. Blaine was Speaker. As the session was near its close and the bill seemed likely to be lost, its friends bespoke Blaine's assistance. He suggested that a certain point of order be raised, which would facilitate the passage of the measure, and also asked General John A. Logan to raise the point. Logan did so, Blaine sustained him and the act was passed. Nearly three months later, Warren Fisher, Jr., a Boston business man, asked Blaine to participate in the affairs of the Little Rock Railroad. Blaine signified his readiness, closing his letter with the words, "I do not feel that I shall prove a dead-head in the enterprise if I once embark in it. I see various channels in which I know I can be useful." When Blaine's enemies got hold of this, they declared that he intended to use his position as Speaker to further the interests of the road, as he had done at the time of the famous point of order; his friends asserted that he intended merely to sell the securities of the road to investors. Whether one of these contentions is true, or both, he did sell considerable amounts of the securities of the road to Maine friends, getting a "handsome commission." Considerable correspondence passed between Blaine and Fisher from 1869 to 1872 when their relations ended. Blaine understood that all their correspondence was mutually surrendered.

In the spring of 1876, the presidential campaign was on the horizon and Blaine was a prominent candidate for the Republican nomination. Meanwhile ugly rumors were flying about concerning the connection of certain members of Congress, Blaine among them, with questionable railroad transactions, and he arose in the House to deny the charges. He did not discuss the matter fully, as he did not wish his Maine constitutents to know that he had received a large commission for selling Little Rock securities. Gossip grew, however, and a congressional investigation resulted in May, 1876. Blaine was one of the witnesses, but was doubtless anxious to bring the investigation to an end, since it clearly reduced his chances of receiving the nomination. Presently gossip said that Warren Fisher and James Mulligan were going to testify. Mulligan had been confidential clerk to one of Mrs. Blaine's brothers and later to Fisher. When Mulligan began his testimony it appeared that he intended to lay before the com-

mittee a package of letters that had passed between Blaine
and Fisher, and thereupon, at Blaine's whispered request,
one of the members of the committee procured an adjournment for the day. That evening Blaine found Mulligan at
the latter's hotel and prevailed on him to surrender the letters temporarily, in order that Blaine might read and then return them. Blaine thereupon consulted two lawyers and on
their advice he refused to restore the package to Mulligan.
Merely to keep silence, however, was to admit guilt. Blaine,
therefore, arose one day in the House of Representatives and
holding the letters in his hand read selections and defended
himself in a remarkable burst of emotional oratory. At the
climax of this defence he elicited from the chairman of the
committee of investigation an unwilling admission that the
committee had suppressed a dispatch which Blaine declared
would exonerate him. Blaine was triumphant, his friends
sure that he had cleared himself and the matter dropped for
the time. Further investigation was prevented by Blaine's
refusal to produce the letters even before the committee and
by his sudden illness shortly afterward. His election to the
Senate soon took him out of the jurisdiction of the House
committee and no action resulted.

The nomination of Blaine in 1884 was a fresh breeze on
the half-dead embers of the Mulligan letters. *Harper's
Weekly* and other periodicals published them with damaging explanatory remarks. Campaign committees spread them
abroad in pamphlet form. Attention was directed to such
phrases as "I do not feel that I shall prove a dead-head" and
"I see various channels in which I know I can be useful."
Hostile cartoonists used the phrases with an infinite variety
of innuendo. But the most powerful evidence was still to
come. On September 15, 1884, Fisher and Mulligan made
public additional letters which Blaine had not posssessed at
the time of his defence in 1876. The most damaging of these
was one in which Blaine had drawn up a letter completely ex-

onerating himself, which he asked Fisher to sign and make public as his own. Blaine had marked his request "confidential" and had written at the bottom "Burn this letter." Fisher had neither written the letter which was requested nor burned Blaine's. Meanwhile it was recalled that Blaine had earlier characterized the reformers as "upstarts, conceited, foolish, vain" and as "noisy but not numerous, pharisaical but not practical, ambitious but not wise," and the already intemperate campaign became more personal than ever.

Thomas Nast's able pencil caricatured Blaine in *Harper's Weekly* as a magnetic candidate too heavy for the party elephant to carry; *Puck* portrayed him as the "tattooed man" covered all over with "Little Rock," "Mulligan Letters" and the like. *Life* described him as a

> Take all I can gettery,
> Mulligan lettery,
> Solid for Blaine old man.

Nor was the contest of scurrility entirely one-sided. *Judge* caricatured Cleveland in hideous cartoons. The New York *Tribune* described him as a small man "everywhere except on the hay-scales." Beginning in Buffalo rumors spread all over the country that Cleveland was an habitual drunkard and libertine. As is the way of such gossip, its magnitude grew until the Governor appeared in the guise of a monster of immorality. The editor of the *Independent* went himself to Buffalo and ran the rumors to their sources. He came to the conclusion that Cleveland as a young man had been guilty of an illicit connection, that he had made amends for the wrong which he had done and had since lived a blameless life. Such religious periodicals as the *Unitarian Review*, however, continued to describe him as a *"debauchee"* and *"roué."* Nearly a thousand clergymen gathered in New York declared him a synonym of "incapacity and incontinency." Much was made, also, of the fact that Cleveland had not served in the war, and John Sherman denounced him as having no sympathy for the Union cause. It did little good in the heated condition of partisan discussion to point out that young Cleveland had two brothers in the service, that he was urgently needed to support his widowed mother and her six other children, and that he borrowed money to obtain a substitute to take the field. On the other side, *Harper's Weekly* dwelt upon the Mulligan scandal; *The Nation,* while deploring the incident in Cleveland's past, considered even so grave a mistake as less important than Blaine's, since the latter's vices were those by which "governments are overthrown, states brought to naught, and the haunts of commerce turned into dens of thieves."

As the campaign neared an end it appeared that the result would turn upon New York, Connecticut, New Jersey, and Indiana, and especially upon the first of these. In New York several elements combined to make the situation doubtful and interesting. Tammany's dislike of Cleveland was well-known, but open opposition, at least, was quelled before election day. Roscoe Conkling, still influential despite his retirement, refused to take the stump in behalf of Blaine, declaring that he did not engage in "criminal practice." The Republicans also feared the competition of the Prohibitionists, because they attracted some Republicans who refused to vote for Blaine and could not bring themselves to support a Democrat. On the eve of the election an incident occurred which would have been of no importance if it had not been for the closeness of the contest. As Blaine was returning from a speaking tour in the West, he was given a reception in New York by a delegation of clergymen. The spokesman of the group, the Reverend Dr. Burchard, referred to the Democrats as the party of "Rum, Romanism and Rebellion." Blaine, weary from his tour, failed to notice the indiscreet remark, but the opposition seized upon it and used it to discredit him in the eyes of the Irish. On the same evening a dinner at

Delmonico's at which many wealthy men were present, provided material for the charge that the Republican candidate was the choice of the rich classes.

Early returns on election night indicated that the Democrats had carried the South and all the doubtful states, with the possible exception of New York. There the result was so close that some days elapsed before a final decision could be made. Excitement was intense and business almost stopped, so absorbed were people in the returns. At length it was officially decided that Cleveland had received 1,149 more votes than Blaine and by this narrow margin the Democrats carried New York, and with it the election.

Contemporary explanations of Blaine's defeat were indicated by a transparency carried in a Democratic procession which celebrated the victory:

The *World* Says the Independents Did it
The *Tribune* Says the Stalwarts Did It
The *Sun* Says Burchard Did It
Blaine Says St. John Did It
Theodore Roosevelt Says it Was the Soft Soap Dinner [1]
We Say Blaine's Character Did It
But We Don't Care What Did It
            It's Done.

None of these explanations took into account the strength of Cleveland, but the closeness of the result made all of them important. From the vantage ground of later times, however, it could be seen that greater forces were at work. By 1884 the day had passed when political contests could be won on Civil War issues. The younger voters had no recollections of Gettysburg and felt no animosity toward the Democratic South. Moreover, Cleveland's success was the culmination of a long-continued demand for reform which he satisfied better than Blaine.

[1] A reference to the Dorsey dinner at which Arthur told how Indiana was carried.

The opening of the first Democratic administration since Buchanan's time excited great interest in every detail of Cleveland's activities and characteristics.[2] Moreover, many who had voted for him distrusted his party and were apprehensive lest it turn out that a mistake had been made in placing such great confidence in one man. The more stiffly partisan Republicans firmly believed that Democratic success meant a triumphant South, with the "rebels" again in the saddle. Sherman declared that Cleveland's choice of southern advisors was a "reproach to the civilization of the age," and Joseph B. Foraker, speaking in an Ohio campaign, found that the people wished to hear Cleveland "flayed" and wanted plenty of "hot stuff."

The President's early acts indicated that the partisans were unduly disturbed. His inaugural address was characterized by straightforward earnestness. The exploitation of western lands by fraudulent claimants was sharply halted. The cabinet, while inexperienced, contained several able men, of whom Thomas F. Bayard, Secretary of State, William C. Whitney, Secretary of the Navy, and L. Q. C. Lamar, the Secretary of the Interior, were best known.[3]

The first great obstacle that Cleveland faced was well portrayed by one of Nast's cartoons, in which the President, with an "Independent" club in his hand, was approaching a snarling, open-jawed tiger, which represented the office-seeking classes. The drawing was entitled "Beware! For He is Very Hungry and Very Thirsty." It was not difficult to foresee grave trouble ahead in connection with the civil service. The Democrats had been out of power for twenty-four years, the offices were full of Republicans, about 100,000 positions were

---

[2] His marriage to Miss Frances Folsom, which occurred in 1886, occasioned lively interest.

[3] Other members were: Daniel Manning, N. Y., Secretary of the Treasury; William C. Endicott, Mass., Secretary of War; A. H. Garland, Ark., Attorney-General; William F. Vilas, Wis., Postmaster-General.

at the disposal of the administration, and current political practice looked with indifference upon the use of these places as rewards for party work. Hordes of office-seekers descended upon congressmen, in order to get introductions to department chiefs; they filled the waiting rooms of cabinet officers; they besieged Cleveland. Disappointed applicants and displaced officers added to the clamor and confusion.

The President's policy, as it worked out in practice, was a compromise between his ideals and the wishes of the party leaders. He earnestly approved the Pendleton act and desired to carry out both its letter and its spirit. He removed office holders who were offensively partisan and who used their positions for political purposes. He gave the South a larger share in the activities of the government, both in the cabinet and in the diplomatic and other branches of the service. When the term of a Republican office holder expired he filled the place with a fit Democrat, if one could be found, in order to equalize the share of the two parties in the patronage. Nearly half of the diplomatic and consular appointments went to southerners, and eventually most of the Republicans were supplanted.

The displacement of so many officials gave the Republicans an opportunity to attempt to discredit the President in the eyes of his mugwump supporters. The Tenure of Office Act as amended in 1869 had given the Senate a partial control over removals, although the constant practice of early times had been to give the executive a free hand. Moreover the law had fallen into disuse—or, as the President put it—into "innocuous desuetude." The case on which the Senate chose to force the issue was the removal of George M. Duskin, United States District Attorney in Alabama, and the nomination of John D. Burnett in his place. The Senate called upon the Attorney-General to transmit all papers relating to the removal; the President directed him to refuse, on the ground that papers of such a sort were not official papers, to which the Senate had a right, and also on the ground that the power of removal was vested, by the Constitution, in the president alone. In the meantime it had been hinted to Cleveland that his nominations would be confirmed without difficulty if it were acknowledged that the suspensions were the usual partisan removals. To do this would, of course, make his reform utterances look hypocritical and he refused to comply:

> I . . . dispute the right of the Senate . . . in any way save through the judicial process of trial on impeachment, to review or reverse the acts of the Executive in the suspension, during the recess of the Senate, of Federal officials.

As he was immovable and was taking precisely the position that such Republican leaders as President Grant had previously taken, the Senate was obliged to give way. Although it relieved its feelings by censuring the Attorney-General, it later repealed the remains of the Tenure of Office Act as it stood after being amended in 1869, leaving victory with the President.

In connection with the less important offices Cleveland was forced to compromise between the desirable and the practicable. Most of the postmasters were changed, although in New York City an efficient officer was retained who had originally been appointed by Garfield. All the internal revenue collectors and nearly all the collectors of customs were replaced. On the other hand, the classified service was somewhat extended by the inclusion of the railway mail service, a change which, with other increases, enlarged the classified lists by 12,000 offices.

It seems evident that Cleveland pressed reform far enough to alienate the politicians but not so far as to satisfy the reformers. When he withstood Democratic clamor for office, the Independents applauded, and the spoilsmen in his own party accused him of treason. When he listened to the demands of the partisans, the reformers became disgusted

and many of them returned to their former party allegiance. Eugene Field expressed Republican exultation at
the dissension in the enemy's ranks:

> . . . the Mugwump scorned the Democrat's wail,
> And flirting its false fantastic tail,
> It spread its wings and it soared away,
> And left the Democrat in dismay,
>   Too hoo!

Aside from the President, official Washington seems to have
had but little real interest in reform. The Vice-President,
Hendricks, was a partisan of the old school, and so many
members of Congress were out of sympathy with the system
that they attempted to annul the law by refusing appropriations for its continuance. On the whole a fair judgment was
that of Charles Francis Adams, a Republican, who thought
that Cleveland showed himself as much in advance of both
parties as it was wise for a leader of one of them to be.

In addition to further improvements in the civil service
laws, Cleveland was interested in a long list of reforms which
he placed before Congress in his first message: the improvement of the diplomatic and consular service; the reduction of
the tariff; the repeal of the Bland-Allison silver-coinage act;
the development of the navy, which he characterized as a
"shabby ornament" and a naval reminder "of the days that
are past"; better care of the Indians; and a means of preventing individuals from acquiring large areas of the public
lands. The fact that Hayes and Arthur had urged similar
reforms shows how little Cleveland differed from his Republican predecessors. It was not likely, however, that the
program would be carried out, for Congress was not in a
reforming mood and the Republicans controlled the upper
house so that they could block any attempt at constructive
policies.

The latent hostility which many of the Civil War veterans

felt toward the Democratic party was fanned into flame by
Cleveland's attitude toward pension legislation. The sympathy of the country for its disabled soldiers had early resulted in a system of pensions for disability if due either to
wounds or disease contracted in the service. Early in the
seventies the number of pensioners had seemed to have
reached a maximum. Two new centers of agitation, however, had appeared, the Grand Army of the Republic and
the pension agent. The former was originally a social organization but later it took a hand in the campaign for new
pension legislation. The agents were persons familiar with
the laws, who busied themselves in finding possible pensioners
and getting their claims established. The agitation of the
subject had resulted in the arrears act of 1879, which gave
the claimant back-pensions from the day of his discharge from
the army to the date of filing his claim, regardless of the time
when his disability began. As the average first payment to
the pensioner under this act was about $1,000, the number of
claims filed had grown enormously and the pension agents
had enjoyed a rich harvest. The next step was the dependent
pensions bill, which granted a pension to all who had served
three months, were dependent on their daily toil, and were
incapable of earning their livelihood, whether the incapacity
was due to wounds and disease or not. President Cleveland's
veto of the measure aroused a hostility which was deepened
by his attitude toward private pension acts.

For some time it had been customary to pass special acts
providing pensions for persons whose claims had already been
rejected by the pension bureau as defective or fraudulent.
So little attention was paid to private bills in Congress that
1454 of them passed between 1885 and 1889, generally without
debate and often even without the presence of a quorum of
members. Two hours on a day in April, 1886, sufficed for
the passage of five hundred such bills. Nobody would now
deny that many were frauds, pure and simple. Cleveland

was too frugal and conscientious to pass such bills without examination and he began to veto some of the worst of them. Each veto message explained the grounds for his dissent, sometimes patiently, sometimes with a sharp sarcasm that must have made the victim writhe. In one case where a widow sought a pension because of the death of her soldier husband it was discovered that he had been accidentally shot by a neighbor while hunting. Another claimant was one who had enlisted at the close of the war, served nine days, had been admitted to the hospital with measles and then mustered out. Fifteen years later he claimed a pension. The President vetoed the bill, scoffing at the applicant's "valiant service" and "terrific encounter with the measles." Altogether he vetoed about two hundred and thirty private bills. Time after time he expressed his sympathy with the deserving pensioner and his desire to purge the list of dishonorable names, and many applauded his courageous efforts. Nevertheless, his pension policy presented an opportunity for hostile criticism which his Republican opponents were not slow to embrace. His efforts in behalf of pension reform were said to originate in hostility to the old soldiers and in lack of sympathy with the northern cause. In 1887 it even became necessary for him to withdraw his acceptance of an invitation to attend a meeting of the Grand Army in St. Louis, because of danger that he might be subjected to downright insult.[4]

Before the hostility due to the pension vetoes had subsided, Adjutant-General Drum called the attention of the President to the fact that flags taken from Confederate regiments by Union soldiers during the war and also certain flags formerly belonging to northern troops had for many years lain packed in boxes in the attic and cellar of the War Department. At

[4] President Cleveland also frequently used his veto power to prevent the passage of appropriations for federal buildings which he deemed unnecessary.

his suggestion Cleveland ordered the return of these trophies to the states which the regiments had represented. Although recommended by Drum as a "graceful act," it was looked upon by the old soldiers with the utmost wrath. The commander of the Grand Army called upon Heaven to avenge so wicked an order and such politicians as Governor Foraker of Ohio gained temporary prominence by their bitter condemnation of it. Eventually the clamor was so great that the President rescinded the order on the ground that the final disposition of the flags was within the sphere of action of Congress only. In February, 1905, however, Congress passed a resolution providing for the return of the flags and the exchange was effected without excitement.

For the reasons already mentioned, little legislation was passed during President Cleveland's administration that was of permanent importance. An exception was the Interstate Commerce Act, which is a subject for later discussion. A Presidential Succession Act, which has earlier been described, provided for the succession of the members of the cabinet in case of the removal or death of the president and vice-president. The Electoral Count Act of 1887 placed on the states the burden of deciding contests arising from the choice of presidential electors. When more than one set of electoral returns come from a state, each purporting to be legal, Congress must decide which shall be counted. If the two houses of Congress disagree, the votes of those electors shall be counted which have been certified by the governor of the state. Of some importance, too, was the establishment of the Department of Agriculture in 1889 and the inclusion of its secretary in the cabinet. The admission of the Dakotas, Montana and Washington as states took place in the same year. The improvement of the navy, begun so auspiciously by Secretary Chandler under President Arthur, was continued with enthusiasm and vigor, and the vessels constructed formed an important part of our navy.

Of less popular interest than many of the political questions, but of more lasting importance, was the rapid reduction of the public land supply. The purpose of the Homestead law of 1862 had been to supply land at low rates and in small amounts to *bona fide* settlers, but the beneficent design of the nation had been somewhat nullified by the constant evasion of the spirit of the laws. Squatters had occupied land without reference to legal forms; cattlemen had fenced in large tracts for their own use and forcibly resisted attempts to oust them; by hook and by crook individuals and companies had got large areas into their possession and held them for speculative returns. Western public opinion looked upon many such violations with equanimity until the supply of land began to grow small. Then came the demand for the opening of the Indian reservations, which comprised 250,000 square miles in 1885. The Dawes act of 1887 provided for individual ownership of small amounts of land by the Indians instead of tribal ownership in large reservations. By this means a considerable amount of good land was made available for settlement by whites. The dwindling supply of western land also called attention to certain delinquencies on the part of the railway companies. Many of them had been granted enormous amounts of land on certain conditions, such as that specified parts of the roads be constructed within a given time. This agreement, with others, was frequently broken, and question arose as to whether the companies should be forced to forfeit their claims. Cleveland turned to the problem with energy and forced the return of some millions of acres. Nevertheless, the fact that it was becoming necessary to be less prodigal with the public land indicated that the supply was no longer inexhaustible, and led the President in his last annual message to urge that the remaining supply be husbanded with great care. Congress was not alert to the demands of the time, however, and no effective steps were taken for many years.

BIBLIOGRAPHICAL NOTE

H. C. Thomas, *The Return of the Democratic Party to Power in 1884* (1919), is most complete and scholarly on the subject; Sparks, Curtis, Dewey, and Stanwood continue useful; H. T. Peck, *Twenty Years of the Republic,* 1885–1905 (1907), is illuminating and interesting; H. J. Ford, *Cleveland Era* (1919), is brief; the files of *The Nation* and *Harper's Weekly* are essential, while those of the New York *Sun, Evening Post* and *Tribune* add a few points. The Mulligan letters are reprinted in *Harper's Weekly* (1884, 643–646).

On the administration, consult the general texts and the special volumes mentioned in chapter V, particularly Robert McElroy, *Cleveland.* See also G. F. Parker, *Recollections of Grover Cleveland* (1909); and *Political Science Quarterly* (June, 1918), "Official Characteristics of President Cleveland," give something on the personal side; J. L. Whittle, *Grover Cleveland* (1896), is by an English admirer; Cleveland's own side of one of his controversies is in Grover Cleveland, *Presidential Problems* (1904); on Blaine, Edward Stanwood, *James G. Blaine* (1905). The *Annual Cyclopedia* has useful biographical articles.

CHAPTER IX

TRANSPORTATION AND ITS CONTROL

Of all inventions, the alphabet and the printing press alone excepted, those inventions which abridge distance have done most for the civilization of our species.

T. B. Macaulay.

For fifty years until 1887 . . . the railroads existed in a state of Nature, knowing no law but the common law and not quite all of that.

Garet Garrett.

Law! What do I care about law? Hain't I got the power?

"Commodore" Vanderbilt.

When . . . one devotes his property to a use in which the public has an interest, he . . . must submit to be controlled by the public for the common good.

The Supreme Court in Munn v. Illinois.

THE most significant legislative act of President Cleveland's administration was due primarily neither to him nor to the great political parties. It concerned the relation between the government and the railroads, and the force which led to its passage originated outside of Congress. The growth of the transportation system, therefore, the economic benefits which resulted, the complaints which arose and the means through which the complaints found voice were subjects of primary importance.

Beginning with the construction of the Baltimore and Ohio Railroad about 1830, the extension of the railways went forward with increasing rapidity so that they soon formed a veritable network: between 1830 and 1850 over 7,000 miles were laid; by 1860 the total was 30,000 miles; the Civil War and the financial depression of 1873 retarded progress somewhat, but such delays were temporary, and by 1890 the total

201

exceeded 160,000 miles. In the earlier decades most construction took place in the Northeast, where capital was most plentiful and population most dense. Later activity in the Northeast was devoted to building "feeders" or branch lines. In the South, the relatively smaller progress which had been made before the war had been undone for the most part by

1860									

Railroad Mileage,
1860-1920, in Thousands
of Miles

1870

1880

1890

1900

1910

1920

25 50 75 100 125 150 175 200 225 250

the wear and tear of the conflict, but the twenty-five years afterward saw greatly renewed construction. The most surprising expansion took place in Texas where the 711 miles of 1870 were increased to 8,754 by 1890. In the Middle West, roads were rapidly built just before the war and immediately after it, and the first connection with the Pacific Coast, as has been shown, was made in 1869.

Many of the circumstances accompanying this rapid expansion were novel and important. Beginning with a federal grant to the Illinois Central in the middle of the century, both the nation and the states assisted the roads by gifts of

millions of acres of land. It was to the advantage of the companies to procure the grants on the best possible terms, and
they exerted constant pressure upon congressmen whose votes
and influence they desired. Frequently the agents of the
roads were thoroughly unscrupulous, and such scandals as
that connected with the Credit Mobilier were the result.
More important still, the fact that the federal and state governments had aided the railroads so greatly gave them a
strong justification for investigating and regulating the activities of the companies.

Mechanical inventions and improvements had no small part
in the development of the transportation system. The early
tracks, constructed of wood beams on which were fastened
iron strips, and sometimes described as barrel-hoops tacked
to laths, were replaced by iron, and still later by heavy steel
rails. By 1890 about eighty per cent. of the mileage was composed of steel. Heavy rails were accompanied by improved
roadbeds, heavier equipment and greater speed. A simple
improvement was the gradual adoption of a standard gauge—
four feet eight and a half inches—which replaced the earlier
lack of uniformity. The process was substantially completed
by the middle eighties, when many thousands of miles in the
South were standardized. On the Louisville and Nashville,
for example, a force of 8,763 men made the change on 1,806
miles of track in a single day. The inauguration of "standard" time also took place during the eighties. Hitherto
there had been a wide variety of time standards and different
roads even in the same city dispatched their trains on different systems. In 1883 the country was divided into five
vertical zones each approximately fifteen degrees or, in sun-
time, an hour wide. Both the roads and the public then
conformed to the standard time of the zone in which they
were. In a word, "the railroads (of Civil War days) with
their fragile iron rails, their little wheezy locomotives, their
wooden bridges, their unheated coaches, and their kerosene

lamps" made way for their more powerful, rapid and
comfortable successors.[1]

Of greater importance was the consolidation of large numbers of small lines into the extensive systems which are now
familiar. The first roads covered such short distances that
numerous bothersome transfers of passengers, freight and
baggage from the end of one line to the beginning of the
next were necessary on every considerable journey. No fewer
than five companies divided the three hundred miles between
Albany and Buffalo, no one of them operating more than
seventy-six miles. In 1853, these five with five others were
consolidated into the New York Central Railroad. Sixteen
years later, in 1869, the Central combined with the Hudson
River, and soon afterwards procured substantial control of
the Lake Shore and Michigan Southern, the Rock Island, and
the Chicago and Northwestern. As the result of this process
a single group of men directed the interests of a system of
railroads from New York through Chicago to Omaha. The
Pennsylvania Railroad began with a short line from Philadelphia to the Susquehanna River, picked up smaller roads here
and there—eventually one hundred and thirty-eight of them,
representing two hundred and fifty-six separate corporations—reached out through the Middle West to Cincinnati,
Chicago and St. Louis, and in 1871 controlled over three thousand miles of track, with an annual income of over forty million dollars. In the eighties a railroad war in northern New
England started the consolidation of the Boston and Maine
system.

The beneficial results of the growth of the transportation
facilities of the nation were immediate and revolutionary.
The fact that average freight rates were cut in halves between
1867 and 1890 helped make possible the economic readjust-
ments after the Civil War to a degree that is not likely to be
overestimated. Not only did railway construction supply

[1] *Cf.* Hendrick, *Age of Big Business*, 2.

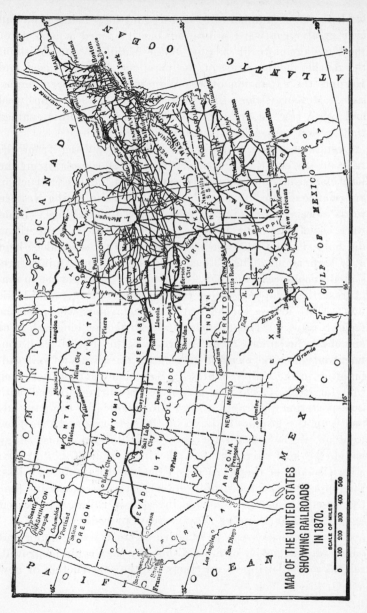

MAP OF THE UNITED STATES
SHOWING RAILROADS
IN 1870.

SCALE OF MILES

work for large numbers of laborers and help bring about an ever greater westward migration, but it opened a market for the huge agricultural surplus of the Middle West. Without the market in the cities of the populous Atlantic Coast and Europe, the expansion of the West would have been impossible. Moreover, the railways brought coal, ore, cotton, wool and other raw materials to the Northeast, and thus enabled that section to develop its manufacturing interests.

Despite the admittedly great benefits resulting from the railroad system, there was a rising tide of complaint on the part of the public in regard to some aspects of its construction and management. It was objected that many of the western roads especially were purely speculative undertakings. Lines were sometimes built into new territory where competition did not exist and where, consequently, the rates could be kept at a high point. The Chicago, Burlington and Quincy presented such a case in 1856. Profits were so great as to embarrass the company, since the payment of large dividends was sure to arouse the hostility of the farmers who paid the freight rates. "This, indeed," declared the biographer of one of the presidents of the road, "was the time of glad, confident morning, never again to occur in the history of railroad-building in the United States." Sometimes lines were driven into territory which was already sufficiently supplied with transportation facilities, in order to compel the company already on the ground to buy out the new road. If, as time went on, traffic enough for both roads did not appear, they had to be kept alive through the imposition of high rates; otherwise, one of them failed and the investors suffered a loss. The opportunities for profit, however, were so numerous that the amount of capital reported invested in railways increased by $3,200,000,000 during the five years preceding 1885.

A practice which was productive of much wrong-doing and which was suggestive of more dishonesty than could be proved, related to the letting of contracts for the construction of new

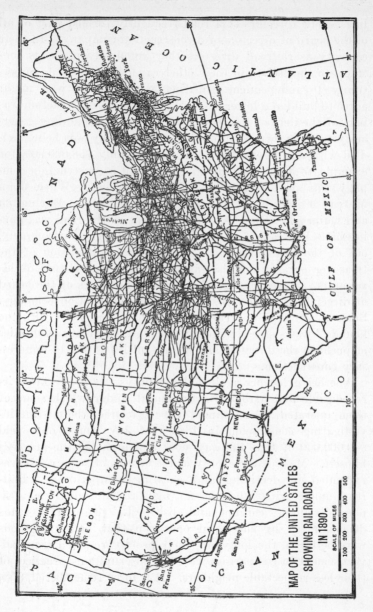

MAP OF THE UNITED STATES
SHOWING RAILROADS
IN 1890.

lines. The directors of a road frequently formed part or all of the board of directors of a construction company. In their capacity as railroad directors they voted advantageous contracts to themselves in their other capacity, giving no opportunity to independent construction companies who might agree to build at a lower cost. As the cost of construction was part of the debt of the road, the directors were adding generously to their own wealth, while the company was being saddled with an increased burden. It cost only $58,000,000, for example, to build the Central Pacific, but a construction company was paid $120,000,000 for its services. When John Murray Forbes was investigating the Chicago, Burlington and Quincy he found that the president of the road was paying himself a salary as president of a construction company, out of the railroad's funds, without the supervision of the treasurer or any one else, and without any auditing of his accounts. Moreover, six of the twelve members of the board of directors were also members of the construction company. Such an attempt to "run with the hare and hunt with the hounds" was suggestive, to say the least, of great possibilities of profit to the directors and a constant invitation to unnecessary construction.

Another grievance against the railways was the reckless, irresponsible and arrogant management under which some of them operated. An eminent expert testified before an investigating commission in 1885 that Jay Gould once sold $40,000,000 of Erie Railway stock and pocketed the proceeds himself. Most of the energy of the officers of some roads was expended in deceiving and cheating competitors. "Railroad financeering" became a "by-word for whatever is financially loose, corrupt and dishonest." If certain roads demonstrated by successful operation that honest methods were better in the long run, their probity received scant advertisement in comparison with the unscrupulous practices of their less respectable neighbors. It is to be remembered, also, that the growth of the railway system had been so rapid and so huge that it was impossible to meet the demand for trained administrators. Naturally, men possessed of little or no technical understanding of transportation problems could not provide highly responsible management.

The dishonest manipulation of the issues and sales of railroad stocks is a practice that was not confined solely to the twenty-five years after the Civil War, but the numerous examples of it which occurred during that period aggravated the exasperation which has already been mentioned. Daniel Drew, the treasurer of the Erie Railway in 1866, furnished an excellent illustration of this type of activity. Drew had in his possession a large amount of Erie stock which had been secretly issued to him in return for a loan to the company. The stock in the market was selling near par and still rising. Drew instructed his agents to make contracts for the future delivery of stock at prices current at the time when the contracts were made. When the time approached for fulfilling his contracts, Drew suddenly threw the secret stock on the market, drove general market prices on Erie stock down from ninety-five to fifty, bought at the low figure, and sold at the high price which was called for in the contracts made by his agents. The effect of such sharp dealing on investors, the railroad or the public seems not to have entered into the calculation. Indeed, the Erie and many another road was looked upon by its owners merely as a convenient piece of machinery for producing fortunes.

Gould, Drew and other railroad men of their time were also expert in the practice of ''stock-watering.'' This consists in expanding the *nominal* capitalization of an enterprise without an equivalent addition to the *actual* capital. The rates which the railway has to charge the public tend to increase by approximately whatever dividends are paid on the water.[2]

---

[2] For example, an investor might contribute $100 in cash to an enterprise. The "paid in capital" or "actual" capital would then be $100.

Then, as later, when a road was prospering greatly it would sometimes declare a "stock dividend," that is, give its stockholders additional stock in proportion to what they already owned. The addition would frequently be water. Its purpose might be to cover up the great profits made by the company. If, on a million dollars' worth of stock, it was paying ten per cent. dividends, the public might demand lower freight and passenger rates; but if the stock were doubled and earnings remained stationary, then the dividends would appear as five per cent.—an amount to which there could be no objection. H. V. Poor, the railroad expert, declared before a commission of investigation in 1885 that the New York Central Railroad was carrying $48,000,000 of water, on which it had paid eight per cent. dividends for fifteen years. He also estimated that of the seven and a half billions of indebtedness which the roads of the country were carrying in 1883, two billions represented water. Others thought that the proportion of water was greater. In any case the unnecessary burden upon business to provide dividends for the watered stock was an item of some magnitude. The investor, however, looked upon stock-watering with other eyes. The building of a new road was a speculation; the profits might be large, to be sure, but there might in many cases be a loss. In order to tempt money into railroad enterprises, therefore, inducements in the form of generous stock bonuses were necessary.

The rate wars of the seventies gave wide advertisement to another aspect of railroad history. The most famous of these contests had their origin in the grain-carrying trade from the Lakes to the sea-board. The entry of the Baltimore and Ohio and the Grand Trunk into Chicago in 1874, stimulated a four-cornered competition among these roads and the Pennsylvania and New York Central for the traffic between the upper

He might receive in return $100 in stock and $100 in bonds, in which case the "nominal capital" would be $200; the additional $100 would be "water." If the enterprise paid interest on the bonds, and dividends on the stock, it would, of course, be paying a return on the water.

Mississippi Valley and the coast. Rates on grain and other products were cut, and cut again; freight charges dropped to a figure which wiped out profits; yet it was impossible for any line to drop out of the competition until exhaustion forced all to do so. A railroad can not suspend business when profits disappear, for fixed expenses continue and the depreciation of the value of the property, especially of the stations, tracks and rolling stock, is extreme. Since the rate wars were clearly bringing ruin in their train, rate agreements and pooling arrangements were devised. The latter took several forms. Sometimes a group of competing roads agreed to divide the business among the competitors on the basis of an agreed-upon percentage. Another plan was to pool earnings at the close of a period and divide according to a prearranged ratio. Sometimes destructive competition was prevented by a division of the territory, each company being allowed a free hand in its own field. In general, pooling agreements were likely to break down, although a southern pool organized by Albert Fink on a very extensive scale lasted for many years and was thought to have had a vital influence in eliminating rate-wars. Their efficacy depended mainly on good faith, and good faith was a rarity among railroad officials in the seventies and eighties. In the eyes of the public, rate agreements and pools were vicious conspiracies which left the rights and well-being of the private shipper completely out of the calculation.

Still another indictment of the railways resulted from their participation in politics. It was inevitable, of course, that the roads should be drawn into the field of legislation—the grants of public land, for example, helped bring about the result. It early seemed advantageous to attempt to influence state legislatures to pass favorable laws, and it seemed a necessity to bring pressure to bear in order to protect the roads from hostile acts. The methods used by the railway agents in their political activity naturally varied all the way from legitimate agitation to crude and subtle forms of bribery. An insidious method of influencing both lawmaking and litigation was the pass system. Under it the roads were accustomed to give free transportation to a long list of federal and state judges, legislators and politicians. For a judge to accept such favors from a corporation which might at any time be haled before his court, and for a legislator to receive a gift from a body that was constantly in need of legislative attention is now held to be improper in the extreme. But in those days a less sensitive public opinion felt hardly a qualm. That the practice was likely to arouse an unconscious bias in the minds of public officials is hardly debatable. The more crude forms of bribery, too, were not uncommon. It was testified before a committee of investigation that the Erie Railway Company in one year expended $700,000 as a corruption fund and for legal expenses, carrying the amount on the books in the "India-rubber account." The manipulation of the courts of New York by the Erie and the New York Central during the late sixties was nothing short of a scandal. Alliances between political rings and railroad officials for the purpose of caring for their mutual interests were so common that reformers questioned whether the American people could be said to possess self-government in actuality. Immediately after the Civil War, Charles Francis Adams, Jr., an acute student of transportation, declared that it was scarcely an exaggeration to say that the state legislatures were becoming a species of irregular boards of railroad direction. The evils of the alliance between the roads and politics were not, of course, due entirely to the former. The receiver of a pass shared with the giver the evil of the system. Many a legislator was corrupt; more shared in practices which were little removed from dishonorable. Adams gives an account of his experiences, as a director of the Union Pacific, in dealing with a United States senator in 1884. The congressman was ready to take excellent care of railroad corporations which retained him as counsel, but was a corrupt and ill-mannered bully toward the Union Pacific, which had not employed him.[3] The most constant grievance was discrimination—that the roads varied their rates for the benefit or detriment of especial types of freight, of individuals and of entire localities. Through business between competing points was carried at a low figure, while the roads recouped themselves by charging heavily in towns where competition was absent. Shippers complained that rates between St. Paul and Chicago, for example, where competition existed were hardly more than half the charges to places at a similar distance where a single road was in a position to demand what it pleased. Manufacturers in Rochester could send goods to New York City and reship them to Cincinnati, back through Rochester, for less than the rate direct to their destination. Yet the direct haul was seven hundred miles shorter than the indirect. Secret arrangements were commonly made with favored shippers by which they secured lower rates than their competitors through a "rebate" or return of part of the rate charged. The mischief of such practices is well stated by Garet Garrett:

The power to make freight rates was and is and must be the power to transfer whole industries from one section of the country to another. Given a high rate on cattle, which are unprofitable and wasteful to haul, and a low rate on meat products, and the meat-packing industry moves bodily from the East to to the Mississippi Valley. A rate in wheat from Kansas into Texas lower than the rate on flour caused a flour-milling industry to appear in Texas. The New England cotton-goods industry lives by virtue of a low freight rate on raw cotton from the South.

In brief, then, it was complained that the growth of the transportation system had placed enormous power in the hands

[3] In this connection Professor Farrand mentions the statement of a railroad magnate that "in Republican counties he was a Republican, and in Democratic counties he was a Democrat, but that everywhere he was for the railroad." *Development of the United States*, p. 290.

of a small group of men, many of whom had indicated by their selfishness, arrogance and questionable practices that they ought not to be entrusted with so great a measure of authority.

The best example of the American railroad president after the war was "Commodore" Cornelius Vanderbilt. Vanderbilt began his career by ferrying passengers and freight between Staten Island and New York City. Later he turned his attention to shipping, in which he made a fortune, and planned the operation of steamships on a large scale. Becoming interested in railroading, he clearly perceived the importance of the western trade and the necessity of consolidation. Vanderbilt was a man of vision, a man who combined magnitude of plan with the vigorous grasp of the practical details necessary for the realization of his ambitions. He was buoyant, energetic, confident, ambitious, determined, despotic. Unhampered by modern conceptions of public duty, undeterred by the hostility of powerful opponents, with eyes fixed upon the combination and control of a great transportation system, Vanderbilt entered courageously upon bitter struggles for supremacy which involved the misuse of the courts, the control of the New York state legislature and a thousand charges of corrupt influence and bribery, but he welded railroads together, replaced wood and iron with steel, and constructed tracks and terminals. At his death in 1877 he left a huge fortune and bequeathed to his successors a great, consolidated railroad enterprise, skilfully and successfully administered. The great weakness of Commodore Vanderbilt and his associates, and of those who later imitated his work was their fundamental conception of the railroad as a private venture. Success consisted in bigness, great profits, crushing or buying out competitors, and administering the business for the best good of the few owners, regardless of the interests of the region through which the railway passed. Vanderbilt and many of his contemporaries

were men of business sagacity and foresight, but their ethical
outlook was restricted and their sense of public responsibility
not well developed.

So considerable a list of grievances naturally bestirred the
people to seek relief at the hands of their legislators. Two
lines of action were followed. In Massachusetts, as early as
1869, a state commission was formed with purely advisory
powers. Under the able leadership of Charles Francis
Adams, Jr., it attained great influence and worked effectively
for the elimination of railroad abuses through conference and
the weight of public opinion. In Illinois, on the other hand,
reliance was placed upon compulsory action. The state constitution of 1870 declared the railroads to be public highways and required the legislature to fix rates for the carriage
of freight and passengers, and to pass laws to correct abuses
connected with the railways and grain warehouses. In compliance with the constitution the state passed the necessary
legislation and placed their execution in the hands of a commission with considerable power. Other western states followed the Illinois model.

On the national scale the agitation for government action
began with the minor parties. In 1872 the Labor Reformers
demanded fair rates and no discrimination; in 1876 the Prohibitionists called for lower rates; in 1880 the Greenbackers
stood for fair and uniform rates; four years later they urged
laws which would put an end to pooling, stock-watering and
discrimination, and in the same year the Republicans promised an act to regulate commerce if they were elected. The
most effective force behind the demand for railroad regulation was the Patrons of Husbandry, better known as the
"Grange." This society was founded by O. H. Kelley, a
government clerk in Washington, in 1867. Its initial purpose was the organization of the agricultural classes for social and intellectual improvement, but later it engaged in the
effort to correct transportation abuses and to arouse coopera-

tion among the farmers in other ways. The movement grew astonishingly, especially in the Middle West, where its membership reached nearly 759,000 in 1875.

Transportation conditions in the West had not reached the relatively stable situation which characterized those of the East. In the West much new work was being done, with the attendant evils of construction companies and unnecessary and speculative undertakings. Much of the railroad stock was in the hands of eastern investors whom the western farmers pictured as living in idle ease on swollen incomes, careless of the high rates and unfair discriminations under which the farmer groaned. The constantly falling prices, which influenced the West in so many other ways, served to heighten the discontent with any abuse which increased the farmer's burden. Moreover, the western states had contributed huge amounts of land to help build the railways and they were not minded to give up the hold which their generosity had justified.

Impelled, then, by such force as the Grange and similar organizations supplied, the western states proceeded to the adoption of laws whose purposes ordinarily included railroad rate-making by the legislature or by a commission, the doing away with such abuses as discrimination, and the prohibition of free passes. The railroads promptly opposed the laws and carried the battle to the courts. The so-called "Granger Cases" resulted. Three of these were representative of the general trend of the decisions.

The famous case Munn v. Illinois, which was decided by the Supreme Court in 1876 was possibly the most vital case in history of the regulation of public service corporations after the Civil War. The legislature of Illinois, in conformity with the state constitution of 1870, had passed a law fixing maximum charges for the storage of grain in warehouses. The owners of a certain warehouse refused compliance with the law on the ground that it was contrary to the Constitution and hence null and void. They argued that when the state fixed rates it deprived the owners of the right to set higher charges and so, in effect, deprived them of their property, in defiance of that portion of the Fourteenth Amendment forbidding a state to "deprive any person of life, liberty, or property, without due process of law."

On examination of the history of the control of such enterprises, the Court found that it had been customary in England for many centuries and in this country from the beginning, to regulate rates on ferries, charges at inns, and similar public enterprises, and that it had never been thought that such action deprived persons of property without due process of law. In other words, the established common law, at the time of the passage of the Fourteenth Amendment, did not look upon rate regulation as a deprivation of property. The Court, therefore, declared the Illinois warehouse law constitutional, and in doing so made the following statement:

Property does become clothed with a public interest when used in a manner to make it of public consequence, and affect the community at large. When, therefore, one devotes his property to a use in which the public has an interest, he, in effect, grants to the public an interest in that use, and must submit to be controlled by the public for the common good, to the extent of the interest he has thus created.

While the Munn case was before the Court, the case Peik v. the Chicago and Northwestern Railway Company was raising a question which struck at the heart of the chief practical impediment in the way of state control of transportation. The central question in the litigation was whether the legislature of Wisconsin could lawfully regulate rates on railroads inside the state. Since the bulk of the traffic on most roads crosses state borders at one time or another in its transit, the regulation of rates within a state normally affects interstate commerce. But the regulation of interstate commerce is vested in Congress by the terms of the Constitution.   The railroad was quick to take advantage of the division of power between the states and the nation.   Indeed, when fighting state legislation, the roads earnestly emphasized the exclusive power of Congress over interstate commerce; but when fighting national regulation, they equally deprecated any interference with the reserved rights of the states.   Acting in accordance with its established practice, the Court decided that the state was authorized to regulate rates within its borders, even though such regulation indirectly affected persons outside, until Congress passed legislation concerning interstate commerce.   Obviously this decision allowed the states to work out their railroad problems unhampered, and constituted one of the chief victories for the Grangers.

In 1886, however, the Court overturned some of the principles which had been established in the Munn and Peik cases. The new development came about in connection with the Wabash railroad.   It appeared that the road had been carrying freight from Peoria, Illinois, to New York for smaller rates than were charged from Gilman, Illinois, to New York, despite the fact that Peoria was eighty-six miles farther away. Since Illinois law forbade a road to levy a greater charge for a short haul than for a long one, a suit was instituted and carried to the Supreme Court.   The company held that the Illinois legislation affected interstate commerce and hence trenched upon the constitutional power of Congress.   This time the court upheld the road.   It decided that the transportation of goods from Illinois to New York was commerce among the states, that such commerce was subject to regulation by Congress exclusively, and that the Illinois statute was void.   It seemed, then, that state regulation was a broken reed on which nobody could safely lean, and attention thereupon turned to the federal government.

Congress had already been discussing federal regulation intermittently for some years.   The so-called "Windom Report" of 1874 had advised federal construction and improvement of transportation facilities in order to lower rates through competition, but no action had resulted. In 1878 the "Reagan bill" had proposed government regulation, and from that time the subject had been almost continuously before Congress. In 1885 the Senate had appointed a select committee of five to investigate and report upon the regulation of freight and passenger transportation. The committee was headed by Shelby M. Cullom, who had been a member of the legislature of Illinois and later governor, in the years when the railroad and warehouse laws were being put into effect. It endeavored to discover all shades of opinion by visiting the leading commercial centers, and by consulting business men, state commissioners of railroads, Grange officials and others. After a somewhat thorough investigation, the committee expressed its conviction that no general question of governmental policy occupied so prominent a place in the attention of the public as that of controlling the growth and influence of corporations. The needed relief might be obtained, the committee thought, through any one of four methods: private ownership and management, with a greater or less degree of government oversight; government ownership and management; government ownership with private management under public regulations; partial state ownership and management in competition with private companies. The widespread opposition to state ownership of railroads, the committee asserted, seemed to point to some form of government regulation and control of the existing situation.

Impressed with the magnitude of the abuses involved, and the hopelessness of regulation through state laws, the committee presented a bill designed to bring about regulation on a national scale through a federal agency. The resulting law was the Interstate Commerce Act of February 4, 1887. It provided that all railway charges should be reasonable and just; forbade the roads to grant rebates, or to give preferences to any person, locality or class of freight, or to charge more for a short haul than for a long one except with the consent of the proper authorities; it made pooling unlawful; and it ordered the companies to post printed copies of their rates, which were not to be altered except after ten days' public notice. The act also created an Interstate Commerce Commission of five members to serve six-year terms, into whose hands the administration of the measure was placed. Persons who claimed that the railways were violating the provisions of the law could make complaint to the Commission, or bring suit in a United States Court. In order that the Commission might know the condition of the roads, it was given power to call upon the carriers for information, to demand annual reports from them, and to require the attendance of witnesses. If the railroads refused to carry out the orders of the Commission, they could be brought before a United States district court.

In forbidding pools, the Act committed the railroads to the policy of enforced competition, a policy which was commonly accepted at the time as the best one for the public interest. Such experts, however, as Professor A. T. Hadley and Charles Francis Adams, Jr., raised important objections. They cited the rate wars to indicate the results of competition and declared that railroads ought to be monopolies. If two grocery stores are established where trade enough exists for only one, they asserted, the weaker competitor can close his doors and the public loss is not heavy; but in the case of the railways a weak competitor must continue business even at disastrously low rates because all his interest charges continue and the depreciation on his property is extreme. The construction of an unnecessary road and its subsequent operation at a loss, its failure or its abandonment, constitute a great drain upon the public. Such objectors contended that pooling combinations did away with many of the evils of cutthroat competition, and they accordingly urged that the carriers be permitted to make such arrangements, under whatever government regulation might be needed to prevent unreasonable charges. By such means the available business of a region might be fairly divided among the roads entering it, without resort to competitive rate-cutting and its consequent evils.

The passage of the law was looked upon with much hostility on the part of the railroad interests. James J. Hill thought that the railroads might survive, although the country would be ruined, and he predicted that Congress would shortly be called in special session to repeal the act. More important than mere hostility was the constant opposition and evasion which characterized the attitude of the carriers toward the operation of the law. Discriminations were commonly practiced and hidden away in accounts under false or misleading headings. Rebates were given and received, a fact which was due in no small degree to the shippers themselves. A large shipper might demand advantageous rates and threaten to turn his trade over to a rival road. As the arrangement would be secret, and the likelihood of discovery small, the temptation to break the law was correspondingly great.

The good results of the passage of the law were disappointingly slight. To be sure, the Commission was gaining experience, administrative precedents were being established and injustice was somewhat less common than before. The first chairman was Judge T. M. Cooley, a noted lawyer whose appointment was considered an admirable one. Most important of all, the principle of government regulation was established. Nevertheless, progress was so slow as to be almost invisible. The courts hampered the activities of the Commission. When cases arose involving its decisions, they allowed a retrial of the entire case from the beginning, permitting the introduction of facts which had been designedly withheld by the carriers in order to undermine the influence of the

Commission, and sometimes they reversed its findings and so dulled the effectiveness of its labors. Eleven years after the Act was passed the Commission declared that abuses were so constant that the situation was intolerable; a prominent railroad president made the charge that "good faith had departed from the railway world"; and an important authority on railroad affairs declared that the Commission had become an impotent bureau of statistics.

BIBLIOGRAPHICAL NOTE

More study has been made of railroad regulation and the technical side of railroading than of the history of transportation and the effects of the roads on the political and economic life of the people. An excellent single volume is John Moody, *The Railroad Builders* (1919), which devotes attention to the important personages of railroad history, discusses the growth of large systems and contains valuable maps; the best concise account of the history of the railways is W. Z. Ripley, *Railroads: Rates and Regulation* (1912), Chap. I; W. Z. Ripley, *Railway Problems* (rev. ed., 1913), is reliable; E. R. Johnson and T. W. Van Metre, *Principles of Railroad Transportation* (1916), has some excellent chapters and several informing maps; C. F. Carter, *When Railroads were New* (1909), is a popular account; C. F. Adams, *Chapters of Erie* (1886), exposes early railroad practices; H. O. Pearson, *An American Railroad Builder* (1911), presents the career of J. M. Forbes as a railroad president; A. T. Hadley, *Railroad Transportation* (1886), is a classic, early account. Consult also E. R. Johnson, *American Railway Transportation* (1903); Frank Parsons, *Heart of the Railroad Problem* (1906); C. F. Adams, Jr., *Railroads: Their Origin and Problems* (1878, rev. ed., 1893); "A Decade of Federal Railway Regulation," in *Atlantic Monthly* (Apr., 1898). On the personal side, the following are valuable: E. P. Oberholtzer, *Jay Cooke, Financier of the Civil War* (2 vols., 1907); J. G. Pyle, *Life of J. J. Hill* (2 vols., 1917); *Memoirs of Henry Villard* (1909). On the subject of land grants and regulation: L. H. Haney, *Congressional History of Railways* (2 vols., 1910); S. J. Buck, *The Granger Movement* (1913), and the same author's *The Agrarian*

Crusade (1920), are best on the relation of unrest among the agricultural classes to the railroad problem. The "Cullom Report" is in Senate Reports, 49th Congress, 1st session (Serial Number 2356), in 2 vols., and is a mine of information on early abuses. The most important Granger cases are in *United States Reports*, vol. 94, p. 113 (Munn v. Ill.), and vol. 118, p. 557 (Wabash case).

CHAPTER X

INDUSTRY AND PUBLIC INTEREST

Corporations, which should be the carefully restrained creatures of the law and the servants of the people, are fast becoming the people's masters.

PRESIDENT GROVER CLEVELAND, Dec. 3, 1888.

The time came when it was possible in some great corporations for the officers . . . to issue with the same nonchalance and certainty of their being complied with, orders for . . . industrial equipment, on the one hand, or for the delivery of delegations in a state, county, or national convention, on the other.

WILLIAM H. TAFT.

[Mark Hanna] was an incarnation of the spirit and methods of the men who seized and cleared the public domain, developed its natural resources, started and organized an industrial and commercial system.

HERBERT CROLY.

Every . . . trust . . . in restraint of trade . . . is illegal.

SHERMAN ANTI-TRUST ACT.

ABOUT the time the Sherman anti-trust law was being passed, in 1890, Henry D. Lloyd was writing his book *Wealth Against Commonwealth,* in which occurred a memorable passage:

A small number of men are obtaining the power to forbid any but themselves to supply the people with fire in nearly every form known to modern life and industry, from matches to locomotives and electricity. They control our hard coal and much of the soft, and stoves, furnaces, and steam and hot-water heaters; the governors on steam-boilers and the boilers; gas and gas-fixtures; natural gas and gas-pipes; electric lighting, and all the appurtenances. You cannot free yourself by changing from electricity to gas, or from the gas of the city to the gas of the fields. If you fly from kerosene to candles, you are still under the ban.

To understand the dangers of the monopolies which Lloyd

feared and denounced, it is necessary to know the principal
features in the development of American industry from the
close of the Civil War to 1890.

It will be remembered that the consolidation of small railroad lines into large systems was accompanied by such advantages to the companies and to the traveling public, as to
demonstrate that combination was the inevitable order of the
day. The similar integration of small industrial and commercial enterprises took place more slowly between 1870 and
1890, but the process was no less inevitable on that account.
The census of 1890 indicated that the production of manufactured articles had greatly increased since 1870; more capital was engaged; the product was more valuable; and more
workmen were employed. Nevertheless the number of establishments which were in operation had shown a considerable decline in many industries. An army of 100,000 employees represented the expansion of the wage-earning force in
the iron and steel works, for example, and $270,000,000 the
increase in the value of their products; yet the number of establishments engaged showed a shrinkage of nearly fourteen
per cent. The workers in the textile mills grew from 275,-
000 to 512,000, and the capital outlay from $300,000,000 to
$750,000,000, but the number of factories declined from
4,790 to 4,114. A cartoon in *Puck* on January 26, 1881, remarked that "the telegraph companies have been consolidated,
which in simple language means that Mr. Jay Gould controls
every wire in the United States over which a telegram can be
sent."

Some of the reasons for the prevalent tendency toward combination were not hard to discover. In the first place, although industrial organizations fought one another with the
utmost bitterness, it was in the nature of things for them to
combine if threatened by any common foe. Moreover, production on a large scale made possible savings and improvements
that were outside the grasp of more modest enterprises;

buying and selling large quantities of goods commanded opportunities for profit; waste products could be made use of and costly scientific investigations conducted in order to discover improved methods, overcome difficulties and open new avenues of activity; large salaries and important positions could be offered to men of executive capacity; and expensive equipment could be purchased and utilized.[1] An effective force which tended to drive industries to combine was the cut-throat competition which prevailed. Herbert Croly in his stimulating book *The Promise of American Life* vividly describes the bitter, warlike character of industrial competition after 1865. Competition was battle to the knife and tomahawk. The leaders were constantly seeking bigger operations, to which the bigger risks only added zest. A company might be making unbelievable profits one year and "skirting" bankruptcy the next. Exciting as all this was, however, the desire for adventure was not as powerful as the desire for profits, and cut-throat competition in industry led as naturally to combination, as rate-wars on the railroads led to pooling agreements.

An important factor in the development of large corporations was the increasing use of the corporation form of industrial organization, as contrasted with the co-partnership plan. If a few men enter a co-partnership, each of them must supply a considerable amount of capital; but if a corporation is formed and stock is sold, the par value of the shares may be placed at a low figure—$100 or less—and thus a large number of persons may be able to establish an industry which is far beyond the financial resources of any individual or small group among them. The corporation, moreover,

---

[1] Charles M. Schwab mentions an unusual example. Under the direction of Andrew Carnegie, the wealthy steel magnate, he had a new mill erected, which seemed likely to meet all the demands which would be placed upon it. But in the process of building it Schwab had seen a single way in which it could be improved. Carnegie at once gave orders to have the mill taken down before being used at all, and rebuilt on the improved plan.

is relatively permanent, for the death of one stock-holder among many is unimportant as compared with that of one member of a co-partnership. In case of disaster to the enterprise the liability of the stock-holder in a corporation is limited to the amount which he has invested, while any member of a partnership may be legally held for all the debts of the organization. With such advantages in its favor the corporation plan largely dominated the organization of industry.

The most famous example of combination before 1890 was the Standard Oil Company, which was the cause of more litigation, more study and more complaint than any other industrial organization that has ever existed in America. In 1865 Rockefeller & Andrews started an oil-refining business in Cleveland, Ohio. Samuel Andrews was a mechanical genius and he attended to the technical end of the industry; John D. Rockefeller had bargaining capacity, and to him fell the task of buying the crude oil, providing barrels and other materials and selling the product. The firm prospered. H. M. Flagler was taken into the company and a branch was established in New York. In 1870 these three with a few others organized the Standard Oil Company of Ohio, with a capitalization of a million dollars. It controlled not over ten per cent. of the business of oil-refining in the United States at that time. But the oil business was so profitable that capital flowed into it and competition became keen. Rockefeller and some associates, therefore, devised the South Improvement Company of Pennsylvania, a combination of refiners, headed and controlled by the Standard, the purpose of which was to make advantageous arrangements with the railroads for transportation facilities. Early in 1872, a most remarkable contract was signed between the company and the important railroads of the oil country—the Pennsylvania, the New York Central, and the Erie. By it the roads agreed to establish certain freight rates from the crude-oil producing region of western Pennsylvania to such refining and shipping centers as New York, Philadelphia, Baltimore, Pittsburgh and Cleveland. From these rates the South Improvement Company was to receive substantial rebates, amounting to forty or fifty per cent. on crude oil and twenty-five to forty-five per cent. on refined. On their side the railroads were promised the entire freight business of the Company, each to have an assured proportion of the traffic, with freedom from rate-cutting competition. All this was the common railroad practice of the times.

But another portion of the contract was not so common. It provided that the roads should give the South Improvement Company rebates on all oil shipped by its competitors and furnish it with full way-bills of all such shipments each day. In other words, the Company was to know exactly the amount of the business of its competitors and with whom it was being done. The contract allowed the roads to make similar rebates with anybody offering an equal amount of traffic, but the likelihood of such an outcome was slender in the extreme. Armed with this powerful weapon, Rockefeller entered upon a campaign to eliminate competition by offering to buy out independent refiners either with cash or with Standard Oil stock, at his estimate of the value of their property. Those who objected to selling were shown that the alliance between the South Improvement Company and the railroads was so strong that they faced the alternative of giving way or being crushed. Of the twenty-six refineries in Cleveland, at least twenty-one yielded. The capacity of the Standard leaped from 1,500 to 10,000 barrels a day and it controlled a fifth of the refining business of the country. When these facts came to be known in the oil country, the bitter Oil War of 1872 began. Independent producers joined to fight for existence, and at length the railroads gave way and agreed to abandon the contract with the South Improvement Company, and the legislature of Pennsylvania annulled its charter, although in one way or another rebates continued and the absorption of rivals went on. In 1882 the entire combination—thirty-nine refiners, controlling ninety to ninety-five per cent. of the product—was organized as the Standard Oil Trust. All stock-holders in the combining companies surrendered their certificates and received in return receipts or "trust-certificates," which showed the amount of the owner's interest in the trust. In order to secure unity of purpose and management, the affairs of the combination were put into the hands of nine trustees, with Rockefeller at the head.

The wonderful success of the Standard Oil Company, however, was not due solely to the alliance with the railroads, although this advantage came at a strategic time when it was fighting for supremacy. Its marketing department gave it an unenviable reputation, but achieved amazing success. The department was organized to cover the country, find out everything possible about competitors, and then kill them off by price-cutting or other means. The great resources of the Company enabled it to undersell rivals, going below cost if necessary, and thus wearing out opposition. Continuity of control, also, contributed to Standard success; the narrow limits of the area in which the crude oil was produced before 1890 rendered the problem of securing a monopoly somewhat easier; the organization was extremely efficient and the constituent companies were stimulated to a high degree of productivity by encouraging the spirit of emulation; men of ability were called to its high positions; the policy of gaining the mastery over the trade in petroleum and its products was kept definitely and persistently to the front; and then there was John D. Rockefeller.

Rockefeller was what used to be called a "self-made" man. He began his business life in Cleveland as a clerk at an extremely modest salary. Capacity for details and for shrewd bargaining, patience, frugality, seriousness, secretiveness, caution, an instinctive sense for business openings, self-control— all these were characteristic both of the Cleveland clerk and

the later oil-refiner. In the bigger field he developed a daring
caution, a quick understanding of the value of new inventions,
a capacity for organization, quick grasp of essentials and a
resourcefulness that dominated the entire Standard combination. He built the barrels that he used, and owned the pipe-
lines, tank-cars, tank-wagons and warehouses. Consolidation,
magnitude and financial returns were his aims, and in achieving these he and his associates were so successful as to make
the Standard a leader in all branches of business, except the
ethics of industry. Litigation has been the constant accompaniment of Standard progress.

Following the Standard Oil Company, other combinations
found the trust form of organization a convenient one. The
cotton trust, the whiskey trust, and the sugar, cotton bagging,
copper and salt trusts made the public familiar with the term.
Moreover, popular suspicion and hostility became aroused,
and the word "trust" began to acquire something of the
unpleasant connotation which it later possessed.

Although it was upon the Standard Oil Company that people turned when they denounced the trusts and feared or
condemned their practices, the principles to which the Standard adhered when under the strain of competition were the
practices which were followed by their contemporaries, both
big and little. When the Diamond Match Company was before the Courts of Michigan in 1889, it appeared that the organization was built up for the purpose of controlling the
manufacture and trade in matches in the United States and
Canada. Its policy was to buy up and "remove" competition, so that it might monopolize the manufacture and sale of
matches. It could then fix the price of its commodity at such
a point that it could recoup itself for the expense of eliminating competitors and also make larger profits than were possible when its rivals were active.

Still more dangerous was the combination of the hard
coal operators. By 1873, six corporations owned both the

hard coal deposits of Pennsylvania and the railroads which made it possible to haul the coal out to the markets. In the same year and later these companies made agreements which determined the amounts of coal that they would mine, the price which they would charge, and the proportion of the whole output that each company would be allowed to handle. Independent operators—that is, operators not in the combination—found their existence precarious in the extreme, for their means of transportation was in the hands of the six coal-carrying railroads, who could raise rates almost at will and find reasons even for refusing service. The states were powerless to remedy the situation because their authority did not extend to interstate commerce, yet it was intolerable for a small group of interested parties to have power to fix the output of so necessary a commodity as coal, on no other basis than that provided by their own desires.

Other abuses appeared which showed that industrial combinations were open to many of the complaints which, in connection with the railroads, had led to the Interstate Commerce Act. Industrial pools resembled railroad pools and were objected to for similar reasons. Bankers and others who organized combinations were given returns that seemed as extravagant as the prices paid to railroad construction companies; the issues of the stock of corporations were bought and sold by their own officers for speculative purposes; and stock-watering was as common as in railroading. The industrial combinations also had somewhat the same effect on politics that the railroads had. Lloyd declared that the Standard Oil Company had done everything with the Pennsylvania legislature except refine it.

One of the most noted cases of corporation influence in politics was that of the election of Senator Henry B. Payne of Ohio. In 1886 the legislature of the state requested the United States Senate to investigate the election of Payne because of charges of Standard Oil influence. The debate over the case showed clearly the belief on the part of many that the Standard, which controlled "business, railroads, men and things," was also choosing United States senators. Senator Hoar raised the question whether the Standard was represented in the Senate and even in the Cabinet. In denying any connection with the Oil Company, Payne himself declared that no institution or association had been "to so large an expense in money" to accomplish his defeat when he was a candidate for election to the lower house. Popular suspicion seemed confirmed, therefore, that the Company was taking an active share in government. Whether the trust was for or against Payne made little difference.

A complaint that brought the trust problem to the attention of many who were not interested in its other aspects was the treatment accorded independent producers. The roughshod methods employed by the Standard Oil Company, the Diamond Match Company and the coal operators were concretely illustrated in many a city and town by such incidents as that of a Pennsylvania butcher mentioned by Lloyd. An agent of the great meat-slaughtering firms ordered the butcher to cease slaughtering cattle, and when he refused the agent informed him that his business would be destroyed. He then found himself unable to buy any meat whatever from Chicago, the meat-packing center, and discovered that the railroad would not furnish cars to transport his supplies. Faced by such overwhelming force, the independent producer was generally compelled to give way to the demands of the big concerns or be driven to the wall. The helplessness of the individual under such conditions was strikingly expressed by Mr. Justice Harlan of the Supreme Court in a decision in a suit against the Standard Oil Company:

All who recall the condition of the country in 1890 will remember that there was everywhere, among the people generally, a deep feeling of unrest. The Nation had been rid of human slavery . . . but the conviction was universal that the country was in real danger from another kind of slavery sought to be fastened on the American people, namely, the slavery that would result from aggregations of capital in the hands of a few . . . controlling, for their own . . . advantage exclusively, the entire business of the country, including the production and sale of the necessaries of life.

Observers noted that fortunes which outstripped the possessions of princes were being amassed for the few by combinations which sometimes, if not frequently, resorted to illegal and unfair practices, and they compared these conditions with the labor unrest, the discontent and the poverty which was the lot of the many.

In the meanwhile there had arisen a growing demand for action which would give relief from the conditions just described. As early as 1879 the Hepburn committee appointed by the New York Assembly had investigated the railroads and had made public a mass of information concerning the relation of the transportation system to the industrial combinations. In 1880 Henry George had published *Progress and Poverty* in which he had contended that the entire burden of taxation should be laid upon land values, in order to overcome the advantage which the ownership of land gave to monopoly. In 1881 Henry D. Lloyd had fired his first volley, "The Story of a Great Monopoly," an attack on the Standard Oil Company which was published in the *Atlantic Monthly* and which caused that number of the periodical to go through seven editions.[2] In 1888 Edward Bellamy's *Looking Backward* had pictured a socialized Utopian state in which the luxuries as well as the necessities of life were produced for the common benefit of all the people. Societies had been formed for the propagation of Bellamy's ideas, and the parlor study of socialism had become popular.

The platforms of the political parties had given evidence of a continuing unrest without presenting any definite pro-

[2] It was not until 1894 that Lloyd published *Wealth Against Commonwealth*, but his pen had been busy constantly between 1881 and 1894.

posals for relief. As far back as 1872 the Labor Reformers had condemned the "capitalists" for importing Chinese laborers; in the same year the Republicans and Democrats had opposed further grants of public land to corporations and monopolies—referring in the main to the railroads; in 1880 the Greenbackers and in 1884 the Anti-Monopolists, the Prohibitionists and the Democrats had denounced the corporations and called for government action to prevent or control them; and in 1888 the Union Labor party, the Prohibitionists and the Republicans had urged legislation for doing away with or regulating trusts and monopolies. By 1890 eight states had already passed anti-trust laws. Among unorganized forces, possibly the independent producers were as effective as any. Although usually overcome by the superior strength of their big opponents, they frequently conducted vigorous contests and sometimes carried the issue to the courts where damaging evidence was made public.

A just evaluation of the industrial problems of the seventies and eighties, however, must take account of the more admirable characteristics of American business. At the outset it must be remembered that even the better magnates of that period were *pioneers*—new to their problems, not yet guided by the soberer conventions of preceding industrial experience, and forced to compete on all sides with the crude energy of other pioneers. Like the explorer, the fur trader, the man who drove the prairie schooner, and the farmer who broke the primeval turf of the Mid-West, the industrial pioneer had to possess the qualities which enabled him to overcome the obstacles which faced him,—the qualities of initiative, energy, fearlessness, and the chance-taking spirit of the born gambler. If such men tended to be ruthless and crude, if they lacked culture and high ethical standards, it may be said by way of explanation, if not of defence, that they were the product of their times.

There are, doubtless, far better examples of the industrial

pioneer of the generation after the Civil War than Marcus
A. Hanna of Ohio, but if so, the facts of their lives have not
been made so conveniently available as his have been in the
pages of Mr. Herbert Croly's discriminating biography. Two
years after the close of the war, "Mark" Hanna entered a
co-partnership in Cleveland. The city was small, but rapidly
growing, and situated at an advantageous point on the Great
Lakes, accessible to the Erie Canal, the Ohio Canal, several
railroads, and the natural resources of the Lake Superior and
Pittsburgh regions. Mr. Hanna helped to build up a commission business in coal and iron, while his surplus energy overflowed into the purchase of a newspaper, the presidency of a
bank, the operation of a theatre and the management of a
street railway company. Into each of these he threw himself with energy and the will to succeed. "He always played
fair, even if he did not always play politely," says Mr. Croly;
"and when he sat in a game he usually won, and he usually
occupied or came to occupy a seat at the head of the table."
Perhaps a later generation might question Hanna's inauguration of his newspaper venture by the purchase of every editor and reporter who was supposed to contribute to the
success of his chief rival; doubtless the level of civic morality
was lowered by his procuring franchises for his street railway
by the direct method of purchasing the city council which had
the power to make the grants. But, again, his standards
were the standards of his time.

In his relations with his employees, Mr. Hanna was direct
and personal. If there were complaints among the employees,
he went straight to the leaders (whom he generally knew in
person), endeavored to discover the source of the trouble,
found his own solution, and acted accordingly and at once.
If a workman met with an accident or fell ill, he cared for
the man as he deemed just,—not because of any law forcing
him to act, but because he knew and liked his subordinates.

If men of the Mark Hanna type stood stiffly against government regulation (which would inevitably restrict their freedom of action), if they held rigidly to the conviction that they could deal more successfully with their employees without the complications of labor union officials and practices, if they felt that the upshot of their work was beneficial to the American public,—perhaps it is not difficult to see some justification for their position. At any rate, their ability, their energy and their activities—right and wrong—made enormously more difficult an already complex problem—that of "trust" or monopoly regulation.

The solution of the problem—if there is any solution—was not easy to discover and apply. The amount of property involved was so great that forceful legislation would be fought to the last ditch. Legislation that was obviously weak, on the other hand, would not satisfy public opinion. Public officials were hopelessly divergent in their views. Cleveland had called attention to the evils of the trusts in his tariff message of 1887, but had laid his emphasis on the need of reduced taxation rather than upon control of the great combinations. Blaine was opposed to federal action. Thomas B. Reed in the House of Representatives had characteristically ridiculed the idea that monopolies existed:

And yet, outside the Patent Office there are no monopolies in this country, and there never can be. Ah, but what is that I see on the far horizon's edge, with tongue of lambent flame and eye of forked fire, serpent-headed and griffin-clawed? Surely it must be the great new chimera "Trust." Quick, cries every masked member of the Ways and Means. Quick, let us lower the tariff. Let us call in the British. Let them save our devastated homes.

More serious was the almost universal lack of knowledge of the elements involved in the situation. Industrial leaders were unenlightened and wrapped up in the attempt to outdo rivals who were equally unenlightened and absorbed; the nation needed instruction and leadership, and neither was to be found. Instead, the poorer classes became more and more hostile to big business; the capitalist class set itself stolidly to the preservation of its interests. The one saw only the abuses, the other only the benefits of combinations. Thoughtful men felt that industrialism was afflicted with a malady which would kill the nation unless a remedy were found.

The legal and constitutional position of the trusts was almost impregnable. Ever since the decision of the Supreme Court in the Dartmouth College case, handed down in 1819, franchises and charters granted by states to corporations had been regarded as contracts which could not be altered by subsequent legislation. Moreover, the Court had so interpreted the Fourteenth Amendment, as has been seen, that the states had found great difficulty in framing regulatory legislation that would pass muster before the judiciary.[3] It was doubtful whether federal attempts at regulation would be more fortunate. More fundamental still, for public opinion underlies even constitutional interpretation, American industrial and commercial expansion had run ahead of our conception of the possible and proper functions of government. Government as the protector of property was an ancient concept and commonly held in the United States; government as the guardian of the individual against the powerful holder of a great deal of property was a new idea and not generally looked upon with favor.

It has already been seen that the prevailing economic theory, *laissez faire*, was diametrically opposed to government regulation of the economic activities of the individual. According to this view, unrestricted industrial liberty would result in adjustment by business itself on honorable lines. Men whose integrity was such that they were in control of great enterprises, asserted an attorney for the Standard Oil Company, would be the first to realize that a fair policy toward competitors and the public was the most successful policy.

[3] *Cf.* above, pp. 94 *ff.* on Fourteenth Amendment.

Combination was declared to be inevitable in modern life, and reductions in the price of many commodities were pointed to as a justification for leaving the trusts unhampered.

Public opinion, however, was reaching the point where it was prepared to brush aside theoretical difficulties. The presidents, Senator Sherman and others urged action. Large numbers of anti-monopoly bills were presented in Congress. The indifference of some members and the opposition of others was somewhat neutralized by the fiery zeal of such men as Senator Jones of Arkansas, who declared that the fortunes made by the Standard Oil Company did not represent a single dollar of honest toil or one trace of benefit to mankind. ''The sugar trust,'' declared the senator, ''has its 'long, felonious fingers' at this moment in every man's pocket in the United States, deftly extracting with the same audacity the pennies from the pockets of the poor and the dollars from the pockets of the rich.''

After much study of the mass of suggested legislation, Congress relied upon its constitutional power to regulate commerce among the several states and passed the Sherman Antitrust Act, which received President Harrison's signature on July 2, 1890. Its most significant portions are the following:

Sec. 1. Every contract, combination in the form of trust or otherwise, or conspiracy, in restraint of trade or commerce among the several States, or with foreign nations, is . . . illegal.

Sec. 2. Every person who shall monopolize, or attempt to monopolize, or combine or conspire with any other such person . . . to monopolize any part of the trade or commerce among the several States, or with foreign nations, shall be deemed guilty of misdemeanor.

Sec. 7. Any person who shall be injured in his business or property by any other person or corporation by reason of anything forbidden . . . by this act, may sue . . . and shall recover three fold the damages by him sustained.

The purpose of the framers of the Act seems clearly to have been to draw up a general measure whose terms should be those usual in the English common law and then rest on the assurance that the courts would interpret its meaning in the light of former practice. For some centuries restraint of trade had been considered illegal in England, but no contract was held to be contrary to law if it provided only a *reasonable* restraint—that is, if the restraint was merely minor and subsidiary. The Sherman act was a Senate measure, was presented from the Judiciary Committee and was passed precisely as drawn up by it. In speaking from the Committee, both Edmunds and Hoar took the attitude which the latter expressed as follows: "The great thing that this bill does, . . . is to extend the common-law principles, which protected fair competition . . . in England, to international and interstate commerce in the United States." Just how far the members of Congress who were not on the Judiciary Committee of the Senate shared in this view or really understood the bill can not be said. Indeed, many members of both chambers absented themselves when the bill came to a vote.[4]

For a long time the Sherman Act like the Interstate Commerce Act was singularly ineffective and futile. Trusts were nominally dissolved, but the separate parts were conducted under a common and uniform policy by the same board of managers. The Standard Oil Company changed its form by selecting the Standard Oil Company of New Jersey as a

[4] The authorship of the Sherman law has often been a source of controversy. Senator John Sherman, as well as other members, introduced anti-trust bills in the Senate in 1888. Senator Sherman's proposal was later referred to the Judiciary Committee, of which he was not a member. The Committee thoroughly revised it. Senator Hoar, who was on the Committee, thought he remembered having written it word for word as it was adopted. Recent investigation seems to prove that the senator's recollection was faulty and that Edmunds wrote most of it, while Hoar, Ingalls and George wrote a section each and Evarts part of a sentence. If this is the fact, it seems most nearly accurate to say that Sherman started the enterprise and that almost every member of the Judiciary committee, especially Edmunds, shared in its completion,

"holding corporation." Stock of the members of the combination was exchanged for stock in the New Jersey organization, leaving control in the same hands as before. The "same business was carried on in the same way but 'under a new sign.'" The wide variety of conditions tolerated under the corporation laws of the several states made confusion worse confounded. In its early attempts to convict corporations of violation of the law, the government was uniformly defeated.

In 1895 came the climax of futility. The American Sugar Refining Company had purchased refineries in Philadelphia which enabled it to control, with its other plants, ninety-eight per cent. of the refining business in the country. The government asked the courts to cancel the purchase on the ground that it was contrary to the Sherman law, and to order the return of the properties to their former owners. The Supreme Court, in United States *v.* E. C. Knight (better known as the Knight case), declared that the mere purchase of sugar refineries was not an act of interstate commerce and that it could not be said to restrain such trade, and it refused to grant the request of the government. Unhappily the prosecuting officers of the Attorney-General's office had drawn up their case badly, making their complaint the purchase, not the resulting restraint. No direct evidence was presented to show that interstate commerce in sugar and the control of the sugar business and of prices were the chief objects of the combination. To the public it seemed that the corporations were impregnable, for even the United States government could not control them.

BIBLIOGRAPHICAL NOTE

The early history of anti-trust agitation centers about Henry D. Lloyd. His earliest article, "The Story of a Great Monopoly," is in *The Atlantic Monthly* (Mar., 1881); his classic account of trust abuses is *Wealth against Commonwealth* (1894); consult also C. A. Lloyd, *Henry D. Lloyd* (2 vols., 1912). Early and valuable articles in periodicals are in *Political Science Quarterly,* 1888, pp. 78–98; 1889, pp. 296–319; W. Z. Ripley, *Trusts, Pools, and Corporations* (rev. ed., 1916), is useful; B. J. Hendrick, *Age of Big Business* (1919), is interesting and contains a bibliography. Ida M. Tarbell, *History of the Standard Oil Company* (2 vols., 1904), is carefully done and a pioneer work. Other valuable accounts are: S. C. T. Dodd, *Trusts* (1900), by a former Standard Oil attorney; Eliot Jones, *The Anthracite Coal Combination in the United States* (1914); J. W. Jenks, *Trust Problem* (1900), contains a summary of the economies of large scale production; J. W. Jenks and W. E. Clark, *The Trust Problem* (4th ed., 1917), is scholarly and complete; J. D. Rockefeller, *Random Reminiscences of Men and Events* (1916), is a brief defence of the Standard Oil Company; W. H. Taft, *Anti-Trust Act and the Supreme Court* (1914), summarizes a few important decisions on the Sherman law. H. Croly, *Marcus Alonzo Hanna* (1912), is valuable for its delineation of a type. Edward Bellamy, *Looking Backward* (1888), describes an economic Utopia. Early proposed anti-trust laws, together with the Congressional debates on the subject are in *Senate Documents,* 57th Congress, 2nd session, vol. 14, No. 147 (Serial Number 4428). No complete historical study has yet been made of the effects of industrial development, immediately after the Civil War, on politics and the structure of American society.

CHAPTER XI

EXTREME REPUBLICANISM

. . . our present tariff laws, the vicious, inequitable, and illogical source of unnecessary taxation, ought to be at once revised and amended.
PRESIDENT GROVER CLEVELAND, Dec. 6, 1887.

I would put the manufacturers of Pennsylvania under the fire and fry all the fat out of them.
PARTY WORKER, 1888.

Altogether I am by no means pleased with what our party, at both the White House and the Capitol, has done about Civil Service Reform.
Civil Service Commissioner THEODORE ROOSEVELT, 1892.

[In 1890 in the House of Representatives] three resolute men could stop all public business, and one-fifth of the House, owing to the right to call the yeas and nays, could . . . use up three hours of public time by the employment of as many minutes.
THOMAS B. REED.

THAT the election of 1888 differed from its predecessors since 1865 was due chiefly to the independence, courage and political insight of President Cleveland. Hitherto campaigns had been contested with as little reference to real issues as conditions rendered possible. Neither party had possessed leaders with sufficient understanding of the needs of the nation to force a genuine settlement of an important issue. That 1888 saw a clear contest made it a memorable year in recent politics.

It will be remembered that the tariff act of 1883 had been satisfactory only to a minority in Congress, because it retained the high level of customs duties that had been established during the Civil War. The congressional election of 1882 had resulted in the choice of a Democratic House of Representatives and had offered another opportunity for downward revision. Early in 1884, therefore, William R.

242

Morrison presented a bill making considerable additions to the free list and providing for a "horizontal" reduction of about twenty per cent. on all other duties as levied under the act of 1883. The measure was defeated by four votes. Opposed to it were substantially all the Republicans and forty-one Democrats, most of them from the industrial states of New York, New Jersey, Pennsylvania and Ohio. The Democratic tariff plank of 1884, as has been seen, was practically meaningless, but the election of Cleveland, and the choice of a Democratic House gave another opportunity for revision. Again Morrison attempted a reduction, and again he was defeated by Samuel J. Randall and the other protectionist Democrats.

The entire matter, however, was about to receive a new and important development at the hands of President Cleveland and John G. Carlisle, who was the Speaker of the House during the four years from 1885 to 1889. Carlisle was a Kentuckian, a man of grave bearing, unflagging industry and substantial attainments. His tariff principles were in accord with those of the President, and his position as Speaker enabled him to determine the make-up of the Committee on Ways and Means, which would frame any tariff legislation. Cleveland had expressed his belief in the desirability of tariff reduction in his messages to Congress of 1885 and 1886, basing his recommendations on the same facts that had earlier actuated President Arthur in making similar suggestions. His recommendations, however, had received the same slight consideration that had been accorded those of his Republican predecessor. He therefore determined to challenge the attention of the country and of Congress by means of a novel expedient.

Previous presidential messages had covered a wide variety of subjects—foreign relations, domestic affairs, and recommendations of all kinds. Departing from this custom, the President made up his mind to devote an entire message to tariff reform. His project was startling from the political point of view, for his party was far from being a unit in its attitude toward reduction, a presidential campaign was at hand, and the Independents, who had had a strong influence in bringing about his success in 1884, sent word to him that a reform message would imperil his chances of re-election. This type of argument had little weight with Cleveland, however, and his reply was brief: "Do you not think that the people of the United States are entitled to some instruction on this subject?"

On December 6, 1887, therefore, he sent to Congress his famous message urging the downward revision of the tariff. The immediate occasion of his recommendation, he declared, was the surplus of income over expenditure, which was piling up in the treasury at a rapid rate and which was a constant invitation to reckless appropriations. The portion of the public debt which was payable had already been redeemed, so that whatever surplus was not expended would be stored in the vaults, thus reducing the amount of currency in circulation, and making likely a financial crisis. The simplest remedy for the situation seemed to Cleveland to lie in a reduction of the income, and the most desirable means of reduction seemed to be the downward revision of the tariff, a system of "unnecessary taxation" which he denominated "vicious, inequitable, and illogical." Disclaiming any wish to advocate free trade, he expressed the hope that Congress would turn its attention to the practical problem before it:

Our progress toward a wise conclusion will not be improved by dwelling upon the theories of protection and free trade. This savors too much of bandying epithets. It is a *condition* which confronts us, not a theory.

The effect of the message was immediate. Men began at once to take sides as if everybody had been waiting for a leader to speak his mind; and the parties adopted the defi-

nite principles to which they adhered for many years afterwards. The Democrats very generally rallied to the support
of their champion; gaps in the ranks were closed up; and
doubtless the usual pressure was applied to obstinate members who were disinclined to follow the leader. The Republican attitude was well expressed in the phrase of one of the
politicians: "It is free-trade, and we have 'em!" The most
prominent Republican, James G. Blaine, was in Paris, but
true to his instinctive recognition of a good political opportunity he gave an interview which was immediately cabled
to America. In it Blaine maintained that tariff reduction
would harm the entire country, and especially the South and
the farmers, and urged the reduction of the surplus by the
abolition of the tax on tobacco, which he termed the poor
man's luxury. The "Paris Message" was generally looked
upon as the Republican answer to Cleveland, and as pointing
to Blaine as the inevitable candidate for the ensuing campaign. On one point, most men of both parties were agreed
—that the President had displayed great courage. "The
presidential chair," declared James Russell Lowell, "has a
MAN in it, and this means that every word he *says* is weighted
with what he *is*."

The chairman of the Ways and Means Committee in the
House of Representatives, Roger Q. Mills, promptly presented
a bill which conformed to the principles for which the President had argued. The discussion of the Mills bill was long
known as the "Great Tariff Debate of 1888." The House
seethed with it for more than a month. Mills and Carlisle
on one side and William McKinley and Thomas B. Reed on
the other typified the new leadership and the new positions
which the parties were taking. Senator Morrill's idea that
the war tariff was a temporary one, President Arthur's advice that the tariff be revised, the recommendations of the
Tariff Commission of 1882 that reductions were necessary,—
all these were no longer heard. Instead, the Republicans up-

held the protective system as the cause of the unexampled
prosperity of the nation. It is not to be supposed that protectionist or reductionist converts were made by the endless
discussion, but the initial prejudices of each side were undoubtedly deepened. Each telling blow on either side was applauded by the partisans of each particular speaker, so that
"applause" fairly dots the dull pages of the Congressional
Record. McKinley enlivened his colleagues by pulling from
his desk and exhibiting a suit of clothes which he had purchased for $10.00, a figure, he asserted, which proved that the
tariff did not raise prices beyond the reach of the laboring
man. Mills tracked down the cost of the suit and the tariff on
the materials composing it, and further entertained the House
by an exhibit showing that it cost $4.98 to manufacture the
suit and that the remainder of the price which the laborer
paid was due to the tariff. In the end, the Mills bill passed
the House with but four Democrats voting against it. ✓Ran-
dall was so ill that he was unable to be present when the final
vote was taken, but a letter from him declaring his opposition
to the bill was greeted with great applause on the Republican
side. Randall's day was past, however, and leadership was
passing to new men.

Meanwhile the Republicans in the Senate, where they were
in control, had prepared a tariff bill which was designed to
give evidence of the sort of act which would be passed if they
were successful in the campaign. Senator Allison and Senator Aldrich were influential in this connection. The passage
of leadership in tariff matters to Senator Aldrich and men of
his type was as significant as the transition in the House.
Aldrich was from Rhode Island, an able man who had had
experience in state affairs, had served in the federal House
of Representatives and had been in the Senate since 1881.
He had already laid the foundations of the great financial
and industrial connections which gave him an intimate, personal interest in protection and which later made him an

important figure in American industry and politics. Since neither party controlled both branches of Congress, it was impossible to pass either the Mills bill or the Senate measure; but the proposed legislation indicated what might be expected to result from the election. Each side had thoroughly committed itself on the tariff question.

In the meanwhile, great interest attached to the question of leaders for the campaign. Opposition to Cleveland was not lacking. His efforts in behalf of civil service reform had not endeared him to the office-seekers, and the hostility of the Democrats in the Senate was shown by their feeble support of him. The West did not relish his opposition to silver coinage, while his vetoes of pension legislation were productive of some hostility, even in his own party. Nor was the personality of the President such as to allay ill-feeling. Indeed, Cleveland was in a position comparable to that of Hayes eight years before. He was the titular party leader, but the most prominent Democratic politicians were not in agreement with his principles, and any step taken by him was likely to arouse as much hostility in some Democratic quarters as among the Republicans. Opposition to his nomination focused upon David B. Hill, Governor of New York, a man who was looked upon as better disposed towards the claims of party workers for office. Other leaders like Bayard, Thurman and Carlisle aroused little enthusiasm, and the gradual drift of sentiment toward Cleveland became unmistakable. If the politicians did not accept him with joy, they at least accepted him; for he was master of the party for the moment at least, and his hold on a large body of the rank and file was not to be doubted. When the Democratic convention met at St. Louis in June, 1888, his nomination was made without the formality of a ballot.[1]

[1] The vice-presidential candidate was Allan G. Thurman of Ohio, affectionately known as the "noble old Roman," one of whose titles to fame was the ownership of a large red bandanna handkerchief which he flourished on all occasions.

The platform was devoted, for the most part, to the question of revenue reform, indorsing the President's tariff message and urging that the party be given control of Congress in order that Democratic principles might be put into effect. Resolutions were also adopted recommending the passage of the Mills bill, which was still under discussion when the convention met.

Among the Republicans the choice of a candidate was a far more difficult matter. The probable choice of the party was Blaine, but his letter from Italy, where he was traveling, early in the convention year, forbade the use of his name and opened the contest to a great number of less well-known leaders. Publicly it was stated that Blaine refused for reasons which were "entirely personal," but intimate friends knew that he would accept a nomination if it came without solicitation and as the result of a unanimous party call. Although the demand for him still continued, there were smaller "booms" for various favorite sons, and as his ill health continued he made known his irrevocable decision to withdraw. Except for Blaine, the most prominent contender was Senator Sherman, whose candidacy reached larger proportions than ever before. The Ohio delegation was unitedly in his favor and considerable numbers of southern delegates were expected to vote for him. On the other hand, his lack of personal magnetism was against him and his career had been connected with technical matters which did not make a popular appeal. On the first ballot in the nominating convention his lead was considerable, although not decisive, but no fewer than thirteen other leaders also received votes. One of these was Senator Benjamin Harrison of Indiana whom Blaine had suggested as an available man and whom the New York delegation considered a strong candidate because he was poor, a reputable senator, a distinguished volunteer officer in the war and a grandson of William H. Harrison of Tippecanoe fame. Further voting only emphasized the lack of unanimity until the eighth ballot, when the delegates suddenly turned to Harrison and nominated him.

The platform was long and verbose. It devoted much attention to the protective tariff which, in imitation of Henry Clay, it entitled the "American system"; it advocated the reduction of internal revenue duties, if necessary to cut down the surplus; and it urged civil service reform, liberal pensions and laws to control oppressive corporations.

Two factions of the Labor party, as well as the Prohibitionists, nominated candidates and urged programs to which no attention was paid, but which were later taken up by both the great parties, such as arbitration in labor disputes, an income tax, the popular election of senators, woman suffrage, and the prohibition of the manufacture of alcoholic beverages.

The campaign deserves attention because of the unusual elements that entered into it. A spectacular feature which, although not new, was developed on a large scale, was the formation of thousands of political clubs, which paraded evenings with flaming torches. In this type of organization the Republicans were more successful than the Democrats and thus steered many young men into the party at a time when they were looking forward to casting their first ballot. The most unwholesome feature was, as before, the methods used to finance the campaign. In this connection both parties were guilty, but the Republicans were able to tap a new source of supply. The campaign was in the hands of Matthew S. Quay, a Pennsylvania senator whose career as a public official left much to be desired. Quay's political methods were vividly described at a later time by his friend and admirer Thomas C. Platt, whose account lost none of its delightfulness in view of the fact that Platt obviously felt that he was complimenting his friend in telling the story. Believing in the "rights" of business men in politics, Platt declared, Quay was always able to raise any amount of money needed, although when funds were raised by business interests against him, he lifted the "fiery cross" and virtuously exposed his opponents before the people. Having calculated with skill the number of votes needed for victory, he found out where he could get them—"and then he got them."

That Quay was able to tap a new source of supply was due to a combination of circumstances. It will be remembered that the Pendleton civil service act of 1883 had forbidden the assessment of office-holders in political campaigns, and had made it necessary to procure funds elsewhere. In the campaign of 1888, business men who believed that the success of Cleveland would hurt their interests, and manufacturers who profited directly by the protective tariff rallied to the defence of Harrison and contributed heavily to his campaign fund.[2]

The use to which the funds thus contributed were put was revealed in a letter written apparently by W. W. Dudley, treasurer of the National Republican Committee, and sent to party leaders in Indiana. The latter were directed to find out who had the "Democratic boodle" and force them, presumably by competition, to pay big prices for their own men. The leaders were also instructed to "divide the floaters into blocks of five and put a trusted man with the necessary funds in charge of these five, and make him responsible that none get away, and that all vote our ticket."

On the other hand, the most wholesome feature of the campaign was its educational aspect. Hundreds of societies, tons of "literature," thousands of stump speeches attacked and defended the tariff. Schoolboys glibly retailed the standard arguments on one side or the other. Attention was eentered, as it had not been since the war, on an important issue.

[2] A party worker who realized the opportunity which this fact presented complained that Pennsylvania manufacturers who made fortunes under protection did not contribute to the Republican campaign fund, and remarked: "If I had my way about it I would put the manufacturers of Pennsylvania under the fire and fry all the fat out of them."

At the close of the campaign the Republicans played a trick which was reminiscent of the Morey letter of Garfield's day. A letter purporting to be from a Charles F. Murchison, a naturalized American of English birth, was sent to the British minister in Washington, Lord Sackville-West. Murchison requested the minister's opinion as to whether President Cleveland's hostile policy in a recent controversy with Canada had been adopted for campaign purposes and whether after election the President would be more friendly toward England. Lord Sackville indiscreetly replied that he believed President Cleveland would show a conciliatory spirit toward Great Britain. The correspondence was held back until shortly before the election and was then published in the newspapers and on hand bills. Republicans triumphantly declared that Cleveland was the "British candidate." The President was at first inclined to overlook the incident but eventually gave way to pressure and dismissed the minister, whereupon the English government refused to fill the vacancy until there was a change of administration.

In the ensuing election the vote cast was unusually heavy; the protectionists felt that a supreme effort must be made to preserve the tariff system, and the Democrats, having experienced the joys of power, were determined not to loosen their grip on authority; the Prohibitionists increased their vote over that of 1884 by 100,000, while the Labor party cast 147,000, almost as many ballots as the Prohibitionists had numbered in the earlier year. Cleveland received somewhat over 100,000 more votes than Harrison, but his support was so placed that his electoral vote was sixty-five less than his opponent's.

From the standpoint of political history the result was unfortunate. The tariff question had been sadly in need of a definite answer, the people had been educated upon it and had given a decision, but the electoral system placed in power a President pledged to the theories of the minority.[3] Aside from the unusual effect of our machinery of election, many small elements entered into the Republican victory. Some of the Independents had become disaffected since 1884 and had returned to the Republican fold. Disgruntled office-seekers opposed a President who did not reward his workers. In New York, which was the decisive factor, Hill was a candidate for re-election as governor and was elected by a small majority, while Cleveland lost the state by 7,000 votes. This gave color to charges that the enemies of the President had made a bargain with the Republicans by which the latter voted for Hill as governor and the Democrats for Harrison as President.

Benjamin Harrison, veteran of the Civil War in which he had attained the rank of brevet brigadier-general, and senator from Indiana for a single term, was hardly a party leader when he was nominated for the presidency. Although he was by no means unknown, he had been sufficiently obscure to be unconnected with factional party quarrels, and his career and character were without blemish. At the time of his accession to the executive chair he was fifty-six years of age, a short man with bearded face, and with head set well down between his shoulders. Accounts of his characteristics, drawn by his party associates, did not differ in any essential detail. As a public speaker, the new President was a man of unusual charm—felicitous in his remarks, versatile, tactful. In a famous trip through the South and West in 1891, he made speech after speech at a wide variety of places and occasions, and created a genuine enthusiasm. His remarks were widely read and highly regarded. Nevertheless there seems to have been some truth in the remark of one of his contemporaries that he could charm ten thousand men in a public speech but meet them individually and send every one away his enemy.

[3] The mandate of the people, moreover, was not absolutely clear, for a Republican House was elected.

His manner, even to senators and representatives of his own party, was reserved to the point of frigidity. When he granted requests for patronage he was so ungracious as to anger the recipients of favor. Although his personal character and integrity were as unquestioned as those of Hayes, and although he was a man of cultured tastes, well-informed, thoughtful and conscientious, it must be admitted that he lacked robust leadership and breadth of vision, and that he did not understand the real purposes of the policies which his party associates were embarking upon, or if he did that he tamely acquiesced in them. The party leaders were soon engaged in initiating practices and passing legislation which would strengthen the organization with certain groups of interested persons. Harrison, conscientious but aloof, provided no compelling force to turn attention toward wider and deeper needs.

Two appointments to the cabinet were important. Since Blaine was the foremost leader of the party and had done much to bring about the election of Harrison, it was well-nigh impossible for the latter to fail to offer him the position of Secretary of State. The appointment was so natural that popular opinion looked upon it as the only possibility, yet the natures of the two men were so diverse and their positions in the party so different that friction seemed likely to result. Even before the administration began it was freely predicted that Blaine would "dominate" the cabinet, a prophecy that might well create a feeling of restraint between the two. The invitation to John Wanamaker to become Postmaster-General was regarded as significant. Wanamaker was a wealthy merchant of Philadelphia, who had organized an advisory campaign committee of business men which contributed and expended large sums of money during the canvass. Critical reformers like the editor of *The Nation* were not slow to connect Wanamaker's large contribution to the campaign fund with his elevation to the cabinet, and to suggest that the business interests were being brought into close relations with the administration. T. C. Platt, expectant of a return for his campaign assistance, in the form of a cabinet position, and in fact understanding that a pledge had been made that he would be appointed, found himself superseded by William Windom of Minnesota in the Treasury and became a bitter opponent of the President.[4]

It was an odd turn of the fortune of politics that brought Benjamin Harrison face to face with the responsibility for furthering the cause of civil service reform—the same Harrison who, as a senator, had sneered at Cleveland for surrendering to difficulties. The party platform had urged the continuation of reform, which had been "auspiciously begun under the Republican administration," and had declared that the party promises would not be broken as Democratic pledges had been; and Harrison had announced his adherence to the party statement. In some respects real progress was made. Secretary of the Navy Tracy introduced reform methods in his department. The appointment of Theodore Roosevelt to the Civil Service Commission was productive of good results. The work of reform was defended forcefully and successfully; its opponents were challenged to substantiate their charges. When Senator Gorman declared that in an examination for letter carriers in Baltimore the candidates were asked to tell the most direct route from Baltimore to China, Roosevelt at once wrote asking him to state the time and place of the examination himself or to send somebody to look over the papers, copies of which were in the commission's office. The senator did not reply.

The removal of office holders, however, proceeded with amazing rapidity. The First Assistant Postmaster-General was J. S. Clarkson, who had been vice-chairman of the Re-

4 The remaining members of the cabinet were: Redfield Proctor, Vt., Secretary of War; W. H. H. Miller, Ind., Attorney-General; B. F. Tracy, N. Y., Secretary of the Navy; J. W. Noble, Mo., Secretary of the Interior; J. M. Rusk, Wis., Secretary of Agriculture.

publican National Campaign Committee. The speed with which he cleared the service of Democrats earned him the title ''headsman'' and is indicated by the estimate that he removed one every three minutes for the first year. When the force of clerks was increased for the taking of the census of 1890, the superintendent of the census office found himself ''waist deep in congressmen'' trying to get places for friends. The Republican postmaster of New York who had been continued by Cleveland was not reappointed. It was soon discovered, also, that the President was placing his own and his wife's relatives in office and giving positions to large numbers of newspaper editors, thus indirectly subsidizing the press. The Commissioner of Pensions, Corporal James Tanner, distributed pensions so freely as to arouse wide-spread comment and was soon relieved of his position.[5]

Curtis, addressing the National Civil Service Reform League, flayed the President because he had despoiled the service. A Republican newspaper, he declared, had said that the administration whistled reform down the wind ''as remorselessly as it would dismiss an objectionable tramp.'' Prominent members of the party went to the President in person to urge on him the redemption of the platform promises.

Although progress was not general, nevertheless there were particular reforms that commended themselves. The offensive Clarkson gave way to hostile criticism and retired. During the last half of the administration, the civil service rules were amended so as to add a considerable number of employees to the classified service, especially in the postoffice department. Quay and Dudley found their methods condemned by public

---

[5] Corporal Tanner is commonly supposed to have been so anxious to have a hand in the generous distribution of government revenue among the old soldiers that he declared one morning as he seated himself at his desk, "God help the surplus." This is a mistake, although the Corporal seems to have been more ready than the President to act quickly and generously on claims.

opinion and resigned their positions on the National Republican Committee.[6] Moreover, the publicity given to blocks of five, frying the fat out of the manufacturers of Pennsylvania, and other aspects of the use of money in the election gave real assistance to the movement for ballot reform. Alarmed by the corruption seen in the election, state after state introduced the secret or Australian ballot which had already been used in Louisville, Kentucky, on February 28, 1888, and in Massachusetts on May 29 of the same year. Under the Australian system, the voter marks his ballot in private in a small booth at the polling place. No longer could blocks of five be marched to the polls and superintended while they voted "right." No longer could workmen be intimidated by the employer, watching at the ballot box to see that "our ticket" was upheld. Elections became more orderly, and more voters were enabled to "split the ticket" or vote for men here and there on the ballot (regardless of party affiliations), whom they regarded as most fit for office.

Aside from his choice of subordinates, Harrison contributed little to the political history of his administration, for the leadership was seized by a small coterie of extreme Republicans in the House of Representatives, of whom the chief figure was the Speaker, Thomas B. Reed. The House which had been elected with Harrison contained 159 Democrats and 166 Republicans. The Republican majority was too slight for safety, for the questions which were coming before Congress were such as to arouse party feeling to a high pitch. The Republicans felt themselves commissioned, by a successful election, to put the party program into force, but so powerful a minority could readily block any legislation under the existing parliamentary rules. Only Reed knew what expedient would be resorted to in the attempt to put through the party pro-

---

[6] Another reform movement was that which resulted in the destruction of the Louisiana lottery. *Cf.* A. K. McClure, *Recollections*, pp. 173–183, and Peck, *Twenty Years*, 215–220.

gram, and not even he could guarantee that the adventure would be successful.

Thomas B. Reed had long represented Maine in the House of Representatives. He was a man of huge bulk, bland in appearance, imperturbable in his serenity, caustic, concise and witty of tongue, rough, sharp, strong, droll. In the cut-and-thrust of parliamentary debate and manœuvre, as well as in his knowledge of the intricacies of procedure, Reed was a past master. He worsted his adversaries by turning the laugh on them, and his stinging retorts, which swept the House "like grapeshot," made him a powerful factor in partisan contests.[7]

The political and economic philosophy of Reed and his associates was unusually important, because it controlled their action during the time when they dominated the House and determined the character of the legislation passed during Harrison's time. When President Cleveland's tariff message welded the Democrats together to demand reduction, it likewise influenced the Republicans to adopt the other extreme. That is not to say, of course, that the Republican attitude was due solely to Cleveland, for the party was already committed to protectionism. Nevertheless, many of its prominent leaders, including its presidents, had urged revision. That recommendation was now no longer heard. Such men as McKinley in the House fairly apotheosized the protective system. The philosophy of the party leaders received full exposition in a volume edited by John D. Long, ex-governor of Massachusetts, and composed of articles written by sixteen of the most prominent Republicans. It had been published during the campaign. The attitude of the party toward its chief

---

[7] An incident which occurred when he was not speaker may serve to illustrate the manner in which he routed his opponents. Representative Springer, of Illinois, who had a reputation for loquacity and insincerity, once asked for unanimous consent to correct a statement which he had previously made in debate. "No correction needed," shouted Reed. "We didn't think it was so when you made it."

tenet was expressed in the phrase, ''The Republican party enacted a protective tariff which made the United States the
greatest manufacturing nation on earth''; and its conception
of the Democratic party in the statement that the Democrats
were mainly old slave-holders, liquor dealers and criminals
in the great northern cities. In the field of national expenditure, also, the party reacted from Cleveland's frugality. Senator Dolph frankly urged the expenditure of the surplus revenue rather than the reduction of taxation. McKinley took
the position that prices might be too low. ''I do not prize the
word cheap,'' he said; ''cheap merchandise means cheap men
and cheap men mean a cheap country.'' Harrison remarked
that it was ''no time to be weighing the claims of old soldiers
with apothecary's scales.'' This philosophy was now to have
its trial, but first the obstructive power of the minority must
be curbed. Reed's plan for accomplishing this result appeared
late in January, 1890.

A contested election case was up for decision in the House.
The roll was called and three less than a quorum of representatives answered. Scores of Democrats were present, but
by merely refusing to answer to their names they could be
officially absent. Unless the Republicans could provide a
quorum—that is, more than half the total membership of the
chamber—of their own number, they were helpless. Clearly
they could not muster their full force at all times and especially on questions upon which the party might be divided.
On the other hand, the right to refuse to vote was a long-
standing one and had been used over and over again by Republicans as well as Democrats. Reed, however, had made
up his mind to cut the Gordian knot. Looking over the
House he called the names of about forty Democrats, directed
the clerk to make note of them and then declared a quorum
present. The meaning of the act was not lost on the opposition. Pandemonium broke loose. Members rushed up
the aisle as if to attack the Speaker, but Reed, huge, fearless

and undisturbed, stood his ground. The Democrats hissed and jeered and denounced him with a wrath which was not mollified by the derisive laughter of the Republicans, who were surprised by the ruling, but rallied to their leader. Two days later, when a member moved to adjourn, the Speaker ruled the motion out of order and refused to entertain any appeal from his decision. He then firmly but quietly stated his belief that the will of the majority ought not to be nullified by a minority and that if parliamentary rules were used solely for purposes of delay, it was the duty of the Speaker to take "the proper course."

The rules committee then presented a series of recommendations designed to expedite business. One of the proposed changes provided that the chair should entertain no dilatory motions. Such motions, whose purpose was merely to obstruct action, had long been common. Opponents of the Kansas-Nebraska bill of 1854 were said to have alternated motions to adjourn and fix a day for adjournment no less than one hundred and twenty-eight times in their attempt to defeat the measure. The second rule allowed the speaker to count members who were present and not voting in determining whether a quorum was present. Other rules systematized procedure and facilitated the passage of legislation. The Democrats raged, denounced Reed as a "Czar," fought against the adoption of the rules—all to no avail. The majority had its way; the Speaker dominated legislation.[8]

The efficacy of the Reed reforms in expediting legislation was quickly demonstrated. One of the earliest proposals to pass the House was Henry Cabot Lodge's federal election law, which was intended to insure federal control at polling places. Theoretically the measure was applicable to the North as well

8 In his *Manual of General Parliamentary Law*, Reed declared that the House prior to 1890 was the most unwieldy parliamentary body in the world. Three resolute men, he asserted, could stop all public business. A few years later, when the Democrats were in power, they adopted the plans which Reed had so successfully used.

as to the South, but no doubt existed that it was really designed to prevent southern suppression of the negro vote. The Democrats rallied to the opposition and denounced Lodge's plan as a "force act." Despite objections it passed the House, but it languished in the Senate and finally was abandoned. The generous expenditure policy which the new philosophy called for brought forth certain increases which were noteworthy. The dependent pension bill which Cleveland had vetoed was passed, and a direct tax which had been levied on the states during the Civil War was refunded. Another extreme party measure was the Sherman silver act which became law on July 14, 1890. By it, 4,500,000 ounces of silver were to be purchased each month. Its partisan character was indicated by the fact that no Republicans voted against it, and no Democrats for it. Since the amount of silver to be purchased was practically the total output of the country, it was evident that the western mine owners were receiving the same attention that was being accorded manufacturers who sought protective tariff laws. Indeed, western Republicans, who were opposed to the high tariff which the eastern Republicans favored, were brought to support such legislation only by a bargain through which each side assisted the other in getting what it desired.[9]

The tariff measure which was thus entwined with the silver bill was intended to carry out the pledge made in the party platform. Harrison had early called the attention of Congress to the need of a reduction of the surplus, had urged the passage of a new tariff law and the removal of the tobacco tax which, he declared, would take a burden from an "important agricultural product." The framing of the bill was in the hands of William McKinley, the chairman of

[9] These acts were part of the general financial history of the period and in that connection demand fuller discussion at a later point. *Cf.* Chap. XIV.

the Committee on Ways and Means. McKinley was a thorough-going protectionist whose attitude on the question had already been expressed somewhat as follows: previous Democratic tariffs have brought the country to the brink of financial ruin; without the protective tariff English manufacturers would monopolize American markets; under the protective system the foreign manufacturer largely pays the tax through lessened profits; under protection the American laborer is the best paid, clothed and contented workingman in the world; since it is necessary, then, to preserve protection, the surplus should be reduced by the elimination of the internal revenues; and protective tariff duties should be raised and retained, not gradually lowered and done away with.

The Committee early proceeded to hold public hearings at which testimony was taken, and to which manufacturers came from all over the country to make known what duties they thought they ought to have. The bill which was finally presented to the House proposed a level of duties which was so high that it has generally been considered the extreme of protection. McKinley himself justified the high rates only on the ground that without them the bill could not be passed. With the help of the Reed rules and the western Republicans the McKinley tariff reached the President and was signed by him on October 1, 1890. It went into effect at once.

The more prominent features of the measure sprang from the tariff creed which had been advocated through the campaign. In order to conciliate the farmers, the protective principle was applied to agricultural products, and tariffs were laid on such articles as cereals, potatoes and flax. On the cheaper grades of wool and woolens and on carpet wools there was a slight rise over even the rates of 1883. On the higher grades of woolen, linen and clothing the increase was marked. The duty on raw sugar was removed and one-half cent per pound retained on the refined product, but domestic sugar producers were given a bounty of two cents a pound in order to protect them against the free importation of the raw material. As the sugar duty had been productive of large amounts of revenue, its remission reduced the surplus by about sixty to seventy millions of dollars. In order to encourage the manufacture of tin-plates, a considerable duty was imposed, which was to cease after 1897 unless domestic production reached specified amounts. As the result of Blaine's urgency, a reciprocity feature was introduced. The usual plan had been to reduce duties on certain products in case concessions to American goods were given by the exporting countries, but in the McKinley act the Senate inserted a novel provision. Instead of being given power to lower duties in case reciprocal reductions were made, the president was authorized to impose duties on certain articles on the free list when the exporting nation levied "unjust or unreasonable" customs charges on American products. It was expected that this plan would be applied to Latin-American countries and would increase our exports to them in return for sugar, molasses, tea, coffee and hides. In general, the McKinley act was the climax of protection. Under the impetus of President Cleveland's reduction challenge, the Republican party had recoiled to the extreme.

The high rates levied by the new tariff act were quickly reflected in retail prices and caused immediate and widespread discontent. The benefits which the farmer had been led to expect did not put in their appearance. Unhappily for McKinley and his associates the congressional elections occurred early in November, scarcely a month after the new law went into effect, and when the dissatisfaction was at its height. The result was a stinging defeat for the Republicans. The 159 Democrats were increased to 235, and the 166 Republicans dwindled to 88. Even in New England the Democrats gained eleven members, in New York eight, and in Iowa five. In Wisconsin not one Republican survived, and among the lost in Ohio was McKinley himself.

Although the Republicans retained control of the Senate after 1890, the Democratic House brought an end for a time to the domination of Reed and the primacy of the lower chamber in the government. Such extreme legislation as had characterized the first half of the Harrison régime stopped abruptly. The rôle played in all this by Harrison himself seems to have been a minor one. Many of his recommendations lacked the solid character of those made by Hayes, Arthur and Cleveland, and he did not make his influence felt in connection with the silver legislation, of which he probably disapproved.

BIBLIOGRAPHICAL NOTE

In addition to the general and special works already mentioned, C. Hedges, *Benjamin Harrison: Speeches* (1892), provides useful material; Cleveland's tariff message of Dec. 6, 1887, is in J. D. Richardson, *Messages and Papers of the Presidents,* VIII, 580–591.

On the administration, and particularly the ascendency of the House of Representatives under Reed, consult: De A. S. Alexander, *History and Procedure of the House of Representatives* (1916); Mary P. Follett, *Speaker of the House of Representatives* (1896); C. S. Olcott, *William McKinley* (2 vols., 1916); J. G. Cannon in *Harper's Magazine* (Mar., 1920); *Annual Cyclopaedia,* 1890, pp. 181–191; S. W. McCall, *Thomas B. Reed* (1914), well written, although adding little to what was already known; H. D. Croly, *Marcus A. Hanna* (1912); W. D. Foulke, *Fighting the Spoilsman* (1919), on Harrison and the civil service; G. W. Curtis, *Orations and Addresses* (2 vols., 1894), summarizes the administration's attitude toward civil service; *Selections from the Correspondence of Theodore Roosevelt and Henry Cabot Lodge* (2 vols., 1925). T. B. Reed, *Reed's Rules, A Manual of General Parliamentary Law* (1894), gives a concise summary of parliamentary conditions from Reed's standpoint; H. B. Fuller, *The Speakers of the House* (1909), excellent on the personal side. The tariff is well treated in

Stanwood, Taussig and Tarbell. On pensions consult W. H. Glasson, *History of Military Pension Legislation in the United States* (1900), or better, the same author's *Federal Military Pensions in the United States* (1918).

CHAPTER XII

DEMOCRATIC DEMORALIZATION

I am supposed to be a leader in my party. If any word of mine can check these dangerous fallacies [about free coinage of silver], it is my duty to give that word, whatever the cost may be to me.

GROVER CLEVELAND, 1891.

I had a very short and cold interview with the President [Harrison].

THEODORE ROOSEVELT.

The national power to create money is appropriated to enrich bondholders.

PEOPLE'S PARTY PLATFORM, 1892.

. . . we were all—Democrats as well as Republicans—trying to get in amendments in the interest of protecting the industries of our respective States.

SENATOR S. M. CULLOM.

IN view of the fact that Harrison had been successful in 1888 and that Cleveland had been the most able Democratic leader since the Civil War, it seemed natural that their parties should renominate them in 1892. Yet the men at the oars in the Republican organization were far from enthusiastic over their leader. It is probable that Harrison did not like the rôle of dispenser of patronage and that he indicated the fact in dealing with his party associates; at any rate, he estranged such powerful leaders as Platt, Quay and Reed by his neglect of them in disposing of appointments. The reformers were no better satisfied; much had been expected of him because his party had taken so definite a stand in 1888, and when his choice of subordinates failed to meet expectations, the scorn of the Independents found forceful vent. Among the rank and file of his party, Harrison had aroused respect but no great enthusiasm.

The friends of Blaine were still numerous and active, and they wished to see their favorite in the executive chair. Perhaps Blaine felt that there would be some impropriety in his becoming an active candidate against his chief, while remaining at his post as Secretary of State; at any rate he notified the chairman of the National Republican Committee, early in 1892, that he was not a candidate for the nomination. The demand for him, nevertheless, continued and relations between him and Harrison seem to have become strained. Senator Cullom, writing nearly twenty years afterward, related a conversation which he had had with Harrison at the time. In substance, according to the senator, the President declared that he had been doing the work of the Department of State himself for a year or more, and that Blaine had given out reports of what was being done and had taken the credit himself. Cullom's recollection seems to have been accurate, at least as far as relations between the two men were concerned, for three days before the meeting of the Republican nominating convention Blaine sent a curt note to the President resigning his office without giving any reason, and asking that his withdrawal take effect immediately. The President's reply accepting the resignation was equally cool and uninforming. If Blaine expected to take any steps to gain the nomination, the available time was far too short. That the act would be interpreted as hostile to the interests of Harrison, however, admitted of no doubt, and it therefore seems probable that Blaine had changed his mind at a late day and really hoped that the party might choose him.

Despite Blaine's apparent change of purpose, it seemed necessary to renominate Harrison in order to avoid the appearance of discrediting his administration, and on the first ballot Harrison received 535 votes to Blaine's 183 and was nominated. The only approach to excitement was over the currency plank in the platform. Western delegates demanded the free coinage of silver, which the East opposed. The plank adopted declared that

The Republican party demands the use of both gold and silver as standard money, with such restrictions and under such provisions, to be determined by legislation, as will secure the maintenance of the parity of values of the two metals.

It was a meaningless compromise, but it seems to have satisfied both sides.

Cleveland, during the Harrison administration, had been an object of much interest and not a little speculation. After seeing President Harrison safely installed in office, he went to New York City where he engaged in the practice of law. He himself thought that he was retiring permanently and not a few enemies were quite willing that this should be the case. The eminent Democratic editor, Henry Watterson, remarked that Cleveland in New York was like a stone thrown into a river, "There is a 'plunk,' a splash, and then silence." He was constantly invited, nevertheless, to addresss public assemblies, which provided ample opportunity for him to express his thoughts to the country. Moreover, the McKinley Act of 1890 and the political reversal which followed brought renewed attention to the tariff message of 1887 and to its author. In February, 1891, Cleveland was asked to address a meeting of New York business men which had been called by the Reform Club to express opposition to the free coinage of silver. The question of the increased use of silver as a circulating medium, as has been seen, was a controverted one; neither party was prepared to take a definite stand, and, indeed, division of opinion had taken place on sectional rather than partisan lines. While the subject was in this unsettled condition Cleveland received his invitation to the Reform Club and was urged by some of his advisors not to endanger his chances of renomination by taking sides on the issue. The counsel had no more effect than similar advice had produced in 1887 when the tariff was in the same unsettled condition. Although unable to attend, Cleveland wrote a letter in which he characterized the experiment of free coinage as "dangerous and reckless." Whether right or wrong, he was definite; people who could not understand the intricacies of currency standards and the arguments of the experts understood exactly what Cleveland meant. Little doubt now existed but that the name of the ex-President would be a powerful one before the nominating convention, for he would have the populous East with him on the currency issue—unless David B. Hill should upset expectations.

Hill was an example of the shrewd politician. Like Platt, whom he resembled in many ways, he was absorbed in the machinery and organization of politics, rather than in issues and policies. Beginning in 1870, when he was but twenty-seven years of age, he had held public office almost continuously. In the state assembly, as Mayor of Elmira, as Lieutenant-Governor with Cleveland and later as Governor, he developed an unrivaled knowledge of New York as a political arena. In 1892 he was at the height of his power and the presidency seemed to be within his grasp. The methods which he used were typical of the man—the manipulation of the machinery of nomination.

The national Democratic nominating convention was called for June 21st, but the New York state Democratic committee announced that the state convention for the choice of delegates would meet on February 22nd. So early a meeting, four months before the national convention, was unprecedented, and at once it became clear that a purpose lay behind the call. It was to procure the election of members to the state convention who would vote for Hill delegates to the nominating convention, before Cleveland's supporters could organize in opposition. Furthermore, it was expected that the action of New York would influence other states where sentiment for

Cleveland was not strong. Hill's plan worked out as he had expected—at least in so far as the state convention was concerned—for delegates pledged to him were chosen. Cleveland's supporters, however, denounced the "snap convention" and a factional quarrel arose between the "snappers" and the "anti-snappers"; outside of New York it was so obvious that the snap convention was a mere political trick that the Hill cause was scarcely benefited by it. Delegates were chosen in other parts of the country who desired the nomination of Cleveland.

The convention met in Chicago on June 21st and proceeded at once to adopt a platform of principles. The silver plank was hardly distinguishable from that of the Republicans, except that it was enshrouded with a trifle more of ambiguity. The adoption of a tariff plank elicited considerable difference of opinion, but the final result was an extreme statement of Democratic belief. Instead of adopting the cautious position taken in 1884, the convention declared that the constitutional power of the federal government was limited to the collection of tariff duties for purposes of revenue only, and denounced the McKinley act as the "culminating atrocity of class legislation."

Although it was evident when the convention met, that the chances of Hill for the nomination were slight indeed, the battle was far from over. Hill was a "straight" party man, a fact which he reiterated again and again in his famous remark, "I am a Democrat." Cleveland was not strictly regular, a charge which Hill apparently intended to emphasize by constant reference to his own beliefs. The oratorical champion of the Hill delegation was Bourke Cockran, an able and appealing stump speaker. For two hours he urged that Cleveland could not carry the pivotal state, New York, and that it was folly to attempt to elect a man who was so handicapped. Eloquence, however, was of no avail. The first ballot showed that the Hill strength was practically confined to New York, and Cleveland was easily the party choice. For the vice-presidency Adlai E. Stevenson, a partisan of the old school, was chosen.

Among the smaller parties there appeared for the first time the "People's Party," later and better known as the "Populists." Their nominee was James B. Weaver, who had led the Greenbackers in 1880. Their platform emphasized the economic burdens under which the poorer classes were laboring and listed a series of extremely definite demands.

The campaign was a quiet one as both Cleveland and Harrison had been tried out before. So unenthusiastic were the usual political leaders that Colonel Robert G. Ingersoll declared that each party would like to beat the other without electing its own candidates. Although the financial issue was kept in the background, the tariff was fought out again somewhat as it had been in 1888. The New York *Sun* shed some asperity over the contest by calling the friends of Cleveland "the adorers of fat witted mediocrity," and the nominee himself as the "perpetual candidate" and the "stuffed prophet"; and then added a ray of humor by advocating the election of Cleveland. The Homestead strike near Pittsburgh, Pennsylvania, somewhat aided the Democrats. The Carnegie Steel Company, having reduced wages, precipitated a strike which was settled only through use of the state militia. As the steel industry was highly protected by the tariff, it appeared that the wages of the laboring man were not so happily affected as Republican orators had been asserting.[1]

The result of the election was astonishing. Cleveland carried not merely the South but Connecticut, New York, New Jersey, Indiana, Illinois, Wisconsin and California, while five of Michigan's fourteen electoral votes and one of Ohio's twenty-three went to him. In the last-named state, which had never gone against the Republicans, their vote exceeded that of the Democrats by only 1,072. For the first time since

---

[1] Below, p. 301, for an account of the strike as an industrial dispute.

Buchanan's day, the Democrats would control all branches of the government, the Chief Executive, the Senate and the House. More surprising and more significant for the future, was the strength of the People's Party. Over a million ballots, twenty-two electoral votes, two senators and eleven representatives were included among their trophies. It was an important fact, moreover, that twenty-nine out of every thirty votes cast for the People's Party were cast west of Pennsylvania and south of Maryland. Something apparently was happening, in which the East was not a sharer. The politician, particularly in the East, was quite content to dismiss the Populists as ''born-tired theorists,'' ''quacks,'' ''a clamoring brood of political rain-makers,'' and ''stump electricians,'' but the student of politics and history must appraise the movement less provincially and with more information.

It was in the nature of things that the Populist movement should come out of the West. From the days of Clay and Jackson the westerner had been characterized by his self-confidence, his assertiveness and his energy. He had possessed unlimited confidence in ordinary humanity, been less inclined to heed authority and more ready to disregard precedents and experience. He had expressed his ideals concretely, and with vigor and assurance. He had broken an empire to the plow, suffered severely from the buffetings of nature and had gradually worked out his list of grievances. One or another of his complaints had been presented before 1892 in the platforms of uninfluential third parties, but not until that year did the dissenting movement reach large proportions.

It has already been seen that the people of the West were in revolt against the management of the railroads. They saw roads going bankrupt, to be sure, but the owners were making fortunes; they knew that lawyers were being corrupted with free passes and the state legislatures manipulated by lobbyists; and they believed that rates were extortionate. The seizure and purchase of public land, sometimes contrary to the letter of the law, more often contrary to its spirit, was looked upon as an intolerable evil. Moreover, the westerner was in debt. He had borrowed from the East to buy his farm and his machinery and to make both ends meet in years when the crops failed. In 1889 it was estimated that seventy-five per cent. of the farms of Dakota were mortgaged to a total of $50,000,000. Boston and other cities had scores of agencies for the negotiation of western farm loans; Philadelphia alone was said to absorb $15,000,000 annually. The advantage to the West, if conditions were right, is too manifest to need explanation. But sometimes the over-optimistic farmer borrowed too heavily; sometimes the rates demanded of the needy westerners were usurious; often it seemed as if interest charges were like "a mammoth sponge," constantly absorbing the labor of the husbandman. The demand of the West for a greater currency supply has already been seen, for it appeared in the platforms of minor parties immediately after the Civil War. Sometimes it seemed as if nature, also, had entered a conspiracy to increase the hardships of the farmer. During the eighties a series of rainy years in the more arid parts of the plains encouraged the idea that the rain belt was moving westward, and farmers took up land beyond the line where adequate moisture could be relied upon. Then came dryer years; the corn withered to dry stalks; farms were more heavily mortgaged or even abandoned; and discontent in the West grew fast.

The complaints of the westerner naturally found expression in the agricultural organizations which already existed in many parts of the country. The Grange had attacked some of the farmer's problems, but interest in it as a political agency had died out. The National Farmers' Alliance of 1880 and the National Farmers' Alliance and Industrial Union somewhat later were both preceded and followed by many smaller societies. Altogether their combined membership began to mount into the millions. When, therefore, the Alliances began to turn away from the mere discussion of agricultural grievances and toward the betterment of conditions by means of legislation, and when their principles began to be taken up by discontented labor organizations, it looked as if they might constitute a force to be reckoned with.

The remedies which the Alliances suggested for current ills were definite. Fundamentally they believed that the government, state and federal, could remedy the economic distresses of the people and that it ought to do so. At the present day such a suggestion seems commonplace enough, but in the eighties the dominant theory was individualism—each man for himself and let economic law remedy injustices—and the Alliance program seemed like dreaded "socialism." The counterpart of the demand for larger governmental activity was a call for the greater participation of the people in the operation of the machinery of legislation. This lay back of the demand for the initiative, the referendum, and the popular election of senators. Currency ills could be remedied, the farmers believed, by a national currency which should be issued by the federal government only—not by national banks. They desired the free coinage of silver and gold until the amount in circulation should reach fifty dollars per capita.[2] Lesser recommendations were for an income tax and postal savings banks. In relation to the transportation system, they declared that "the time has come when the railroad corporations will either own the people or the people must own the railroads." In order to prevent the waste of the public land and to stop its being held for speculative purposes, they urged that none be allowed to remain in the hands of aliens and that all be taken away from the railroads and corporations which was in excess of actual needs.

The power of the new movement first became evident in

[2] The amount in circulation in 1890 was slightly less than twenty-three dollars per capita. In 1920 it first went beyond the amount desired by the Populists, reaching $50.11 at that time.

1890 and distinctly disturbed both the Republican and the
Democratic leaders. Determined to right their wrongs, the
farmers deserted their parties in thousands, flocked to conventions and crowded the country schoolhouses for the discussion
of methods and men. Perhaps it was true, as one of their
critics asserted, that they put a "gill of fact and grievance
into a gallon of falsehood and lurid declamation" so as to
make an "intoxicating mixture." If so, the mixture took immediate effect. Alliance governors were elected in several
southern states; many state legislatures in the South and
West had strong farmer delegations; and several congressmen
and senators were sent to Washington. Success in 1890 made
the Alliances jubilant and they looked to the possibility of a
country-wide political organization and a share in the campaign of 1892. The first national convention was held in
Omaha in July, 1892, at which many of the farmers' organizations together with the Knights of Labor and other groups
were represented. The name "People's Party" was adopted,
the principles just mentioned were set forth in a platform and
candidates nominated. In the ensuing election the party exhibited the surprising strength which has been seen.

It has taken more time to describe the Populist movement
than its degree of success in 1892 would justify. But it deserves attention for a variety of reasons. Its reform demands
were important; it was a striking indication of sectional economic interests; it gave evidence of an effective participation
in politics by the small farmers, the mechanics and the less
well-to-do professional people—the "middle class," in a word;
it was a long step toward an expansion of the activities of the
central government in the fields of economic and social legislation; and finally it emphasized the significance of the West,
as a constructive force in American life. If the Populists
should capture one of the other parties or be captured by it,
nobody could foresee what the results would be on American
political history.

The second administration of Grover Cleveland, from 1893 to 1897, was the most important period of four years for half a century after the Civil War. For twenty-five years after 1865 American politicians had been sowing the wind. Issues had rarely been met man-fashion, in direct combat; instead, they had been evaded, stated with skilful ambiguity, or beclouded with ignorance and prejudice. Politics had been concerned with the offices—the plunder of government. It could not be that the whirlwind would never be reaped.

The situation in 1893 was one that might well have shaken the stoutest heart. International difficulties were in sight that threatened unusual dangers; labor troubles of unprecedented complexity and importance were at hand; the question of the currency remained unsettled, the treasury was in a critical condition, and an industrial panic had already begun. Each of these difficulties will demand detailed discussion at a later point.[3]

To no small degree, the settlement of the political and economic issues before the country was complicated by the unmistakable drift toward sectionalism, and by the particular characteristics of the President. If the administration pressed a tariff reduction policy, it would please the South and West but bring hostility in the East. The demands of the West, so far as the Populists represented them, were for the increased use of the powers of the federal government and the application of those powers to social and economic problems; but the party in power was traditionally attached to the doctrine of restricted activity on the part of the central authority. The sectional aspects of the silver question were notorious; and only the eastern Democrats fully supported their leader in his stand on the issue.

The personal characteristics of President Cleveland have already appeared.[4] He had a burdensome consciousness of

[3] Below, Chaps. XIII, XIV XVI.
[4] Above, Chap. VIII.

his own individual duty to conduct the business of his office
with faithfulness; a courageous sense of justice which impelled him to fight valiantly for a cause that he deemed right,
however unimportant or hopeless the cause might be; a reformer's contempt for hypocrisy and shams, and a blunt
directness in freeing his mind about wrong of every kind.
He had the faults of his virtues, likewise. Sure of himself and
of the right of his position, he had the impatience of an unimaginative man with any other point of view; he was intran-
sigeant, unyielding, rarely giving way a step even to take two
forward. It seems likely that his political experience had accentuated this characteristic. For years he had thrown aside
the advice of his counsellors and had shown himself more
nearly right than they. As Mayor of Buffalo he had used the
veto and had been made Governor of the state; as Governor he
had ruggedly made enemies and had become President; as
President he had flown in the face of caution with his tariff
message and his Reform Club letter and had three times received a larger popular vote than his competitor. And each
time his plurality was greater than it had been before. If he
tended to become over-sure of himself, it should hardly occasion surprise. Furthermore he looked upon the duties and
possibilities of the presidential office as fixed and stationary,
rather than elastic and developing. He was a strict constructionist and a rigid believer in the checks and balances of the
Constitution. Although constantly aware of the needs and
rights of the common people, such as composed the Populist
movement, his adherence to strict construction was so complete that he was unable to advocate much of the federal legislation desired by them. It was only with hesitation and constitutional doubts that he had been able to sign even the Interstate Commerce Act. In brief, then, the western demand
for social and economic legislation on a novel and unusual
scale was to take its chances with an honest, dogged believer
in a restricted federal authority.

The experience of the administration with the patronage question illustrates how much progress had been made in the direction of reform since the beginning of Cleveland's first term in 1885. In the earlier year it had required a bitter contest to make even the slightest advance; in his second term he retained Roosevelt, a Republican reformer, on the Commission and gradually extended the rules so as to cover the government printing office, the internal revenue service, the pension agencies, and messengers and other minor officials in the departments in Washington. Finally on May 6, 1896, he approved an order revising the rules, simplifying them and extending them to great numbers of places not hitherto included, "the most valuable addition ever made at one stroke to the competitive service." The net result was that the number of positions in the classified service was more than doubled between 1893 and 1897, making a total of 81,889 in a service of somewhat over 200,000.[5] By the latter year the argument against reform had largely been silenced. The dismal prediction of opponents who had feared the establishment of an office-holding aristocracy had turned out to have no foundation. Agreement was widespread that the government service was greatly improved. There were still branches of the service for the reformers to work upon but the great fight was over and won.[6]

Although the Democrats came into power in 1893 largely on the tariff issue, Cleveland felt that the most urgent need at the

[5] The sweeping reform order of Cleveland late in his second term illustrated the most common and effective method of making advance. Late in his administration the president adds to the classified service; his successor withdraws part of the additions, but more than makes up at the end of his term,—a sort of two steps forward and one backward process.

[6] Cleveland's second cabinet was composed of the following: W. Q. Gresham, Ill., Secretary of State; J. G. Carlisle, Ky., Secretary of the Treasury; D. S. Lamont, N. Y., Secretary of War; R. Olney, Mass., Attorney-General; W. S. Bissell, N. Y., Postmaster-General; H. A. Herbert, Ala., Secretary of the Navy; Hoke Smith, Ga., Secretary of the Interior; J. S. Morton, Neb., Secretary of Agriculture.

beginning of the administration was the repeal of the part of the Sherman silver law that provided for the purchase of 4,500,000 ounces of silver each month. The financial and monetary aspects of this controversy demand relation at another point.[7] Politically its results were important. Western and southern Democrats, friendly to silver, fought bitterly against the repeal, and became thoroughly hostile to Cleveland whom they began to distrust as allied to the "money-power" of the East. Despite his success, therefore, in achieving repeal, the President found that he had divided his party into factions at the very moment when he stood in greatest need of united partisan support.

Other circumstances which have been mentioned combined to make the time inauspicious for a revision of the tariff—the slight Democratic majority in the Senate, the deficit caused by rising expenditure and falling revenue, the imminent industrial panic and the prevailing labor unrest. Nevertheless it seemed necessary to make the attempt. If the results of the election of 1892 meant anything, they meant that the Democrats were commissioned to revise the tariff.

The chairman of the House Committee on Ways and Means was William L. Wilson, a sincere and well-read tariff reformer who had been a lawyer and a college president, in addition to taking a practical interest in politics. The measure which he presented to the House on December 19, 1893, was not a radical proposal, but it provided for considerable tariff reductions and a tax on incomes over $4,000. There was a slight defection in party support, but it was unimportant because of the large majority which the Democrats possessed, and the bill passed the House without unusual difficulty.

In the Senate a different situation presented itself. The Democratic majority over the Republicans, provided the Populists voted with the former, was only nine; and in case the

[7] Below, pp. 321 ff.

Populists became disaffected, the Democrats could outvote the opposition only by the narrow margin of three, even if every member remained with his party. Such a degree of unanimity, in the face of prevailing conditions, was extremely unlikely. The Louisiana senators were insistent upon protection for their sugar; Maryland, West Virginia and Alabama senators looked out for coal and iron ore; Senator Hill of New York was unalterably opposed to an income tax; Senator Murphy, of the same state, obtained high duties on linen collars and cuffs; and Senators Gorman and Brice were ready to aid the opposition unless appeased by definite bits of protection which they demanded. Many years later Senator Cullom, a Republican, explained the practical basis on which the Senate proceeded: "The truth is, we were all—Democrats as well as Republicans —trying to get in amendments in the interest of protecting the industries of our respective States."

The 634 changes made in the Senate were, therefore, mainly in the direction of lessening the reductions made by the House. After the bill had passed the Senate, it was put into the hands of a conference committee, where further changes were made. At this stage of the proceedings, Wilson read to the House a letter from the President condemning the form which the bill had taken under Senate management, and branding the abandonment of Democratic principles as an example of "party perfidy and party dishonor." The communication had no effect except to intensify differences within the party, and senators made it evident that they would have their way or kill the measure. The House thereupon capitulated and accepted what became known as the Wilson-Gorman act—a law which was only less protectionist than the McKinley act. The President, chagrined at the breakdown of the party program, allowed the act to pass without his signature, but expressed his mingled disappointment and disgust in a letter to Representative T. C. Catchings:

There are provisions in this bill which are not in line with honest tariff reform. . . . Besides, there were . . . incidents accompanying the passage of the bill . . . which made every sincere tariff reformer unhappy. . . . I take my place with the rank and file of the Democratic party . . . who refuse to accept the results embodied in this bill as the close of the war, who are not blinded to the fact that the livery of Democratic tariff reform has been stolen and worn in the service of Republican protection, and who have marked the places where the deadly blight of treason has blasted the counsels of the brave in their hour of might.

A few phases of the attempt at tariff reduction indicate the extent to which political decay and especially Democratic demoralization had gone. As it passed the House, the Wilson bill left both raw and refined sugar on the free list. This was unsatisfactory to the Louisiana sugar growers, who desired a protective duty on the raw product, and was objected to by the Louisiana senators. On the other hand, the American Sugar Refining Company, usually known as the "Sugar Trust," desired free raw materials but sought protective duties on refined sugar. In the Senate, a duty was placed on raw sugar, partly for revenue and partly to satisfy the Louisiana senators. On refined sugar, rates were fixed which were eminently satisfactory to the Trust. Rumors at once began to be spread broadcast over the country that the sugar interests had manipulated the Senate. The people were the more ready to believe charges of this sort because of experience with previous tariff legislation and because the Sugar Trust had been one of the earliest and most feared of the monopolies which had already caused so much uneasiness. A Senate committee was appointed, composed of two Democrats, two Republicans and a Populist, to investigate these and other rumors. Their report, which was agreed to by all the members, made public a depressing story. It appeared that one lobbyist had offered large sums of money for votes against the tariff bill on account of the income tax provision. Henry O. Havemeyer, president of the American Sugar Refining Company, testified that the company was in the habit of contributing to the campaign funds of one political party or the other in the states, depending on which party was in the ascendency; that these contributions were carried on the books as expense; and that they were given because the party in power "could give us the protection we should have." Further, one or more officers of the company were in Washington during the entire time when the tariff act was pending in the Senate and had conferred with senators and committees. Senator Quay testified that he had bought and sold sugar stocks while the Senate was engaged in fixing the schedules and added: "I do not feel that there is anything in my connection with the Senate to interfere with my buying or selling the stock when I please; and I propose to do so." Finally the committee summarized the results of its investigation, taking the occasion to

strongly deprecate the importunity and pressure to which Congress and its members are subjected by the representatives of great industrial combinations, whose enormous wealth tends to suggest undue influence, and to create in the public mind a demoralizing belief in the existence of corrupt practices.

Yet one more drop remained to fill the cup of Democratic humiliation to overflowing. The constitutionality of the income tax had been assumed to have been settled by previous decisions of the Supreme Court, especially that in the case Springer v. United States, which had been decided in 1880, and in which the Court had upheld the law. The new tax was brought before the Court in 1894, in Pollock v. Farmers' Loan and Trust Company. The argument against the tax was pressed with great vigor, not merely on constitutional grounds, but for evident social and economic reasons. Important financial interests engaged powerful legal talent and it became clear that the question to be settled was as much a class and sectional controversy as a constitutional problem. Counsel urged the Court that the tax scattered to the winds the fundamental principles of the rights of private property. Justice Field, deciding against the tax, declared it an "assault upon capital" and a step toward a war of the poor against the rich. There was fear among some that the exemption of the smaller incomes might result in placing the entire burden of taxation on the wealthy. Justice Field felt that taxing persons whose income was $4,000 and exempting those whose income was less than that amount was like taxing Protestants, as a class, at one rate and Catholics at another. The sectional aspects of the Controversy were brought out in objections that the bulk of the tax would fall on the Northeast. The most important point involved was the meaning of the word "direct" as used in the Constitution in the phrase "direct Taxes shall be apportioned among the several States . . . according to their respective Numbers." If an income tax is a direct tax, it must be apportioned among the states according to population. Unhappily the framers of the Constitution were not clear as to what they meant by the word direct, and specifically they could not have told whether an income tax was direct or not, because no such tax existed in England or America at that time. Hence the Supreme Court was placed in the awkward position of defining a word which the framers themselves could not define, although the uniform practice hitherto had been to regard the income tax as indirect and therefore constitutional, even if not apportioned according to population.

The Pollock case was heard twice. The result of the first trial was inconclusive and on the central point the Court divided four to four. After a rehearing, Justice Jackson, who had been ill and not present at the first trial, gave his vote in favor of constitutionality, but in the meantime another Justice had changed his opinion and voted against it. By the narrow margin of five to four, then, and under such circumstances, the income tax provision of the Wilson-Gorman act was declared null and void. Probably no decision since the Dred Scott case, with the single exception of the Legal Tender cases, has put the Supreme Court in so unfortunate a light. Certainly in none has it seemed more swayed by class prejudice, and so insecure and vacillating in its opinion.

Before the question regarding the constitutionality of the income tax was settled, the Democrats reaped the political results of the Wilson-Gorman tariff act. The law went into force on August 27, 1894; the congressional elections came in November. The Democrats were almost utterly swept out of the House, except for those from the southern states, their number being reduced from 235 to 105. Reed was replaced in the speaker's chair; tariff reform had turned out to be indistinguishable from protection; and the Democracy, after its only opportunity since 1861 to try its hand at government, was demoralized, discredited, and in opposition again.

BIBLIOGRAPHICAL NOTE

The election of 1892 is described in the standard histories of the period, and especially well in Peck.

The rise and growth of the Populist movement resulted in a considerable literature of which the following are best: F. E. Haynes, *James Baird Weaver* (1919); S. J. Buck, *The Agrarian Crusade* (1920), is founded on wide knowledge of the subject and contains bibliography; F. J. Turner in The *Atlantic Monthly* (Sept., 1896), gives a brief but keen account; other articles in periodicals are F. E. Haynes, in *Quarterly Journal of Economics,* X, 269, W. F. Mappin in *Political Science Quarterly,* IV, 433, and F. B. Tracy, in *Forum,* XVI, 240; F. E. Haynes, *Third Party Movements* (1916), is detailed; M. S. Wildman, *Money Inflation in the United States* (1905), presents the pyschological and economic basis of inflation; J. A. Woodburn, *Political Parties and Party Problems* (1914); F. L. Paxson, *New Nation* (1915).

Cleveland's administration is well discussed by D. R. Dewey, *National Problems* (1907), and by H. T. Peck, who also presents

an unusual analysis of Cleveland in *The Personal Equation* (1898).
The income tax is best handled by E. R. A. Seligman, *The Income
Tax* (1914). Cleveland's own account of the chief difficulties of
the administration are in his *Presidential Problems;* consult Robert
McElroy, *Grover Cleveland.*

CHAPTER XIII

THE RISE OF THE WAGE EARNER

... the concentrated massing of the forces of capitalism and the forces of labor, in which two figures—those of John D. Rockfeller and Samuel Gompers—will always stand out ... as the most representative and significant leaders of their time.

JOHN R. COMMONS.

One most consummate piece of humbuggery ever suggested in connection with the "labor question" is the so-called "eight hour movement." The thing is really too silly to merit the attention of a body of lunatics. ... No legislative body on earth can properly have anything to do with the subject. *Illinois State Register,* Mar. 13, 1880.

Blood! Lead and Powder as a cure for dissatisfied workmen! *Arbeiter Zeitung* of Chicago, May, 1886.

IN their handling of the labor problem, the governments of the states and the nation showed greater ignorance and less foresight than characterized their treatment of any of the other issues of the quarter century following the Civil War. Yet the building of the railroads and their consolidation into great systems, the development of manufacturing and its concentration into large concerns, and the growth of an army of wage earners brought about a problem of such size and complexity as to demand all the information and vision that the country could muster. However unpalatable it might be, the plain fact was that distinct social classes were forming in the United States, based in the main on economic possessions. Each class had its ideals and its ambitions, and each was preparing,—unconsciously, to be sure, but in reality nevertheless—for a bitter class struggle, not to say economic warfare. Even a brief and superficial account of this aspect of recent American history must take into account these several successive stages: (1) the origin and growth of the two main classes; (2) the period of the organizing or marshaling of forces; (3) a recital of the demands of one class, and the opposition thereto on the part of the other; and (4) the resort to force.

The phenomenal accumulation of wealth in the fields of mining, transportation and manufacturing which characterized the new industrial America formed the basis of a powerful propertied class. The men who made their way to the top— men like Gould, Fisk, Vanderbilt, Rockefeller and Carnegie— were pioneers whose courage, foresight, and daring were combined with sufficient ruthlessness to enable them to triumph where others failed. A few of them, like Carnegie, had some slight conception of the meaning of the labor problem; most of them did not. Linked to the industrial pioneer by community of interest was the holder of the war bonds of the federal government. These securities were purchased with depreciated paper currency but increased very greatly in value after the successful outcome of the struggle, and formed an investment whose value it is extremely difficult to estimate. The owners of the stocks and bonds of the railroads and manufacturing combinations further swelled the ranks of the propertied class. Stability, continuous business and large earnings were the immediate considerations to this group. Anything which interfered was, naturally, a thing to be fought. Never before, unless in the South in slavery days, had a more powerful social class existed in the United States. A large fraction of the group was composed of men who had risen from poverty to wealth in a short time. From one point of view such a man is a "self-made" man, industrious, frugal, able, energetic, bold. From another point of view he is a *parvenu*, narrow, overbearing, ostentatious, proud, conceited, uncultivated. The relatively small size of the propertied class and an obvious community of interest tended to make its members reach a class consciousness even during the Civil War. The success of the group in preventing all tariff reduction after 1865 was a striking example of the solidarity of its membership and its readiness for action.

Class consciousness among the wage earners developed much more slowly, and in the nature of things was much less definite. Nevertheless the history of the industrial turmoil of the quarter century after the Civil War is the history of a class groping for political, social and economic recognition.

At the close of the war the labor situation was confused and complicated. A million and a half of men in the North and South had to be readmitted to the ranks of industry. Approximately another million had died or been more or less disabled during the conflict. A stream of immigrants, already large and constantly increasing, was pouring into the North and seeking a means of livelihood. As has been seen, most of these settled in the manufacturing and mining sections of the northern and eastern states, helped to crowd the cities, and overflowed into the fertile, free lands of the Mid-West. Nearly 800,000 of them reached the United States in one year, 1882. Most of them were men—an overwhelming portion of them men of working age, unskilled, frequently illiterate and hence compelled to seek employment in a relatively small number of occupations. The danger of unemployment, of irregular employment and of a lowered standard of living were all increased by immigration.

From about 1830 to the late eighties and early nineties, the army of the wage earner was growing faster than the population. Between 1870 and 1890 the population increased sixty-three per cent., while the number of laborers engaged in manufacturing increased nearly 130 per cent. By the latter year, 6,099,058 persons, about a tenth of the total population, were employed in transportation, mining and manufacturing.

It was noticeable, also, that the wage earners tended to concentrate. The laborers engaged in manufacturing were to be found, for the most part, in the Northeast, and especially in such leading industrial cities as New York, Chicago and Philadelphia. Furthermore, the development of the factory system and the consolidation of many small companies into a few great ones tended to localize the labor problem still further —in a relatively small number of plants. The concentration of industry in great factories where large numbers of workers labored side by side ended the paternal care which the old-time employer had expended upon his employees.

The greater use of machinery during the progress of the war has already been alluded to, but some of its results demand further mention.[1] Most evident was the huge increase in the volume and value of the products of the factories. The labor of a single worker increased in effectiveness many times; in other words, the labor cost of a unit of production greatly diminished with the improvement of mechanical devices. The labor cost of making nails by hand in 1813 was seventy fold the cost of making them by machinery in 1899; loading ore by hand was seventy-three times as expensive in 1891 as machine loading was in 1896. Increased production encouraged greater consumption, enhanced competition for markets, and opened the world to the products of American labor. Moreover, the introduction of machinery emphasized the importance of capital. When iron was rolled by hand, when cloth was produced by the use of the spinning wheel and hand-loom, when fields were tilled by inexpensive plow and hoe, relatively small amounts of capital were needed by the man who started in to work. Mechanical inventions revolutionized the situation. A costly power-loom enabled its owner to eliminate handworking competitors. If a workman could raise sufficient money or credit to purchase a supply of machines he could "set up in business," employ a number of "hands" and merely direct or manage the enterprise. Under such a system the employer must make enough profit

[2] *Cf.* above, p. 68.

to pay interest on his investment and to repair and replace his equipment. His attention was fixed on these elements of his industrial problem and the well-being of the laborer sank to a lower plane of importance. If the employer found the labor supply plentiful he had the upper hand in setting the wage-scale; the unorganized employee was almost completely at his mercy, because the employer could find another workman more easily than the workman could find another job. Meanwhile the workman knew the increased product which he was turning out, and became discontented because he did not see a corresponding increase in his remuneration. Moreover, the danger of accidents due to the ignorance or carelessness of fellow workmen increased. The use of mechanical appliances gave opportunity for the employment of women and 'children, and thus raised the question whether any restrictions ought to be placed upon the employment of these classes of people. The construction of factories, their ventilation, sanitary appliances, and safe-guards for health and comfort became subjects of importance.

With the example of consolidation before them that was presented by the railroads and the corporations, it was inevitable that the wage earners should organize for their protection and advancement. Labor organizations of wage earners have, in fact, existed in the United States since 1827, and between that time and 1840 came a considerable awakening among the laboring classes which was part of a general humanitarian movement throughout the country. Robert Owen, an English industrial idealist, had visited this country about 1825 and provided the initiative for a short-lived communistic settlement at New Harmony, Indiana. Similar enterprises were established at other points, the most famous being that at Brook Farm in Massachusetts, which enlisted the interest and support of many of the literary people of New England. The expanding humanitarian and idealistic movement was cut short by the Civil War, but the development of

industrialism went on uninfluenced by the spirit of social
progress which might have permeated it.   After reconstruction
was over, a new generation had to become impressed with the
evils which needed correction and to set itself to the task which
civil strife had thrust aside.

The need of a responsible organization of wage earners was
indicated by the career of the Molly Maguires.   The Molly
Maguires constituted an inner circle of Irish Catholics who
controlled the activities of the branches of the Ancient Order
of Hibernians in the hard-coal counties of eastern Pennsylvania.   During the war and immediately after it the group
gained a little power in local politics, and also undertook to
punish mine owners, bosses and superintendents who offended
members of the Order.   Intimidation became common, and
even murder was resorted to until the region was fairly
terrorized.   It seemed impossible to combat the Mollies because their activities were shrouded in secrecy.   Usually, for
example, when a murder was to be committed, a member would
be brought in from an outside district in order that he might
not be recognized if discovered, and he would be aided in
escaping after the crime.   Finally the president of the Philadelphia and Reading Railroad procured a Pinkerton detective
named James McParlan who went into the region and remained for two years.   During this time he posed as a fugitive
from justice and as a counterfeiter, became a member of the
Order, a confidant of the Molly Maguires, and collected
evidence.   Armed with the knowledge acquired by McParlan,
the officials were able to arrest and convict twenty-four criminals, of whom ten were executed, and the career of the Mollies
came to an end.

The activities of the Molly Maguires were symptomatic of
what might occur throughout the ranks of labor during the
confused period of adjustment after the war, and yet they
were temporary and local in their effect on the development
of the labor movement.   The history of the great labor con-

troversies after the war properly begins with the Knights of Labor, an association which originated in Philadelphia in 1869 as the result of the efforts of a garment cutter named Uriah S. Stephens.[2] In the beginning, the affairs of the Knights were veiled in dense secrecy; even the name of the society was never mentioned but was indicated by five stars *****. As the number of members increased, however, all manner of disquieting and untruthful rumors spread concerning its purposes, so that the element of secrecy was done away with in 1881 and a declaration of principles was made public. The fundamental purpose of the Knights was the formation of an order which should include all branches of the wage earners and which should aim to improve their economic, moral, social and intellectual condition. Emphasis was placed, that is to so say, on the welfare of the laboring classes as a whole, rather than upon that of any particular trade or craft. The organization was centralized and the interests of the group were developed on a national scale. The growth of the association was extremely rapid at times, reaching a climax in the middle eighties when about 700,000 members, both men and women, made it a power in industrial disputes. Some of the members taken in at this time were extremists—European anarchists, for example—who urged a violent policy and got almost if not quite out of control of the officers during 1886. In the late eighties the membership dwindled rapidly, owing to the failure of strikes instituted by the order, and its place and influence were largely taken by the American Federation of Labor.

The latter body was the outgrowth of a convention held in Pittsburgh in 1881, but it did not adopt its final name until 1886. Its purpose was to group labor organizations of all kinds, leaving the government of each affiliated body with the body itself. Each of the members of the Federation is com-

[2] Two earlier organizations had a brief existence, the National Labor Union and the Industrial Brotherhood.

posed of workers in a given trade or industry, like the International Typographical Union, the United Mine Workers, and many others. The annual convention is composed of delegates from the constituent societies. The growth of the organization was rapid and continuous. Coincidently with the expansion of the Knights of Labor and the growth of the American Federation came the great development of the labor press. Professor Ely estimated late in the eighties that possibly five hundred newspapers were devoted to the needs of the labor movement. The numerous farmers' organizations, typified by the Patrons of Husbandry, are other examples of the growing tendency toward cohesion among the less powerful classes. Indeed, the Grange originated only a year earlier than the Knights of Labor, and like it was a secret order.

The wage earners, then, were rapidly becoming class conscious. They had found conditions which seemed to them intolerable, had formed organizations on a national scale and had drawn up a definite program of principles and reforms. The exact grievances which inspired the Knights, the Federation and other less important organizations are therefore of immediate importance.

In order to secure for the wage earner a sufficient money return for his work, and sufficient leisure for the education of his intellectual and religious faculties, and to enable him to understand and perform his duties as a citizen, the Knights demanded the establishment of bureaus of labor for the collection of information; the reservation of the public lands for actual settlers; the abrogation of laws that did not bear equally on capital and labor; the adoption of measures for the health and safety of the working classes; indemnity for injuries due to the lack of proper safeguards; the recognition of the incorporation of labor unions; laws compelling corporations to pay laborers weekly; arbitration in labor disputes; and the prohibition of child labor. The Knights of Labor also favored state ownership of telegraphs and railroads, as well as an eight hour working day   The purposes of the American Federation scarcely differed from this program, although its methods and its form of organization were quite distinct.

Two illustrations will throw light upon some of the demands which the wage earners frequently presented. Writing in August, 1886, Andrew Carnegie, the prominent steel manufacturer, discussed the proper length of the working day. Every ton of pig-iron made in the world, with the exception of that made in two establishments, he asserted, was made by men working twelve hours a day, with neither holiday nor Sunday the year round. Every two weeks it was the practice to change the day workers to the night shift and at that time the men labored twenty-four hours consecutively. Moreover, twelve to fifteen hours constituted a day's work in many other industries. Working hours for women and children had almost equally slight reference to their physical well-being.

The "truck-system" was a less widespread abuse, but one that caused serious trouble at certain points. Under this plan, a corporation keeps a store at which employees are expected to trade, or are sometimes forced to do so. Obviously such a store might be operated to the great benefit of the workman and without loss to the employer, but the temptation to make an unfair profit and to keep the laborer always in debt to the company was very great. A congressional committee which investigated conditions in Pennsylvania in 1888 found that prices charged in company stores ran from ten per cent. to 160 per cent. higher than prices in other stores in the vicinity, and that a workman was more likely to keep his position if he traded with the company.

The most insistent cause of industrial conflict was the question of wages. Forty-one per cent. of all the strikes between 1881 and 1900 were for more pay; twenty-six per cent., for shorter hours. Between the close of the war and the early nineties, industrial prosperity was widespread except for the period of prostration following 1873 and the less important depression of 1884. Not unnaturally the laborer desired to have a larger share of the product of his work. The individual, however, was impotent before a great corporation, when the wage-scale was being determined; hence workmen found it advantageous to combine and bargain collectively with their employer, in the expectation that he would hesitate to risk the loss of all his laboring force, whereas the loss of one or a few would be a matter of indifference.

At the present time, when most of these demands have been met in one degree or another, it is difficult to see why there should have been delay and contention in agreeing to a program which, so far as it deals with labor problems pure and simple, appears both modest and reasonable. But the state of mind of a large fraction of the nation was not in accord with ambitions which doubtless seemed excessively radical. Fundamentally a great portion of the propertied classes held a low estimate of the value and rights of the laboring people, as well as of the possibilities of their development, and feared that evil results would follow from attempts to improve their condition. The employment of children in factories, it was thought, would inculcate in them the needed habits of industry, and the reduction of the working hours would merely provide time which would be spent in the acquirement of vicious practices. If, in addition, the employers opposed such changes as the abolition of child labor and the reduction of the working day to eight hours on the ground of the financial sacrifice which seemed to be involved, their attitude was in keeping with the ruthless exploitation of the human resources of the country which was common during this period. It should be remembered, too, that the lofty conception which most Americans held of the opportunities and customs of their country stood in the way of a frank study of conditions and an equally frank admission of abuses. For decades we had reiterated that America was the land of opportunity, that economic, political and social equality were the foundations of American life and that the American workingman was the best fed and the best clothed workingman in the world. In the face of this view of industrial affairs it was difficult to be alert to manifold abuses and needed reforms. To one holding this view of affairs—and it was a common view—the laborer who demanded better conditions was unreasonable and unappreciative of how "well off" he was. Hence the blame for the labor unrest was frequently laid on the foreigner, who was supposed to bring to America the opposition to government which had been fostered in him by less democratic institutions abroad. Undoubtedly immigration greatly complicated industrial conditions, as has been indicated, yet essentially the labor question arose from the upward progress of a class in American society and was as inevitable, foreigner or no foreigner, as the coming of a new century.

During the sixties and seventies a little ameliorative labor legislation was passed by the state assemblies and by Congress. The mention of a few such enactments is instructive— not only because it shows how slight the progress was, but because it suggests the conditions that must have existed even in the most progressive states before these hesitating experiments in social legislation were made.

A Massachusetts law of 1866 forbade the employment of children under ten years of age in manufacturing establishments, prohibited the employment of children between the ages of ten and fourteen for more than eight hours per day, and provided that children who worked in factories must attend school at least six months in the year. In 1868 a federal act constituted eight hours a day's work for government laborers, workmen and mechanics, but some doubt arose as to the intent of part of it and the law was not enforced. In many states eight hour bills were introduced, but were defeated in all except six, of which Connecticut, Illinois and California were examples, and even in these cases the laws were not properly drawn up or were not enforced. In 1869 a Bureau of Statistics of Labor was established in Massachusetts which led the way for similar enterprises in other states. It collected information concerning labor matters and reported annually to the legislature. In 1874 a Massachusetts ten hour law forbade the employment of women and minors under eighteen for more than sixty hours a week, although refraining from the regulation of working hours for men. In 1879, in imitation of English factory acts, Massachusetts passed a general law relating to the inspection of manufacturing establishments. It provided that dangerous machinery must be guarded, proper ventilation secured, elevator wells equipped with protective devices and fire-escapes constructed. Other states followed slowly.

During the eighties Congress concerned itself slightly—and only slightly—with the labor problem. In 1884 a Bureau of Labor was established to collect information on the relation of labor and capital. Two years later, just before the distressful Haymarket affair,[3] President Cleveland sent a message to Congress in which he adverted to the many disputes which had recently arisen between laborers and employers, and urged legislation to meet the exigency. Considerations of justice and safety, he thought, demanded that the working classes be looked upon as especially entitled to legislative care. While Cleveland deprecated violence and condemned unjustifiable disturbance, he believed that the discontent among the employed was due largely to avarice on the part of the employing classes and to the feeling among workmen that the attention of the government was directed in an unfair degree to the interests of capital. On the other hand, he suggested that federal action was greatly limited by constitutional restrictions. He accordingly urged that the Bureau of Labor be enlarged and that permanent officers be appointed to act as a board of arbitration in industrial disputes. The legislative branch was not inclined to follow Cleveland's lead, although

[3] Cf. below p. 299 ff.

he returned to the subject after the Haymarket affair, for it was commonly felt that his suggestion was too great a step in the direction of centralization of government. Two years later, in 1888, a modest act was passed which provided for the investigation of differences between railroads and their employees, but only when agreed to by both parties, and no provision was made for the enforcement of the decision of the investigators. The practical results were not important. Similar action had already been taken in a few states. By 1895 fifteen states had laws providing for voluntary arbitration, but the results were slight in most cases.

Very little progress was being made in the states in the passage of other industrial legislation. In Alabama and Massachusetts in the middle eighties acts extended and regulated the liability of employers for personal injuries suffered by laborers while at work.[4] At the same time the attitude of the legislatures and the courts in some states toward strikes underwent a slight modification. In many states where the legislatures had not passed definite statutes to the contrary, it had been held by the courts that strikers could be tried and convicted for conspiracy. In a few cases, states passed acts attempting to define more exactly the legal position of strikers. A New York court in 1887, for example, held that the law of the state permitted workmen to seek an increase of wages by all possible means that fell short of threats or violence. Before the close of Cleveland's second administration in 1897, considerable progress had been made in state legislation concerning conditions and hours of labor for women and children, protection of workers from dangerous machinery, the payment of wages, employer's liability for accidents to workmen, and other subjects.

The total results, however, were much less imposing in practice than on the pages of the statute books. Ignorant,

[4] For the legal side of this matter, consult Wright, *Industrial Evolution*, pp. 278–282.

short-sighted and grasping employers opposed the passage of laws which would now be termed salutary, and evaded them after their enactment. Too few government officials had the knowledge and experience necessary for proper law enforcement. On the other hand, unreasonable or ill-considered actions on the part of the unions or their active agents—the "walking delegates"—turned popular sentiment against them. Particularly was this true in cases of violence and of strikes or boycotts by unions in support of workmen in other trades at far distant points.

Having passed through the stages of development, organization, and the formulation of purposes, the class struggle then entered the period of the resort to force.[5]

It will be remembered that the great railroad strikes of 1877 extended over many of the northern roads, but caused most trouble in Martinsburg, West Virginia, Pittsburgh and other railway centers. Much property was destroyed, lives were lost, and the strikers failed to obtain their ends.[6] Other effects of the controversy, moreover, made it an important landmark in the history of the labor question. The inconvenience and suffering which the strike caused in cities far distant from the scene of actual conflict indicated that the transportation system was already so essential a factor in welding the country together that any interruption to its operation had become intolerable. The hostility of some of the railway managers to union among their laborers and the rumors that they were determined to crush such organizations augured ill for the future. The hordes of unemployed workmen and the swarms of tramps which had resulted from the continued industrial depression of 1873 insured rioting and

[5] This is not, of course, to say that the beginning and end of each stage of this evolution was clear-cut and uniform all over the country. Not only did the periods overlap, but the stages of development differed widely in different sections of the country and in different industries.

[6] Above, p. 145 *ff.*

violence during the strike, whether the strikers themselves favored it and shared in it or not. The destruction of property which resulted from the strike caused many state legislatures to pass conspiracy laws directed against labor; more attention was paid to the need of trained soldiers for putting down strikes, and the construction of many armories followed; and the courts took a more hostile attitude toward labor unions. Equally important was the effect on the workmen themselves. When the strike became violent and the state militia failed to check it, the strikers found themselves face to face with federal troops. President Hayes could not, of course, refuse to repress the rioters; nevertheless his action aligned the power of the central government against the strikers, and seemed to the latter to align the government against the laborers as a class. Of a sudden, then, the labor problem took on a new and vital interest; workingmen's parties "began to spring up like mushrooms"; and the laboring men saw more clearly than ever the essential unity of their interests.

Industrial unrest increased rather than diminished during the prosperous eighties; for the first five years of the decade, strikes and lockouts together averaged somewhat over five hundred annually. The climax came in "the great upheaval" of 1884 to 1886. In the latter year nearly 1600 controversies involved 610,024 men and a financial sacrifice estimated at $34,000,000. Early in May, 1886, occurred the memorable Haymarket affair in the city of Chicago. The city was a center of labor agitation, some of it peaceful, some of it in the hands of radical European anarchists whose methods were shown in a statement of one of their newspapers, *The Alarm*, on February 21, 1885:

Dynamite! Of all the good stuff, this is the stuff. Stuff several pounds of this sublime stuff into an inch pipe . . . plug up both ends, insert a cap with a fuse attached, place this in the immediate neighbourhood of a lot of rich loafers . . . and light the fuse. A most cheerful and gratifying result will follow.

On May 1 strikes began for the purpose of obtaining an eight hour day. During the course of the strike some workmen gathered near the McCormick Reaper Works; the police approached, were stoned, and retorted by firing upon the strikers, killing four and wounding many others. Thereupon the men called a meeting in Haymarket Square to protest against the action of the police; in the main they were orderly, for Mayor Carter Harrison was present and found nothing objectionable. Later in the evening, when the Mayor and most of the audience had left, remarks of a violent nature seem to have been made, and at this point a force of 180 police marched forward and ordered the meeting to disperse. Just then a bomb was thrown into the midst of the police, killing seven and wounding many others. The entire nation was shocked and terrified by the event, as hitherto anarchy had seemed to be a far-away thing, the product of autocratic European governments. The thrower of the bomb could not be discovered, but numerous anarchists were found who themselves possessed such weapons or had urged violence in their speeches or writings. Eight of them, nearly all Germans, were tried for murder on the ground that the person who threw the bomb must have read the speeches or writings of the accused anarchists and have been thereby encouraged to do the act. The presiding judge, Joseph E. Gary, was of the opinion that the disposition in the guilty man to throw the bomb was the result of the teaching and advice of the prisoners. The counsel for the accused declared that since the guilty person could not be found it was impossible to know whether he had ever heard or read anything said or written by the prisoners, or been influenced by their opinions. Eventually eight anarchists were convicted, of whom four were hanged, one committed suicide, and three were imprisoned. In 1893 the Governor of Illinois, John P. Altgeld, pardoned the three prisoners, basing his action mainly on the ground that no proof had been brought forward to show that they were in any way acquainted with the unknown bomb-thrower. The result of the conviction was the break-up of the radical anarchistic movement and also the temporary discrediting of the general agitation for an eight hour day, although neither the Knights of Labor nor the Federation of Labor had any connection with the anarchists, and both deprecated violence.

During the presidential campaign of 1892 a violent strike at the Carnegie Steel Company's works in Homestead, Pennsylvania, arose from a reduction in wages and a refusal of the Company to recognize the Iron and Steel Workers' Union. An important feature of this disturbance was the use of armed Pinkerton detectives by the Company for the protection of its buildings. Armed with rifles they fell into conflict with the workmen, a miniature military campaign was carried on, lives were lost and large amounts of property destroyed. Eventually the entire militia of the state had to be called out to maintain peace.

It remained, however, for Chicago and the year 1894 to present one of the most far-reaching, costly and complex labor upheavals that has ever disturbed industrial relations in America. So ill understood at the time were the real facts of the controversy that it is doubtful whether it is possible even now to distinguish between truth and rumor in regard to some of its aspects.

The town of Pullman, near Chicago, was the home of the Pullman Palace Car Company, a prosperous corporation with a capital of $36,000,000. It provided houses for its employees, kept up open stretches of lawn, flower beds and lakes. In 1893 and 1894, when general business conditions were bad, the Company reduced the wages of its workmen about twenty-five per cent. A committee of the men asked for a return to former rates, but they were refused, three members of the committee were laid off, and the employees then struck. Late in June, 1894, the American Railway Union, to which many of the workmen belonged, took up the side of the men, and the General Managers' Association, comprising officials of twenty-four roads entering Chicago, took the side of the Company. Through the entry of the Union and the Association, the relatively unimportant Pullman affair expanded to large proportions. Violence followed; cars were tipped over and burned; property was stolen and tracks ruined; and eventually the United States government was drawn into the controversy.

Numerous complaints having reached Washington that the mails were being obstructed and interstate commerce interfered with, President Cleveland decided to send troops to Chicago. The Constitution requires that the United States protect states against domestic violence on the application of the legislature, or of the executive when the legislature is not in session. Moreover the statutes of the United States empower the president to use federal force to execute federal laws. The position taken by the Governor of Illinois, John P. Altgeld, was expressed in his telegram to President Cleveland protesting against the action of the executive:

Should the situation at any time get so serious that we can not control it with the State forces, we will promptly and freely ask for Federal assistance; but until such time I protest with all due deference against this uncalled-for reflection upon our people, and again ask for the immediate withdrawal of these troops.

The President replied that troops were being sent in accordance with federal law upon complaint that commerce and the passage of the mails were being obstructed. A somewhat acrimonious correspondence between the Governor and the President resulted but the troops were retained and assisted in bringing the strike to a conclusion.

The attitude of the courts, meanwhile, had brought up a serious situation. On July 2 a "blanket injunction" was issued by the United States District Court of Illinois and posted on the sides of the cars. It forbade officers, members of the Union and all other persons to interfere in any way with the operation of trains or to force or persuade employees to refuse to perform their duties. Under existing law, anybody who disobeyed the injunction could be brought before the Court for contempt, and sentenced by the judge without opportunity to bring witnesses and to be tried before a jury. When Eugene V. Debs, the president of the Union, and other officers continued to direct the strike they were arrested for contempt of court and imprisoned.[7] With federal troops against them and their officers gone, the strikers could hardly continue and gave up in defeat. The loss in property and wages had already reached $80,000,000.

The apportionment of the blame for so appalling a controversy was not a simple task. On the one hand, a writer in the *Forum* declared that

The one great question was of the ability of this Government to suppress insurrection. On the one side was the party of lawlessness of murder, of incendiarism, and of defiance of authority. On the other side was the party of loyalty to the United States.

But this was a superficial view. A commission of investigation appointed by President Cleveland looked into the matter more deeply. Its unanimous report made important assertions: the Pullman Company, while providing a beautiful town for its employees, charged rents twenty to twenty-five per cent. higher than were charged in surrounding towns for similar accommodations, and the men felt a compulsion to reside in the houses if they wished to retain their positions;

[7] The Court based its action mainly on the provisions of Section 2 of the Sherman anti-trust law, which thus had an unforeseen effect. The Supreme Court upheld the action, although on broader grounds. Above, p. 238, *cf.* 159 *U. S. Reports*, 564.

when wages were reduced, the salaries of the better paid officers were untouched, so that the burden of the hard times was placed on the poorest paid employees; there was no violence or destruction of property in Pullman, and much of the rowdyism in Chicago, but not all of it, was due to the lawless adventurers and professional criminals who filled the city at that time;[8] when various public officials and organizations attempted to get the Company to arbitrate the dispute, the uniform reply was that the points at issue were matters of fact and hence not proper subjects for arbitration; and the Managers' Association selected, armed and paid 3,600 federal deputy marshals who acted both as railroad employees and as United States officers, under the direction of the Managers.

In view of the amount of labor disturbance after the Civil War, it was noteworthy that it attracted the interest of political parties to so slight a degree previous to 1896. In general the national platforms of the two large parties reflected an indefinite if not remote concern with the welfare of the wage earner. It was urged, to be sure, by both protectionists and tariff reformers that customs duties should be framed with the welfare of the laborer in mind, but the sincerity of this concern was sometimes open to question. The smaller parties, as usual, were far less vague in their demands. The Labor Reformers in 1872 demanded the eight hour day; the Greenbackers had a definite program for relief in 1880; the Anti-Monopolists in 1884 and the Union Labor and the United Labor parties in 1888. By 1892 the great parties found themselves face to face with a growing labor vote. The labor planks in the two platforms of that year were strikingly similar. Each called for federal legislation to protect the employees of transportation companies, but looked to the states for the relief of employees engaged in manufacturing.

[8] In 1893 the "World's Fair" in Chicago had celebrated the four hundredth anniversary of the landing of Columbus, and many of the criminals attracted by the event had remained in the city.

Neither the Socialist Labor party nor the Populists, however, were greatly troubled by the question of the proper distribution between state and nation of the responsibility for the welfare of the wage earner. Both proposed definite action; both urged the reduction in length of the working day. The Populists condemned the use of Pinkertons in labor disputes and the Socialists urged arbitration, the prohibition of child labor, restrictions on the employment of women in unhealthful industries, employers' liability laws and the protection of life and limb.

The inadequacy of the measures used by both sides in the class struggle is more evident now than it was in the thirty years after the Civil War. To be sure, the laborer gradually compelled his reluctant employer to grant his demands, whether reasonable or unreasonable. But the presence of lawless, not to say criminal elements in all the cities, almost guaranteed the outbreak of violence in strikes, whether the strikers themselves sympathized with it and abetted it or not. Violence compelled the state and federal governments to step in with troops and quell the disturbance, thus complicating the issues at stake and diverting attention entirely away from the question of justice to the workman and to the employer. So nearly inevitable was the outbreak of rowdyism, that the employers could confidently wait for it (or even secretly incite it), and then call upon the government to fight their battles. Under such circumstances, either class warfare or political action seemed the most probable solution of the difficulty. That out-and-out war did not result was due to a wide variety of fundamental considerations, too numerous to discuss here. Relief through legislative action, nevertheless, was difficult to attain. The leaders of the two large parties had given no evidence of an effective and immediate interest in labor unrest. The other political parties were too small to afford chances of success. If less reliance was to be placed upon the strike and more upon political action, either a third party must be constructed or the leadership in one of the old ones must be seized. When the conference of labor officials met in Chicago and concluded that the Pullman strike was lost, it issued an address to the members of the American Railway Union advising a return to work, closer organization of the laboring class and the correction of industrial wrongs at the ballot box. If this advice should be taken, and if the wage earner should attempt to control legislation for his economic interest, as the propertied class had long been doing for its benefit, the struggle might be shifted to the political arena. The interest of the workers in the South and West in the Populist movement suggested the possibility that such a shift might occur.

BIBLIOGRAPHICAL NOTE

Surprisingly little attention has been paid to the social aspects of the growth of the laboring classes before 1896. There is ample material, however, on the more obvious sides of the labor movement, such as the growth of the organizations and the use of the strike.

The *Documentary History of American Industrial Society* (10 vols., 1910–1911), contains a little documentary material on the period after 1865; J. R. Commons and others, *History of Labor in the United States* (2 vols., 1918), is the best and most recent historical account; T. S. Adams and H. L. Sumner, *Labor Problems* (1905), is useful; consult also R. T. Ely, *Labor Movement in America* (3rd ed., 1890); C. D. Wright, *The Industrial Evolution of the United States* (1897), by a practical expert; G. E. McNeill, *The Labor Movement* (1887); J. R. Buchanan, *Story of a Labor Agitator* (1903); S. P. Orth, *The Armies of Labor* (1919), contains a good bibliography; John Mitchell, *Organized Labor* (1903); T. V. Powderly, *Thirty Years of Labor* (1890); *Quarterly Journal of Economics* (Jan., 1887), Knights of Labor; J. H. Bridge, *Inside History of the Carnegie Steel Co.* (1903). On the Haymarket affair, compare *Century Magazine* (Apr., 1893), and J. P. Altgeld, *Reasons for Pardoning Fielden, Neebe and Schwab;* on the Pullman strike, Grover Cleveland, *Presidential Problems,* and the report of the commission of investigation in Senate Executive Documents, 53rd Congress, 3rd session, vol. 2 (Serial Number 3276). See also W. R. Browne, *Altgeld of Illinois* (1924); *Centennial History of Illinois* (1922), vol. IV; E. Berman, *Labor Disputes and the President of the United States* (1924). Edward Stanwood, *History of the Presidency*, contains political platform planks on labor. The reports of the Commissioner of Labor (1886–), and of the state bureaus of statistics of labor in such states as Massachusetts (1870–), and New York (1884–), are essential for the investigator. S. Gompers, *Seventy Years of Life and Labor* (2 vols., 1925), is by the late president of the A. F. of L.

CHAPTER XIV

MONETARY AND FINANCIAL PROBLEMS

It is little less than a National disgrace that a large number of Senators belonging to both old political parties can be found willing to obey the dictation of the President in a brutal attempt to coerce the friends of silver into acquiescence in the dangerous and destructive single gold standard theory.

Denver Republican, Oct. 13, 1893.

This cause to which the crisis of 1893 is directly and wholly attributable consisted of a wide-spread fear . . . that the United States would not be able to maintain a gold standard of payments.

W. J. LAUCK.

I think it may here be frankly confessed that it never occurred to any of us to consult [at the time of the bond sale to J. P. Morgan] farmers, doctors, lawyers, shoe-makers, or even statesmen. We could not escape the belief that the prospect of obtaining what we needed might be somewhat improved by making application to those whose business and surroundings qualified them to intelligently respond.

GROVER CLEVELAND.

THE critical monetary and financial situation during Cleveland's second administration is understandable only in the light of a series of acts which were passed between 1878 and 1893. It will be remembered that in the former year the Bland-Allison act had provided for the purchase and coinage of two million to four million dollars' worth of silver bullion per month, and that the force behind the measure had been found chiefly among westerners who wished to see the volume of the currency increased and among mine owners who were producing silver.

The passage of the law did not end all opposition to the greater use of silver, nor did it solve all our monetary difficulties. In the first place, the United States sent delegates to an International Monetary Conference in Paris, in conformity

with one of the provisions of the Bland-Allison act, to discuss a project for the utilization of silver through an agreement among the commercial nations of the world. No tangible results were obtained, however, so that it was plain that
for the time, at least, the United States would be alone in its
attempt to bring about the greater use of the white metal. In
the meantime the law was put into operation, and the secretary of the treasury exercised his option by purchasing the
minimum amount, two million dollars' worth of bullion. It
was impossible to keep the coins in circulation, however,
mainly because of their weight, and the policy was therefore
adopted of storing part of the silver in the government
vaults and issuing paper "silver certificates" in its place.
As these were of small denominations and circulated on a par
with gold, no immediate difficulty was experienced in making
them part of the currency supply of the country.

The currency question, nevertheless, remained as complicated as ever and the differences of opinion upon it as diverse
as before. The market price of silver steadily declined
through the eighties and the bullion value of the metal in a
dollar sank from ninety-three cents in 1878 to less than
seventy-one cents in 1889. Both Republican and Democratic
secretaries of the treasury gave warning that the inflow of
silver into the currency supply was too great. President
Arthur urged the repeal of the Bland-Allison act in his first
annual message; President Cleveland again and again reiterated the same advice, warning Congress of the danger that
silver would be substituted for gold. The argument of the
opponents of silver could hardly be stated in more concise
or complete terms. As soon as the supply of currency became too great, he asserted, the unnecessary portion would go
out of circulation;[1] it was the experience of nations that the

---

[1] According to the principle known as Gresham's law, bad money
tends to drive out good; or overvalued money to drive out undervalued
money. If the face value of a coin is more than its worth as bullion,

more desirable coin—gold, in this case—would be hoarded by banks and speculators; it would then become apparent that the bullion value of the gold dollar was greater than that of the silver dollar and the two coins would part company; those who, in such a contingency, could get gold dollars would demand a premium for them, while the laboring man, unable to demand gold, would find his silver dollar sadly shrunken in value.

Although the coinage of silver in the twelve years during which the Bland-Allison act was in force amounted to $378,-000,000, the danger that Cleveland's prophecy would come to pass was lessened by several facts. The country was, in the first place, passing through a period of industrial expansion that required an enlarged circulating medium; the revenues of the government were exceeding expenditures, and part of the surplus was being stored in the vaults in Washington and the volume of the national bank notes shrank more than $158,-000,000 between 1880 and 1890. Falling prices for agricultural products continued to keep western discontent alive and far from being convinced by Cleveland's warnings, western conventions and representatives in Congress continued to urge legislation to increase the amount of silver to be coined, and free-coinage bills were constantly introduced and frequently near passage. Manifestly the demand that something more be done for silver was not at an end.

Although agitation over the use of silver currency resulted in no further important legislation for the time being, the general financial situation was complicated by a series of important acts. During the eighties the federal revenues

it is "overvalued." Thus, if coins of equal face value, but of different bullion value, circulate side by side, there will be a tendency for the possessors of the coins to pass on the currency with the smaller bullion value and to withdraw the others for sale as bullion and for use in the arts.

mounted to an unprecedented height and as expenses did not
increase proportionately, a surplus of large and finally of embarrassing and dangerous size appeared.

Between 1880 and 1890 it averaged more than $100,000,000
annually. Although part of it was used to reduce the public
debt, the remainder began to accumulate in the treasury and
thereby seriously reduced the amount of currency available
for the ordinary needs of business. In 1888, for example, the

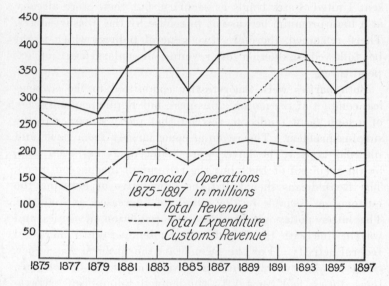

*Financial Operations
1875–1897 in millions*
——·—— *Total Revenue*
------- *Total Expenditure*
——·— *Customs Revenue*

surplus in the treasury was one-fourth as great as the entire
estimated sum outside. The one device for doing away with
the surplus upon which all leaders could unite was the reduction of the national debt. Between 1879 and 1890 over
$1,000,000,000 were thus disposed of. Yet even this process
raised difficulties. Although a portion of the debt came due
in 1881 and could be redeemed at the pleasure of the government, other bonds were not redeemable until 1891 and 1907,

unless the federal authorities chose to go into the market and buy at a premium. Eventually this was done for a time, although prices were thereby forced up to 130 in 1888, and as a result the redemption of $95,000,000 during the year cost more than $112,000,000. The treasury also adopted the expedient of depositing surplus funds in banking institutions, but the plan was open to serious objections. In order to qualify for receiving government deposits the banks had to present United States bonds as security, but these were already at a high premium because of purchase by the treasury itself. There remained, therefore, two general policies which might be followed—reduction of revenue or enlargement of expenditure.

Both parties were theoretically committed to the economical conduct of the nation's business, but Republican advocacy of a high tariff tended to restrict that party's answer to the surplus problem. The revenue came largely from tariff and internal taxes. The latter were reduced, as has been seen, by the tariff act of 1883, but the redundant income continued. The Republicans then faced the alternative of lowering the customs or turning to the policy of increased expenditure. The latter policy would delay the reduction of duties and was in line with the Republican tendency toward increased federal activity. For the Democrats the problem was easier. Since the party was tending toward advocacy of low customs duties, had constantly condemned Republican extravagance in administration and was traditionally the party of a restricted national authority, it was logical to turn to severe reduction of revenue in order to solve the problem of the surplus.

President Cleveland's political and personal philosophy led toward economy in expenditure and therefore toward revenue reduction. By nature he was frugal; in politics, a strict constructionist. In vetoing an appropriation bill he succinctly set forth his creed:

A large surplus in the Treasury is the parent of many ills, and among them is found a tendency to an extremely liberal, if not loose, construction of the Constitution. It also attracts the gaze of States and individuals with a kind of fascination, and gives rise to plans and pretensions that an uncongested Treasury never could excite.

The Republicans were becoming committed to the policy of large expenditures. President Harrison, to be sure, in his first annual message urged the reduction of receipts, declaring that the collection of money not needed for public use imposed an unnecessary burden upon the people and that the presence of a large surplus in the treasury was a disturbing element in the conduct of private business. Nevertheless such party leaders as Reed and McKinley, who effectively controlled the legislation of the Harrison administration, acted on the philosophy of Senator Dolph:

If we were to take our eyes off the increasing surplus in the Treasury and stop bemoaning the prosperity of the country, . . . and to devote our energies to the development of the great resources which the Almighty has placed in our hands, to increasing (our products) . . . to cheapening transportation by the improving of our rivers and harbors, . . . we would act wiser than we do.

Congress was more inclined to follow the policy suggested by Dolph than that proposed by Cleveland. One project was the return of the direct tax which had been levied on the states at the outbreak of the Civil War. At that time Congress had laid a tax of $20,000,000 apportioned among the states according to population. About $15,000,000 had been collected, mainly, of course, from the northern states. It was suggested that the levy be returned, a plan which would give the northern states a return in actual cash and the southern states "the empty enjoyment of the remission from a tax which no one now dared to suggest was ever to be made good." President Cleveland had vetoed such a bill, during his first administration, believing it unconstitutional and also objectionable as a "sheer, bald gratuity." Under the Harrison administration the scheme was revived and carried to completion, March 2, 1891.

Pension legislation was even more successful as a method of reducing the unwieldy surplus. Garfield had declared in 1872, when introducing an appropriation bill in the House of Representatives, "We may reasonably expect that the expenditures for pensions will hereafter steadily decrease, unless our legislation should be unwarrantably extravagant," and in fact the cost of pensions for 1878 had been lower by more than $7,000,000 than in 1871. The Arrears act of 1879 had given a decided upward tendency to pension expense, which amounted to over $20,000,000 more in 1880 than in 1879. The surplus was a constant invitation to careless generosity. Liberality to the veteran was a patriotic duty which lent itself to the fervid stump oratory of the time and presented an opportunity to the undeserving applicant to place his name on the rolls of pensioners along with his more worthy associates. Besides, an administration which seemed niggardly in its attitude toward the veterans was certain to lose the soldier vote, and neither party was willing to incur such a risk. Hence, despite Cleveland's vetoes of private pension legislation, hundreds of such measures passed during his first term. The Harrison administration proceeded upon the President's theory that it "was no time to be weighing the claims of old soldiers with apothecary's scales." A dependent pension bill like that which President Cleveland vetoed in 1887 was passed in 1890. The list of pensioners more than doubled in length; the number of applications for aid increased tenfold in two years. It became necessary for President Harrison to displace his over-liberal commissioner of pensions, but the mischief was already done. The total yearly pension expenditure quickly mounted beyond the one hundred million mark, where it has remained ever since. Indeed, the cost of pensions in 1872 when Garfield made his prophecy was less than one-sixth as great as in 1913. Large pension expenditure was clearly a permanent charge.[2]

The improvement of the rivers and harbors of the country has always been a ready means of disposing of any embarrassing surplus and of assisting Congressmen to get money into their districts. "Promoters of all sorts of schemes, beggars for the widening of rivulets, the deepening of rills," clustered about the treasury during the eighties. During the early seventies expenditure on this account had not reached $6,500,000 annually, although in 1879 it exceeded $8,000,000. In 1882, the year of the mammoth surplus, Congress passed over Arthur's veto a bill carrying appropriations which amounted to almost nineteen million dollars.[3] Expenditures were somewhat reduced in the years immediately following, and Cleveland continued the repressive policy of his predecessor. Harrison in his first message to Congress in December, 1889, recommended appropriations for river and harbor improvement, although deprecating the prosecution of works not of public advantage. The recommendation fell upon willing ears and appropriations for undertakings of this sort at once increased again. Expenditure for rivers and harbors, like that for pensions, remained at a high level, the wise and necessary portions of such measures being relied upon to carry the unwise and unnecessary ones.

A project which lacked many of the unpleasant features of river and harbor legislation was the Blair educational bill, which proposed to distribute a considerable portion of the surplus among the states. As discussion of the Blair bill proceeded, it became clear that its results might be more far-reaching than had been anticipated. A gift from the national government seemed sure to retard local efforts at raising

[2] The Commissioner of Pensions reported June 30, 1925, that there were still twenty-one widows of the War of 1812 on the pension rolls, and seventeen soldiers and 12,257 widows of the War with Mexico.

[3] Above, p. 174.

school funds and would initiate a vicious tendency to rely on federal bounty. Hence although the Senate passed the bill in 1884, 1886, and 1888, it never commended itself sufficiently to the House and eventually was dropped.

A small portion of the increased expenditure in the eighties was due to improvements in the navy, in which both parties shared. Presidents Arthur and Cleveland urged upon Congress the need of modern defences. Progress was slow and difficult. Although the day of steel ships had come, the American navy was composed of wooden relics of earlier days. The manufacture of armor and of large guns had to be developed, and skill and experience accumulated. Results began to appear in the late eighties when the number of modern steel war vessels increased from three to twenty-two in four years. Expenditures mounted from less than $14,000,-000 in 1880 to over $22,000,000 in 1890.

As effective as new expenditure was the McKinley tariff act of 1890, the details of which from the point of view of tariff history have already been noted.[4] The extremely high rates levied under that legislation caused a slight reduction in customs revenue in 1891 and a sharp decline in 1892. Moreover the coincidence of instability in the currency system, business depression and the relatively high Wilson-Gorman tariff schedules of 1894 continued the decline of income from customs during the middle nineties.

In the meantime the silver agitation, which had been somewhat repressed by the well-known attitude of Cleveland during his first administration, revived with increased vigor. The election of 1888, it will be remembered, had turned wholly on the tariff and had been a victory for the Republicans. The western states had almost uniformly supported Harrison in the election and during 1889 four more were admitted to the Union. Their representatives in Congress were mainly

4 Above, p. 260 *ff.*

silver advocates. In his first message to Congress the President declared that the evil anticipations which had accompanied the use of the silver dollar had not been realized but he feared nevertheless that either free coinage or any "considerable increase" of the present rate of coinage would be "disastrous" and "discreditable." He announced that a plan would be presented by the Secretary of the Treasury, to which he had been able to give only a hasty examination. The scheme for expanding the silver coinage which the Secretary, William Windom, presented was not acceptable to Congress, but the result of the agitation was the law generally known as the Sherman silver purchase act, which was passed on July 14, 1890. It directed the secretary of the treasury to purchase 4,500,000 ounces of silver bullion per month and to issue in payment "Treasury notes of the United States." These notes were legal tender for all debts and were receivable for customs and all public dues. Further, the secretary was directed to redeem the notes in gold or silver at his discretion, "it being the established policy of the United States to maintain the two metals on a parity with each other."

The silver to be purchased was substantially the total output of the American mines. Fearing the strength of the silver element in the Senate and doubtful of the position which the President might take, former Secretary Sherman, now in the Senate, supported the act, although confessing that he was ready to vote for repeal at any time when it could be done without substituting free coinage. The provision for the purchase of four and one-half million ounces instead of four and one-half million dollars' worth was introduced at Sherman's suggestion. This clause kept the amount to be absorbed at a uniform level, whereas the purchase of a fixed number of dollars' worth would have increased the coinage when the price of bullion fell. The vote on the Sherman act was strictly partisan—no Republicans opposing it and no Democrats fav-

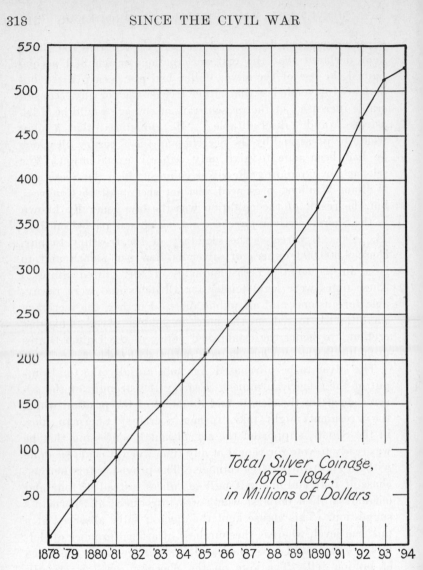

Total Silver Coinage,
1878–1894,
in Millions of Dollars

NOTE: BY THE ACT OF 1890 THE SILVER PURCHASED WAS PAID FOR IN TREASURY NOTES. AFTER THAT DATE, THEREFORE, THE CHART INDICATES THE TOTAL COINAGE OF SILVER TOGETHER WITH TREASURY NOTES ISSUED FOR THE PURCHASE OF BULLION oring it when the measure was finally passed, although 116 members of the House failed to answer to their names on the roll-call.

In view of the fact that the industrial and commercial countries of Europe were almost universally reducing their silver coinage, the passage by the United States of an act which substantially doubled the amount of silver purchased under the Bland-Allison law seems extraordinary. Moreover, only six years later a presidential campaign was fought almost wholly on the silver issue and at that time the Republican party resolutely opposed free coinage. It is obvious that powerful forces must have been at work to align the party so unitedly in behalf of the Sherman law. It was to be expected that western Republicans would support it, but the eastern members were found voting for it as well. Doubtless many things contributed to the result. Some perhaps agreed with Sherman that the silver advocates were so strong that free coinage would result in case Congress refused to pass legislation of any kind. Some may have feared with Platt of Connecticut, that a party split would ensue unless the wishes of the westerners were acceded to—hence an act which gave liberal assistance to silver to please the West and South but stopped short of free coinage so as to please the East. That opportunist politics had an influence with certain members is indicated by the remarks of a Massachusetts Republican representative who later favored the gold standard:

It is pure politics, gentlemen; that is all there is about it. We Republicans want to come back and we do not want you (to the Democratic side) to come back in the majority, because, on the whole, you must excuse us for thinking we are better fellows than you are. That is human nature, that is all there is in this silver bill (laughter on the Republican side); pure politics.

A Democrat who favored free coinage denounced the act as

"Janus-Faced," moulded so as to look like silver to the West and gold to the East. Important, also, seems to have been the attitude of the western members on the tariff. The party had returned to power on the tariff issue and it seemed necessary to pass some sort of legislation on the subject. Yet the party majority in Senate and House was slight and the westerners were understood to be ready to defeat the McKinley bill which was then pending, unless something was done for silver. Harrison seems to have been unwilling to endanger successful tariff legislation by opposing the considerable extension of the coinage of silver.[5]

Contrary to the expectations of the proponents of the act, the price of silver fell gradually until the value of the bullion in a dollar was sixty cents in 1893 and forty-nine cents in 1894. They who had opposed the law saw their fears verified; as they had prophesied, silver began to replace gold in circulation; the latter was hoarded and used for foreign shipments; customs duties, which had hitherto been paid largely in gold, were now paid in paper currency; since gold was now more desired than silver, large amounts of paper were presented to the government for redemption in the more valuable metal. To be sure, the Sherman law allowed the secretary of the treasury to redeem the treasury notes of 1890 in gold or silver at his discretion, but it contained a proviso that the established policy of the United States was to maintain the two metals on a parity or equality. The secretary believed that if he refused to redeem the treasury notes in whatever coin the holder desired, that is, if he insisted on redemption in silver only, a discrimination would be made in favor of gold and the equality of the two metals would be destroyed. Parity would be maintained, the government held, only when

---

[5] The law remained in force about three years. During that interval nearly $156,000,000 worth of silver bullion was purchased with the new treasury notes. The government began retiring these notes in 1900.

any kind of money could be exchanged for any other kind, at the option of the holder.

For the redemption of the greenbacks, the government had since 1879 maintained a fund known as the gold reserve. No law fixed its amount, but custom had set $100,000,000 as the minimum. Hitherto a negligible amount of paper had been presented for redemption, but as soon as the Sherman law came into effective operation the demand for gold became increasingly great and the level of the reserve promptly fell. Between July 1, 1890, and July 15, 1893, the supply of gold in the treasury decreased more than $132,000,000, while the stock of silver increased over $147,000,000. Evidently silver was replacing gold in the treasury, and it was equally clear that a continuation of the process would result in forcing the government to pay its obligations in silver and to refuse to redeem paper in gold—in other words, go upon a silver standard.

The situation when Cleveland's second administration began on March 4, 1893, was complex and critical. The annual expenditures had increased by $119,000,000 between 1880 and 1893, while the revenue had expanded by only half that amount; the surplus had decreased every year during Harrison's administration and a deficit had been avoided only by the cessation of payments on the public debt; the supply of currency in circulation was being heavily increased by the operation of the Sherman law; and the gold reserve had been kept at the traditional amount only through extraordinary efforts on the part of Harrison's Secretary of the Treasury as the administration came to a close.

Cleveland's attitude toward the Sherman law was well-known. He had long urged the repeal of the Bland-Allison act; before the election of 1892 he had predicted disaster in case the nation entered upon "the dangerous and reckless experiment of free, unlimited, and independent silver coinage";

it was his belief that the distresses under which the country labored were due principally to the Sherman silver purchase law. He therefore called a special session of Congress for August 7 (1893), sent a message giving a succinct account of the operation of the law and urged its immediate repeal.[6] In the House, repeal was voted with surprising promptness, although a strong free-silver element fought vigorously to prevent it. That party lines were broken was indicated by the fact that two-thirds of the Democrats and four-fifths of the Republicans voted in accord with the President's request.

In the Senate the silver advocates were stronger. The entire history of coinage was discussed at length. Members who favored repeal disliked to overturn the tradition of the Senate which allowed unlimited debate, and the silver senators therefore filibustered through the summer and early fall. Senator Jones of Nevada made a single speech that filled a hundred dreary pages of the *Congressional Record*. Senator Allen of Nebraska quoted more than thirty authorities, ranging from the Pandects of Justinian to enlivening doggerel poetry. Feeling ran high. In the West, Jones, Allen and others were looked upon as heroes; in the East, as villains. To a satirical onlooker it seemed that the nation had become insanely obsessed with the question of repeal:

All men of virtue and intelligence know that all the ills of life— scarcity of money, baldness, the comma bacillus, Home Rule, . . . and the Potato Bug—are due to the Sherman Bill. If it is repealed, sin and death will vanish from the world, . . . the skies will fall, and we shall all catch larks.

[6] The call for the extra session, together with news of the suspension of free-coinage in India, sent the bullion price of silver down twenty-one cents per ounce in two weeks. The President was seriously handicapped at this time by a cancerous growth in the jaw, necessitating an operation, news of which was withheld from the public for fear of its ill effect on the financial situation. *Cf. Saturday Evening Post*, 22 Sept., 1917.

Not until October 30 were the silver supporters overcome. Including members who were paired, twenty-two Democrats and twenty-six Republicans favored repeal, and twenty-two Democrats, twelve Republicans and three Populists opposed. Again the West and South were aligned against the North and East. The Democratic party was divided and charges and countercharges had been made that augured ill for party successes, as has been seen, in dealing with the tariff and other important problems.[7] Worst of all, the chief question—the volume and content of the currency—was still unanswered. Something had been done for silver—and undone—but there was no scientific settlement of the problem.

The disastrous financial and industrial crisis of 1893 made yet more complex the already tangled skein of economic history during President Cleveland's second administration. The catastrophe has been ascribed to a variety of causes but the relative importance of the various factors is still a matter of disagreement. Rash speculation on the part of industrial interests here and abroad seems to have made weak links in the international commercial chain; financial conditions both in Germany and in Great Britain were precarious during the early part of 1890; the collapse of the Philadelphia and Reading Railroad in February, 1893, and of the National Cordage Company soon afterwards were warnings of what was to follow; the silver purchase law produced widespread fear that the United States would not be able to continue the redemption of paper currency; and the change of political control had produced the usual feeling of uncertainty. The dwindling of the gold reserve, which has already been mentioned, assisted in causing a critical situation. Foreign investors, fearful of financial conditions here, sold their American railroad and other securities and received payment in gold. The one

[7] Above, p. 278.

place where the yellow metal could be readily obtained was the United States treasury and upon it the strain centered. People attempted to turn property of all kinds into gold before the existing standard should change to a depreciated silver basis. At the same time there was a rush to the banks to withdraw funds, and the visible supply of currency therefore was seriously reduced. "Under these conditions gold seemed scarce. In reality gold was only relatively scarce in comparison with the abnormal offering of property for sale on account of the fear of the silver standard." In an incredibly short time, currency became so scarce as to create a genuine panic and was purchased like any commodity at premiums ranging from one to three per cent. In order to enable their families to pay the running expenses of every day at the summer resorts, business men were compelled to buy bills and coin and send them in express packages. The national banks were unable to supply the demand for currency so quickly, and 158 of them failed in 1893 and hundreds of state and private financial institutions were forced to close their doors. Industrial firms were affected by the uncertainty and panic and over 15,000 failures resulted, with liabilities amounting to $347,-000,000 in the single year. Production of coal and iron fell sharply; railway construction nearly ceased and the value of securities shrank to a fraction of their former value. The distress among the wage earners became extreme; unemployment was common; strikes, like that beginning in Pullman in 1894, were bitter and prolonged. "Coxey's army," composed of unemployed workmen, marched to Washington with a petition for relief.

As is usually the case in our politics, the blame for the industrial disturbance was laid at the door of the party in power. The argument of an Ohio congressman in the debate over the repeal of the Sherman law typified the political use made of the crisis of 1893. Until November, 1892, the orator declared, prosperity was undimmed. "Iron furnaces throughout the country were in full blast, and their cheerful light was going up to heaven notifying the people of the United States of existing prosperity and warning them against change of conditions.'' Then came the election of the party ''which had declared war on the system upon which our whole industrial fabric had been erected.'' ''One by one the furnaces went out, one by one the mines closed up, one after another the factories shortened their time.'' Business interests, he asserted, were fearful of Democratic rule and especially of tariff reform; hence prosperity and confidence could be renewed only by leaving the Sherman law intact and by refusing to undertake any sweeping revision of the protective tariff.

Further to complicate the financial trials of the burdensome mid-nineties, the depletion of the gold reserve demanded immediate attention. During the closing months of President Harrison's administration, in fact, the Secretary of the Treasury had ordered the preparation of plates for engraving an issue of bonds by which to borrow sufficient gold to replenish the redemption fund. By a personal appeal to New York bankers, however, he was able to exchange paper for gold and so keep the level above the one hundred million mark, and when Cleveland succeeded to the chair, the reserve was $100,-982,410. In the meantime the scarcity of gold continued, and the combination of large expenditures and slender income severely embarrassed the government in its attempts to obtain a sufficient supply of gold to keep the reserve intact. The administration, indeed, was all but helpless. Paper presented for redemption in gold had to be paid out to meet expenses and was then turned in for gold again. Hence, as Cleveland ruefully reminded Congress, ''we have an endless chain in operation constantly depleting the Treasury's gold and never near a final rest.'' On April 22, 1893, the reserve fell momentarily below $100,000,000 and later in the year it was apparent that the reduction was likely to become permanent. By January, 1894, the reserve was less than $70,000,000, while $450,-000,000 in paper which might be presented for redemption

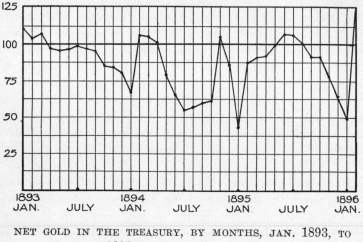

NET GOLD IN THE TREASURY, BY MONTHS, JAN. 1893, TO
FEB. 1896, IN MILLIONS OF DOLLARS

were in actual circulation. Only one resource seemed available—borrowing gold. The treasury therefore sold bonds to the value of $50,000,000. Even this, however, did not remedy the ill. Bankers obtained gold to purchase bonds by presenting paper currency to the government for redemption. Relief was temporary. On the last day of May the reserve amounted to only $79,000,000; in November, to $59,000,000. Another issue of bonds was resorted to in November, but the results were not better than before. At the same time the Pullman strike during the summer months, the Wilson-Gorman tariff fiasco and an unfortunate harvest seemed to indicate that man and nature were determined to make 1894 a year of ill-omen.

By February, 1895, the treasury found itself confronted with a reserve of only $41,000,000. It seemed useless to attempt borrowing under the usual conditions, and Cleveland therefore resorted to a new device. A contract was made with J. P. Morgan and a group of bankers for the purchase of 3,500,000 ounces of gold to be paid for with United States four per cent. bonds. In order to protect the reserve from a renewed drain, the bankers agreed that at least half the gold should be obtained abroad, and they promised to exert all their influence to prevent withdrawals of gold from the treasury while the contract was being filled. The terms of the contract were favorable to the bankers, but the President defended the agreement on the ground that the promise to protect the reserve entitled the bankers to a favorable bargain. The fact, however, that the Morgan Company was able to market the bonds with the public and make a large profit, increased the demand that the administration sell directly to the people and make the profit itself. In January, 1896, occured a fourth sale—to the public, this time—and 4,640 bids were received, for a total several times greater than the $100,000,000 called for. By this time, business conditions were improving, confidence was restored among the financial classes and gold again began to flow out of hiding and into the treasury. The endless chain was broken.

The denunciation which Cleveland received for the untoward monetary and industrial events of his administration was unusual even for American politics in the middle nineties. Such extreme silver men as Senator Stewart of Nevada declared that Cleveland's second administration was probably the worst administration that ever occurred in this or any other country; that he was a bold and unscrupulous stock-jobber; that he deliberately caused the panic of 1893 and that he sent the Venezuela message in order to divert the attention of the people from the silver question. The New York *World* described the transaction between the government and the Morgan Company as a "bunco" game, and charged that Cleveland had dishonest, dishonorable and immoral reasons for bringing about the transaction and that he did it for a "consideration." Representative W. J. Bryan, who belonged to the President's party and who ordinarily was chivalrous to his opponents, declared that Cleveland could no more escape unharmed from association with the Morgan syndicate than he could expect to escape asphyxiation if he locked himself up in a room and turned on the gas. The Democratic party, he thought, should feel toward its leader as a confiding ward would feel toward a guardian who had squandered a rich estate, or as a passenger would feel toward a trainman who opened a switch and precipitated a wreck.

BIBLIOGRAPHICAL NOTE

The standard works, mentioned under Chapter V, by Dewey, Hepburn and Noyes continue valuable. The attitude of Hayes and of succeeding presidents is found in J. D. Richardson, *Messages and Papers of the Presidents;* F. W. Taussig, *The Silver Situation in the United States* (1892), is concise; *Political Science Quarterly,* III, 226, discusses the surplus revenue; *Quarterly Journal of Economics,* III, 436, on the direct tax; W. H. Glasson, *Federal Military Pensions,* has already been mentioned. W. J. Lauck, *Causes of the Panic of 1893* (1907), lays the blame for the industrial distress of 1893 wholly on the silver law of 1890. On the gold reserve, consult Grover Cleveland, *Presidential Problems;* D. R. Dewey, *National Problems* (1907); *Political Science Quarterly,* X, 573; and *Quarterly Journal of Economics,* XIII, 204. "The Silver Debate of 1890," in *Journal of Political Economy,* I, 535, contains a detailed account of the discussion in Congress. W. J. Bryan, *First Battle* (1897), should be consulted. On Coxey's "army" and similar demonstrations, see "The Industrial Armies and the Commonweal," by D. L. McMurray, in *Mississippi Valley Historical Review,* Dec., 1923.

CHAPTER XV

1896

The man on the rented farm who is raising corn at fifteen cents per bushel to pay interest on a mortgage is apt to be bitter.

HAMLIN GARLAND.

We beg no longer; we entreat no more; we petition no more. We defy them.

WILLIAM J. BRYAN.

The restoration of the Republican party to power and the election of McKinley assumed in [Hanna's] eyes the character of a patriotic mission.

HERBERT CROLY.

THE political situation in 1896, when the parties began to prepare for the presidential election, was more complex than it had been since 1860. The repeal, in 1893, of the purchase clause of the Sherman silver act had divided the Democrats into factions; the financial and industrial distress in the same year had been widely attributed to fear of Democratic misgovernment; the Wilson-Gorman tariff act of 1894 had discredited the party and aroused ill-feeling between the President and Congress; the Pullman strike and the use of the injunction had aroused bitterness in the labor element against the administration; the income tax decision of 1895 had done much to shake popular confidence in the Supreme Court; the Hawaiian and Venezuelan incidents had caused minor dissent in some quarters;[1] and the bond sales had made Cleveland intensely unpopular in the West and South. The Democratic party was demoralized and leaderless. The Republicans were better off because they had been out of power during the years of dissension and panic, but

[1] See below, pp. 362, 370.

they had been without a leader since the death of Blaine in 1893 and were far from united in regard to the most pressing issues. Indeed, the sectional differences in both parties, and the unexpected strength of the Populist movement caused no little anxiety among the political leaders. And finally, the volume and character of the currency was still undetermined. The Democrats had divided on the question. The Republicans were almost as little united; they had played politics in passing the Sherman silver act and three years later had assisted a President of the opposite party in accomplishing the repeal of its most important provision. From the standpoint of the silver supporters neither party organization was to be trusted. The outstanding political questions of 1896, therefore, were whether the supporters of silver could capture the machinery of one of the parties and whether the other unsettled issues could ride into the campaign on the strength of the financial agitation. The answers to these questions gave the campaign and election its peculiar significance.

The background of 1896 is to be found in the South and West, where the farmers' alliances and the Populist party continued their success in arousing and directing the ambitions of the discontented classes. In 1892, it will be remembered, the Populists had cast more than a million ballots and had chosen twenty-two presidential electors, two senators, and eleven representatives. In 1894, at the time of the congressional election, they had increased their voting strength more than forty per cent., and had elected six senators and six members of the House, besides several hundreds of state officials. In the Senate it happened that the two great parties had been almost equally strong, after the election of 1894, so that the Populist group had held the balance of power. The insistence of the South and West that Congress do something further for silver had not lessened. A measure providing for the coinage of a portion of the silver bullion in the treasury had been defeated in 1894 only through the President's veto.

Indeed the only hope of the East and of the supporters of the gold standard was the unflinching determination of the head of a party to which the East and the gold supporters were, in the main, opposed.

The growing enthusiasm for silver which was sweeping over the South and West and rapidly developing into something resembling frenzy was difficult for the more stolid East to comprehend. Not merely the politician, but the man on the street and in the store, the school-teacher, the farmer and the laborer, in those portions of the country, fell to discussing the virtues of silver as currency and the effect of a greater volume of circulating medium upon prices and prosperity. The two metals became personified in the minds of the people. Gold was the symbol of cruel, snobbish plutocracy; silver of upright democracy. Gold deserted the country in its hour of need; silver remained at home to minister to the wants of the people. Such arguments as those presented in *Coin's Financial School,* published in 1894, brought financial policy within the circle of the emotions of its readers even if they did not satisfy the more critical student of monetary problems. This influential little volume, written by W. H. Harvey, acted as a hand-book of free coinage, cleverly setting forth the major arguments for the increased use of silver and bringing forward objections which were triumphantly demolished. Simple illustrations enforced the lessons taught by its pages: a wood-cut of a cripple with one leg indicated how handicapped the country was without the free coinage of two metals; in another, Senator Sherman and President Cleveland were depicted digging out the silver portion of the foundations of a house which had been erected on a stable basis of both gold and silver; in a third, western farmers were seen industriously stuffing fodder into a cow which capitalists were milking for the benefit of New York and New England.[1] With the en-

[1] I have drawn at this point upon Peck, *Twenty Years of the Republic,* pp. 453–456.

thusiasm and the sincerity of the early crusaders, the people
assembled in ten thousand schoolhouses to debate the absorbing subject of the currency. Indeed the South and West had
become convinced that the miseries inflicted upon mankind by
war, pestilence and famine had been less "cruel, unpitying,
and unrelenting than the persistent and remorseless exaction"
which the contraction of the volume of the currency had made
upon society. Low prices, the stagnation of industry, empty
and idle stores, workshops and factories, the increase of crime
and bankruptcy—all were laid at the door of the gold
standard.

The East looked upon the rising in the West at first with
amusement, and was quite ready to accept the diagnosis of a
western newspaper man, quoted by Peck in his *Twenty Years
of the Republic:*

What's the matter with Kansas?

We all know; yet here we are at it again. We have an old moss-
back Jacksonian who snorts and howls because there is a bath-tub
in the State House. We are running that old jay for Governor. . . .
We have raked the ash-heap of failure in the State and found an
old human hoop-skirt who has failed as a business man, who has
failed as an editor, who has failed as a preacher, and we are going
to run him for Congressman-at-large. . . . Then we have discovered
a kid without a law practice and have decided to run him for
Attorney-General.

Later the East looked upon tendencies in the West with more
concern: Roosevelt, although admitting the honesty of the
Populists, characterized their ignorance as "abysmal"; others
were more inclined to doubt their sincerity; their conventions were supposed to be made up of cranks and unsexed
women; and their principles were looked upon as "wild and
crazy notions."

In fact it was no simple task to distinguish between the
legitimate grievances and ambitions of the westerners, and

their eccentricities and errors. Nor was this difficulty lessened by the reputation with which some of the proponents of silver were justly or unjustly credited. "Sockless Jerry" Simpson and Mrs. Lease were among them—the Mrs. Lease to whom was ascribed the remark "Kansas had better stop raising corn and begin raising hell!"[2] Benjamin R. Tillman was another—a rough, forceful character, leader of the poor whites and small farmers of South Carolina, organizer of the "wool hats" against the "silk hats" and the "kid gloves"— Governor of the state and later member of the federal Senate. Although a Democrat, he was thoroughly at odds with Cleveland, and publicly declared it was his ambition to stick his pitchfork into the President's sides.[3] Richard P. Bland, of Missouri, had the disadvantage of having been one of the earliest of the silver supporters, since he had initiated the bill which resulted in the Bland-Allison act, and was looked upon in the East as a thorough-going, free-silver radical. Governor Altgeld, of Illinois, leader of the Democrats of that state from 1892 to 1896, was a successful lawyer who was looked upon by his friends as a liberal-minded humanitarian, the friend of

> The mocked and the scorned and the wounded,
> the lame and the poor,

whose sympathies with the laboring classes had given him the support of the reformers and the wage earners. But his pardon of the Haymarket anarchists and his attitude during the Pullman strike had led the East to regard him as a dangerous revolutionist and an enemy to society.[4]

The free-silver movement nevertheless continued to gather momentum. For some years influential silver advocates had been associated in the Bimetallic League, an organization

---

[2] Peck, pp. 451–453.
[3] For brief accounts of Tillman, see Leupp, *National Miniatures*, p. 117; N. Y. *Times*, July 4, 1918; N. Y. *Evening Post*, July 3, 1918.
[4] *Cf.* Whitlock, *Forty Years of It*, p. 64 ff.; Altgeld, *Live Questions* and *The Cost of Something for Nothing*.

which supported the free coinage of both gold and silver. Among its members were prominent Democrats, Republicans and Populists, especially from the western states, and some of the foremost labor leaders. At one of its meetings in 1893 it was determined to invite every labor and industrial organization in the country to send delegates. A few experts, even in the East, gave some scientific support to the argument for the greater use of silver. Eastern Republicans like Senator Henry Cabot Lodge proposed free coinage of both metals by an international agreement, which, they thought, might be brought about through threats of tariff discrimination against nations refusing to adhere to the arrangement. A silver convention in Nebraska in 1894 was attended by a thousand delegates. From the point of view of party harmony the subject was a nuisance. Democratic state conventions were badly divided. Thirty of them adopted resolutions distinctly favorable to free coinage and fourteen opposed. Ten of the latter committed themselves definitely to the gold standard. The fourteen included all the northeastern states, together with Michigan, Wisconsin and Minnesota. Such gold Democrats as President Cleveland sought to stem the tide, but Cleveland's control over his followers was rapidly dwindling, and it seemed likely that the silver element of the party might reach out to seize the organization and displace the former leaders.

The Republican professional politicians were as ignorant of technical monetary problems as the Democrats, and moreover did not wish to risk popular disapproval in any section by utterances which might be offensive to that part of the country. The first Republican state convention during 1896 was that in Ohio. Its financial plank was awaited with interest, because of the early date of the meeting and because its proceedings were in the hands of friends of the most prominent candidate for the Republican presidential nomination. The convention dodged the issue by demanding that all our currency be ''sound as the Government and as untarnished as its honor," and that both metals be used as currency and kept at parity by legislative restrictions. The New York *Tribune* thought that this could mean nothing but a gold standard; the *Times* was fearful that it would lead to silver; the *Springfield Republican* condemned it as "chock full of double-dealing." Its ambiguity, however, was in line with the purposes and ambitions of two men who were actively preparing for the campaign of 1896—Marcus A. Hanna and Major William McKinley.

Marcus A. Hanna, or "Mark" Hanna as he was universally known, was an Ohioan, born in 1837.[5] As a young man he entered upon a business career in Cleveland, first in a wholesale grocery company, later in a coal and iron firm and finally in a variety of industrial and commercial enterprises which his energy and ability opened to him. The expansion of industrial America after the Civil War was coincident with the greater part of Hanna's career and he was a typical product of that period in his political, economic and social philosophy. After he had attained a degree of business success he became actively interested in politics and took a prominent part in placing Joseph B. Foraker in the governor's chair in Ohio in 1885. Strained relations between the two turned Hanna's attention to the fortunes of John Sherman. When it became apparent in 1888 that the presidential campaign would turn upon President Cleveland's tariff principles, Hanna, who looked upon the protective tariff as synonymous with industrial expansion and even of industrial safety, threw his weight upon the side of Sherman, who was again seeking the Republican nomination. The failure of Sherman was a blow to Hanna, but it called to his attention the pleasing personality of a more prominent protectionist, William McKinley. He was an important agent in McKinley's successful campaign for the governorship of Ohio in 1891. Two years later the Governor

---

[5] In connection with the following pages, consult Croly, *Marcus A. Hanna*, one of the few satisfactory biographies of this period.

met serious financial reverses, and again Hanna proved to be a firm friend. Aided by other men of means he rescued McKinley from bankruptcy. Between the two there sprang up a mutual admiration of unusual strength, and finally, in 1894–1895, Hanna withdrew from his business enterprises in order to devote his entire time to the political fortunes of his friend.

Mark Hanna had extraordinary capacity for leadership. Sociable, open-handed, full of energy, direct, aggressive, shrewd, daring, a hard fighter, a loyal friend, an organizer and a man of his word, he was essentially a man of action. In politics he was practical and straight-forward. He wanted results, not reforms, and results meant accepting the prevailing methods and using them. When he wished a street-railway franchise in Cleveland, he bought enough influence with the city government to get what he wanted, as others of his day did. He was a strict party man; good government and safety to industry, he believed, were dependent upon Republican control. Patriotism therefore demanded his utmost energy in getting Republicans elected. In political campaigns his counsel, his energy and his money were always available. A protective customs tariff, a "sound" currency system and a free hand in the conduct of business were the things which he most desired from the government.

William McKinley would have been a formidable competitor for the presidential nomination in 1896 even without the assistance of his rugged friend. His personality was attractive, in a pleasing, soothing, tactful, ingratiating way. His military career had been honorable even if not famous. For most of the time from 1877 to 1891 he had been a member of the House of Representatives, becoming identified particularly with the high protective tariff and acting as sponsor for the McKinley act of 1890. After being defeated for re-election, just subsequent to the passage of the tariff law, he had become Governor of Ohio for two terms. The panic of 1893 and the ill-fated Wilson-Gorman tariff act during the time when he was Governor caused the tide of popular favor to swing away from the Democrats; McKinley, as the apostle of protection, appeared in a more favorable light; and his partisans began to press him forward as the logical nominee for 1896 and as "the advance agent of Prosperity." The fact that his home was in a populous state in the Middle West was also in his favor, because the Republicans had frequently chosen their candidate from this debatable ground rather than from the Northeast, where success was to be had without a struggle.

Hanna's first care upon determining to devote himself to the interests of McKinley was to keep the candidate before the people as the one man who could rescue the nation from industrial depression. To that end he widely circulated the Cleveland *Leader*, a strong McKinley organ, for eighteen months at his own expense; he rented a house in Georgia, entertained Governor McKinley there and brought numbers of southern politicians to meet the candidate; and experienced political workers were sent all over the country and especially to the South to prepare the way for the election of delegates to the nominating convention. Hanna himself went to the East to discover on what terms the support of some of the states in that section could be obtained. On his return he reported that aid would be assured by a guarantee that the patronage of the administration would go to certain powerful politicians; Hanna thought the bargain a desirable one, but the candidate objected and Hanna acquiesced. The campaign of publicity and of personal canvass for delegates and influence continued. First and last, it is estimated, Hanna contributed over $100,000 for this purpose, urging his assistants always to use funds only for legitimate ends, although promising McKinley partisans who aided in the work that they would be "consulted" in the disposition of patronage.

Two difficulties stood in the way of completely ensuring the choice of McKinley as the candidate by the convention. Several states had "favorite sons" whom they would be sure to present, and if so many of these should appear as to prevent McKinley's nomination on the first ballot or at least on an early one, there might be a stampede to an unknown man—a "dark horse"—and then Hanna's ambitions would be frustrated. Thomas B. Reed of Maine was an especial source of anxiety as he possessed considerable strength throughout New England. To guard against such a danger, Hanna sedulously cultivated the popular demand for Governor McKinley and also fought in the state conventions for delegates even against favorite sons. A crucial state was Illinois, where Senator Cullom was powerful. The Senator says that a representative of McKinley offered him "all sorts of inducements" to withdraw, but McKinley's biographer mentions no such attempt at a bargain. Eventually Cullom made the fight and was defeated, and from then on, the nomination of McKinley seemed sure unless he should be tripped by the currency issue.

The silver question was the second obstacle in the way of success. Not only was the party divided, but McKinley's record on the subject was far from consistent. He had voted for the Bland free-silver bill in 1877, for the Bland-Allison act in 1878 and for the passage of that act over President Hayes's veto. In 1890 he had urged the passage of the Sherman silver purchase law, intimating that he would support a free coinage measure if it were possible to pass it. Hardly more than a year later he was campaigning for the governorship of Ohio, and there he denounced the free coinage of silver and advocated international bimetallism. In 1896 McKinley feared that a definite public utterance on the one side or the other of the question would widen the division in the party, prevent his nomination and lose the election. Hence the ambiguous currency plank in the Ohio state convention and hence, also, the refusal of the candidate to commit himself openly. Nevertheless he commissioned a friend to go to the East and explain his attitude privately to certain leaders and prominent business men, urging them not to force a declaration for gold before the convention met. In this way, he thought, the currency issue might be subordinated, the tariff emphasized and the party held together. In this state of uncertainty the currency situation was allowed to rest until the convention met at St. Louis on June 16.

The platform adopted was, for the most part, of the usual sort. It urged popular attention to the matchless achievements of thirty years of Republican rule and contrasted that period of "unequalled success and prosperity" with the "unparalleled incapacity, dishonor, and disaster" of Democratic government; it promised the "most ample protection" to the products of mine, field and factory; generous pensions, American control of Hawaii, a Nicaragua canal, the Monroe Doctrine, restricted immigration and the arbitration of labor disputes affecting interstate commerce received the support of the party.

It was the currency plank, however, that differentiated the platform of 1896 from that of other campaigns. Many Republican leaders and business men, particularly in the East, were disposed to call for a definite party statement in favor of a gold standard and had reached the point where they could not be put off by the usual meaningless straddle. Thomas C. Platt, Henry Cabot Lodge, Joseph B. Foraker, Charles W. Fairbanks and other party chiefs were among them. Hanna was ready to declare for gold after he had been assured of the nomination of his candidate. McKinley was willing to stand for gold, although he preferred not to mention that word in the plank and hoped to make the contest on the tariff. Moreover so many silver delegates had already been elected to the Democratic convention, which was soon to be held, that a definite utterance from that party seemed a certainty. The Prohibitionists had already divided into halves over the dominant issue. It was almost imperative, therefore, for the Republican convention to be more explicit than it had hitherto ventured to be. As leader after leader arrived who was insistent upon a gold standard, it became increasingly evident to Hanna that he must proceed with caution. If McKinley committed himself to gold, the silver advocates would balk at his candidacy, and perhaps unite on somebody else; if he committed himself to silver, he would lose the eastern leaders. The astute Hanna therefore allowed sentiment in favor of the gold plank to gather force, although holding the discussion as far as possible under cover, and kept McKinley from making a definite statement. Then at the last minute, when the McKinley delegates were numerous enough to ensure the nomination of the Major and when it was too late for the silver forces to agree upon an opposition candidate, Hanna gave way to the pressure for gold and agreed to the plank which he had always favored.[6]

Despite the canny management of Hanna a defection took place over the decision on the currency issue. As soon as the platform was read, Senator Henry M. Teller, of Colorado, moved to replace the gold plank by one advocating the free coinage of silver. The earnestness with which Teller urged the adoption of the substitute was an indication of the sincerity of the western wing of the party. He had been a strict Republican since the formation of the party in the mid-fifties, yet he now found himself forced to accept a policy which he believed to be pernicious or break the political bonds which had held him for forty years. The majority of the convention,

[6] As finally adopted, the gold plank asserted: "We are unalterably opposed to every measure calculated to debase our currency or impair the credit of our country. We are, therefore, opposed to the free coinage of silver, except by international agreement with the leading commercial nations of the world, which we pledge ourselves to promote, and until such agreement can be obtained the existing gold standard must be preserved. All our silver and paper currency must be maintained at parity with gold, and we favor all measures designed to maintain inviolably the obligations of the United States and all our money, whether coin or paper, at the present standard, the standard of the most enlightened nations of the earth." Several leaders claimed to have been the real author of the gold plank. It seems more nearly true that many men came to the convention prepared to insist on a definite statement and that each thought himself the originator of the party policy.

however, was determined to adopt the gold plank and overwhelmingly defeated the Teller amendment, whereupon the Senator and thirty-three other silver supporters solemnly withdrew from the hall.

The way was now clear for the nomination of a candidate. Thomas B. Reed, Senator Quay and other favorite sons received but scant support, and McKinley was nominated by an overwhelming majority on the first ballot. Garrett A. Hobart, a lawyer and business man whose reputation was confined to New Jersey, his home state, was nominated for the vice-presidency. The platform and the candidate were generally hailed with favor in the East. To be sure, critical newspapers were inclined to look askance upon McKinley's past. The New York *Evening Post* favored a gold standard but decried the candidate's "absence of settled convictions about leading questions of the day, and his want of clear knowledge on any subject." Yet on the whole, the platform and the candidate were popular, and, in view of the serious factional disputes among the Democrats, the Republicans seemed likely to make good their boast that victory would be so easy that they could nominate and elect a "rag baby" if they chose. The redoubtable Hanna was appointed chairman of the National Republican Committee, from which office he was to direct the campaign. McKinley still believed that the contest would be of the old-fashioned sort and that it would turn on the tariff, despite the platform utterance of the party. And so it might have proved had it not been for an important change of purpose and leadership in the opposition.

The friends of free silver coinage went to the Democratic convention at Chicago on July 7 with the same determination to get a definite statement on the currency question that had characterized the eastern leaders at the Republican convention. Without the loss of a moment they wrested the control of the organization from the former leaders by defeating Senator Hill of New York, a gold Democrat, for the temporary chairmanship and electing Senator Daniel of Virginia, a recognized proponent of free silver. Hill's support came mainly from the Northeast; Daniel's, from the West and South. Senator White of California, a representative of the silver wing, was then chosen permanent chairman and the convention was ready for the contest over the platform. While it awaited that document, however, it listened to several favorite leaders, of whom Senator Tillman and Governor Altgeld of Illinois were the best known. From the sentiments expressed by these men it was clear that the radical Democrats believed that they were speaking for the masses of the people and that they were bent upon making far-reaching changes both in the organization and the creed of the party.

A disquieting feature was a degree of turbulence beyond that which usually characterizes our nominating conventions. The official proceedings record the following, for example, while Senator Tillman was addressing the delegates:

I hope that when this vast assembly shall have dispersed to its home the many thousands of my fellow-citizens who are here will carry hence a different opinion of the pitchfork man from South Carolina to that which they now hold. I come to you from the South—from the home of secession—from that State where the leaders of—(the balance of the sentence of the speaker was drowned by hisses). Mr. Tillman (resuming): There are only three things in the world that can hiss—a goose, a serpent, and a man . . .

In the last three or four or five years the Western people have come to realize that the condition of the South and the condition of the West are identical. Hence we find to-day that the Democratic party of the West is here almost in solid phalanx appealing to the South, and the South has responded—to come to their help.' . . . Some of my friends from the South and elsewhere have said that this is not a sectional issue. I say it is a sectional issue. (Long prolonged hissing).

At length the platform was presented. It was a summary of the complaints against the East which had been forming

in the West and South ever since the days of the Greenbackers
and the "Ohio idea." It recognized first that the money
question was paramount to all others; laid hard times at the
door of the gold standard, which it denounced as a British
policy; and demanded the free coinage of both metals at the
existing legal ratio, under which sixteen parts of silver by
weight were declared equivalent to one part of gold in mint-
ing coins. Nor would the party wait for the consent of any
other nation. It opposed the issuance of interest-bearing
bonds in time of peace, condemned the bond transactions of
the Cleveland administration and denounced the national
bank-note system. The McKinley tariff was declared a prolific
breeder of trusts which enriched the few at the expense of
the many. The plank concerning the income tax, which had
so recently been declared unconstitutional by the Supreme
Court, excited much condemnation among Republicans and
conservative Democrats, who denounced it as an attack on
the Court. It noted that the Court had uniformly sustained
income taxes for nearly a hundred years and declared it to
be the duty of Congress

to use all the constitutional power which remains after that decision, or which may come from its reversal by the court as it may
hereafter be constituted, so that the burdens of taxation may be
equally and impartially laid, to the end that wealth may bear its
due proportion of the expenses of the government.

The reaction of the party on the labor disputes of recent years
and especially the Pullman strike was clearly in evidence.
Arbitration of such controversies was called for; "interference" by federal authorities in local affairs was condemned;
government by injunction was objected to; and the passage
of such laws was demanded as would protect all the interests
of the laboring classes.

A minority of the platform committee now presented the
opposing point of view. It objected to many of the planks;

complained that some were ill-considered, others revolutionary; and offered two amendments, one advocating the gold standard, the other expressing commendation of Cleveland's administration. The contest was then on. Tillman excoriated Cleveland and declared that the East held the West and South in economic bondage; Hill denounced the currency, income tax and Supreme Court planks as furiously as any Republican could have wished. The currency plank, he thought, was unwise, that on the income tax unnecessary, that on the Court assailed the supreme tribunal, and the entire program was "revolutionary." As yet, nobody had quite expressed the feelings of the convention. Tillman was too crude; Hill had no remedy for long-standing ills. At this juncture William J. Bryan stepped upon the platform. He was a young man— only thirty-six years of age—and known but slightly as a representative from Nebraska who possessed many of the arts and abilities of an orator. Bryan began with a modest and tactful declaration that his opposition to the gold wing of the party was based solely on principles and not at all on personalities. The convention had met, he insisted, not to debate but to register a judgment already rendered by the people. Old leaders had been cast aside because they had refused to express the desires of those whom they aspired to lead. Briefly he outlined the reply of the radicals to the objections made by Hill and the gold wing to the proposed platform. The conservatives, Bryan declared, had complained that free silver coinage would disturb business:

We say to you that you have made the definition of a business man too limited in its application. The man who is employed for wages is as much a business man as his employer; the attorney in a country town is as much a business man as the corporation counsel in a great metropolis; the merchant at the cross-roads store is as much a business man as the merchant of New York; the farmer who goes forth in the morning and toils all day—who begins in the spring and toils all summer—and who by the application of brain and muscle to the natural resources of the country creates wealth, is as much a business man as the man who goes upon the board of trade and bets upon the price of grain; the miners who go down a thousand feet into the earth, or climb two thousand feet upon the cliffs, and bring forth from their hiding places the precious metals to be poured into the channels of trade are as much business men as the few financial magnates who, in a back room, corner the money of the world. We come to speak for this broader class of business men.

The time was at hand, Bryan insisted, when the currency issue must be squarely met:

We have petitioned and our petitions have been scorned; we have entreated, and our entreaties have been disregarded; we have begged, and they have mocked when our calamity came. We beg no longer; we entreat no more; we petition no more. We defy them.

The radical wing of the Democracy had now found its orator. Every word was driven straight to the hearts of the sympathetic hearers. The income tax law had been constitutional, Bryan complained, until one of the judges of the Supreme Court had changed his mind; the tariff was less important than the currency because "protection has slain its thousands, the gold standard has slain its tens of thousands." Fundamentally, he insisted, the contest was between the idle holders of idle capital and the struggling masses who produce the capital:

If they come to meet us on that issue we can present the history of our nation. More than that; we can tell them that they will search the pages of history in vain to find a single instance where the common people of any land have ever declared themselves in favor of the gold standard. They can find where the holders of fixed investments have declared for a gold standard, but not where the masses have . . .

You come to us and tell us that the great cities are in favor of the gold standard; we reply that the great cities rest upon our broad and fertile prairies. Burn down your cities and leave our farms, and your cities will spring up again as if by magic; but destroy our farms and the grass will grow in the streets of every city in the country . . .

Having behind us the producing masses of this nation and the world, supported by the commercial interests, the laboring interests, and the toilers everywhere, we will answer their demand for a gold standard by saying to them: You shall not press down upon the brow of labor this crown of thorns, you shall not crucify mankind upon a cross of gold.

The frenzy of approval which this brief speech aroused was proof that the West and South had found a herald. Whether wisely or not, the radicals acclaimed their leader and the party was embarked upon a program that made the campaign of 1896 a memorable one. Without further ado, the amendments of the conservatives were voted down—the vote being sectional, as before. Proposals that changes in the monetary standard should not apply to existing contracts and that if free coinage should not effect a parity between gold and silver at a ratio of 16 to 1 within a year, it should bo suspended, were both voted down without so much as a division. The platform was then adopted by an overwhelming majority and radical democracy had the bit in its teeth. In the East the platform was viewed with amazement. The New York *World*, a Democratic newspaper, expressed the opinion that the only doubt about the election would be the size of McKinley's victory. The Republican *Tribune* thought that the party was afflicted with "lunacy"; that it had become the "avowed champion of the right of pillage, riot and train-wrecking"; that the platform was an anarchist manifesto and a "call to every criminal seeking a chance for outrage."

Before Bryan's speech it had been impossible to foretell who the party candidate for the presidency would be, although the veteran free silver leader, Richard P. Bland, had been looked upon as a logical choice in case his well-known principles should become those of the convention. After the speech, however, it was clear that Bryan embodied the feelings of many of his colleagues and on the fifth ballot he was chosen as the candidate. The vice-presidential choice was Arthur Sewall, of Maine, a shipbuilder and banker who believed in the free coinage of silver.

The gold Democrats were now in a quandary. Many of them had refrained from voting at all in the convention after the silver element had gained control. Strict partisans, however, adopted the position of Senator Hill who was asked after the convention whether he was a Democrat still. "Yes," he is said to have retorted, "I am a Democrat still—very still." Some frankly turned toward the Republican party, while others organized the National Democratic party and adopted a traditional Democratic platform, with a gold plank. After considering the possibility of nominating President Cleveland for a third term, the party chose John M. Palmer for the presidency and Simon B. Buckner for the vice-presidency. Soon after the Democratic convention, the People's party and the Silver party met in St. Louis. Both nominated Bryan for the presidency, and thereafter the Democrats and the Populists made common cause.

At the opening of the campaign, then, it was evident that class and sectional hatreds would enter largely into the contest. The Populists and the radical Democrats felt that they were fighting the battle of the masses against "plutocracy"—the subtle and corrupting control of public affairs by the possessors of great fortunes; they thought that they saw arrayed against them the forces of wealth and the corporations, seeking to enslave them. The conservative Democrats and the gold Republicans, saw in their opponents an organized attempt to carry out a program of dishonesty and socialism. The one side believed that the creditor class desired to scale debts upward; the other, that the debtor class wished to scale them down. The radicals believed that the Supreme Court was in the control of the wealthy; the conservatives, that their opponents sought to assail the highest tribunal in the land. The peculiar circumstances preceding the year 1896, however, focussed attention on the monetary standard rather than upon the other demands of the Populist-Democratic fusion.

Each candidate adopted a plan of campaign that was suited to his individual situation. Bryan was relatively unknown and he therefore decided to appeal directly to the people, where his powers as a speaker would have great effect. The usual "notification" meeting was held in Madison Square Garden, in New York City, so as to carry the cause into the heart of "the enemy's country." During the few months of the campaign the Democratic candidate traveled 18,000 miles, made 600 speeches and addressed nearly five million people. The effect was immediate. The forces of social unrest, hitherto silent in great measure, were becoming vocal and nobody could measure their extent. McKinley had prophesied that thirty days after the Republican convention nothing would be heard about the currency. When the thirty days had passed, on the contrary, scarcely anything was heard except that very question. Whatever his personal wishes, McKinley must meet the problem face to face, and in alarm, Hanna and the Republican campaign leaders put forth unparalleled efforts to save the party from defeat.

The share of McKinley in these efforts was a novel one. Instead of going upon the stump, he remained at his home in Canton, Ohio. A constant stream of visiting delegations of supporters from all points of the compass came to hear him speak from his front porch. Some of the delegations came spontaneously; the visits of others were prearranged; but in all cases the speeches delivered were looked over beforehand with great care. The candidate memorized or read his own remarks and carefully revised those which the spokesman of the visitors planned to offer. In this way, any such untoward incident as the Burchard affair was avoided and the accounts of the front-porch speeches which went out through the press contained nothing which would injure the chances for success. The effectiveness of the plan was attested on all sides.

In addition, extraordinary attempts were put forth to instruct the people on various aspects of the currency question. A small army was organized to distribute literature and address rallies; 120,000,000 documents were distributed from the Chicago and New York headquarters; newspapers were supplied with especially prepared matter; posters and buttons were scattered by the carload. At the dinner-table, on the street corner, in the railroad train, in store, office and shop, the people gave themselves over to a heated discussion of the merits of gold and silver as currency and to the feasibility of free coinage at a ratio of 16 to 1. The amount of money which these efforts required was unusually large. Business men and banking institutions, especially in New York, contributed liberally. The Standard Oil Company gave $250,000; large life insurance companies helped freely, although the fact was well concealed at the time. Business men were fearful that Bryan's election would mean a great shrinkage in the value of their properties. Many feared that the Democrats would assail the Supreme Court and that their leader would surround himself with advisors of a reckless and revolutionary character. Funds therefore poured into the Republican war-chest to an amount estimated at three and a half million dollars.

Before the close of the campaign a feeling akin to terror swept over the East; contracts were made contingent upon the election of McKinley; employees were paid on the Saturday night before election day and notified that they need not return to work in the event of Democratic success. Although caution and good manners characterized the utterances of the two candidates, their supporters were hardly so restrained. The following, for example, is typical of the editorial utterances of the New York *Tribune;*

Let us begin with the Ten Commandments. "Thou shalt not take the name of the Lord thy God in vain." The Bryan campaign from beginning to end has been marked with such a flood of blasphemy, of taking God's name in vain, as this country, at least, has never known before. "Thou shalt not steal." The very foundation of the Bryan platform is wholesale theft. "Thou shalt not bear false witness." In what day have Bryan and his followers failed to utter lies, libels and forgeries? "Thou shalt not covet." Why, almost every appeal made by Bryan, or for him, has been addressed directly to the covetousness, the envy, and all the unhallowed passions of human nature. A vote for Bryan is a vote for the abrogation of those four Commandments.

At the close of the campaign *The Nation* sagely observed, "Probably no man in civil life has succeeded in inspiring so much terror, without taking life, as Bryan."

The result of the election was decisive. McKinley and a Republican House of Representatives were elected, and the choice of a Republican Senate assured. The successful candidate received seven million votes—a half million more than his competitor. All the more densely populated states, together with the large cities—where the greatest accumulations of capital had taken place—were carried by the Republicans. Not a state north of the Potomac–Ohio line and east of the Mississippi was Democratic, and even Kentucky, by a narrow margin, and West Virginia crowded their way into the Republican column. On the other hand Bryan's hold on the South and West was almost equally strong. Never before had any presidential candidate received so great a vote and not for twenty years did a Democratic candidate surpass it. Moreover, although the Democratic vote on the Atlantic seaboard was less than that received by Cleveland in 1892, Bryan's support in the Middle West showed considerable gains over the earlier year, while Kansas, Nebraska and all the mining states except California were carried by the silver cause. On the whole the election seemed to indicate that the voters of the country, after unusual study of the issues of the campaign, clearly distrusted the free-silver program, but that class and sectional discontent had reached large proportions. The political results of the election of 1896 were important. It definitely fixed the attitude of the Republican party on the currency question; it gave the party control of the executive chair and of Congress at an important time, and it ensured the domination of the propertied classes and the *laissez faire* philosophy in the party organization. On the other hand, the Democratic party had incurred the suspicion and hostility of the East, with hardly a compensating increase of strength in the West; its principles had become radical for that day and had abruptly changed from those of previous years; its membership included more of the discontented classes than before; and its leadership had been snatched from the hands of an experienced and conservative leader and placed in the care of an untried radical. It remained to be seen whether the victors would attempt to study and meet the complaints of the farmer and the wage earner; whether the new Republican leaders would be able to preserve the *laissez faire* attitude toward the railroads and the corporations; and whether the forces of dissent represented in Populism and radical Democracy had received a death blow or only a rebuff.

BIBLIOGRAPHICAL NOTE

Peck contains one of the most illuminating accounts of the rising in the West, together with the campaign of 1896. H. Croly, *Marcus A. Hanna* (1912), is one of the few critical biographies of leaders who have lived since the Civil War. W. J. Bryan, *The First Battle* (1897), is indispensable; C. S. Olcott, *William McKinley* (2 vols., 1916), is uncritical and eulogistic, but makes important material available; C. A. Beard, *Contemporary American History* (1914), contains a good chapter; W. H. Harvey, *Coin's Financial School* (1894), is mentioned in the text; Carl Becker's clever essay in *Turner Essays in American History* (1910). throws light on Kansas

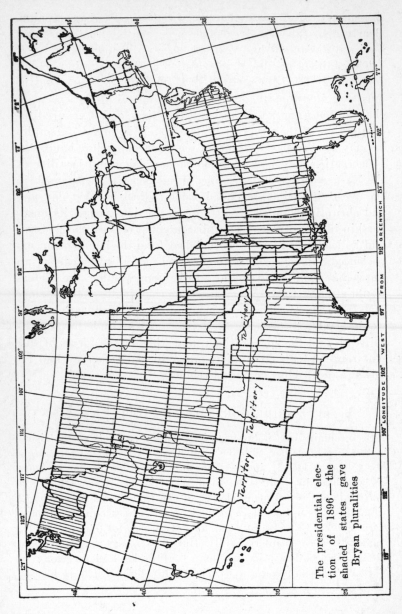

The presidential election of 1896 — the shaded states gave Bryan pluralities

psychology; S. J. Buck, *Agrarian Crusade* (1920), is excellent. Consult also D. R. Dewey, *National Problems* (1907); H. H. Kohlsaat, *From McKinley to Harding,* (1923); F. E. Haynes, *James Baird Weaver* (1919). J. A. Woodburn, *Political Parties and Party Problems* (1914); *Quarterly Journal of Economics,* X, 269; and F. E. Haynes, *Third Party Movements* (1916). The files of *The Nation,* and the New York *Tribune* and *Sun* well portray eastern opinion. The references to the rise of the populist movement under Chap. XII are also of service.

CHAPTER XVI

THE TREND OF FOREIGN RELATIONS

The foreign trade of the United States was in 1865, $404,775,000 in 1872, $1,071,000,000; in 1900, $2,244,000,000.

STATISTICAL ABSTRACT OF THE UNITED STATES, 1924.

. . . down to the time of the Spanish War it was not worth the while for any public officer of the United States to familiarize himself with foreign affairs unless it was the Secretary of State.

ELIHU ROOT.

. . . our situation in this [Samoan] matter was inconsistent with the mission and traditions of our Government, in violation of the principles we profess, and in all its phases mischievous and vexatious.

GROVER CLEVELAND.

Let the fight [with Great Britain over Venezuela] come if it must; I don't care whether our sea coast cities are bombarded or not; we would take Canada.

THEODORE ROOSEVELT.

AFTER the international issues arising from the Civil War were settled, and before foreign relations began to become more important late in the nineties, our diplomatic history showed the same lack of definiteness and continuity that stamped the history of politics during the same years. Eleven different men held the post of Secretary of State during the thirty-four years from 1865 to 1898, one of them, Blaine, serving at two separate times. The political situation in Washington changed frequently, few men of outstanding capacity as diplomatists were in the cabinets, and most of the problems which arose were not such as would excite the interest of great international minds. That any degree of unity in the conduct of our foreign relations was attained is due in part to the continuous service of such men as A. A. Adee, who was connected with the state department

354

from 1878 to 1924, and Professor John Bassett Moore, long in the department and frequently available as a counsellor. Despite the relative unimportance of most of the diplomatic incidents which caught the public attention, and despite the evanescent character of the public interest in them, there were deep-seated forces at work which were destined to affect American life profoundly. The extension of trade to every portion of the earth was the most pervasive and far-reaching of these forces.

Never had the total foreign trade of the United States reached so high a figure as one billion dollars until 1872. Never, after that year, did it fall below. In 1900 it reached two billion dollars,—which it has never since failed to exceed. So large a volume of traffic involved the government in a thousand ways. Traders traveling abroad must be protected. New sources of materials and new markets for exports must be discovered and opened. Facilities for coaling and refitting naval vessels had to be found. These activities and others of a like character fell to the State Department, with its diplomatic and consular service, and to the Navy Department.

The consular service had been created in an unsystematic and elementary form in 1792, but not until 1856 had the rights and duties of consuls been clearly defined, and an attempt made to establish a service composed of trained men. The attempt was far from successful, measured according to more recent standards, because the appointments of the men and their advance in rank and pay were altogether too haphazard and dependent on political influence. There was, nevertheless, a tolerable consular service composed of men stationed in the principal centers of the world's trade. Their duties were by no means restricted to commercial matters, but their most important function was the promotion of the export and import business. Beginning in 1856 a yearly

Commercial Relations of the United States was published, containing reports from the consuls on the trade situation in the countries to which they were assigned. Annual reports, however, were inadequate to meet the demands of the manufacturer and the farmer who were seeking an outlet for their surplus, and in 1880 the publication of the *Monthly Consular Report* was inaugurated. In 1898 the State Department began the publication of daily reports containing information regarding trade opportunities which must be taken advantage of immediately. It is distributed freely to firms and associations interested in foreign commerce. The purpose of the several reports is to publish ways and means for extending American trade, to pass along ideas which may serve to improve methods and processes, and to give information relating to currency changes, freight and tariff rates, port regulations and the like. It is significant that both Grant and Hayes, the first presidents after the close of the Civil War, pledged their devotion to the expansion of the foreign market in their opening messages to Congress; and that Arthur, at the outset of his administration, urged a better navy to protect "the varied interests of our foreign trade."

EARLY INTERESTS IN THE PACIFIC OCEAN

Even before the Civil War, Americans had been interested in the affairs of the nations whose shores were touched by the Pacific Ocean. Missionaries and traders had long visited China and Japan. Grant, in 1869, recognizing "the necessity of looking to other markets for the sale of our surplus," urged upon Congress especial attention to China and Japan, and among other things recommended that the mission to the former power be raised to the first class. During the years when the transcontinental railroads were being built, as has been seen, the construction companies looked to China for a labor supply, and there followed a stream of Chinese immigrants who were the cause of a difficult international problem. Our relations with Japan were extremely friendly. Until the middle of the nineteenth century the Japanese had been almost completely cut off from the remainder of the world, desiring neither to give to the rest of humanity nor to take from them. In 1854 Commodore Matthew C. Perry of the United States Navy had succeeded in obtaining permission for American ships to take coal and provisions at two Japanese ports. Townsend Harris shortly afterwards had been appointed consul-general to Japan and his knowledge of the East and his tactful diplomacy had procured increased trade rights and other privileges. In 1863 a Japanese prince had sought to close the strait of Shimonoseki which connects the inland sea of Japan with the outside ocean. American, French and Dutch vessels had been fired upon, and eventually an international expedition had been sent to open the strait by force. Seventeen ships of war had quickly brought the prince to terms. An indemnity had been demanded, of which the United States had received a share. The fund remained in the treasury untouched until 1883 when it was returned to Japan. The latter received the refund as "a strong manifestation of that spirit of justice and equity which has always animated the United States in its relations with Japan."

The purchase of Alaska in 1867, stretched a long, curved finger out towards the Asiatic coast, but there was little interest in the new acquisition and no knowledge of its size or resources.[1] Its peculiar geographical configuration, however, brought the United States into a diplomatic controversy from which it emerged with little credit. An arm or peninsula of the possession extends far out into the Pacific and is continued by the Aleutian Islands, which resemble a series of stepping-stones reaching toward Siberia.[2] Bering Sea is al-

[1] Cf. Fish, American Diplomacy, 398.
[2] Cf. map. p. 11.

most enclosed by Alaska and the Islands. Within the Sea and particularly on the islands of St. Paul and St. George in the Pribilof group, large numbers of seals gathered during the spring and summer to rear their young. In the autumn the herds migrated to the south, passing out through the narrow straits between the members of the Aleutian group, and were particularly open to attack at these points. As early as 1870 the United States government leased the privilege of hunting fur seals on St. Paul and St. George to the Alaska Commercial Company, but the business was so attractive that vessels came to the Aleutian straits from many parts of the Pacific, and it looked as if the United States must choose between the annihilation of the herds and the adoption of some means for protecting them. The revenue service thereupon began the seizure in 1886 of British sealing vessels, taking three in that year and six during the next. The British government protested against the seizures on the ground that they had taken place more than three miles from shore —three miles being the limit to the jurisdiction of any nation, according to international law. The Alaskan Court which upheld the seizures justified itself by the claim that the whole Bering Sea was part of the territory of Alaska and thus was comparable to a harbor or closed sea (*mare clausum*), but Secretary Blaine disavowed this contention. The United States then requested the governments of several European countries, together with Japan, to cooperate for the better protection of the fisheries, but no results were reached.

Continuance of the seizures in 1889 brought renewed protests from Lord Salisbury, who was in charge of foreign affairs. Blaine retorted that the destruction of the herds was *contra bonos mores* and that it was no more defensible even outside the three mile limit than destructive fishing on the banks of Newfoundland by the explosion of dynamite would be. Lord Salisbury replied that fur seals were wild animals, *ferae naturae*, and not the property of any individual until captured. An extended diplomatic correspondence ensued, which resulted in a treaty of arbitration in 1892.[3] A tribunal of seven arbitrators was established, two appointed by the Queen of England, two by the President, and one each by the rulers of France, Italy and Sweden and Norway, the last two being under one sovereign at that time. Several questions were submitted to the tribunal. What exclusive rights does the United States have in the Bering Sea? What right of protection or property does the United States have in the seals frequenting the islands in the Sea? If the United States has no exclusive rights over the seals, what steps ought to be taken to protect them? Great Britain also presented to the arbitrators the question whether the seizures of seal-hunting ships had been made under the authority of the government of the United States.

The decisions were uniformly against the American contention. It was decided that our jurisdiction in the Bering Sea did not extend beyond the three mile limit and that therefore the United States had no right of protection or property in the seals. A set of regulations for the protection of the herds was also drawn up. Another negotiation resulted in the payment of $473,000 damages by the United States for the illegal seizures of British vessels.[4]

Another indication that the United States was extending its interests into the sphere of the Pacific Ocean appeared as

[3] J. W. Foster, who was intimately connected with the case, suggests that the defects in the American argument were due partly to following briefs prepared by an agent of the Alaska Commercial Company in Washington. The agent was interested in getting everything possible for his company but his knowledge of the law in the case was slight. Cf. Foster, Memoirs, II, p. 26 f.; Moore, American Diplomacy, pp. 97–104.

[4] The attempts to protect the herds by government regulation failed to have any important results. In 1911 a convention was entered into by which Great Britain, Russia, Japan and the United States agreed to prohibit their citizens from "pelagic" sealing (killing in the open sea) in the waters of the North Pacific. The United States also prohibited its citizens in 1912 from killing on land, mainly the Pribilof islands, for five years. Under these restrictions the herds rapidly increased and in 1925 contained 723,050 seals.

early as 1872, when a Samoan chief expressed to an American
naval commander a desire to grant the United States the
privileges of a naval station in the harbor of Pagopago on the
island of Tutuila. Tutuila is far from American shores, being below the equator on the under side of the world, but the
harbor of Pagopago is an usually good one and its relation
to the extension of American commerce in the South Pacific
was readily seen. In 1878 the agreement was placed on a
treaty basis. Not long afterward, similar trading privileges
were granted to Germany and Great Britain. Conditions in
the islands had by no means been peaceful even before the
advent of the foreigners with their intrigues and jealousies,
and in 1885 the Germans, taking advantage of a native rebellion, hauled down the Samoan flag on the government building
in Apia and seemed about to take control. In the following
year, at the request of the Samoan king, the American consul
Greenebaum proclaimed a protectorate and hoisted the United
States flag. The act was unauthorized and was disavowed at
once by the government at Washington. In the hope of establishing order in the Islands, Bayard, Secretary of State in
President Cleveland's first administration, suggested a triple
conference of Germany, Great Britain and the United States
in Washington. During a recess in the conference a native
rebellion overturned the Samoan government and Germany
assumed virtual control. While civil war raged among native
factions, the Germans landed armed forces for the protection
of their interests. The American and British governments,
fearful of danger to their rights, already had war vessels in
the harbor of Apia and armed conflict seemed almost inevitable when a sudden hurricane on March 16, 1889, destroyed
all the vessels except one. The *Calliope* (English), steamed
out to sea in the teeth of the great storm and escaped in safety.
In the face of such a catastrophe all smaller ills were forgotten and peace reigned for the moment in Samoa.

Meanwhile, just as Cleveland was retiring from office for the first time, another conference of the three powers was arranged which provided a somewhat complicated triple protectorate. After a few years of quiet, another native insurrection called attention to the islands. Cleveland was again in the presidential chair, and in a message to Congress on December 3, 1894, he expressed his belief that the United States had made a mistake in departing from its century-old policy of avoiding entangling alliances with foreign powers:

The present government (he asserted), has utterly failed to correct . . . the very evils it was intended to prevent. It has not stimulated our commerce with the islands. Our participation in its establishment against the wishes of the natives was in plain defiance of the conservative teachings and warnings of the wise and patriotic men who laid the foundations of our free institutions, and I invite an expression of the judgment of Congress on the propriety of steps being taken by this Government looking to the withdrawal from its engagements with the other powers.

A year later, in 1895, he returned to the subject more earnestly than ever. A report from the Secretary of State presented the history of our Samoan relations and ventured a judgment that the only fruits which had fallen to the United States were expense, responsibility and entanglement. Nothing came of Cleveland's recommendation, but the continuance of native quarrels later necessitated another commission to the islands. The American member reported that the harbor of Apia was full of war vessels and the region about covered with armed men, but that "not the sail or smoke of a single vessel of commerce was to be seen there or about the coasts of these beautiful islands." In 1899, the triple protectorate was abandoned, as it had complicated the task of governing the islands. The United States received Tutuila with the harbor of Pagopago, Germany took the remainder of the group, and England retired altogether.[5] The trend of Samoan relations was significant: our connection with the islands began with the desire to possess a coaling station; the possession first resulted in entanglements with other nations, and later in the question whether we ought not to withdraw; and eventually we withdrew from some of the responsibilities but not from all. Despite its traditional policy of not contracting entangling alliances, the United States was in the contest for the commerce of the Pacific to stay.

Among the many troublesome questions that faced President Cleveland when he entered upon the Presidency in 1893 for the second time, the status of the Hawaiian Islands was important. Since the development of the Pacific Coast of the United States in the forties and fifties, there had been a growing trade between the islands and this country. Reciprocity and even annexation had been projected. In 1875 a reciprocity arrangement was consummated, a part of which was a stipulation that none of the territory of Hawaii should be leased or disposed of to any other power. In this way a suggestion was made of ultimate annexation. Moreover the commercial results of the treaty were such as to make a friendly connection with the United States a matter of moment to Hawaii. The value of Hawaiian exports increased, government revenues enlarged, and many public improvements were made. In 1884 the grant of Pearl Harbor to the United States as a naval station made still another bond of connection between the islands and their big neighbor.

The King of Hawaii during this period of prosperity was Kalakaua. During a visit to the United States, and later during a tour of the world he was royally received, whereupon he returned to his island kingdom with expanded theories of the

---

[5] In 1920 the possessions of Germany in the group were given to New Zealand to be controlled under a mandate from the League of Nations.

position which a king should occupy. Unhappily he dwelt more on the pleasures which a king might enjoy than upon the obligations of a ruler to his people. At his death in 1891 Princess Liliuokalani became Queen and at once gave evidence of a disposition to rule autocratically. The white population of the islands had, meanwhile, been growing both in numbers and in power as compared with the natives, and were not willing to tolerate an increase in the authority of the crown. They thereupon assembled, appointed a committee of public safety and organized for resistance. On January 17, 1893, the revolutionary elements gathered, proclaimed the end of the monarchial régime and established a provisional government under the leadership of Judge S. B. Dole. The new authorities immediately proposed annexation to the United States and a treaty was promptly drawn up in accord with President Harrison's wishes, and presented to the Senate. At this point the Harrison administration ended and Cleveland became President.

Cleveland immediately withdrew the treaty for examination and sent James H. Blount to the islands to investigate the relation of American officials to the recent revolution. The appointment of Blount was made without the advice and consent of the Senate and was denounced by the President's enemies, although such special missions have been more or less common since the beginning of our history.[6] Blount reported that the United States minister to Hawaii, J. L. Stevens, had for some time been favorably disposed to a revolution in the islands and had written almost a year before that event asking how far he and the naval commander might deviate from established international rules in the contingency of a rebellion. "The Hawaiian pear is now fully ripe," Stevens had written to the State Department, early in 1893, "and this is the golden hour for the United States to pluck it." Blount also informed the President that the monarchy

[6] *Cf. Political Science Review,* Aug., 1916, pp. 481–499.

had been overturned with the active aid of Stevens and
through the intimidation caused by the presence of an armed
naval force of the United States.

The blunt language which Cleveland employed in his message to Congress on the subject, left no doubt about his opinion
of the transaction. ''The control of both sides of a bargain
acquired in such a manner is called by a familiar and unpleasant name when found in private transactions.'' Believing that an injustice had been done and that the only honorable course was to undo the wrong, he sent A. S. Willis as
successor to Stevens to express the President's regret and to
attempt to make amends. One of the conditions however
which President Cleveland placed upon the restoration of the
Queen was a promise of amnesty to all who had shared in the
revolution. The Queen was at first unwilling to bind herself
and when she later agreed, a new obstacle appeared in the
refusal of the provisional government to surrender its authority. Indeed it began to appear that the President's sense of
justice was forcing him to attempt the impossible. The provisional government had already been recognized by the
United States and by other powers, the deposition of the
Queen was a *fait accompli* and her restoration partook of the
nature of turning back the clock. Moreover, force would
have to be used to supplant the revolutionary authorities,—
a task for which Americans had no desire. The President,
in fact, had exhausted his powers and now referred the whole
affair to Congress. The House condemned Stevens for assisting in the overturn of the monarchy and went on record as
opposed to either annexation or an American protectorate.
Sentiment was less nearly uniform in the upper chamber.
The Democrats tended to uphold the President, the Republicans to condemn him. Although a majority of the committee
on foreign relations exonerated Stevens, yet no opposition appeared to a declaration which passed the Senate on May 31,
1894, maintaining that the United States ought not to inter-

vene in Hawaiian affairs and that interference by any other
government would be regarded as unfriendly to this country.

In the outcome, these events merely delayed annexation;
they could not prevent it. In Hawaii the more influential
and the propertied classes supported the revolution and desired annexation. In the United States the desire for expansion was stimulated by the fear that some other nation
might seize the prize. The military and naval situation in
1898 increased the demand for annexation, and in the summer
of that year the acquisition was completed by means of a
joint resolution of the two houses of Congress.[7] While negotiations were in progress Japan protested that her interests in the Pacific were endangered. Assurances were given,
however, that Japanese treaty rights would not be affected
by the annexation and the protest was withdrawn. The
United States was now "half-way across to Asia."

THE NORTHEASTERN COAST FISHERIES

When Cleveland came into power the first time, he found
a long-standing disagreement with Canada over the fisheries
of the northeastern coast. An arrangement which had resulted from the Treaty of Washington in 1871 came to an
end in 1885, and the rights of American fishermen in Canadian
waters then rested upon a treaty of 1818. This treaty was
inadequate owing to various changes which had taken place
during the nearly seventy years that had elapsed since it was
drawn up. Several difficulties lay in the way of the arrangement of a new treaty, an important one being the readiness
of the Republican Senate to embarrass the President and thus
discredit his administration. Matters came to a critical point
in 1886 when Canadian officials seized two American vessels

[7] *Cf.* below, p. 384 *ff.* Hawaii was brought into the Union as a territory in 1900.

engaged in deep-sea fishing. Cleveland then arranged a treaty which provided for reciprocal favors, and when the Senate withheld its assent the administration made a temporary agreement (*modus vivendi*), under which American ships were allowed to purchase bait and supplies and to use Canadian bays and harbors by paying a license fee.[8]

THE ITALIAN IMBROGLIO

Blaine was compelled to face another embarrassing situation in dealing with Italy in 1891–1892. In October, 1890, the chief of police of New Orleans, D. C. Hennessy, had been murdered, and circumstances indicated that the deed had been committed by members of an Italian secret society called the Mafia. A number of Italians were arrested, of whom three were acquitted, five were held for trial and three were to be tried a second time. One morning a mob of citizens, believing that there had been a miscarriage of justice, seized the eleven and killed all of them. The Italian government immediately demanded protection for Italians in New Orleans, as well as punishment of the persons concerned in the attack, and later somewhat impatiently demanded federal assurance that the guilty parties would be brought to trial and an acknowledgment that an indemnity was due to the relatives of the victims of the mob. Failing to obtain these guarantees, the Italian government withdrew its minister. When a grand jury in New Orleans investigated the affair, it excused the participants and none of them was brought to trial.

The government at Washington was hampered by the fact that judicial action in such a case lies with the individual state under our form of government, whereas diplomatic action is of course entirely federal. If the states are tardy or derelict in action, the national government is almost help-

[8] For later aspects of the controversy, see below, p. 574 *ff.*

less. President Harrison urged Congress to make offenses against the treaty rights of foreigners cognizable in federal courts, but this was never done. Diplomatic activity, however, brought better results, and an expression of regret on the part of the United States, together with the payment of $24,000 closed the incident.

RELATIONS WITH LATIN AMERICA

Relations with the Latin American countries south of the Mexican border had been unstable since the Mexican War, an unhappy controversy that left an ineradicable prejudice against us. John Quincy Adams and Henry Clay had hoped for a friendly union of the nations of North and South America, led by the United States, but this ideal had turned out to have no more substance than a vision. Moreover, the increasing trade activity of Great Britain and later of Germany had made a commercial bond of connection between South America and Europe which was, perhaps, stronger than that which the United States had established. Yet some progress was made. Disputes between European governments and the governments of Latin American countries were frequently referred to the United States for arbitration. An old claim of some British subjects, for example, against Colombia was submitted for settlement in 1872 to commissioners of whom the United States minister at Bogota was the most important. The problem was studied with great care and the award was satisfactory to both sides. In 1876 a territorial dispute between Argentina and Paraguay was referred to the President of the United States. In the case of a boundary controversy between Costa Rica and Nicaragua, President Cleveland appointed an arbitrator; Argentina and Brazil presented a similar problem which received the attention of Presidents Harrison and Cleveland.

It fell to James G. Baine to revive the idea of a Pan-

American conference which had been first conceived by Adams and Clay. As a diplomat, Blaine was possessed of outstanding patriotism and enthusiastic imagination, even if not of vast technical capacity or of an international mind. As Secretary of State under President Garfield in 1881 he invited the Latin American countries to share with the United States in a conference for the discussion of arbitration. The early death of Garfield and the ensuing change in the state department resulted in the abandonment of the project for the time being. Blaine, however, and other interested persons continued to press the plan and in 1888 Congress authorized the president to invite the governments of the Latin American countries to send delegates to a conference to be held in Washington in the following year. By that time President Harrison was in power. Blaine was again Secretary of State and was chosen president of the conference. Among the subjects for discussion were the preservation of peace, the creation of a customs union, uniform systems of weights, measures and coinage, and the promotion of frequent inter-communication among the American states. Little was accomplished, beyond a few recommendations, except the establishment of the International Bureau of American Republics. This was to have no governmental power, but was to be supported by the various nations concerned and was to collect and disseminate information about their laws, products and customs. The Bureau has become permanent under the name Pan American Union and is a factor in the preservation of friendly relations among the American republics. The reciprocity measure which Blaine pressed upon Congress during the pendency of the McKinley tariff bill was designed partly to further Pan American intercourse.

In the case of a disagreement with Chile, Blaine was less successful. A revolution against the Chilean President, Balmaceda, resulted in the triumph of the insurgents in 1891. The American minister to Chile was Patrick Egan, an Irish agitator who sympathized with President Balmaceda against the revolutionists and who was *persona non grata* to the strong English and German colonies there. While Chilean affairs were in this strained condition, the revolutionists sent a vessel, the *Itata*, to San Diego in California for military supplies, and American authorities seized it for violating the neutrality laws. While the vessel was in the hands of our officers, the Chileans took control of it and made their escape. The cruiser *Charleston* was sent in pursuit, but the revolutionists voluntarily surrendered the *Itata* before anything further occurred. Not long afterward, a United States Court decided that the pursuit had been without justification under international law. The result was that the United States seemed to have been over-ready to take sides against the revolutionists, and the latter became increasingly hostile to Americans.

Relations finally broke under the strain of a street quarrel in the city of Valparaiso in the fall of 1891. A number of sailors from the United States ship *Baltimore* were on shore leave and fell in with some Chilean sailors in a saloon. A quarrel resulted—just how it originated and just who was the aggressor could not be determined—but at any rate the Americans were outnumbered and one was killed. The administration pressed the case with vigor, declining to look upon the incident as a sailors' brawl and considering it a hostile attack upon the wearers of an American uniform. For a time the outbreak of war was considered likely, but eventually Chile yielded, apologized for its acts and made a financial return for the victims of the riot. Later students of Chilean relations have not praised Egan as minister or Blaine's conduct of the negotiations, but it is fair to note that the Chileans were prejudiced against the American Secretary of State because of an earlier controversy in which he had sided against them, and that the affair was complicated by the presence of powerful European colonies and by the passions which the revolution had aroused.

Most dangerous in its possibilities was the controversy with Great Britain over the boundary between British Guiana and Venezuela. British Guiana lies on the northern coast of South America, next to Venezuela and extends inland, with its western boundary roughly parallel to the valley of the Orinoco River. A long-standing disagreement had existed about the exact position of the line between the two countries—a disagreement which harked back to the claims of the Dutch, who had acquired Guiana in 1613 and had turned it over to the British in 1814. In 1840 England commissioned a surveyor named Schomburgk to fix the boundary but his decision was objected to by the Venezuelans who claimed that he included a great area that rightfully belonged to them. Gradually the British claims included more and more of the territory claimed by Venezuela, and the discovery of gold in the disputed region not only drew attention to the necessity of a settlement of the boundary but also attracted prospectors who began to occupy the land. In 1876 Venezuela began negotiations for some means of deciding the dispute and came to the conclusion that arbitration was her only recourse. On the refusal of Great Britain to heed her protests, the Venezuelan government suspended diplomatic relations in 1887, although the United States attempted to prevent a rupture by suggesting the submission of the difference to an arbitral tribunal. This offer was not accepted by Great Britain, and repeated exertions on the part of both Venezuela and the United States at later times failed to produce better results. When Cleveland returned to the presidency in 1893 he again became interested in the Venezuelan matter and Secretary of State Gresham urged the attention of the British government to the desirability of arbitration.

President Cleveland was a man of great courage and had a very keen sense of justice. In his opinion a great nation was playing the bully with a small one, and the injustice stirred his feelings to the depths. With the President's approval Secretary Olney, who had succeeded Gresham on the death of the latter, drew up an exposition of the Monroe Doctrine which was communicated to Lord Salisbury. This despatch, which was dated July 20, 1895, brought matters to a climax. In brief the administration took the position that under the Monroe doctrine the United States adhered to the principle that no European nation might deprive an American state of the right and power of self-government. This had been established American policy for seventy years. The Venezuelan boundary controversy was within the scope of the doctrine since Great Britain asserted title to disputed territory, substantially appropriating it, and refused to have her title investigated. At the same time Secretary Olney disclaimed any intention of taking sides in the controversy until the merits of the case were authoritatively ascertained, although the general argument of the despatch seemed to place the United States on the side of Venezuela. Moreover, Secretary Olny adopted a swaggering and aggressive, not to say truculent tone. He drew a contrast between monarchical Europe and self-governing America, particularly the United States, which "has furnished to the world the most conspicuous . . . example . . . of the excellence of free institutions, whether from the standpoint of national greatness or of individual happiness." The United States, he asserted, is "practically sovereign on this continent" because "wisdom and justice and equity are the invariable characteristics" of its dealings with others and because "its infinite resources combined with its isolated position render it master of the situation . . . as against any or all other powers."

Lord Salisbury did not reply to Secretary Olney for more than four months. He then asserted that President Monroe's message of 1823 had laid down two propositions: that America was no longer to be looked upon as a field for European colonization; and that Europe must not attempt to extend its political system to America, or to control the political condition of any of the American communities. In Lord Salisbury's opinion Olney was asserting that the Monroe Doctrine conferred upon the United States the right to demand arbitration whenever a European power had a frontier difference with a South American community. He suggested that the Monroe Doctrine was not a part of international law, that the boundary dispute had no relation to the dangers which President Monroe had feared and that the United States had no "apparent practical concern" with the controversy between Great Britain and Venezuela. He also raised some objections to arbitration as a method of settling disputes and asserted the willingness of Great Britain to arbitrate her title to part of the lands claimed. The remainder, he declared, could be thought of as Venezuelan only by extravagant claims based on the pretensions of Spanish officials in the last century. This area he expressly refused to submit to arbitration. The language of the Salisbury note was diplomatically correct, a fact which did not detract from the effect of the patronizing tone which characterized it.

President Cleveland doggedly proceeded with his demands. On December 17 (1895), he laid before Congress the correspondence with Lord Salisbury, together with a statement of his own position on the matter. Disclaiming any preconceived conviction as to the merits of the dispute, he nevertheless deprecated the possibility that a European country, by extending its boundaries, might take possession of the territory of one of its neighbors. Inasmuch as Great Britain had refused to submit to arbitration, he believed it incumbent upon the United States to take measures to determine the true divisional line. He suggested therefore that Congress empower the executive to appoint a commission to investigate and report. His closing words were so grave as to arouse the country to

a realization of the dangerous pitch to which negotiations
had mounted:

When such report is made and accepted it will in my opinion
be the duty of the United States to resist . . . the appropriation
by Great Britain of any . . . territory which after investigation
we have determined of right belongs to Venezuela. In making these
recommendations I am fully alive to the responsibility incurred,
and keenly realize all the consequences that may follow. I am
nevertheless firm in my conviction that while it is a grievous thing
to contemplate the two great English-speaking peoples . . . as being otherwise than friendly . . . there is no calamity . . . which
equals that which follows a supine submission to wrong and injustice.

Congress at once acceded to Cleveland's wishes and appropriated $100,000 for the proposed investigation. For a
brief moment neither Great Britain nor America quite realized the meaning of the President's warlike utterance. In
America it had generally been felt previously that his foreign policy was conciliatory rather than aggressive and, besides, the Venezuelan dispute had but little occupied popular
attention. When it became evident that war was a definite
possibility, public interest followed every step with anxiety.
Newspaper sentiment divided. A few periodicals like *The
Nation* insinuated that the President was actuated by the
desire to make political capital for a third term campaign and
characterized his action as "criminally rash and insensate,"
"ignorant and reckless," "impudent and insulting." The
press generally, however, judged Cleveland's stand strong and
"American." Influential citizens in both countries made
energetic attempts to prevent anything that might make war
inevitable. The Prince of Wales and Lord Roseberry threw
their influence on the side of conciliation. A. J. Balfour declared that a conflict with the United States would carry some-

thing of the "horror of civil war" and looked forward to the time when the country would "feel that they and we have a common duty to perform, a common office to fulfill among the nations of the world."

The President appointed a commission which set to work to obtain the information necessary for a judicial settlement of the boundary, and both Great Britain and Venezuela tactfully expressed a readiness to cooperate. Their labors, however, were brought to a close by a treaty between the two disputants providing for arbitration. A prominent feature of the treaty was an agreement that fifty years' control or settlement of an area should be sufficient to constitute a title, a provision which withdrew from consideration much of the territory to which Venezuela had laid claim. In October, 1899, the arbitration was concluded. The award did not meet the extreme claims of either party, but gave Great Britain the larger share of the disputed area, although assigning the entire mouth of the Orinoco River to Venezuela.

Besides giving new life to the Monroe Doctrine as an integral part of our foreign policy, the incident served to illustrate the dangers of settling international disputes in haphazard fashion. In January, 1897, therefore, Secretary Olney and the British Ambassador at Washington, Sir Julian Pauncefote, negotiated a general treaty for the settlement of disputes between the two countries by arbitration. Even with the example of the possible consequences of the Venezuelan controversy before it, however, the Senate failed to see the necessity for such an expedient, defeated the treaty by a narrow margin and left the greatest problem of international relations—the settlement of controversies on the basis of justice rather than force—to the care of a future generation.

On the whole, as has already been noted, the history of American diplomacy from 1877 to 1897 is scarcely more than an account of a series of unrelated incidents. Not only did the foreign policy of Blaine differ sharply from that of Cleveland, but there was no great question upon which public interest came to a focus, except temporarily over the Venezuelan matter, and no lesser problems that continued long enough to challenge attention to the fact that they remained unsolved. There were visible, nevertheles, several important tendencies. Our attitude toward Samoa and Hawaii indicated that the instinctive desire to annex territory had not disappeared with the rounding out of the continental possessions of the United States; American interest in arbitration as a method of settling disputes was expressed again and again; the place of the Monroe Doctrine in American international policy was clearly shown; and the determination of the United States to be heard in all affairs that touched her interests was demonstrated without any possibility of doubt. Time could tell— and only time—whether the American instinct for expansion had spent its force or not. But before pursuing that subject further, it is necessary to have in mind the political background of the closing years of the nineteenth century.

BIBLIOGRAPHICAL NOTE

The most complete and reliable authority is J. B. Moore, *A Digest of International Law* (8 vols. 1906), by one who was intimately connected with many of the incidents of which he wrote; the text of the treaties is in W. M. Malloy, *Treaties, Conventions, International Acts, etc., between the United States of America and other Powers* (2 vols., 1910). Valuable volumes are: J. B. Moore, *American Diplomacy* (1905); and C. R. Fish, *American Diplomacy* (1915); H. James, *Richard Olney and His Public Service* (1923); R. G. Adams, *A History of the Foreign Policy of the United States* (1924); and the chapters in McElroy, *Cleveland.* W. F. Johnson, *America's Foreign Relations* (2 vols., 1916), is interesting but somewhat marred by the author's tendency to take sides on controversial points; see also J. B. Henderson, *American Diplomatic Questions* (1901). J. S. Bassett, *Short History of the United States* (1913), contains a brief and compact chapter.

Essential material on particular incidents is found in the following. On Japan, "Our War with One Gun," in *New England Magazine*, XXVIII, 662; J. M. Callahan, *American Relations in the Pacific and the Far East* (1901); W. E. Griffis, *Townsend Harris* (1896). On Samoa, J. W. Foster, *American Diplomacy in the Orient* (1903); R. L. Stevenson, *Eight Years of Trouble in Samoa* (1892). On the seal fisheries, J. W. Foster *Diplomatic Memoirs* (2 vols. 1909). On Hawaii, Cleveland's message in J. D. Richardson, *Messages and Papers of the Presidents*, IX, 460. On Venezuela, Grover Cleveland, *Presidential Problems*, Chap. IV.

CHAPTER XVII

REPUBLICAN DOMINATION AND WAR WITH SPAIN

Of course the President [McKinley] is a bit of a jollier.

THEODORE ROOSEVELT.

The underlying fact of all is that we never have a sufficient army and are always caught unprepared when we go to war. . . . Not since the campaign of Crassus against the Parthians has there been so criminally incompetent a General as Shafter.

THEODORE ROOSEVELT.

When [war] came the American government was ready. Its fleets were cleared for action. Its armies were in the field, and the quick and signal triumph of its forces on land and sea bore equal tribute to the courage of American soldiers and sailors and to the skill and foresight of Republican statesmanship.

REPUBLICAN CAMPAIGN PLATFORM, 1900.

THE ceremonies attendant upon the inauguration of William McKinley on March 4, 1897, were typical of the care-taking generalship of Mark Hanna. The details of policing the crowds had been foreseen and attended to; the usual military review was effectively carried out to the last particular; "the Republican party was coming back to power as the party of organization, of discipline, of unquestioning obedience to leadership." [1]

The political capacity, the characteristics and the philosophy of the new President were sufficiently representative of the forces which were to control American affairs for the next few years to make them matters of some interest. McKinley was a traditional politician in the better sense of the word. As an executive he was patient, calm, modest, wary. Ordinarily he committed himself to a project only after long consideration, and with careful propriety he avoided entangling

[1] Cf. Peck, p. 518.

377

political bargains. His engaging personality, his consummate tact and his thorough knowledge of the temper and traditions of Congress enabled him to lead that body, where Cleveland failed to drive it. As a speaker he seldom rose above an ordinary plane, but he was simple and sincere. His messages to the Congress breathed an atmosphere of serenity and of deferential reliance upon the wise and judicious action of the legislative branch. Their smug and genial tone formed a sharp contrast with his predecessor's anxious demands for multifarious reforms; while Cleveland inveighed against narrow partisanship and selfish aims, McKinley benignantly observed: "The public questions which now most engross us are lifted far above either partisanship, prejudice, or former sectional differences."

The political philosophy of McKinley typified that of his party. The possibilities which he saw in protective tariffs, which occupied the foremost position among his principles, were well set forth in his message to Congress on March 15, 1897. Additional duties should be levied on foreign importation, he asserted,

to preserve the home market, so far as possible, to our own producers; to revive and increase manufactures; to relieve and encourage agriculture; to increase our domestic and foreign commerce; to aid and develop mining and building; and to render to labor in every field of useful occupation the liberal wages and adequate rewards to which skill and industry are justly entitled.

Like most American presidents, McKinley was a peace-lover, pleasantly disposed toward the arbitration of international difficulties and prepared to welcome any attempt to further that method of preserving the peace of the world. His conception of the presidential office differed somewhat sharply at several points from that of his predecessor. Like Cleveland he looked upon himself as peculiarly the representative of the people, but he was far less likely either to lead public opinion

or to attempt to hasten the people to adopt a position which
he had himself taken. This fact lay at the bottom of the
complaints of his critics that he always had his "ear to the
ground" in order that he might be prepared to go with the
majority. On the other hand, although he was aware of
constitutional limitations upon the functions of the executive,
he was not so continually hampered by the strict constructionist view of the powers of the federal government as Cleveland had been. McKinley's attitude towards Congress was
far more sagacious than Cleveland's. He distributed the
usual patronage with skill; he approached Congressmen individually with the utmost tact; he appointed them to serve
on commissions and boards of arbitration, and later, when
matters upon which the commissions had been engaged came
before Congress in the form of treaties or legislation, these
men found themselves in a position to lead in the adoption
of the principles which the President desired. All this indicated an ability to "touch elbows" with Congress that has
rarely been exceeded. When coupled with the organizing
power of Hanna, the harmonizing sagacity of the President
soon brought about a notable degree of party solidarity. As
a political organization, the Republican party reached a
climax.

McKinley was hardly an idealist, and distinctly not a
reformer. Although sensitive to pressure from the reform
element, he was not ahead of ordinary public opinion on
matters of economic and political betterment. Leaders in
federal railroad regulation found the President cold toward
projects to strengthen the Interstate Commerce law; the Sherman Anti-trust Act was scarcely enforced at all during
McKinley's administration, and the parts of his messages
which relate to the regulation of industry are vague and lacking in purpose. One searches these documents in vain for
any indication that the Republican leader had either vigorous sympathy with the economic and social unrest which had

made the year 1896 so momentous or even any thorough understanding of it. Even if he had possessed both sympathy and understanding, however, it is doubtful whether he could have made real progress in the direction of economic legislation and the enforcement of the acts regulating railroads and industry, in view of his long-continued and close affiliation with business leaders of the Mark Hanna type and his deep obligation to them at the time of his financial embarrassments in 1893.

McKinley's cabinet was composed of men whose advanced age and conservative characteristics indicated that his advisers would commend themselves to the business world and would instinctively avoid all those radical proposals that were coming to be known as "Bryanism." The dean of the cabinet in age and experience as well as in reputation and ability was John Sherman, who was now almost seventy-four years of age and had been occupying a position of dignity and honor in the Senate. Two reasons have been given for his appointment to the post of Secretary of State. In the first place, important diplomatic affairs were on hand, in the settlement of which his long experience as a member of the Senate Committee on Foreign Relations would be of obvious advantage. The second reason was the ambition of Hanna to enter the Senate. Since Sherman and Hanna were both from Ohio, it was possible to call the former to the cabinet and rely upon the Governor of the state to appoint the latter to the Senate. The propriety of this course of action depended somewhat on the question of Sherman's physical condition. Rumor declared that he was suffering from mental decay, due to his age, but McKinley believed the rumor to be baseless, summoned him to the cabinet, and Hanna was subsequently appointed to the Senate. When Sherman took up the duties of his office it appeared that the rumor had been all too true, and a serious lapse of memory on his part in a diplomatic matter forced his immediate replacement

by William R. Day. Somewhat more than a year later Day
retired and John Hay assumed the position. Many critics
have asserted that McKinley was aware of the precise condition of Sherman and that he made the choice despite this
knowledge, but it now seems likely that he was guilty only
of bad judgment and carelessness in failing to inform himself
about Sherman's infirmities. Another error of judgment was
made in the choice of Russell A. Alger as Secretary of War.
Alger failed to convince popular opinion that he was an effective officer and he resigned in 1899. As in the case of Sherman, McKinley then somewhat retrieved his mistake by
appointing a successor of undoubted ability, in the person of
Elihu Root.[1] It thus came about that the political and economic theories which had been characteristic of the leaders of
both parties during the seventies and eighties, but more particularly of the Republican party, were again in the ascendancy.
The President and his cabinet were uniformly men who had
grown up during the heyday of *laissez faire,* and Hanna, who
would inevitably be regarded as the mouthpiece of the administration in the Senate, was the embodiment of that philosophy.

McKinley's experience with the distribution of the offices
emphasized the progress that had been made since civil
service reform had been inaugurated. One of the steps which
President Cleveland had taken during his last administration,
it will be remembered, was to increase the number of positions
under control of the Civil Service Commission. The immediate result, of course, was to increase the demand for
places in the unclassified service. John Hay picturesquely
described the situation in the State Department a few years
later:

---

[1] Other members of the cabinet were: Lyman J. Gage, Ill., Secretary
of the Treasury; Joseph McKenna, Calif., Attorney-General; J. A. Gary,
Md., Postmaster-General; J. D. Long, Mass., Secretary of the Navy;
C. N. Bliss, Secretary of the Interior; James Wilson, Ia., Secretary of
Agriculture.

All other branches of the Civil Service are so rigidly provided for that the foreign service is like the topmost rock which you sometimes see in old pictures of the Deluge. The pressure for a place in it is almost indescribable.

Both in his inaugural address and in his message to Congress on December 6, 1897, McKinley expressed his approval of the prevailing system, but suggested the possibility of exempting some positions then in the classified service. President Cleveland had, indeed, admitted to the Civil Service Commission that a few modifications might be necessary. The Senate promptly ordered an investigation and discovered 10,000 places which it believed could be withdrawn, but because of other events further action was delayed. In 1899 the President returned to the subject and promulgated an order authorizing the withdrawal of certain positions from competitive examination and the transfer of others from the Commission to the Secretary of War—a total of somewhat less than 5,000 changes.[2] It appeared, in view of the circumstances under which the change had occurred, that a retrograde step had been taken, and McKinley received the condemnation of the reformers.

The first legislation undertaken by the administration was that relating to the tariff. The election of 1896, to be sure, had been fought out on the silver issue, but it was not deemed feasible to proceed at once to legislation on the subject, because of the strong silver contingent within the party. Several other considerations combined to draw attention away from the currency question and towards the tariff. The Wilson-Gorman Act of 1894 had been passed under circumstances that had caused the Democratic President himself to express his shame and disappointment; the period of industrial depression following the panic of 1893 had been attributed

2 The National Civil Service Reform League estimated the changes at 10,000.

so widely to Democratic tariff legislation that a Republican tariff act could be hailed as a harbinger of prosperity; and the annual deficit which had continued since 1893 indicated a genuine need of greater revenue, if the current scale of expenditures was to be continued. The President and the party leaders in Congress were men who were prominently identified with the protective system, and it was not likely that the business interests which profited from protection, which believed in its beneficent operation, and which had contributed generously to the Republican war-chest would remain inactive in the presence of an opportunity to revise the tariff.

Immediately after his succession to office, therefore, McKinley called a special session of Congress to legislate upon the chosen subject. His message urged an increase in revenue to be brought about by high import duties which, he suggested, should be so levied as to be advantageous to commerce, manufacturing, agriculture, mining, building and labor. The projected bill was already in hand. Republican success in the election had insured the return of Thomas B. Reed to the speaker's chair and Nelson Dingley to the Committee on Ways and Means. The latter was as devoted to the high-tariff cause as the Speaker and the President, and had laboriously constructed a bill which was distinctly protective. The legislative history of the Tariff Act of 1897—more commonly known as the Dingley act—was in several respects much like that of similar measures of earlier years. Its passage through the House was expedited by the masterful personality and vigorous tactics of the Speaker—a process which consumed less than a fortnight. In the Senate, bargain and delay ruled procedure; a few of the silver Republicans held the balance of power and demanded a *quid pro quo* for their support, and the Secretary of the Wool Manufacturers' Association preserved a suggestively close connection with the Finance Committee which had charge of the bill. After amending the House draft in 872 particulars, the Senate entrusted its interests to the usual conference committee, and there, as had happened before, the rates were in many cases raised above those desired by either the Senate or the House. The bill became law in July, 1897.

The Dingley act added little to the settlement of the tariff problem. The ordinary consumer was as little able as before to present his demands effectively and at the time and place at which the rates were really determined. The requirements of the silver Republicans were met by the imposition of high duties on wool. For one reason or another, duties were restored or raised upon hides, silks and linens, although those on cotton goods were slightly lowered. The duty on sugar was retained at a point favorable to the trust. In brief, then, the act of 1897 was aggressively protectionist. An abortive section of the act empowered the president to conclude treaties providing for reductions, as great as twenty per cent., in return for commercial concessions from other countries. Such reciprocity arrangements, however, must be made within two years of the passage of the law and might not remain in force more than five years, and each treaty must be ratified by the Senate. The President was favorable to reciprocal adjustments and several were arranged but were uniformly rejected by the Senate.

Business was prosperous after the enactment of the Dingley tariff and little agitation for a change was observable for a decade. Prosperity, being world wide, was doubtless not due in its entirety to the American tariff, yet the coincidence of protection and good times gave the Dingley act a pleasant reputation. For many years enthusiastic stump speakers placed the beneficence of Providence and the tariff of 1897 on an equality as causes of American well-being.

The President's first message to Congress had extended congratulations upon the fact that peace and good will with all the nations of the earth continued unbroken. Nevertheless it was necessary for him to devote much attention to the relations between Spain and its most valuable American possession—the island of Cuba.

American interest in Cuba was by no means of recent growth. The situation of the island—dominating the narrowest portion of the waterway between the Atlantic seaboard and the Gulf of Mexico—insured the importance of Cuba as a strategic position. The traditional attitude of Spain toward her colony had been one of exploitation, a policy which was sure to be looked upon with suspicion by a nation which had itself revolted from oppression. Riots and rebellions in the island, having their origin in Spain's colonial policy, had long engaged American sympathy and attention. American statesmen—Jefferson, John Quincy Adams, Clay and Webster—had pondered upon the wisest and most advantageous disposition of Cuba. In 1859 the Senate Committee on Foreign Relations had even concluded that "The ultimate acquisition of Cuba may be considered a fixed purpose of the United States." From 1868 to 1878 the "Ten Years' War" between Cuba and Spain had raised American feeling to a high pitch. The struggle was characterized by a barbarity that rivaled mediæval warfare; islanders who escaped to the United States sent ships to Cuba laden with arms and men; American trade rights were interfered with and American citizens seized by the Spaniards and shot; the *Virginius* was captured—a ship carrying the American flag—and many of her crew were executed. Indignation meetings were held, the navy was put in order and war was in sight. Cautious diplomatic negotiations delayed hostilities, however, and subsequently exhaustion caused the restoration of peace between Spain and her distracted colony.

With the recurrence of insurrection in 1895, interest in the United States was renewed, and this time circumstances combined to bring about a climax in American relations with Spain. On both sides the contest between Spain and her colony was carried on with unutterable cruelty. The island leader, Maximo Gomez, conducted guerrilla warfare, devastating the country, destroying plantation buildings and forcing laborers to cease work, in order to exhaust the enemy or to bring about American intervention. Spanish procedure was even more barbaric. A "reconcentration" order, promulgated by Valeriano Weyler, Governor-general of the island and General-in-Chief of the army, compelled the rural population to herd together in the garrisoned towns. Their buildings were then burned and their cattle driven away or killed; hygienic precautions were disregarded and the people themselves were insufficiently clothed and fed. The extermination of the inhabitants proceeded so rapidly as to promise complete devastation in a short time.

President Cleveland had been deeply affected by the Cuban situation. His last annual message to Congress had noted the $30,000,000 to $50,000,000 of American capital invested in the island, the volume of trade amounting yearly to $100,000,000, the use of American soil by Cubans and Cuban sympathizers for raising funds and purchasing equipment, and the stream of claims for damages done to American property in Cuba. In spite of his well-known disinclination to share in the internal affairs of other peoples, he had voiced a suggestive warning that American patience could not be maintained indefinitely.

Rumors of these conditions were substantiated by Senator Redfield Proctor, who went to Cuba and, on his return, set forth his conclusions in a notable speech to the Senate. After describing the distress which the natives were undergoing because of the reconcentration policy, he declared:

Torn from their homes, with foul earth, foul air, foul water, and foul food or none, what wonder that one-half have died and that one-quarter of the living are so diseased that they can not be saved?

The succession of McKinley seemed likely to result in a change in the attitude of America toward the Cuban problem. He was more responsive to public opinion than his predecessor had been, public opinion was more and more coming to favor intervention, and his party had committed itself in its platform to Cuban independence through American action. Moreover, two events early in 1898 greatly irritated the United States.

On February 9 a New York newspaper published a letter written by Señor Enrique Dupuy de Lôme, Spanish minister to the United States, to a personal friend in Havana. The letter had been given to the press by Cuban sympathizers. It referred to President McKinley as a "would-be politician who tries to leave a door open behind himself while keeping on good terms with the jingoes of his party." It further revealed the intention of the Minister to carry on a propaganda among senators in the interest of a commercial treaty. On all sides it was seen that the usefulness of Señor de Lôme was at an end and his government immediately recalled him. On February 15 the whole world was shocked by the destruction of the United States battleship *Maine* in Havana harbor, with the loss of 260 officers and men. News of the disaster was accompanied by the appeal of Captain Sigsby, commander of the vessel, that popular judgment of the causes of the disaster be suspended until a court of inquiry could investigate and report. Nevertheless on March 9, Congress placed $50,000,000 at the President's disposal for the purposes of national defence and the navy prepared for a conflict that seemed inevitable. Both the Spanish and American authorities conducted examinations. The American court reported that the ship had been destroyed by the explosion of a submarine mine, which had caused the partial explosion of two or more of her magazines. No evidence could be found which would fix the responsibility on any individual. The Spanish court came to the conclusion that the catastrophe was due solely to an explosion of the ship's magazines. American opinion naturally supported the findings of the

American court, and feeling ran high; newspapers demanded war; "Remember the *Maine*" summarized much of popular discussion.[3]

Under such circumstances, diplomatic negotiations looking toward peace were difficult, and accentuated the disagreements and delays which had already marked the discussions with Spanish officials. Moreover, a large fraction of McKinley's supporters in Congress were keenly in favor of war, and a quarrel within the party might result if the President restrained them longer. "Every Congressman," asserted Mr. Boutelle of Maine, "has two or three newspapers in his district, most of them printed in red ink and shouting for blood." Accordingly, McKinley determined to lay the matter before Congress—a step which was equivalent to a declaration of war, in view of the well-known sentiments of that body. As he was about to transmit his message, he received official information that the Spanish government had ordered a suspension of hostilities in Cuba "in order to prepare and facilitate peace." Without waiting to determine whether such a breathing-spell might or might not present a means of peaceful settlement, McKinley sent his message to Congress on April 11. In it he set forth the sufferings of the people of Cuba, the injury to Americans and to American property and trade, and the menace to American peace which was entailed by continuous conflict at our very threshold. "The issue is now with Congress," he concluded; "I await your action." A more self-reliant president or one who was less sensitive to the dangers of a party schism might have made a further attempt to delay or prevent the resort to war. But not McKinley.[4] Congress was not minded to continue nego-

[3] In 1911 the wreck of the *Maine* was raised and examined. The evidence found was such as to substantiate the findings of the American court of inquiry. It is perfectly possible that the explosion was planned by a Cuban sympathizer who desired American intervention. *Scientific American*, January 27, 1912.

[4] James Ford Rhodes in his *McKinley and Roosevelt Administrations* asserts "we may rest assured that if Mark Hanna had been President

tiations, and on April 19 it resolved that the people of Cuba were and ought to be independent, demanded that Spain withdraw from the island and directed the President to use the force of the nation to achieve the results desired. The approval of the Executive on the following day completed the severance of peaceful relations with Spain. At daylight on April 22 Admiral Sampson and his fleet were crossing the narrows between Florida and Cuba on the way to establish a blockade of the greater part of the island. Within three days more, Commodore George Dewey, who was in command of a fleet at Hong-Kong, had been instructed to proceed at once to the Philippine Islands and capture or destroy the Spanish fleet there. On April 25 Congress formally declared war upon the kingdom of Spain.[5]

It was not by mere chance, of course, that Admiral Sampson and Commodore Dewey were prepared to act with such celerity. Authorities in the Navy Department had long felt that a collision with Spain was inevitable and had been preparing for such an eventuality. With as little publicity as possible the Department completed and commissioned ships that were already under construction; it hastened the repair of vessels which were in any way defective; it ordered target practice and fleet manœuvres; and it prepared plans for the conduct of a naval war. Commanders of squadrons were instructed to keep in service men whose terms of enlistment were about to expire; supplies of ammunition were procured

there would have been no war with Spain." In view of the many circumstances which pressed the United States toward war, it seems doubtful whether McKinley could have done more than delay the conflict.

[5] It has commonly been felt among certain classes in the United States since 1898 that the business interests whose property and trade were mentioned by President McKinley had an undue share in bringing about the declaration of war. While it can not be doubted that the President was swayed more by business interests than most of our executives since the Civil War have been, yet it is also true that the sufferings of the Cubans aroused genuine sympathy in the United States.

and shipped to points where they would be needed; the *Oregon,* which had been stationed on the Pacific coast, was ordered to return to Key West by way of the Straits of Magellan and so began a voyage whose closing days were watched with interest by a whole nation. A Northern Patrol Squadron was organized to guard New England; a Flying Squadron was assembled at Hampton Roads for service on the Atlantic coast or abroad; and a formidable array gathered at Key West under Rear-Admiral Sampson for duty in the West Indies. Foreign shipyards were scoured for vessels in process of building and several were purchased, completed and renamed for American service. Greater additions were made through the purchase of merchantmen and their transformation into auxiliary cruisers, gunboats and colliers. In these ways the attempt was made, with some success, to improvise a navy on the eve of war.

The people of the country had scarcely become accustomed to the thought that war with Spain had actually come to pass when word was received in Washington of the exploit of Commodore Dewey in the Philippine Islands. Attention for the moment was focussed on the Far East, and the press dilated upon the first test of the new American navy.

The story of the test proved to have points of interest and importance. When Commodore Dewey received the orders already mentioned, on April 25, he finished immediately the preparations for conflict which had been initiated and turned his flagship, the *Olympia,* in the direction of Manila. His available force consisted of four protected cruisers, two gunboats, a revenue cutter, a collier and a supply ship. The city of Manila is on Manila Bay, a body of water twenty miles or more wide, and is reached only through a narrow entrance. Dewey judged that the channel was too deep to be mined successfully except by trained experts and that both contact and electrical mines would deteriorate so rapidly in tropical waters as to be effective only for a short time. He therefore decided to steam through the channel at night, disregarding the mines, and on May 1, to attack the Spanish fleet which lay within. The plans worked out even better than he had hoped. With all lights masked and the crews at the guns, the squadron moved silently through the passage with no other opposition than three shots from a single battery. Once within the Bay Dewey steamed slowly toward the city of Manila and then back to a fortified point, Cavite, where he found his quarry arranged in an irregular crescent and awaiting the conflict. Oblivious of the hasty and inaccurate fire from the batteries on shore, he deliberately moved to a position within two and a half miles of the Spanish ships and said to the captain of the *Olympia*, "You may fire when you are ready, Gridley."

Three times westward and twice eastward the American squadron ran slowly back and forth, using the port and starboard batteries in turn, and in a short time the shore batteries

THE PHILIPPINES

and the Spanish fleet were masses of ruins. Of the American forces, only eight were injured, and they only slightly, while 167 of the Spanish were killed and 214 wounded. News of the victory was as unexpected as it was welcome in the United States. President McKinley appointed Dewey an acting Rear-Admiral and on all sides discussion began of the situation and possibilites of the Philippines.

In the meantime, the position of the American squadron was far from safe. To be sure, all resistance from the batteries in and around Manila was quickly suppressed by a threat to destroy the city; nevertheless Admiral Dewey was in command of too slight a force to enable him to occupy both the town and its environs. He accordingly notified Washington that more troops were necessary if it were intended to seize and retain Manila, and expeditionary forces were dispatched, the first of which arrived on June 30. Indeed it was high time that assistance be forthcoming, for new possibilities of conflict had appeared in the presence of a powerful force of German warships.

As soon as the defeat of the Spanish squadron had been effected, Admiral Dewey established a blockade of Manila Bay and, according to custom, the war vessels of interested nations went thither to observe the effectiveness of the blockade and to care for the well-being of their nationals. Among the early arrivals were the British, the French and the Japanese, all of whom observed the formalities of the situation and reported to the American Admiral before venturing into the harbor. The Germans, however, omitted the proprieties until sharply reminded by a shot across the bow of the *Cormoran*. By mid-June five German men-of-war under command of Vice Admiral von Diederichs were in the Bay—a force nearly if not quite the match of the American squadron. When the Germans continued their disregard of the regulations controlling the blockade, indicating a potential if not an actual hostility, it became necessary for Admiral Dewey to have done with the Teutonic peril at once. He sent a verbal message to von Diederichs which effectually ended all controversy. Admiral Dewey never disclosed the exact phraseology of the message, nor did he send a record of it to the Navy Department. A newspaper correspondent who was acting as one of the Admiral's aides asserted that the protest was against von Diederichs' disregard of the usual courtesies of naval intercourse and that it closed with the words, "if he wants a fight he can have it right now." The disclosure by Captain Edward Chichester, in command of the English force, that he had orders to comply with Admiral Dewey's restrictions and that his sympathies were with the Americans, together with the arrival of the expeditionary force, assured American supremacy and a peaceful blockade. On August 13 a joint movement of the naval forces and the infantry under General Wesley Merritt resulted in the speedy surrender of the city of Manila. The Americans were now in control of the capital of the Philippine Islands and would, perforce, face the question of the ultimate disposition of the archipelago in case of the eventual defeat of Spain. In the meanwhile, popular attention turned toward stirring events which were taking place in the Caribbean Sea.[6]

On April 28—a week after Admiral Sampson started for Cuba—the Spanish Admiral Cervera left the Cape Verde Islands. His force was a considerable one; his goal was unknown, though naturally believed to be some point in the Spanish West Indies. On the assumption that this hypothesis was a correct one, Sampson patrolled the northern coast of Cuba, extending his movement as far as Porto Rico, and scouts were placed out beyond Gaudeloupe and Martinique. The entire nation anxiously awaited the outcome of the impending encounter.

On May 19 Cervera slipped into Santiago, a town on the eastern end of Cuba which had rail connections with Havana, the capital of the island. Commodore W. S. Schley who was in command of a squadron on the southern coast soon received information of the enemy's whereabouts and established a blockade of the city, while Sampson hastened to the scene

[6] Professor L. B. Shippee, after a thorough investigation of the episode of the Germans reached the conclusion that the government was keenly alert for any advantages which the war might present for Germany, but "that there was never any real danger of war." *American Historical Review*, July, 1925, pp. 754–777.

and assumed command of operations. The American force now included four first-class battleships, one second-class battleship and two cruisers. They were arranged in semi-circular formation facing the harbor, and at night powerful search-lights were kept directed upon the channel which

THE SPANISH AMERICAN WAR IN THE WEST INDIES

Admiral Cervera must take in case of an attempt to escape. The main part of Santiago Bay is between four and five miles long and is reached through a narrow entrance channel. Elevated positions at the mouth of the channel rendered the vigorous defense of the harbor a matter of some ease. Early in the progress of the blockade the Americans attempted to sink a collier across the entrance, but fortunately, as it turned out, this daring project failed, and Admiral Sampson settled down to await developments.

It was apparent that the capture of Santiago, and the destruction of the fleet could be brought about only through a joint movement of the army and navy. Hitherto the war had been entirely on the sea. Nevertheless over 200,000 volunteers had been called for, in addition to somewhat over 50,000 regular troops and the "Rough Riders"—the last a regiment of volunteer cavalry which had been raised by Colonel Leonard Wood and Theodore Roosevelt and which was largely composed of cowboys, ranchmen, Indians and athletes from eastern colleges. The regulars, together with a few volunteers and the Rough Riders, were sent to Tampa, Florida, while most of the volunteers were trained at Chickamauga Park, in Georigia. It had been expected that the important military operations would take place around Havana and for that reason the officer commanding the army, General Nelson A. Miles, with most of the regular troops, were retained for the larger service. The command of the expedition to Santiago fell to General William R. Shafter. Sixteen thousand eight hundred and eighty-seven officers and men set sail for Tampa on June 14 and began to disembark eight days later at Daiquiri, sixteen miles to the east of Santiago.

Advancing from this point General Lawton, commanding a division of infantry, moved parallel to the shore and seized Siboney. General Wheeler, a former Confederate who was now in command of the cavalry, met and defeated a Spanish force at Las Guasimas. Further advance met difficulties that were more serious. On the left of the American line was San Juan Hill, an eminence which commanded the country toward the east; on the right was El Caney, a fortified village held by a small force of Spaniards. The country between the two points was a jungle, the roads hardly better than trails, where troops frequently had to go in single file. The fight at El Caney was severe, the enemy being well-entrenched, well-armed, and protected by wire entanglements and block houses, and General Lawton suffered a loss of more than 400 killed and wounded before driving the Spaniards out of their position. San Juan Hill was still more stubbornly defended, and an American advance was impeded by the heat, the tropical growth and the uneven character of the country. Under these circumstances officers became separated from their men and victory was gained through the determination and re-

Campaign about Santiago
— Roads. ---- Trails.

El Caney
Santiago
Kettle Hill
San Juan Hill
Heavy Undergrowth
Las Guasimas
Siboney
Daiquiri
5 miles   Caribbean Sea

sourcefulness of the individual. The Spaniards then fell back upon Santiago.

The continued success of the Americans compelled the Spanish authorities to make an immediate decision in regard to the fleet. To remain in the harbor seemed to mean being encircled and starved; to go out through the narrow channel seemed to lead to sure destruction. Yet the latter venture appealed to the commander-in-chief of Cuba, Captain General Blanco, as the more honorable one and on July 2 orders were sent to Admiral Cervera to make the attempt. Early next morning, while Admiral Sampson was away at a conference with General Shafter, lookouts on the American battleships descried the *Infanta Maria Teresa* feeling her way out of the harbor, followed by the remainder of the Spanish fleet, three armored cruisers and two torpedo-boat destroyers. The Americans instantly closed in, directing their fire first against the *Teresa* and later against the rest of the fleet as they tried to follow their leader out to safety. Once out of the harbor the entire Spanish fleet dashed headlong toward the west, parallel to the coast, while the Americans kept pace, pouring a gruelling fire from every available gun. The Spaniards returned the fire and thus "the action resolved itself into a series of magnificent duels between powerful ironclads." One by one the enemy's vessels were sunk or forced to run ashore—the *Cristobal Colon* last, at two o'clock in the afternoon. The Spanish losses, besides the fleet, were 323 killed and 151 wounded; the Americans lost one killed and one wounded. The city of Santiago, deprived of its fleet, found itself in a desperate plight and surrendered on July 16. Shortly afterwards General Miles led an expedition into Porto Rico, but operations were soon brought to a close because of the suspension of hostilities, and from a military point of view the importance of the campaign was negligible.

The succession of overwhelming defeats drove home to Spain the futility of further conflict. The despatch of American troops to the Philippines and to Porto Rico, moreover, indicated that Spain would soon suffer other losses. Hence the Spanish government, acting through Jules Cambon, the French ambassador to the United States, sought terms for the settlement of the war. The President's reply of July 30 made the following stipulations: Spain to relinquish and evacuate Cuba and to cede Porto Rico and one of the Ladrone Islands; the United States to occupy the city and Bay of Manila, pending the conclusion of peace and the determination of the final disposition of the Philippines. Spain wished to restrict negotiations to the Cuban question, but was forced to accept the conditions laid down by the victor. A preliminary agreement or proctocol was therefore signed, which provided for a conference at Paris concerning peace terms.

The uniform success of the American arms could not obscure the popular belief that the Department of War had been guilty of many shortcomings. It will doubtless be always a subject for dispute as to whether the major portion of the blame is to be laid at the door of the traditional American disinclination to be prepared for warfare, or upon Secretary Alger and his immediate advisors. That the conduct of the military affairs was inexpert, however, is admitted on all sides. The facilities for taking care of the troops at Tampa were inadequate. When transports reached Tampa to take the troops to Santiago, officers wildly scrambled to get their men on board. The Rough Riders made their way into a transport intended for two other regiments, one of regulars and the other of volunteers, with the result that the volunteers and half of the regulars were left on shore.

When we unloaded our regiment at Tampa, wrote Colonel Roosevelt, we had to go 24 hours without food and not a human being met us to show us our camp or tell us anything about what we were to do. When we were ordered to embark here it took us twelve hours to make the nine miles of railroad, and on the wharf not one shadow of preparation had been made to receive any regiment; no transports had been assigned in advance, and there was actually no office for either the commissary or Quartermaster. We had to hunt all over the dock among ten thousand people before, by chance we ran across first one and then the other . . . Under these circumstances it . . . took over three days to embark the troops. . . . The steamer on which we are contains nearly one thousand men, there being room for about five hundred comfortably.

The clothing supplied for the Cuban campaign was better suited to a cold climate than to summer in the tropics. The health of the troops during the Santiago campaign was such that the general officers expressed the opinion that the army must immediately be removed from Cuba or suffer severe and unnecessary losses from malarial fever. When the men were removed, however, they were taken to Montauk Point on Long Island, where the climate was too cool and bracing. Unsanitary conditions in the training camps within the borders of the United States were the cause of fatalities estimated at several times the number killed in battle. A controversy over the quality of the beef supplied to the troops led to an executive commission of investigation. Both unnecessary and unfortunate was the Sampson-Schley controversy, which originated in a difference of opinion about the proportion of credit which each of these officers should have for the success of Santiago and which was continued in charges that the latter had made serious mistakes in the conduct of his share of the operations. Subsequently a Court of Inquiry investigated the accusations and made a decision which did not completely satisfy either side.

The weaknesses in the military system which had been uncovered by the Spanish War were turned to good account by Elihu Root, Secretary of War, during the five years immediately after peace was declared. Among the changes which he was instrumental in bringing about, two stand out as most important. Beginning in 1899 he urged the establishment of an Army War College—which was eventually opened in 1907. The College was intended to act as an advanced training school for the instruction of army officers in the theory and practice of handling troops. The second accomplishment was the formation of the General Staff, which was brought about at Root's suggestion by the act of February 14, 1903. The General Staff was to consist of forty-five officers, headed by a Lieutenant-General. Its purpose was to provide the information and well-thought-out plans which are so necessary for successful military actions, and which had been so conspicuously lacking in the campaign against Cuba.

The political effect of the war was distinctly favorable to the administration. The successful prosecution of a popular war, combined with widespread prosperity and the demoralization of the opposition party greatly heightened the prestige of the Republicans. McKinley appeared to have been in truth, the "advance agent of prosperity"; and his party obtained a dominating control of public policy.

BIBLIOGRAPHICAL NOTE

H. Croly, *Marcus A. Hanna* (1912), and C. S. Olcott, *William McKinley* (2 vols., 1916), discuss the politics of the period, subject to the limitations already mentioned. W. D. Foulke, *Fighting the Spoilsman* (1919), describes the relation of the administration to the civil service; for the Dingley tariff, Stanwood, Tarbell and Taussig.

The literature on the Spanish war is extensive. Most detailed and reliable is F. E. Chadwick, *Relations of the United States and Spain; I, Diplomacy, II, III, The Spanish War* (1909, 1911). J. H. Latané, *America as a World Power* (1907), has several good chapters; H. E. Flack, *Spanish American Diplomatic Relations (Preceding the War of 1898* (1906), E. J. Benton, *International Law and Diplomacy of the Spanish-American War* (1908), and B. A. Reuter, *Anglo-American Relations during the Spanish-American War* (1924), take up the diplomatic side. On naval preparations, J. D. Long, *New American Navy* (2 vols., 1903), is by McKinley's Secretary of the Navy; see also E. S. Maclay, *History of the United States Navy* (rev. ed., 3 vols., 1901–1902). Good autobiographical accounts are: C. E. Clark, *My Fifty Years in the Navy* (1917); George Dewey, *Autobiography* (1913); Theodore Roosevelt, *Auto biography;* W. S. Schley, *Forty-five Years under the Flag* (1914); L. S. Mayo, *America of Yesterday* (Journal of John D. Long, 1923). See also A. T. Mahan, *Lessons of the War with Spain* (1899); and E. Root, *The Military and Colonial Policy of the United States* (1916).

On the episode of the Germans in Manila Bay see L. B. Shippee, "Germany and the Spanish-American War" in *American Historical Review,* July, 1925.

CHAPTER XVIII

IMPERIALISM

... the war has brought us new duties and responsibilities which we must meet and discharge as becomes a great nation. ... Incidental to our tenure of the Philippines is the commercial opportunity. ...
PRESIDENT WILLIAM McKINLEY.

... the subjugation of the Philippine Islands, the acquisition of a dependency to be held in subjection by the United States, the overthrow of the great doctrine that Governments rest on the consent of the governed. ...
SENATOR GEORGE F. HOAR.

BESIDES destroying the naval forces of Spain in the Philippines and Cuba, the victories of Dewey, Schley and Sampson had raised unforeseen questions,—as war commonly does. Ought the United States to carry off the spoils of war in the form of territory outside the limits of continental North America? Would it be wise policy to attempt to administer the affairs of peoples whose languages, racial characteristics and forms of government were utterly strange? Assuming that the policy was wise, was it constitutional? Would such annexations beget "Imperialism," and place the United States on a level with the land-grabbing states of Europe? Such misgivings assailed the minds of many Americans as the conference assembled at Paris on October 1 to settle the terms of peace.[1]

[1] The American commissioners were W. R. Day, Secretary of State; Whitelaw Reid, editor of the New York *Tribune;* and Senators C. K. Davis, W. P. Frye and George Gray. Senator Hoar remonstrated with McKinley for placing senators on such commissions as this, on the ground that the independence of the Senate was thereby lessened when the question of ratifying the treaty came before that body. He declared that McKinley admitted that the practice was wrong. *Cf. Autobiography*, II, pp. 46–51.

401

The chief controversies between the Spanish and the American negotiators related to Cuba and the Philippines. The Spanish commissioners early proposed to transfer Cuba to the United States, the latter to turn it over to the Cuban people in due time. With the sovereignty of Cuba was to go the debt of the island. On the refusal of the Americans to accede to this, the Spanish commissioners urged the transfer of Cuba to the United States without any promise as to its future. Instructions from Washington both on possession and on debt, however, were explicit and in the end Spain had to relinquish all claim to Cuba and assume responsibility for its indebtedness.

The proper disposition of the Philippines presented far greater difficulty. In the first place, the capture of the city of Manila had taken place after the proctocol had been signed and after hostilities had been ordered suspended, but before news of these facts had reached Admiral Dewey. The Spanish commissioners were not slow to point out how these facts compromised any American claim to the sovereignty of the islands. Moreover, the American government was far from sure that it desired to annex the Philippines, and grave diversity of opinion on the subject existed both in the peace commission and among the people at large. The original instructions of President McKinley to the peace commissioners were to the effect that the outcome of the war had placed new duties and responsibilities on the United States, that the commercial opportunity which possession of the Philippines would present could not be overlooked and that the island of Luzon at least must be ceded. So little was known about the people and the possibilities of the islands that the American commission was compelled to go far afield to obtain information from writers and investigators in regard to questions of defense, the political capacity of the inhabitants, the danger that another nation might step in if the United States should evacuate, commercial prospects, and so on. President McKinley eventually came to the opinion that the proper course was to take the entire archipelago. To give them back to Spain would mean anarchy and misrule, for the Spanish government in the Philippines was in a state of demoralization. To leave them to themselves would be worse, for the great majority of the Filipinos were incapable of self-government, and some foreign power—Germany, for example—would be sure to step in and take possession. On the other hand, the opportunity for trade in the Orient was alluring. Several European powers were, at that moment, obtaining territorial and commercial advantages in China. Why should not the United States avail itself of its good fortune and acquire islands which would not only give us a valuable Philippine trade, but also provide convenient ports for the development of commerce with China. Hence President McKinley came to the conclusion that the only thing for the United States to do was to take the Philippines and "educate the Filipinos, and uplift and civilize and Christianize them."

The American commissioners therefore demanded the Philippines, but realizing the defect in their case, since the conquest of Manila had taken place after the conclusion of the protocol, agreed to pay Spain $20,000,000. The Spanish commissioners thereupon yielded to necessity and reluctantly agreed.

As finally signed, the treaty of December 10, 1898, contained the following points: Spain agreed to relinquish Cuba, and the United States was to protect life and property during its occupancy of the island; Spain also ceded Porto Rico and the other Spanish West Indies, Guam in the Ladrones, and the Philippines on payment of $20,000,000; the United States agreed to return to Spain, at its own cost, all Spanish prisoners taken at the time of the capture of Manila; the civil and political rights of the inhabitants of the ceded territories were to be determined by Congress; and freedom of religion was guaranteed.

The reference of the treaty to the Senate for ratification elicited many divergences of opinion, the ablest opposition being presented by members of the President's own party. In particular, the position taken by Senator Hoar, a rigid Republican and a close friend of President McKinley, made a strong impression. That there can be no just government without the consent of the governed, he asserted, was the central doctrine of the Declaration of Independence. Moreover, the acquisition of foreign lands, he believed, would lead us into competition with European powers for territory, and thus tempt us away from the international policy which had been laid down by the "fathers" and followed by the nation ever since. Most of the Democrats held similar views, but some of them heeded the advice of Bryan, who urged that the treaty be ratified in order to end the war, and that the ultimate disposition of the new possessions be decided in the next presidential campaign. The point of view which seems to have prevailed with most Republicans was that the United States, being a sovereign nation, possessed power to acquire territory and to determine its future status, and that as a matter of expediency it was better to take the Philippines than to risk the dangers which lay in leaving them alone. Shortly before the final vote was taken, an insurrection broke out in the Philippines against American control, which may have influenced some senators to accept the President's settlement. Even with this aid, however, ratification was brought about by the narrow margin of one vote more than the required two-thirds majority.[2]

The congressional election of 1898 increased the advantage which the supporters of a gold standard had gained in 1896. Although the number of Republicans in the House of Representatives was considerably reduced, the party still pre-

[2] Of the President's party, T. B. Reed, the powerful Speaker of the House, retired from public life for personal reasons and because of his dissent from the imperialist policy of his party. McCall, *Reed*, pp. 237–8.

served a majority, the number of Populists declined, and the strength of the opposition to the free coinage of silver was increased. In the Senate, eight supporters of silver were replaced by gold men.

It became feasible, therefore, to crystallize public opinion on the monetary question in the form of legislation. A gold standard act was accordingly passed on March 14, 1900, under the provisions of which,

. . . the dollar consisting of twenty-five and eight-tenths grains of gold nine-tenths fine, . . . shall be the standard unit of value, and all forms of money issued or coined by the United States shall be maintained at a parity of value with this standard . . .

Furthermore, $150,000,000 in gold is set aside in the treasury for redemption purposes only, and the Secretary is instructed to maintain the reserve. In addition, the act provided for the retirement of the "Treasury Notes" which had been issued under the Sherman Silver Purchase law of 1890. There was an end, then, to the agitation for the expansion of the currency supply by means of the increased use of silver.

Conditions were auspicious for the Republicans, therefore, at the approach of the presidential election of 1900. The gold standard act had relieved the financial and commercial classes of the dread of a currency upheaval, and hence allied them even more closely with President McKinley and his party than they had been before. The world-wide prosperity which has already been mentioned and in which the United States shared was in striking contrast with the business depression of the recent Democratic administration. American foreign trade was in the midst of a distinct and lasting upward swing,—increasing from $1,650,000,000 in 1890 to $3,300,-000,000 in 1910. The discoveries of gold in the Klondike and the improvement of methods of extracting the metal from the ore increased the annual coinage of the precious metal by fifty per cent. This addition to the currency, together with the additions to other forms of money, brought about the very inflation which the Populists and the western Democrats had attempted to accomplish through the free coinage of silver. The price level went gradually up, giving the western farmer a greater feeling of prosperity, and largely lessening his complaints. Within the Republican organization, the President's soothing personality and Hanna's meticulous attention to the details of the party machinery continued undiminished the momentum which had been gathered.

The renomination of McKinley at the Republican Convention in Philadelphia, on June 19, 1900, was unanimous. The vice-presidency, contrary to tradition, occupied the center of interest. Several men of prominence were mentioned in this connection but the name which evoked most enthusiasm was that of Theodore Roosevelt. Roosevelt's career during the war with Spain had been a prominent factor in making him Governor of New York. As Governor he had shown energy and independence, especially in connection with measures for taxing street railway and other franchises, and had come into conflict with Senator Thomas C. Platt, the boss of the state, and many of the powerful New York business men with whom Platt was connected. This group, therefore, desired to divert the vigorous Governor into the vice-presidency, an office which usually casts a "species of political oblivion" over its occupant. McKinley and Hanna were both opposed to the plan.

Roosevelt himself scorned the inactivity which usually falls to the lot of the presiding officer of the Senate, and besides he desired to put into effect further plans which he had made as Governor. Nevertheless both he and his political advisor, Senator Henry Cabot Lodge, hoped that he might use the vice-presidency as a stepping stone for higher honors—the presidency in 1904 was the ultimate object—and he therefore refrained from committing himself to a flat-footed refusal. When the convention met, sentiment in behalf of Roosevelt.

especially from the West, was so strong as to over-rule both the administration and the wishes of the Governor. McKinley sent emphatic word that he was neither for nor against any man, but would accept the decision of the delegates. Hanna then withdrew his objections and Roosevelt was nominated without opposition.

The Republican platform emphasized the prosperity which had resulted from the accession of the party to power; it pointed out the danger which would ensue if the opposition were allowed to conduct public affairs; and it dwelt upon the growth of the export trade, and the beneficence of the Dingley tariff. An anti-trust plank deprecated combinations designed to create monopolies, and promised legislation to prevent such abuses. Imperialism was briefly dismissed.

No other course was possible than to destroy Spain's sovereignty throughout the West Indies and in the Philippine Islands. That course created our responsibility before the world . . . to provide for the maintenance of law and order, and for the establishment of good government and for the performance of international obligations.

The dissension which had existed within the Democratic party since the second administration of Cleveland was still the important fact about the organization. Having been out of power, the party could take only the negative position of hostile criticism; there had been no reorganization and clarification of purposes, and no new leader had appeared who combined the personal prestige of Bryan with those qualities of conservatism and solidity which the East demanded, so that from the beginning there was no doubt that Bryan would again be the candidate and that he would take the lead in framing the platform. The convention met in Kansas City, on July 4. The platform placed most emphasis upon three issues. The first, which was declared the "paramount" one, was imperialism. The reasons given for opposing territorial expansion were mainly those brought forward by Senator Hoar at the time when the peace treaty was under discussion:

We declare again that all governments instituted among men derive their just powers from the consent of the governed; that any government not based upon the consent of the governed is a tyranny; and that to impose upon any people a government of force is to substitute the methods of imperialism for those of a republic.

The second issue, the evils of big business, received renewed attention, although an old complaint, because of the many industrial consolidations of the years immediately preceding. The "trusts" were condemned for appropriating the fruits of industry for the benefit of the few, and the Republican party was charged with fostering them in return for campaign subscriptions and political support. The Dingley act was denounced as a "trust-breeding" measure. The remedies proposed were severely definite in comparison with the vague plank which had been offered by the Republicans: they included publicity as to the affairs of corporations doing an interstate business; the prohibition of stock-watering and attempts at monopoly; and the use of all the constitutional powers of Congress over interstate commerce and the mails for the enactment of comprehensive and effective legislation. That the silver issue was mentioned was due to the insistence of Bryan, who believed that the stand which had been taken by the party in 1896 was a right one. Notwithstanding the objections of many influential leaders, therefore, a free silver plank was inserted, although in brief terms and in an inconspicuous place.

As a political contest, the campaign of 1900 lacked the spirited personal controversies that marked the elections of 1884 and 1896. Defections from the Republican party on the score of imperialism were distinguished more for quality than for numbers. Such men as George F. Hoar and Thomas

B. Reed denounced their party, but would not go over to the enemy. Less strongly partisan leaders like Charles Francis Adams, Carl Schurz, Moorfield Storey and W. G. Sumner took the attitude of opposition which may be guessed from the title of Sumner's essay, "the Conquest of the United States by Spain." The average man, however, seems to have been more impressed by the dangers involved in giving up our newly acquired possessions and the desirability of expansion, than by the perils of imperialism. Interest in the subject waned visibly as the weeks wore on. Prosperity and the increased money supply sapped the strength of earlier discontent with the currency situation, so that the choice presented to the voters simmered down to imperialism and Bryan. A bit of vigor was infused into the campaign through the energetic speaking tours of Roosevelt and the Democratic leader. Hanna, as Chairman of the Republican National Committee, organized everything with his usual skill, and raised, his biographer tells us, $2,500,000 from the important business men of the country—one-fifth of it from two companies. The result of the election was the choice of McKinley, whose plurality over Bryan exceeded 860,000 in a total vote of less than 14,000,000; Bryan received less support than had been accorded him in 1896.

While imperialism as a political issue was being discussed and decided, the history of American control in Cuba, Porto Rico, the Philippines and Hawaii was rapidly being written.[3] Economic conditions in the first of these islands at the time of the American occupation were little short of appalling. The streets, houses and public institutions were filthy and in disrepair; anarchy ruled, for lack of any stable and recognized government; and the people were half-clothed, homeless and starving. At noon on January 1, 1899, the Spanish flag

[3] Although the Hawaiian Islands were not acquired by the treaty closing the Spanish war, the war itself had much to do with annexation, and their final disposition was part of the problem of imperialism. *Cf.* p. 418.

was hauled down in Havana, the American flag was hoisted in its place, and representatives of Spain relinquished all rights to the sovereignty and public property of the island. General John R. Brooke, and later General Leonard Wood controlled affairs as military governors.

The first task was to feed the hungry, and care for the sick and dying. The customs service was revived under command of Colonel Tasker H. Bliss and began to supply needed revenue. The penal institutions were investigated—noisome holes in which were crowded wretched prisoners, many of whom had been incarcerated for no ascertainable reason. Education was reorganized, equipment provided, teachers found, and schools repaired or rebuilt. Most remarkable, was the work of sanitation. Heaps of rubbish were cleared away; houses washed and disinfected; sewers were opened and streets cleaned. Scientific investigation disclosed the fact that the mosquito disseminated the yellow fever and steps were taken to prevent the breeding of these pests. So successful were the efforts that in a few years the fever had become a thing of the past.[4]

It was seen that the economic rehabilitation of Cuba must come about mainly through the production of sugar, and since the United States was the chief purchaser of the product, the tariff schedule was of vital importance. In 1901 Congress was urged to reduce the tariff on imports from Cuba, but the opposition was formidable. The American Beet Sugar Association complained that their industry, which had been recently established, would be ruined by allowing reductions to Cuban growers; the cane-sugar planters of Louisiana were allied with them; and the friends of protection feared the effect of any break in the tariff wall. On the other hand, the American Sugar Refining Company, popularly called

[4] For details concerning this splendid service, see "Yellow Fever Meets its Master" in *World's Work*, Apr., 1924; and Mark Sullivan, *Our Times*.

the "Sugar Trust," merely refined raw sugar and desired an increase in the supply. Lobbyists of all descriptions poured into Washington to influence committees and individuals, and General Leonard Wood, then the Governor of Cuba, even expended Cuban funds in the spread of literature favorable to a reciprocal reduction of duties. In the meantime, a reciprocity treaty was made and submitted to the Senate, where it hung fire for somewhat more than a year, and was finally ratified on December 16, 1903. It provided for the admission of Cuban products into the United States at a reduction of twenty per cent., and a reciprocal reduction on American goods entering Cuba of twenty-five to forty per cent.

The establishment of a policy in regard to permanent relations between the United States and Cuba was brought about in 1901–1902. When Congress had demanded the withdrawal of Spain from the island in 1898, its action had been accompanied by the Teller Resolution:

That the United States hereby disclaims any disposition or intention to exercise sovereignty, jurisdiction, or control over said Island except for the pacification thereof, and asserts its determination when that is accomplished to leave the government and control of the Island to its people.

After the close of the war President McKinley and his closest advisors in Congress had determined that the pledge should be kept, and public sentiment had been in agreement with them. As soon, therefore, as American control was an established fact, plans were formulated for relinquishing Cuba to the people of the island. A constitutional convention was held, and a form of government, modeled on that of the United States, was framed and adopted on February 21, 1901.

While the Cuban convention was deliberating, it became apparent that the constitution would not include any statement of policy in regard to future relations with the United States. The American Senate, therefore, under the leadership of Senator O. H. Platt, passed the so-called "Platt Amendment." Its several provisions were as follows: the Cuban government shall never enter into agreements with other powers which tend to impair the independence of the island; it shall not contract public debts of such size that the ordinary revenues would be inadequate to pay interest charges and provide for a sinking fund; it shall permit the intervention of the United States when needed to preserve Cuban independence and the maintenance of an adequate government; and it shall sell or lease necessary coaling stations to the United States.[5] When satisfied that the purpose of the Amendment was not to enable the United States to meddle in affairs in Cuba, but merely to secure Cuban independence and set forth a definite understanding between the two nations, the convention incorporated it in the final constitution. On May 20, 1902, the control of Cuba was formally relinquished to the people of the island, with the good wishes of the people of the United States.

At divers times the oversight of the United States, exerted in accord with the Platt Amendment, has saved Cuba from serious difficulties. In 1906 there was a political uprising which assumed the proportions of a small rebellion. When the Cuban army was unable to quell it, the United States sent down an expeditionary force of 5600 men and restored quiet. A provisional government under Secretary of War Taft and Governor Charles E. Magoon conducted affairs until a president was peacefully elected in 1909. On three occasions in 1912, American intervention seemed possible. One of them was a negro uprising which became so serious that 700 American marines were landed at Guantanamo, and warships were assembled at Key West. In 1917, following an election, another political revolution under a former president was suppressed by the Cuban government

[5] A naval station was subsequently established at Guantanamo, near the eastern end of the island.

with the aid of American troops and a warning from the American government. In 1919, General Enoch Crowder was sent to the islands to advise with the authorities about the revision of the election laws; in 1920 intervention again seemed possible, but was averted; and yet again in 1921 a combination of political and administrative difficulties required the expert skill of General Crowder, together with a body of troops. In all these cases the plan followed has been to warn the Cuban government that order must be maintained, and then to supplement the efforts of the authorities in power. In no case has the United States indicated any purpose to make intervention an excuse for annexation, and, on the whole, Cuba has enjoyed relative quiet and prosperity under American protection.[6]

The task of the United States in Porto Rico was far simpler than in Cuba. The island was small; the people well-disposed towards American occupation; nearly sixty-two per cent. of its 953,243 people were white; and only slight damage had been done by the troops during the war because of the cessation of hostilities at the outset of the Porto Rican expedition.

On October 18, 1898, United States officials assumed control of the island, and until May 1, 1900, the government was in the hands of the War Department. On the latter date a civil government was established under the "Foraker Act," an organic law or constitution passed by Congress on April 12, 1900. Since Porto Rico was not fitted for the degree of self-government accorded either a state or a territory under the American system, its people were made, by the Foraker Act, "citizens of Porto Rico" (not of the United States), were

[6] The treaty of 1898, by which Spain relinquished Cuba to the United States did not specifically mention the Isle of Pines, off the western end of the island of Cuba. In 1904 a treaty was drawn up between the United States and Cuba, by which all American claims to the Isle of Pines were transferred to Cuba. Not until March 13, 1925, after twenty-one years of intermittent deliberation, did the United States Senate succeed in ratifying it.

declared entitled to the protection of the United States, and were constituted "a body politic under the name of The People of Porto Rico." The laws of the United States, where applicable, were extended to the island, and a framework of government set forth. This latter provided for a governor who was to be appointed by the president of the United States and was to be the chief executive officer of the island. The people of Porto Rico were allowed a voice in the government through the power to elect the lower house of the legislature; but control by the United States was assured by giving the president authority to choose the members of the upper house, and by giving both the governor and Congress a veto on legislation passed by the island legislature.

This peculiar status—neither territory, nor state, nor self-governing dominion—did not long satisfy the people of Porto Rico. Agitation began for a greater degree of autonomy, which was granted by the act of March 2, 1917. This law made the people citizens of the United States, and allowed them to elect both houses of the legislature. There are indications, however, that even this degree of self-government will not be permanently satisfactory.

The economic well-being of Porto Rico has received constant attention. Under the provisions of the Foraker Act only fifteen per cent. of the usual duties were to be paid on goods passing between the island and the United States, and since July 25, 1901, complete free trade has existed. Commerce with the United States has grown from $12,500,000 in 1901 to a yearly average of about $125,000,000 since 1917—mainly in sugar, tobacco and fruits.[7] Seven hundred and eighty-three miles of highway were built between 1898 and 1920,—new construction under Spanish rule having been almost negligible. At the beginning of American occupation, there were almost no public schools. These conditions were remedied to

---

[7] Except that in the two years 1920–1921 the value of Porto Rican commerce reached the record height of more than $200,000,000.

such an extent that in 1922 over 226,000 pupils were enrolled in an educational system which ran all the way from elementary schools to a University. Sanitary conditions have been greatly improved; nevertheless, about ninety per cent. of the people suffer from the dreaded hook-worm disease.

The first difficulty met by the United States in the Philippines was an inheritance from Spanish rule. In 1896 the Filipinos, led by Aguinaldo, had risen against the government in order to secure more liberal treatment and to eliminate the influence of the Catholic friars from politics. The "embers of dissatisfaction" were still aglow when the American war intervened. Relations between the revolutionists and the United States forces became strained when the former were not allowed to cooperate with the Americans against the Spanish, and in February, 1899, open warfare followed. Not until July, 1902, was quiet restored, and during the process enough cruelties were practiced by American soldiers to make the anti-imperialists doubly fearful of military control.[8]

McKinley and his Secretary of War—at this time Elihu Root—desired to supplant military government with civil rule as quickly as possible and to this end the President appointed the first Philippine Commission on January 20, 1899, with Jacob G. Schurman, of Cornell University, as Chairman. It was instructed to investigate the situation in the islands and to recommend any action that seemed wise. The unsettled condition of affairs seriously hampered the work of the Commission but it gathered a fund of information which it later published. A second Commission was sent out in 1900, with Judge William H. Taft at the head. The instructions given to the Commission by President McKinley embodied an enlightened colonial policy, the core of which was

[8] The Philippine group is about 7,000 miles southwest of San Francisco; the chief island, Luzon, is almost exactly the size of Ohio, 40,000 sq. miles; the largest city, Manila, contained over 250,000 people at the time of the American occupation, and about 285,000 in 1918.

that the government being established was "designed not for our satisfaction, or for the expression of our theoretical views, but for the happiness, peace, and prosperity of the people of the Philippine Islands." The Commission wielded such large powers that gradually the area controlled by the civil government increased at the expense of the military authorities, and by 1902 only the wild Moros were under military control.

By this time a definite form of government could be planned for, built upon the labors of the second Commission. The Philippine Act of July 1, 1902, provided for a governor appointed by the president, with the advice of the Senate; executive departments; and a legislature, the lower house of which was elected by the people. From the beginning the Filipinos, like the Porto Ricans, have desired a greater range of self-government, and in 1916 long steps were taken in the direction desired by them. The Jones act of that year materially increased the powers of the Philippine government and gave the Filipinos power to elect the upper as well as the lower house of the legislature. The passage of the law met with enthusiastic approval in the islands.

The purpose of American rule in the Philippines has been to fit the people for self-government, although opinions have differed as to how soon the final outcome could be brought about. An early and bothersome problem was found in the friars' lands, which consisted of about 425,000 acres, for the most part in the vicinity of Manila. The possession of so great an area, together with the religious power and the considerable political authority which the friars exercised under Spanish rule, gave the Church a domination which might threaten trouble after the American occupation. The solution of the problem was found in the purchase of the lands for about $7,000,000 by the United States. Efforts have been made to introduce a complete system of education—physical and industrial, as well as academic—with such success that when the Jones bill was being discussed in Congress in 1916 it was asserted that every member of the Philippine legislature at that time was a college graduate. In 1922 the Filipino student body numbered more than a million, with a corps of teachers, nearly all of whom were Filipinos. There is, besides, a University of the Philippines, with about 5,000 students. Political education has also been a part of the American idea. Elementary self-government was gradually introduced, starting in the more civilized local municipalities and provinces and confining the suffrage to the educated people, the official classes and property owners. The preservation of order has been more and more entrusted to a Philippine constabulary; civil service officers and school teachers have been increasingly chosen from the Filipinos; and the courts have been partly manned with native judges. Work in sanitation has followed the lines marked out in Cuba and Porto Rico. First and last over 10,000,000 vaccinations were performed before 1914; smallpox has been controlled; attention has been paid to the building of highways and railroads, water supply, the disposal of sewage, and allied problems.

The first attempt to revise the customs laws in the Philippines was made by the Commission during the governorship of William H. Taft. These schedules were revised in Washington in such a way as to discriminate against Philippine interests, but they had remained in force only a short time when Congress passed the act of March 8, 1902, allowing goods grown or produced in the Philippines to enter the United States under a twenty-five per cent. reduction. In 1909, the tariff makers were induced to relent to the extent of allowing the free importation of goods grown, produced or manufactured in the Philippines, except that only a specified annual amount of Philippine sugar and tobacco might be brought in. In 1913 the wall was entirely removed on all trade between the United States and the Philippines in articles made or grown in either of the two countries.

The chief remaining question concerning the Philippines is the one which all nations with colonial possessions have had to answer since history began,—to what extent shall they be given self-government? It has always been assumed that complete independence would some day be granted if the Filipinos desired it. Presidents of both parties have indicated such an expectation, and Congress committed itself in the preamble of the Jones Act of 1916:

Whereas it is, as it always has been, the purpose of the people of the United States to withdraw their sovereignty over the Philippine Islands and to recognize their independence as soon as a stable government can be established therein . . .

On the other hand, many competent observers feel that the people are not yet fitted for self-government, and will not be for an indefinite time in the future. Moreover, the trade between the United States and the Philippines increased between 1898 and 1920 from about $4,000,000 to approximately $200,000,000, thus creating a sort of bond which usually makes nations loath to part with their colonies.

In the meantime, the agitation for immediate independence continues in the Philippines, led by the powerful "Nationalist" Party. General Leonard Wood, appointed governor in 1921, has been bitterly opposed by the Nationalists, who declare that he has curtailed their powers of self-government. In 1923 the Filipinos sent a commission to Washington to ask for the appointment of a Filipino governor, but without result.

Although the acquisition of Hawaii was not due to the treaty closing the War with Spain, its annexation in 1898 was distinctly hastened by the events of the conflict.[9] It therefore constituted a part of the imperialistic problem which the United States has had to face ever since,—a problem made

[9] *Cf.* p. 362.

somewhat difficult in the case of Hawaii because a large fraction of its inhabitants were Asiatics.

The organic act of April 30, 1900, erected a form of government slightly different from those given to Porto Rico and the Philippines. It made Hawaii a territory, placed it under the safeguards of the Constitution and made its people citizens of the United States. A governor is appointed by the president, and must be a citizen of Hawaii. The territorial legislature is elected by the people, but voting is restricted to citizens who are able to speak, read and write the English or Hawaiian language,—thus excluding the Asiatic element. According to the census of 1920, the population of the islands was 255,912, most of whom were Chinese (23,507) and Japanese (109,274), with smaller numbers of Americans, Hawaiians, Portuguese, Filipinos and others.

Trade with the United States is the main economic reliance, amounting to about $180,000,000 in 1924,—the greater part being sugar and tropical fruits.

While Congress and the President were concerning themselves with the practical problems of military control, sanitation and the like, the Supreme Court was laboriously considering the less tangible but equally perplexing question of the constitutionality of the several acts which the legislative and executive departments had committed. The power of Congress to acquire territory and the right of the executive to control new territory under the war power had long been conceded. Admittedly, however, government under the war power was temporary and transitional. In earlier times such acquisitions as those effected by the Louisiana purchase and the annexation of Texas had been consummated with the distinct understanding that these regions should immediately or eventually become territories or states in the Union. The status of Porto Rico and the Philippines was novel. ''The civil rights and political status of the native inhabitants of the territories hereby ceded to the United States," ran the words of the treaty of peace closing the War with Spain, "shall be determined by the Congress." Did this mean that Congress might govern the new acquisitions independently of the Constitution? Could it abridge freedom of speech, and permit cruel and unusual punishments, or establish slavery? Could Congress permanently govern these lands without giving their citizens the rights of citizens of the United States, and with no intention of ever making them territories or states? On the other hand, if Congress must act within the limits prescribed by the Constitution, would the wild Moros of the Philippines be the beneficiaries of the amendment preserving the right of trial by jury? In the popular language of the day, did the Constitution follow the flag?

It was not long before the Supreme Court was called upon in the "Insular Cases" to express itself upon these constitutional questions. The first case was De Lima v. Bidwell. It was a suit to recover duties paid on goods sent from Porto Rico to the United States during the interval between the cession of the island and the passage of the Foraker Act. The duties had been paid under the Dingley law, which levied customs of specified amounts upon all goods imported "from foreign countries." Was Porto Rico a "foreign" country? The majority of the nine members of the Court thought that it was not foreign, that there was scarcely a "shred of authority" for the view that a "district ceded to and in the possession of the United States remains for any purpose a foreign country." Since Porto Rico was not a foreign country, the duties were wrongfully collected and must be returned. The remaining four justices dissented. One of them delivered a dissenting opinion in which he held that Porto Rico occupied middle ground between that of a foreign country and domestic territory. As such its status could be determined by Congress only and therefore its products were subject to duties levied by the Dingley act.

In Downes *v.* Bidwell the Court was compelled to determine the constitutionality of the part of the Foraker Act which provided for a tariff between Porto Rico and the United States equal to fifteen per cent. of that levied by the Dingley act. Again the Court divided five to four. Mr. Justice Brown delivered the majority opinion. It was to the effect that the Constitution applied only to *States;* that Congress possessed unlimited power over the political relations of the *territories;* that Porto Rico was a "territory appurtenant to and belonging to the United States"; and that the part of the Constitution which says that duties shall be uniform throughout the United States did not apply to Porto Rico unless Congress so willed. Hence the customs clause of the Foraker Act was valid. Four of the majority, however, who agreed with Mr. Justice Brown in his conclusion that the tariff clause of the Foraker Act was constitutional did so for reasons which they asserted to be "different from, if not in conflict with, those expressed" by him.

From the point of view of constitutional law, the decisions were unsatisfactory, because of the balanced division of opinion. Yet to have declared all the provisions of the Constitution in force in all the acquisitions would have been embarrassing. Logic and the Constitution went to the winds, while the executive and legislative departments administered the territories on the convenient and flexible theory that certain constitutional provisions must be heeded and that others need not.

While the colonial policy of the United States was being developed, the possession of the Philippines added interest in the United States to an unusual international situation in China which immediately involved several European nations and eventually affected America. The Chinese-Japanese War, which came to a close in 1895, had uncovered to the world the weakness of China as a military power and had weakened the hold of the reigning monarch upon the people of the Empire. Thereupon the leading commercial nations of Europe began to seize portions of China in order to extend their trade relations in the Far East. Russia first attempted to obtain a seaport, but retired when an uproar of protest arose from the remainder of Europe. Not long afterwards, two German missionaries in the province of Shantung were murdered. The outrage formed a sufficient pretext for aggressive action, as a result of which China leased Kiaochau to Germany in 1898 for ninety-nine years, including in the grant railway and mining privileges and an indemnity; Russia then renewed her attempt and succeeded in leasing Port Arthur and Talienwan for twenty-five years. Great Britain followed with the acquisition of rights in Weihaiwei similar to those of Russia in Port Arthur; and France found its share in Kwangchaouwan. In each case, moreover, the leasing power designated a large area around its holdings as a "sphere of interest" in which its economic mastery was complete. In this way, thirteen of the eighteen provinces of China, including the most desirable harbors, waterways and mines, were partially controlled by the powers.

American foreign affairs had been, since October 1, 1898, in the skilful hands of John Hay, who was possessed of an intimate knowledge of conditions in Europe. Hay perceived the danger to American commercial interests in China, and accordingly in September, 1899, he addressed a circular note to the powers requesting each of them to give formal assurances that in its sphere of influence: (1) it would not interfere with any treaty port or vested interest; (2) it would agree that the Chinese tariff should apply equally to all goods shipped to ports in the spheres, and be collected by the Chinese officials; and (3) it would charge no higher harbor and railroad rates for citizens of other nations than for its own. The powers having agreed more or less directly, Hay informed them by a note of March 20, 1900, that all had acceded to his propositions and that the United States considered their assent as "final and definitive." There could be, of course, no effectual guaranty that the powers would fully observe this "Open Door" policy, but the economic penetration of China, which would soon result in complete political possession, was at least retarded for the moment.

Domestic affairs in China, meanwhile, had been seething under the surface. An ill-starred reform movement, initiated by the Emperor, had failed, the government was discredited, and the Empress Dowager seized the throne for herself. All China interpreted the event to presage a return to the old order of things—a general anti-foreign movement. Economic distresses, bad crops, a disastrous flood and hatred of foreign missionaries, combined with a deep resentment at the European partition of their country, caused the Chinese to break out in a score of scattered attacks on the hated aliens. The culmination was the Boxer Rebellion. The Boxers was a society which had long existed in China for various religious, patriotic and other purposes. It took up the cry "Drive out the foreigners and uphold the dynasty." Government officials by their disinclination to quell the Boxer uprising, showed that their sympathies were with the rioters.

The climax of the outbreak came in and around Pekin, the capital of China. The railroad from the city to the coast was seized, telegraphic connection cut off, and the representatives of the foreign powers were compelled to fortify themselves within the city. On June 19, 1900, all foreigners were ordered to leave within twenty-four hours, and the German minister was shot when he attempted to visit the proper officer in order to protest. The Chinese army poured out to surround the quarter of the city where the legations were situated and cut them off from the rest of the world. All foreigners fled to the British legation, where they constructed

bomb proof cellars, raised barricades and planted artillery.[10]
The powers, including the United States, combined to send a
punitive expedition to Pekin, while the legationers settled
down to a state of siege, determined to hold out as long as
possible. At last on August 14, when the surviving foreigners were reduced to eating horse flesh and when scores had
been killed or wounded, the relief column reached the capital.
It was high time. The foreign quarters and much of the business portion, the banks, and the theatres had been burned, and
the entire city threatened with destruction.

By the time that the uprisings in Pekin and elsewhere had
been suppressed, it was evident that the powers would have a
stern accounting with China. Hay had already openly announced the policy of the United States in his note of July 3,
1900; it was that the United States would seek a solution
which should bring about permanent safety and peace to
China, preserve the territorial entity of the country, protect
the rights of friendly powers and insure an equal opportunity
for all nations in the commerce of China. Hay continued
through the negotiations to urge joint action on the part of
the powers, and procured from them a statement disclaiming
any purpose to acquire any part of China. At length in
December, 1900, the demands upon China were formulated,
to which that unhappy nation was compelled to accede. The
most important were, punishment for the guilty rioters, safeguards for the future, indemnities for losses and the improvement of commercial relations. The financial indemnity finally
placed upon China was $333,000,000, of which $24,000,000
was for the United States. The latter sum proved to be more
than sufficient to satisfy all claims and China was relieved
from the payment of about $12,000,000. As a mark of ap-

10 It was on the occasion of despatching troops to avenge the death of
Von Ketteler, the German minister, that the Emperor gave instructions
to "give no quarter and to (act) so like Huns that for a thousand years
to come no Chinese would dare to look a German in the face."

preciation for this act, the Chinese government determined to use the fund in sending students to the United States for education.

The conduct of American colonial affairs has been dominated by four main considerations: (1) In the beginning, the United States was not controlled by any legal limitations except such as were found in the treaty with Spain; (2) The country, however, felt a moral obligation to govern the acquisitions with due consideration for their inhabitants;[11] (3) The inhabitants were not fitted for self-government, and must be held in a status for which this country had no constitutional precedents; (4) The dependencies had great commercial possibilities,—especially in tropical products of which the United States has need.

It is fair to say that the United States has attempted to protect the people of the dependencies with the safeguards of the Constitution and to carry out its moral obligations. Nevertheless the Constitution has had to be strained in order to make it function under circumstances which were never anticipated by its framers. Trade with Cuba and Porto Rico have made necessary an interest in the stability and domestic affairs of other countries in and around the Caribbean Sea, and in European nations which own colonies there. Hawaii and the Philippines have brought connections with China and Japan and with problems of the Pacific Ocean.[12] Any armed conflict which threatens any of these American interests would be a cause for entanglement. The Spanish War, then, has brought the United States into a position where it possesses outlying dependencies and a growing colonial commerce,—objects which have caused many of the international difficulties of the world's history.

[11] *Cf.* Root. *Military and Colonial Policy of the United States,* pp. 161 *ff.*

[12] *Cf.* p. 551 *ff.*

BIBLIOGRAPHICAL NOTE

The framing, contents and ratification of the treaty of 1898 are well described in Chadwick, Latané and Olcott. The treaty itself is conveniently found in William MacDonald, *Documentary Source Book of American History* (new ed., 1916). The negotiations are in *Senate Document* No. 62, Pt. I, 55th Congress, 3d session (Serial Number 3732).

The best accounts of the election of 1900 are in Stanwood, Croly and Latané.

The island possessions have given rise to a considerable body of special volumes of a high order. Especially useful are: (Cuba), Elihu Root, *Military and Colonial Policy of the United States* (1916), by McKinley's Secretary of War; L. A. Coolidge, *O. H. Platt* (1910); A. G. Robinson, *Cuba and the Intervention* (1905); C. E. Magoon, *Republic of Cuba* (1908), by the provisional governor during the second intervention. (Porto Rico), W. F. Willoughby, *Territories and Dependencies of the United States* (1905), by a former treasurer of Porto Rico; L. S. Rowe, *United States and Porto Rico* (1904). The most complete work on the Philippines is D. C. Worcester, *Philippines: Past and Present* (2 vols., 1914), by a member of the Commission; the valuable report of Commissioner Taft is in *Report of the Philippine Commission,* 1907, part 3, printed also as *Senate Document* 200, 60th Congress, 1st session, vol. 7 (Serial Number 5240). The reports of the governors of Porto Rico and the Philippines, found in the *War Department, Annual Reports,* are essential. "The Case for Immediate Philippine Independence," by M. L. Quezon, President of the Philippine Senate, is in *Current History,* Sept., 1924.

General accounts are in W. F. Johnson, *America's Foreign Relations* (1916), II, Chaps. XXXII–XXXIII; and R. Cortissoz, *Life of Whitelaw Reid* (2 vols. 1921).

The legal and constitutional aspects of imperialism are best followed in the *Harvard Law Review,* vols. XII, XIII; W. W. Willoughby, *Constitutional Law of the United States* (2 vols., 1910); C. F. Randolph, *The Law and Policy of Annexation* (1901); the "insular cases" are in *United States Reports* vol. 182, pp. 1, 244.

The most complete account of affairs in China is P. H. Clements,

The Boxer Rebellion (1915); J. B. Moore, *Digest,* vol. V (1906), is useful, as always; J. W. Foster, *American Diplomacy in the Orient* (1903), is clear and concise; W. R. Thayer, *John Hay* (2 vols., 1915), is disappointing.

On the policy of imperialism: L. A. Coolidge, *An Old-Fashioned Senator, O. H. Platt* (1910); G. F. Hoar, *Autobiography of Seventy Years,* 2 vols.; A. C. Coolidge, *United States as a World Power* (1916); W. G. Sumner, *War and Other Essays* (1913), "The Conquest of the United States by Spain." On the economic side, Faulkner, *American Economic History* (1924), chap. XXV.

CHAPTER XIX

THE THRESHOLD OF THE TWENTIETH CENTURY

The aggregate net profits of the United States Steel Corporation, April 1, 1901, to December 31, 1924, were $2,108,848,640.11.
TWENTY-THIRD ANNUAL REPORT OF THE UNITED STATES STEEL CORPORATION, DEC. 31, 1924.

On October 9, 1876, Dr. Bell talked from Boston to his associate, Thomas Watson, in Cambridge, over two miles of telegraph line.
INFORMATION DEPARTMENT, A. T. AND T. CO.

The scientific revolution which began with the last quarter of the nineteenth century will doubtless have a greater effect on the world's history than the industrial revolution which began at the close of the eighteenth.

Expectation of life in years, at birth, in Massachusetts:

1890—42.5
1900—46.0
1910—49.3
1920—54.0

THE conditions under which the average American lived changed between 1890 and 1920 more rapidly, perhaps, than in any previous thirty years in the history of the country. To be sure, most of the tendencies which had characterized the growth of population, the expansion of the West, the concentration of the people in cities, the development of manufacturing and agriculture, and the extension of the railway system, from 1870 to 1890, were equally significant during the three decades following the latter year. In other phases of life, however, the changes were more spectacular and revolutionary. The year 1890 was only,—the year 1890. 1920 seemed more than thirty years forward as measured in political, economic, social, scientific and cultural existence.

428

POPULATION CHANGES

The rate of growth of population slowed up slightly from 1890 to 1910, being twenty-one per cent. per decade, as contrasted with twenty-five per cent. from 1870 to 1890. After 1914 Europe was engaged in a devastating war, and immigration to America diminished abruptly, so that the increase in population from 1910 to 1920 was only fifteen per cent. The increases, however, were distributed over a larger area than was the case between 1870 and 1890. No fewer than thirteen states added more than a million inhabitants,—industrial states like New York, Pennsylvania, Illinois and Ohio; fast-developing states like Texas and California; and new states like Oklahoma. On the other hand large areas showed a tendency to slow up or even to decline. What growth there was in northern New England continued slowly. In the five states Iowa, Missouri, Nebraska, Kansas and Colorado, the great rush of settlers which characterized the years before 1890 dwindled to a modest increase after 1910. Such a purely agricultural state as Mississippi suffered an actual loss in population from 1910 to 1920, while the neighboring industrial state of Alabama increased more than 200,000.

Immigration continued to be large until 1914, and concentrated in the North, especially in the cities. In New Bedford, in 1920, forty-two per cent. of the inhabitants were foreign born, and forty-one per cent. more were of foreign or mixed foreign and native parentage. Factory cities like Lawrence, Massachusetts, and Passaic, New Jersey had hardly a larger percentage of native born citizens than New Bedford, and in New York City alone were massed one-third of all the Russians in the United States. The chief European contributors to the population of America in 1920 in the order of their importance were Germany, Italy, Russia, Poland, Great Britain and Ireland. In some states the foreign element was especially strong. Forty per cent. of all the German-Americans

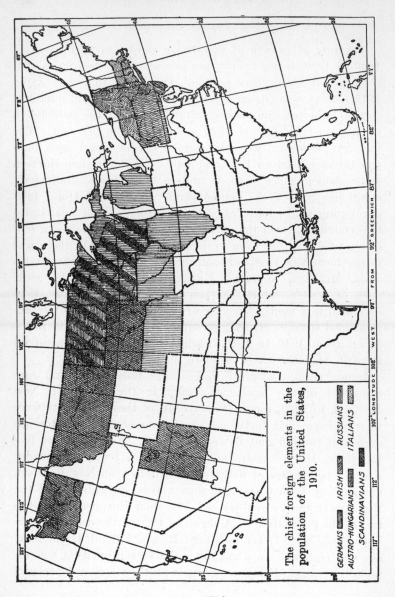

The chief foreign elements in the population of the United States, 1910.

GERMANS   IRISH   RUSSIANS
AUSTRO-HUNGARIANS   ITALIANS
SCANDINAVIANS

in 1920 were in the states of New York, Illinois and Wisconsin; the Italians concentrated in New York, Pennsylvania, and New Jersey; and the Poles in New York, Pennsylvania and Illinois.

Interstate migration showed new tendencies. The population movement within the United States has always been predominantly westward. During the twelve decades from 1790 to 1910 the center of population moved toward the West at the average rate of forty-six miles every ten years. Between 1910 and 1920, however, it moved less than ten miles. In part this was due to rapidly growing states like Oklahoma and Texas, which drew heavily on the upper Mississippi Valley; Florida, which attracted many from northern states; and to the growth of eastern cities which called to their borders hundreds of thousands of southerners and westerners. A noticeable aspect of interstate migration between 1910 and 1920 was the movement of negroes to the industrial cities. The numbers of negroes migrating were not so important as their concentration in particular districts, and the resulting danger of race friction. Akron, Ohio, for example, increased its negro population nearly 750 per cent.; Detroit, more than 600 per cent.; and Cleveland over 300 per cent.

By all odds the most significant population change following 1890, however, was the continued and rapid growth of the cities. So far-reaching were its effects that its statistical outlines are well worth attention:

Census Year	Percentage of Urban Population [1]	Number of Cities of Over 100,000 Inhabitants
1890	35.4%	26
1900	40.0	37
1910	45.8	50
1920	51.4	68

[1] By "urban population" is meant that living in towns or villages of 2,500 inhabitants or more.

In a word, the population of the United States in 1890 was almost two-thirds rural; in 1920 it was more than half urban. The causes of this growth seem to have been the same as in earlier years, except that the immigrant stream after 1890 tended to go more to the industrial areas and less to the farms than had hitherto been the case, and therefore was a greater factor in city life than formerly.

So great an expansion necessitated, of course, a corresponding territorial enlargement; and this in turn required more expeditious means of transportation. During the late eighties and early nineties the old-fashioned horse-drawn street car and the omnibus began to give way to the electric trolley car, and the suburbs were enabled to pour their contribution of factory workers and office employees into the shops and stores of the cities with what was then thought to be miraculous speed.

For those who did not find housing in the suburbs, the apartment building was developed. This type of dwelling was not of American origin, and was to be seen in New York as early as President Grant's time, but it became increasingly common after 1890. The same pressure for space that sent people into the suburbs and made apartment houses a necessity, caused the construction of the most American of all buildings,—the "sky-scraper" Beginning in 1890 in Chicago and New York, tall office structures were erected on a steel skeleton or framework, as wood and brick were incapable of carrying the terrific weight of a tall building. Grave questions of health and public safety likewise originated in the speed with which the cities grew. Houses were built, as we have seen [2] without proper safeguards against fire; rooms were constructed without adequate attention to the necessity of light and air; and families were crowded into such small spaces as to invite epidemics of disease. Laws were passed, against great pressure from land-owners, to reform

[2] *Cf.* p. 62.

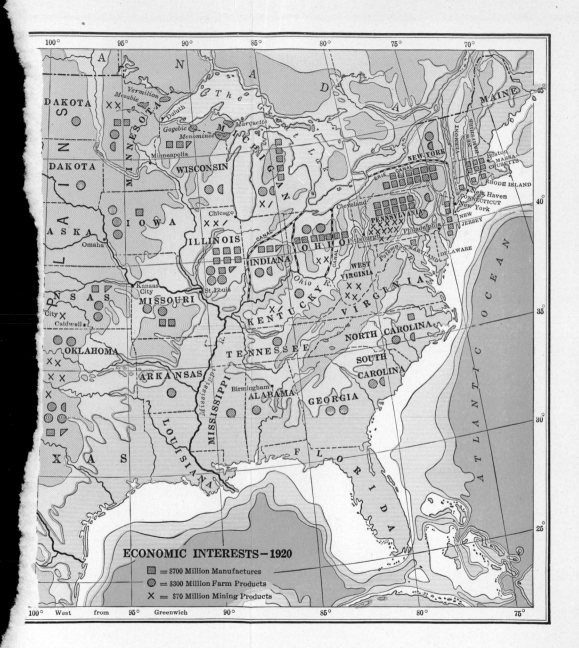

ECONOMIC INTERESTS—1920

⬛ = $700 Million Manufactures
⬤ = $300 Million Farm Products
✕ = $70 Million Mining Products

such conditions. The cities had to find out how to dispose of refuse and waste, and how to ensure adequate water, and pure milk and food supplies for a population that was increasing at a rate which no human ingenuity could predict.

If the family of wealth or moderate means faced constantly changing conditions, in the cities of the eighties and nineties, the ignorant proletariat often faced the most dire distress. Particularly, of course, was this true in those "slum" areas where swarms of immigrants were huddled together,—poor, ignorant of the American language, frequently vicious, and commonly a prey to a greedy landlord. It was to combat these conditions that settlement houses were established. The first of these was founded in New York in 1887, in imitation of Toynbee Hall in London; another in 1889, also in New York; and most famous of all, Hull House in Chicago in the same year. The settlement idea was to provide buildings in the poorer districts of the cities where altruistic men and women could live among the "submerged tenth," and give them the benefit of "trained intelligence and friendly sympathy." Sometimes this meant alleviating hunger and poverty; sometimes, teaching kindergarten or sewing classes; and sometimes providing amusement and recreation.

In order to modify the fundamental conditions which cause slums, poor housing and unsanitary conditions, numerous municipal reforms were attempted after 1890. Following Bryce's famous indictment of city government in the United States,[3] American writers and reformers called attention to the urgent need of action. A wide variety of new forms of city government were experimented with. Galveston, for example, after a disastrous storm in 1900 which destroyed a great part of the city, did away with the usual mayor and city legislature, and placed its affairs in the hands of a board of five commissioners. These men conduct the city's business as if they were both the managers and the di-

[3] *Cf.* p. 63.

rectors of a corporation. Several hundreds of cities have adopted the plan since that time. Another expedient for the reformation of misgovernment was the "city manager" plan which originated in Sumter, South Carolina, in 1913 and in Dayton, Ohio, at about the same time, and has been tried in more than 300 other places. Under this scheme, the people elect a small commission to act as a city legislature or council. The commission appoints an executive officer or general manager for the city's business,—frequently a business man or an expert in municipal affairs,—who is expected to care for the city as if it were an industrial organization and not a patronage prize for the politicians to fight for.

The latest improvement in the history of the city is "city planning." The first step in city planning is the study of the laying out of streets and parks, the construction of public buildings, the control of traffic, and in fact all matters which affect the well-being of the whole community. The second step is the use of the information in future construction in such a way as to prevent further mistakes. The movement in the United States had its inspiration in the World's Fair in Chicago in 1893, but it did not achieve much until after the beginning of the twentieth century. All these developments in municipal life cost so much money that some of the cities rival the states in their financial operations. The annual budget of New York, to mention an extreme case, increased from $35,000,000 in 1890, to almost $400,000,000 for 1925.

The effect of the development of the city has extended far beyond the limits of the cities themselves, and is much greater than is indicated by any statistics. The great electric light and power plant is made possible only by the large demand of a city, but it may supply electricity to a score of small villages and a thousand isolated houses outside; the splendidly equipped hospital with its staff of specialists is a product of the city, but rapid transit and the telephone place them at the disposal of the family on the farm; and the discovery of methods of providing an ample pure water supply free from typhoid contamination is a task for highly paid scientists in the employ of a city,—but when their work is done, the results may be at the call of the most distant hamlet. From this point of view the United States is more thoroughly urbanized than its 51.4 per cent. of city population would indicate.

The relation of the growth of the cities to the development of athletic sport before 1895 has already been made apparent.[4] After 1895, and especially after 1900 another effect appeared. As men engaged more in "white collar" work at offices, stores and factories, and less in manual labor on the farms, they discovered the necessity of out-of-door recreation and vacations. Large corporations adopted definite systems by which employees of certain classes received a leave of absence during a part of the summer. Business men began to lengthen the traditional holidays into two or three if they came near the week-end. Sunday itself became used as a day of recreation. Summer camps were opened in growing numbers, where boys and girls who lived in the city might learn something of the woods and the country, how to swim and how to handle a canoe.

MANUFACTURING AND AGRICULTURE

Manufacturing increased its importance as the foremost economic activity of the country. The number of persons engaged in it doubled between 1890 and 1920, although the entire population was increasing during that time only about sixty-six per cent.

Prices have mounted so rapidly since 1900 that it is impossible to describe accurately the changes in the value of American manufacturing. Nevertheless it is apparent that the United States has become more and more an industrialized nation. In 1890 the value of the manufactures of the country was nearly $9,400,000,000; in 1910 it was about twenty-one

[4] *Cf.* p. 63.

billions, and in 1919 nearly sixty-two and a half billions.

The center of the manufacturing industry has tended to move west with the population. In 1850 it was in central Pennsylvania; between 1880 and 1890 it crossed into Ohio, and by 1920 it had nearly reached the western boundary.

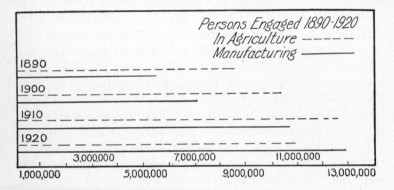

Persons Engaged 1890-1920
In Agriculture − − − − −
Manufacturing ————

Ohio, Illinois, Michigan and Indiana have been shifting their interest from agriculture to manufacturing, and finding their points of view increasingly like those of the eastern states. In the Far West, the chief manufacturing states are California, Washington and Oregon. The strides which these states have taken in recent years is indicated by the fact that Washington increased the value of its manufactured goods nearly twenty fold between 1890 and 1920, and the other two states about nine fold. In none of these cases is the main economic reliance placed on the mining of precious metals. In California, petroleum refining, the canning of fruit, ship building and meat packing have become the leading industries; in Washington, lumber and timber, ship building and grist mill products; and in Oregon, lumber, flour and foundry products. Ship building is a new interest which has arisen in the main since 1913. The production of lumber and timber has taken a prominent place as a result of the search for new forests.

At the close of the Civil War the Northeast was producing

more than one-third of the lumber used in the country; by
1880 it was pretty well cut over, and the region around the
Great Lakes took its place; by 1900 the South forged to the
front and has maintained that position; by 1920, however,
the Rocky Mountain and the Pacific Coast states were increasing their cut faster than the South, and again the lumberman
prepared to migrate. The rapidity with which the available
supply of timber was being cut off was the main cause of a
movement to be more frugal with what was left.

The growth of manufacturing in the South was slightly more
rapid than in the United States as a whole. The number
of wage earners increased nearly three fold and the values of
the product almost nine times. In 1890 the textile interests
of the South were almost negligible except in one or two states.
Several powerful factors changed this condition with the in-
evitability that attaches to economic transitions. In the first
place the South was nearer to the sources of cotton supply
than New England,—the traditional home of the textile industry. For a variety of reasons, also, the problems of labor,
working hours and taxes were not so pressing. New England
textile corporations transferred a part of their operations
to the cotton producing states; where new plants were constructed, with new and improved machinery, they were frequently built near the source of raw material. By 1920,
therefore, there were almost as many spindles at work in the
cotton growing states as in New England. Of the five leading states in the manufacture of cotton goods in 1920, New
England states were first and fifth (Massachusetts and Rhode
Island), but the remaining three were North Carolina, South
Carolina and Georgia. The extraction of valuable materials
from the soil in the South was largely confined before 1890
to the mining of coal and iron in a few states, more especially
Alabama. The slow and steady development of this industry has made Alabama one of the heavy producers of iron and
steel. More rapid has been the production of petroleum

in West Virginia, Oklahoma and Texas,—chiefly since 1910. These three states in 1909 extracted about one hundred and thirteen million dollars' worth of raw materials from the ground. In ten years this had grown to nearly seven hundred and thirty-eight million dollars; fortunes were being made overnight, and "boom" times were again showering their combined blessings and curses on the Southwest.

The census of 1920 made evident the fact that agriculture, like the population and the manufacturing industry, was moving westward. In 1890 the center of farm values was in mid-Illinois; in 1920 it was in the center of Missouri. The farmers of the eastern states were either turning their energies into industry, or migrating westward to take possession of the more attractive soil of the Mississippi Valley.

New England contained scarcely more than half as much improved farmland in 1920 as in 1890; the improved area in New York, New Jersey and Pennsylvania declined after 1880; Ohio tilled fewer acres after 1900, and Indiana and Illinois fewer after 1910. The great increases in tilled land between 1890 and 1910 had been on the Plains, which had lost their earlier unique and picturesque characteristics as the cattle country, and had given way to the homesteader. During those twenty years a vast empire was turned over by the plow,—24,000,000 acres in Oklahoma and Texas alone; nearly eighty-six and a half million acres between the Mississippi River and the Rocky Mountains (more than two and a half times the area of England). After 1910 the process of opening new land slowed down even on the plains. The pioneer-farmer turned his face further westward once more, and found virgin soil in the valleys of the Rocky Mountains. Here, between 1910 and 1920, 14,000,000 acres were new or additional improved land,—nearly as much as in all the rest of the United States put together. The contest between the husbandman with his plow on the one side, and the Indian, the wild animal and the wilderness on the other, was about over.

Several of the southern states have experienced a considerable agricultural development since 1890. The increased use of tobacco in all parts of the country has revived its production in Virginia, kept it up in Kentucky and nearly quadrupled it in North Carolina. The development of rapid transit to Florida has made an outlet for huge crops of oranges and other fruits; and the inflow of northern capital and winter visitors from the North has brought about a real estate boom and an agricultural expansion. The boundless area of Texas has enabled that state to lead the country in the growth of cotton,—producing nearly three million bales in 1920.

An economic fact of no little importance was a change in the downward tendency of the price level after 1896. It will be remembered that the constant fall in prices from 1873 to 1896 had brought distress to the farmers of the West and

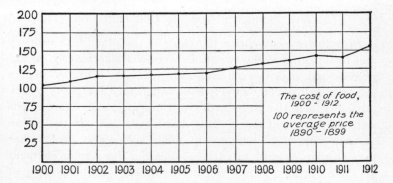

The cost of food, 1900 - 1912.
100 represents the average price 1890 - 1899

had been one of the causes of the Populist revolt. After 1896 the process was reversed. Between that year and 1913 the quantity of gold in circulation considerably increased, as has been seen; bank deposits subject to check trebled in volume, and the use of checks became more common; altogether it was estimated by Professor Irving Fisher that the quantity of money in circulation increased two fold. The cost of food was fifty per cent. higher in 1913 than in the earlier year, and accordingly the complaints of the farmer were less frequently heard. The wage earners in the factories, however, most people living on salaries which were more or less fixed, and practically all persons who lived on the income of investments were differently affected. The prices which the wage earner and the salaried man had to pay for the necessities of life were increasing faster than their incomes, so that their standard of living tended to decline. People whose income was obtained from investments received the same amount of money as formerly but its purchasing power was growing relentlessly smaller. Inasmuch as the numbers of people in these several groups was becoming constantly larger, it seemed inevitable that the problem of rising prices after 1896 would constitute as great a problem as the problem of falling prices had done before that year.[5]

THE TENDENCY TOWARD CONSOLIDATION

In industrial enterprise the close of the nineteenth century and the opening of the twentieth were characterized by an unprecedented rush toward consolidation. To a milder degree the process had, of course, been under way for many years, during which the Standard Oil Company and other trusts were the subject of much study and legislation. In the course of time some of these concerns made such great profits that their leaders sought attractive openings for the investment of their surplus. They began to appear on the boards of directors of railways, banks, electric lighting companies and other industrial organizations.[6] Before 1900 two powerful

[5] For later aspects, *cf.* pp. 669, 691.

[6] Shortly after 1900, for example, Chauncey M. Depew was a director or officer in fifty-six transportation companies, W. K. Vanderbilt in fifty-one; and George J. Gould in thirty-five. Meyer, *History of the Northern Securities Case*, p. 240.

groups had definitely formed. The Standard or Rockefeller group was obtaining large interests in such railways
as the Missouri, Kansas and Texas, the Delaware, Lackawanna
and Western, and the Chicago, Milwaukee and St. Paul. It
was reaching out to the gas and electric companies in New
York, and had an alliance with the National City Bank and
others, and was in touch with great life insurance companies
such as the Equitable and the Mutual of New York. Such
connections enabled them to determine the policies and direct
the investments of those important concerns. The Morgans
extended their influence over the Philadelphia and Reading,
the New York, Lake Erie and Western, the Lehigh Valley and
others. Morgan himself also entered the industrial field as
organizer of the Federal Steel Company and the National Tube
Company.

From every point of view the tendency after 1890 was
emphatically toward large commercial and industrial plants,
toward huge capitalizations and armies of employees. The
census of 1920 proved that the number of very small establishments was not so great as it had been twenty years earlier,
while the number of very large ones,—those employing more
than a thousand wage earners—was rapidly on the increase.
The pace was faster during some years and was more pronounced in some sections of the country than others,—but it
was undoubtedly the spirit of the age.

The organization of mammoth corporations came to a climax about 1900. The census taken in that year noted ninety-
two that had been formed between January 1, 1899, and June
30, 1900. Early in 1904 the editor of Moody's *Manual of
Corporation Securities* recorded the existence of 440 large
industrial and transportation combinations whose capitalization as measured by the par value of their stocks and bonds
was nearly $20,500,000,000. The securities—stocks and bonds
—of the new companies were eagerly taken up by the investing
public. Prosperity was widespread and the financial strength

behind the organizations seemed unlimited. Speculation became common. A few individuals amassed wealth through the shrewd purchase and sale of stocks, and countless others sought unsuccessfully to imitate them. Where sales of 400,000 shares on the stock exchange had formerly been looked upon as a good day's business, the record jumped to a million, then two, and even three.[7]

A threatened competitive struggle among the steel manufacturers in 1901 led to the formation of the United States Steel Corporation, the most famous consolidation of the period. It was, strictly speaking, a "holding corporation" which did not manufacture at all, but merely held the securities and directed the policies of the group of companies of which it was composed. It integrated all the elements of the industry— ore deposits, coal mines, limestone, a thousand miles of railroads, ore vessels on the Great Lakes, furnaces, steel works, rolling mills and other related interests. The value of the tangible property which was thus brought under the control of a single group of men was estimated by the United States Commissioner of Corporations at about $700,000,000. The company issued securities, however, to somewhat over twice this amount. In other words, about $700,000,000 of the capitalization was "water," that is, securities issued in excess of the value of the tangible properties owned. The prices paid to those who controlled the constituent companies were such as to make them multi-millionaires over night, and the commission given to the financiers who organized the Corporation was unparalleled in size, amounting to $62,500,000.

The appreciation of the value of the ore deposits controlled by the Steel Corporation later replaced some of the water in its securities, but in many other cases no such process came about. Investors therefore discovered that the paper which they had purchased did not represent real property, but

---

[7] The shrinkage of the value of these securities caused the "rich men's panic" of 1903. Consult Noyes, *Forty Years,* pp. 308–311.

merely the hope of a company that its profits would be large enough to provide returns upon all its securities. One hundred of the leading industrial stocks shrank in value $1,750,-000,000 within eighteen months. In the case of the Steel Corporation it was noticeable that its supremacy depended to a large extent on the possession of resources of ore on land much of which had originally belonged to the public, a fact which, the Commissioner of Corporations remarked, made the affairs of the company a matter of public interest.

The growth and consolidation which characterized the history of industry were also taking place in the railway system, although somewhat more slowly. It has already been noted that the length of the railroads had reached 164,000 miles by 1890. For the next two decades the rate of construction diminished slightly, yet the total in 1914 was 252,231 miles, and the par value of all railroad securities was estimated at $20,500,000,000. Nearly four and a half million persons, a railroad president estimated in 1915, were at that time interested in the industry as employees, as workmen in shops making railroad supplies, or through the ownership of stocks and bonds. The management of the roads is, of course, continually changing; alliances are made and broken; groups form and dissolve. About the time that the United States Steel Corporation was being organized, however, nearly ninety-five per cent. of the important lines were in the control of six groups of influential persons, which were dominated by fourteen individuals. Each group had obtained the upper hand in the roads of one or more sections. The group headed by J. P. Morgan and James J. Hill held the Chicago, Burlington and Quincy, the Northern Pacific, the Great Northern, the Southern, the Atlantic Coast Line, the Erie and others, amounting to 47,206 miles. E. H. Harriman, chairman of the board of directors of the Union Pacific, succeeded in obtaining control of so many lines that by 1901 the Interstate Commerce Commission asserted that the consummation of plans

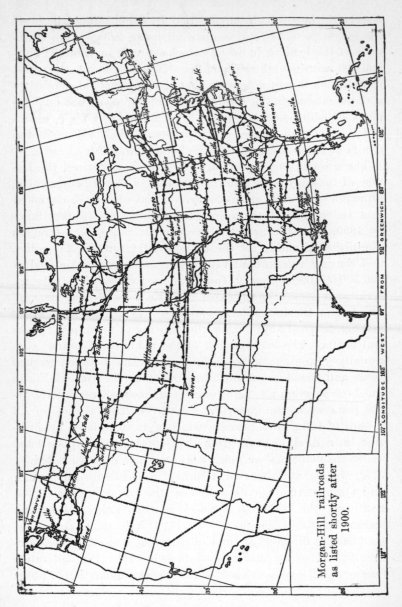

Morgan-Hill railroads as listed shortly after 1900.

which he then had in mind would subject nearly one-half the territory of the United States to the power of a single will. Before his death in 1909 he had obtained practical control of a system of roads running from coast to coast and passing through the most important cities of the country and had planned to continue indefinitely the process of acquiring new lines.

The concentration of the banking interests of the country went hand in hand with consolidation in industry and railway control. The unprecedented operations which have just been mentioned demanded unprecedented amounts of capital and credit, and the concentration of these necessities occurred in New York City. The Standard Oil group and the Morgan group dominated the banking interests to such an extent that it was doubtful whether any great business enterprise demanding large capital could be started without the aid of one or the other of them. Some years later a congressional investigation was started, to discover whether the control of a few men over the financial affairs of the nation amounted to a "money trust," and at that time it was found that the members of four allied financial institutions in New York City held 341 directorships in banks, insurance companies, railroads, steamship companies and trading and public utility corporations, having aggregate resources of $22,245,000,000.

The financial power thus placed in the hands of a small number of men was the cause of much legislation passed by the states and by Congress in connection with the railroads and trusts. Opinions varied widely in regard to the effects of concentration. On the one hand it was argued that the men of greatest ability and vision naturally came to the top; that industry received the necessary stabilizing influence; that production and demand were compelled to harmonize; that scientific research directed toward the discovery of new processes and products, and the better utilization of old ones could be successfully carried on only by concerns with large resources; and that efficiency and economy resulted from large-scale operation. On the other hand it was pointed out that a small number of persons who were responsible to nobody could dominate the fortunes of hundreds of thousands of wage earners, manipulate production, make or break a region or a rival, bring about financial crises and, in a controversy or for private gain, use a great industry or a railroad as a weapon and wreck it regardless of the welfare of the public at large.[8]

THE SCIENTIFIC REVOLUTION

In the fields of scientific invention and progress, the fifty years after 1875 was a half century of such unprecedented ac- tivity as to constitute a scientific revolution.

Most important of all, the United States began to reap the accumulated benefits of the world's advances in medicine and surgery. These took the form of a three-fold campaign against disease, through quarantine regulations, through stamping out the source of disease and by rendering people insusceptible to particular maladies. In the first place, quarantine laws were designed to keep out tropical and other epidemics which might get a foothold in this country through immigration. The second expedient,—the destruction of the sources of disease—was based largely on the work of Louis Pasteur, the eminent French chemist. Pasteur discovered that many diseases are caused by minute organisms which enter the body through contact or in food, milk and water. The world's scientists thereupon began the attempt to find out what germs cause individual diseases and what agencies will destroy them.

---

[8] For an illustrative battle between great railroad interests, see Pyle, *Life of James J. Hill*, II, chaps. XXVII–XXIX; Kennan, *E. H. Harriman*, I, chaps. XI–XII.

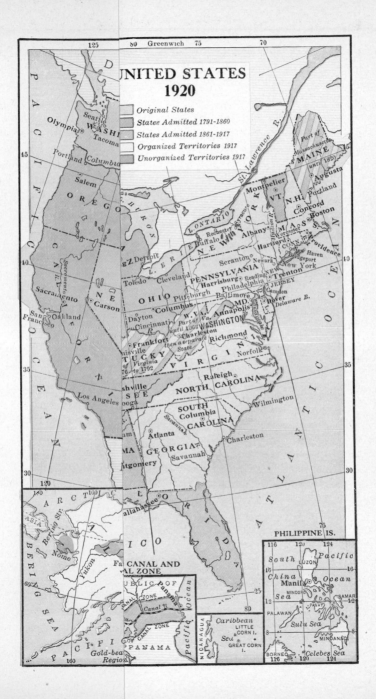

UNITED STATES
1920

Original States
States Admitted 1791-1860
States Admitted 1861-1917
Organized Territories 1917
Unorganized Territories 1917

One such effort uncovered the fact that the malaria germ was carried to human beings by the bite of the mosquito. The malaria—or fever and ague—had for decades been the dreaded scourge of the Mississippi Valley, and the cause of infinite suffering and loss of life. The yellow fever, likewise, had for centuries been epidemic in the lower Mississippi Valley, as well as in Central and South America. In 1900 and 1901 it was discovered that this disease is also transmitted by the bite of a certain type of mosquito. The draining of swamps, the oiling of water surfaces to prevent mosquito growth, and the use of screens on windows have largely done away with the mosquito, and malaria and yellow fever are in retreat. The effect of the germ theory on surgery was likewise important. Hitherto many surgical operations had ended in disaster because infection set in after the surgeon had done his work. After the validity of the germ theory had been demonstrated, the surgeon took care to sterilize his instruments and keep the wound protected from any organisms that might enter it. Infection thereupon became less common and human life so much the safer.[9]

The third weapon in the cause of preventive medicine was the use of serums which render the individual immune to special diseases. Smallpox, for example, whose ravages used to terrify all parts of the world, was all but eradicated through vaccination.[10] Pasteur found similar preventatives for hydrophobia and anthrax, and Emil von Behring for diphtheria.

[9] The English scientist, Huxley, said that Pasteur's discoveries in the prevention of diseases in sheep and oxen in France were worth enough to pay the whole cost of the indemnity paid to Germany by France after the Franco-Prussian war.

[10] Dr. Jenner, an English physician who died in 1823, discovered that smallpox could be prevented by inoculating people with a serum obtained from cattle having the relatively harmless cowpox. It was not until much later, however, that European nations began to make compulsory the general vaccination against smallpox,—Germany, for example, in 1870 and France in 1902. In the United States the laws vary from state to state.

City and federal governments expanded their activities to include, on a large scale, the functions of disease prevention. Health departments were organized in cities and towns. Water and milk supplies were looked into, in order to insure their freedom from disease germs. A thousand ordinances were passed which were intended to prevent the accumulation of disease-spreading dirt and the communication of infection from person to person. Campaigns were instituted for the conservation of child health; and the schools were utilized for spreading information and inculcating healthful habits.[11] It is impossible to state how many years have been added to the average lifetime by the advances made in medicine and surgery since 1865. Statistics indicate, however, that the addition is a very real one.

The traditional American capacity for invention and mechanical improvements was continuously active during the decades immediately before and after 1900. From 1890 to 1910, every year showed a steady increase in the number of patents issued by the Patent Office, reaching nearly a million in the latter year.

It was in 1876 that Alexander Graham Bell made a bit of crude apparatus which enabled him to talk through wires. In doing so he placed himself at the front of one of the most important scientific advances of recent times,—the rapid transmission of ideas. As late as 1890, however, only about 200,000 telephones were in use in the entire country, but from that time on the telephone became more and more a necessity. In 1900 there were 700,000 of them; in 1910, 5,000,000; and in 1924, more than 15,000,000. In fact the number changes so rapidly that to-day's statistics are out of date to-morrow.

The study of the problem of sending messages without wires almost paralleled the invention and improvement of the tele-

---

[11] The expenditure for public health in New York City alone for 1924 was greater than the cost of operating the government of the United States during the first year of Washington's administration.

phone, and many scientists worked at the tempting project. It was not until 1901, however, that Guglielmo Marconi succeeded in sending the letter S (. . .) in the Morse code—from Cornwall in England to St. John's in Newfoundland. Within a few years, press despatches were being sent across the Atlantic by "wireless" or radio-telegraphy. In 1909 two steamships collided at sea and by means of wireless were able to summon help which rescued the passengers from the sinking vessels. Thereafter, the improvements in the instruments and the uses to which they were put succeeded one another so fast as to be known only to the specialist. Within a short time wireless telephones and telegraphs were so common that the last word seemed to have been reached in the speed with which ideas could be transmitted.

In the census of 1890 there appeared a new industry which produced goods worth somewhat more than three and one half million dollars,—it was the manufacture of typewriting machines. Like many other scientific projects, a writing machine had long been in many minds. One made by an American was shown in 1876 at the Centennial Exhibition. By the early eighties a few were being used in government offices, and during the nineties they were commonly seen everywhere.

In the utilization of forms of energy which had hitherto been scientific playthings, the years about 1900 were revolutionary. Electricity had, of course, been studied and experimented with for centuries, but it was not until the late seventies that its practical possibilities were discovered. In 1879 Thomas A. Edison introduced a loop of platinum wire into a glass globe, which was sealed and exhausted of air, and then passed an electric current through the wire. The result was an incandescent lamp of twenty-five candle power. As soon as Edison was able to find a material for his filament which was less costly than platinum, electricity quickly drove out oil and gas for street-lighting purposes and more gradually for illumination in the home. The development of the dynamo and electric motor followed at once, making possible the electrification of street car lines all over the United States between 1890 and 1900, and the utilization of electricity for all sorts of power needs. The industry was not sufficiently developed to be reported in the census of 1880, and the statistics for 1890 were fragmentary. By 1900, however, electrical energy was being developed on a considerable scale; by 1905 it was rivaling the old-time waterwheel; and by 1910 was only less important than steam as a source of power. The falls at Niagara were being harnessed and hydro-electric plants were being built or projected wherever large sources of water power were to be found. Sites near water-falls were being snapped up by corporations. As many of these were on public lands in western states, a question of policy arose. Should the development of power resources be irrevocably released to private corporations, or should the federal government in some way keep a hold on it?

Electrical energy, however, was not to be left in sole possession of the field. For several centuries experimenters had tinkered with the power possibilities in the explosions of various gases. Nevertheless no practical internal combustion engine was forthcoming until about 1860. At that time a Frenchman built an engine in which a moving flywheel drew forward a piston, which in turn drew a charge of gas and air into a cylinder. When the stroke was about half accomplished, valves closed, an explosion was caused by an electric spark, the piston returned and the waste gases were expelled. From that time onward the primary ideas have been improved by thousands of experimenters in ten thousand ways. The use of the internal combustion engine for the propulsion of carriages on a highway attracted the attention of scientists in Europe and America. In this country, Elwood Haynes in Kokomo, Indiana, and Charles B. Duryea in Springfield,

Massachusetts, were pioneers. Not until after 1900, however, was the automobile more than a curiosity and not until after 1910 did the production begin to reach such proportions as to affect American life profoundly. The year 1916 was the first million-car year, and so fast thereafter did the industry grow that in 1920 the manufacture of automobiles was one of the three greatest industries in the country.

Flying through the air is one of mankind's most ancient dreams, but not until the day of the perfected internal combustion engine could the dream take tangible form. As with electricity, the automobile and other scientific and mechanical improvements, many experimenters labored with the problem of a heavier-than-air flying machine. In the United States Samuel P. Langley began about 1895, and the Wright Brothers—Wilbur and Orville—somewhat later. In 1903 the Wrights succeeded in making a short flight after endless experiments and adjustments. In 1908 they were giving public exhibitions, and thereafter the permanence of the airplane was assured. Improvement succeeded improvement; records for speed and distance were made and shattered almost daily. Fliers crossed the Atlantic, went from the Atlantic to the Pacific across the United States between dawn and dusk, braved the polar snows and even made their way around the world.

The uses to which the internal combustion engine can be put have not yet been exhausted. Motor trucks and motor conveyances increase in importance every year. Motor tractors of various kinds have lessened the labor of the man with the plow and reaper, and have greatly increased the speed with which he can work. The demand for gasoline,—the most commonly used fuel for motor vehicles of all kinds— has correspondingly increased. The production of the crude petroleum (from which gasoline is distilled), doubled in the United States alone between 1908 and 1918, and again between 1918 and 1923. The available sources of fresh supplies are sought from the poles to the equator, and in every known land.

Underlying most of the scientific advances of the time was the discovery of methods of producing steel of high quality and low price. Heavy steel rails and bridges had to precede fast express service on the railroads. Structural steel was essential for the sky-scraper. Motor cars and airplanes and agricultural machinery and steel ships all had to wait upon a supply of cheap and durable steel. The most important single development in the manufacture of steel was in the discovery of the Bessemer process by William Kelly in the United States and Henry Bessemer in England shortly before the Civil War. This process consists in forcing a blast of air through the impure molten iron, thus burning out any impurities, and then introducing such quantities of carbon or other elements as are needed to make the quality of steel desired. After the war, improvements were made in the direction of speed and cheapness; the Bessemer process was largely superseded by the "open-hearth" process, and the United States became one of the world's steel producing nations.

The importance of the scientific revolution should not be so obscured by confusing statistical information as to distract attention from its economic, social and political implications.

(1) The several industries founded on the revolution provided a livelihood for some millions of wage earners, and gave a field for financial investment to some millions of others.

(2) Preventive medicine reduced the hazards of the tendency toward the urbanization of the United States, made life happier and longer, and increased the working capacity of the average individual.

(3) The new methods of transmitting information and goods caused distances to shrink with unprecedented speed. The nations of the world were brought so much closer to one

another that they are now attempting to learn how to live together,—just as bringing people together in cities forced them to discover how to live under an urban social economy.

(4) The telephone, the typewriter and rapid transit lie at the foundation of big business.

(5) The motor car has compelled the construction of better highways, has destroyed millions of dollars' worth of electric street railroads, and even threatened the steam railways. Its yearly toll of lives vies with the great battles of the Civil War.

(6) The great growth of the American city was in no small measure made possible by the scientific revolution.

(7) And in general life has been made more complex and costly. Standards of living and comfort have been changed. The age at which people marry, and the choice of the professions which they will enter depend largely on economic considerations. If they can not marry early and live according to the prevailing social standards, they will delay; if particular professions or types of business do not provide sufficient financial returns to satisfy the complicated necessities of to-day, those activities will find difficulty in recruiting their ranks. In a word, the scientific revolution which began with the close of the nineteenth century will doubtless have a greater effect on the world's history than the industrial revolution which began at the close of the eighteenth.

THE FEMINIST MOVEMENT

An important aspect of the transition after 1890 was the modification of the economic and legal status of women. As has been seen, the opening of opportunities for the higher education of women had for some time been an accomplished fact,—and a fact which presaged a demand on woman's part to be allowed to go into such professions as medicine and the law, which had traditionally been closed to her.[12] The organi-

[12] *Cf.* p. 106.

zation of the General Federation of Women's Clubs took place in 1890, and offorded a means for propaganda on a national, as well as on a local scale, on behalf of any reform that interested its members. Most important of all, women were, in growing numbers, entering more active economic life. The 4,000,000 employed women in 1890 increased to more than 8,500,000 by 1920. The greater use of the telephone opened an opportunity for operators,—an opportunity which was seized and almost monopolized by women. The invention of the typewriter, and the growth of large-scale business created a demand for stenographers, clerks and bookkeepers. Men almost abandoned teaching in the public grammar schools, leaving their places to women. Domestic service became, accordingly, less popular as a means of earning a livelihood, and women increasingly entered economic activities that brought them into competition with other wage earners.

There had been constant agitation before 1890 for changes in the status of women in connection with voting and holding office, the practice of the several professions, and the control of property. It was not until after 1880, and especially after 1890, however, that the complete results of the agitation began to appear. Such modifications as were made differed widely, of course, in the different states; and states adopted laws which were liberal in theory, but which were not adhered to in practice. Nevertheless,—varied as the changes were, definite tendencies were observable. These may deserve some attention.

Voting powers were earliest conferred on women in the election of members of school boards—as early as 1879 in Massachusetts—although this was by no means the universal practice even as late as the opening of the twentieth century. During the eighties and nineties laws began to allow women to serve on boards of trustees of libraries and state asylums. In Massachusetts by a law of 1896 a woman could serve as a town clerk *pro tempore,* but not apparently as a permanent officer.   Not until the nineties were matrons required at jails, and then only in the larger cities of a few states.   Wyoming, to be sure, gave women equal political rights as early as 1869, but in practice women seem to have held as few elective positions as they did in other states.[13]   The doors to the professions were opened to women earlier and more easily than those to the privileges of the suffrage and office holding. Nevertheless there were states in which women could not legally act as physicians or lawyers as late as 1901.

It was in connection with property rights, however, and the control of children that the feminist movement made its most important advances about the year 1900,—advances which far outweigh the importance of the suffrage and which indicate an earlier situation surprising to the student of more recent times.   Before the last two decades of the nineteenth century, the English common law still prevailed in most states in regard to a married woman's ownership of property and the guardianship of her children.   She could not buy or sell any property whatever.   All that she had belonged to her husband,—even property which she had possessed, previous to her marriage.   The husband could sell it without her consent,—or even give it away in some states.   If she worked for a salary or conducted a business enterprise, all her earnings were his.   Any children, also, belonged to him.   He was entitled to their services and earnings, and could keep them or give them away at his will.   Although modifications of this condition were made as early as 1848, it was not until the late eighties and nineties that any widespread change was brought about,—and then the change was rapid indeed.   By the close of the century, about three-fourths of the states allowed a wife to own and control her separate property, and in two-thirds of them she was allowed to keep wages which she had earned.

The guardianship of the children remained, as late as 1900,

[13] For later developments, see p. 519.

almost everywhere with the father alone.[14] In some states the father could in his will appoint a guardian over his children, thus preventing the mother from exercising any control even after the husband's death. The possibilities which lay in the situation were illustrated in Massachusetts in 1901. The father of six children decided to give them away,—as he had a legal right to do. The mother, hearing of his intention, went insane and killed all her offspring. Public opinion was aroused and in 1902, against vigorous opposition, the state legislature passed an act making the father and the mother equally guardians of the children.

The Intellectual and Cultural Background

Among the intellectual forces underlying American history after 1890, a prominent place should be given to the expansion of the public library, the growth of public education and the development of the press. Many libraries, of course, had been established long before the Civil War—the library of Congress having been founded in 1800—but the great growth of the public library supported by taxation and open to all citizens alike occurred after 1865. Between that year and 1900 no fewer than thirty-seven states passed laws enabling the towns within their borders to levy taxes for the support of public libraries; private bequests amounted to fabulous sums, the outstanding example of which were the gifts of Andrew Carnegie, amounting to $62,500,000 between 1881 and 1915. By 1924 every state had many small public libraries and practically all of them had collections as large as 40,000 volumes. The library of Congress contained more

---

[14] In 1902 the situation was described as follows: "Fathers and mothers are given equal guardianship of children in the District of Columbia, and nine States—Colorado, Connecticut, Illinois, Kansas, Maine, Massachusetts, Nebraska, New York and Washington." Anthony and Harper, *History of Woman Suffrage,* IV, p. 458.

than three million books and several college and public libraries possessed more than one million each.

The significant features in the growth of education in the North between 1865 and 1890 had been the improvement of the public grammar school, the establishment of high schools, and the founding of the great state universities. The South, meanwhile, was so prostrated by the War that the public school system was in less satisfactory condition in 1900, even, than it was in 1860.[15]

After 1890 in the North and after 1900 in the South, by all odds the most vital fact is the increasingly huge number of boys and girls, young men and young women going to school and college. 12,700,000 youngsters were in the public schools in 1890; 23,200,000 in 1922, a rate of increase considerably greater than the increase in population. The expenditures grew from one hundred and forty millions of dollars a year to over a billion and a half in 1922. (This was roughly equal to the entire cost of operating the United States government, wars and all, from the inauguration of Thomas Jefferson to the inauguration of Abraham Lincoln.) The change in the enrollment of the colleges was more extreme. Between 1890 and 1922 the number of students in the colleges increased six fold,—doubling even in the brief ten years after 1912. In the South, the same general tendencies were visible.[16] As late as 1900, even, the public school system of the South was distinctly inferior to that of the remainder of the country. The school term was short, the teachers underpaid, the school buildings inadequate in most cases, and the administration in the hands of political appointees rather than experts. With the increased wealth, however, that accompanied the industrial expansion of the South, came a desire for better schools. The

15 *Cf*. p. 104.
16 On this point see *Public Education in the South*, by E. W. Knight, Professor of Education in the University of North Carolina.

middle classes asserted themselves as they had in the North and demanded for their children the advantages of "book-learning." Taxes for school purposes were doubled in ten years. Better school buildings were constructed; attendance increased; and illiteracy in the South—always too large—took a decided drop.[17]

The character of the curriculum of the school changed sharply as the number of pupils increased. The demands of business offices for book-keepers, clerks and stenographers were so great as to cause a demand for business and commercial departments in the schools. Various kinds of manual and domestic training were added,—a sort of education which the boy and girl on the farm had received at home. The states, as well as the federal government, interested themselves in vocational training, to the end that education might not be entirely academic or theoretical, but might lead to bread-winning professions or trades.

The effects of the public school system are admittedly far-reaching, even if difficult to evaluate. More than any one agency, the public school assimilated the immigrant stream which was so huge after 1880. Striking evidence of this is found in the sharp decrease in illiteracy between the foreign-born population and their children of the next generation. It is difficult to conceive the effect of the immigration of the eighties and nineties without the Americanizing service of the public school. The school, moreover, helped attract the rural parent to the city where his children could receive a better education. It reduced illiteracy all over the United States from 13.3 per cent. in 1890 to 6.0 per cent. in 1920. It laid the foundations for the growing consumption of newspapers, magazines and books, as well as the economic prosperity which, most of the time, marked the decades after 1890.

A large proportion of the political, social and economic

[17] An "illiterate" is defined in the census as a person more than ten years of age who is unable to *write* in any language, English or other.

changes and reforms that have taken place in the United States since 1890 have done so because public opinion was educated, quietly influenced or noisily bestirred by the press. Governors and presidents ·appealed to their constituents through the newspaper and the periodical. Political campaigns have become increasingly matters of publicity; candidates for office have their press bureaus; corporations, abandoning their traditional policy of silence, explain their practices; and railroads defend their policies by means of advertisements in the newspapers. Newspaper correspondents go out through the country months before candidates for the presidency are nominated, and discover and publish sentiment favorable to the individual whom the particular organ desires to see placed in office.

In 1921 the circulation of the daily newspapers amounted to approximately 34,000,000 copies for each issue. In the North, the Middle West and on the Pacific Coast the number published was sufficient to provide every family with one copy. The South and the Rocky Mountain regions were less well supplied. The great metropolitan newspapers circulated widely, not only in the immediate vicinity of the publisher's office, but over a wide area outside and also exercised a great influence over the character of newspapers throughout the country. Half a million copies of each issue became not uncommon, while consolidations and the establishment of chains of newspapers gave individual editors a greater number of readers than had ever been known before.

Cooperation among newspapers in the gathering of information is no novelty in the United States, but the greatest strides have been taken since 1890, and particularly since the incorporation of the present Associated Press in 1900. As early as 1915 the association had leased 50,000 miles of telegraph wires forming a net all over the country. It had its representatives not only in obvious centers of interest such as London, Paris and Berlin, but in Fez, Madeira, Colombo, Tsingtau, Sydney

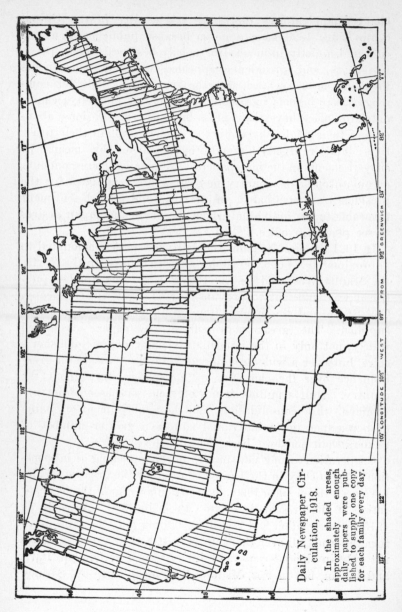

Daily Newspaper Circulation, 1918.

In the shaded areas, approximately enough daily papers were published to supply one copy for each family every day.

and a host of others.   In addition it has agents in the offices
of the other three great news gatherers of the world,—the
Wolff Agency, which serves the Teutonic, Slav and Scandinavian countries; the Reuter Company of London, which
finds the news all over the British Empire, China, Japan
and Egypt; and the Agence Havas of Paris, which operates
in the Latin countries:

Thus, if a fire should break out in Milan, the *Secolo,* the leading
newspaper of the city, would instantly telegraph a report of it
to the Stefani Agency at Rome.   Thence it would be telegraphed
to all of the other Italian newspapers, and copies of the *Secolo's*
message would also be handed to the representatives, in the Stefani
headquarters, of the Reuter, Wolff, Havas, and the Associated
Press Agencies.[18]

So good is the service rendered by the Associated Press that
perhaps a half of the news printed in American papers is provided by it.

The rise of the "muck-rake" magazines was typical of the
ten years at the opening of the twentieth century.[19] These
periodicals printed articles which portrayed a side of American life not commonly discussed in the newspapers.   One of
the earliest serials of this type was Miss Ida M. Tarbell's
History of the Standard Oil Company, published in *McClure's
Magazine* in 1902–1903.   Instead of the ordinary eulogy of
the size and success of the Company, Miss Tarbell presented
many of its unfair practices.   At the same time and in the
same publication Lincoln Steffens was exposing the seamy
side of municipal affairs in "The Shame of the Cities."   *Mun-
sey's Magazine, Collier's* and others took up the crusade.
The activities of the railroads in politics, the adulteration of
foods and drugs,—anything that hurt the public—became the

---

[18] M. E. Stone, *Fifty Years a Journalist*, pp. 363–4.
[19] The word originated in 1906 with President Roosevelt, who likened
certain sensational journalists to the man with the Muck-Rake in
Bunyan's *Pilgrim's Progress.* Bishop. *Roosevelt,* II, p. 10.

popular theme of countless magazine articles and of novels "with a purpose." Between 1901 and 1906 one of the muck-rake periodicals increased its sales three fold, another four and another seven.

The great changes at the threshold of the twentieth century were not solely scientific and economic, although they were mainly so. After 1876 there was a period of progress in painting, sculpture and music. It is an odd circumstance that the Centennial Exhibition of 1876 helped bring this about. American machinery, engines and scientific inventions took a prominent position at the exposition, but the display of American artistic productions was a cause for chagrin. Some of the younger painters were much impressed by the comparative excellence of foreign pictures, and were inspired to improve their own technique. The work of these and other men did not amount to a distinctive "school" of American painting, but a few of them deserve mention.

George Inness (1825–1894), painted landscapes of genuine merit, although his work was so greatly affected by the French masters that it could scarcely be placed in the front rank. The work of James A. M. Whistler (1834–1903), was more original and better known, although most of his life was spent in England and France, where the artistic atmosphere was more congenial. His picture "The artist's mother" is perhaps as well known as any American painting. John La Farge (1835–1910), and Edwin A. Abbey (1852–1911), did mural painting in the Boston Public Library and elsewhere which is considered meritorious. Although Abbey was born in Philadelphia, most of his life was spent in England. In the public schools and in numerous art schools, drawing and painting have been somewhat widely taught, but little progress has been made toward the production of great artists. The appreciation of good pictures, however, developed rapidly after 1876. The Metropolitan Museum of Art in New York

City, opened in 1880, contains one of the great collections of the world. Its treasures, like those of the museums at Boston, Chicago and other cities, are visited by thousands of people every year. Men of wealth have spent fabulous sums of money gathering these objects of art from all over the world, —but only a comparatively small number of them are of American origin.

American sculptors seem more nearly able to stand comparison with the best that Europe has to offer. The "Minute Man" at Concord, by Daniel C. French (1850–), the work of Frederick MacMonnies (1863–), for the World's Fair at Chicago in 1893, and especially that of Augustus St. Gaudens stand that hardest of all tests,—the test of time. St. Gaudens was born in Ireland in 1848 but was brought as a small child to America because his parents wished to escape the famine of that year. His "Lincoln" in Chicago, the "Shaw Memorial" in Boston, and the "Adams Monument" in Washington were epoch-making in the history of American artistic effort.

Architecture was at a low ebb during the generation following the Civil War, both in the United States and in Europe. In the cities, the governments were in the hands of the Tweeds, and cheap shoddy construction and inferior taste were the rule. The turning point came with the World's Fair, which celebrated the four hundredth anniversary of the landing of Columbus. In order to make the buildings and grounds as beautiful as possible, the best artists in America were summoned to the task. The landscape architecture was planned by the veteran Frederick Law Olmstead (1822–1903); some of the statuary by MacMonnies and St. Gaudens; and the architects were led by Daniel H. Burnham (1846–1912). The artistic influence of the World's Fair lasted for many years after 1893, especially in the fields of architecture and city planning. Burnham and his friends started the movement which led to the vast improvements made in the public buildings, avenues and parks of Chicago, Washington, Cleveland

and San Francisco. Later public buildings, private homes, monuments, parks and even medals and coins showed the influence of the new movement toward a greater appreciation of the significance of the fine arts.

The native American stock is as nearly lacking in musical genius as it is in the use of the palette and brush. The early Puritans looked upon music and musical instruments with no little disquietude. Only the most distinctly foreign colonies, like the Moravians in Bethlehem, Pennsylvania, paid any considerable attention to music. Hence the best orchestras of to-day were founded later than the Civil War, with the single exception of the New York Philharmonic Orchestra which was started in 1842. The most famous, the Boston Symphony, was founded in 1881 and was made possible through the financial aid of a wealthy patron, Henry L. Higginson, rather than by the support of a musical public.[20] Following the example of the Boston Orchestra, similar organizations were founded before 1900 in Philadelphia, Chicago, San Francisco, Cincinnati and Los Angeles. The Metropolitan Opera House in New York, the most pretentious enterprise in American musical circles, began its history in 1883. All of these orchestras, as well as the opera companies, have been compelled to rely on European musicians and composers. A few men,—such as Edward MacDowell, George W. Chadwick and Horatio Parker—have given promise of a school of American composers, but it is a promise only. On the other hand,

[20] The difficulties in building up a music-loving public are indicated in the biography of Theodore Thomas, a native of East Friesland, who led symphony orchestras in New York and Chicago and attempted to present music of a high quality. Shortly after the Civil War Thomas gave a series of out-door concerts in New York, holding his audience where necessary by novelties or tricks. On one occasion, as Thomas tells it in his autobiography: "In the 'Carnival of Venice' the tuba player had been sent . . . back of the audience into the shrubbery. When he began to play the police mistook him for a practical joker who was disturbing the music, and tried to arrest him! I shall never forget the comical scene, as the poor man fled toward the stage, pursued by the irate policeman, and trying to get in a note here and there, as he ran." Theodore Thomas, *A Musical Autobiography*, I, p. 54.

the American folk song has everywhere maintained its appeal. The best of these, however, are products of an earlier period —"Swanee River" and "Old Kentucky Home" by Stephen C. Foster (1826–1864), and "Dixie" by Dan Emmett (1815–1904). These were accompanied or followed by less well-known cowboy songs and negro spirituals.

American artistic development, therefore, since 1865 has been a promise and a beginning rather than a distinct attainment. The European influence is stronger and more easily demonstrable than the immigrant influence in any other field of American history. The attempts to make music and drawing a part of the education of children in the public schools imply an understanding of the value of artistic things and a determination to appreciate them. Moreover, the support of musical organizations, the collection of the best paintings and antiquities, and the encouragement of architecture and mural decoration provide a means for expending American fortunes which.is in pleasing contrast to the cruder ways of the decades before 1890.

BIBLIOGRAPHICAL NOTE

The literature is voluminous and not easy to evaluate. On population changes, immigration, developments in manufacturing and agriculture, and the growth of cities, the best source is the *Abstract of the Fourteenth (1920) Census* (1923). F. A. Ogg, *National Progress* (1918), has a good chapter; see also Joseph Schafer, *A History of the Pacific Northwest* (rev. ed., 1918); H. T. Lewis and S. I. Miller, *Economic Resources of the Pacific Northwest* (1923).

The consolidation in industry, railroads and finance may be studied in: A. D. Noyes, *Forty Years of American Finance* (1909); J. Moody, *The Truth about the Trusts* (1904); *Report of the Commissioner of Corporations on the Steel Industry* (3 parts, 1911), on the United States Steel Corporation; A. P. Youngman, *Economic Causes of Great Fortunes* (1909); E. R. Johnson and T. W. Van Metre, *Principles of Railroad Transportation* (1916); J. Moody, *The Railroad Builders* (1919), and *The Masters of Capital* (1919);

and *Report of the Committee Appointed Pursuant to House Resolutions 429 and 504 to Investigate the Concentration of Control of Money and Credit* ("Pujo Committee") 1913. On special phases see B. J. Hendrick, *The Age of Big Business* (1919); J. G. Pyle, *James J. Hill,* 2 vols. (1917); Kennan, *E. H. Harriman,* 2 vols. (1922); C. Hovey, *The Life Story of J. Pierpont Morgan* (1912); Stehman, *Financial History of the American Telephone and Telegraph Company* (1925).

Some phases of the urbanization of America may be seen in: C. A. Beard, *American City Government* (1912); H. G. James, *Municipal Functions* (1917); C. C. Maxey, *An Outline of Municipal Government* (1924); N. P. Lewis, *The Planning of the Modern City* (1923); J. A. Riis, *Making of an American* (1901), and *Battle with the Slums* (1902); A. C. Holden, *The Settlement Idea* (1922); L. D. Wald, *The House on Henry Street* (1915); J. Addams, *Twenty Years at Hull House* (1920).

On the influence of the press: M. E. Stone, *Fifty Years a Journalist* (1921). Suggestive articles are: *World's Work* (Oct. 1916), "Stalking for Nine Million Votes"; *Arena* (July, 1909), "The Making of Public Opinion"; *Atlantic Monthly* (Mar., 1910), "Suppression of Important News", Walter Lippmann in *Atlantic Monthly* (Nov., Dec., 1919). The statistics of newspaper circulation may be found in N. W. Ayer, *American Newspaper Annual and Directory.* See also "The Muck-Raking Campaign," in *Historical Outlook,* Jan., 1924.

On the scientific revolution, L. B. Shippee, *Recent American History* (1924), chap. XVII, is good. See also H. U. Faulkner, *American Economic History* (1924); A. B. Paine, *In One Man's Life* (Theodore N. Vail) (1921); H. G. Prout, *Life of George Westinghouse* (1921); F. L. Dyer, *Edison* (2 vols., 1910); W. Kaempffert, *A Popular History of American Invention* (2 vols., 1924). Statistics are available in the *Abstract of the Fourteenth (1920) Census* (1923) and in the annual *Statistical Abstract of the United States.* Articles of value containing some account of the historical side are in the *Encyclopædia Britannica,* "Aeroplane," "Pasteur," etc. The *Encyclopædia Americana* has excellent material on "Preventive Medicine." See also *Annual Report of the Rockefeller Foundation* 1922.

On the feminist movement see the references after Chapter IV. Volume IV of *The History of Woman Suffrage* (1902), S. B. Anthony and I. H. Harper eds., contains a state-by-state summary of the legal situation in 1900.

On education, consult the references already mentioned under Chapter IV.

On artistic progress: C. H. Caffin, *American Masters of Painting* (1918), and *American Masters of Sculpture* (1913); L. C. Elson, *History of American Music* (1904); A. H. Granger, *Charles Follen McKim* (1913); M. A. DeW. Howe, *The Boston Symphony Orchestra* (1914); R. Hughes and A. Elson, *American Composers* (1914, rev. ed.); E. V. Lucas, *Edwin A. Abbey* (2 vols., 1921); C. Moore, *Daniel H. Burnham* (2 vols., 1921); W. S. Pratt, *History of Music* (1910); *Reminiscences of Augustus St. Gaudens* (2 vols., 1913); L. Taft, *History of American Sculpture* (1917). There are numerous volumes of recollections, such as those by Damrosch, Auer, Tetrazzini, Theodore Thomas, C. L. Kellogg, and others.

CHAPTER XX

THEODORE ROOSEVELT

Public interest is "a new intellectual perspective through which we view all moral issues affecting society."

WILLIAM J. TUCKER.

. . . in the interest of the whole people, the Nation should, without interfering with the power of the States in the matter itself, also assume power of supervision and regulation over all corporations doing an interstate business.

THEODORE ROOSEVELT.[1]

CHANGES in political philosophy seem to follow upon changes in economic interests. Men expect their government to respond to the major needs of the time,— and the major needs are likely to be economic. It came about, in accord with this general principle, that some of the underlying bases of American government were changed rather abruptly after 1900. That the change came was due in part to slow-moving forces which had been gathering momentum for some years. But it was due in part also to human agencies which formed themselves in harmony with the new ideas and were able to put themselves into positions of effective leadership. It was the collocation of the new ideas and new leaders that gave American politics after 1900 their peculiarly interesting character.

It will be remembered that *laissez faire* was the prevailing theory in regard to the proper relation between government and industry during the twenty-five years after the close of the Civil War, except in so far as industrial organizations desired protective tariffs. In brief the upholders of this creed

[1] For Roosevelt's foreign policies, see Chapter XXIII.

contended that legislation should concern itself as little as possible with the regulation of trade, that it should restrict itself to protecting commerce from interference, and that business men should be permitted to work out their own problems with the least possible reference to such artificial forces as were supplied by legal enactments.[2] It would be inaccurate to say that the theory of *laissez faire* had completely given way by the end of the half century after the Civil War. Nor would it be wholly correct to say that any other theory has yet demonstrated its permanent reliability. Nevertheless the distinctive philosophy upon which later legislation has been built is the theory of public interest. The theory needs definition in some detail, because it forms the philosophy which underlies most of the political developments and much of the legislation of the early twentieth century.

As the men of the eighties and nineties contemplated the vast amounts of wealth created during those decades they saw it concentrated to a great extent in the hands of the few. The few believed that the public good was best cared for in this way, but an increasing majority of the people looked upon the tendency with greater and greater alarm. They complained that the railroads discriminated in favor of the powerful few; that corporations were achieving monopoly; and that the government itself often assisted the process by framing tariff schedules primarily for the interest of the manufacturers. When the reaction against this situation started, it was of course found that the seats of power were already occupied by the adherents of *laissez faire*,—the party committees, the legislatures, the executive offices and the courts. There ensued, therefore, a long struggle for power and for a new theory of government. The land-marks of the controversy were to be found in interstate commerce acts, anti-trust laws, income taxes, bureaus of labor and factory legislation.

[2] *Cf.* p. 99 *ff.* above.

The proponent of *laissez faire* would allow the few to accumulate large fortunes which they might share with the many through benefactions, gifts to education, libraries, and other public enterprises; the adherent of public interest would inquire why the many are poor, and attempt so to change economic conditions as to reduce the number of the poor to a minimum. Instead of framing laws so that wealth and power would get into the hands of a small number of individuals, in the expectation that prosperity would filter down to the many, the advocate of public interest would aim his legislation directly at what he considers the needs of the less powerful classes. He would interfere with the railroads, for example, to compel them to charge uniform rates, prevent corporations from electing public officers by means of large contributions to campaign funds, force industry even at some cost to protect employees through safety devices, and would hold the great forests on the public lands for the direct good of the whole people. The transfer of emphasis from *laissez faire* to public interest was based upon a steady growth in the value placed upon the worth of the individual man, and upon a shift from legislating for the few to legislating directly for the multitude. The change was greater than can be indicated by citing any one law or group of laws. It was "a new intellectual perspective through which we view all moral issues affecting society." [3]

Underlying many of the difficulties in the way of replacing *laissez faire* with a new theory, was the attitude of the courts toward certain parts of the Fourteenth Amendment. A portion of section one of the Amendment forbids the states to "deprive any person of life, liberty, or property, without due process of law." The majority of the Supreme Court in early

[3] I have drawn largely at this point upon Dr. W. J. Tucker's article "The Progress of the Social Conscience" in the *Atlantic Monthly*, Sept., 1915, pp. 289–303. The clearest idea of the transition from *laissez faire* to public interest is gained by reading the biography of *M. A. Hanna* by Croly, and La Follette's and Roosevelt's autobiographies.

decisions interpreting the Amendment had expressed the belief that its purpose was the protection of the negro. By 1890, however, the Court had come to hold that the word "person" as used in the first section included corporations, and thus had given the language of the Amendment a greatly widened application. Of 528 decisions given by the Court on the Amendment between 1890 and 1910, only nineteen concerned the negro race, while 289 affected corporations. In the decision of the case Lochner v. New York, a state law regulating hours of labor in bakeries was declared to conflict with the Amendment, because the right of the laborer to work as many hours as he pleased was part of the "liberty" which was protected by the Amendment. Laws regulating railroad rates through commissions were held to deprive corporations of property without due process. Until recently changed, the statutes did not allow appeal to the Supreme Court in cases where state courts declared state laws in conflict with the United States Constitution, and the Fourteenth Amendment therefore acted as a protective bulwark in state as well as nation. In brief, then, the legal position of the big industrial organizations was almost impregnable because of the fortuitous circumstance that the words of a part of the Constitution might be held to mean something which probably did not enter the minds of the Congress or the state legislatures which placed the words in the document.

The people of the United States have usually avoided hostile criticism of the Constitution and the decisions of the Supreme Court, and they have reflected this feeling in their acquiescence in the unexpected turn given to the meaning of the Fourteenth Amendment. The members of the Court, however, have frequently expressed disquietude. Dissenting opinions opposing the view which the Court has taken, have been common. Mr. Justice Harlan declared that the scope of the Amendment was being enlarged far beyond its original purpose; Mr. Justice Holmes asserted that the word "liberty" was being "perverted" and that the Constitution was not intended to embody *laissez faire* or any other economic theory.[4]

The most prominent pioneers in replacing the old by the new theory were William J. Bryan, Robert M. La Follette and Theodore Roosevelt. Bryan's leadership in 1896 has already been mentioned. With courage and sincerity he attempted to solve the social and economic problems of his day, but his youth, his inexperience, his radicalism, and the fact that he did not choose issues that were immediately practicable made it impossible for him to command the confidence of the majority. Unable himself to scale the heights of reform, he nevertheless pointed them out to others. With a voice that has been likened to an organ with a hundred stops, with persistence, energy and good nature he spread far and wide a new conception of social obligation. He insisted that the social and economic discontent of the South and West were real, and that they could not be laughed out of court or frightened into silence.

La Follette's constructive pioneer work was done for the most part in Wisconsin. During the ascendency of the *laissez faire* theory, the state was largely controlled by the lumber, railroad and other interests, using the Republican party as their political agency; and a small but powerful group controlled the election of state and federal officials, the press and state legislation. Between 1885 and 1891 La Follette, who was himself a Republican, was a representative in the federal House. In the latter year he came into collision with Senator Sawyer, a wealthy lumber merchant who was the leader of the dominant party in the state. For years the state treasurers had been lending the state's money to favored banks without interest. Senator Sawyer had acted as bondsman for the treasurers and was sued by the attorney-general of the state for

---

4 Usually cases involving the Fourteenth Amendment have also involved other parts of the Constitution. The main reliance, however, in such cases has been the Amendment mentioned.

back interest. La Follette threw himself into this controversy on the side of the state; and being unable to obtain a hearing through the usual medium of the press, he and his supporters went directly to the people, speaking from town to town before interested audiences; and subsequently the state won.

In the Sawyer controversy were visible all the elements of the later creed and methods of La Follette. Except for the last political campaign of his career, he always remained with the Republican party, preferring to attempt change from within; and he always opposed the "interests" and found his strength in direct appeals to the people of his state. Out of those years came the "Wisconsin idea,"—a program which included the taxation of railroads and corporations, primaries in which the people could nominate their own candidates for office, the prohibiting of the acceptance of railroad passes by public officials, and the conservation of the forests and water power of the state. The conflict between *laissez faire* and public interest in Wisconsin was long and bitter, but it led to a series of triumphs for La Follette, who was elected governor in 1900, 1902, and 1904, and chosen to the federal Senate in 1905. In the meanwhile there was a widespread demand throughout the West for legislation along the lines marked out by Wisconsin; interest in the East was keen, although less widespread.

The trial of the public interest theory on a national scale was undoubtedly hastened by the act of an assassin. On September 6, 1901, President McKinley was attending the Pan-American Exposition in Buffalo, when he was shot by a young fanatic. He died eight days later and was succeeded by the Vice-President, Theodore Roosevelt.

Seldom, in times of peace, is the personality of a single individual so important as that of Theodore Roosevelt during the early years of the twentieth century. At the time of his accession to the presidency, he lacked a month of being forty-three years old, but the range of his experience in politics had been far beyond his age. In his early twenties, soon after leaving Harvard, he had entered the Assembly of the state of New York. President Harrison had made him Civil Service Commissioner in 1889, and he had been successively President of the Board of Police Commissioners of New York City, Assistant Secretary of the Navy, an important figure in the War with Spain, and Governor of New York. He had been known as a young man of promise—energetic, independent and progressive—and in addition to his political activities he had found time to write books on historical subjects, see something of life on a western ranch and develop a somewhat defective physique into an engine of physical power.

Brimming with energy, nimble of mind, impetuous, sure of himself, quick to strike, a fearless foe, frank, resourceful, audacious, honest, versatile—Roosevelt possessed the qualities which would challenge the admiration of the typical American. One who frequently saw him at work described thus the way in which he prepared a message to be sent to the Senate:

He storms up and down the room, dictating in a loud and oratorical tone, often stopping, recasting a sentence, striking out and filling in, hospitable to every suggestion, not in the least disturbed by interruption, holding on stoutly to his purpose, and producing finally, out of these most unpromising conditions, a clear and logical statement, which he could not improve with solitude and leisure at his command.

The breadth of his interests, the democratic character of his friendships—for he was equally at home with blue-stocking, politician, cowboy and artisan—his complete loyalty to his friends and his disregard of conventionalities gave him a grip upon popular favor that had not been duplicated since the days of Andrew Jackson, unless by Lincoln. The effectiveness of so compelling a personality was in no way diminished by Roosevelt's possession of what a journalist would call "news sense." He was made for publicity; he had an instinct for the dramatic. His speeches were removed from mediocrity by his evident sincerity, his abounding interest in every occasion at which he was called upon to talk and the phrases that were half victories which he coined almost at will. "Mollycoddle," "muckraking," "the square deal," "the big stick" became familiar idioms in the vernacular of politics and the street. The political leadership of Roosevelt rested mainly upon his personal prestige and upon his attributes as a reformer. With unerring prescience he chose those political issues which would make a wide appeal and which could be pressed quickly to a successful conclusion. His complete integrity saved him from mere opportunism; his ruggedly practical common sense saved him from that combination of high purpose and slight accomplishment which has characterized many other reformers.

In his choice of subordinates, Roosevelt was uncommonly successful. Courage, honesty and a desire to serve the people, he insisted upon,—or as he expressed it himself: "My view was that every executive officer, and above all every executive officer in high position, was a steward of the people bound actively and affirmatively to do all he could for the people, and not to content himself with the negative merit of keeping his talents undamaged in a napkin." His own buoyant energy, unconventionality and directness of purpose were like a reviving breeze through the sultry atmosphere of executive Washington. The heads of departments worked hard and happily, proud to have their names associated with the work that Roosevelt was doing.

No estimate of the deficiencies in Roosevelt's personality and leadership would be agreed upon at the present time. In some cases—as in the realm of international relations—only the future can decide whether he was a prophet or a chauvinist; in all cases, opinions have differed widely, for Roosevelt could scarcely explore a river, describe a natural phenomenon or urge a political innovation without thereby arousing a controversy in which his friends and his opponents would participate with equal intensity. His identification of himself with his purposes was as complete as that of Andrew Jackson; opposition to his proposals was reckoned as opposition to him as an individual. Like many leaders of the fighting type, he was frequently weak when judging the motives of those who disagreed with him. One of his admirers declared that his greatest political defect was an impatience of any interval between an expressed desire for an act and the accomplishment of the deed itself—an inability to stand through years of defeat for the future success of an ideal. A keener and equally sympathetic critic dubbed him the ''sportsman'' in politics—honest, hard-hitting, but playing the issue which had an immediate political effect.

At the outset of his administration Roosevelt was apparently an adherent of the prevailing Republican creed—protective tariff, gold standard, imperialism, *laissez faire* and the rest. His first official utterance after becoming President was an indication that he would continue unbroken the policies of his predecessor, and to this end he insisted that the cabinet should remain intact.[5] His foreign policy was aggressive; his interest in the military and naval establishments, real and constant. Roosevelt was more venturesome than McKinley, and more ready to experiment with new ideas. He took up the duties of his position with an unaffected zest and enthusiasm; he looked upon the presidential office as an exhilarating adventure in national and even international affairs. As time went on, therefore, it became more and more evident that he was prepared to play a big rôle on a great stage. Moreover, few doubts concerning the constitutional powers of the executive position seem ever to have assailed him. What-

[5] In view of the later activities of President Roosevelt, there is point in the remark of a satirist that Roosevelt did carry out the policies of McKinley—and bury them. *Atlantic Monthly*, CIX, p. 164.

ever may have been his theory at the outset of his presidency, he came eventually to believe that the executive power was limited only by the specific restrictions and prohibitions appearing in the Constitution, or imposed by Congress in laws which it had constitutional authority to pass. The scope which this theory presented for the exercise of his energetic originality is evident when contrasted with the theory of his predecessors, who had, in times of peace, held to the belief that the executive possessed only the powers specifically designated by the Constitution.

Not until some future time, when the events of the early twentieth century are better understood, will it be possible to judge accurately the value of President Roosevelt's régime in its relation to the control of railroads and corporations. There can be no doubt, however, that one of the most serious problems that faced the American people during that time was the position which the government ought to occupy toward the business interests of the nation. Not only were the railroads and the great corporations the center of the economic life of the people, but their social and political effects were momentous.

Neither the Interstate Commerce Act of 1887 nor the Sherman Anti-trust law of 1890, it will be remembered, had accomplished what had been expected of them. The Interstate Commerce law had met with grave obtacles in the courts; the Sherman act had been seldom invoked by the federal executive, and in the most prominent case, United States v. E. C. Knight Co., the government had failed to obtain the decision it desired. Government regulation seemed like a broken reed.[6] A few cases, however, had indicated the possibility that strength might be discovered in the law. In United States v. the Trans-Missouri Freight Association, the Supreme

[6] The case concerned the purchase of refineries by the American Sugar Refining Company. See above, p. 240.

Court had declared that the Anti-trust act applied to rail-roads and that it forbade agreements among them to maintain rates; two years later, in 1899, the Court pronounced illegal a combination of iron pipe manufacturers in the Middle West, on the ground that its result was to restrain interstate commerce.

Roosevelt, like Bryan and La Follette, had been groping his way to an understanding of the importance of the new problem. During his term as Governor of New York he had clashed with the older political leaders when he supported an act looking to the heavier taxation of railway franchises. The first recommendations in his message to Congress on December 3, 1901, concerned the subject of the relation of government and industry. The accumulation of wealth in recent years in the United States, he asserted, had been due to natural causes, and much of the antagonism aroused thereby was without warrant. Nevertheless grave evils had attended the process: overcapitalization was one; untruthful representations concerning the value of the properties in which business asked the public to invest was another. Such evils should be attacked; with extreme care, to be sure, but also with resolution. Combination and concentration, he thought, should be supervised and, within reasonable limits, controlled. The remedies which the President suggested were simple: in the interest of the public the government should have the right to inspect the workings of organizations engaged in interstate commerce; because of the lack of uniformity in corporation legislation within the states, the federal government should so extend its power as to include supervision of corporations; a Department of Commerce and Industries should be established, whose head should be a cabinet officer; the Interstate Commerce law should be amended; railway rates should be just, and should be the same to all shippers alike. It was typical of his philosophy and of his practical nature to urge a definite means to these ends. *The government, he thought, should be the agent to provide the remedies.*

The enthusiastic reception accorded the message by the press indicated that one or another of its numerous recommendations had met with approval. The effect on Congress, however, of the portion dealing with interstate commerce was represented by a cartoon in the New York *World*. Uncle Sam was there portrayed stowing away for later attention a bundle of manuscript labeled "President's Message 1901. 30,000 words," while he smilingly remarked "When I git time!" But Roosevelt was not content to let the matter drop, and in the following summer he took the unusual step of carrying his message directly to the people. In the New England states first, and later in the West, he declared his creed on the federal regulation of industry. The effectiveness of the campaign was increased by the moderation of the President, by his increasing popularity and by the many telling phrases, with which he enforced his main thesis. The Sherman act looked less like a broken reed when the chief executive of the nation declared: "As far as the anti-trust laws go they will be enforced . . . and when (a) suit is undertaken it will not be compromised except upon the basis that the Government wins." Here and there objection was raised that the program was not sufficiently definite; now and then a critic hazarded a conjecture that Roosevelt had not consulted the leaders of his party; but in the main he succeeded in obtaining a sympathetic hearing. At this juncture the coal strike of 1902 gave him one of those fortunate opportunities which were commonly referred to as a part of "Roosevelt's luck." With no uncertain hand he seized the opportunity which chance presented.

Before 1899, there had been no organization of the anthracite miners with sufficient strength to force any changes in the conditions under which the men performed their work. During that year the United Mine Workers of America began to send organizers into the Pennsylvania region. In 1900 the men struck, but an agreement was reached with the operators and work was resumed. The settlement, however, was not satisfactory to either side, and in 1902 the workers asked for a conference. They complained that wages were low, and being still further depressed by unskilled immigrant labor from Poland, Hungary and Italy. They objected that the operators compelled them to load 3000 pounds of coal on a car as a "ton"; and they pointed to the abuse of the company stores at which the miners were frequently forced to trade. Sometimes the men were paid in orders on the company store, not in money, and the prices which they had to pay were exorbitant. "As the mine workers themselves expressed it, many of the companies earned the money not only by mining coal but by mining miners." The fundamental demand, however, was the recognition of the union,—the workmen insisting on collective bargaining because they were helpless as individuals against the rich, powerful operators.

The presidents of the coal companies and the coal-carrying railroads replied that they were always ready to meet their own employees, but would have no dealings with a general labor organization. They would have no interference by politicians, and no compromise. Mark Hanna, who talked with men on both sides, was surprised to discover how determined the operators were to refuse any accommodation short of complete victory. "It looks," said he, "as if (the coal strike) was only to be settled when the miners are *starved* to it." When attempts at conference failed, the miners struck and from May 12 until October 23 nearly 147,000 of them remained idle. The total loss to miners and operators was nearly $100,000,000.

Since the Pennsylvania fields were almost the sole source of supply for anthracite coal, discomfort was soon felt in the North and West, and as the cooler weather came on, suffering became acute and public feeling bordered on panic. A winter without hard coal could scarcely be contemplated without grave misgivings. Popular opinion, meanwhile, went increasingly to the side of the miners. The refusal of the operators to confer, and the propriety of the conduct of the workmen made a wide impression that was favorable to the union. Moreover, George F. Baer, president of the Philadelphia and Reading Company, spoke of himself and his associates in a letter to a correspondent as those ''Christian men to whom God in His infinite wisdom has given the control of the property interests of the country.'' The remark was widely quoted and generally looked upon as evidence of a selfish and uncompromising individualism.[7]

The strike had now become a matter of national importance. President Roosevelt believed that he had no legal responsibility for the settlement of the trouble, but its political bearings were not to be ignored—the congressional elections were hardly more than a month away—and he keenly realized the suffering which the country would soon be compelled to endure. Hence he requested the operators and representatives of the miners to meet him in Washington, October 3. At the conference the spokesmen for the operators showed plainly that they resented the President's course of action. They declared that all trouble would cease if the government would send troops to keep the miners in order, and suggested that the Attorney General institute suits against the miners under the Sherman anti-trust law. When the leader of the United Mine Workers, John Mitchell, proposed arbitration and pledged the workmen to accept it, the operators refused. Plainly the theory of public interest and the philosophy of *laissez faire* had come to grips.

Roosevelt's next move was the application of pressure on

---

[7] It was later denied that Baer made the statement, but a photographic copy of the letter was printed in Lloyd, *Henry D. Lloyd*, II, p, 190. See also Mitchell, *Organized Labor*, p. 384; Peck, *Twenty Years*, pp. 693–6.

the operators to force them to accept his conciliatory proposal. He obtained the consent of Grover Cleveland to act as
chairman of a commission of investigation, and sent Elihu
Root, his Secretary of War, to see the eminent financier, J. P.
Morgan. Morgan agreed with Root that the President should
appoint a commission, and succeeded in getting the assent of
the operators, with the proviso that Cleveland should not
serve. Subsequently Roosevelt appointed Judge George Gray
as chairman, the miners immediately returned to work, coal
began again to flow to the North, and public rejoicing was
extreme.[8] The President's Commission at once repaired to
Pennsylvania, heard 558 witnesses, visited the mines, and in-
spected machinery and the homes of the miners. It concluded that neither side was completely in the right, and
therefore made an award that satisfied some of the complaints
of both parties. The miners were given a ten per cent. raise
in wages, and future disputes were to be referred to a Board
of Conciliation of six members, three to be chosen by the mine
owners and three by the workmen,—a provision which practically gave the miners the collective bargaining which they
had demanded.

In the history of the relation between the federal government
and the business interests of the nation, the anthracite strike
of 1902 is of marked significance. The operators had given
evidence of a failure to understand that their business so concerned the nation that the interest of the public in it must be
heeded. The successful outcome enhanced the prestige of the
government and of the President, and an example of the need
of greater control over corporations received wide publicity at

[8] In case the operators had resisted Morgan's pressure, President
Roosevelt planned to appoint a commission of investigation nevertheless, throw troops into the anthracite region and work the mines,
regardless of what the owners might say or do, until the commission
made its report. Perhaps news of this plan leaked out to the operators
and influenced them to accept the proposed plan, or perhaps Cleveland's willingness to cooperate with Roosevelt influenced them.

the precise moment when the general subject was uppermost in the popular mind.

So completely did Roosevelt's campaign for more effective government regulation of industry receive public approbation that the single year 1903 saw five important steps in the new direction. The first was an act approved on February 11, 1903, by which any suit brought in a Circuit Court by the United States government under the Sherman Anti-trust act or the Interstate Commerce law, could be given precedence over other cases at the desire of the Attorney-General. Three days later a law was passed which established a Department of Commerce and Labor, whose chief was to be a cabinet officer. Included in the Department was a Bureau of Corporations headed by a Commissioner, who was authorized to investigate the organization and conduct of the business of corporations. Within another five days the Elkins Act had been passed—a law designed to eliminate rebating. Despite the Interstate Commerce act, the practice of rebating had continued. Agreement was general that railroad men who, in other respects, were perfectly scrupulous, commonly violated the law in order to get business in competition with their rivals.[9] Among the railroad men who had violated the law but who deprecated the necessity of so doing, was Paul Morton, president of the Santa Fé system. Morton volunteered to assist Roosevelt in stamping out the evil, and the Elkins law was designed to aid in this process. It forbade any variation from published rates, made both a corporation and its agents punishable for offenses against the law, prohibited the receiving of rebates as well as giving them, and made the penalty for failure to observe the provisions of the Act a fine of one thousand to twenty thousand dollars. Furthermore, during February,

9 A railroad president, who had himself made rebates for many years, once went so far as to say that "there is not a city of 100,000 people in the United States where I could not put my finger on an ample fortune made by rebating." Rainsford, *Story of a Varied Life*, p. 423.

19C3, Congress appropriated $500,000 to be expended under the direction of the Attorney-General for the better enforcement of the anti-trust and interstate commerce laws.

The last of the five steps was an important judicial proceeding in the direction of the enforcement of the Sherman law. The Great Northern Railway Company and the Northern Pacific Railway Company operated parallel competing lines of road extending from the region of Lake Superior to the Pacific Coast. Early in 1901 an unsuccessful attempt had been made by the Union Pacific, under E. H. Harriman, to get a controlling interest in the Northern Pacific. In order to prevent a repetition of this danger, the Northern Securities Company was founded at the suggestion of James J. Hill, who had been the leading spirit in building the Great Northern, and with the cooperation of J. P. Morgan, whose main interest was in the Northern Pacific. The Company was to purchase at least a majority of the stock of the Northern Pacific and the Great Northern—these two also controlled the Chicago, Burlington and Quincy—and might—besides, hold shares of coal and other companies which were of value to the railroads.[10] By such a plan the lines concerned would be operated as one, their policies would harmonize instead of clash, and a virtual consolidation would be effected. Its capitalization—$400,000,000—was so great as to make it unlikely that anybody could go into the market and purchase a controlling share of its securities. Hill and his associates had studied with care the legal situation, and felt assured that they were not transgressing the Sherman anti-trust law. In view of the decision in the Knight case, it seemed altogether likely that the Supreme Court would agree with them.

At the request of President Roosevelt, however, the Attor-

[10] The Northern Securities was a "holding company,"—that is, it held the securities of other companies and directed their policies, but did not actually operate them. Like so many other corporations, it was chartered under New Jersey law.

ney General, Philander C. Knox, investigated the situation, and proceedings were instituted against the Company. The decision of the Supreme Court given in 1904, was by the narrow margin of five to four and upheld the government's contention that the Northern Securities was a combination in restraint of trade. Roosevelt was jubilant, as the decision indicated that future prosecutions under the Sherman law might run the gauntlet of the courts.

Nineteen hundred and four, the year of the presidential election, found Roosevelt in a strong position. His success in handling the coal strike and his energetic preparations for the crusade against trust evils had struck a responsive chord in the popular mind. Late in 1903 he had announced to Congress that frauds had been discovered in the post office and land office, and urged the appropriation of funds for the prosecution of the offenders. The result was a house-cleaning which involved the conviction of many officials, including two United States senators. Roosevelt's popularity became greater than ever.

It was to be expected, however, that some opposition would appear to the nomination of Roosevelt for a continuation of his term of office, and it was around the forceful Mark Hanna that the opposition began gradually to center. Hanna had attained remarkable influence as a senator, was highly trusted by the business interests and was popular among southern Republicans. But his death in February, 1904, effectively ended any opposition to Roosevelt, since it was then too late to focus attention upon any other competitor.

The Republican nominating convention, therefore, which met in Chicago on June 21, lacked any semblance of a contest, and the President was renominated without opposition. The platform was of the traditional sort. The history of the party was approved; its achievements in giving prosperity to the country and peaceful government to the island possessions were recounted; the protective tariff, the gold standard, an

isthmian canal, the improvement of the army and navy, the
continuation of civil service reform and a vigorous foreign
policy,—on all these the party utterance was that of other days.
Surprisingly little was said upon the subject of the regulation
of corporations. The few steps already taken were approved,
but as to the future, the platform was almost colorless:

Combinations of capital and of labor are the results of the
economic movement of the age, but neither must be permitted to
infringe upon the rights and interests of the people. Such combinations, when lawfully formed for lawful purposes, are alike entitled to the protection of the laws, but both are subject to the laws,
and neither can be permitted to break them.

The Democratic convention met in St. Louis on July 6, and
the excitement which marked its proceedings compensated
for the lack of interest at the Republican meeting. As drawn
up by a sub-committee of the Committee on Resolutions, the
platform was, in many of its planks, a distinct return to the
programs of the days before 1896. It urged a reduction of the
tariff, generous pensions and civil service reform, together
with the enforcement of the anti-trust laws and the popular
election of senators. In the main, it was devoted to a condemnation of the existing Republican administration, which
it denounced as "spasmodic, erratic, sensational, spectacular
and arbitrary." It also contained a paragraph declaring that
the question of the money standard had ceased to be an issue,
on the ground that recent discoveries of gold had enormously
increased the supply of currency in the country. Bryan did
not approve. With characteristic energy he threw himself
into an all-night fight in the Committee in behalf of a silver
plank. His defeat indicated that the convention was in the
hands of his opponents and the platform as adopted contained
no reference to the currency.

The delegates had, in fact, come to the meeting with the
distinct purpose of returning to the "safe and sane" democ-

racy of Grover Cleveland. To that end, the platform was to
drop the silver issue and Bryan was to be replaced by a more
conservative leader. The radical forces centered their
strength upon William R. Hearst, but they were in a distinct minority, and in the end, the Cleveland wing succeeded in nominating Judge Alton B. Parker of New York.
As soon as he was notified of his nomination, Judge Parker
telegraphed to the convention that he regarded the gold standard as irrevocably established and that he must decline to be
the party candidate if his attitude on the currency was unsatisfactory to the delegates. Thereupon the convention replied
that the platform was silent on the question of a monetary
standard because it was not regarded as a campaign issue.
Parker was satisfied with the reply, and the last word was
written upon a question that had disturbed politics for many
years.

The succeeding campaign was unusually listless. Parker
did not inspire enthusiasm, although a man of undoubted integrity and ability, and the personality of Roosevelt was the
controlling force. Only at the close of the canvass did a
passing interest appear in some charges made by Parker. He
called attention to the fact that Secretary Cortelyou of the
Department of Commerce and Labor had been charged with
the duty of examining the acts of corporations and had then
resigned to become chairman of the National Republican Committee. Parker insinuated that Cortelyou was using information about corporate misdoing, which he had discovered, in
order to force large contributions from the business interests.
He also declared that the Republican campaign was being
financed by the corporations. Roosevelt did not answer the
charges until three days before the election, and then he asserted that the statements made by Parker were ''unqualifiedly
and atrociously false.'' Later investigations have shown that
in general Parker was correct in his complaint as to the activities of the corporations, although he would have found diffi-

culty in proving his charges in detail. The same investigations, however, indicated that some of the Democratic campaign fund had come from similar sources.

The election resulted in the choice of President Roosevelt, whose popular vote was 7,600,000 to Parker's 5,000,000. In the more populous sections of the country, which were normally Republican, the party vote scarcely exceeded that of 1900, but in the Far West, the increases were notable. Beyond the Mississippi River, except in the southern states, hardly a county gave a majority for Parker, showing that the region which had gone to Bryan in 1896 was substantially solid for Roosevelt. Indeed, the policies to which Roosevelt was committed bore a greater resemblance to the principles of Bryan than to the *laisse faire* philosophy to which many important Republican leaders adhered. Despite their dissent, however, his victory in the election was so overwhelming that he could carry out his program with the irresistible pressure of public opinion behind him.

During the campaign year, the Commissioner of Corporations was busy investigating the activities of the so-called "beef-trust," and a suit against the combination was pressed to a successful conclusion in January, 1905. In its decision in the case (Swift & Company *v.* United States), the Supreme Court dwelt at some length on the charges made against the Company. A dominant proportion—six-tenths—of the dealers in fresh meat in the United States were alleged to have agreed not to bid against one another in the live-stock markets; to restrict the output of meat in order to raise prices; to keep a black-list; and to get illegal rates from the railroads to the exclusion of competitors. To the objection of the members of the trust that the charges against them were general and did not set forth any specific facts, the Court retorted that the scheme alleged was so vast as to present a new problem in pleading. The decision was against the combination, which

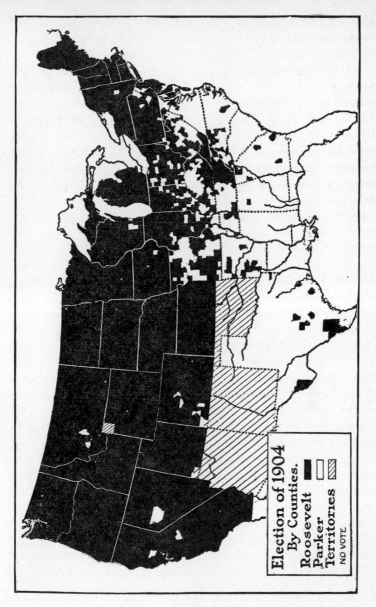

Election of 1904
By Counties.
Roosevelt
Parker
Territories
NO VOTE

was ordered to dissolve. The publicity given to the case and to the methods of the meat packers assisted in the passage of legislation requiring government inspection of meats.

An unexpected phase of the Sherman act appeared in 1908, in the case Loewe v. Lawlor. The American Federation of Labor, acting through its official organ, had declared a boycott against D. E. Loewe, a hat manufacturer of Danbury, Connecticut. The Court decided that a combination of labor organizations designed to boycott a dealer's goods was a combination in restraint of trade and that the manufacturer might maintain an action against the Hatters' Union for damages.[11]

In the meantime, another prominent trust had played into the hands of the administration. The American Sugar Refining Company imported large amounts of raw sugar, on which it paid tariff duties. In November, 1907, it was discovered that the Company had tampered with the scales on which the incoming sugar was weighed, in such a manner as to defraud the government. In the resulting legal actions, over $4,000,000 were recovered from the Company, criminal prosecutions were carried on against the officials and employees, and several of them were convicted. The close relation between the railroads and the great corporations was indicated when the Standard Oil Company of Indiana was brought into court on the charge of receiving rebates on petroleum shipped over the Chicago and Alton Railroad. The decision by Judge K. M. Landis was that the Company was guilty on 1,462 separate counts and must pay a fine of $29,240,000. On appeal to a higher court the case was dismissed, partly on a question concerning the meaning of the law.

The efforts of Roosevelt in the direction of control of the railroads resembled his activities in relation to industrial com-

[11] In 1917, fourteen years after Loewe's first suit, he recovered damages from the Union.

binations. A variety of circumstances had combined to arouse a popular demand for the reinforcement of existing legislation: the discovery of grave abuses in connection with the transportation of petroleum; the continuance of favoritism and rebating, together with increasing public knowledge of their existence; the rise in freight rates; and the consolidation of the railroads into a few large systems, with the accompanying concentration of power in the hands of a small number of persons. In his public speeches and in his messages to Congress in 1904 and 1905, President Roosevelt made himself the spokesman of the popular will. In particular—and it was here that the conflict was destined to rage—the President called for the transfer to the Interstate Commerce Commission of the power to determine the rates which the roads should be allowed to charge. The project was not a new one, having already taken shape in previous years, but at no time was Congress prepared to pass definite legislation. The railroad executives—none too friendly toward Roosevelt since the action against the Northern Securities Company—fought the proposal with all their power. An energetic lobby worked insistently upon Congress, first to prevent action and later, when action was seen to be inevitable, to weaken the legislation wherever possible. The railroad's campaign of popular education, however, helped to convince the popular mind that new laws were needed, and came coincidently with the disclosures of corporate mismanagement and wrong-doing. Moreover, the muck-rake press had prepared the public mind to view capitalist activities with alarm and to support the President in his demands upon Congress. The outcome was the Hepburn act of June 29, 1906.

Its major provisions were five in number. It enlarged the scope of the Interstate Commerce act so as to include control of express and sleeping car companies, pipe lines, switches, spur tracks and terminals. Free passes, which had hitherto been productive of much favoritism and the source of political corruption, were strictly forbidden, except to a few specified groups. The "commodity clause" forbade railroads to carry goods, other than timber, in which they had an interest, except such as they were going to use themselves. This provision was designed mainly to check the activities of those companies which owned both coal mines and railroads, and which used their advantageous position to crush independent operators.[12] The Hepburn law also enabled the Commission to prescribe the methods of book-keeping which the roads must follow, to call for monthly or special reports and to employ examiners who should have access to the books of the carriers. The roads were even denied the right to keep any records except those approved by the Commission. These drastic features of the law were due in part to the practices of certain roads which hid away corrupt expenditures in their accounts in such a manner that detection was almost impossible. Most important, however, among the provisions of the act was that in relation to rate-making, which not only empowered the Commission to hear complaints that rates were unjust or unreasonable, but even enabled it to determine what would be a just and reasonable charge in the case, and to order the carrier complained of to adhere to the new rate. The rate-making section in the Hepburn Act immediately resulted in a large increase in the number of complaints entered by shippers against the carriers. Previously, few cases had been taken to the Commission—only 878 in eighteen years—because relief was seldom obtained and then only at great cost in time and money. Under the new law more than 1500 cases were entered within two and a half years, and several thousand others were informally settled out of court.

[12] The enforcement of this provision met with unexpected complications. In earlier decisions, the courts took the stand that ownership of coal company stock by a railroad did not prevent the latter from lawfully carrying the coal company's product. In later cases, more emphasis has been placed on the rather obvious intent of the law, and the tendency has been to order the separation of the railroads from the coal companies. *Cf.* Miller, *Railway Transportation,* pp. 772–775.

The example of the federal government in adopting restrictive railway legislation was followed by the states, on a
nation-wide scale. Hours of labor were regulated, liability
for accidents defined, railroad commissions given larger
powers, and freight and passenger rates determined. The result was a tangle of local regulations, many of which were designed to embarrass the roads and others of which were passed
with slight knowledge of the practical questions involved.

Aside from his connection with the anti-trust campaign and
the movement for railroad regulation, Roosevelt's most significant activities during his second administration related to
conservation. As early as 1880 the Superintendent of the
Census had called attention to the exhaustion of the best public lands. The truth of his assertion had been exemplified in
the rush of settlers to Oklahoma when the former Indian
Territory was opened to settlement on April 22, 1889. At
noon on that day the blast of a cavalry bugle was the signal
that any settler might enter and stake out his claim. On foot,
on fleet horses, in primitive wagons, an excited, jostling mob
rushed toward those lands that seemed most desirable. Trains
were crowded to the roofs; tools, furniture, and portable
houses were carried in from Texas, Nebraska and Kansas.
By nightfall a stretch of waving prairie became Guthrie, with
a population of 10,000 persons; by the evening of the first day
Oklahoma possessed a population of 50,000; thirty years
later it had over two million, contained flourishing cities,
many public enterprises, and a beautiful state university.

The fact that desirable land was becoming so rare called
attention to the waste and dishonesty in connection with our
public land system.[13] In his annual report for 1884 the Sec-

13 The drain which modern civilization makes on the supply of raw
materials is indicated in the following illustration cited by Faulkner,
American Economic History, p. 657 n.: "The Public Service Bureau
of the *Chicago Tribune* gives 'the approximate figures on the materials
that are required to publish the Sunday edition of the Chicago *Tribune*'

retary of the Interior had complained that large amounts of land had been acquired under fictitious names or by persons employed for the purpose. Their holdings were then passed over to speculators who retained huge areas for a rising market. Railroads had kept lands granted to them, without fulfilling the conditions of the grants. Titled Englishmen and English land companies had gained control of tracts of unbelievable size, one of them being estimated at 3,000,000 acres. Too much of the standing timber had been given to private concerns and cut down without provision for reforestation or for protection against fires. Coal had been mined, oil wasted and wild animals killed as if there were no end to nature's bounty.

A few far-sighted individuals had long urged caution in the disposal of the public resources. An act of 1891, for example, had enabled the president to set apart as public reservations any lands bearing forests. All the presidents, from Harrison down, had availed themselves of their power, and had established numbers of reservations, most of them in states west of the Mississippi.

One of the first problems that challenged Roosevelt's interest was the best use of the remaining natural resources. By instinct he was a lover of the out-of-doors, and through his life in Dakota he had become somewhat acquainted with the problems of the western farmer and ranchman. With his usual enthusiasm and energy he threw himself into the conservation movement, putting to the fore the economic advantage of the common man, the farmer and the homesteader, rather than the great timber, land and power companies.

The careless disposal of the public land was promptly checked in order that more might be left for *bona fide* settlers who would remain upon the land and establish homes.

as follows: 'Standing timber, 54 acres; sulphur, 21 tons; coal, 665 tons; electric horsepower, 63,000; water, 18,200,000 gallons; limestone, 28 tons; paper 800 tons.' "

Frauds were stopped,—saving 250,000 acres in a single case and involving the prosecution and conviction of a senator from Oregon. The withdrawal of timber lands from public sale was so rapidly extended that altogether Roosevelt set aside nearly 150,000,000 acres.[14] Side by side with the expansion of the public forest area went the development of the Division of Forestry in the Department of Agriculture. Some beginnings, in fact, had already been made there, where Gifford Pinchot was actively interested in forest preservation. Protection against fires was devised, timber cut and reforestation carried on.[15] In 1906 an act of Congress was passed which granted the use of water-power sites in southern California to the Edison Electric Power Company. Hitherto such grants had been made outright. Now, at the suggestion of the forestry service, the sites were *leased* for a period limited to forty years, and the Company was to pay an annual rental to the government. Later legislation extended the principle to other types of public land.[16]

Another project in the conservation program was the addition of five national parks. On these and other public reservations, attempts were made to protect birds, and such wild animals as the buffalo which were in imminent danger of complete extinction.

In 1907 President Roosevelt appointed a commission to

[14] By 1910 the number of the national forests had reached 149, containing nearly 193,000,000 acres; in 1923, there were 146 forests, which contained 157,000,000 acres.

[15] The quickness with which the economic resources of the country were consolidated in a few hands is strikingly illustrated in a Report of the Bureau of Corporations. Not long after the Civil War, according to the Report, three-fourths of the standing timber of the country was on public land; forty years later, in Roosevelt's administration, four-fifths was in private hands, and three corporations, the Southern Pacific Railway, the Northern Pacific and the Weyerhaeuser Timber Company held one-twenty-fifth of the entire supply. The developed water power was being similarly monopolized. Ten groups of men, the Bureau declared, controlled nearly sixty per cent, of it. *Cf.* Roosevelt, *Autobiography* (1920 ed.), p. 418.

[16] *Cf.* below p. 705,

study the inland waterways, which after careful investigation recommended a convention for the discussion of conservation problems. Thereupon the President invited the governors of the states to Washington for a conference, at which conservation questions were thoroughly discussed. The resulting recommendations composed a complete, although general plan of reform : the natural resources of the country to be used for the prosperity of the American people; reclamation of arid lands; conservation of forests, minerals and water-power; the protection of the sources of the rivers; and cooperation between Congress and the states in developing a conservation program. Inspired by the leadership of the federal government, thirty-six states appointed conservation commissions, and on June 8, 1908, the National Conservation Commission was named. It coordinated the work of organizing the movement, and made an exhaustive inventory of the nation's natural resources.

The conservation movement also called attention to the possibilities of the arid region between the western parts of Kansas, Nebraska and the Dakotas, and the eastern border of California. Within this vast area were large tracts of land that would be fertile if sufficiently supplied with water. The most important legislation in a series of acts designed to meet this need was the Reclamation act of 1902. Under its provisions the federal government set aside the proceeds of the sale of public land in sixteen states and territories as a fund for irrigation work. By 1911, three projects were completed and twenty-two more were under way. Huge dams were built—like that at Shoshone in Wyoming, and the Roosevelt dam in Arizona—which made possible the storage of sufficient water to irrigate hundreds of thousands of acres. Private companies and western states also carried out numerous projects. Altogether, more than 19,000,000 acres of irrigated land were being cultivated in 1920, the most valuable crops being alfalfa, rice, cereals and fruits. The Department of Agriculture after its establishment in 1889 had also conducted many undertakings which, in effect, were conservation enterprises. It helped educate the American farmer in scientific methods, sought new crops in every corner of the globe, discovered and circulated means of combating diseases and insects, studied soils, distributed seeds and gathered statistics. In the arid and semi-arid regions the discovery of dry farming was of great value. This consists in planting the seed deep and keeping a mulch of dust on the surface by frequent cultivation, in order to retard the evaporation of the moisture in the ground underneath.[17]

Nothing can be more apparent than the complete change of position which was brought about during the eight years after the death of President McKinley. At the end of that period, both the industrial corporations and the railways were on the defensive, and the public had secured the whip hand. Industry, especially the railroads, was tamed and hobbled— some thought, crippled. Many factors contributed to the revolution. President Roosevelt was its most active agent, to be sure,—its "gigantic advertiser" and popularizer. But it could hardy have taken place—at least at the time and in the way it did—without the great upheaval of 1896, without the publicity which the "muck-rake" magazines and daily newspapers were able to offer, without the industrial consolidations of 1898 and later, and without the refusal of industry and the railways to obey earlier and less drastic laws, and their skilled and insistent attempts to find loop-holes in legislation.

From the standpoint of public morals, the influence of Roosevelt's accomplishments may perhaps have been more

[17] The territory of Alaska contains immense stores of natural resources which are being conserved with more wisdom than characterized the disposal of our continental supplies. The area of the territory, 586,400 square miles, constitutes a kingdom. It has uncounted wealth in fish, furs, timber, coal and precious metals. At present the federal government is building a railroad which will tap some of the resources of the region.

important than they were from the standpoint of economic history. Whether the enforcement of the Sherman anti-trust act has benefited the country as a whole, is a question on which honest men still differ. Probably there would be agreement, however, that the ethics of big business were bad and needed correction, and that standards of conduct in economic life sharply improved during Roosevelt's administration. Many unfair practices became less common; railroad rebating has to a great extent been given up,—much to the relief of railway companies and shippers alike; and the discovery of frauds and the punishment of the offenders tended to inculcate virtue, even if for no other reason than that of common prudence.

From the standpoint of politics, the effect of the Roosevelt administrations had a continuing interest. As has been seen, the Republican party had become largely the party of the business and commercial classes, conservative and unyielding to the new demands of the late nineteenth century. Its leadership had been sharply challenged by the forces of unrest in 1896. On an issue other than a monetary one, the success of Bryan would have been possible. The failure of the attempt to get control of the federal government in the interest of the Populist program was only a temporary defeat, for the revival of unrest, although checked by the War with Spain, was sure soon to reappear. In President Roosevelt, the forces of discontent, especially in the Middle and Far West, saw their hoped-for champion, and their support of him was instant and complete. The dominant leadership and much of the rank and file of the Republican party had become liberal. The situation was anomalous, however, for no great political party can experience a thorough-going change of philosophy in a few years. Only the future, therefore, could tell whether the newer and more liberal element would continue to control the party, or whether a reaction against its leadership would take place. Before pursuing that part of the investigation, it may

help to an understanding of the fundamental points at issue if
the political ideals of the two groups are defined and evaluated.

BIBLIOGRAPHICAL NOTE

Roosevelt can be partly understood through a critical reading of
his writings, especially his *Addresses and Presidential Messages*
(1904), and his *Autobiography* (1913), although portions of the latter were written in considerable political heat. J. B. Bishop, *Theo-*
dore Roosevelt and His Time (2 vols., 1920) was written for the most
part under Roosevelt's supervision, and is a sort of enlarged autobiography. *Selections from the Correspondence of Theodore*
Roosevelt and Henry Cabot Lodge (2 vols., 1925) contains many
self-revealing passages. The following are also available: L. F.
Abbott, *Impressions of Theodore Roosevelt* (1919); Lord Charn-
wood, *Theodore Roosevelt* (1923); H. H. Kohlsaat, *From McKinley*
to Harding (1923); F. E. Leupp, *The Man Roosevelt* (1904);
W. D. Lewis, *The Life of Theodore Roosevelt* (1919); W. R. Thayer,
Theodore Roosevelt (1919); C. G. Washburn, *Theodore Roosevelt;*
the Logic of His Career (1916).

The emergence of the theory of public interest is best seen
in the autobiographies of La Follette and Roosevelt. A profound
article is W. J. Tucker, "The Progress of the Social Conscience,"
in *Atlantic Monthly* (Sept., 1915). On the Fourteenth Amendment,
consult the volumes already mentioned under Chap. IV. There
are no thorough estimates of Bryan and La Follette. On the
former: *Atlantic Monthly* (Sept., 1912), and *Nineteenth Century*
(July, 1915); H. Croly, *Promise of American Life* (1914); W. J.
Bryan, *First Battle* (1897). La Follette's narrative as given in his
Autobiography should be read with care, as it was written in the
midst of partisan controversy. See also F. C. Howe, *Wisconsin*
an Experiment in Democracy (1912), and C. W. Alvord, "La Follette and the Wisconsin Idea," *Contemporary Review* (Oct., 1924).

The Northern Securities Case may be studied in B. H. Meyer,
A History of the Northern Securities Case in "Bulletin of the
University of Wisconsin," vol. 1, 1906; J. G. Pyle, *The Life of*
James J. Hill (2 vols., 1917); G. Kennan, *Life of E. H. Harriman*
(2 vols., 1922); and in Roosevelt's *Autobiography*. The decision

of the Supreme Court is in the *United States Reports,* vol. 193, pp. 197 *ff.*

On the coal strike, consult Roosevelt; *Senate Reports* 58th Congress, special session, Document No. 6 (Serial Number 4556), the report of the President's Commission; J. Mitchell, *Organized Labor* (1903).

The election of 1904 is discussed in Latané, Croly and Stanwood. The new railroad acts may be studied in W. Z. Ripley, *Railroads: Rates and Regulation* (1912); F. H. Dixon in *Quarterly Journal of Economics* XXI, p. 22; S. L. Miller, *Railway Transportation* (1924).

The literature of conservation is very large. Excellent single chapters are in K. Coman, *Industrial History of the United States* (rev. ed., 1910), and Roosevelt, *Autobiography.* C. R. Van Hise, *The Conservation of Natural Resources in the United States* (1913), is a standard work. See also R. P. Teele, *Irrigation in the United States* (1915). For documents concerning the conference of governors, *House of Representatives Document* No. 1425, 60th Congress, 2nd session (Serial Number 5538).

On the anti-trust campaign, consult the various books by and about Roosevelt. See also the references at the close of Chapter X.

CHAPTER XXI

TWO DECADES OF ECONOMIC AND POLITICAL TRANSITION, 1896–1916

The pressure is so great, so steady and so all-sided towards the expansion, intensification and centralization of governmental power, that it sweeps everything in its course.

JOHN W. BURGESS.

Whether you like it or not, the arbitrary settlement of labor matters by the employer without taking the employee into conference is no longer possible.

THE PRESIDENT OF THE STANDARD OIL COMPANY OF NEW JERSEY.

For a couple of years I have felt that you and I were heading opposite ways as regards internal politics

THEODORE ROOSEVELT TO HENRY CABOT LODGE.

THE economic unification of the United States after 1865 and particularly after the great railroad and industrial expansion of the eighties is one of the most important facts in American history since the Civil War,—if not the most important. The passage of the Interstate Commerce act in 1887 was an early recognition of the fact that the transportation problem of the nation transcended state bounds; and the Sherman Anti-trust law of 1890 arose from the realization that commercial and industrial unity were rapidly coming about. In addition to passing general legislation of new types, the federal government itself entered the economic field with a Post Office Savings Bank in 1910, a parcel post service in 1912, and a complete federal banking system in 1913.

The executive was not less active than Congress in reaching out into new spheres of power. President Roosevelt, as has been seen, acted boldly on the principle that the chief execu-

tive should do those things for the public welfare that were
not forbidden by the Constitution and the laws, that he should
have the affirmative force of an active agent and not the negative character of one who merely prevents illegal things from
being done. His popular successes in connection with the
coal strike of 1902 and the anti-trust campaign were notable
precedents in politico-economic unification.

The scientific revolution added its momentum to the process.
Distances were shortened by steel rails and fast express trains,
by the telephone and the automobile. More people crossed
state lines than had ever done so before in American history.
Newspapers circulated over greater distances and came more
promptly than ever to the reader's door. Advertising and
rapid transportation made possible the huge mail order department stores. The unparalleled corporations, which were
so distinctly a mark of the opening of the new century, sold
their products in every state of the Union. Instead, then, of
remaining a federation of diverse economic sections, we became increasingly homogeneous. Much of the economic and
political legislation enacted after 1896, and many of the practices and standards which were adopted by leaders in economic and political life were an outgrowth of the new
conditions.

It will be remembered that the eighties and early nineties
had been years of labor unrest. Costly and bitter strikes on
the part of the workmen, and resolute and powerful resistance
on the part of the employers were the commonplaces of the
history of labor,—strikes that too closely resembled downright
war, with rifles, barricades and troops, with pickets, spies and
heavy loss of life, as in the Carnegie labor upheaval at
Homestead.[1]   The culmination was the Pullman strike of 1894.
Its cost in money and suffering was appalling; it placed the
federal military power in the hands of the employers; and

[1] Cf. above, p. 301.

although it was a failure as far as the strikers were concerned, yet an impartial investigation after the struggle was over established the justice of much of which the men had complained. If discriminating justice were to be measured out to both sides, instead of victory to the side of the strongest battalions, and if intolerable waste and discomfort were to be avoided, some remedies for industrial unrest must be discovered which would replace strikes and violence. Happily, signs were not wanting that such a change was slowly taking place.

A combination of influences tended to place the labor problem on a new footing after 1896. One of the most important of these forces was the increasing entry of the wage earners into trade unions. A few of these, like the Railway Conductors, the Railroad Trainmen, the Locomotive Engineers, and the Locomotive Firemen, with a total membership of 358,000 in 1916, devoted themselves chiefly to the improvement of conditions in particular industries. More important was the American Federation of Labor which exercised a widespread influence in nearly all branches of manual work. Although this organization never reached more than 275,000 members before 1896, its size and influence grew rapidly after 1900, with the consolidation of the great corporations. By 1916 it included over 2,000,000 wage earners in its ranks. From 1882 to 1924, with the single exception of the year 1885, the president of the Federation was Samuel Gompers, an able, resourceful leader who gave the organization continuity of purpose and experience. With labor thus thoroughly organized in unions, there was an increasing acceptance of the principle of trade agreements, whereby the employer and the employees determined the conditions of labor by direct negotiation. Although a radical, socialistic element broke away in 1905 and formed the Industrial Workers of the World, yet the defection was not immediately serious and in general schisms have been avoided.

Moreover, after 1896 and especially after the coal strike of

1902 there was an increasing recognition on the part of the public that a labor problem existed and that it must be solved in some way other than by force of arms. Physicians and scientific experts called attention to the lack of proper care for the health of workmen in dangerous industries; the movement for the preservation of the forests and mineral supplies emphasized the need of efforts for the conservation of human lives; social reformers, economists, writers and educators upheld the needs and rights of the neglected classes; and the press and the muck-rake periodicals found it profitable to expose extreme abuses. Distress that had hitherto been unnoticed or disregarded became important, and remedies were demanded. Change was in the air, and not alone in America, for England and France were experiencing the same problems, and attempting to devise new expedients to solve them. After the beginning of the new century, also, the employing class came to a better realization of the needs and rights of the employee:

Labour, said John H. Patterson, founder and president of the National Cash Register Company,—labour is suspicious—and has a right to be. Generally speaking, it is not fairly treated and it has not been given either its rightful share in industry or its proportion of income. The idea has been to get everything that is to be had out of a man, keep him down, regulate his wages by the smallest amount he will take and not by what he is worth, and when he is worn out, to throw him off like an old shoe.

Although it had been the policy of the American Federation of Labor to keep out of politics, it was almost inevitable that the policy should receive some modifications. Organizations of employers were influential at Washington, and had long been so. Accordingly in 1908 the Democratic platform was endorsed on account of its labor planks, and again in 1910 and 1912. By the latter year all parties were earnestly striving to capture the labor vote, and the platforms contained most of what the wage earner had been seeking for the previous generation.

The major demands in the labor program of earlier years—higher wages, shorter hours, settled conditions of employment, and the like—were not altered after 1896, but a few striking advances were made. The attempt to legislate concerning hours of employment had been continually obstructed by the clauses in the Fifth and Fourteenth Amendments forbidding any legislation depriving the individual of "life, liberty, or property, without due process of law." The courts had usually interpreted these phrases as prohibiting laws restricting hours of labor, on the ground that the liberty of the workman to contract freely regarding his own working hours was thereby infringed. A Massachusetts law of 1874, nevertheless, which limited a day's work for women and children to ten hours, had followed the long-continued assertion that regulatory legislation could be based on the "police power"—a somewhat indefinite authority which was gradually conceded by the courts to the states and the federal government, and under which it was possible to pass legislation concerning the conservation of the health and morals of the people without violating the Constitution.[2] Not until 1908, however, was the constitutionality of such legislation finally settled by the Supreme Court, in upholding an Oregon ten-hour law. "As healthy mothers are essential to vigorous offspring," the de-

---

[2] The police power is an indefinite and flexible authority which has been assumed by both state and federal governments. It has been defined by the Supreme Court as the power "to prescribe regulations to promote the health, peace, morals, education, and good order of the people, and to legislate so as to increase the industries of the State, develop its resources, and add to its wealth and prosperity." Under this authority, the states have frequently restricted personal rights in the interests of public safety and morals,—e. g., by requiring the heating of railway coaches, safety appliances in factories, etc. The federal government has debarred objectionable material from the postoffice and suppressed lottery companies by refusing them the privilege of the mails. The extent to which the power may be used depends obviously on the political and economic philosophy of the courts. *Cf.* Barbier *v.* Connolly, 113 U. S. 31.

cision asserted, "the physical well-being of women becomes an object of public interest and care in order to preserve the strength and vigor of the race." In other words, the Court was prepared to approve limitations on the freedom of contract in order to further the public interest. The Massachusetts law was imitated far and wide, so that at the present time an almost negligible number of states have failed to restrict the length of the working day for women.

Recently, also, substantial progress has been made in restricting working hours for children. As long ago as 1866 Massachusetts had restricted the employment of children, but neither this law nor similar laws passed by other states had been fully enforced. Greater progress has been made since 1903, when Illinois, followed by the majority of the important industrial states, established the eight-hour standard for children under sixteen. Impressed with the need of federal legislation to coerce backward states, the reformers took their case to Congress where a federal act was passed in 1916. On account of constitutional limitations, the measure was framed so as to forbid shipment, on interstate railways, of the products of factories employing children under fourteen years of age. It was estimated that 150,000 out of nearly 2,000,000 working children might be affected by the act. Its fate, however, was that of many another piece of economic legislation; by a vote of five to four, the Supreme Court declared the law unconstitutional on the ground that it was not an attempt to regulate commerce, but an attempt to regulate the conditions of manufacture. Early in 1919 the effort to regulate child labor was renewed through the imposition of a tax of ten per cent. on the net profits of factories employing children under fourteen years of age. In 1922 this law was also declared unconstitutional on the ground that the purpose of the law was not the raising of revenue (and therefore a valid use of the taxing power), but the regulation of child labor. Such control, the Court thought, belonged to the states. Thereupon a constitutional amendment was drawn up which expressly empowered Congress to limit and prohibit the labor of persons under eighteen years of age. By this time a wide variety of elements combined to arouse public opinion against such action,—among them the feeling that a halt should be called to the centralizing tendency of American government, and it was found impossible to gain the assent of the requisite thirty-six states. The regulation of child labor, therefore, remains for the time at least outside the control of Congress.

It will be noted that all the foregoing legislative attempts to reduce the working day affected women and children only; in general, little attempt has been made to limit the working day for men. Nevertheless, large numbers of cities, more than half the states, and the federal government provide for an eight-hour day on public work; and western states have followed the lead of Utah in passing eight-hour laws for miners. Hours of labor for railway employees have also been the subject of study and legislation. Cases had not been unknown where employees were kept at their posts for thirty, fifty and even one hundred hours; frequently such workmen fell asleep and disastrous accidents occurred. In 1907 this situation was met by a congressional act limiting the hours of railway engineers to sixteen and providing that periods of work must be followed by specified rest periods. Train-despatchers, telegraphers, and others were similarly protected. A majority of the states imitated these federal statutes. In a few cases, state laws have been passed which were intended to limit working hours in other especial industries.

The shifting attitude of the Supreme Court on legislative regulation of the length of the working day is well illustrated in three cases, one near the beginning, one midway, and one at the close of the two decades 1896-1916. In Holden *v.* Hardy, which was decided in 1898, the Court reviewed the Utah law restricting hours of labor in mines and smelters to eight. The law, declared the Court, was "a valid exercise of the police power of the state." In 1905 the same tribunal gave its decision in Lochner v. New York on a state law providing that bakers should not work more than ten hours a day. The opinion, by a majority of five to four was as follows:

We think the limit of the police power has been reached and passed in this case. There is, in our judgment, no reasonable foundation for holding this to be necessary or appropriate as a health law. . . .

In 1917 the Court had to decide upon the validity of an Oregon law which provided that nobody should be employed "in any mill, factory or manufacturing establishment" in the state for more than ten hours a day. The statute was upheld as a valid health regulation.[3]

Whether court decisions were favorable or unfavorable, however, the length of the working day continued to grow less. The insistence of the trade unions had much to do with it. So did the changing opinion of industrial executives who found that eight hours of labor under improved conditions were more productive than ten hours where dissatisfaction ruled. Public opinion, as typified in religious and philanthropic organizations, demanded a reduction of hours on general humanitarian grounds. A notable case was that of the steel industry in which the working day was traditionally twelve hours in length.[4] For several years stockholders in the United States Steel Corporation, church organizations and finally the President of the United States urged a radical change in the situation, and at length in 1923 it was announced that the twelve-hour working day would be reduced to eight as rapidly as possible.[5] Census statistics for the years 1909 and 1919 prove that the change which was brought about in the Steel Corporation was general throughout the

---

[3] Bunting v. Oregon, 243 U. S. 426; Holden v. Hardy is in 169 U. S. 366, and Lochner v. N. Y. in 198 U. S. 45.

[4] Above, p. 293.

[5] Cf. Gulick, Labor Policy of the U. S. Steel Corp., chap. I.

country. As late as 1909, less than eight per cent. of the
wage earners of the country were working under eight hour
conditions; by 1919 nearly fifty per cent. were at work eight
hours or less. In fact the tendency toward a forty-four hour
week—five eight-hour days, and a half day on Saturday—
seemed to indicate that the long fight of the trades union for
an eight-hour day had been won—and more than won.

The early twentieth century also saw progress on the subject of compensation for industrial accidents. As far back
as 1884 Germany had enacted a law which put the blame for
all accidents on the employers, except when the victim was
wilfully negligent; and in 1897 England had passed the
British Workman's Compensation Act which virtually made
the employer the insurer of his workmen against all accidents.
The theory underlying these laws was that casualties were like
wear and tear, and should be made a charge on the industry,
like the depreciation of buildings and machinery. The United
States, however, lagged behind other industrial nations, despite the astonishing number of accidents which yearly occurred. In 1919 according to the Interstate Commerce Commission, 2,000 railroad employees were killed, and more than
130,000 injured; and in the ordinary course of manufacturing, although estimates differ widely, injuries certainly occur annually in hundreds of thousands, and probably in millions.[6] Under previous practice in this country compensation
for industrial accidents had been awarded in accord with
common law principles, under which the employer was not responsible for an employee who was injured through the negligence of a fellow servant. Any workman who entered haz-
ardous employment was assumed under the common law to
know the dangers and to be ready to run the risks, and no
compensation could be recovered unless it could be shown that
the master had been negligent and the employee had not also

---

[6] In New York state alone in 1923, 346,845 accidents were reported
to the state Department of Labor. *Cf. World Almanac*, 1925, p. 213.

been negligent. It came widely to be thought that the common law did not justly apply to the complex industrial system of modern times. It did not seem equitable, for example, that the fellow servant doctrine should hold in case of a railway employee killed through the negligence of a train despatcher many miles away, whom he did not know and had never even seen.

The first workmen's compensation act in the United States was passed in Maryland in 1902. Its scope was narrow and it came to nothing as it was declared unconstitutional. In course of time, however, legislation was framed in such language as to pass muster before the courts, and moreover judicial decisions changed, as time went on, in the direction desired by popular opinion. Beginning in 1911 there was an avalanche of liability and compensation laws and by 1920 forty-two states, together with Porto Rico, Alaska and Hawaii, had passed acts that placed the burden more or less completely on the employer, and provided schemes of compensation. The federal government also took action. At the suggestion of President Roosevelt an act was passed in 1908 making interstate railroads responsible for injuries to employees and expressly doing away with former common law practices.[7] At the same time a similar liability was placed upon the United States for accidents occurring to certain classes of government employees and a plan of compensation was established. In 1916 another act brought all civil servants under the system.

Several other types of social legislation have made considerable progress in Europe, but have found little or no foot-hold in this country, such as minimum wage laws, health insurance, old age and widows' pensions, and unemployment insurance. The minimum wage law, establishing a level below which wages must not go, has been adopted by Massachusetts and a few

7 An act of 1906 had been declared unconstitutional.

other states in a restricted form.[8]   The unemployment problem
has hardly been touched, although the federal Department of
Labor since its establishment in 1913 has gathered and made
public information in regard to opportunities for work.

Recent years have likewise seen a vast number of laws which
together have made a new era in American industrial life,
although separately no one of them was revolutionary. For
example, matches containing white phosphorous were subjected to a prohibitive tax because of the harmful effect of the
phosphorous on workmen in match factories; greater care
was exercised in guarding dangerous machines, elevator wells
and the like; fire protection, harmful or poisonous fumes and
dust, ventilation and safety devices in mines, safety appliances
on railway trains, together with numberless other accompaniments of modern industry were the subject of state legislation.[9]
Almost as important as legislative enactments were the changes
in working conditions voluntarily made by the most progressive corporations. One who compares a factory built within
twenty-five years of the close of the Civil War with a building
erected since 1900 discovers revolutionary changes. Later
buildings are constructed with much more care for convenience,
safety and health. Steel and concrete skeletons have made
possible wall-space which is eighty per cent. glass, giving

[8] The Massachusetts minimum wage act of 1912 provides for a board
to fix the wages of women and children in any occupation in which
the wages paid to any considerable number of workers are believed to be
inadequate to maintain an American standard of living or to maintain
health. The law forbids the payment of wages less than the minimum
fixed by the board. Failure to comply, however, is punished only by
publication of the facts in the press. *Cf. New International Year Book,*
1912, p. 417.

[9] The new idea of health preservation is well illustrated in the
following case. A workman in an Ohio storage battery company suddenly died from no explainable cause. At the request of the company,
the employees were all examined and 33 per cent. found to be suffering from lead poisoning. Measures were then taken to prevent future
trouble. *Cf.* Rehm, "Human Conservation in Industry," in *Smith
Alumnæ Quarterly,* Feb., 1924.

floods of sunshine, and greatly reducing eye-strain. Ventilation, and even the temperature of the workrooms is a matter for painstaking attention; ''welfare'' work is now a commonplace, with rest rooms, lunch rooms, recreation fields and factory social activities. Factory or store committees that confer with higher officers in relation to hours and the needs and desires of the employees are by no means uncommon. Corporations enable their employees to share in the profits of the industry through the purchase of stock, under advantageous conditions, and in some cases thorough-going pension systems have been established. That of the United States Steel Corporation, which was inaugurated in 1910, provides a fund of $12,000,000 for the retirement of employees who have been long in the service of the company.[10]

On the other hand, laws and statute books did not always guarantee performance. Laws were continually avoided both by the employers and the employees; workmen transgressed rules laid down for their welfare; the passage and execution of many laws were hampered to the last degree by shortsighted employers; the courts invalidated much legislation on the ground of unconstitutionality; and progress was frequently confined to leading states or corporations and was by no means universal. It nevertheless is true that the tendencies in social and economic legislation since 1896 have been widely different from those prevalent before that year.

In several cases the influence of the labor element in federal legislation has been decisive. The use of the injunction, it will be remembered, was one of the grievances most frequently mentioned at the time of the Pullman strike. In the campaign of 1908 both parties strove to attract the labor vote by

[10] In 1916, employees of the Steel Corporation purchased 49,538 shares. In 1921, which was a ''peak'' year, 241,785 shares were purchased. *Cf.* Gulick, *op. cit.*, p. 181. By 1925, 245 firms had pension systems in operation—all but three having been inaugurated since 1896; 2,815,512 employees are covered in the systems. National Industrial Conference Board, *Industrial Pensions in the U. S.*, pp. 5–6.

proposals of reform, but not until 1914 was the issuance of injunctions forbidden, "unless necessary to prevent irreparable injury to property . . . for which injury there is no adequate remedy at law." At the same time the labor unions were exempted from the operation of the anti-trust laws.[11] The influence of the labor organizations was also a factor in the agitation for the restriction of immigration which continued from 1897 to 1917. In the former year a bill was passed which contained a literacy test—that is, a provision excluding persons who were unable to read or write English or some other language. President Cleveland exercised his veto, as did later presidents when similar measures were carried in 1913, 1915 and 1917, but in the latter year Congress was able to muster sufficient strength to pass the act over the President's veto. One of the main purposes of the measure seems to have been the restriction of the labor supply, and hence it enlisted the support of the American Federation of Labor and other similar organizations.[12]

The ameliorative measures already mentioned have by no means prevented the boycott and the strike. Indeed they have not, except in rare cases, directly affected the two great causes of industrial disputes—hours and wages for adult male laborers. Many formidable and violent strikes have occurred since 1896, such as those of the shirt-waist makers in New York in 1909, the textile operatives in Lawrence, Massachusetts, in 1912, and the Colorado coal miners in 1913. On the whole, however, it seems that the labor unions have developed somewhat greater conservatism and that their influence has been against violence in strikes.

Few aspects of the labor problem have been the cause of more earnest thought than the search for peaceful methods

[11] It should be said, however, that the meaning of this law is far from clear and is yet to be fully interpreted by the courts.

[12] Presidents McKinley and Roosevelt also favored it. See Ogg, *National Progress*, pp. 123–130. For later aspects of the immigration matter, see below p. 696.

of settling industrial controversies. In 1898, by the Erdman Act, the federal government provided a means for arbitrating disputes on interstate railways. The Newlands Act of 1913 superseded this by the creation of a formal Board of Mediation and Conciliation, and many disputes were decided under the terms of these laws. The Department of Labor mediated in many industrial disputes, and in 1916 when the four railway brotherhoods threatened to strike for an eight-hour day, Congress itself intervened with a piece of special legislation, the Adamson law, which was framed to settle the questions under dispute.[13] In some cases, profit-sharing plans have been put into force; in others, disputes have been referred to impartial boards of outsiders; and in yet others, machinery has been established for continuous conference between representatives of the employees and employers. Neither federal and state boards and commissions, however, nor the efforts of individual employers have been sufficient fully to insure industrial peace.

The increased activity of the state and federal governments in the fields of economic legislation, as indicated in the passage of labor laws, was also illustrated in two important measures passed in 1906. The adulteration of foods had been brought to a state of dangerous perfection, and drugs had been commonly advertised and sold all over the country which had none of the powers ascribed to them by their makers. Since the eighties, many states had forbidden the sale of impure or tainted food, but the laws were varied and difficult to enforce, and it appeared that reliance must be placed on the federal government. As early as 1890 a federal law had provided for the inspection of meats which were to be exported, but otherwise little progress had been made. In 1906 Upton Sinclair published *The Jungle,* a novel which purported to describe the ghastly conditions under which the meat packers

13 Below, p. 615.

of Chicago conducted their business. Sinclair's book, together with a campaign of education conducted by the muckrake periodicals against harmful patent medicines, aroused public interest to such a degree, that two important laws were passed. One provides for federal inspection of meats intended for interstate commerce, so as to make sure that they are obtained from healthy animals and slaughtered under sanitary conditions. The other act forbids the manufacture or sale of adulterated, misbranded, poisonous or harmful foods, drugs and medicines. Drugs fall under the ban if below a certain prescribed strength, or if they contain harmful ingredients not mentioned on the label. In 1911 the law was made stronger by an amendment which forbids labeling drugs with false statements concerning their curative effects. As a result, many "quack" patent medicines were driven out of existence.

Innovations in the field of politics and government since 1896 have been as marked as in the field of social and economic legislation. Possibly the most outstanding development has been the rapid expansion of the range and variety of the activities of the federal government. The unification of the economic life of the nation, as has been shown, compelled a program of federal economic legislation, and helped inculcate a feeling of greater political solidarity. When fires and floods and other disasters occurred which were too great for a single city or state to take care of, when state laws became confusing because of their variety, when railroads crossed a dozen states and corporations that were chartered in New Jersey did business in Maine, Florida and California, only at the federal capital could the requisite authority be found, which would give the needed relief. As the theory of *laissez faire* gradually broke down, moreover, giving way to the belief that the government ought to be the servant of the mass of the people, it was inevitable that the people should themselves turn more to legislation as a remedy for their grievances. To Washington, therefore, hurried the proponents of every reform.

This tendency was not only counter to the probable intention of the framers of the Constitution, but it trenched upon the powers specifically granted to the states. The tenth amendment stated in so many words that "The powers not delegated to the United States . . . are reserved to the States." It was necessary for the federal government to act, however, or else to leave problems that had become national in character to the chaos that results from legislation in nearly fifty states. State laws concerning railroads as well as marriage and divorce, child labor and trusts are even now in a maze. No solution of the problem seemed possible other than constant stretching of the terms of the Constitution. In 1906, one of the most conservative statesmen in the country, Elihu Root, even went so far as to utter a warning that if the states did not use their powers to better advantage a "construction of the Constitution will be found to vest the power where it will be exercised—in the National Government." In 1910 Roosevelt called attention to what he termed the "twilight zone" between federal and state control. When railroads fought regulative legislation in the state courts, they emphasized the idea that interstate commerce lay within federal jurisdiction; and when combating similar federal legislation, they shifted their contention to the reserved rights of the states.[14] The solution of the matter, according to Roosevelt, lay in the extension of federal authority into the twilight zone, to the end that powerful law-breakers should be brought to book.

The burden thus shifted from state to nation was somewhat lightened by the appointment of numerous commissions to which was entrusted the administration of specific laws or

[14] *Cf.* above, p. 217, on the Peik and Wabash cases.

the accumulation of specific data. The earliest of these was the Interstate Commerce Commission; later, others were appointed to administer laws concerning banking, the tariff and the trusts.

With the expansion of the power of the federal government went the elevation of the office of chief executive. Cleveland's use of the veto power had given an indication of the possibilities of the presidential office in obstructing undesirable legislation; his action in bringing about the repeal of the purchase clause of the Sherman silver law in 1893 had shown the more positive force which a determined officer could exert. Roosevelt's activity in carrying his anti-trust program to the people, and his mediation in the coal strike carried the prestige of the presidency to greater heights. His successors augmented rather than diminished the powers of the presidential office.

The Senate, on the contrary, lost both in power and in prestige. Many reasons for the increasing popular distrust of the Senate after the middle nineties can be given. There was a widespread belief that a controlling fraction of the body had achieved membership through wealth, through the assistance of corporate interests and because of skill in the manipulation of political wires. The charge was common that a small coterie of powerful strategists held the Senate in their hands and with it the control of important legislation. Most of all, and especially in the West, many thoughtful people believed that the state legislatures were easily influenced to choose inferior or untrustworthy men as senators. Whatever the reasons, however, there grew increasingly after 1870 and particularly after 1893 a demand for the popular election of senators. Between the latter year and 1911, at six different times resolutions were presented to Congress proposing an amendment to the Constitution which should secure popular election. At length Congress gave way, proposed the Seventeenth Amendment and sent it to the states. Within ten months thirty-six states had agreed, and after May 31, 1913, senators were elected by the people.

The demand for greater popular control over the choice of senators was a part, merely, of a somewhat general political trend. Distrust of the state legislatures had long been observable, and new state constitutions had been notable for detailed prohibitions placed upon law-making bodies. The West, which had gone to greatest extremes in framing new state constitutions, was also the testing-ground for the initiative, referendum and recall. The first of these devices—the initiative—is a plan by which a specified percentage of the voters may initiate legislation—that is, propose a law and require the officials of the state to submit it to the electorate. If the people accept the proposal, it becomes law as if enacted by the legislature. Under the referendum system, any measure already accepted by the legislature is held in abeyance on petition of a specified number of voters, until presented to the people for approval or rejection. Both the initiative and the referendum had been commonly used in Switzerland before being adopted in South Dakota in 1898. In two decades they had been accepted in twenty states, most of them west of the Mississippi River. After 1918, however, interest in the scheme rapidly dwindled. In Oregon was made the most complete trial of these methods of legislation, after their adoption in 1902. An unusual feature was a law providing for the distribution of the arguments for and against any proposed change. "In 1908, the measures referred to the voters and the arguments favoring and opposing certain of them constituted a booklet of 124 pages, a copy of which was sent by the secretary of state to every voter." [15]

The recall is a process by which any public official may be withdrawn from his office by popular vote before the expiration of his term. Los Angeles adopted the plan in 1903 and

[15] See Beard, *American Government and Politics*, (rev. ed.), p. 464.

was imitated by a small number of other western cities; Oregon in 1908 applied the device to all state officers, and in one form or another it was adopted in ten states in about as many years. In 1912 Roosevelt went so far as to advocate "a recall of judicial decisions." The plan was aimed at pronouncements of the courts which declared invalid acts passed by the states under the police power. The people were to be given an opportunity to vote on the question whether they desired the acts to become law despite the decisions. The results of the proposal were negligible.

More significant than the recall as an indication of the prevailing desire to increase popular control over the processes of government was the adoption of direct primaries. Under this expedient the nominees of a party for office are chosen directly by the party voters, rather than by a party convention. Wisconsin first used the system in 1903 and from that state it spread rapidly. At the present time most states have some form of direct nomination. The peculiar circumstances surrounding the campaign for the Republican nominations in 1912 gave force to the demand for presidential preference primaries which were held in about a fourth of the states.

The agitation for woman suffrage was another example of the increasing desire for the more democratic control of government. Suffrage for women was first granted by Wyoming in 1869 when its territorial government was organized. Colorado in 1893, and Utah and Idaho in 1896 followed the lead of Wyoming. For ten years thereafter, popular interest in the subject was markedly dormant. Several factors then combined to change the situation somewhat abruptly. The successful campaign for changes in local laws relating to the legal status of women, and permitting women to vote on school matters gave promise of further victories in the field of suffrage.[16] The entry of increasing numbers of women into economic competition with men, and the growth of the move-

[16] *Cf.* above p. 455.

ment for more direct government and for the greater participation of Congress in social and economic legislation, enlisted
the interest of women in politics. Finally, the suffrage became a burning question in many European countries, particularly in England.

The suffrage enthusiasts in the United States succeeded in
getting their project referred to a popular vote in state after
state in 1910 and the years immediately following. On the
whole, the western states accepted it and those in the East
opposed. By 1916 eleven states had given way,—but only one,
Illinois, was east of the Mississippi River. Blocked in this
way, the proponents of suffrage turned to the expedient of
a federal amendment. Both chief presidential candidates in
that year favored women's suffrage,—although in different
ways—and Roosevelt had advocated it for several years. In
1919 Congress proposed a constitutional amendment expressly
stating that sex should not be a bar to the suffrage. 1920
was to be a presidential year, and both major parties were
disinclined to take any risks by opposing the women. Under
such favorable circumstances, the Nineteenth Amendment was
ratified by the required number of states and proclaimed in
force August 26, 1920.[17]

Accompanying the increased popular control of government after 1896 was a gradual demand for a higher level of
political ethics. The revelations of the insurance investigations of 1905 were significant of this change. Early in that
year certain newspapers made charges against the Equitable
Life Assurance Company which were taken up by the New
York legislature and referred to a committee for investigation.
The committee's task was the examination of the affairs of
life insurance companies doing business in the state of New

[17] The Nineteenth Amendment reads: Section 1. The rights of
citizens of the United States to vote shall not be denied or abridged
by the United States, or by any State, on account of sex. Section 2.
Congress shall have power, by appropriate legislation, to enforce the
provisions of this article.

York; its attorney was Charles E. Hughes.   The results of the
investigation amazed the country.   The exorbitant salaries
paid to officers, the unreasonable expenses incurred and the
disregard of the rights of the policy holders were of concern
chiefly to persons doing business with the companies.   But it
also appeared that several of the larger concerns had divided
the country into districts, and had systematically influenced
legislation affecting either insurance or financial interests to
which they or their officers were related; enormous sums were
expended and records not kept, or so kept as to conceal the
real purposes of the expenditure.   The contributions of the
companies to the Republican campaign funds were very heavy
—$50,000 by one company in 1904.   It appeared from testi-
mony that Democrats also sought contributions from the companies but were refused.   The final report of the committee
unsparingly condemned these abuses and embodied a program
of legislation for their reform, which was put into effect.   The
public received an education in the connection of corporations
with politics, and Hughes himself at once became a figure of
national importance, the favorite of the reform element, and
was launched upon a career that made him governor of New
York, a member of the United States Supreme Court and
candidate for the presidency.[18]

Laws regulating campaign expenditures had long been on
the statute books although they had been little heeded, but
as the result of the insurance investigation, New York in
1906 forbade contributions by corporations for political purposes.   In 1907 Congress passed a similar law concerning
federal campaigns, and most of the states have since passed
laws placing restrictions on the use of campaign funds.   In
the campaign of 1908 Bryan requested that the Democratic
National Committee receive no contributions from corpora-

[18] The election of Senator Isaac Stephenson of Wisconsin occasioned
another outbreak of reform sentiment.   Investigation betrayed the fact
that he had expended $107,793.05 in his primary campaign.   The salary
of a senator at that time was $7,500 per annum.

tions, that no sums in excess of $10,000 be received from any source and that a list of contributors be published in advance of the election. By a law enacted in 1911 Congress compelled a statement of the amounts of money spent by committees, and limited the amounts which might be spent by candidates for Congress. In 1919 the Chairman of the Republican National Committee announced that the party would raise funds for the next campaign in amounts from $1 to $1,000. Both parties were discovering that public sentiment opposed large contributions from individuals and corporations, because they expect a *quid pro quo* after the election.[19]

The several political and economic changes which have just been mentioned had, of course, different effects on different sections and classes. On the whole, the West was inclined to accept them more readily than the East. In the latter section, however, certain types and classes of people accepted the innovations with enthusiasm. Such were the social welfare workers, who desired legislation for the bettorment of the wage earners and the prohibition of child labor; such also were many students of government and others interested in public affairs who had confidence in the efficacy of legislation

[19] An investigation of federal campaign expenditures conducted in 1912–1913 by a committee headed by Senator Moses Clapp uncovered much that had hitherto been only the subject of rumor. The Standard Oil Company, for instance, contributed $125,000 in 1904. Archbold, the vice-president of the company, testified that he told Bliss, the Republican treasurer, "We do not want to make this contribution unless it is thoroughly acceptable and will be thoroughly appreciated by Mr. Roosevelt"; and that Bliss "smilingly said we need have no possible apprehension on that score." Archbold complained later when the administration attacked the company, but Roosevelt declared that he was unaware of the contribution at the time. The Republican fund in 1908 was $1,655,000. The testimony of Norman E. Mack, Chairman of the Democratic National Committee, indicated his perfect willingness to accept money wherever he could get it, and that he refused to receive contributions from corporations only because of Bryan's scruples. Roosevelt declared, on the authority of an insurance officer, that the Democrats in the campaign of 1904 were after all the corporation funds they could get.

for the accomplishment of reforms, and who had succeeded
in getting state laws passed, only to find that federal statutes
were essential for the accomplishment of their objects. More
important perhaps in the East were the admirers of Roosevelt,
who followed him in his advocacy of the innovations as they
would have followed him in anything. By 1910 the proponents of the new ideas were being called insurgents, liberals
and more commonly progressives. The opponents were coming
to be known as conservatives, stand-patters, and the old guard.
When Theodore Roosevelt wrote to Senator Henry Cabot
Lodge in 1912, "For a couple of years I have felt that you
and I were heading opposite ways as regards internal politics,"
it was to these changes that he referred. Not only were
Roosevelt and Lodge heading in different directions; millions
of other people were doing the same. It was this schism that
made politics from 1908 to 1912 both interesting and significant.

BIBLIOGRAPHICAL NOTE

Several of the subjects mentioned in this chapter have been treated
in recent monographs of high quality. General accounts may be
found in the several text-books already mentioned, and in the biographies of Roosevelt and La Follette.

On the growth of the power of the federal government, see W.
Thompson, *Federal Centralization* (1923), and E. Berman, *Labor
Disputes and the President of the United States* (1924). J. W.
Burgess, *Recent Changes in American Constitutional Theory* (1923),
is a vigorous indictment of recent changes.

On hours and conditions of labor, J. R. Commons and J. B.
Andrews, *Principles of Labor Legislation* (1916) ; S. Gompers,
Seventy Years of Life and Labor (2 vols., 1925) ; R. W. Babson,
Recent Labor Progress (1924) ; L. Wolman, *The Growth of Amer-
ican Trade Unions 1880–1923* (1924) ; C. A. Gulick, Jr., *Labor Policy
of the United States Steel Corporation* (1924) ; S. Crowther, *John
H. Patterson* (1923) ; National Industrial Conference Board, *Indus-
trial Pensions in the United States* (1925). For the courts and

police power, the cases cited on p. 508; C. G. Haines, *American Doctrine of Judicial Supremacy* (1914); E. Freund, *The Police Power* (1904). Accounts of the workmen's compensation idea are in A. F. Weber in *Political Science Quarterly* (June, 1902); and *National Industrial Conference, Research Report Number 1*, "Workmen's Compensation Acts in the United States" (1919). Ida M. Tarbell, *New Ideals in Business* (1917), describes the accomplishments of the industrial leaders rather than of the rank and file.

Some of the political innovations are discussed in A. L. Lowell, *Public Opinion and Popular Government* (1913); *Proceedings of the American Political Science Association*, V, 37, "The Limitations of Federal Government"; Elihu Root, *Addresses on Government and Citizenship* (1916), "How to Preserve the Local Self-Government of the State." The most complete account of the historical development of the power of the president is in Edward Stanwood, *History of the Presidency*, II (1916), Chap. V. The fullest account of the movement for popular election of senators is G. H. Haynes, *The Election of Senators* (1906). The initiative, referendum and recall have given rise to a literature of their own. Convenient volumes are: C. A. Beard and B. E. Shultz, *Documents on the State-wide Initiative, Referendum and Recall* (1912); W. B. Munro, *The Initiative, Referendum and Recall* (1912); J. D. Barnett, *Operation of the Initiative, Referendum, and Recall in Oregon* (1915). See also R. J. Swenson, *The National Government and Business* (1924). General texts in political science, such as those by Beard, Kimball and others, give brief accounts.

American Political Science Review (Aug., 1915), "Presidential Preference Primaries." The articles in A. C. McLaughlin and A. B. Hart, *Cyclopaedia of American Government* (3 vols., 1914), are a convenient source on most topics considered in this chapter.

On the use of money in politics: *Report of the Legislative Insurance Investigating Committee* (10 vols., 1905–1906), Armstrong-Hughes committee; *Testimony before a Sub-committee of the Committee on Privileges and Elections, United States Senate, 62d Congress, 2d session, pursuant to Senate Resolution 79* (Clapp Report).

CHAPTER XXII

POLITICS, 1908–1912

I have never come so close to tariff making before, and the amount of ruthless selfishness that is exhibited on both sides surpasses anything I have ever seen.

HENRY CABOT LODGE, writing about the Payne-Aldrich bill.

. . . any man who goes out from this convention with a nomination secured by the votes of these men [whose right to vote was disputed by the Roosevelt group] will bear a tainted nomination and will never deserve nor receive the support of the American people. [Yells of delight, cries of "That's right!" cheers, yells of derision; laughter, cries of "That's what we think of your man!" &c. for nearly three minutes.]

ACCOUNT OF GOV. H. S. HADLEY'S
SPEECH IN REPUBLICAN CONVENTION
OF 1912, AS REPORTED IN NEW YORK
Sun, June 19, 1912.

. . . both the old parties . . . have become the tools of corrupt interests which use them impartially to serve their selfish interests.

PROGRESSIVE PLATFORM, 1912.

BY 1908, the year of the presidential election, an influential portion of the Republican members of Congress, particularly in the Senate, were bitterly opposed to President Roosevelt. His attitude on the trusts and the railroads was offensive to many, and on several occasions he had gained the upper hand over Congress by means which were coming to be known as "big-stick" methods. The so-called "constructive recess" of 1903 was an example.

Under the provisions of the Constitution, the president appoints many officials with the advice and consent of the Senate, when it is in session, and fills vacancies that happen during a recess by granting commissions which expire at the end of the next session. On December 2, 1903, at noon, one session of Congress came to an end and another began. Precisely at 12 o'clock, according to the official statement, the President issued new commissions to W. D. Crum, a negro, to be collector of the port of Charleston, and also to 168 army officers, of whom the President's close friend Brigadier-General Leonard Wood was one. General Wood was to be promoted to a major-generalship and the remaining promotions were dependent upon his advance. The President's theory was that a "constructive recess" intervened between the two sessions, during which he could make recess appointments. Although the Senate was hostile to both Crum and Wood, it reluctantly succumbed to Roosevelt's wishes rather than withhold promotion from the 167 officers to whom it had no objection.

In 1908, Senator Tillman, an outspoken Democratic critic of the President, declared that senators vigorously denounced Roosevelt's radical ideas in private but that in public they opposed merely by inaction. Party loyalty was sufficient to keep these Republicans, in most cases, from open and continued rebellion. Hardly less hostile to the President were many of the business men of the country, who objected to his economic policies, but the only alternative to Roosevelt was Bryan, who, as one of the earliest proponents of radical legislation, was even more offensive. On the other hand, a large majority of the rank and file of the party, especially in the North and West, upheld the President with unfeigned enthusiasm and made his position in the party so strong that he could practically name his successor. Several candidates had more or less local support for the nomination—Senator Knox, of Pennsylvania, Governor Hughes, of New York, Speaker Cannon, of Illinois, Vice-President Fairbanks, of Indiana, Senator La Follette, of Wisconsin and Senator Foraker, of Ohio. The President's prestige and energy, however, were frankly behind the candidacy of his Secretary of War, William H. Taft.

The Republican convention of 1908 met in Chicago on June 16. Early in the proceedings the mention of Roosevelt's name brought an outburst of enthusiasm which indicated the possibility that he might be nominated for a third term, despite his expressed refusal to allow such a move to be made. In the platform the achievements of the retiring administration were recounted in glowing terms; tariff reform was promised; and a postal savings bank, the strengthening of the Interstate Commerce law and the Sherman Anti-trust act, the more accurate definition of the rules of procedure in the issuance of injunctions, good roads, conservation, pensions and the encouragement of shipping, received the stamp of party approval. Planks pledging the party to legislation requiring the publicity of campaign expenditures, the valuation of the physical property of railroads and the popular election of senators were uniformly rejected. The closing paragraph declared that the "trend of Democracy is toward Socialism, while the Republican party stands for wise and regulated individualism." The contest over the nomination was extremely brief, as Taft received 702 out of 979 votes on the first ballot. James S. Sherman of New York was nominated for the vice-presidency.

The Democrats, meanwhile, were in a quandary. A considerable fraction of the party desired the nomination of somebody other than Bryan, whose defeats in 1896 and 1900 had cast doubts upon the wisdom of a third trial. Nevertheless the failure of Parker in 1904 had been so overwhelming that the nomination of a conservative seemed undesirable and, moreover, no candidate appeared whose achievements or promise could overcome the prestige of Bryan. The national convention was held in Denver, July 7–10, and Bryan dominated all its activities. The platform welcomed the Republican promise to reform the tariff, but doubted its sincerity; promised changes in the Interstate Commerce law, a more elastic currency, improvements in the law of injunctions, generous pensions, good roads and the conservation of the national resources. In the main, however, the platform was an emphatic condemnation of the Republican party as the party of "privileges and private monopoly." It declared that the Republican speaker of the House of Representatives exercised such absolute domination as to stop the enactment of measures desired by the majority. It demanded the termination of the "partnership which has existed between corporations of the country and the Republican party," by which the business interests contributed great sums of money in elections in return for an unmolested opportunity to "encroach upon the rights of the people." It promised the enactment of laws preventing corporation contributions to campaign funds and providing for the publication before election of all contributions by individuals. Detailed and definite planks in relation to trusts indicated that the framers of the platform possessed at least the courage of their convictions. Three laws were promised: one preventing the duplication of directors among competing corporations; another establishing a license system which would place under federal authority those corporations engaged in interstate commerce which controlled as much as twenty-five per cent. of the product in which they dealt, and which should likewise protect the public from watered stock and prohibit any single corporation from controlling over fifty per cent. of the total amount of any commodity consumed in the United States; and, third, a law forcing corporations to sell to purchasers in all sections of the country on the same terms, after making due allowance for transportation costs.

As soon as the platform was out of the way, the convention turned to the nomination of the candidate. Only George Gray, of Delaware, and John A. Johnson, of Minnesota, contested the leadership of Bryan, but their support was so slight that he was chosen on the first ballot. John W. Kern, of Indiana, was nominated for the vice-presidency.

Of the smaller parties which shared in the election of 1908, the People's party and the Socialists should be mentioned. The Populists adopted a program of economic reforms many parts of which had been prominent in their platforms of 1892 and 1896. Both the Republicans and the Democrats, however, had adopted so many of these earlier demands that the Populists rapidly lost strength and disappeared after 1908. The Socialists likewise advocated economic reforms, together with government ownership of the railroads, and of such industries as were organized on a national scale. The candidate nominated was Eugene V. Debs, a labor leader who had gained prominence at the time of the Pullman strike.

The only novelty in the campaign was Bryan's stand in regard to campaign funds. By calling upon his supporters for large numbers of small individual contributions, he drew attention to the fact that the corporations were helping generously to meet Taft's election expenses. At their leader's direction the Democratic committee announced that it would receive no contributions whatever from corporations, that it would accept no offering over $10,000 and that it would publish a list of the contributors before the close of the campaign.

The result of the election was the triumph of Taft and his party. The Republican popular vote was 7,700,000; the Democratic, 6,500,000; the Socialist, 420,890. The election also gave the Republicans control of Congress, which was to be constituted as follows during 1909–1911: Senate, Democrats, 32, Republicans, 61; House of Representatives, Democrats, 172, Republicans, 219.

Few men in our history have had a wider judicial and administrative experience before coming to the presidency than that of William H. Taft. He was born in 1857 in Ohio, graduated from Yale University with high rank in the class of 1878 and later entered upon the study of law. A judicial temperament early manifested itself and Taft became successively judge of the Superior Court in Cincinnati and of a United States Circuit Court. From the latter post he was called to serve upon the Philippine Commission, was later Governor of the Philippines and Secretary of War in Roosevelt's cabinet. During the period of his connection with the Philippines and his membership in the Cabinet he visited Cuba, Panama, Porto Rico, Japan and the Papal Court at Rome in connection with matters of federal importance. Personally Taft is kindly, unaffected, democratic, full of good humor, courageous. As a public officer he was slow and judicial, rather than quick and executive like his predecessor. Although in sympathy with the reforms instituted by Roosevelt, Taft was less the reformer and more conscious of considerations of constitutionality. Roosevelt thought of the domain of the executive as including all acts not *specifically forbidden* by the Constitution or by the laws of the nation; Taft thought of it as including only those which were *specifically granted* by the Constitution and laws. The one was voluble, a dynamo of energy, quick to seize and act upon any innovation that gave promise of being both useful and successful; the other thought and acted more slowly and was less sensitive to the feasibility of change. One possessed wellnigh all the attributes necessary for intense popularity; the other inspired admiration among a smaller group. Roosevelt had a peculiarly keen perception of the currents of public opinion, enjoyed publicity and knew how to achieve it; Taft was less quick at discovering the popular thing and less adept at those tricks of the trade that heightened the popularity of his predecessor.

He is all we believed him to be (wrote Henry Cabot Lodge confidentially to Roosevelt shortly after Taft's inauguration), and I have great affection and respect for him, but I am surprised that he has not, in all his years of public life, learned more about politics, and you will understand that I do not mean this in any bad sense of the word but as one of the conditions with which a man has to deal, especially a President.

Despite the patent differences of temperament and philosophy between Taft and Roosevelt, both expected that the new administration would be an extension of the old one. Roosevelt indicated this in his frank preference for Taft as his successor; Taft indicated it in his thorough acceptance of the policies of the preceding seven years and in his intention, expressed at the time of his inauguration, to maintain and further the reforms already initiated. His first act, however, the appointment of his official advisors, caused some surprise among the friends of his predecessor who expected that he would retain most if not all of the Roosevelt cabinet. When he did not do so, it seemed as if the attempt to further the Roosevelt policies would lack continuity.[1]

The immediate problem that faced the new executive was the revision of the tariff. The task was one which has frequently resulted in political disaster, but the platform left no choice to the President:

The Republican party declares unequivocally for a revision of the tariff by a special session of Congress immediately following the inauguration of the next President. . . . In all tariff legislation the true principle of protection is best maintained by the imposition of such duties as will equal the difference between the cost of production at home and abroad, together with a reasonable profit to American industries.

The precise meaning of this declaration will perhaps always remain a matter of dispute, although it is certain that the public in general understood it to mean a distinct lowering of the tariff wall, and Taft committed himself to downward revision in his inaugural address. Moreover, whether it was intended by the framers to commit the party to downward revision or not, the method of defining the amount of protec-

[1] The cabinet was composed of: P. C. Knox, Pa., Secretary of State; F. Mac Veagh, Ill., Secretary of the Treasury; J. M. Dickinson, Tenn., Secretary of War; G. W. Wickersham, N. Y., Attorney-General; F. H. Hitchcock, Mass., Postmaster-General; G. vL. Meyer, Mass., Secretary of the Navy; R. A. Ballinger, Wash., Secretary of the Interior; J. Wilson, Ia., Secretary of Agriculture; C. Nagel, Mo., Secretary of Commerce and Labor. Meyer and Wilson had been in Roosevelt's cabinet.

tion to be granted was both novel and unsatisfactory, as Professor Taussig has pointed out. How could the costs of production at home or abroad be determined? To what extent would the principle announced in the platform be carried? Almost any commodity can be produced almost anywhere if the producer is guaranteed the cost of production, together with a reasonable profit. The wise revision of the tariff is difficult enough under any circumstances; under so vague a theory as was proposed in 1908, the chances of success became remote.

The drafting of the tariff bill proceeded in the usual manner. The Ways and Means Committee of the House, the chairman of which was Sereno Payne, held preliminary public "hearings," which were open to any who desired to offer testimony or make requests. Naturally, however, the great body of the consuming public was little represented; most of those who appeared were manufacturers, importers and other interested parties. The bill drawn up by the Committee and passed by the House revised existing duties, on the whole, in the downward direction. The Senate Finance Committee, however, under the leadership of Nelson W. Aldrich, an experienced and able proponent of a high protective tariff, made 847 amendments, many of them important and generally in the direction of higher rates. The Senate, like the House, contained several Republicans, usually called "insurgents," who were inclined to break away from some of the party doctrines. Senators Bristow, Cummins, Dolliver and La Follette were among them. This contingent had hoped for a genuine downward revision, and when they saw that the bill was not in accord with their expectations, they prepared to demand a thorough debate. Each of the insurgents made an especial study of some particular portion of the proposed measure so as to be well prepared to urge reductions. Their efforts were unavailing, however, and the bill passed—the insurgents vot-

ing with the great majority of the Democrats in the negative.
The bill then went to a conference committee. Up to this
point, the President had taken little share in the formation of
the bill. Yet as leader of the party he had pledged himself
to a downward revision and the result seemed likely not to be
in the promised direction. He therefore exerted pressure on
the conference committee and succeeded apparently in getting
some reductions, chiefly the abolition of the duty on hides.
The bill was then passed by both houses and signed by the
President on August 5, 1909.

The question whether the Payne-Aldrich act redeemed the
pledge embodied in the platform of 1908 will doubtless remain
a debatable question. On the one hand, a prominent Republican member of the Committee on Ways and Means and of the
Conference Committee, declared that the act repesented the
greatest reduction that had been made in the tariff at any
single time since the first revenue law was signed by George
Washington. Roosevelt also defended the act. Experts outside of Congress sharply differed. Professor Taussig analyzed
the act in all its aspects and concluded that no essential change
had been made in our tariff system. "It still left an extremely high scheme of rates, and still showed an extremely in-
tolerant attitude on foreign trade." General public opinion
was most affected by the fact that duties on cotton goods were
raised, and those on woolen goods left at the high rates levied
under the Dingley act. It also appeared that many silent influences had been at work—the duty on cheap cotton gloves,
for example, being doubled through the efforts of an interested individual who procured the assistance of a New England senator.[2]

Not long after the passage of the act President Taft de-

[2] Other features of the act were the establishment of a Court for
the settlement of tariff disputes, provisions for a tariff commission and
a tax on corporation incomes.

fended it in a speech at Winona, Minnesota, as the best tariff
bill that the Republican party had ever passed. In regard to
the woolen schedule he frankly said:

Mr. Payne in the House, and Mr. Aldrich, in the Senate, although
both favored reduction in the schedule, found that in the Republican
party the interests of the wool growers of the Far West and the
interests of the woolen manufacturers in the East and in other
States, reflected through their representatives in Congress, were
sufficiently strong to defeat any attempt to change the woolen tariff
and that, had it been attempted, it would have beaten the bill
reported from either committee. . . . It is the one important defect
in the present Payne tariff.

The response of the press and the insurgent Republicans to the
passage of the bill and to the Winona speech were ominous
for the future of the party. Although not unanimous, condemnation was common in the West, even in Republican
papers. Particular objection was made to the high estimate
which the President placed upon the act and to his defense of
Senator Aldrich, who had come to be looked upon as the fore-
front of the "special interests"; and western state Republican
platforms in 1910 declared that the act had not been in accord
with the plank of 1908.[3]

Coincidently with the disagreement over the Payne-Aldrich
act, there raged the unhappy Pinchot-Ballinger controversy.
One of the last acts of President Roosevelt had been to withdraw from sale large tracts of public land which contained
valuable water-power. The purpose and the effect of the
order was to prevent these natural resources from falling into
private hands and particularly into the hands of syndicates or

[3] Mr. Dooley, who was well known as a humorous character created
by F. P. Dunne, made merry with the claim that the tariff had been
reduced, by reading to his friend Mr. Hennessy the "necessities of life"
which had been placed on the free-list and which included curling
stones, teeth, sea-moss, newspapers, nuts, nux vomica, pulu, canary bird
seed, divy divy and other commodities.

corporations who would develop them mainly for individual interests. President Taft's Secretary of the Interior, Richard A. Ballinger, took the attitude that the withdrawals were without statutory justification and he therefore revoked the order for withdrawals immediately after coming into office. Upon further investigation, however, he re-withdrew a part of the land, although somewhat doubtful of his power to do so.

During the summer of 1909, Gifford Pinchot, the Chief Forester, addressed an irrigation Congress in Spokane and asserted that the water-power sites were being absorbed by a trust. Much interest was aroused by the charge, which was looked upon as an attack upon the Secretary of the Interior and his policy. Within a short time the idea became widespread, through the press, that Ballinger was associated with interests which were desirous of seizing the public resources and that this fact lay back of his partial reversal of the policy of his predecessor. This impression was deepened by the charges of L. R. Glavis, an employee of the Department of the Interior, concerning the claims of a certain Clarence Cunningham, representing a group of investors, to some exceedingly valuable coal lands in Alaska. Glavis asserted that the Cunningham claims were fraudulent, that many of the Cunningham group were personal friends of Ballinger and that the latter had acted as attorney for them before becoming Secretary of the Interior. President Taft, with the backing of an opinion from Attorney-General Wickersham, upheld Ballinger and dismissed Glavis. The press again took the matter up and the controversy was carried into Congress, where an investigation was ordered. About the same time Pinchot was removed for insubordination, and additional heat entered into the disagreement. The majority of the congressional committee of investigation later made a report exonerating Ballinger, but his position had become intolerable and he resigned in March, 1911. The result of the quarrel was to weaken the President, for the idea became common that his administration had been friendly with interests that wished to seize the public lands.[4]

Republican complaint in regard to the tariff and the Pinchot-Ballinger controversy were surface indications of a division in the party into conservative or "old-guard," and progressive or insurgent groups. The same line of demarcation appeared in a quarrel over the power of the Speaker of the House of Representatives, Joseph G. Cannon. Cannon had served in the lower branch of Congress almost continuously for twenty-seven years, and in 1910 was filling the position of speaker for the fourth consecutive time. Much of his official influence rested on two powers: he appointed the committees of the House and their chairmen, a power which enabled him to punish opponents, reward friends and determine the character of legislation; and he was the chairman and dominant power of the Committee on Rules which determined the procedure under existing practice and made special orders whenever particular circumstances seemed to require them. It was widely believed that Cannon, like Aldrich in the Senate, effectually controlled the passage of legislation, with slender regard to the wishes or needs of the people. "Cannonism" and "Aldrichism" were considered synonymous. For several years an influential part of the Republican and Independent, as well as the Democratic, press had attacked Speaker Cannon as the enemy of progressive legislation. Many of them laid much of the blame for the character of the Payne-Aldrich act at his door. *The Outlook* decried "government by oligarchy"; *The Nation* declared that he belonged to another political age; Bryan queried what Cannon was selling and how much he got; Gompers, the head of the American

---

[4] Henry Cabot Lodge, who was close to Roosevelt, wrote to the latter on Jan. 15, 1910: "Taft is going to urge, and Ballinger has recommended, legislation in regard to Conservation which Pinchot himself told me went beyond anything he had recommended. The general feeling in the country is that Pinchot represents the people and your policy of Conservation, which is true, and that Ballinger and the administration represent opposition to it, which is not true."

Federation of Labor, pointed him out as the enemy of all reforms.

The outcry against the Speaker in the House itself, reinforced by the gathering opposition outside, found effective voice in a coalition of the Democrats and the insurgent Republicans. In mid-March, 1910, an insurgent presented a resolution designed to replace the old Committee on Rules by a larger body which should be elected by the House, and on which the speaker would have no place. The friends of Cannon rallied to his defense; other business fell into the background; and debate became sharp and personal. One continuous session lasted twenty-six hours, parliamentary fencing mingling with horse-play while each side attempted to get a tactical advantage over the other.[5] Eventually about forty insurgent Republicans joined with the Democrats to pass the resolution. The result of the change was to compel the speaker to be a presiding officer rather than the determining factor in the passage of legislation. About the time that Cannon's domination in the House was being broken, the announcement that Senator Nelson W. Aldrich and his staunchly conservative associate, Eugene Hale, of Maine, were about to retire indicated a similar change in the Senate. These men had served for long periods in Congress and were looked upon as the ablest and most influential of the "reactionary" element in the upper house.

Coincidently with the partial disintegration of the conserva-

---

[5] A sample of the jocosity that partially relieved the tension is the following portion of the *Congressional Record* for March 18:

The Speaker *pro tempore*: The House will be in order. Gentlemen will understand the impropriety of singing on the floor, even though the House is not at this moment transacting any business. The House is not in recess.

Chorus. "There'll be a hot time in the old town to-night."

The Speaker *pro tempore*. That was last night, not to-night. (Laughter.) The House will be in order.

Mr. Shackleford. Mr. Speaker, I made the point of order that the tap-tapping of the Chair's gavel interferes with the music. (Laughter.) *Cf.* Atkinson, *Committee on Rules*. p. 115.

tive wing of the Republican party in Congress, there was passed a large volume of legislation of the type desired by the insurgents. The public land laws were improved; acts requiring the use of safety appliances on railroads were strengthened; a Bureau of Mines was established to study the welfare of the miners; a postal savings bank system was erected; and an Economy and Efficiency Commission appointed to examine the several administrative departments so as to discover wasteful methods of doing business. Of especial importance was the Mann-Elkins Act of June 18, 1910, which further extended the powers of the Interstate Commerce Commission. Experience had brought out serious defects in the rate-fixing procedure set up by the Hepburn Act. By that law, to be sure, a shipper could complain that the roads were charging him an unreasonable rate and the Commission might, in course of time, uphold him and order relief; but in the meantime the shipper, especially if he were a small one, might be crushed out of existence through the large rates, and the consuming public would have paid increased prices for commodities with no possibility of a remuneration to them, even if the commission decided that the rates levied were unreasonably high. The Mann-Elkins law, therefore, provided that the Commission might suspend any proposed change in rates for a period not greater than ten months, and decide during that time whether it was reasonable and should go into effect or not. In this way the burden of proving the justice of a suggested change was placed upon the railroads.[6]

An act of June 25, 1910, which was amended a year later, required the publication of the names of persons contributing to the federal campaign funds of the political parties, and the amounts contributed, as well as a detailed account of the expenditures of the committees and the purposes for which the

[6] A Commerce Court was also provided, so as to expedite the decision of appeals from orders of the Commission. Its career was brief, for Congress was not well-disposed toward the project, and the Court was abolished in 1913.

expenses were incurred. President Taft also urged the passage of an income tax amendment to the federal Constitution and indicated that he was in favor of an amendment providing for the popular election of senators. Amendments for both these purposes passed Congress; but they were not ratified and put into effect until 1913.

In June, 1910, Roosevelt returned from Africa whither he had gone for a hunting trip, after the inauguration of President Taft. Both elements in the Republican party were anxious for his sympathy and support. Roosevelt himself seems to have desired to remain outside the arena, at least for a time, but for many reasons permanent separation from politics was impossible. He became a candidate for the position of temporary chairman of the New York Republican State Convention against Vice-President James S. Sherman. The contest in the convention brought out opposition to him on the part of the old guard, and his triumph left that wing of the party dissatisfied and disunited. During the summer and autumn of 1910 he made extensive political tours. At Ossawatomie, Kansas, he developed the platform of the "New Nationalism," which included more thorough control of corporations, and progressive legislation in regard to income taxes, conservation, the laboring classes, primary elections at which the people could nominate candidates for office, and the recall of elective officials before the close of their terms. He urged such vigorous use of the powers of the federal government that there should be no "neutral ground" between state and nation, to serve as a refuge for law-breakers. Critics pointed out that these proposals had been urged by the insurgents and the followers of Bryan, and there could be no doubt where the sympathies of Roosevelt lay in the factional dispute within the Republican party.

While conditions within the organization were such as were indicated by the hostile criticism of the Payne-Aldrich act, by the Pinchot-Ballinger controversy, the overturn of Speaker

Cannon and the disintegration of the Aldrich-Hale group, the congressional election of 1910 took place. Signs of impending change had already become evident. Insurgent Republicans were carrying the party primaries; and the Democrats, who were plainly confident, emphasized strongly the tariff act, Cannonism and the high cost of living as reasons for the removal of the Republicans. The result was a greater upheaval than even the Democrats had prophesied. In nine states the Republicans were ousted from legislatures that would elect United States senators; the new Senate would contain forty-one Democrats and fifty-one Republicans—too narrow a Republican majority in view of the strength of the insurgents. In the choice of members of the lower branch of Congress there was a still greater revolution; the new House would contain 228 Democrats, 161 Republicans and one Socialist, while Cannon would be retired from the speakership. In eastern as well as western states, Democratic governors were elected in surprising numbers. Maine, Masachusetts, Connecticut, New York, New Jersey, Ohio and Oregon were among them. Of particular importance, as later events showed, was the success in New Jersey of Woodrow Wilson, former president of Princeton University.

Not long after the election of 1910 the President sent to Congress a special message urging the adoption of a reciprocal trade agreement with Canada. The arrangement provided for freedom of trade in many raw materials and food products, and for substantial reductions on some manufactured articles. He believed that the project would benefit both countries economically and improve the already friendly relations existing between them, and he set his heart upon its adoption. Opposition appeared at once: the farmers' organizations protested vigorously at the reduction of the tariff on agricultural products; the high protectionists were fearful of an entering wedge which might lead to further tariff reductions; and the paper and wood pulp interests also objected.

Although the agreement eventually passed both houses of Congress by large majorities, the opposition was composed chiefly of Republicans. Objection to the arrangement in Canada turned out to be stronger than had been anticipated. The fear that commercial reciprocity might make the Dominion somewhat dependent on the United States seems to have caused a manifestation of national pride, and Sir Wilfrid Laurier, who had led the forces in favor of the agreement, was driven out of power and reciprocity defeated. The result for the administration was failure and further division in the party.

Democratic control of the House during the second half of Taft's term effectually prevented the passage of any considerable amount of legislation. A parcel-post law, however, was passed, a Children's Bureau was established for the study of the welfare of children, and a Department of Labor provided for, whose secretary was to be a member of the cabinet. Aided by the insurgents, the Democrats attempted a small amount of tariff legislation. Although a general revision of the entire tariff structure would be a long and laborious task, specific schedules could be revised which would indicate what might be expected in case of Democratic success in 1912. The sugar, steel, woolen, chemical and cotton schedules were taken up in accord with this plan and bills were passed which were uniformly vetoed by the President.

In his attitude toward the regulation of big business, President Taft was in harmony with his predecessor and was in thorough sympathy, therefore, with suits brought under the Sherman law against the Standard Oil Company, and the American Tobacco Company. In May, 1911, the Supreme Court decided that both of these companies had been guilty of combining to restrain and to monopolize trade, and ordered a dissolution of the conspiring elements into separate, competing units. The Court also undertook to answer some of the knotty questions that had arisen in relation to section 1 of the

act, which declares illegal "every contract, combination in
the form of trust or otherwise, or conspiracy, in restraint of
trade." Did the prohibition against every contract or combination mean precisely *every* contract, whether important or
not? Or did it refer merely to large and unreasonable restraints? The phraseology of the statute seems to prohibit
restraints of all kinds, and the previous decisions of the Court
had been in line with this view. When, then, the decisions in
these two cases erected the "rule of reason" and declared that
only those restraints were forbidden that were unreasonable,
the attention of some opponents of the trusts was focussed on
the *obiter dictum*, rather than upon the decisions themselves.
In taking this position, they had the support of Mr. Justice
Harlan who agreed to the decision but condemned the *obiter
dictum*, asserted that the exact words of the law forbade *every*
contract, and deprecated what he believed to be the amendment
of statutes by the courts. The dissolution of the companies
into competing units, however, had no apparent effect that.
was of benefit to the public. In fact, immediate increases in
the value of Standard Oil stocks indicated that the decision
was of slight consequence.

In the meantime the widening of the breach in the Republican party was indicated by the formation of the National
Progressive Republican League on January 21, 1911. Its
most prominent leaders were Senators Bourne, Bristow and
La Follette; and leading progressives in different states were
invited to join—among them ex-President Roosevelt. The
later had for some months been becoming more and more dissatisfied with Taft. Exactly when and why this divergence
began is not yet fully known, but a letter of Roosevelt's written
on April 11, 1910, throws some light on the subject:

You do not need to be told that Taft was nominated solely on my
assurance to the Western people especially, . . . that he would
carry out my work unbroken; not (as he has done) merely work-

ing for somewhat the same objects in a totally different spirit, and with a totally different result, but exactly along my lines with all his heart and strength.

It was hoped by the leaders of the Progressive League that Roosevelt would join and thus place himself in opposition to the Taft administration. The purpose of the organization was the passage of progressive economic and political legislation, especially acts providing for the election of senators by vote of the people, direct primåries for the nomination of elective officers, direct election of delegates to national conventions, the initiative, referendum and recall in the states, and a thorough-going corrupt practices act.

Early in 1912 the factions in the Republican party began to consider the question of a leader for the coming presidential campaign, some of the progressive element looking to La Follette as the natural candidate, and others to Roosevelt when it was seen that he would not support Taft for a renomination. On February 21, Roosevelt addressed a constitutional convention in Columbus, Ohio, and expressed a political creed that closely resembled the program of the National Progressive Republican League. In the meantime the demand for Roosevelt as a candidate had been incessant on the part of numerous Republicans of insurgent sympathies, who realized how many more progressive principles he had accepted than Taft. Finally on February 24 he replied to an appeal from a group of his supporters, including seven state governors, that he would accept a nomination. Thereupon most of the progressives transferred their allegiance from La Follette to the ex-President. President Taft's fighting spirit had become aroused, in the meanwhile, and he had declared that only death would keep him out of the fight.

The call had already been issued for the Republican nominating convention to be held in Chicago, in June, and the contest began for the control of the 1,078 delegates who would compose its membership. The supporters of Taft, being in possession of the party machinery, were able to dictate the choice of many of these delegates, especially from the South, by means that had been usual in politics for many years. The friends of Roosevelt, in order to overcome this handicap, began to demand presidential preference primaries, in which the people might make known their wishes, and in which his personal popularity would make him a strong contender. During the pre-convention campaign, twelve states held primaries and the others held the usual party conventions. At first Taft did not actively enter the contest, but the efforts of Roosevelt were so successful and his charges against the President so numerous that he felt compelled to take the stump. The country was then treated to the spectacle of a President and an ex-President touring the country and acrimoniously attacking each other. The progressives, Taft asserted, were "political emotionalists" and "neurotics"; Roosevelt, he complained, had promised not to accept another nomination, had broken his agreement, and had not given a fair account of the policies which the administration had been following. Roosevelt charged Taft with being a reactionary, a friend of the "bosses" and with using the patronage in order to secure a renomination. And he grated on the sensibilities of the nation by referring to his influence in getting Taft elected in 1908 and remarking, "it is a bad trait to bite the hand that feeds you." The result of the presidential preference primaries in the few states that held them was overwhelmingly in favor of Roosevelt; in the states where conventions chose the delegates, Taft obtained a majority; in the case of over 200 delegates, there were disputes as to whether Taft or Roosevelt men were fairly chosen. These contests, as usual, were decided by the National Republican Committee, with the right of appeal to the convention itself. The Committee decided nearly all the contests in favor of Taft's friends, and since all the delegates thus chosen would sit in the convention and vote on one another's cases, the decision seemed likely to be final.

The scene of action then shifted to Chicago where the convention assembled on June 18. Aroused by the action of the Committee in the contests, Roosevelt went thither to care for his interests.[7] The election of a temporary chairman resulted in the choice of Elihu Root, who was favorable to Taft. The Roosevelt delegates, declaring that the contests had been unfairly decided, enlivened the roll-call by shouts of "robbers," "thieves"; and when Root thanked the convention for the confidence which it reposed in him, his words were greeted with groans. Upon the failure of an attempt to revise the decision of the National Committee in the cases of the contested delegates, Roosevelt announced that he was "through." One of his supporters read to the convention a statement from him charging that the Committee, under the direction of Taft, had stolen eighty or ninety delegates, making the gathering no longer in any proper sense a Republican convention. Thereafter most of the Roosevelt delegates refused to share either in the nomination of the candidate or in the adoption of a platform. The choice of Taft as the candidate was then made without difficulty.

The platform contained the usual planks concerning the party's past, the protective tariff and the civil service; and it reflected something of the rising interest in economic and political reforms in its advocacy of laws limiting the hours of labor for women and children, workmen's compensation acts, reforms in legal procedure, a simpler process than impeachment for the removal of judges, additions to the anti-trust law, the revision of the currency system, publicity of campaign contributions and a parcel-post.

As the Republican convention was drawing its labors to a close, the dissatisfied adherents of Roosevelt met and invited

[7] When Roosevelt arrived in Chicago, he remarked that he felt like a "bull moose," an expression which later gave his party its popular name. The expression was an old one with him, dating back to 1894 at least.

him to become the candidate of a new organization. Upon his acceptance, a call was issued for a convention of the Progressive Party, to be held in Chicago on August 5. The discord among the Republicans was viewed with undisguised content by the Democratic leaders, for it seemed likely to open to them the doorway to power. Yet the same difference between liberals and conservatives that had been the outstanding feature of the Republican convention was evident among the Democrats, and nobody could be sure that a schism would not take place.

There was no lack of aspirants for the presidential nomination. J. B. ("Champ") Clark, Speaker of the House of Representatives, Governor Judson Harmon, of Ohio, O. W. Underwood, Chairman of the House Committee on Ways and Means, and Governor Woodrow Wilson, of New Jersey, all had earnest supporters. In contests in the state conventions and primaries, Speaker Clark was most successful, although not enough delegates were pledged to him to secure the nomination.

The convention met in Baltimore on June 25, and for the most part centered about the activities of Bryan. On the third day he presented a resolution declaring the convention opposed to the nomination of any candidate who was under obligations to J. P. Morgan, T. F. Ryan, August Belmont, or any of the "privilege-hunting and favor-seeking class." An uproar ensued, but the resolution was overwhelmingly adopted. Balloting for the candidate then began. Speaker Clark had a majority, but was far from having the two-thirds majority which Democratic conventions require; Governor Wilson was more than a hundred votes behind him. While the fourteenth ballot was being taken, Bryan created a new sensation by announcing that he should transfer his vote from Clark to Wilson, on the ground that the New York delegates were in the hands of Charles F. Murphy, the leader of Tammany Hall, and that Murphy was for the Speaker. The relative positions of the two leading candidates remained unchanged, however, for five ballots more. Then the tide began to turn. At the thirtieth, Governor Wilson led for the first time, and on the forty-sixth Clark's support broke and Wilson was nominated.

The platform resembled that of 1908. It called for immediate downward revision of the tariff, the strengthening of the anti-trust laws, presidential preference primaries, prohibition of corporation contributions to campaign funds, a single term for the president and the revision of the banking and currency laws.

The organization of the Progressive party, in the meantime, was rapidly proceeding, and on August 5 the national convention was held. It was an unusual political gathering both in its personnel—for women delegates shared in its deliberations—and in the emotional fervor which dominated its sessions. At the Democratic convention the delegates had awakened the echoes with the familiar song "Hail! Hail! The gang's all here"; the Progressives expressed their convictions in "Onward, Christian Soldiers." Roosevelt's speech was called his "confession of faith"; his charge that both of the old parties were boss-ridden and privilege-controlled epitomized the prevailing sentiment among his hearers. Without a contest Roosevelt was nominated for the presidency and Hiram Johnson of California for the vice-presidency.

The platform adopted was distinctly a reform document. It advocated such political innovations as direct primaries, the direct election of senators, the initiative, referendum and recall, a more expeditious method of amending the Constitution, women's suffrage, and the limitation of campaign expenditures. A detailed program of social and economic legislation included laws for the prevention of accidents, the prohibition of child labor, a "living wage," the eight-hour day, a Department of Labor, the conservation of the nation's resources, and the development of the agricultural interests. The third portion of the platform dealt with "the unholy alliance between

corrupt business and corrupt politics." It declared the test
of corporate efficiency to be the ability "to serve the public";
it demanded the "strong national regulation of interstate corporations," a federal industrial commission comparable to the
Interstate Commerce Commission and the protection of the
people from concerns offering worthless investments under
highly colored and specious appearances.

The results of the election indicated how complete the
division in the Republican party had been. In the electoral
college Wilson received 435 votes to Roosevelt's 88 and Taft's
8. Yet Wilson's popular vote—6,300,000—fell far short of
the combined Roosevelt-Taft vote—7,500,000—and was less
than that of Bryan in 1896, 1900, and 1908.[8] The fact that
the combined Roosevelt-Taft vote was less than that received
by Taft in 1908 seems to indicate that many Republicans
refused to vote. The control of Congress, in both houses, went
to the Democrats, even such a popular leader as Speaker
Cannon failing of re-election. In twenty-one of the thirty-
five states where governors were chosen, the Democrats were
triumphant. Whether, then, the schism in the Republican
party was responsible for the success of the opposition, or
whether the electorate was determined upon a change regardless of conditions in the party which had hitherto controlled
popular favor, the fact was that the overturn was complete.
And circumstances that could not have been forseen and that
affected the entire world were destined to make the political
revolution profoundly significant. In order to understand
these circumstances in their several aspects, it is necessary
to have in mind the main outlines of America's relations with
the rest of the world since the accession of Theodore Roosevelt.

BIBLIOGRAPHICAL NOTE

In the main, periodical literature written with more or less
partisan bias must be relied upon.

[8] Roosevelt, 4,000,000; Taft, 3,500,000.

For the election of 1908, F. A. Ogg, *National Progress* (1918), and the better newspapers and periodicals. W. H. Taft may be studied in his *Presidential Addresses and State Papers* (1910), *Present Day Problems* (1908), and *Our Chief Magistrate and His Powers* (1916).

On the Payne-Aldrich tariff: S. W. McCall in *Atlantic Monthly*, vol. CIV, p. 562; G. M. Fisk in *Political Science Quarterly*, XXV, p. 35; H. P. Willis in *Journal of Political Economy*, XVII, pp. 1, 589, XVIII, 1; in addition to Tarbell and Taussig.

The documents in the Pinchot-Ballinger controversy are in *Senate Documents*, 61st Congress, 2nd session, vol. 44 (Serial Number 5643), and 3rd session, vol. 34 (Serial Numbers 5892–5903).

For other incidents: C. R. Atkinson, *Committee on Rules and the Overthrow of Speaker Cannon* (1911); Canadian reciprocity in *Senate Documents*, 61st Congress, 3rd session, vol. 84 (Serial Number 5942); Appleton's *American Year Book* (1911). The decisions in the Standard Oil and American Tobacco cases are in *United States Reports*, vol. 221, pp. 1, 106; a good discussion will be found in W. H. Taft, *Anti-Trust Act and the Supreme Court* (1914). For the rise of the insurgent movement and the election of 1912, F. E. Haynes, *Third Party Movements* (1916); R. M. La Follette, *Autobiography;* B. P. De Witt, *Progressive Movement* (1915); W. J. Bryan, *Tale of Two Conventions* (1912); besides Ogg, Beard and Stanwood. A mine of information on the progressive period is volume II, of *Selections from the Correspondence of Theodore Roosevelt and Henry Cabot Lodge* (2 vols., 1925).

The *American Year Book* (1910—), becomes serviceable in connection with major political events. Its articles are usually nonpartisan and may be relied upon to bring continuing tendencies and practices up to date.

CHAPTER XXIII

LATER INTERNATIONAL RELATIONS [1]

"You are afraid," says Mr. Oswald today, "of being made the tools of the powers of Europe." "Indeed I am," says I. "What powers?" said he. "All of them," said I.

DIARY OF JOHN ADAMS, Nov. 18, 1782.

Why, by interweaving our destiny with that of any part of Europe, entangle our peace and prosperity in the toils of European ambition, rivalship, interest, humour, or caprice?

GEORGE WASHINGTON, 1796.

Our people here in the United States are probably more ready to assent to [an international court] than the people of any other country in the world.

ELIHU ROOT, 1910.

We are provincials no longer.

WOODROW WILSON, 1917.

THE recent foreign policy of the United States has to a large extent resulted from the impact of two antagonistic forces. One of the forces arises from the comparative remoteness of the country from the conflicts of Europe, and from such opportunities for colonial expansion as those provided by Africa and Asia. This force is expressed in Washington's admonition against becoming involved in the "toils of European ambition, rivalship, interest, or caprice"; in Jefferson's warning against "entangling alliances"; and in a deep-seated disinclination on the part of the American people to divert attention from their own

[1] The Presidents and Secretaries of State during this period were as follows:
McKinley, 1897–1901; John Sherman, William R. Day, John Hay.
Roosevelt, 1901–1909; John Hay, Elihu Root, Robert Bacon.
Taft, 1909–1913; P. C. Knox.
Wilson, 1913–1921; W. J. Bryan, Robert Lansing, B. Colby.

economic and political affairs. The other force arises from the shrinkage of the size of the world which the railroad, the steamship and the cable have brought about, together with an instinctive desire for more territory. It accompanies the merchant and financier who seek world markets for surplus agricultural and manufactured products; the imperialist who welcomes the acquisition of Samoa, Hawaii and the Philippines; and, as well, the missionary who wishes to spread American Christianity, and the idealistic patriot who yearns to see his country take a leading rôle on the international stage.

The trend of diplomacy from the Civil War to the War with Spain had considerably strengthened the last named force.[2] Colonies had been acquired;—even colonies beyond the limits of continental America. Armies had been sent to the far rim of the Pacific. The Constitution was so interpreted after 1898 as to enable the United States to possess political entities which were neither "states" nor "territories," but a *tertium quid* of an indefinite sort. *After 1898 the traditional policy of isolation was destined still further to be modified by a continuing series of international contacts.*

AMERICAN POLICY IN THE PACIFIC

American relations with China were determined in the main by financial considerations. Citizens of European countries which had earlier obtained spheres of influence in China had loaned that unhappy nation large sums of money for the building of railroads and the development of internal resources. As usual, the security of these loans became a matter of international concern. Individuals applied to their governments for backing. In short, the national income and expense account became to such a degree subject to foreign control that Chinese independence was seriously restricted.

Philander C. Knox, President Taft's Secretary of State,

[2] *Cf.* below, Chapter XVI.

was fully committed to the policy of promoting loans, contracts and concessions for American investors abroad,—to such an extent, indeed, that his foreign policy was commonly dubbed "dollar diplomacy." Taft and Knox urged that dollar diplomacy opened new fields for the use of American capital, and thus indirectly benefited the whole people. The President was also desirous of increasing American investments in China on the ground that they would extend the beneficent influence of the United States abroad and react favorably in continuing the open-door policy which had been successfully asserted by Secretary Hay.

An opportunity for large investments in China was presented during 1912–1913. In the former year a revolution in that distracted country had come to an end and a republic had been set up with Yuan Shih-kai as President. Since the new government was in need of funds, it undertook to borrow through an associated group of bankers from six foreign nations, the United States among them. The financial interests agreed to the loan, but insisted on having control of some of the sources of revenue, in order that they might insure the safety of their funds. The objection most commonly made was that the United States government would become bound up in the interests of the investors, and might be compelled to interpose with armed force if difficulties arose between the bankers and China. Such an action was obviously contrary to the principle of "no entangling alliances." It was opposed likewise to the usual American policy of refusing to assume any responsibility for the successful outcome of investments in backward countries.

At this point President Wilson's administration began. The bankers at once asked him whether he would request them to participate in the "six-power" loan, as President Taft had done. Wilson believed that the conditions which were attached to the loan threatened the administrative independence of China, and he accordingly declined to make the request.

Thereupon the American bankers withdrew and the six-power group subsequently disintegrated.

Relations with Japan had traditionally been friendly.[3] During the first years of the twentieth century, however, friction points became dangerously evident. The Russo-Japanese War came to a close in 1905. Japan had fought a successful contest against a much larger power, and hence gained the enthusiastic admiration of the American public. In the meantime the Japanese government as well as the Emperor of Germany had secretly requested President Roosevelt to attempt to bring about a peaceful settlement. Roosevelt acted upon the suggestion, and the peace conference was held in Portsmouth, New Hampshire. During the course of the sessions, American sympathy shifted somewhat to the Russian side, and when Japan did not receive the heavy indemnity which the Japanese people expected, they laid the blame in part on Roosevelt and in part on the people of the United States.

A subject which at times contained distinctly unpleasant possibilities was the restriction of Japanese immigration into the United States. The western part of the country, especially California, has objected vigorously to the presence of the Japanese on the coast. In 1906, for example, the Board of Education of San Francisco separated the Japanese children in the public schools from the American children, and forced them to attend separate school buildings. Inasmuch as the friendliness of the United States toward Japan was almost a tradition, and because Japan had recently contributed heavily to the sufferers from an appalling earthquake in San Francisco, the Japanese people were thoroughly indignant. The most effective remedy for the objections of the Californians was the complete stopping of Japanese immigration. Under the circumstances, however, Japan refused to agree to such a treaty as that which restricts the entry of the Chinese. Recourse

[3] *Cf.* Chapter XVI.

was then had to the "gentleman's agreement" of 1907 between Secretary Root and Baron Takahira, the Japanese ambassador at Washington. By this arrangement the Japanese government itself undertook to prevent the emigration of laborers to the United States. It was more difficult to reach an agreement concerning Japanese who were already living in the United States.

In 1913 the legislature of California had before it a law forbidding certain aliens from holding land in the state. As the act would apply almost solely to the Japanese, the federal government was placed in an embarrassing position. Under existing treaties the Japanese were granted equal rights with other aliens, but the states were able to modify the practical operation of treaty provisions, as California planned to do, by declaring certain aliens ineligible to citizenship and then placing particular restrictions upon them. The Secretary of State, William J. Bryan, went to California and attempted to persuade the state authorities to alter their land laws. Although the law was eventually passed, it was modified to the extent of allowing Japanese to lease agricultural lands for terms not greater than three years.[4]

The attitude of the American people toward Japan, however, and of the Japanese toward the United States, has not been determined merely by what *did* occur, but by what many people feared *might* occur. And thereby hangs the influence of the "yellow" press. After Japan's successful war against Russia, the jingoistic journals of both countries began to print sensational prophecies in regard to the possible next move of the victorious empire. It was said that the Japanese might turn upon America's colonial possessions and attempt to seize the Philippines and Hawaii, or that they might even invade the Pacific Coast. It was due in great part to the forebodings of such irresponsible journals that the long-continued friendly relations between the United States and Japan were visibly

[4] For later aspects of this subject, see below, p. 696.

strained,—relations that had continued amicable since the days of Commodore Perry and Townsend Harris.[5]

An interesting illustration of the difference between the real and the imaginary relations between the two countries was an exploit of the navy which was undertaken at the command of President Roosevelt. In order to test and train the navy on a grand scale, he determined to send a fleet of battleships across the Pacific and around the world. Among other objections, the fear that Japan would look upon the cruise as a threatening gesture was prominently emphasized. Despite objections, a fleet of sixteen battleships left Hampton Roads on December 16, 1907, went down the eastern and up the western coast of South America, across the Pacific to Japan and other Asiatic countries, and back home in February, 1909, by way of the Suez Canal. Everywhere the officers and men were greeted with great hospitality, and nowhere with more than in Japan. Indeed, Roosevelt said, ''I may add that every man of them came back a friend and admirer of the Japanese.''

In 1917 Robert Lansing, the American Secretary of State, and Viscount Ishii, special ambassador of Japan, reached an important agreement concerning relations in the Orient, which was intended to remove any causes of irritation in that quarter. By it the United States admitted the interest of Japan in China, but the two placed themselves on record as mutually opposed to the acquisition by any government of special rights in China that would affect the independence or the territorial integrity of that country. Nevertheless Japan had already forced China in 1915 to grant her territorial and economic concessions that constituted a grave menace to Chinese independence, and final settlement between the two awaited later events.

One further question in the Pacific area contained some elements of trouble. It was the boundary between Alaska

[5] Cf. above, p. 356.

and Canada. A treaty of 1825 between Russia and Great Britain had established the line in terms that were somewhat ambiguous, the most important provision being that the line from the 56th degree of north latitude to the 141st degree of west longitude should follow the *windings of the coast*, but should be drawn not more than ten marine leagues inland. The coast at this point is extremely irregular, and the few important towns of the region are at the heads of the bays. With the discovery of gold in the Klondike region in 1897 and the consequent rush of population to the coast settlements, the question of jurisdiction became important.

The claim of Great Britain was that the word "coast" should be interpreted to include adjacent islands. Hence the ten league line would follow the general direction of the shore but would cut across the inlets and headlands and thus leave the towns in the possession of Canada. The American contention was that the line should follow closely the windings of the shore of the mainland, thus giving the United States a continuous strip of coast. The controversy was referred in 1903 to a board composed of three Americans, two Canadians and the Lord Chief Justice of England. Since the Americans and the Canadians were firmly committed to their respective sides of the case, no arbitration was to be expected,—unless on the part of the Lord Chief Justice, Baron Alverstone. As he concurred with the Americans on all the important points, a line was subsequently drawn in general conformity with their demands.

RELATIONS WITH LATIN AMERICA

The extension of American economic and political interests in the Caribbean Sea brought about significant modifications in the policy of the United States in Central and South America. Traditionally this policy had been briefly summed up in the Monroe Doctrine. Opinions differ widely about the proper implications of Monroe's statement, but it is safe to say that in its origins it set forth two important assertions: (1) that it is contrary to American policy to take part in the wars of European powers ''in matters relating to themselves''; and (2) that the American continents are not to be considered as subjects for future colonization by any European power.

The modification, or more accurately the extension of the Monroe Doctrine was due to three advances made into the Caribbean area: (1) the infiltration of American capital; (2) the establishment of a protectorate over Cuba, and the acquisition of Porto Rico; and (3) the construction of the Panama Canal. American economic interest in the Caribbean was no novelty before 1898, but it increased at an astonishing rate after the War with Spain. Increasing amounts of manufactured articles were exported to Latin American countries; and greater quantities of their food supplies were sent to be consumed in the United States. It became evident that this country was a serious rival to those European nations who were already deep in South American enterprises. American capital began to vie with European capital in the development of sugar production, fruit and coffee growing, and in prospecting for oil and asphalt. Branches of American banks and commercial houses were established, and American business men began a fight for their share in a lucrative trade. With the islands and shores of the Caribbean Sea alone, American commerce doubled in the decade after 1903.

Orderly governments, which could and would discharge their financial obligations, became of prime importance to the American investor. Moreover,—and it is here that the Monroe Doctrine came into question—unstable governments might cause European nations to intervene in defense of their commercial classes. If to interfere, then perhaps to blockade harbors or seize custom houses, and possibly retain control over territory,—and thus to transgress the Monroe Doctrine. Under such circumstances would not the United States be well advised to assume oversight of the unstable Latin American governments *before* European intervention came about? Ought not the Monroe Doctrine to be so interpreted as to deprecate acts which might *in the future* lead to those extensions of the European system that President Monroe had feared?

The effects of the American protectorate over Cuba and the possession of Porto Rico we already know.[6] The United

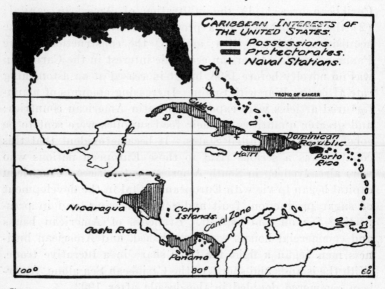

States committed itself to a Cuba which was to be not merely independent, but also free from entanglement with other countries through political or economic obligations. Porto Rico became American territory,—and nations do not voluntarily give up or see endangered the possession of land once obtained.

The third advance was brought about by the desire for a canal across the Isthmus of Panama. The project was as old

[6] *Cf.* p. 409 *ff.*

as colonization in America. For present purposes, however, it is not necessary to go farther into the past than the Clayton-Bulwer treaty of 1850, by the terms of which the United States and Great Britain agreed that neither would obtain any control over an Isthmian canal without the other. As time went on, American sentiment in favor of a canal built, owned and operated by the United States alone grew so powerful that the Hay-Pauncefote treaty of 1901 was arranged with Great Britain. This agreement permitted a canal constructed under the auspices of the United States. Sentiment in Congress was divided between a route through Nicaragua and one through that part of the Republic of Colombia known as Panama, but in 1902 an act was passed authorizing the president to acquire the rights of the New Panama Canal Company, of France, on the isthmus for not more than $40,000,000, and also to acquire a strip of land from Colombia not less than six miles wide.[7] In case the president was unable to obtain these rights "within a reasonable time and upon reasonable terms," he was to turn to the Nicaragua route. President Roosevelt was himself in favor of the Panama project.

The Hay-Herran convention with Colombia was accordingly drawn up and signed in January, 1903, giving the United States the desired rights on the isthmus, but the Senate of Colombia rejected the treaty. Thereupon the New Panama Canal Company became alarmed because it would lose $40,000,000 in case the United States turned from Panama to Nicaragua, and its agents busied themselves on the isthmus in the attempt to foment a break between Colombia and its province of Panama; the people of Panama became aroused because their chief source of future profit lay in their strategic position between the two oceans; and the President was concerned because Congress would soon meet and might insist on the Nicaragua route or at least greatly

[7] The French company had a concession on the isthmus and had already done considerable work.

delay progress. He hoped for a successful revolt in Panama which would enable him to treat with the province rather than with Colombia, and he even determined to advise Congress to take possession forcibly if the revolt did not take place.

The administration meanwhile kept closely in touch with affairs in Panama, and having reason to suspect the possibility of a revolution sent war vessels to the isthmus on November 2, 1903, to prevent troops, either Colombian or revolutionary, from landing at any point within fifty miles of Panama. Since the only way by which revolution in Panama could be repressed was through the presence of Colombian troops, the action of the American government made success highly probable in case a revolt was attempted. On the next day the plans of the Canal Company agents or of some of the residents of Panama came to a head; early in the evening a small and bloodless uprising occurred; and while the United States kept both sides from disturbing the peace, the insurgents set up a government which was recognized within two days and Philippe Bunau-Varilla, a former chief engineer of the Company, was accredited to the United States as Minister. A treaty was immediately arranged by which the United States received the control of a zone ten miles wide for the construction of a canal, and in return was to pay $10,000,000 and an annuity of $250,000 beginning nine years later, and to guarantee the independence of Panama. The Secretary of State, John Hay, described the process of drawing up the treaty in a private letter of November 19, 1903:

Yesterday morning the negotiations with Panama were far from complete. But by putting on all steam, getting Root and Knox and Shaw together at lunch, I went over my project line by line, and fought out every section of it; adopted a few good suggestions: hurried back to the Department, set everybody at work drawing up final drafts—sent for Varilla, went over the whole treaty with him, explained all the changes, got his consent, and at seven o'clock signed the momentous document.

The ratification of the treaty by the Senate, and the purchase of the equipment and rights of the French canal company cleared the way for action on the isthmus.

The manner in which the President had acquired the canal strip, however, was the cause of a long and bitter controversy. His critics called attention to the unusual haste that surrounded every step in the "seizure" of Panama; condemned the disposition of war vessels which prevented Colombia from even attempting to put down the uprising; and insinuated that the administration was in collusion with the insurgents.[8] In self-defense Roosevelt condemned Colombia's refusal to ratify the Hay-Herran treaty and asserted that no hope remained of getting a satisfactory agreement with that country; that a treaty of 1848 with Colombia justified his intervention; and that our national interests and those of the world at large demanded that Colombia no longer prevent the construction of a canal.[9]

[8] Roosevelt, after his retirement from office was widely reported as having said in an address at the University of California: "If I had followed traditional, conservative methods, I would have submitted a dignified state paper of probably two hundred pages to Congress, and the debate on it would have been going on yet; but I took the Canal Zone and let Congress debate." *Cf.* Jones, *Caribbean Interests*, pp. 238–239.

[9] A treaty of 1848 with Colombia (then called New Granada) contained the following provisions: "The Government of New Granada guarantees to the government of the United States that the right of way . . . across the Isthmus of Panama . . . shall be open and free to the . . . United States. . . ."

" . . . the United States guarantees, positively and efficaciously, to New Granada, . . . the perfect neutrality of the before-mentioned isthmus, with the view that the free transit . . . may not be interrupted . . . ; the United States also guarantees, . . . the rights of sovereignty and property which New Granada has and possesses over said territory."

Roosevelt claimed that these provisions justified the United States in keeping order on the isthmus, even if the sovereignty of Colombia was somewhat impaired, because "only the active interference of the United States had enabled her to preserve so much as a semblance

Roosevelt's successors in the presidency felt that there was some degree of justice in the claim of Colombia that she had been unfairly treated, and several attempts were made to negotiate agreements which would carry with them a money payment to Colombia. At length in 1922 a treaty was ratified by which the United States agreed to pay $25,000,000.

The work of constructing the waterway was delayed by changes of plan until 1906, when a lock canal was decided upon, and shortly afterward a start was made. So huge an undertaking—the isthmus is forty-nine miles wide at this point—was an engineering task of unprecedented size, and involved stamping out the yellow fever, obtaining a water supply, building hospitals and dwellings and finding a sufficient labor force, as well as the more difficult problems of excavating soil and building locks in regions where landslides constantly threatened to destroy important parts of the work. At length, however, all obstacles were overcome and on August 15, 1914, the canal was opened to the passage of vessels. Ten years later nearly 27,000,000 tons of cargo were annually going through the canal and about $24,000,000 in toll charges being collected.

The final diplomatic question relating to the canal concerned the rates to be charged on traffic passing through. By the terms of the Hay-Pauncefote treaty with Great Britain, the United States agreed that the canal should be free and open to all nations "on terms of entire equality." In 1912 Congress enacted legislation exempting American coast-wise vessels from the payment of tolls, despite the protest of Great Britain. As President Wilson was of the opinion that our action had been contrary to our treaty agreement, he urged the repeal of the act and succeeded in accomplishing his purpose on June 15, 1914.

of sovereignty." *Autobiography,* p. 516. His critics thought that the treaty could hardly be interpreted to mean that the United States would prevent Colombia's upholding its sovereignty against an insurrection.

While the project for a canal was engaging attention, a complicated controversy in Venezuela was illustrating the problems presented by the economic penetration of the Caribbean area by European and American investors.

Venezuela had long granted concessions to foreign investors —Germans, English, Italians and others—in order to develop her mines, timber and railroads, but unsettled conditions in the country frequently resulted in the non-fulfillment of the obligations which had been entered into. Germany claimed that the government of Venezuela had guaranteed dividends on the stock of a railroad built by German subjects and had failed to live up to the contract. Having in mind the pos- sible use of force to compel Venezuela to carry out her al- leged obligations, Germany consulted our state department to discover whether our adherence to the Monroe Doctrine would lead us to oppose the contemplated action. The atti- tude of President Roosevelt in 1901 was that there was no connection between the Monroe Doctrine and the commercial relations of the South American republics, except that pun- ishment of those nations must not take the form of the acquisi- tion of territory. In 1902 no fewer than ten powers were making demands for the payment of debts due their citizens. Germany, Great Britain and Italy proceeded to blockade some of the ports of Venezuela, and the latter thereupon agreed to submit her case to arbitration. Apparently, how- ever, Germany was unwilling to relinquish the advantage which the blockade seemed to promise, and in the meantime Roosevelt became fearful that the result of the blockade might be the more or less permanent occupation of part of Venezuela. He therefore told the German ambassador that unless the Emperor agreed to arbitration within ten days, the United States would send a fleet to Venezuela and end the danger which Roosevelt feared. The pressure quickly produced the desired results, and during the summer of 1903 many of the claims were referred to commissions. The three blockading powers believed themselves entitled to preferential treatment in the settlement of their claims, over the non-blockading nations, while the latter held that all of Venezuela's creditors should be treated on an equality. This portion of the controversy was referred to the Hague tribunal, which subsequently decided in favor of the contention raised by Germany, Great Britain and Italy, and eventually all the claims were greatly scaled down and ordered paid.[10]

The Venezuela case made evident the possibility that European creditors of backward South American nations might use their claims as a reason for getting temporary control over harbors or other parts of these countries. A new policy was therefore adopted in relation to Santo Domingo. That country was frankly bankrupt,—with annual expenditures more than twice its normal income. Its foreign creditors—including the United States—were insistent. In 1905 President Roosevelt made an arrangement with the Dominican government under which an official designated by him administered the custom houses of the Republic, giving the government forty-five per cent. of the income to use in the payment of current expenses, and retaining the remainder for the satisfaction of foreign claims. The effect was immediate. Revenues became greater than before. Forty-five per cent. under businesslike American management was greater than 100 per cent. had been under Dominican control. Obligations were met. The danger of European intervention was averted and the independence of the country assured. Unhappily, however, political conditions remained unstable. American and foreign investments were again menaced, and in 1916 United States troops were sent to restore order. They were not withdrawn until 1924,—after bitter complaints in Santo Domingo about American militarism, and much

---

[10] For the Roosevelt "threat," together with another version of the story, cf. Thayer, *Hay*, II, pp. 284–289 and *North American Review*, Sept., 1919, pp. 414–417, 418–420.

doubt in the United States as to the wisdom of the military occupation. American administration of the custom houses, however, still remains (1926).

Haitian difficulties began with the same problem of European pressure for the payment of debts, complicated by a succession of revolutionary upheavals. During one of these disturbances the President of Haiti seized a number of influential citizens and had them put to death,—after which the people killed him and carried his body through the streets. This diverting episode occurred in 1915. Next year a treaty was arranged and put into force by which the United States agreed to control the collection of customs and organize a Haitian constabulary under American officers. Some of the provisions of the Platt amendment were also adapted to Haiti, such as the stipulation that no agreements should be entered into with foreign powers which tend to impair the sovereignty of the Republic. The treaty might remain in force for twenty years. The results have been two fold. Revenues have been larger, living conditions better and the independence of the island from foreign control assured. On the other hand, Haitians have complained that the United States marines have treated the natives with cruelty, that prisoners have been executed unlawfully and that American military rule has resulted in restricting their self-government. And the United States is still in Haiti (1926).[11]

The latest acquisition of territory by the United States in the Caribbean region is the Virgin Island group, purchased from Denmark in 1917 for $25,000,000. There are three principal islands, St. Croix, St. Thomas and St. John. St. Thomas has one of the best harbors in the West Indies and is of strategic importance in connection with the Panama Canal.

[11] Oversight of other Latin-American countries has been established from time to time. For example, a small guard of marines was stationed in Nicaragua from 1912–1925.

For good or for ill the "United States aims to control the Panama Canal as well as any other canal which may connect the Atlantic with the Pacific; to hold the military approaches to them; to give reasonable protection to legitimate American investments; and to encourage and, in certain cases, to maintain peace and political and financial stability throughout the region." The Monroe Doctrine aimed to prevent the territorial extension of European possessions in America; the "Caribbean policy" aims to *control circumstances which might sooner or later lead to such an extension.*

The policy has not been greatly modified by changes in the presidency from Roosevelt to Taft, or from Taft to Wilson, nor by their several secretaries of state. President Wilson, aware of the distrust of the United States which was widely felt in Latin-American countries, stated his policy in language that was conciliatory and evidently designed to allay suspicion. He constantly expressed the view that the American states were cooperating equals. He asserted that the United States had no designs on territory, and nothing to seek except the lasting interests of the peoples of the two continents. The opposition to the *political* effects of American occupation, as distinct from the financial and other benefits bestowed has nevertheless continued to be serious. American officials seem too frequently to lack the capacity to carry out policies with the necessary combination of forcefulness in administration and tactfulness in method.

The size and wealth of Mexico, together with its proximity to the United States, make American relations with that country a difficult problem,—the most difficult in the Caribbean area.

The masterful hand of Porfirio Diaz had ruled Mexico from 1877 to 1880 and from 1884 to 1911. Although enjoying the title "president," he was in reality a benevolent despot. Political elections awaited his nod. The resources of Mexico (which are so huge that the country has been called the "storehouse of the world"), he developed through concessions to foreign investors. Mining, ranching and plantation companies made attractive profits. Mammoth stores of petroleum were discovered and exploited; 15,000 miles of railroad were constructed. In 1912 President Taft said that American investments alone had been estimated at a billion dollars.

But there was another side of the picture. The wealth of Mexico was in the hands of a few. There was a widespread belief that too great a part of Mexico's natural resources had been relinquished to the control of foreigners. The great mass of the people lived in a condition bordering on slavery. Restive under a long-continued, one-man government, confused by a system where so much wealth was created and so little distributed, the people were ready material for a revolution. It came in 1910 when Francisco Madero organized a revolt, compelled Diaz to flee to Europe in 1911, and was himself chosen chief executive. The collapse of political and economic order as soon as Diaz had gone was the best proof that his government had been fundamentally unsound.

President Taft meanwhile had sent troops to the border, stray bullets from across the line killed a few American citizens and the demand for intervention began. Madero was soon overthrown by General Victoriano Huerta, who became provisional president. Shortly afterward Madero was shot under circumstances that pointed to Huerta as the instigator of the assassination, but his friends kept the fires of revolt alive, and Governor Carranza of Coahuila, the state across the border from northwest Texas, refused to recognize the new ruler. It was at this juncture that Wilson succeeded Taft. General Huerta was promptly recognized by the leading European nations but President Wilson refused to do so, on the ground that the new government was founded on violence, in defiance of the constitution of Mexico and contrary to the dictates of morality. He then sent John Lind to Mexico to

convey terms to Huerta—peace, amnesty and a free election
at which Huerta himself would not be a candidate. When
the latter refused the proposal, President Wilson warned
Americans to leave Mexico and adopted the policy of "watch-
ful waiting," hoping that Huerta would be eliminated
through inability to get funds to administer his government.
In the meanwhile the destruction of lives and property
continued.

War was barely avoided in the spring of 1914 when a boat's
crew of American marines was imprisoned in Tampico. An
apology was made by the Huerta government, but Admiral
Mayo demanded in addition a salute to the United States
flag. Wilson preferred to ignore the affair after the apology,
but felt constrained to support the action of Mayo. When
Huerta refused the salute, troops were landed at Vera Cruz
and slight encounters ensued. At this juncture Argentina,
Brazil and Chile, "the ABC powers" made a proposal of
mediation which was accepted. The conference averted war
between the United States and Mexico, and perhaps somewhat
reassured the South American republics that the United States
had no ulterior motive, but it failed to solve the questions at
issue. Shortly afterward (on July 15, 1914), Huerta retired
from the field unable to continue his dictatorship, and the
American troops were soon withdrawn.

The end was not yet however. Carranza and his associate,
Villa, fell to quarreling. Bands of ruffians made raids across
the border, and Mexico became more than before a desolate
waste peopled with fighting factions. At President Wilson's
suggestion six Latin-American powers met in Washington in
1915 for conference, and decided to recognize Carranza as the
head of a *de facto* government. Diplomatic relations were
then renewed after a lapse of two and a half years. In a
message to Congress the President reviewed the imbroglio,
but expressed doubts whether Mexico had been benefited.

His fear soon proved to be well founded. In 1916 Villa

crossed into New Mexico and raided the town of Columbus. The situation which then came about was so complex that its main elements are well worth reviewing. In the first place, the Latin American republics were prepared to be apprehensive and scornful of actions of any kind taken by the United States in relation to Central American affairs. Mexican public opinion was particularly sensitive and irritated over the events of the previous five years. Europe was at war, the United States was in imminent danger of being dragged into it, and Germany was in the midst of an intrigue by which she hoped to set Mexico and possibly Japan at loggerheads with the United States. The year 1916, moreover, was the year of a hard-fought political campaign during which every positive assertion of power and every omission to act was sure to be the object of bitter controversy in partisan circles. And finally—and this is by no means least important —American and foreign investors were keen'y aware of the danger in which their billions were placed, and some of them hoped even if they did not intrigue for American intervention in Mexico.

A repetition of the Villa raid upon Columbus might well crystallize public sentiment in the United States in favor of a declaration of hostilities, and the administration therefore sought some forceful move short of actual warfare. The method employed was an expedition into Mexico under the command of General John J. Pershing. Its purpose was the prevention of further attacks along the border of Arizona, New Mexico and Texas. It was consented to—or more accurately, perhaps, tolerated by Carranza. The expedition was almost completely successful—successful because the raids ceased and intervention was avoided, and lacking completeness only because Villa was not captured.

Pershing's task, it should be said in passing, was as delicate and difficult as may be imagined. Equipped as he was, he could have penetrated far into Mexico, if not to Mexico City itself. Scarcely a day passed when he might not have so irritated the Mexicans as to precipitate war. And yet— war, or even a genuine threat of war would have nullified the whole purpose of the expedition, would have instigated new raids and have compelled intervention. The skill and tact with which Pershing accomplished his task, without over- doing it, marked him as a possible commander in case of later warfare, and his troops received a field training which would stand them in good stead in case of further trouble.[12]

The next clash arose over the exploitation of Mexican nat- ural resources. Article XXVII of a new constitution adopted in 1917 provided that the ownership of all minerals and petroleum should be vested in the state. Only Mexicans were to be allowed to obtain concessions for the production of these materials. Foreigners might, to be sure, obtain the same privileges, but only on condition that they agree to submit disputes to Mexican justice—in other words, not to call upon their own governments for the protection of their investments. All concessions made since the beginning of the Diaz régime were to be subject to revision. A billion dollars of American property was seen immediately to be in jeopardy. Investors organized to protect their rights and to protest against any attempt to make Article XXVII retroactive.

Another revolution in 1920 ended the career of Carranza and placed General Obregon in the presidential chair. Not until 1923, however, was the vexed question of Article XXVII satisfactorily settled. In that year a commission composed of delegates from the two countries sat in Mexico City and agreed that the Article should not be retroactive. Property titles acquired previous to the adoption of the constitution of 1917 were confirmed, and a commission was established to settle questions in dispute between the two countries. With these settlements, with the weathering of a revolution against

[12] In connection with this expedition I am indebted to Newton D. Baker, Secretary of War from 1916 to 1921.

Obregon in 1924, the appointment of an ambassador to Mexico, and the inauguration of President Calles on December 1, 1924, the Mexican problem subsided—for the time.

AMERICAN INTEREST IN EUROPE

International peace, particularly through the practice of arbitration, is an ideal which has always been held by a large portion of the American people. The great hopes raised by the two Hague Conferences were striking proofs of this fact. In 1899, at the suggestion of Czar Nicholas II of Russia, twenty-six leading powers conferred at The Hague, in order to discover means of limiting armaments and ensuring lasting peace. A second conference was held in 1907 at the suggestion, in part, of President Roosevelt. At this gathering forty-four states were represented including most of the Latin-American republics. During the two conferences many questions relating to international law were discussed, and the conclusions reached were expressed in the form of "Conventions," which the several powers signed. In the main these agreements related to the rights and duties of nations and individuals in time of war. Most important among the agreements was one for the pacific settlement of international disputes, according to which, in certain less important controversies, the states concerned would appoint a "commission of inquiry" which would study the case and give its opinion of the facts involved. It was also agreed to organize a Permanent Court of Arbitration to be available at all times for the peaceful settlement of differences. Strictly speaking this body was not a Court, but a list of judges to which each nation was to contribute four, and when any countries became involved in a controversy they could draw arbitrators from the list. Moreover the powers agreed "if a serious dispute threatens to break out between two or more of them, to remind these latter that the Permanent Court is open to them."

The United States was a party to four of the fifteen cases presented to the Court between 1902 and 1913. The first controversy was between the United States and Mexico and involved "The Pious Fund," a large sum of money which was in dispute between Mexico and the Roman Catholic Church of California, and the second concerned claims of the United States, Mexico and eight European countries against Venezuela. As the Court was successfully appealed to in case after case, high hopes began to be entertained that the "Parliament of Man" had at last been established. Elihu Root, the Secretary of State, asserted in a communication to the Senate in 1907 that the Second Conference had presented the greatest advance ever made at a single time toward the reasonable and peaceful regulation of international conduct, unless the advance made at the Hague Conference of 1899 was excepted.

In the meantime, in 1904, under President Roosevelt's leadership, treaties were arranged with France, Germany, Great Britain and other nations, under which the contracting parties agreed in advance to submit their disputes to the Hague Court, although excepting questions involving vital interests, independence or national honor. While the Senate was discussing the treaties, it fell into a dispute with the President in regard to its constitutional rights as part of the treaty-making power, and although there was general agreement on the value of the principle of arbitration, yet the Senate insisted upon amending the treaties, whereupon the President refused to refer them back to the other nations. Secretary Root revived the project, however, in 1908 and 1909 and secured amended treaties with a long list of nations, including Austria-Hungary, France and Great Britain. President Taft signed treaties with France and England in 1911 which expanded the earlier agreements so as to include "justiciable" controversies even if they involved questions of vital interest and honor, but again the Senate added such amendments that the project was abandoned. Bryan, Secretary of State from 1913 to 1915, undertook still further to expand the principles of arbitration, and during his term of office many treaties were submitted to the Senate, under which the United States and the other contracting parties agreed to postpone warfare arising from any cause, for a year, in order that the facts of the controversy might be looked into. Many of these treaties were ratified by the Senate.

The attitude of the American people toward the pacific settlement of international disputes found expression in many ways in addition to the arrangement of treaties. At Lake Mohonk, yearly conferences were held at which leading citizens discussed phases of international peace. Andrew Carnegie and Edwin Ginn, the publisher, devoted large sums of money to country-wide education and propaganda on the subject. The leaders of the movement and the membership of the organizations included so many of the most prominent persons of their time—public officials, university presidents and men of influence—as to prove that the traditional American reliance upon international arbitration was more firmly rooted in 1914 than ever before in our history.

The attitude of the United States toward European political controversies was illustrated in our action on the Morocco question. In 1905 Germany protested to President Roosevelt that France and Spain desired to divide Morocco between them, and exclude other nations from her markets. The German Emperor insisted upon a conference of the powers to settle the dispute—lacking which, a general European war seemed likely, since Austria approved Germany's position, and England was expected to stand with France. Roosevelt was extremely anxious to further international good-will, and was engaged at the very moment in the settlement of the Russo-Japanese war. At the same time he recognized that the United States had no important interests in Morocco, and that our traditional policy had been one of aloofness from

European affairs except in connection with movements looking
toward arbitration and peace. His resulting action took account of all these factors. In the first place, he helped bring
about the desired international conference—which met at
Algeciras in Spain in 1906—through the exercise of diplomatic shrewdness and energy. In the next place, he and
Secretary Root took a hand in drawing up the *agenda* or
program for the conference, which gave France and Spain
an international mandate to police Morocco and to preserve
an open door for all other nations. The French and Spanish
policing forces were to report annually to Italy as a third
power in regard to their handling of the mandate. Roosevelt
kept in direct touch with the conference, allaying irritation
on the one side and on the other, and finally helping to bring
about the adoption of his program. And lastly,—the United
States did not *seem* to have departed from her traditional
policy of isolation, for the leadership of Roosevelt was kept
a profound secret from all except a handful of officials until
1920.[13] The "Act" which set forth the conclusions of the
Conference was placed before the Senate for its approval,
and that body in ratifying asserted that its assent was not
to be considered a departure from our traditional policy of
aloofness from European questions.

The most complicated negotiation of the period, as well
as one of the most complicated in our history, concerned the
North Atlantic Coast fisheries. Under the treaty of 1818
relating to matters remaining over from the War of 1812, the
United States possessed the right to take fish on the coast of
Newfoundland and Labrador. All claims to fishing privileges
outside of these grounds were relinquished,—except, of course,
beyond the three mile limit. From that time on there was
intermittent negotiation concerning the meaning of the terms
of the treaty and the justice of fishing regulations made by

---

[13] Bishop, *Theodore Roosevelt,* vol. I, tells the whole story for the
first time.

Canada. Sometimes the negotiations were unimportant and amicable, but at other times feeling ran high. In 1908 the United States and Great Britain made a general arbitration treaty, under the terms of which the fisheries question was referred to members of the Court of Arbitration at The Hague.[14] The award was made in 1910. It recognized the right of Great Britain to make regulations concerning American fishing under the treaty of 1818, it upheld the rights of American fishermen on the coast of Newfoundland, and recommended the establishment of a permanent fishery commission to settle all future controversies. Thus was settled, on the basis of reasonable negotiation, a dispute which had lasted nearly a century.

COMMERCE AS AN INTERNATIONAL RELATION

The constant presence of investments as the bone of contention in Caribbean and Asiatic affairs indicate that foreign trade itself may well be considered an international relation, —and a most fundamental one.

It was after 1890 that foreign commerce and especially the export trade began to assume its most important proportions. Between that year and 1915, imports increased more than two fold and exports more than three,—the total growing from $1,600,000,000 to nearly four and a half billions.[15]

The mainspring of the increased export trade was the industrialization of America. Some of the raw materials for expansion in the field of manufactures had been supplied by the discovery of unlimited supplies of petroleum in the region around Pittsburgh. The opening of the agricultural West

[14] The American member of the tribunal was Judge George Gray. The closing argument for the United States was made by Elihu Root. Robert Lansing was one of the associate counsel.

[15] It must be noted that a portion of this increase was more apparent than real, being due to the general rise in the price level. *Cf.* p. 439.

and the utilization of the ore supplies of the Great Lakes area after 1865 had provided basic necessities. The extension of the railway net after the war, and especially after the recovery from the panic of 1873 had supplied essential means

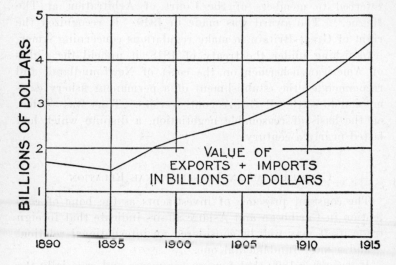

of transport. By 1900, manufactured articles were being produced in such quantities, and fluid capital was so abundant that Americans looked increasingly abroad for new fields for the investment of their surplus. In 1890, manufactured articles composed about one-fifth of our exports, and agricultural products about three-fourths; in 1915, manufactures had increased to one-half and the products of the farms provided only forty-three per cent. of the total. Cotton goods, iron and steel, meat products, wheat and flour, petroleum, and the manufactures of copper, wood and leather were sent all over the world,—most of all to Great Britain, Germany, Canada, France, the Netherlands and Italy,—all but one of them in Europe.

The technique of foreign trade was first developed by the

large corporations. The Standard Oil Company entered the export field as early as 1880. Branch offices were established, advertising started, and a corps of trained men built up. In 1914, it was declared that more Standard Oil wagons were to be seen in Europe than in America. The United States Steel Corporation constructed its export organization between 1900 and 1914, and by the latter year had its representatives in sixty countries. In 1914 the National City Bank began establishing foreign branches, and in ten years had fifty of them in various parts of the world. In 1918 the Webb-Pomerene act authorized the formation of export associations by manufacturers of competitive products and exempted them from the provisions of the Sherman anti-trust law.

As leadership in the export field shifted from agricultural products to manufactured goods, imports became increasingly materials in a raw or semi-raw state which were to be used in the factories. Such were rubber, hides, and raw silk and wool. Nearly half of the imports were from European countries, even the products of the tropics being frequently shipped by way of European ports.

The reasons for so rapid an expansion—beyond those already mentioned—were more important in the mass than in detail. The transatlantic cable, opened in 1867, was the forerunner of 270,000 miles of submarine telegraph wires that made possible rapid international communication. In 1901, wireless telegraphic messages were sent across the ocean, and within a few years private and press notices were being sent across the Atlantic, vessels were commonly equipped with instruments, and international regulations concerning radio-telegraphy were adopted by the chief powers of the world. The government aided by the improvement of water-ways and harbors, and the expansion of the activities of the consular service.

The growth of American commerce was not accomplished, of course, without a struggle. European exporters were already, for the most part, in command of world trade. They knew the demands of the consumer in foreign countries; and they controlled most of the commercial avenues, such as steamship lines and banking facilities. Japanese goods had seized a position of leadership in parts of the Far East. American exporters, therefore, had to face bitter competition. Hence arose the rivalry for new or undeveloped markets like China and South America. And in a similar manner the contest for sources of needed raw materials, such as oil, rubber and phosphates. All this concerned not merely the ordinary commercial classes—ship-owners, exporters and investors —but the much larger number of producers, manufacturers, miners, meat-packers and farmers who directly and indirectly supplied the materials for export. Hence the continual recurrence of the interests of investors in later diplomatic history.

The international relations of the United States for the twenty years immediately preceding 1914 may be briefly summarized. The one international problem which interested the greatest numbers of people was the best method of arriving at international peace. Other problems, except the Mexican question, were simple and inconspicuous, and the majority of Americans knew little of European politics or international relations. In Roosevelt's time, it is true, the United States not merely *participated* in Asiatic and European affairs—as in the Russo-Japanese war and at Algeciras —but even assumed *leadership*. These acts, however, were personal rather than official, and did not commit the United States as a nation to a new international philosophy. Only in the fields of communication and commerce was the United States becoming increasingly and intimately related to the remainder of the world, and the extent to which this change supplemented the effect of the War with Spain in broadening the American international outlook was a matter of conjecture.

BIBLIOGRAPHICAL NOTE

The general texts mentioned at the close of Chapter XVI continue to be useful. In addition, Blakeslee, *Recent Foreign Policy of the United States* (1925) is invaluable.

On Asiatic relations: S. K. Hornbeck, *Contemporary Politics in the Far East* (1916); P. J. Treat, *Japan and the United States 1853-1921* (1921); T. Roosevelt, *An Autobiography* (1920), 377–384, 548–559; T. Dennett, *Roosevelt and the Russo-Japanese War* (1925); and *Americans in Eastern Asia* (1922).

Alaska boundary: Latané, *America as a World Power* (1907) has an excellent chapter with a good map; J. W. Foster, *Diplomatic Memoirs* (2 vols., 1909); *Alaska Boundary Tribunal* (3 vols., 1903), contains the case of the United States.

On Panama, see an excellent chapter in Latané; Roosevelt's side is upheld in his *Autobiography;* Bishop, *Theodore Roosevelt*, I, chaps. XXIV, XXV (1920); M. C. Gorgas and B. J. Hendrick, *W. C. Gorgas: His Life and Work* (1924); I. J. Cox in *Journal of International Relations* XI, 549 on the Colombia treaty.

An account of the Venezuela arbitrations is in *Senate Documents*, 58th Congress, 3rd session, No. 119 (Serial Number 4769).

A considerable body of material relating to the Caribbean has recently appeared. In addition to Blakeslee, the following are scholarly and valuable: C. L. Jones, *Caribbean Interests of the United States* (1916); H. G. James and P. A. Martin, *Republics of Latin America* (1923); W. S. Robertson, *Hispanic-American Relations with the United States* (1923); G. H. Stuart, *Latin America and the United States* (1922); P. M. Brown, *American Journal of International Law* XI, 394, "San Domingo Protectorate"; C. Kelsey, "American Intervention in Haiti and the Dominican Republic" in *Annals of the American Academy,* Mar., 1922; G. A. Finch, "Treaty between the United States and Haiti of Sept. 16, 1915," in *American Journal of International Law*, X, 859; A mass of information is also to be found in *U. S. Congress, Senate, Select Committee on Haiti and Santo Domingo, Hearings* (2 vols., Washington, 1922). W. Westergaard, *Danish West Indies* (1917).

On Mexico consult Robertson, James and Martin, and Stuart

mentioned above; G. H. Blakeslee, ed., *Mexico and the Caribbean* (1920).

For foreign trade statistics, *Statistical Abstract of the United States 1923*, 799 *ff.*; L. C. and T. F. Ford, *Foreign Trade of the United States* (1922); R. W. Dunn, *American Foreign Investments* (1926); E. R. Johnson and T. W. Van Metre, *History of Domestic and Foreign Commerce of the United States* (vol. II, 1915); Faulkner has a good chapter (XXV).

On the Hague Conference reliance may be placed on G. F. W. Holls, *The Peace Conference at The Hague* (1900), by the secretary of the American delegation; A. D. White, *Autobiography* of *Andrew D. White* (2 vols., 1905), by a member of the delegation; *J. W.* Foster, *Arbitration and the Hague Court* (1904); P. S. Reinsch, in *American Political Science Review*, II, 204 (Second Conference).

The proceedings in the North Atlantic Coast Fisheries Arbitration are in *Senate Document* No. 870, 61st congress, 3rd session (12 vols., 1912–1913); more briefly in G. G. Wilson, *Hague Arbitration Cases* (1915).

On Algeciras, J. B. Bishop, *Theodore Roosevelt and His Time* (2 vols., 1920).

On Wilson, E. E. Robinson and V. J. West, *Foreign Policy of Woodrow Wilson* (1917).

CHAPTER XXIV

WOODROW WILSON

. . . we have grown more and more inclined . . . to look to the President as the unifying force in our complex system, the leader both of his party and of the nation.

WOODROW WILSON, 1908.

President Wilson has brought his party out of the wilderness of Bryanism. It has been a great exhibition of leadership.

New York *Tribune*, Dec. 24, 1913.

. . . the peace of Europe was at the mercy of a chapter of unforeseen and unforeseeable accidents.

H. H. ASQUITH.

I intend to handle this situation in such a manner that every American citizen will know that the United States Government has done everything it could to prevent war. Then if war comes we shall have a united country, and with a united country there need be no fear about the result.

WOODROW WILSON.

IT is now apparent that the international position of the United States in the year 1913 contained many dangerous possibilities,—near-war with Mexico, controversies with European countries over their Caribbean interests, and the necessity of protecting travelers, investors and traders all over the globe. There was no thought, however, of foreign entanglements or of unusual diplomatic difficulties when the Democrats came into power on March 4. The election of 1912 had been fought out entirely on domestic issues, and had resulted in Democratic success because of the schism in the Republican party.

President Wilson had been chosen by a distinct minority of the popular vote, and his practical political experience had been less than that of any chief executive since Grant. His party had been in power so little since the Civil War that it

581

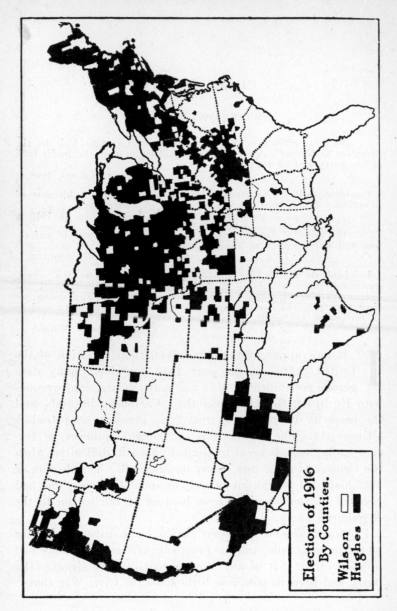

Election of 1916
By Counties.

Wilson ☐
Hughes ■

had no body of experienced administrators from which to pick cabinet officers, and no corps of parliamentary leaders practiced in the task of framing and passing a constructive program. The party as a whole was lacking in cohesion and had perforce played the rôle of destructive critic most of the time for more than half a century; its principles were untested in actual experience, and although its majority in the House was large, in the Senate its margin of control was so narrow as to suggest the near possibility of the failure of a party program. Wilson was under no illusions as to the circumstances of his election and he realized that both he and his party were on probation. Yet the accident—if it was such—was a fateful one. Both the President and Congress were to be confronted with problems the solution of which would vitally affect not only the people of America, but the people of the world; never before had their decisions been so subject to the possibilities of mistakes which would certainly be momentous and might be tragic. The characteristics of the chief executive, therefore, soon became matters of extraordinary importance in American history.

Woodrow Wilson was born in Staunton, Virginia, in 1856. His ancestors were Scotch-Irish and his father an educator and Presbyterian clergyman. After graduating from Princeton University he practiced law, studied history and politics, and taught these subjects at several different institutions. Subsequently he became a professor at Princeton and later its president. He was a prolific and successful writer. His book on *Congressional Government* went through twenty-four impressions before he became President of the United States. *The State*, an account of the mechanism of government in ancient and modern times, and some of his portrayals of American history were hardly less in demand. His election as Governor of New Jersey in 1910 and his election to the presidency two years later have already been mentioned.

Before coming to the presidency he had long pondered on

the proper and possible functions of that office, and had drawn in imagination the outlines and many of the details of the rôle which he was to play. Years of careful study had drilled him in the accumulation of facts. As a specialist in politics and history he was accustomed to make up his mind on the basis of his own researches, and to change his judgments without embarrassment when new facts presented themselves. His literary style was characterized by precision, a close texture and frequently by suppressed emotion. An unbending will, an alert conscience, stubborn courage, restrained patience, political sagacity, a thorough-going belief in democracy and above all an instinctive understanding of the spiritual aspirations of the common people made him the most powerful political figure in America within a brief time after his accession to the presidency. His enemies and political opponents charged him with resenting counsel which ran counter to his own views, with deliberately surrounding himself with small men in order that he might domineer over them, and with an intense determination to do everything himself, thus disregarding the members of Congress and other persons who might have a right to present their views for consideration. On the other hand, Republicans like Grosvenor Clarkson, Director of the Council of National Defense, declared that he was distinctly receptive to ideas; Charles H. Grasty, a prominent newspaper correspondent, asserted that he was more tolerant of frankness than Roosevelt; and such a financial expert as Thomas W. Lamont "never saw a man more ready and anxious to consult," or more ready to give credit to others. A partial explanation of the divergence of opinion is suggested by the journalist David Lawrence who reported the activities of Wilson most of the time from 1906 to the end of his career:

The President . . . figured out that he could handle a problem . . . more effectively if he got all phases before him in writing than if he received various individuals interested in the same thing. . . . They wanted to see him in person. They claimed to be unable to write it; they must deliver themselves of a speech to him. But Mr. Wilson had the same thing presented to him by a dozen other people, and he believed it would be a waste of his time to grant the interview.[1]

In his personal contacts, Wilson frequently exhibited a restraint or reserve like that with which Washington offended Jefferson and his associates. During the latter years of his presidency, especially, he somehow lacked the power to capitalize his personality, to advertise his emotions, to interpret himself to the people. Probably the New York *World* supported him as enthusiastically as any newspaper; nevertheless, the editors asserted, during the eight years in which Mr. Wilson was in the White House he never sought a favor from *The World*, he never asked for support either for himself or any of his policies, he never complained when he was criticised, he never offered to explain himself or his attitude on any issue of government.

His conception of the part which the chief executive ought to play was a definite one. He looked upon the president as peculiarly the representative of the whole people in the federal government, as the leader of the party in power and as commissioned by the voting population to carry out the platform of principles upon which the party and its leader were elected. He believed that the unofficial leaders who are better known as "bosses" existed partly because of the absence of official leaders. As Governor of New Jersey he had acted on the principles that he had outlined for the chief executive of the nation, and upon his accession to the presidency he began at once to put into effect a similar program.

At the outset of the administration, President Wilson found awaiting him a troublesome political problem. As the new Democratic leader he was compelled to cultivate either the support or the opposition of William J. Bryan, the one

[1] N. Y. *Times*, Jan. 29, 1925; *Atlantic Monthly*, Jan., 1920, p. 1; Seymour and House, *What Really Happened at Paris*, pp. 272–273.

member of the party who had a large and devoted personal following. Bryan's influence in nominating Wilson had been very great, and the adherence of his admirers was necessary if the party was to be welded into an effective organization. Unhappily for this purpose Wilson placed a low estimate on Bryan's wisdom, and had even expressed a wish that the "Great Commoner" might be knocked into a "cocked hat." Despite these things, Wilson offered Bryan a cabinet position as Secretary of State. In 1915 Bryan resigned because of serious differences of opinion with his chief, but continued to give his complete political support. The other members of the official family were much less well-known, only Franklin K. Lane (Secretary of the Interior), and W. G. McAdoo (Secretary of the Treasury), having achieved a national reputation. The South was represented heavily in the appointments of A. S. Burleson, of Texas, as Postmaster General; Josephus Daniels of North Carolina, as Secretary of the Navy; J. C. McReynolds, of Tennessee, as Attorney General; D. F. Houston, a native of North Carolina, who had long lived in Texas, as Secretary of Agriculture; and Secretary McAdoo of Georgia. On the whole they seem to have had the ability to cooperate with one another and provide the "teamwork" which the President desired to obtain.[2]

True to his systematic and aggressive spirit, his inaugural went beyond the usual expressions of patriotic good-will, and outlined the program to which his party had committed itself:

[2] The cabinet, 1913–1921, was as follows: Secretary of State, W. J. Bryan (to 1915), R. Lansing (to 1920), B. Colby; Secretary of the Treasury, W. G. McAdoo, C. Glass, D. F. Houston; Secretary of War, L. M. Garrison, N. D. Baker; Attorney-General, J. C. McReynolds, T. W. Gregory, A. M. Palmer; Postmaster-General, A. S. Burleson; Secretary of the Navy, J. Daniels; Secretary of the Interior, F. K. Lane, J. B. Payne; Secretary of Agriculture, D. F. Houston, E: T. Meredith; Secretary of Commerce, W. C. Redfield, J. W. Alexander; Secretary of Labor, W. B. Wilson.

We have itemized with some degree of particularity the things that ought to be altered and here are some of the chief items: A tariff which cuts us off from our proper part in the commerce of the world, violates the just principles of taxation, and makes the Government a facile instrument in the hands of private interests; a banking and currency system based upon the necessity of the Government to sell its bonds fifty years ago; . . . an industrial system which . . . holds capital in leading strings, restricts the liberties and limits the opportunities of labor.

Congress was called for a special session on April 7, 1913, in order to revise the tariff. It was a dangerous task—one which had discredited the Democrats in 1894 and divided the Republicans in 1909—but plans had been laid with care in order to avoid previous mistakes. The Chairman of the Committee on Ways and Means in the House, Oscar W. Underwood, had begun the preparation of a bill during the session before and had discussed it with Democratic members of the Senate Committee on Finance, and with the President.

At the opening of the session Wilson broke the precedent established by Jefferson in 1801, and read his message personally to Congress, instead of sending it in written form to be read by a clerk. In substance the message expressed the President's conviction that the appearance of the chief executive in Congress would assist in developing the spirit of cooperation, and outlined the tariff problem which they were together called upon to settle. He declared that the country wished the tariff changed, that the task ought to be completed as quickly as possible and that no special privileges ought to be granted to anybody. He advocated a tariff on articles which we did not produce and upon luxuries, but he urged that otherwise the schedules be reduced vigorously but without undue haste. Other considerations were more important, however, than the substance of the message. Previous documents of this kind had been long and filled with a wide variety of recommendations concerning both international and domestic relations; Wilson's speech occupied but a few moments, it focused the attention of Congress upon one subject, and fixed the eyes of the country upon the problem. The nation knew that one task was in hand, and knew where to lay the blame if delay should ensue. It was a great responsibility that the President had assumed, but he assumed it without hesitation.

Underwood presented his bill at once and it passed the House without difficulty, but in the Senate the Democratic majority of six was too small to guarantee success in the face of the objections of Louisiana senators to the proposal for free sugar, and the usual bargaining for the protection of special interests. When the lobby appeared—the group that had so mangled the Wilson-Gorman bill and discredited the Payne-Aldrich Act—the President issued a public statement warning the country of the "extraordinary exertions" of a body of paid agents whose object was private profit and not the good of the public. So vigorous an action resulted in hostility to Wilson, but Congress found itself unusually free from objectionable pressure. Hence while experts differed in regard to the wisdom of one part or another of the bill, it was not charged that its schedules bore the imprint of favoritism for any particular private interests. Discussion in the Senate was so extended that the Underwood act did not finally pass and receive the President's signature until October 3.

The general character of the measure is indicated by the number of changes made in the tariffs as they existed at the time of the passage of the act. On 958 articles the duties were reduced; on 307 they were left unchanged and on eighty-six (mainly in the chemical schedule), they were increased. Despite the numerous reductions, the Underwood law retained much of the protective purpose of preceding enactments. Attempts were made to decrease the cost of living by considerable reductions on some agricultural products and by placing others on the free list; wool was to be free after December 1, 1913, and the duty on sugar was to be reduced gradually and taken off completely on May 1, 1916; duties on cotton goods and on woolens ("Schedule K") were heavily reduced. Underwood represented an iron manufacturing section of Alabama, but he showed an uncommon attention to the general interest by favoring large reductions on pig-iron and placing iron ore and steel rails on the free list. An important part of the law was a provision for an income tax, which had been made possible by the Sixteenth Amendment to the Constitution proclaimed on February 25, 1913. Incomes over $3,000 ($4,000 in the case of married persons), were to be taxed one per cent., with an additional one per cent. on incomes of $20,000 to $50,000, and similar graded "surtaxes" on higher incomes, reaching six per cent. on those above $500,000. The board which the Republicans had established for the scientific study of the tariff had been allowed to lapse by the Democrats, but was revived in 1916 through the appointment of a bi-partisan Commission of six members with twelve-year terms.

On June 23, 1913, after the tariff bill had been piloted around the chief difficulties in its way, the President again addressed Congress—this time on currency legislation. Again he laid down certain principles—a more elastic currency, some means of mobilizing bank reserves, and public control of the banking system. Before mentioning the further history of this recommendation, however, it is necessary to have in mind the main facts in the development of the monetary issue since 1900. Complaint had been common since that year. One difficulty lay in the fact that the volume of the currency could not quickly increase and decrease as busy times demanded more or quiet times required less of the circulating medium. At those parts of the year, for example, when the crops were being moved there was a greater demand for currency than the banks could conveniently meet. They could, to be sure, buy United States bonds and issue national bank notes upon them as security, but this was a slow and costly process. The dangers of the existing inelastic arrangement were illustrated in the panic of 1907.

In that year occurred a financial crisis which resulted in business failures, unemployment and the indictment of prominent figures in the commercial world; it was precipitated by a gamble in copper stocks. An unsuccessful attempt to corner the stock of a copper company led to the examination of the Mercantile National Bank of New York, with which the speculators had intimate connections. Meanwhile the president of the bank and all the directors were forced to resign. One of the associates of a director in the Mercantile was the president of the Knickerbocker Trust Company, and depositors in the latter bank thereupon became frightened, and $8,000,000 were withdrawn in three hours. The alarm then spread to the depositors of the Trust Company of America—the president of the Knickerbocker was one of its directors—and $34,000,000 were withdrawn by the now thoroughly anxious depositors, who stood in line at night in order to be ready for the next day. The panic spread to other parts of the nation; country banks withdrew funds from the city banks, and they from New York; and at length the government came to the aid of the distressed institutions and deposited $36,000,000 between October 19 and 31. Nevertheless, at the time when depositors were trying to get their money there was sufficient currency in existence to satisfy all needs. The defect lay in the lack of machinery for pooling resources in such a way as to relieve any institution that was in temporary straits. The experts pointed also to the unscrupulous manipulation of the supplies of currency by New York financiers. There was widespread comment on the fact that if the magnates did not actually constitute a ''money trust'' they were nevertheless able to expand and contract the available supply to such an extent as to serve their own ends and embarrass the public. In the meanwhile many experts, among them Senator Nelson W. Aldrich, had been studying the entire banking system. The result of this work was the Aldrich-Vreeland Act of 1908. It permitted national banks to form associations for the issuance of temporary circulating notes on the security of commercial paper, and it also arranged for a National Monetary Commission to investigate the currency and banking systems in this and other countries. The Commission published thirty-eight volumes of information and recommendations, which were a storehouse of facts concerning the problem, although no legislation resulted. All that Taft did was to pass the task along to Wilson.

As has been seen, President Wilson seized the opportunity at once. Senator Owen and Carter Glass, Chairmen of the Senate and House Committees on Banking and Currency, together with William G. McAdoo, the Secretary of the Treasury, and the President himself drafted the Federal Reserve bill. This measure received careful attention, being the cause of extended hearings and debate in Congress and of discussion in banking circles.[3] The special session wore on and came to an end, but the regular session began at once (December 1), and consideration of the measure continued without interruption. At length on December 22 the House acted favorably, thirty-four Republicans, eleven Progressives, and one Independent assisting the Democrats in passing the bill; on the following day the Senate passed it, one Progressive and three Republicans voting with the majority. In many details the act as passed differed from the original plan, but in its essential points it was not amended. Although its precise form was the work of a few men, the project in general, of

[3] A confidential friend of the President gathered the banking laws of every nation in Europe, and reports from experts in economics and banking, as well as consulting "every banker . . . who knows the subject practically." Seymour, *Intimate Papers of Col. House*, I, pp. 160 *ff.*

course, represented the labors of many persons extending over many years, and for that reason embodied the best that American experts could give.

The Act provided for the establishment of Federal Reserve Banks, to be placed in districts—the number being eventually fixed at twelve. The capital for each Reserve Bank was to be supplied by the banks in its district which became member banks. In other words the Reserve Banks were to act as banks for their members, but not for private individuals. In control of the twelve was a Federal Reserve Board, composed of the Secretary of the Treasury, the Comptroller of the Currency and five persons (a sixth was added in 1922), appointed by the president for terms of ten years. It was at this point that the chief controversies raged between the bankers and the proponents of the administration measure. The bankers desired one central bank, which the administration opposed because it feared centralized control over the currency supply; and the bankers disliked the proposal for a Reserve Board appointed by the president, because they apprehended the entrance of politics into the appointments. The President and his supporters were determined, however, not to allow the bankers to appoint the Board or any portion of it, because they wished the system to be operated solely in the public interest.

Greater elasticity was given to the currency supply through the issuance of federal reserve notes, at the discretion of the Federal Reserve Board, to the several regional Federal Reserve Banks.[1] When a local bank requires more currency it may deposit with the Federal Reserve Bank such valuable commercial paper as may be acceptable—for example, promissory notes of reliable business firms—and receive at once a supply of federal reserve notes. When business is brisk and large supplies of currency are demanded, the local banks will

[1] Federal reserve *bank* notes were also issued which were expected to replace the *national* bank notes.

deposit whatever paper may be necessary to meet their needs; when the emergency has passed they will withdraw notes from circulation, return them to the reserve bank and receive their paper again. The second great purpose of the new system was to supply central reservoirs for the storage of the reserves of the member banks. Each local bank is required to keep certain prescribed balances in the reserve bank of its district, and the federal government may also deposit funds in it. In conformity with strict regulations the reserves thus accumulated in a Federal Reserve Bank may be directed here and there in the district as needed, and even from district to district, under the control of the Federal Reserve Board. Moreover they are not available for those speculative ventures which have caused so much trouble in the past. The operation of the law has apparently more than met the expectation of its friends. It had hardly been established when a war broke out in Europe, but the unusual financial situation which resulted in America was cared for without great strain.[4]

The third major plank in the Democratic platform of 1912 called for legislation concerning trusts, and the President accordingly turned his attention to that topic in his address to Congress on January 20, 1914. He declared that there was no intent to hamper business as conducted by enlightened men, but that, on the contrary, the antagonism between business and government had passed. He recommended the prohibition of interlocking directorates by which railroads, banks and industrial corporations became allied in one monopolistic group, and he suggested that the processes

[4] The degree to which the supply of Federal Reserve notes expands and contracts in response to the demands of business may be illustrated in the following statement of notes in circulation:

January, 1921, $3,177,656,000
February, 1924, $2,034,540,000

Cf. *Federal Reserve Bulletin*, Apr., 1924, p. 303.
For a brief statement of the services of the Federal Reserve system during the war, see Chapman, *Fiscal Functions of the Federal Reserve Banks*, pp. 188–9.

and methods of harmful restraint of trade be forbidden item
by item in order that business men might know where they
stood in relation to the law.   Finally, he believed that the
country demanded a commission which should act as a clearing house for facts relating to industry and which should do
justice to business where the processes of the courts were inadequate.   The results of this undertaking were the Federal
Trade Commission act of September 26, 1914, and the Clayton
Anti-trust act of October 15.

The former of these laws created a Commission of five persons to administer the anti-trust laws and to prevent the use
of unfair methods by any persons or corporations which
were subject to the anti-trust laws.   Whenever it had reason
to believe that any corporation was using unfair methods, the
Commission was to issue an order requiring the cessation of
the practice.   If the order was not obeyed, the Commission
was to apply for assistance to the circuit court of appeals in
the district where the offense was alleged to have been committed.   The purpose of the provision was evidently to prevent unfair practices rather than to punish them.[5]   Another
section of the law empowered the Commission to gather information concerning the practices of industrial organizations,
to require them to file reports in regard to their affairs, and
to investigate the manner in which decrees of the Courts
against them were carried out.   Under direction of the president or Congress, the Commission could investigate alleged
violations of the law, and on its own initiative it might report recommendations to Congress for additional legislation.[6]

[5] Between 1915 and 1924 the Commission received 8632 requests for
action.   Such acts as the following were condemned as "unfair" competition: misbranding commodities, e. g., selling goods as "silk" or
"ivory" which were composed of substitutes; bribery of buyers or
other employees of customers in order to secure patronage; procuring
trade secrets of competitors by espionage or bribery; false claims to
patents; tampering with machines sold by a competitor for the
purpose of discrediting them; and price discrimination.   Cf. Federal
Trade Commission, *Annual Report*, 1925, p. 14.
[6] The Commission superseded the Bureau of Corporations.

The Clayton act specifically prohibited many of the practices common to industrial enterprises. Sellers of commodities were forbidden to discriminate in price between different purchasers—after making due allowance for differences in transportation costs; corporations were forbidden to acquire any of the stock of other similar industries, where the effect would be substantially to lessen competition; and directors of banks and corporations were prohibited, with stated exceptions, from serving in two or more competing organizations. The Clayton act also settled, at least for the time, several of the complaints raised by the labor interests, especially at the time of the Pullman strike. Labor and agricultural organizations were specifically declared not to be conspiracies in restraint of trade; injunctions were not to be granted in labor disputes unless necessary to prevent irreparable injury; and trials for contempt of court were to be by jury, except when the offense was committed in the presence of the court. The law also prohibited the railroads from dealing with concerns in which their directors were interested, except under specified conditions.

The success of the President in pushing his party program made his prestige the outstanding fact in politics. His leadership was indisputable and it was evident that he regarded a party platform as a serious program, to the fulfilment of which the party was committed by its election. While the trust legislation was under discussion, however, he asked for an act which required all the strength he could muster.

It will be remembered that the Panama Canal act of 1912 had exempted American coast-wise traffic through the canal from the payment of tolls. The law had been passed under a Republican, President Taft, and both the Progressive and Democratic platforms of 1912 had favored exemption. On March 5, 1914, Wilson appeared before Congress and urged the repeal of the act on the ground that it was a violation of that part of the Hay-Pauncefote treaty of 1901 in which this country agreed that the canal should be open to all nations upon an equality, and that it was based on a mistaken economic policy. At the close of his address, the President said:

I ask this of you in support of the foreign policy of the administration. I shall not know how to deal with other matters of even greater delicacy and nearer consequence if you do not grant it to me in ungrudging measure.

It was well known, of course, that English opinion looked upon the exemption act as a piece of dishonorable legislation. The meaning of the President's vague reference to ''other matters of even greater delicacy,'' however, was not known until the publication of the *Intimate Papers of Colonel House* in 1926. The secret lay in the attitude of England toward Wilson's Mexican policy. The spring of 1914 was the time when the administration was attempting to rid itself of Huerta. The British ambassador to Mexico was known to be in sympathy with Huerta, and the United States assumed that England would oppose the Wilson policy of refusing to recognize him. On being assured privately, however, that the President favored the repeal of the exemption act, the English government instructed its ambassadors not to interfere with the anti-Huerta policy. ''It is hardly an exaggeration to say that the abdication and flight of Huerta, in July, 1914, was directly related to the withdrawal of British support.'' [7]

Congress, however, ignorant of the international implications of the President's request, presented an uncommonly formidable opposition. The Speaker of the House, Champ Clark, and the chairman of the Ways and Means Committee, O. W. Underwood, made vigorous attacks on the President's policy. Such powerful Republicans, however, as Senator Root and Senator Lodge believed that Wilson was right and

[7] *Cf.* Seymour, *Intimate Papers of Colonel House*, I, pp. 192 *ff*.

that the exemption was contrary to our treaty obligations.
The members of the cabinet, moreover, especially Burleson
and McAdoo, used their influence with wavering Congressmen,
and in the outcome the repeal was voted June 15, 1914. The
President's leadership received a signal triumph. The rift in
the party was promptly healed, and soon forgotten.

The Congressional election of 1914 greatly reduced the
Democratic majority in the House, although leaving control
with that party, but they slightly increased its margin in the
Senate. European affairs and the election of 1916 occupied
political attention during the second half of the administration, nevertheless the President and Congress proceeded with
their program of legislation. Important acts were those providing for the development of the resources of Alaska, the
Newlands act for the arbitration of disputes among railway
employees, a law providing for federal aid in the building
of state highways and measures giving a larger amount of
self-government to the Philippines and Porto Rico. The importance of the agricultural classes was recognized in the
Farm Loan Bank system which was launched by an act
of July 17, 1916. The purpose of the law was the relief of
the farmer from ruinous interest rates. In many parts of the
country money could not be borrowed on the security of farm
land and property except at unreasonable interest charges.
In order to remedy this, the Farm Loan system established
twelve banks in as many sections of the country, the whole to
be administered by a Board composed of five members, including the Secretary of the Treasury. These banks loan
money to farmers at fair rates, up to fifty per cent. of the
value of their land. The major items, as well as the smaller
ones in the Democratic program were in line with many of
the proposals made by the Progressives in their platform in
1912. Attracted by these accomplishments and by the forceful leadership of the President large numbers of the Progres-

sives made the transition into the Democratic party, and from 1913 to 1916 much of the political strategy of both Democrats and Republicans was devoted to attracting the insurgent wing of the Republican organization.[8]

The enactment of such a body of legislation, with the resulting appointment of many officials and clerks, brought the President face to face with the same civil service problem that had caused so much trouble for Cleveland. Upon their accession in 1913 the Democrats had been out of power so long that they exerted the pressure, usual under such circumstances for a share in the offices. The merit system, however, was even more firmly entrenched than in 1897 when Cleveland had made such additions to the classified lists, for both Roosevelt and Taft had extended the merit principle to parts of the consular and diplomatic service. Roosevelt had also made considerable extensions in the application of the system to deputy collectors of internal revenue, fourth-class postmasters, and carriers in the rural free-delivery service; Taft had also increased the number of employees who were appointed under the merit system, notably about 36,000 fourth-class postmasters not touched by his predecessor. Some of the acts passed early in President Wilson's administration—the Federal Reserve law, for example—expressly excepted certain employees from civil service examinations. Bryan, as Secretary of State, showed a lack of devotion to the cause of reform in the conduct of his department. On the other hand the President took a most important step in relation to postmasters of the first, second and third classes, which had always been appointed by the president with the advice and consent of the Senate, and had been among the plums in the gift of the ex-

---

[8] The appointment of Louis D. Brandeis to the Supreme Court brought to that body a well-known proponent of the newer types of social and economic theory. At first the opposition to confirming his nomination in the Senate, based upon certain facts in his career and allegations concerning them, was uncommonly pronounced. Dissent diminished, however, in the face of investigation, and the nomination was confirmed by a large majority on June 1, 1916.

ecutive that had been most sought after. On March 31, 1917, Wilson announced that thereafter the nominees for postmasters of the first three classes would be chosen as the result of civil service examination.

While the United States was absorbed, in these various ways, in the task of internal construction, an event was occurring in a town in Bosnia which was destined to affect profoundly the course of American history. The people of Serbia were ambitious to extend their boundaries so as to include in a "greater Serbia" those of their nationality who lived under the flag of Austria. Some of the more radical of these expansionists gathered in a secret society, the Black Hand, and determined to achieve their ends by violence. In 1914 the Austrian Archduke, Franz Ferdinand, and his wife— the Archduke was heir-apparent to the Austro-Hungarian monarchy—went to Bosnia to attend some army manœuvres. On June 28 they were in Serajevo. Thither also went three youthful members of the Black Hand. One of them threw a bomb at the royal pair—which failed of its mark—and thereupon another of the conspirators fatally shot both the Archduke and his wife with a revolver.[9]

Austria demanded not merely the punishment of the assassins, but the adoption of methods of suppressing all anti-Austrian propaganda—methods which seemed to Serbia to impair her sovereignty. She thereupon agreed to those parts of Austria's ultimatum that did not affect her independence, and offered to refer the remainder to the Hague tribunal or to a conference of the powers. Austrian authorities asserted that the reply was unsatisfactory, and promptly declared war on Serbia. In a brief time, such was the state of the European alliances, Austria and Germany were opposed to Serbia, Russia, Belgium, France, Montenegro and Great Britain in a devastating war. In August, Japan joined the "Allies," as

9 *Cf.* S. B. Fay, "The Black Hand Plot" in *Current History*, Nov., 1925.

the nations on Serbia's side were known, and Turkey, in November, took the side of the Central powers. The act that brought Belgium into the war was of interest to the United States. Germany had declared war on Russia, the friend of Serbia, and expected that France, Russia's ally, would step into the fray. Being thoroughly prepared for war, Germany believed that she could crush France before the latter could take any effective steps. The most convenient path into France lay through Belgium, a small, neutral nation with no interest in the conflict, and the German armies were thereupon poured across the boundary. High German authority freely admitted the wrong of the act, but excused it on the ground of military necessity. Belgium felt that she could not do otherwise than resist the invader and was thus drawn into the vortex. Her danger helped bring Great Britain into the conflict.

Nothing apparently could be more remote from American interests than a political assassination in the Balkans where wars, plots and violence seemed to be almost daily occurrences. President Wilson accordingly issued the usual proclamation of neutrality on August 4. Fifteen days later he issued another in which he urged the people to be "neutral in fact as well as in name." Two considerations were clearly expressed. In the first place—

The people of the United States are drawn from many nations, and chiefly from the nations now at war. It is natural and inevitable that there should be the utmost variety of sympathy and desire among them with regard to the issues and circumstances of the conflict. Some will wish one nation, others another, to succeed in the momentous struggle. It will be easy to excite passion and difficult to allay it. Those responsible for exciting it will assume a heavy responsibility. . . .

In the second place he wished to keep the United States so free from any commitment in the controversy as to enable it "to do what is honest and disinterested and truly serviceable for the peace of the world."

The neutrality of the people of the United States "in fact as well as in name" was of such short duration, and later criticism of the attitude of neutrality was so bitter, that the public opinion of the time is worth recalling. To be sure, stories of the ruthlessness of the German soldiery in Belgium poured into the columns of American periodicals, but the people were naturally skeptical as to their reliability. The German immigrant had always been welcomed in America. The German nation had been lauded for efficiency and virility. Scarcely a year before the war broke out, ex-Presidents Roosevelt and Taft had extolled the German Emperor as an apostle of peace. On September 23rd, more than a month and a half after the invasion of Belgium, Roosevelt published an article in *The Outlook* in which he expressed pride in the German blood in his veins, asserted that either side in the European conflict could be sincerely taken and defended, and continued, referring to the invasion of Belgium:

The rights and wrongs of these cases where nations violate the rules of abstract morality in order to meet their own vital needs can be precisely determined only when all the facts are known and when men's blood is cool. . . . It is certainly eminently desirable that we should remain entirely neutral, and nothing but urgent need would warrant breaking our neutrality and taking sides one way or the other. . . . We have not the smallest responsibiltiy for what has befallen [Belgium].[10]

[10] Bishop in his authorized life of Roosevelt, II, p. 372, asserts that the latter's private letters were more representative of his opinion than *The Outlook* article. Bishop quotes from a letter written to Sir Cecil Spring-Rice, British Ambassador in Washington on Oct. 3, 1914: "If I had been President, I should have acted on the thirtieth or thirty-first of July,—calling attention to the guaranty of Belgium's neutrality and saying that I accepted the treaties as imposing a serious obligation which I expected not only the United States but all other neutral nations to join in enforcing. Of course I would not have made such a statement unless I was willing to back it up." President Eliot of Harvard University, to be sure, wrote to Wilson as early

Wilson's determination to keep the United States neutral and ready for the rôle of mediator was not a new project, but the continuation of an adventure which he had earlier undertaken with Colonel E. M. House.[11]

Because of our racial diversities, however, it was inevitable that complete neutrality should be a temporary condition. Increasing concern in the war was due to a variety of causes. England, France and Russia published selections from the diplomatic correspondence which had taken place with Germany and Austria during the month before the outbreak of hostilities. The central point of the documents was that the Allies had earnestly attempted to bring about an accommodation between Austria and Serbia, and that the attempts

as August 6, urging a combination of the United States, the British Empire, France, Japan, Italy and Russia to punish Austria and Germany for their outrages, but on second thought he withdrew his proposal and commended neutrality. *Cf.* Seymour, *House,* I, pp. 286–291.

[11] This extraordinary character was a Texan by birth, educated, well-read on international as well as domestic politics, shrewd, tactful, a patient negotiator,—who knew when to talk and when to keep silent. "Last night I had a conference with the Austrian Ambassador," he wrote to President Wilson on September 6, 1914. "He talked very indiscreetly and, if one will sit still, he will tell all he knows. I sat very still." More remarkable yet, he sought no office for himself, and none for his friends. Honors he would have none of. Although he had exercised a great influence in bringing about the nomination and election of Wilson, he refused to go with the President and his wife to the inauguration. "I went instead to the Metropolitan Club and loafed around. . . . Functions of this sort do not appeal to me and I never go." To all these uncommon characteristics, he added the quality of agreeing so completely with the President that Wilson had the utmost confidence in him even when personal conferences were months apart.

Shortly before the outbreak of the World War,—on May 16, 1914— House set out for Germany and England on what he called "the Great Adventure." It was nothing less than an attempt, as the President's unofficial advisor, to interest the German Emperor, and the officials of France and England in a plan for international disarmament, to be followed by a cooperative international movement to clean up the tropics and develop the waste areas of the earth. The success which House seems to have had with the Kaiser was as astonishing as the plan was visionary. Then came the World War and the end of the Great Adventure,—or rather, the Great Adventure merged into the project to keep America neutral, so as to be prepared at any moment for the rôle of mediator.

had been frustrated by a determination on the part of the Teutonic powers to have war. The correspondence was widely read and convinced many that England, France and Russia had been the real peace lovers and that Germany had been the aggressor.

Tendencies in foreign trade helped make public opinion favorable to the Allies. The immediate economic effect of the war, to be sure, had been the unsettlement of American financial and industrial affairs. But when the English navy obtained the mastery of the seas, the vessels of the Teutonic powers were driven to cover in neutral ports or kept harmlessly at home, and American trade with neutral nations and the Allies took on new life. Moreover the latter were in need of food, munitions and war materials of all kinds and they turned to American factories. Manufacturers who could accept "war orders" began at once to make fortunes; wages and prices rose. Exports of wheat increased from $89,000,000 during the year before the war, to about $300,000,000 in 1917; explosives from $5,000,000 to $803,000,000. According to international practice, both sides in the European conflict might purchase munitions from neutrals, of which the United States was the largest, but on account of her weakness on the sea Germany was unable to take advantage of this opportunity, while the Allies constantly purchased whatever supplies were needed. At first, the German government protested through diplomatic channels, but our government was able to show not only that international practice approved the course followed by the United States, but also that Germany had herself followed it in previous wars. The practical effect, nevertheless, was to pour American-made munitions into the war on the side of the Allies,—to the disturbance of the peace of mind of many who desired to be neutral, and to the intense irritation of the large groups who favored the German side. In Germany the feeling was even more bitter. They seem to think, wrote one observer, "that every German that is being killed or wounded is being killed or wounded by an American rifle, bullet or shell.''

There then followed propaganda on a large scale by German agents under the direction of Dr. Bernhard Dernburg, which was intended to influence public opinion to demand the prohibition of the shipment of munitions to the Allies. As this activity failed of its purpose, resort was then had to fraudulent clearance papers by which military supplies for German use were shipped from the United States without conforming to our customs regulations; bombs were placed in ships carrying supplies to England; fires were set in munitions factories; strikes and labor difficulties were fomented by German agents and at length the government had to ask for the recall of the Austrian Ambassador, Dr. Dumba, and the German military and naval *attachés* at Washington, Captain Franz von Papen and Captain Karl Boy-Ed.

Relations with the Allies, in the meantime, were becoming unpleasant. The unprecedented scale on which the war was being fought made huge supplies of munitions, food and raw materials such as copper and cotton absolute necessities. England was able to shut off the direct shipment into Germany of stores having military value, but this advantage was of little use so long as the ports of Holland and the Scandinavian countries were open to the transit of such supplies indirectly to Teutonic soil. When England attempted to regulate and restrict trade with these countries, the United States was the chief sufferer. Ships were held up and their cargoes examined—during 1915, for example, copper valued at $5,500,000 was seized while on the way from the United States to neutral nations. On December 26, 1914, the United States protested against the number of vessels that were stopped, taken into British ports and held, sometimes, for weeks; and in reply England pointed out the large increase in the amount of copper and other materials sent to countries near Germany, and declared that the presumption was strong that these stores were being forwarded to the enemy. It could scarcely be doubted that the English were correct in their contention. American exports to the Netherlands, Denmark and Sweden increased from a yearly $157,000,000 just before the war to $301,000,000 in 1915.

The greater the stake, the greater the determination of American shippers to press their rights under international law. Protests from southern cotton growers, from eastern importers, from western export houses poured into the State Department. Shippers complained that the administration was afraid of England and unwilling to care for American interests. The English public, meanwhile, felt that their government was being unreasonably nagged and hammered with complaints about ships and cargoes when they were undergoing frightful privations and sufferings in a life and death struggle in which the welfare of the world was concerned. Sir Edward Grey, the British Secretary of State for Foreign Affairs, whose friendliness toward the United States was well-known wrote confidentially to Colonel House:

After fifteen months of practical experience of war under modern conditions, I am convinced that the real question is not one of legal niceties about contraband and other things, but whether we are to do what we are doing, or nothing at all. . . . As it is, it looks as if the United States might now strike the weapon of sea-power out of our hands, and thereby ensure a German victory.

With her navy driven from the seas, Germany began to feel the effects of the British blockade, and accordingly turned to the submarine as the hope for victory. The decision was a fateful one. American opinion, which had shifted from its neutrality to a partisan interest in the economic and political effects of the war, was now about to take a third position,—a deep and growing concern for the safety of American travelers. On February 4, 1915, Germany declared the English channel and the waters around Great Britain a war zone, in which enemy merchant vessels would be destroyed "even if it may not be possible always to save their crews and passengers." Great Britain replied on March 11th by an order that merchant vessels going into Germany or out of her ports, as well as merchant vessels bound for neutral countries and carrying goods bound for the enemy, must stop at a British or allied port. At these points the cargoes were looked over and any war materials or goods which were regarded as "contraband" were seized. Even though the owners were eventually reimbursed for the cargoes taken, the delay and the interference with trade were burdensome, and the United States accordingly protested that England was establishing an illegal blockade and that the United States would champion the rights of neutrals. Retaliatory legislation aimed at the Allies was threatened by Congress, but for the most part interest in this controversy died in the face of the growing irritation with Germany. The German declaration of February 4, 1915, in regard to submarine warfare caused an energetic protest by the United States on the ground that an attack on a vessel made without any determination of its belligerent character and the contraband character of its cargo would be unprecedented in naval warfare. The American note declared Germany would be held to a "strict accountability" for any injury to American lives and property. Nevertheless, the results of the submarine campaign began to appear at once, and in ten weeks sixty-three merchant ships belonging to various nations were sunk, with a loss of 250 lives.

On May 7th the United States was astounded to hear that the passenger ship *Lusitania* had been torpedoed, and 1,153 persons drowned, including 114 Americans. This fiendish act was no chance occurrence,—it had been planned long beforehand. New York newspapers had even carried advertisements from the German embassy warning passengers of the danger of crossing the Atlantic in the face of the submarine. From that moment there grew an increasing demand for war with Germany. President Wilson himself believed that the sinking of the *Lusitania* was deliberate. He nevertheless felt that emotion ought not to stampede the country into the maelstrom, and he accordingly called upon the German government for a disavowal of the acts by which the *Lusitania* and other vessels had been sunk, all possible reparation, and steps to prevent the recurrence of similar deeds.

A few days after the *Lusitania* catastrophe and before the protest of our government was made public, President Wilson spoke in Philadelphia, and in the course of his remarks said, "There is such a thing as a man being too proud to fight." The address had no relation to the international situation, and moreover the objectionable phrase carried an unexpected and different meaning when separated from its context and linked to the *Lusitania* affair. The words were seized upon by the President's critics, however, as an indication of the policy of the government in the crisis and were severely condemned. On the other hand the formal protest was received with marked satisfaction. It was understood to be the work of Wilson himself, who practically took over the conduct of the more important foreign affairs. When the German government replied without meeting the demands of the President, he framed a second note which brought the possibility of war so near that Secretary Bryan retired from the cabinet rather than sign it. A second reply merely prolonged the controversy and Wilson thereupon renewed his demands and declared that a repetition of submarine attacks would be regarded as "deliberately unfriendly." The statement brought the nation appreciably nearer war, but if the comments of the newspaper press may be relied upon as an index of public opinion, the President had again expressed the feelings of the people. In the meanwhile German submarine warfare was modified in the direction desired by the United States. Instead of sinking merchant vessels on sight and without warning, the commanders of submarines made it their usual practice to stop them, visit and search them, and give the passengers and crews opportunity to escape. On August 19, 1915, the *Arabic* was sunk without warning, but the German government in conformity with its new policy disavowed the act, apologized and agreed to pay an indemnity for American lives lost. The negotiations concerning the *Lusitania* continued to drag on, but otherwise relations between Germany and the United States had reached the point where peace could be maintained if no further accident or provocation intervened.

Despite the general approval of the President's firm stand against Germany, there was an inclination in some quarters to to do everything possible to avoid a conflict, even if the effort necessitated the relinquishment of rights that had hitherto been well recognized. In February, 1916, Representative McLemore introduced a resolution requesting the President to warn American citizens to refrain from traveling on armed belligerent vessels, whether merchantmen or otherwise and to state that if they persisted they would do so at their own peril. The House, according to the Speaker, was prepared to pass the resolution. The positions taken on this subject by the administration had not been entirely consistent, but the President now declared that Americans had the right under international law to travel on such vessels and that the government could not honorably refuse to uphold them in exercising their right. "Once accept a single abatement of right," he asserted, "and many other humiliations would certainly follow, and the whole fine fabric of international law might crumble under our hands piece by piece." Moreover he felt that the conduct of international relations lay in the hands of the executive and that divided counsels would embarrass him in dealing with Germany. He therefore asked the House to discuss the McLemore resolution at once and come to a vote. Under this pressure the House gave way and tabled the resolution,

275 to 135 (ninety-three Republicans joining with 182 Democrats against thirty-three Democrats and 102 Republicans).

On March 24th the French channel steamer *Sussex* was sunk, with the loss of several Americans, and the submarine issue was thus brought forward again. The President accordingly appeared before Congress and reviewed the entire controversy. "Again and again," he reminded his hearers, "the Imperial German Government has given this Government its solemn assurances that at least passenger ships would not be thus dealt with, and yet it has again and again permitted its undersea commanders to disregard those assurances with entire impunity." He asserted that America had been very patient, while the toll of lives had mounted into the hundreds, and informed Congress that he was presenting a warning that "unless the Imperial German Government should now immediately declare and effect an abandonment of its present methods of warfare against passenger and freight carrying vessels this Government can have no choice but to sever diplomatic relations with the Government of the German Empire altogether." The reply of Germany was almost satisfactory, —since it declared that submarine commanders had been ordered to act in accordance with the principles of visit and search. At the same time, however, the German note expressed the expectation that the United States would demand that England observe the rules of international law in respect to the blockade. In response the United States asserted that the new German policy could not be contingent upon the result of American negotiations with any other power. With this interchange the submarine controversy came temporarily to an end. If Germany kept to her promise and no new event occurred to disturb peaceful relations, the United States might keep out of the European war and play the rôle of peacemaker,—unless the presidential campaign should bring about a new American policy.

International relations were in a critical condition when the presidential election of 1916 came on. The Republicans and the Progressives planned to meet in Chicago on June 7 for the nomination of candidates, in the hope that the two parties might unite upon a single nominee and platform, and thus defeat Wilson who was sure to be the Democratic candidate. At first, however, the two wings of the Republican party were in complete disagreement. As far as principles went they had not thoroughly recovered from the schism of 1912. For their candidate the Progressives looked only to Roosevelt, whom the Republicans would not have. Roosevelt urged both parties to accept his long-time friend Henry Cabot Lodge, but the proposal fell on deaf ears. As for himself he refused to enter any fight for a nomination and announced, "I will go further and say that it would be a mistake to nominate me unless the country has in its mood something of the heroic." After conferences between Republican and Progressive leaders which failed to bring about unanimity, the Republican convention nominated Justice Charles E. Hughes of the Supreme Court, and the Progressives chose Roosevelt. Hughes was a reformer by nature, recognized as a man of high principles, courageous, able and remembered as a vigorous and popular governor of New York.

The Republican platform called for neutrality in the European war, peace and order in Mexico, preparedness for national defense, a protective tariff and women's suffrage. It also advocated some of the economic legislation favored by the Progressives in 1912. The Progressive platform laid most emphasis on preparation for military defense—a navy of at least second rank, a regular army of 250,000 and a system for training a citizen soldiery. It also urged labor legislation, a protective tariff and national regulation of industry and transportation. The Republican platform severely denounced the administration, but the Progressives stated merely their own principles.

In the course of his actions after the nomination, however, Roosevelt indicated his belief that the public welfare demanded the defeat of the Democrats. He declared that he did not know Hughes's opinions on the vital questions of the day and suggested that his "conditional refusal" be put into the hands of the National Progressive Committee and that a statement of the Republican candidate's principles be awaited. If these principles turned out to be satisfactory then Roosevelt would not run; otherwise a conference could be held to determine future action. Subsequently Roosevelt issued a declaration expressing his satisfaction with Hughes, condemning Wilson and urging all Progressives to join in defeating the Democrats. Such an action would, of course, spell the doom of the Progressives as a political organization, but he declared that the people were not prepared to accept a new party and that the nomination of a third party candidate would merely divide the Republicans and ensure a Democratic victory. The action of Roosevelt commended itself to a majority of the National Committee, but a minority were displeased and supported Wilson.

The Democrats met at St. Louis on June 14 and renominated President Wilson in a convention marked by harmony and enthusiasm. For the first time in many years the party could point to a record of actual achievement and it challenged "comparisons of our record, our keeping of pledges, and our constructive legislation, with those of any party at any time." After recalling the chief measures passed during the administration, the party placed itself on record as favoring labor legislation, women's suffrage through the action of the states, the protection of citizens at home and abroad, a larger army and navy and a reserve of trained citizen soldiers.[12]

---

[12] Despite Roosevelt's refusal to run, the Progressive vice-presidential candidate continued the campaign. The Socialist Labor party, the Socialist party and the Prohibitionists also presented candidates.

The campaign turned upon the question whether the country approved Wilson's foreign policy, rather than upon the record of the Democratic party and its platform of principles, and in such a contest each side had definite advantages. As the candidate of the party which had been in power most of the time for half a century, Hughes had the support of the two living ex-presidents and the backing of a compact organization with plenty of money. He had been out of the turmoil of politics for six years as a member of the Supreme Court and hence had not made enemies. His party was normally strongest in the East, the most populous section of the country, and there the anti-Wilson sentiment reached unparalleled proportions. The financial classes, which are so often referred to as "Wall Street," had felt a keen resentment toward him as far back as 1911 when he was Governor of New Jersey,—a resentment which had expanded into a bitter personal antipathy. The manufacturing and commercial groups were at odds with his tariff and anti-trust legislation. The strong pro-German elements considered him favorable to the allies; while the powerful pro-ally elements on and near the Atlantic seaboard denounced him for timidity in refraining from urging war with Germany, and scornfully condemned his notes to that power. The manner in which the tense feelings engendered by the war added to the usual bitterness of political campaigns is typified by a scathing indictment entitled "To Woodrow Wilson" by Owen Wister, which appeared in the Philadelphia *Public Ledger* on February 22, 1916:

> Not even if I possessed your twist in speech,
>   Could I make any (fit for use) fit you;
> You've wormed yourself beyond description's reach;
>   Truth if she touched you would become untrue.
> Satire has seared a host of evil fames,
>   Has withered Emperors by her fierce lampoons;
> History has lashes that have flayed the names
>   Of public cowards, hypocrites, poltroons;

You go immune. Cased in your self-esteem,
    The next world cannot scathe you, nor can this;
No fact can stab through your complacent dream,
    Nor present laughter, nor the future's hiss.
But if its fathers did this land control,
    Dead Washington would wake and blast your soul.

On the other hand, Wilson had the advantage of being in power, so that he could, as the expression is, "make the news." He had a foreign policy, the general outlines of which the people knew about. In such uncertain times his supporters could strongly urge the danger of "swapping horses while crossing a stream." He had vigorously upheld American rights in his public statements, without at the same time leading the country into a war,—in both of which cases the sentiment of the people, more particularly in the West, gave him their support. And lastly, his "progressive" domestic legislation had commended itself to many Republicans,—although in the main, the campaign turned but little on domestic issues.

The particular characteristics of the campaign were mainly the results of the activities of Hughes, Roosevelt and Wilson. In his speech accepting the nomination Hughes attacked the record of the administration in regard to the civil service, charged the President with interfering in Mexican affairs without protecting American rights, and asserted that if the government had shown Germany that it meant what it said by "strict accountability" the *Lusitania* would not have been sunk. He also announced that he favored a constitutional amendment providing for women's suffrage. Later he made extended stumping tours in which he reiterated his attacks on the administration, but he disappointed his friends by failing to reveal a constructive program. Roosevelt, meanwhile, assisted the Republican candidate by a series of speeches, one of the earliest of which was that of August 31st, in Maine. That state held its local elections on September

11th and it was deemed essential by both parties to make every effort to carry it so as to have a good effect on party prospects elsewhere. Roosevelt's speech typified his criticisms of the administration. He declared that Wilson had ostensibly kept peace with Mexico but had really waged war there; he asserted that the President had shown a lack of firmness in dealing with Mexico and had kissed the hand that slapped him in the face although it was red with the blood of American women and children; he compared American neutrality in the European War with the neutrality of Pontius Pilate and believed that if the administration had been firm in its dealings with Germany there would have been no invasion of Belgium, no sinking of vessels and no massacres of women and children.

Wilson followed the example of McKinley in 1896 and conducted his campaign chiefly through speeches delivered from the porch of "Shadow Lawn," his summer residence in New Jersey. In this way he emphasized the legislative record of the Democrats, defended his foreign policy and attacked the Republicans as a party, although not referring to individuals. An important part of his strategy was an attempt to attract the Progressives to his support. He met his opponent's vigorous complaints in regard to his attitude toward Mexico and the European war by pressing the question as to the direction in which the Republicans would change it. Unfortunately for Hughes, this was his most vulnerable spot. Although he condemned Wilson's Mexican policy, he could not make clear just how he would change it. His criticism of the attitude of the administration toward the European conflict was scathing,—nevertheless he was unwilling to commit himself to an immediate declaration of war against Germany if elected. He was, therefore, compelled to fall back on the rather negative assertion that if Wilson had taken a firm stand in the beginning and had showed that the administration meant what it said,—all the trouble would have been averted. Wilson's supporters, however, had no need of evasion. They quite approved his foreign policy, summing it up in the telling phrase "He kept us out of war."

Foreign policy as a political issue was pressed temporarily into the background by the sudden demand of the railroad brotherhoods for shorter hours and more pay, threatening a nation-wide strike if their plea was unheeded. Neither party wished to risk the labor vote by opposing the unions, and the public did not desire a strike, much as it deprecated the attitude of the labor leaders in threatening trouble at this juncture. The President took the lead in pressing a program of railroad legislation, part of which was the "Adamson Act" granting the men what they desired.[13] This was immediately passed, although the remaining recommendations were laid aside. In the House the Republicans joined with the Democrats in putting the law through, although nearly thirty per cent of the members refrained from voting at all, but in the Senate party lines were more strictly drawn. In many quarters the President was vigorously condemned on the ground that he had "surrendered" to a threat. Hughes joined in the dissent, but somewhat dulled its effect by giving no evidence of opposition until the law was passed and by stating that he would not attempt to repeal it if elected. During the closing days of the campaign Hughes issued a statement declaring that he looked upon the presidency as an executive office and stated that if chosen he would consider himself the administrative and executive head only, and not a political leader commissioned with the responsibility of determining policies. At the close of the campaign, also, the benefits of a protective tariff were urged as a reason for electing Hughes.

The result of the balloting on November 7 was in doubt for several days because the outcome hinged on the votes of

[13] *Cf.* p. 514.

California and Minnesota, either of which would turn the scale.[14] In the end Wilson was found to have received 9,128,-837 votes and Hughes, 8,536,380. The vote of the electoral college was 277 to 254. The outcome was remarkable in several respects. Each candidate received a larger popular vote than had ever before been cast; Wilson won without New York or any of the other large eastern states, finding his support in the South and the Far West;[15] each side was able to get satisfaction from the result, the Republicans because their party schism was sufficiently healed to enable them to divide the House of Representatives evenly with their opponents, and the Democrats because their candidate was successful in states which elected Republican senators and governors by large majorities.

BIBLIOGRAPHICAL NOTE

In the nature of the case, any bibliography which concerns the events of so recent and important a period is of temporary value only. Ogg presents an excellent one, but many important volumes have been printed since 1917, his date of publication.

A reliable account of the chief events is contained in the *American Year Book*. The numerous biographies of President Wilson are written under the difficult conditions that surround the discussion of recent events. Available ones are: E. C. Brooks, *Woodrow Wilson as President* (1916), eulogistic, but contains extracts from speeches; W. B. Hale, *Woodrow Wilson, The Story of His Life* (1912); H. J. Ford, *Woodrow Wilson* (1916); A. M. Low, *Woodrow Wilson, an Interpretaton* (1918), a friendly and substantial analysis

[14] The situation in California was extraordinary. The Republican candidate for senator, Hiram Johnson carried the state by nearly 300,000 votes, while Hughes lost by 3,800. The explanation seems to be in part that the latter, in a campaign visit to California, largely ignored Johnson and his progressive Republican friends.

[15] The West heartily supported Wilson's "progressive" domestic legislation and his pacific foreign policy. It seems to be assumed that the entire West was quite different from the East in its outlook on the European war. Possibly a study of specific areas might modify this assumption somewhat. *Cf.* W. A. White, *Woodrow Wilson*, pp. 312 *ff.*

by an English newspaper correspondent; W. E. Dodd, *Woodrow Wilson and His Work* (1920); J. P. Tumulty, *Woodrow Wilson as I Know Him* (1921); J. Daniels, *The Life of Woodrow Wilson* (1924); D. Lawrence, *The True Story of Woodrow Wilson* (1924); W. A. White, *Woodrow Wilson*. W. J. and M. B. Bryan, *Memoirs of W. J. Bryan* (1925); A. W. Lane and L. H. Wall, eds., *Letters of F. K. Lane* (1922). Better than any biography is a careful study of Wilson's addresses and speeches, editions of which have been prepared by A. B. Hart, J. B. Scott, A. Shaw, R. S. Baker and others.

Periodical literature concerning the legislative program of the first Wilson administration is especially abundant. On the tariff, in addition to Taussig, consult: *Quarterly Journal of Economics* (1913), "The Tariff Act of 1913"; *Journal of Political Economy* (1914), "The Tariff of 1913." On the federal reserve system, *Political Science Quarterly* (1914), "Federal Reserve System"; *Quarterly Journal of Economics* (1914), "Federal Reserve Act of 1913"; *American Economic Review* (1914), "Federal Reserve Act"; *Journal of Political Economy* (1914), "Banking and Currency Act of 1913"; H. P. Willis, *The Federal Reserve* (1915); E. W. Kemmerer, *The A B C of the Federal Reserve System* (1918); J. M. Chapman, *Fiscal Functions of the Federal Reserve Banks* (1923); W. P. G. Harding, *The Formative Period of the Federal Reserve System* (1925). On the anti-trust acts, *Political Science Quarterly* (1915), "New Anti-Trust Acts"; *Quarterly Journal of Economics* (1914), "Trust Legislation of 1914"; *American Economic Review* (1914), "Trade Commission Act." The activities of the Federal Trade Commission are best followed in its *Annual Reports;* G. C. Henderson, *The Federal Trade Commission* (1924); Eliot Jones, *The Trust Problem in the United States* (1922), Chap. XV. On the Canal tolls repeal, Seymour, *Intimate Papers of Colonel House* (1926), I, 192-206; E. Root, *Addresses on International Questions* (1916), 207–312. For the early stages of the European conflict see Seymour, *The Intimate Papers of Colonel House* (2 vols., 1926); B. J. Hendrick, *The Life and Letters of Walter H. Page* (3 vols., 1924, 1925); W. C. Redfield, *With Congress and Cabinet* (1924).

The best accounts of the election of 1916 are in the *American Year Book,* and in Ogg. Other readable accounts are: *Nineteenth Century* (Dec., 1916), "The Re-Election of President Wilson"; W. E. Dodd, *Woodrow Wilson* (1920).

CHAPTER XXV

THE UNITED STATES AND THE WORLD WAR

No man can support Mr. Wilson without at the same time supporting a policy of criminal inefficiency as regards the United States navy, of short-sighted inadequacy as regards the army, of abandonment of the duty owed by the United States to weak and well-behaved nations, . . .

THEODORE ROOSEVELT.

It is easy enough for one without responsibility to sit down over a cigar and a glass of wine and decide what is best to be done.

EDWARD M. HOUSE.

Under modern conditions, wars are not made by soldiers only, but by nations. . . . The army is merely the point of the sword.

NEWTON D. BAKER.

My standpoint was that we must either treat England as invincible and accept our defeat, . . . or else that we must use every political and military means to shake her position.

ADMIRAL VON TIRPITZ.

An American Army was an accomplished fact.

GENERAL PERSHING, describing the St. Mihiel operation.

THE APPROACH TOWARD WAR

THE campaign and election of 1916 constituted a discordant political episode in a period of comparative calm in American international relations. In April of that year, to be sure, the outlook had appeared so dangerous that a memorandum had been drawn up dismissing Bernstoff, the German ambassador, but the people in general were unaware of this fact. On May 11th the German government had given assurance, after the sinking of the *Sussex*, that the use of the submarine would be limited according to the principles of visit and search. The promise was ad-

618

hered to, in the main, for about nine months. During the remainder of 1916 the United States had no new cause for entering the European conflict. The American people were, nevertheless, divided into two hostile camps.

A dwindling majority wished to keep clear of the war, either because they considered it outside of American interest, or because they had some sympathy with the German side, or because of dislike of England, or because they hoped that the United States might soon act as a mediator and bring the struggle to a close. President Wilson and his immediate advisors sympathized with the project to keep free for mediation. Nor did the administration merely indicate a general willingness to act as a peace-maker. Colonel House was instructed with great secrecy to inform leading French and English officials that President Wilson was prepared, with their assent, to demand a peace conference. If Germany refused to accept terms to be outlined in the proposal, then he would advise Congress to enter the war on the side of the Allies.[1] The plan came to nothing, partly because of French opposition. Having suffered severely from German aggression, France believed that her best chance of giving her ancient enemy a lasting defeat lay in the vigorous prosecution of the war,—not in a project for peace. The effect on Wilson of the allied failure to seize the opportunity for peace was distinctly unfortunate. It left him with the impression that the governments of the Allies had motives which were being withheld from the world. These purposes, he suspected, would involve ruthless indemnities and trouble-making transfers of territory in the event of allied success.[2]

The President's pacific policy, meanwhile, commended it-

[1] The terms included: the restoration of Belgium; the transfer of Alsace and Loraine to France; the acquisition by Russia of an outlet to the sea; and some concessions to Germany outside Europe.

[2] How well founded the suspicions were is evident in the "secret treaties" which, it later appeared, had been entered into by Great Britain, France, Italy and Russia. *Cf.* p. 672.

self to a majority of the American people. The election of 1916 was an indubitable manifestation of that fact.[3] In an address which he delivered in New York, Wilson said that he received a great many letters from unknown and uninfluential people whose one prayer was, "Mr. President, do not allow anybody to persuade you that the people of this country want war with anybody." As late even as February, 1917, the head of the General Motors Company, returning from a trip to the West, declared that he had met only one man between New York and California who wanted war. Even the most outstanding of Wilson's enemies—Ex-President Roosevelt—unwillingly agreed that "he kept us out of war" had attracted a majority of the people. No slight contribution to this result was the irritation caused by England's restrictions on the American carrying trade. Continued efforts were made to induce the Senate to threaten some action against the Allies—even an embargo on munitions—in order to compel England and France to heed American complaints. In brief, then, the proponents of a pacific foreign policy comprised a majority of the American people, but were composed of several different elements.

On the other hand, a growing minority had for some time been demanding the relinquishment of neutrality and earnest preparations for war. The National Security League, organized on December 1, 1914, was one of the earliest influential associations, composed of private citizens. It proposed to obtain authentic information in regard to the national defenses, to find out what appropriations would be required to attain greater efficiency and to bestir the country to a realization of the need of adequate national defense. Theodore Roosevelt

[3] President Wilson felt that the interval of four months between the election in November and the inauguration in March was too great a period between administrations during such uncertain times. He therefore determined to make Hughes Secretary of State in case the latter was elected president. Then Wilson and Marshall, the Vice-President, would resign at once, automatically making Hughes President. Seymour, *House*, II, pp. 378–380.

was the most prominent of a group who urged preparedness for war and entry into the European conflict. The sinking of the *Lusitania* gave a considerable impetus to a campaign of addresses, magazine articles and books which was carried on with the utmost vigor.

The President meanwhile was taking a far more belligerent attitude than his opponents appeared to think. In his message to Congress December 7, 1915, he proposed three measures of great moment,—an enlarged army, a construction program for the navy and the creation of an advisory council to provide for the mobilization of the nation's economic resources. In furtherance of his plans, during the winter of 1915–1916, he made preparation for defense the outstanding feature of his public addresses. In January, 1916, in New York, he admitted his own conversion to the idea of more adequate military preparations; [4] in Cleveland he declared that the country must prepare as effectively and as promptly as possible; in St. Louis,

Either we shall stand still and wait for the necessity for immediate national defense to come and then call for raw volunteers who for the first few months would be impotent as against a trained and experienced enemy, or we shall adopt the ancient American principle that the men of the country shall immediately be made ready to take care of their own Government . . . speaking with all solemnity, I assure you there is not a day to be lost.

Congress acted with much deliberation, but it acted. On June 3 (1916), the *National Defense Act* was passed increasing the regular army to 186,000; establishing Reserve Officers

---

[4] A little over a year before, in December, 1914, in a message to Congress, President Wilson had mildly advocated making *volunteer* military training "as attractive as possible." He added, however, that the time and occasion did not especially call for such measures, and that there was no new need to discuss defense. In the New York address, January 27, 1916, he referred to his earlier position and said: " . . . more than a year has gone by since then and I would be ashamed if I had not learned something in fourteen months." *Cf.* Shaw, *President Wilson's State Papers*, pp. 78–79, 158.

Training Corps at colleges and universities; providing for enlargements for the National Guard until it numbered 425,-000 men; and appropriating $20,000,000 for the production of nitrates necessary for explosives. On August 29th the necessary appropriations for such an enlarged program were passed. A portion of this law called for a *Council of National Defense* composed of six members of the cabinet. This important innovation was intended to organize and develop the industrial resources of the country in case of actual conflict. On the same day the President signed a *Naval Appropriations Act* which authorized the expenditure, within three years, of more than $300,000,000 for battleships, submarines and destroyers, and the building of plants for the production of armor plate and projectiles.

The three acts combined,—for the army and the navy—constituted by far the largest and most costly defense program ever passed by Congress. The opponents of the administration, nevertheless, referred to it as a "shadow" program, and declared that the President's conversion to preparedness was a tardy recognition of an obvious duty, and that he had acted because of "pressure" and "criticism" rather than because of a definite and positive purpose of his own. "The American people," said Theodore Roosevelt, "have forced him to belated and half-hearted action. After eighteen months he has begun feebly to advocate an imperfect preparedness." [5]

The President had, in fact, frankly shifted his position not only on the need of military preparations but also on the relation of the United States to the European conflict,—or more

[5] The Secretary of War, Lindley M. Garrison, resigned on February 10, 1916, and Newton D. Baker was appointed. Mr. Garrison earnestly favored an increased "continental" army, completely controlled by the federal government. The chairman of the House Committee on Military Affairs, Mr. Hay, favored increasing the militia of the states and giving federal aid for the purpose. As President Wilson would not go as far as Mr. Garrison wished, in advocating the continental army, the Secretary resigned.

accurately he had publicly stated his recognition of the fact
that a controversy which had once been merely a Balkan imbroglio had become a matter that deeply affected the world.
On May 27, 1916, while the debate on the defense measures
was going on, he addressed a meeting of the League to Enforce Peace. Three statements which he made in the course
of his remarks were of great importance.

(1) With the causes and objects of the war, he asserted, we
were not concerned. ''The obscure fountains from which its
stupendous flood has burst forth we are not interested to
search for or explore.''

(2) In its spread, however, the war had profoundly affected
our liberties, privileges and property. ''We are not mere dis-
connected lookers-on. . . . We are participants, whether
we would or not, in the life of the world. The interests
of all nations are our own also. We are partners with the
rest.''

(3) America held to three principles in international relations: (a) that people have a right to choose the sovereignty
under which they will live; (b) that small nations have a
right to expect their sovereignty and territorial integrity to
be respected; and (c) that the world has a right to be free
from aggressive wars.

Unhappily the nerves of the world were on edge in 1916—
as has been seen in connection with the presidential campaign
of that year. Attention in the allied countries and among
Wilson's opponents focused upon the first of these three statements, and translated it to mean a lack of sympathy with those
ideals for which the Allies were fighting *at the time the address was delivered.* Once more allied opinion became bitterly critical of American leadership. The significant points
of the speech, however, as far as the course of American history was concerned were the other two statements,—the concern of the United States in the spread of the war, and the
principles of international intercourse for which it would

stand.   In case Wilson should urge America to enter the war, it would be on account of these latter facts.

Between December 18, 1916, and April 2, 1917, events moved so quickly that a summary of the situation at the beginning of this period may not be amiss.

(1) President Wilson had pressed the rights of neutral trade upon the Allies to the point where they were bitter in their criticism of the United States.

(2) He had become convinced of the necessity of defensive measures,—tardily according to the opinion of many—and had succeeded in getting Congress to act.

(3) On May 4, 1916, he had succeeded in getting a promise from Germany to restrict her use of the submarine, and the promise was still being kept.

(4) He had confidentially and unavailingly attempted mediation in the European war and had come to suspect that the Allies had secret and undesirable war aims which they were unwilling to have brought out into the light.

(5) The presidential election of November, 1916, had given him a popular mandate for the continuation of his attempts to keep the United States out of the war.

(6) He had reached a determination that the people of the United States must understand the purposes of the war if they entered it, and had roughly outlined a set of war aims in his speech of May 27, 1916.

And now for the events of December, 1916, to April, 1917.

On December 12 Germany proposed a conference for the discussion of possible peace terms.   Thereupon President Wilson sent to all the belligerents a note which had already been in his mind.   In it he called attention to the fact that the leaders of the two sides had expressed their war aims in general terms only:

But, stated in general terms, they seem the same on both sides. Never yet have the authoritative spokesmen of either side avowed the precise objects which would, if attained, satisfy them and their people that the war had been fought out.

Each power, he said, had expressed the desire to make secure the rights of small states, to end the danger of the repetition of a general European War and to consider the formation of a league of nations. He therefore proposed an interchange of views to clear the way for a conference. Again the Allies were embittered. Although the language of the note was accurate when read with care, they assumed that Wilson intended to place their war aims on a level with those of the hated Teutons. Everywhere in the belligerent countries the people had been excited to a pitch of patriotism where they resented the least suggestion that they were fighting for anything less than high principle. Nevertheless, the good opinion of the United States as the greatest of neutrals was too big a stake to be cast lightly away. Both sides made response.

On January 22 (1917) the President again addressed the Senate and presented the results of his action. The reply of the Germans, he said, had stated merely their readiness to meet their antagonists in conference to discuss terms of peace; the Allies had detailed more definitely the arrangements, guarantees and acts of reparation which would constitute a satisfactory settlement. So far, Wilson's contribution to peace was merely the negative one of the friend of both sides, —the umpire or stake-holder. He now went farther, to make a positive and constructive statement of the sort of settlement that would satisfy America:

(1) There must be a just and permanent peace, not a mere re-alignment of the European nations in a new balance of power;

(2) Small and weak nations must have equal rights with large and powerful ones;

(3) Governments derive their just powers from the consent of the governed and therefore peoples can not be handed

about from sovereignty to sovereignty as if they were property;

(4) So far as possible great nations should have an outlet to the sea;

(5) ". . . the paths of the sea must alike in law and in fact be free";

(6) The limitation of armament on sea and on land must be faced with candor and the spirit of accommodation.

The reception accorded the speech indicated that the President of the United States had become the spokesman of the world. For the most part the Allies condemned it with unconcealed bitterness, because of a single phrase which it contained. Wilson feared that a complete defeat of one side would result in "a victor's terms imposed upon the vanquished. It would be accepted in humiliation, under duress, at an intolerable sacrifice, and would leave a sting, a resentment, a bitter memory upon which terms of peace would rest, not permanently, but only upon quicksand." Peace, therefore, must be "a peace without victory." To an allied world which was undergoing the direst sufferings in order to achieve as thorough-going a victory as lay in them, this seemed like a blow in the face. To people who were under less of a strain, it seemed that Wilson had outlined an enduring settlement.[6]

---

[6] Perhaps no leader ever suffered more from popular misunderstanding of unfortunate phrases which were susceptible of unexpected meanings when taken from their contexts. "Too proud to fight" and "peace without victory" were the most harmful of these, as they lost to the President the support of countless thousands of Americans. In fairness, however, it has to be remembered, as a recent writer points out, that the entire world was keyed up to an unprecedented pitch of hatred, ambition and fear. Under such circumstances some phrases were almost certain to be overemphasized and misunderstood. *The unhappy effect of the phrases*, however, is the historical fact, whether the blame lies with Wilson or with a war-weary world. Mr. Wilson afterward explained that the words "peace without victory" were introduced "as a warning against vindictive triumph such as too many seemed at that time to desire as an outcome of the war. . . . What I meant to say, therefore, was that we must beat them for the sake of the prin-

In the meanwhile German official circles were being torn by
an internal dissension which was at least the equal of any
controversy in the allied countries or America. Led by Admiral von Tirpitz, a powerful militaristic faction had long
urged the ruthless use of the submarine,—and had been held
in check only by the Chancellor (von Bethmann-Hollweg),
and Emperor William. During the summer of 1916 the German submarine fleet was largely augmented, and in the meantime the British blockade was slowly bringing about a dire
shortage of food throughout central Europe. Von Bernstoff,
the German Ambassador at Washington, continually urged his
government to realize that the renewal of unrestricted submarine warfare would throw the resources of the United
States into the conflict on the side of the Allies. The reply
of the German militarists was short and convincing: before
America's weight could become important, a vigorous submarine campaign would raise the English blockade, isolate
England herself and bring victory to the German arms. The
choice seemed to be the unrestricted submarine and a quick
victory,—or the restricted submarine, famine and defeat.

The die was cast on January 31st, when Germany announced an extension of her submarine warfare. A wide area
surrounding the British Isles, France, and Italy, and including the greater part of the eastern Mediterranean Sea was declared to be a barred zone. All sea traffic, neutral as well as
belligerent, the note warned, would be sunk, except that one
American ship would be allowed to pass through the zone
each week provided that it followed a designated, narrow
lane to the port of Falmouth, England, that it was marked
with broad red and white stripes, and carried no contraband.
The President promptly broke off relations with Germany,
sent the German ambassador home and appeared before Congress to state to that body and to the people the reasons for

ciples involved, but not in order to humiliate and destroy them."
Cf. New York *Times,* Mar. 9, 1924.

his decision. He recounted the substance of his earlier correspondence with Germany in regard to submarine warfare and recalled the promise of the German government that merchant vessels would not be sunk without warning and without saving human lives. He declared that the American government had no alternative but to sever relations, although refusing to believe that Germany would ruthlessly use the methods which she threatened, until convinced of her determination by "overt acts." Information of the move made by the United States was sent to American diplomatic representatives in neutral countries with the suggestion that these nations take similar action.

The effect on American shipping was immediate. Shipowners were unwilling to run the risks to vessels and crews that confronted navigation in European waters. Goods for export backed up at the coast cities, and the congestion grew greater day by day. Thereupon the President requested Congress to give him authority to supply merchant vessels with defensive arms to protect vessels and crews on the seas. This, as Wilson pointed out, would place the United States in a position of armed neutrality in regard to the European war. A bill was immediately introduced in Congress, where all but a small minority in the Senate were in favor of its passage. Under existing rules, which permitted unlimited debate, the senatorial few were able to prevent action. Authority was found, however, in existing statutes, and the administration was able to proceed.[7]

Every important event of March, 1917, tended toward war with Germany. On the first day of the month the administration published a remarkable message which had been sent to the German minister in Mexico by Zimmermann, the German Secretary of State for Foreign Affairs. In case the

[7] As a result of this incident the Senate decided to modify somewhat its rule allowing unlimited debate. Under the "closure" rule adopted March 8, 1917, a two-thirds majority may limit discussion on any measure to one hour for each member.

United States entered the European war, the minister was to propose an alliance between Germany and Mexico. They were to make war and peace together; Germany was to lend generous financial support; and it was to be understood that in case of success Mexico would recover Texas, New Mexico and Arizona. The president of Mexico was also to be urged to invite Japan to leave the Allies and join the Mexico-German group. And finally, the minister was to call the attention of President Carranza to the expectation of Germany that the ruthless use of the submarine would bring England to terms within a few months. Even in times when sensations followed one another rapidly, the Zimmermann telegram stirred the anti-German feeling profoundly—especially in the western and southwestern parts of the country, where interest in the European war was least.[8]

On March 5th, President Wilson was inaugurated for the second time and took occasion to state again the attitude of the United States toward the war. Although disclaiming any desire for conquest or advantage, and reaffirming the desire of the United States for peace, he expressed the belief that we might be drawn on, by circumstances, to a more active assertion of our rights and a more immediate association with the great struggle. Once more he stated the things for which the United States would stand whether in war or in peace: the interest of all nations in world peace; equality of rights

[8] Information of the Zimmerman plot was uncovered by the British Intelligence Service. The German Secretary sent the message to his minister in Mexico by three channels. (1) It was transmitted by wireless from Nauen, Germany, to Sayville, Long Island, for Bernstoff, to be sent by him to Mexico. British wireless operators caught the message. (2) It was sent to Mexico by way of the Swedish Foreign Office which was pro-German. The British caught this also. (3) It was also sent to Bernstoff by way of the American State Department! The British did not fail to catch this, either, and in addition purchased a copy from some "approachable" person in Mexico. All the messages, of course, were in a cipher, but the British Intelligence Service had been in possession of the key to the cipher since early in the war. See the whole astonishing story in *Life and Letters of W. H. Page*, III, Chap. xii; and in *World's Work*, Nov. 1925, pp. 23-26.

among nations; the principle that governments derive their just powers from the consent of the governed; the freedom of the seas; and the limitation of armaments.

Later in the month information reached America that there had been a revolution in Russia, that the Czar had been compelled to abdicate and that a republican government had been established. The news was gladly heard in the United States as it seemed to presage the overthrow of autocracy everywhere. For many decades the American people had thought of Russia as the symbol of tyranny, the archetype of repression—and now she had taken her stand among the democratic nations of the world. Another obstacle in the way of cooperation with the Allies was thus removed. On March 22nd, the new Russian government was formally recognized by the United States and later a loan of $100,000,000 was made.

In the meanwhile the "overt acts" which the President and the American people hoped might not be committed became sufficiently numerous to prove that Germany had indeed entered upon the most ruthless use of the submarine. Seven American vessels were torpedoed, with the loss of thirteen lives, and many more vessels of belligerent and neutral nations were sunk, in most cases without warning. The President accordingly summoned Congress to meet in special session on April 2d. When that body assembled he again and for the last time explained the character of German submarine warfare, charging that vessels of all kinds and all nations, hospital ships as well as merchant vessels were being sunk "with reckless lack of compassion or of principle." International law, he asserted, was being swept away; the lives of noncombatant men, women and children destroyed; America filled with hostile spies and attempts made to stir up enemies against us; armed neutrality had broken down in the face of the submarine, and he therefore urged Congress to accept the state of war which the action of Germany had thrust upon the United States. Such action, he believed, should in-

volve the utmost cooperation with the enemies of Germany—
liberal loans to them, an abundant supply of war material of
all kinds, the better equipment of the navy and an army
of at least 500,000 men chosen on the principle of universal
liability to service. An important part of the President's
address was that in which he distinguished between the German people and the German government. With the former,
he asserted, we had no quarrel, for it was not upon their im-
pulse that their government acted in entering the war. But
the latter, the Prussian autocracy, ''was not and never could
be our friend.'' Once more he disclaimed any desire for conquest or dominion:

> We are glad, . . . to fight thus for the ultimate peace of the
> world and for the liberation of its peoples, the German peoples
> included: for the rights of nations great and small and the privilege
> of men everywhere to choose their way of life and of obedience.
> The world must be made safe for democracy. Its peace must be
> planted upon the tested foundations of political liberty.

The response of Congress was prompt and nearly unanimous. In the House by a vote of 373 to fifty, and in the
Senate by eighty-two to six, a resolution accepting the status
of war was quickly passed and proclaimed by the President on
April 6.[9] His position was a strong one. His patience and
self-control, to be sure, had been carried to the extreme where
they seemed like cowardice and lack of policy to the more
belligerent East; but they had convinced the more pacific West
that he could not be hurried into war without adequate reasons. All sections and all parties were united as the country
had never been united before. His insistence that the United
States had no ulterior motives in entering the war and his

[9] The United States was followed immediately by Cuba and Panama,
and before the close of the year by Siam, Liberia, China and Brazil.
Many other Central and South American states severed relations with
Germany and before the close of the struggle several of them declared
war. War was declared against Austria on December 7, 1917.

constant emphasis on ideals and the moral issues of the conflict placed the struggle on a lofty plane, besides giving him and his country at that time a position of leadership in the world such as no man or nation had ever hitherto enjoyed. Moreover the evolution through which the President went, from adherence to the traditional aloofness from European affairs to throwing himself enthusiastically into the conflict, was an evolution through which most of his countrymen were passing. Every public address which the President delivered, every message to Congress, every request to the legislative branch of the government was read widely, disagreed with or received with enthusiasm in one quarter or another and discussed everywhere with interest and energy. The result was the education of America in a new foreign policy. It was no slight matter to discard the traditions of a century and a quarter, and the brevity and inconsiderable size of the controversy was the marvel, rather than its length and bitterness.[10]

THE PREPARATIONS OF A NATION FOR WAR

The entry of the United States into the war was the signal for a titanic contest,—nothing less than a race between American reinforcements for the Allies on the one side, and the German submarines, seeking to eliminate England from the war, on the other.

The months of 1917, following our declaration of war in April, found the Allies facing despair. During the first five months of the unrestricted use of the submarine, Germany

---

[10] The purpose and effect of Wilson's patient foreign policy were briefly expressed by Joseph H. Choate, a Republican advocate of early entry into the war, in a speech in New York on April 25, 1917. Choate declared that a declaration of war after the sinking of the *Lusitania* would have resulted in a divided country and remarked: "But we now see what the President was waiting for and how wisely he waited. He was waiting to see how fast and how far the American people would keep pace with him and stand up for any action that he proposed."

had destroyed more than three and a quarter million tons of allied shipping. So serious were the losses that the English Admiral Jellicoe declared that his country could not go on with the war if they continued. During the autumn of that year Russia staggered and then collapsed, leaving her burden to be shouldered by the remaining Allies. Italy, almost at the same time, suffered severe reverses from an Austro-German advance, ending in a general Italian retreat. Money and supplies were becoming exhausted; reenforcements were insufficient; discouragement seized both the military and the civilian population. "It cannot be said that German hopes of final victory were extravagant, either as viewed at that time or as viewed in the light of history."

The military preparations of the United States were hurried forward in accordance with two principles on which President Wilson and Secretary of War Baker seem to have been thoroughly agreed. In the first place, the war was to be conducted on the theory that modern warfare demands all the efforts of all the people, both military and civilian; and in the second place, the judgment of experts was to be followed so far as possible, thus avoiding the worst mistakes of the Civil War and the War with Spain.[11]

The most important legislation—the army act of May 18, 1917, was founded on these principles. It was drafted by the General Staff. It provided for the increase of the regular army to approximately 237,000, the maximum allowed by law; for taking the militia of the states into federal service; and for the drafting of an army of 500,000 (or 1,000,000 at the discretion of the President). The selective draft was to apply to all male citizens between the ages of twenty-one and thirty, both inclusive; there were to be no bounties; and no provision was made for the purchase of substitutes. The determination to raise the army by draft was based upon the

---

[11] Both these principles are worked out at length in Secretary Baker's *Frontiers of Freedom*.

belief that in this way successive and adequate supplies of men could be found without disproportionate calls on any section of the country and without undue disturbance of the industrial life of the nation, but it ran counter to American practice during most of our history. The conscription feature was opposed by prominent leaders in Congress. "Men came into my office," wrote Secretary Baker, "and said 'The streets of this country will run with blood on the day of the draft.'"

In June all men within the stated ages were required to register. Nearly 10,000,000 did so, in the 4557 registration districts into which the country had been divided. Each man in each district was then given a number, ranging from 1 to 10,500. The numbers 1 to 10,500 were written in red ink on slips of paper, placed in black celluloid capsules and thrown into a great glass bowl. On July 20 the drawing began. The Secretary of War, blindfolded, reached into the bowl, withdrew a capsule and handed it to an assistant who broke it, 258 was the red ink number, and man number 258 in every one of the 4557 districts was drafted. In a similar manner the draw continued until 1,374,000 names were obtained. The men thus designated were called before examining boards to determine their fitness for duty, and in September the first contingents were called into camps.[12]

Officers for the new army were supplied mainly through training camps, sixteen in number. They were scattered throughout the United States, so as to afford opportunity for training with least inconvenience and expense for travel. The first of them, at Plattsburg, New York, had already worked out experimentally a system of officer training, largely

[12] In conformity with its policy of using the civilian population, the War Department caused local civilian boards to be formed to enroll registrants, examine the drafted men for physical fitness and pass on exemptions. The machinery for the administration of the conscription system was constructed by the Provost Marshal General. *Cf.* Baker, *Frontiers of Freedom,* p. 121.

at the suggestion of General Leonard Wood. To the sixteen camps all reserve officers were immediately called and in addition 30,000 other candidates were selected from a much larger number who sought the opportunity. After three months of intensive instruction, most of the men were commissioned as officers, and the camps again and again filled up.

For the housing and training of the enlarged National Guard, sixteen tent camps were established in the South; and for the conscripted, or "National Army," sixteen cantonments, built of wood and capable of caring for 40,000 men each. A cantonment comprised 1,000 to 1,200 buildings, and was virtually a city with highways, sewers, water supply, laundries, hospitals and theatres.[13]

At the camps and cantonments the civilian population gave evidence of its unprecedented unity and interest in the war, as it had in its acceptance of compulsory military service. Organizations like the Y. M. C. A., the Commissions on Training Camp Activities, and churches of all denominations lent their aid in making the transition from business and professional life to military service as pleasant as possible. Within and around the camps, entertainments were given, libraries and writing rooms established, and athletic games and sports conducted. As far as legislation could do it, the most flagrant vices were kept away from the camps and the regions around them. The Red Cross conducted extensive relief work both for enlisted men and their families at home, in order to relieve the military forces of worry about the people who were left behind. The legislation which established the system of allotments, allowances and War Risk Insurance was also designed in part to maintain the *morale* of the army and navy. The pay of the "enlisted man" or private was $30.00 per month. In the case of men with dependents, an

[13] An official of the War Department estimated that the lumber used in the sixteen cantonments if made into sidewalks would go four times around the world.

"allotment" of $15.00 was to be sent home and the government thereupon contributed an "allowance" which normally amounted to $15.00 or more, and was graded according to the number of a man's dependents and the closeness of their relationship to him. Provision was made also for compensation for officers and men injured or disabled in the line of duty, and for training injured men in a vocation. In addition, the War Risk Insurance plan provided means by which both officers and men could at low cost take out government insurance against death or total disability. The latter idea both in its conception and in its details was the work of Samuel Gompers, president of the American Federation of Labor. It occurred to him as an application of some of the underlying principles of the legislation providing for workmen's compensation in case of industrial accidents. It was hoped to alleviate some of the distresses of war, so far as possible, and to guard somewhat against a repetition of the pension abuses of the Civil War.[14]

In the meanwhile, the Allied nations, and particularly Great Britain and France, sent groups of experts to Washington—strategists, mechanical experts, and specialists in supplies, manufacture and industry, who were distributed through the War Department to give the United States the benefit of nearly three years of experience "over there." The one most important contribution which America could make, according to the visitors, was a fresh supply of fighting men. "The Allies," they said, "were bleeding to death. Germany was winning, nothing less. The morale of the French was running out like water through a sieve." Men should be sent at once, they urged, no matter how small the number, for the encouragement of the weary Allies, and more should be sent as quickly as possible.

Hence the American Expeditionary Force,—the "A. E. F."

[14] I am indebted for this point to Newton D. Baker, former Secretary of War.

as it was usually called—for service in Europe. General John J. Pershing, a West Pointer of the class of 1886, with a long and honorable record as an Indian fighter, in the War with Spain, in the Philippines and in Mexico, was appointed to the command. The orders given to Pershing by the War Department were brief but inclusive. He was to command all the troops of the United States in the field of European conflict, and to establish all necessary lines of communication and bases of supply in France. It was made clear, moreover, that there would be no meddling with Pershing's authority, no appointment of political personages to military positions. The war was to be one of experts.[15] On May 28 Pershing set sail from New York. He was followed by a division of the regular army in June, and soon afterwards by the "Yankee Division" from New England, the "Sunset Division" from the West and the "Rainbow Division" of the National Guard, composed of troops from various states widely scattered throughout the country. The purpose of the Rainbow Division, the Secretary of War stated, was to distribute the honor of early participation in the war over a wide area and thus to satisfy in some part the eagerness of the state forces to get across to Europe. As soon as he had seen and considered conditions abroad, Pershing cabled the War Department (on July 6) that plans ought to be made to send at least 1,000,000 men across by May, 1918.[16]

No country in history had ever attempted a task of such size as that contemplated in sending 1,000,000 soldiers to battle fields 3,000 miles away, within ten months. That task, however, or something approximating it, was faced by a nation which had, until a few weeks before, buried itself in the pursuits of peace. Into Washington there poured a be-

[15] How well the promise was kept was expressed afterward by the General himself when he remarked that no commander-in-chief in American history had been so loyally supported by his superior.

[16] A "division" as reorganized for the war consisted of about 28,000 men.

wildering stream of offers of assistance. Organizations had
to be built up over night to take hold of problems that were
new to every man in the group. Men found themselves hurried into tasks for which they must prepare as best they
might, and under crowded working conditions, changing circumstances and confusion of effort that beggar description.

It was inevitable that controversy should arise, as it had
done in 1898 and in 1861, as to whether the War Department
was properly accomplishing its work. In part this was due
to the intense and impatient desire of the country to do its
share—and more—in the war; and in part to the secrecy
usually observed when nations are in conflict, which results
in ignorance on the part of their own supporters and therefore a misunderstanding and complaint. Ex-President Roosevelt wished to raise a volunteer division and lead it himself
to France. The President and the Secretary of War were
both personally well-disposed toward Roosevelt but felt that
they ought to act "at every step and in every particular under expert and professional advice." They therefore acted
according to the recommendation of the General Staff and
refused Roosevelt's request,—thereby increasing the ill-will
which the latter felt for the administration. Another cause
of complaint was the incident of General Leonard Wood.
Wood was an experienced and deservedly popular officer who
had every expectation of going to France and was all but
ready to embark when permission to go was refused. Again
condemnation was visited on the head of the administration.
No authoritative official statement has ever been given as to
the reason for Wood's retention in this country. The refusal
of Pershing to have Wood seems to have been determined and
emphatic, and apparently the administration preferred to
shoulder the hostile criticism itself and uphold its officer
rather than turn the hostility of Wood's admirers toward the
commander of the A. E. F.

More important was the criticism in Congress which focused in a statement by Senator George E. Chamberlin, Chairman of the Senate Committee on Military Affairs. The military establishment, said the Senator, "has . . . almost stopped functioning because of inefficiency in every bureau and every department of the government." In the resulting Congressional investigation, Secretary Baker defended the department in clear and convincing fashion. It seems to be true that the War Department was not organized to handle so huge an enterprise, that it took time to expand, rearrange and consolidate the several bureaus and services, and that the reorganization was already on the way.[17] When the reorganization was completed, the flow of troops and supplies across the Atlantic went on increasingly and without interruption.

The task of the Department of the Navy was, in the nature of things, much simpler. Rear Admiral W. S. Sims was already in Great Britain (having been sent there at the time when it was determined to place armed guards on merchant ships), and had been keeping the Department informed on problems connected with the possible entry of the United States into the conflict. After April 6th, when Congress passed the resolution accepting the status of war, the Admiral was placed in charge of the naval forces of the United States abroad, and thereafter worked in close cooperation with our European associates. On April 11th a conference of American, British and French naval officials was held in Washington. The British and French requested that one or two destroyers be sent at once to aid the British fleet in meeting the submarine danger. Six were sent under Commander Taussig, arriving at Queenstown, in Ireland, on May 4.[18] They were quickly followed by others until, at the close of the war, 5,000

[17] *Cf.* Crowell and Wilson, *The Giant Hand*, XI–XXVII. The authors believe that the Department should have started reorganization sooner, but also emphasize the magnitude of the job to be done.

[18] When the flotilla reached Queenstown, the Commander-in-Chief of the Coasts of Ireland asked Taussig, "When will you be ready to go to sea?" "We are ready now, sir," was the heartening reply, "that is, as soon as we finish refueling."

officers and 70,000 enlisted men were serving abroad. The three-year naval construction program which had been adopted in 1916 was pushed forward and somewhat expanded; new craft were commandeered wherever they could be found; private citizens loaned vessels or leased them at nominal sums; and German ships interned in American ports were taken over. Existing stations for the training of seamen were enlarged and new ones established, and schools were set up in colleges and at other points for radio operators, engineers and naval aviators. By such means the number of vessels in commission was increased from 197 to 2,003 and the personnel from 65,777 to 497,030.

The most dreaded enemy of the navy, the submarine, was successfully met by two devices. When transports and merchant-vessels were being sent across the ocean, they were gathered into groups or convoys and were protected by war vessels, especially torpedo-boat destroyers. The depth charge was also used with telling effect. This consisted of a heavy charge of explosive which was placed in a container and dropped into the sea where the presence of a submarine was expected. The charge was exploded at a pre-determined depth by a simple device, and any under-seas craft within 100 feet was likely to be destroyed or to have leaks started that would compel it to come to the surface and surrender.

Aside from combating the submarine, the greatest activity of the navy was the transportation of men and supplies to France. First and last more than 2,000,000 troops were carried to Europe, and although Great Britain transported more than half the men, yet four-fifths of them made the passage through the danger zones under the escort of United States cruisers and destroyers. The cargo fleet was substantially all American. The transportation of supplies alone required the services of 5,000 officers and 29,000 enlisted men, and involved the accumulation of a vast fleet, the acquisition of docks, lighters, tugs and coaling equipment, as well as the establishment of an administrative organization, at the precise time when the shipping facilities of the world were being strained to the breaking point by submarines.

On the other side of the ocean, naval bases were established in England, Ireland, Scotland, France and Italy; a considerable force operated from Gibraltar and others from Corfu, along the Bay of Biscay, in the North Sea and at Murmansk and Archangel. Besides cooperating with the navy of the Allies in keeping the Germans off the seas, the American navy laid about four-fifths of the great mine barrage which extended from the Orkney Islands to Norway, a distance of 240 miles, and extended 250 feet below the surface of the ocean. This astonishing enterprise—America alone laid 56,000 mines —together with a similar chain laid across the Strait of Dover was intended to pen the submarine within the North Sea.

While the army and navy were being prepared for offensive and defensive action, an unprecedented number of people were taking a civilian's share in helping to win the war. "This isn't one man's war," asserted Secretary Baker, "or several men's war, or an army's war, but it is a war of *all* the people of the United States." To an unprecedented degree this sweeping statement was a fact. The demand came upon every man, woman and child in the belligerent countries because of the sheer size and duration of the war. But the demands on the civilian population of the United States were due in part to 3000 miles of distance between the home base-of-supplies and the fighting ground in Europe. The unbelievable numbers of shoes required may serve as an example. Under the strain of military service, shoes naturally wore out quickly—hence reserve supplies had to be on hand in Europe, other reserves on board ship crossing the Atlantic, and still others in storage at ports in this country awaiting shipment. Stocks must be on hand at the camps, on the way to the camps and at supply depots. Furthermore, Pershing was calling for a program contemplating 100 divisions overseas by 1919. So great an army would require approximately 8,000,000 men, including auxiliary services and services of supply in France, and the necessary replacement troops in training in this country. Owing to the early close of the war, Pershing's enlarged program was never put fully into effect, but the orders for supplies had, of course, to be made while the program was in its early stages.[19]

The most important step had already been taken in the creation of the Council of National Defense on August 29, 1916. This body was composed of six members of the Cabinet, with the Secretary of War as chairman, and was assisted by an Advisory Commission of seven experts in the several industries that would be most essential in the prosecution of the war. On account of the rapid increase in the size and complexity of the industrial problems which faced the administration after our entrance into the war, much of the work of the Council and the Advisory Commission was given to six war agencies. Their activities must be accounted as equal in importance to those of the army and navy.

The first of these, the War Industries Board, was not known under that name until July 8, 1917, and was headed after March 4, 1918, by Bernard M. Baruch. Previously it had been

[19] *Cf.* Quartermaster General's Report, 1918, Chart No. 1. In pursuance of the policy of making the war the affair of the entire nation, the President established a Committee on Public Information on April 14, 1917. Its central purpose was to keep the country informed about the purposes and progress of the war. Through a "news division" the Committee placed war news at the disposal of all correspondents. An *Official Bulletin* printed all orders, official proclamations and the like. A "foreign division" explained America's purposes in allied and neutral countries, and combated German propaganda. The "Four-Minute Men" helped in bringing about the success of liberty-loan and other campaigns; and still another part of the Committee published informational pamphlets which were sent to clubs, schools and the public in general. Altogether the Committee sent out about 125,000,000 pieces of printed material. G. S. Ford, in *Historical Outlook*, March, 1920, pp. 97–100. The Committee came under fire from some who thought it showed partisanship for the administration, and from others who felt that it expended too much money.

a portion of the Council. The vital task of the Board was to bring together the industries of the country so as to make sure that materials needed for the war should be produced in the quantities and at the times needed; and that labor and raw materials should not be wasted on goods which would not contribute to military success. Moreover,—for the Allies had, since 1914, been purchasing their war materials in the United States—the needs of England, France and Italy, as well as of the United States government and our own public had to be analyzed, brought together, altered and met.

Steel was one of the necessities, for the armies were moved and the World War was fought on steel. Raw materials, workmen, furnaces and mills that had been devoted to peace-time production had to be turned to the making of steel plates for ships, steel for projectiles, motor cars and rails. Similarly with copper, explosives, lumber, dyes, leather, rubber and woolen and cotton goods,—the industries of the nation were forced to relinquish the idea of doing "business as usual," and turn their energies to the service of the war machines of America and her associates.[20]

"Among the absolute essentials for the successful prosecution of the war none took precedence over shipping suitable for overseas voyages." A failure to secure sufficient shipping would have meant disaster. Happily a United States Shipping Board had been established by act of Congress in September, 1916, to construct, purchase or lease vessels and make provision for their operation. It was also given power to form corporations for carrying out these duties. As time went on, the Shipping Board took complete control of the overseas-shipping phase of the war. It organized the United States Shipping Board Emergency Fleet Corporation to which it gave the task of finding and operating ships; it seized ninety-one vessels belonging to Germany or to German

[20] The activities of the Council of National Defense are well set forth in Clarkson, *Industrial America in the World War* (1923).

citizens; it assumed control of ship-building yards all over the United States; as early as December 1, 1917, it was supervising the construction of 1,118 vessels; it trained officers, enlarged port facilities, and requisitioned needed ships wherever found. Finally, it cooperated with the Allies by means of an Allied Shipping Council so as to use all the shipping facilities of the allied nations to the best advantage.

The exhausted condition of the supplies of food among the Allies, and the size of the armies which America decided to raise, made the Food Administration one of importance. At the time when the United States entered the war there was a dangerous shortage of food in Europe due to the decrease in production and to the lack of the vessels necessary to bring supplies from distant parts of the world. The problem centered mainly in wheat, meat, fats and sugar. The demand upon the United States was not only large but increasing. Accordingly, legislation was passed on August 10, 1917, which made it unlawful to destroy or hoard food; it provided for the stimulation of agriculture; and it authorized the president to purchase and sell foods and fix the price of wheat. Wilson appointed as the chief of the Food Administration Herbert C. Hoover, whose experience with the problem of Belgian relief enabled him to act promptly and effectively. Hoover's one great purpose was to utilize all food supplies in such a way as would most help to win the war. He cooperated with the Department of Agriculture which had already started a campaign for stimulating the cultivation of farms and gardens on all available land. Food administrators were appointed in the states and local districts. Speakers, posters, libraries and other agencies were utilized to urge the people to eat less wheat, meats, fats and sugar in order that more might be exported to the Allies. Millions of housewives hung cards in their windows to indicate that they were cooperating with the United States Food Administration. "Wheatless" and "meatless" days were set apart. These

voluntary efforts were supplemented by government regulation, and dealers in food products were compelled to take out
federal licenses which enabled the Administration to control
their operations and to prevent prices from going to panic
levels. The Food Administration established a Grain Corporation which bought and sold wheat; it placed an agency
in Chicago to buy meat for ourselves and the Allies; it called
a conference of the sugar refiners, who agreed to put in its
hands the entire supply of that commodity. In a word, by
stimulating voluntary efforts and by means of government
regulations, the Food Administration increased production,
decreased consumption, and coordinated the purchase of food
for the army, the navy, the Allies, the Red Cross and Belgian
relief. The Food Administration was hardly established before it became necessary to organize a Fuel Administration
to teach economy in the use of coal, to stimulate production,
adjust disputes between employers and employees, fix prices
and control the apportioning of the supply among the several
parts of the country.

On October 12, 1917, the War Trade Board, headed by
Vance C. McCormick was established, to coordinate and carry
out a number of powers which had been placed in the hands
of the executive. Its purposes were to control exports, imports and trading with the enemy. Commodities which were
much in demand in the United States were not to be exported
unless under unusual circumstances and then with the permission of the Board. American needs must first be met before the requirements of neutral nations were heeded. Especial efforts were made to prevent commodities reaching enemy
ports either directly or indirectly. Firms all over the world
were blacklisted if of an enemy character or if engaged in
trading with such firms. Vessels leaving the United States
were not allowed even to take on coal until the Board was
assured that the cargo to be taken and the destination to which
it was to go were such as not to harm the war prospects of

the United States and the Allies. Neutral countries like the Netherlands, Sweden and Denmark were put on a rationing system, by which they were allowed only such quantities of goods as would meet their necessities without giving them any surplus for export to the enemy.

The vital relation of the transportation system of the country to the winning of the war was apparent at the start. As soon as war was declared, therefore, nearly 700 representatives of the railroads formed a Railroads' War Board to minimize the individual and competitive activities of the roads, coordinate their operation, and produce a maximum of transportation efficiency. The attempt of the railroad executives, however, quickly broke down. In the first place, as has been seen, our entire body of railroad legislation is based upon the idea of separating the several systems and compelling them to compete rather than cooperate. The habits and customs thus formed could hardly be done away with in an instant. In the second place the cost of labor and materials was constantly mounting and the demand for more equipment was insistent. The railroads could meet these greater costs only by raising rates, a process which involved obtaining the assent of the Interstate Commerce Commission and required a considerable period for its accomplishment. The roads were also embarrassed by an unprecedented congestion of traffic on the eastern seaboard, from which men and cargoes must be shipped to Europe. Accordingly, on December 26, 1917, the President took possession of the railroad system for the government and appointed the Secretary of the Treasury, William G. McAdoo, as Director General. As rapidly as possible the railroads were merged into one great system. The entire country was divided into districts at the head of which were placed experienced railroad executives. Terminals, tunnels and equipment were used regardless of ownership in the effort to get the greatest possible service out of existing facilities. The passenger service was greatly reduced in order to free locomotives and crews for freight trains, duplication of effort was done away with where possible, officials who were not necessary under the new plan were dropped, and equipment was standardized. Existing legislation allowed the government to change freight and passenger rates, and on May 25, 1918, these were considerably raised. The winter of 1917–1918 was memorable for its severity, and placed great difficulties in the way of the railroads; nevertheless, between January 1, 1918, and November 11 of the same year nearly six and a half million actual and prospective soldiers were carried for greater or smaller distances.[21]

An important part of the problem of production, as regards munitions, supplies, fuel, transportation—everything that entered into modern warfare—was, of course, the attitude of the workmen in the factories and mines, and on the railroads. Fortunately the unity of the laborers in the war effort was as great as that of any other group, and was indicated in unmistakable fashion at the outset. Samuel Gompers, President of the American Federation of Labor, was one of the members of the Advisory Commission of the Council of National Defense. Under his leadership, organized labor announced itself solidly behind the President in the prosecution of the war, and urged that every effort be made both by capital and labor to prevent interruptions through strikes and lockouts. It also urged that neither side take advantage of the abnormal situation to change the working conditions under which modern industry was accustomed to operate. Numerous committees worked on the problem of harmonizing the interests of labor and capital in conformity with this pro-

[21] Beginning in March, 1918, the President had regular meetings of the so-called War Cabinet which consisted of representatives of the War and Navy Departments and the heads of the six great civilian agencies: Bernard M. Baruch, for the War Industries Board; E. N. Hurley, of the Shipping Board; Herbert Hoover, for the Food Administration; H. A. Garfield, representing the Fuel Administration; Vance C. McCormick, the head of the War Trade Board; and W. G. McAdoo, Director General of the Railroads.

gram. Most important were the National War Labor Board, headed by ex-President Taft and Frank P. Walsh, which settled disputes in essential industries; and the National Labor Policies Board which determined questions involving the distribution of labor, wages, hours and working conditions. Due to the activities of these and other agencies, the laboring classes lost none of the ground gained since the Pullman strike. Collective bargaining, the principle of the eight-hour day, the protection of women and children in industry, and all the rest of the advances which had been made remained substantially unimpaired.

On the financial side, the World War was unprecedented, as it was in other respects. The total direct money cost from April, 1917, to April, 1919, was estimated by the War Department at $21,850,000,000, an average of over a million dollars an hour, and an amount sufficient to have carried on the Revolutionary War a thousand years. In addition, loans were extended to the Allies at the rate of nearly half a million dollars an hour. This huge amount was raised in part through increased taxes. Income taxes were heavily increased; levies were made on such profits of corporations as were in excess of profits made before the war, during the three years 1911–1913; additional taxes were laid upon spirits and tobacco, on amusements and luxuries; and the postage rates were raised. In part, also, the cost of the war was defrayed through loans. A portion of the amount borrowed was by the sale of War Savings Stamps. This expedient was designed doubtless not merely to encourage persons of small means to aid in winning the war—a beginning could be made with twenty-five cents—but also to encourage thrift among all classes. Most of the borrowed money, however, was raised through the five "Liberty Loans," a series of popular subscriptions to the needs of the government. In each case the government called upon the people to purchase bonds, ranging from two billions at first to six billions at the time of the

fourth loan. There were four and a half million subscribers
for the first loan, but after a little experience the number was
readily increased until 21,000,000 people responded to the
fourth call. Popular campaigns such as never had been seen
in America, campaigns of publicity, house-to-house canvassing
and appeals to the win-the-war spirit resulted in unprecedented financial support. Isolated communities in the back
country and people of slender means in the cities, no less than
the great banks and wealthy corporations cooperated to make
the Liberty Loans of social and economic as well as financial
importance.

Modernizing America's Military Machine

The activities of the civilian population of the country
provided, obviously, the essential foundations for any great
military effort. "The point of the sword," nevertheless, was
the A. E. F. in France. The precise details of the military
effort,—the kind of sword to be used and the manner in which
it was to be wielded,—depended on another simple condition,
one of those conditions which are most obvious after they had
been called to our attention. It was the fact that the United
States was to *cooperate* in the prosecution of a war 3000 miles
away which had *already been going on for nearly three years*.
Almost the entire American program had to be fitted to this
fundamental fact.

In the first place, the United States had been sending food
and explosives to the enemies of Germany. It was most essential that the stream should not only continue but increase. In
the next place the Allies had already established plants for
the making of certain types of equipment, especially artillery,
and had reached the stage of quantity production. Hence
they urged that American divisions be equipped for the time
being with English and French artillery, so as to save shipping space and so that the energies of the United States might

first be diverted into projects where the demand was more immediate. It was more important, therefore, to dovetail the American military program into that of the Allies than for the United States to equip its army *ab initio*. In the third place the war had dug itself down to trench combat rather than fighting in the open field. Hence a part of the training of new troops must be for that type of conflict. And finally it was expected by all hands that the full force of the American effort would be reserved for the latter part of the year 1918, and especially for 1919, when the resources of both sides in Europe would be about exhausted.

Participation by the United States in the World War was further complicated by the inclusion of new branches of service and by the unexpected expansion of old ones. The ordinary problem of providing the fighting man with food, clothing, equipment and arms,—the task, that is, of preserving a line of communications—was made enormously more difficult by the conditions under which the war was being fought. So new and important was this part of the war operations that the "Service of Supply" became only less vital than the combat army itself. For this reason the "S. O. S." deserves particular mention.

The A. E. F. was being sent almost wholly to France. But the landing facilities of the French ports were already strained to the utmost. Ports on the English channel were reserved for England's use. The French themselves had been compelled to set aside the remaining well-equipped harbors for their own needs. To the United States, then, were assigned ports on the Bay of Biscay, such as St. Nazaire, La Pallice and Bassens. Docks had to be constructed; dock-handling machinery to be made in this country and shipped abroad; warehouses built; piles, cranes, tools, lumber sent 3000 miles, assembled and put into operation.[22] At their maximum

---

[22] In addition, large quantities of raw material were purchased in Switzerland, Spain, Holland and the allied countries.

efficiency, the new port facilities handled 45,000 tons of supplies each day.

The carriage of men and supplies from the Atlantic ports to the interior of France required another mammoth construction job. Of railroads, approximately 1,000 miles were built; and on the highways, 10,000 or more men were frequently at work. 20,000,000 square feet of storage space had to be made; hospital cities erected,—one of them composed of 700 buildings; and other structures, chiefly barracks, enough to extend 730 miles, according to the estimate of General Pershing. In the warehouses were stored reserve supplies:—in the "base depots" near the ports, reserves for forty-five days; in the intermediate depots for thirty days; and near the front for fifteen days.

The railways had to be relied upon, ordinarily, to carry supplies to within the reach of motor or horse-drawn transport,—twenty-five carloads every day for each division. It was here that approximately 106,000 animals were being used at the height of American participation in the war,—only about half enough, Pershing complained. The demand for the more rapid transfer of men and supplies led to a new branch of the service, the Motor Transport Corps. This organization set up and repaired cars and furnished transportation, just as any other commodity was supplied.

The Signal Corps, which was likewise a part of the Service of Supply, installed and operated telephone, telegraph and radio service wherever the army was to be found.

In developing new branches of the military service, the United States found aviation one of the most important, for the airman had made himself indispensable in modern fighting. Not only did he drop bombs and operate machine guns on enemy lines, and destroy their airplanes, but he took pictures of enemy positions, regulated artillery fire, kept our forces advised of opponent moves, and flew in contact with the advancing armies. Without superiority in the air, it seemed doubtful whether the Allies could win a final victory.

In April, 1917, the aviation section of the army was a part of the Signal Corps and consisted of 1200 officers and men. There were fewer than 300 airplanes in our possession, and many of these were unfitted for actual combat. So numerous and important had been the developments in aircraft during the course of the war in Europe that it is scarcely an exaggeration to say that the American aviation program had to be built up as a totally new project. In the meantime men were dispatched to aviation centers abroad to find out what had been done; and planes for practice flying as well as for actual service were ordered from France. When in July, 1917, Congress appropriated $640,000,000 for aviation purposes it seemed that nothing ought to prevent the immediate construction of adequate supplies. The task, however, was not quite so simple as it seemed. The necessary quantities of spruce and fir had to be found in the Northwest—174,000,-000 feet and new processes for kiln drying it rapidly enough had to be discovered. Linen for covering the wings was not to be had in sufficient amounts, so that cotton had to be adapted to the service. Even the lubricating oil was not to be had, and castor beans were purchased in India and 239,000 acres planted in order that adequate supplies might be forthcoming. Most important of all, as far as the American contribution to aviation was concerned, a new and effective type of motor, the Liberty Engine, was developed to provide maximum power with minimum weight. It was not until May, 1918, that the first American-built planes were landed in France, and not until August did fliers completely equipped with American-made materials cross over the German lines. By November of the same year, the Air Service (separated from the Signal Corps in May), was composed of 190,000 officers and men, 13,600 Liberty engines had been built, and the best (De Havilland) planes were being turned out at the rate of more than 1100 a month.[23]

Much the same story might be told of the development of machine guns, tanks and chemical warfare. Several kinds of machine guns or rapid-fire rifles had demonstrated their great usefulness in the war, but the United States had not accepted any single type as its permanent standard. Hence the war found this country in the possession of only 1453 such weapons, and these were of four different makes. French machine guns were accordingly relied on for the earlier divisions of the A. E. F. It was soon seen, however, that a standard gun, superior to those used in Europe could be invented, and manufactured in quantity. In May, 1917, two machine guns, the work of John M. Browning, were accepted, but it was not until 1918 that the necessary manufacturing facilities could be constructed, and guns turned out in large numbers. By October, 27,000 were being made each month.

The tank was a late invention—a small, steel-plated fortress equipped with artillery and machine guns, and motor driven on caterpillar tractors. It was not until February, 1918, that the Tank Service was organized, and only sixty-four six-ton tanks were produced in the United States.

Another novelty was the use of toxic or poisonous gases, first tried on a large scale by Germany against the Canadians at Ypres in April, 1915, and later developed by all nations in various ways. Sometimes bombs were thrown filled with liquefied gas which vaporized and smothered or burned all with whom it came into contact. Another method was to launch a wave of poisonous gas when a favorable wind blew toward the trenches of the enemy. Most of the gases pro-

[23] The fact that so huge an amount of money failed to land American-made airplanes in France until thirteen months after the declaration of war gave rise to widespread dissatisfaction. For a concise exposition of the difficulties met and the work accomplished, see Crowell and Wilson, *Armies of Industry*, Chaps. XVII–XXII.

duced merely temporary effects, like burns in the eyes or lungs; but the efficacy of this sort of warfare in disabling men for a short time was extreme. A third of the American "wounded" were the victims of gas warfare, despite the fact that the Allies had been experimenting with protective devices for more than two years.

The American Chemical Warfare Service was established on June 28, 1918, although earlier organizations had been attempting to cope with the problem. Fortunately the Bureau of Mines of the Interior Department had for some time been experimenting with masks to safeguard miners against poisonous gases. It was possible therefore to build on this experience, and the production of gas-masks proceeded early on a large scale,—4,000,000 being sent overseas. So efficacious were these that the only American soldiers injured by gas were those who were unaware of danger or unable to get on their masks in time.

Fortunately these increases in the effectiveness of offensive warfare were somewhat offset by improvements in the fields of medicine, surgery and disease prevention. In general, all the revolutionary advances in medical science made in recent years were at the disposal of the American army. "Up to the end of July" (1918), said Secretary Baker, "about 15 per cent of the entire civilian medical profession of the United States went into active duty as medical officers of the Army. Probably no working force has ever been organized which contained more distinguished men of a single profession than are to-day enrolled in the Medical Department of the United States Army." From mental hygiene to the care of the feet, every known branch of medical science was called upon for its assistance. In the training camps as well as in the A. E. F., general sanitation, water purification and vaccination brought about a striking change over previous experience in time of war. A single example from the Report of the Surgeon General for 1918 may typify the changes made. On the basis of the War with Spain 136,000 cases of typhoid fever might have been expected; only 297 occurred. In the A. E. F., as the fighting fraction of the army, eighty-five per cent. of the wounded were restored to active duty.[24]

Such then were the conditions surrounding the A. E. F. when its first representative, General Pershing, sailed for Europe on May 28, 1917, followed in a short time by a division of regulars and the first divisions of the national guard. The rapid growth of the Expeditionary Force and its exploits in France form the remainder of the story of American participation in the World War.

"THE POINT OF THE SWORD"

When divisions of the A. E. F. began to flow into France, it was assumed that the basic training in discipline, drill, and the use of the rifle and bayonet had been completed in the camps in the United States. The men had then to receive an intensive instruction in the details of actual fighting in France. In general, one month was devoted to the instruction of small units from battalions (1000 men) down; a second month was allotted to experience in a quiet sector on the battle front; and a third month to field practice in open warfare by divisions (28,000), including artillery and all the services of modern combat.[25]

The history of American military participation in the World War divides itself naturally into three parts: (1) from the beginning until April, 1918, the assistance of the

[24] An unforeseen ememy appeared, however, in the autumn of 1918 in an epidemic of influenza. So widespread and so malignant was its attack that during eight weeks there were more than twice as many deaths as in the entire army for the year preceding.

[25] General Pershing was insistent that the troops must receive training in "open warfare" as contrasted with trench fighting, believing that the Germans would not be beaten until forced to fight in the open field. *Cf.* with the later experience of American troops, p. 661.

United States was mainly psychological,—the Allies felt the promise of substantial help in the near future, and were encouraged accordingly; (2) from April to August, 1918, American divisions were used in the trenches here and there wherever they were needed to assist or relieve the French and English; and (3) from August onwards the American troops were gathered into a separate army under its own leaders, and were entrusted with a large sector of the fighting front, and with military operations of the foremost importance.

The weakening of Russia became sufficiently apparent in the summer of 1917 to give the Allies cause for worry if not for more profound concern.[26]   Accordingly on July 26 a conference of British, French and Italian military leaders determined to strengthen the western front as far as feasible and hold fast until American forces arrived in sufficient numbers to give the ascendancy.   It took time, however, for the United States to prepare, and by the end of 1917 only one division was in the line, and only 176,155 troops altogether in France. The Germans were quite aware both of the size of the American preparations, and of their slowness, and were determined to lose no time in following up the advantage which resulted from the collapse of Russia and the retreat of Italy.   They accordingly began a series of tremendous thrusts or drives on March 21, 1918.   The German army, so General Pershing declared, was by far the most formidable fighting force the world had ever seen.   Its terrific offensive, falling against the right of the British line and on the point where the British and French armies joined, carried everything before it for a depth of about thirty-five miles.   Allied losses were so serious that the United States was urgently requested to give priority to infantry and machine gun units, and England made ex-

[26] As the United States entered the war independently of the European opponents of Germany—e. g., without any treaty commitments—and as it wished to preserve its aloofness as far as consistent with the necessities of the situation, the group of Germany's enemies came to be called "the allied and associated powers."

traordinary efforts to supply additional shipping facilities to carry them across. As the result of the first German offensive, also, the Allies became impressed with the disadvantage of divided command, and a conference was held to consider the question of a commander-in-chief. On April 3rd, the important step was taken of appointing General Foch to coordinate the action of the British, French and American armies on the western front. The commander of each of these armies was to have immediate direction of his own troops, but the strategy of the entire front was confided to Foch.

In the meantime the flow of American troops to France was becoming impressive. On March 1st, 1918, they numbered 253,000; on April 1st, 320,000; and on May 1st, 424,000. The A. E. F. was now entering upon the second phase of its history. Secretary of War Baker and General Pershing were in agreement that the military forces of the United States ought to be kept as a unit under American officers and the American flag; so serious was the drain, however, on the man power of England and France that the allied leaders were energetic in their insistence that the American divisions should continue to be placed in the line wherever needed. The second German offensive, beginning on April 9th, wrought such havoc in the allied line and threatened such complete disaster that Sir Douglas Haig issued his famous appeal for a back-to-the-wall stand and gave the order, "Every position must be held to the last man." Under these circumstances Pershing delayed the formation of a distinctly American army, but with the specific understanding that he could withdraw the American units at any time after consultation with Foch. On April 25 the First Division relieved two French divisions, (the French divisions at this time, owing to losses, being about half the size of the American divisions), and on May 28th captured some important observation stations on the heights of Cantigny, with the help of French artillery, aviators and tanks.

The third German drive began on May 27th, and again the American troops were used where the need was greatest.　The

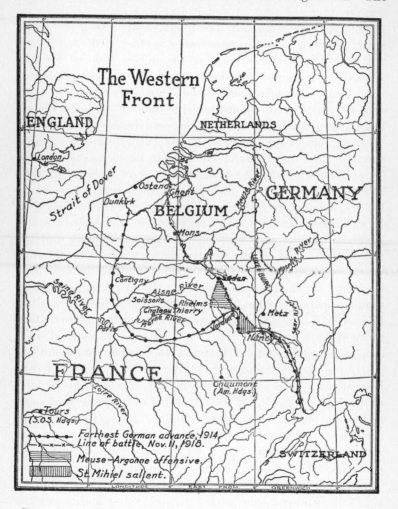

Second and Third Divisions helped the French stem the attack at Château-Thierry, and afterwards the Second Division

wrested Belleau Wood from the enemy. Five other divisions were withdrawn from the English lines to the support of the French.

On July 15th began the last of the great German efforts,—this time on the Champagne front. It was their hope to make this the decisive blow and conclude the war with a victorious peace. Happily the French suspected the point of attack and even discovered the exact hour—about midnight—when the artillery preparation would begin. General Gouraud decided to anticipate the bombardment and at half-past eleven launched a heavy fire by French and American artillery. Despite their surprise the Germans carried out their plans. At quarter of four in the morning their infantry poured out of the trenches and began the assault. The French and Americans held—and then more than held,—prepared for an offensive. One French division and two American divisions (the First and Second) were used as the point of the spear in a counter-attack near Soissons. A conference of all the commanders-in-chief was held to consider the next operation, and it was decided to continue the offensive. *The turning point of the war had been reached.* It was a turning point likewise in the history of the A. E. F., which now entered upon its third phase.[27]

The American army, scattered from the English channel to Switzerland, was brought together, given a separate sector in the front, and charged with its first great independent task,

27 In the face of the extremity overseas and the successes of the Germans, the United States demanded a yet greater army. The "Man Power" act of August 31, 1918, was the result. It changed the draft ages and added more than 13,000,000 registrants to the available supply of men. A clause of this law, designed in part to provide further supplies of officer material, allowed the Secretary of War to send soldiers to educational institutions at the public expense, thus establishing the Students' Army Training Corps, generally known as the "S. A. T. C." The so-called "Training Detachments" had already been established, providing for the training of mechanics, carpenters, electricians, telegraphers, and other necessary skilled artisans at a number of colleges and scientific institutions.

—the reduction of the St. Mihiel salient. This was a dent which extended into the allied line for about twenty miles. It had been held by the enemy since September, 1914, and was well protected both by nature and by artificial fortifications. Under cover of night the American forces were gradually concentrated in the vicinity of St. Mihiel. Every unit was thoroughly instructed in the part it was to play. French, British and American aviators were collected to make the greatest assemblage of air forces that the war had seen. At one o'clock in the morning of September 12 the artillery began raining steel and gas shells on the German lines.

"For four hours, without cessation, the tremendous concentration of fire on the German positions continued, and then at five o'clock, just as day was breaking, the American infantrymen in the first line climbed out of their trenches and started forward. With them went the tanks, lumbering along through the fog of the early morning, crashing through barbed wire, straddling trenches, lurching and twisting but always waddling ahead, opening up gaps in the wire, sweeping nests with machine-gun and small-shell fire. At the same time the light artillery raised its fire and the line of falling steel swept slowly along toward the north, progressing at the predetermined rate of one hundred meters in four minutes." [28] A half million men (430,000 Americans and 70,000 French) supported by such destructive fire were irresistible. By the next afternoon, September 13, the task was done. 16,000 prisoners had been taken, 443 guns and valuable military stores. Railway communications from Paris to the war zone were freed from enemy danger and further offensives were made practicable. "An American Army was an accomplished fact, and the enemy had felt its power."

The next offensive had already been planned by Foch and

---

[28] The intensity of the artillery fire is indicated by the fact that thirty times as many rounds of ammunition were used in four hours as the Union army expended at Gettysburg in three days.

Pershing before that at St. Mihiel was launched.   It was nothing less than to drive the Germans out of the Meuse-Argonne
sector.   This strong position had, like that at St. Mihiel,
been held by the enemy most of the time for four years.   It
had been elaborately fortified to a depth of about thirteen
miles and was of especial strategical importance to the
Germans.   About thirty miles back of the Argonne forest ran
a railroad of which the line from Carignan to Sedan to
Mézières was essential to the enemy for the carriage of supplies and the transfer of troops.   By September 26, when the
Meuse-Argonne offensive was launched, the A. E. F. had
reached impressive proportions.   About 1,800,000 soldiers
were in France, of whom 1,200,000 were available for the
drive; 2,700 guns, 189 small tanks and 821 air planes were
ready to give support to the infantry.   The ensuing action
lasted almost continuously from September 26th to November
11th, and was less a battle than a tremendous war concentrated into seven weeks of furious combat.[29]

The first phase of the offensive, beginning on September
26th, lasted for three days and a half, during which the Germans were gradually pushed back.   Then the troops were
given a breathing spell, replacements were brought up, and
the roads repaired through the region recovered from the
enemy.   On October 4th at daybreak the attack was renewed
on a front approximately seventy-five miles in width.   In
this desperate drive the troops were held in line until they
were exhausted, and artillery kept at the front until "practically all the animals were casualties and the guns were towed
out of line by motor trucks."   The enemy was rushing in his
already slender reserves in order if possible to stem the tide,
but this was made difficult and dangerous by the action of
Foch in keeping up an unceasing attack all along the front,

[29] That this is in no sense an exaggeration is shown by the fact
that the weight of the ammunition used by the American forces in the
Meuse-Argonne was greater than that used by the Union armies in
the entire Civil War.

—Belgian, English and French. During this phase, the American army captured the Argonne Forest and 19,000 prisoners.

On November 1st the relentless pressure continued. The Germans again retreated. On the second and third our heavy artillery was brought to bear on the final objective—the Carignan-Sedan railroad. By the seventh the enemy had been pushed back twenty-five more miles, his line of communications was about to be cut and disaster faced him. Foch, meanwhile, sent word that the German armies were in retreat on the entire front, and on November 11th he announced that an armistice had been signed calling for a cessation of fighting at eleven o'clock that morning.[30]

THE MORALE OFFENSIVE

While the allied armies were first stemming the German advance and later making their counter-offensive, the statesmen were attempting to preserve the morale of the Allies and break down that of the enemy by means of a wide-spread peace offensive. Because of his position as President of the United States and his skill in the expression of the purposes of the Allies, Wilson became by common consent the spokesman of the enemies of Germany, much as he had earlier been the representative of the neutral nations. In August, 1917, the Pope proposed peace on the basis of "reciprocal condonation" for past offenses, and the reciprocal return of territories and colonies. In reply Wilson contended that the suggested settlement would not result in a lasting peace. Peace, he believed, must be between peoples, and not between peoples on the one hand and "an ambitious and intriguing

[30] In addition to the main body of the A. E. F. in France, one regiment was sent to Italy and three battalions of infantry and three companies of engineers to Russia.

The losses of the entire A. E. F. up to November 18, 1918, were by death 53,160; the wounded numbered 179,625.

government" on the other. "We cannot," he declared, "take the word of the present rulers of Germany as a guarantee of anything that is to endure unless explicitly supported by such conclusive evidence of the will and purpose of the German people themselves as the other peoples of the world would be justified in accepting." The reply continued, of course, the attempt made in the address to Congress calling for a declaration of war,—the attempt to drive a wedge between the German people and their rulers,—but for the moment the attempt was fruitless.

On January 8, 1918, President Wilson again explained the attitude of the United States, in an address to Congress in which he gave expression to the famous "fourteen points." "The program of the world's peace," he stated must include: the beginning of an era of "open diplomacy," and the end of secret international understandings; the freedom of the seas in peace and war; the removal of economic barriers between nations; the reduction of armaments; the impartial adjustment of colonial claims; the evacuation of territories occupied by Germany, such as Russia, Belgium, France and the Balkan states; the righting of the wrong done to Alsace-Lorraine, the provinces wrested from France by Germany in 1871; an opportunity for peoples subject to Austria and Turkey to develop along lines chosen by themselves; the establishment of a Polish state which should include territories inhabited by indisputably Polish populations; and an association of nations to guarantee the safety of large and small states alike. Both Austria and Germany replied to this address, but not in a manner to make possible a cessation of warfare. In setting these replies before Congress, as well as in later speeches both to that body and to public audiences, the President reiterated the peace program of the Allies.[31]

[31] Even such a statement of war aims as this was used to increase the growing schism between the rulers of Germany and the German people. Col. House was in close touch with some of the ideals expressed by German liberal thinkers. These he passed on to Wilson, who used

In the meanwhile conditions in the Teutonic countries were reaching a serious point. Germany, Austria, Bulgaria and Turkey were facing an enraged world. Their man-power was almost exhausted, the numbers of killed and wounded in Germany alone being estimated at 6,000,000 men; famine, agitation and mutiny were at the door and revolution on the horizon; food was scarce and of poor quality; Austria was disintegrating; signs were evident of dissensions in the German government and suggestions were even made that the Kaiser abdicate. Allied pressure in the field together with insistent emphasis on the Allied distrust of the German government were at last having their combined effect; *the Teutonic morale was breaking down.* On October 4th the German Chancellor requested President Wilson to take steps toward peace on the basis of the "fourteen points." An interchange of notes ensued which indicated that the Teutonic powers were humbled and that the Chancellor was speaking in behalf of the people of Germany. The Inter-Allied Council then met at Versailles and drew up the terms of an armistice which were delivered to Germany on November 7th. That nation was already in a tumult, in the midst of which demonstrations in favor of a republic were prominent, and while the German government was considering the terms of the armistice the Kaiser abdicated and fled to Holland, and a new cabinet was formed with a Socialist at the head. The end was evidently at hand and on November 11th the world was cheered with the news that Germany had signed the armistice and the war was over.[32]

them in his addresses. Thus the idea of "self-determination" was one of them,—the same idea that was suggested in the Fourteen Points where the demand was made that peoples subject to Austria and Turkey be allowed to develop along lines chosen by themselves. *Cf.* Seymour, in *Atlantic Monthly*, June, 1924, "America's Responsibility to Germany."

[32] An Armistice had been signed with Turkey on October 31st, and with Austria on November 4th.

BIBLIOGRAPHICAL NOTE

The opposition to the Wilson foreign policy is best expressed in Theodore Roosevelt, *Fear God and take Your Own Part* (1916). Roosevelt's condonation of the invasion of Belgium is in *The Outlook* (Sept., 1914), "The World War." Wilson's changing attitude toward the war is best followed in his addresses and messages. See also J. Daniels, *The Life of Woodrow Wilson* (1924); D. Lawrence, *The True Story of Woodrow Wilson* (1924); J. P. Tumulty, *Woodrow Wilson as I Know Him* (1921); W. C. Redfield, *With Congress and Cabinet* (1924). The early stages of the war and American interest in it are described in Ogg; *The American Year Book;* J. B. McMaster, *The United States in the World War* (1918); J. W. Gerard, *My Four Years in Germany* (1918), written by the American Ambassador; Brand Whitlock, *Belgium* (2 vols., 1919), verbose, but well written by the United States minister to Belgium; Count Bernstoff, *My Three Years in America* (1920); Grand Admiral von Tirpitz, *My Memoirs* (2 vols., 1919); Dodd already mentioned; J. S. Bassett, *Our War with Germany* (1919), written in excellent spirit; B. J. Hendrick, *Life and Letters of W. H. Page* (3 vols., 1924–1925); on the Zimmerman letters *World's Work,* Nov., 1925, pp. 23–36; G. Creel, *How We Advertized America* (1920); N. D. Baker, *Frontiers of Freedom* (1918) contains war addresses by the Secretary of War; C. Seymour, "War Time Relations of America and Great Britain" in *Atlantic Monthly,* May, 1924. The President's address calling for a declaration of war is contained in the various editions of his addresses, and in *War Information Series,* No. 1, "The War Message and Facts Behind it," published by the Committee on Public Information.

The subject of federal agencies for the prosecution of the war is fully discussed in W. F. Willoughby, *Government Organization in War Time and After* (1919); and E. L. Bogart "Economic Organization for War" in *American Political Science Review,* 1920, p. 587; G. B. Clarkson, *Industrial America in the World War* (1923), is authoritative. See S. Gompers, *Seventy Years of Life and Labor* (2 vols., 1925), on labor's function in the war. There is no adequate account of the Committee on Public Information, but an excellent brief statement is by G. S. Ford in *The Historical Outlook* (March, 1920, pp. 97–100). E. L. Bogart, *Direct and Indirect Costs of the Great World War* (1918), is useful.

Combat operations are described in the general histories of the war already mentioned, and in "Report of General Pershing" in War Department, *Annual Report*, 1918. The annual reports of the War Department, the Navy Department, and such organizations as the Red Cross are invaluable. See also T. G. Frothingham, *A Guide to the Military History of the World War* (1921); B. Crowell and R. F. Wilson, *How America Went to War* (6 vols., 1921); C. H. Hayes *Brief History of the Great War* (1923); W. S. Sims, *The Victory at Sea* (1920); S. Thomas, *The History of the A. E. F.* (1920); L. P. Ayres, *The War with Germany, a statistical Summary* (1919), is by the chief of the Statistical Branch of the General Staff; C. G. Dawes, *A Journal of the Great War* (2 vols., 1921).

CHAPTER XXVI

RECONSTRUCTION—AGAIN

Probably to no other human being in all history did the hopes, the prayers, the aspirations of so many of his fellows turn with such poignant intensity as to him [President Wilson] at the close of the war.

GENERAL J. C. SMUTS.

There was another object which I had very much at heart, and that was that if we were successful in putting on reservations we should create a situation where, if the acceptance of the treaty [of Versailles] was defeated, the Democratic party, and especially Mr. Wilson's friends, should be responsible for its defeat.

HENRY CABOT LODGE.

We pledge ourselves to a carefully planned readjustment to a peace-time basis and to a policy of rigid economy.

REPUBLICAN PLATFORM, 1920.

Present industrial conditions make this time particularly opportune for employers to take a forward step in the matter of industrial relations . . . it is time to abandon the methods of opposition and strife and to set up the machinery of friendly intercourse and cooperation between employers and employees.

COMMITTEE ON INDUSTRIAL RELATIONS OF THE MERCHANTS' ASSOCIATION OF NEW YORK, MARCH 8, 1921.

With his products not selling on a parity with the products of industry, every sound remedy that can be devised should be applied for the relief of the farmer.

PRESIDENT CALVIN COOLIDGE, December 6, 1923.

INTERNATIONAL AND POLITICAL RECONSTRUCTION

"UPON the signing of the armistice," said Secretary of War Baker, "it was necessary to throw into reverse the machinery which was at that time working at maximum capacity in pushing troops to France." In addition to the more than 2,000,000 men in the A. E. F., nearly 2,250.000 other soldiers and sailors had to be discharged; and 11,400,000 civilian war workers, both men and women, gradually returned to their usual peace-time pursuits. As quickly as possible the members of the A. E. F. were brought to debarkation ports, given a careful physical examination, provided with fresh clothing, transported to America and finally discharged at camps in or near the states from which they had come. By August, 1919, General Pershing and the 1st. Division of regulars sailed home from Brest— the last of the combat troops—leaving about 11,000 officers and men to share with the Allies the responsibility of keeping Germany to the terms of the armistice.[1] The return of more than fifteen and a half million participants in the war constituted a difficult economic problem. Most of them, of course, were quickly absorbed in the pursuits which had engaged them before the war began. In addition, the War Department cooperated with the Department of Labor and with business organizations everywhere in the attempt to find places for men who could find no employment.

In its industrial relations the War Department faced another huge process of readjustment. During the war the government had assumed control of the essential raw materials— all of the wool, for example—and had strictly regulated the production, transportation and sale of many other commodities. Contracts had been let, calling for the procurement of several billions of dollars' worth of war supplies. All these activities had to be reduced as quickly as possible without completely dislocating the economic life of the country. Within a year 22,600 government contracts out of 25,000 were settled which affected agreements amounting to $2,000,000,000. In addition to its contracts calling for the future delivery of sup-

[1] By the terms of the armistice, Germany was to evacuate all invaded countries; surrender a great quantity of artillery, planes and other war material; withdraw its troops beyond the Rhine; deliver 5,000 locomotives and 150,000 cars to the Allies; and surrender all submarines, and seventy-four warships and destroyers. Many smaller provisions were also included. The entire text may be found in Bassett, *U. S. and the World War*, II, pp. 450–458.

plies the government found itself in the possession of several
more billions of dollars' worth of surplus material of all kinds.
Much of it was in France, and consisted of docks and warehouses, as well as movable goods. The United States Liqui-

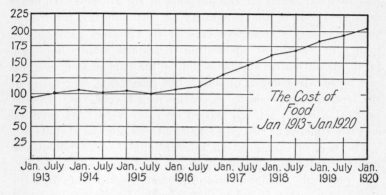

The Cost of
Food
Jan. 1913–Jan. 1920

dation Commission was appointed to dispose of the properties
abroad. Within two years, more than $800,000,000 worth
were sold, about half of it to the French government. In the
United States over $1,000,000,000 worth were sold. Alto-
gether the surplus cost probably twice as much as it brought
in the market.

In addition to caring for the unemployed veteran, the government made an attempt to reconstruct the sick and wounded.
All known branches of medicine, surgery and physical training were called upon for assistance in repairing the injured.
Electro-therapy, calisthenics, mental and manual work and a
host of other expedients were tried. Occupational activities
were given the men in order to keep their minds busy, repair physical damage and, if possible, teach them trades
which might enable them to earn a livelihood even though
physically impaired. At the beginning of 1920 over 20,000
patients were receiving special vocational training, of whom
nearly three-fourths were discharged by the close of the year.

In 1921 the United States Veterans' Bureau was established to handle the claims of soldiers for pay and insurance, and to continue the care and reconstruction of the sick and wounded. Up to the close of the fiscal year 1925, over three billion dollars had been expended for the purposes of the Bureau. In order further to show the generosity of the country toward its soldiers, many states gave each of its veterans payments of money or "bonuses" amounting to several hundreds of dollars. Agitation for similar action on the part of Congress was met by the determined opposition of presidents, secretaries of the treasury and even by ex-service men themselves. Finally in 1924 a bonus act was passed over the veto. Its eventual cost is estimated at two and a half to three billions of dollars.

The task of inaugurating international reconstruction was unprecedented in its magnitude, as the war itself had been. The political, economic and diplomatic affairs of half the world were either in ruins or facing the imminent danger of catastrophe. In order to have a reckoning with Germany and her allies, and to launch an effort to stabilize the affairs of the world, a Peace Conference was called at Versailles. "New States had to be created, territories redistributed, indemnities secured and all upon a scale incomparably greater than any international conference or congress had ever before attempted to deal with."

The representatives of the United States were President Wilson, Robert Lansing (the Secretary of State), Henry White (former ambassador to Italy and France), Edward M. House and General Tasker H. Bliss. A numerous body of experts, ("The Inquiry"), was also taken—geographers, historians and others—who had been studying the ethnic, economic and political affairs of the warring countries since 1917. These men constituted a new element in the settlement of international relations, and were of vast assistance to the American peace commission in its attempt to find the facts about controverted questions.

Unhappily Mr. Wilson did not carry with him the undivided support of his fellow citizens. In November, 1918, just before the close of the war, there had occurred the usual Congressional elections. Foreseeing the great advantage of a strong political backing, the President had urged the country to elect a Democratic Congress, declaring that the Republican leaders in Washington, although favorable to the war, had been hostile to the administration, and that the election of a Republican majority would enable them to obstruct a legislative program. Although Roosevelt had made a similar request during his presidency, the action was almost unprecedented. The Republicans asserted that Wilson had challenged the motives and fidelity of their party. In the ensuing election, the control of both branches of Congress was won by the Republicans. It is impossible to judge whether the President's appeal recoiled seriously against his party or whether the tendency to reaction against the administration at mid-term, which has been so common since the Civil War, was the decisive force. In any case, however, Wilson was compelled to go to Paris hampered with political defeat. Moreover, the Chairman of the Senate Committee on Foreign Affairs, Henry Cabot Lodge, was to be his bitter enemy, and the majority of the remaining members were also opposed to the administration's foreign policy.

In the meanwhile the American commission proceeded to Europe, where Wilson was received with boundless enthusiasm. Never perhaps have the hopes of a weary world turned quite so unanimously to a single figure. Wilson, it was understood, represented a "right" settlement, a settlement based on justice and the principle of self-determination. The war, it had been said on all sides, was to be the world's last combat— "the war to end war." To Wilson the world looked for the touch which should transmute these ideals into golden reality.

The difficulties in the way of satisfying even the simplest of these hopes were scarcely short of insurmountable. Four years of the most savage war had prepared the world for revenge, for retribution and for indemnity, not for a peace based on conciliation and clemency. As soon would Charles Sumner and Thaddeus Stevens have joined Abraham Lincoln in a reconstruction program founded on "charity for all." Would not justice for France demand the spoliation and crippling of Germany? Would not recompense for Belgium mean a crushing indemnity placed upon her foes? Would not a fair-minded Wilson help Italy and Serbia, Poland and Czecho-Slovakia get all the territory which they severally believed was theirs by right? In short, the world was far from agreed as to what was in fact fair and right. Lloyd George, the Prime Minister of England, had carried his party to victory on the principle that Germany should be compelled to pay the entire cost of the war. Italy had entered the lists with the Allies as the result of the secret Treaty of London in 1915, which promised the Italians, in the event of victory, large additions of territory north and east of the Adriatic Sea. As much of this land was inhabited by peoples who were not Italians at all, it was evident that spoils and not justice were the fundamental considerations. Japan had in like manner been promised the rights of Germany in Chinese Shantung. Obviously the transfer of such territories in calm disregard of the wishes of the inhabitants defied completely the American contention of self-determination. And yet—although these secret agreements were cast in the mold of secret diplomacy, they were nevertheless the sworn obligations of England, France and the rest of the Allies. Would a "just" peace turn these commitments into "scraps of paper"?

The old and the new diplomacy, the passing and the coming order in international relations were in reality locking horns for a great conflict. The armistice had been signed and the war brought to a close on the understanding that the peace negotiations would be founded on the "Fourteen Points"— the end of secret understandings, an opportunity for subject peoples to develop along lines chosen by themselves, and an association of nations to guarantee the safety of large and small nations alike.[2] As soon as the armistice was signed, however, the idealism which had somewhat characterized the allied statement of war aims began to wear through, and to show underneath the solid substratum of a natural, human instinct to seize the spoils of victory.

The deliberations of the Peace Conference consumed the entire six months from January to June of 1919, and even a superficial account of all the problems it was compelled to face would require a shelf-full of volumes. The results of the work, however, may be judged by a brief survey of a few outstanding questions. One was the disposal of Germany's colonial possessions, which some of the leaders desired to distribute among the Allies in accord with well-worn practice in such cases. Instead, the principle of "mandates" was originated, by which the colonies were to become the property of a league of the states of the world, and be administered by trustee nations for the benefit of the colonies. The second question was the disposal of the Saar valley, a portion of Germany rich in coal fields, near the French border, but inhabited entirely by Germans. France desired the Saar as compensation for the German destruction of French mines. The solution was novel. The coal fields were awarded to France, but the valley itself was to be placed under the control of the league for fifteen years. At the end of that time the inhabitants will vote where they will place their allegiance.

More contentious was the disposal of Shantung. During the controversies over other questions, the Japanese preserved an immobile silence, preferring apparently to allow the most interested participants to have their way. But when it came to the leases of Germany in China, the Japanese would have their Shantung. To refuse categorically seemed likely to

[2] *Cf.* p. 663. The Allies had expressly reserved, however, the point about the freedom of the seas, and had secured Wilson's approval of compensation for damage done to civilians by Germany.

wreck the conference, and with it the peace of the world.   Five
nations had taken the lead at Paris—the United States, Great
Britain, France, Italy and Japan.   The Italians had already
left because their full claims under the secret Treaty of London had not been granted; if now the Japanese left, as they
threatened to do, the risk of a breakdown was too great.
Nevertheless, Wilson procured a promise that Japan would retire under certain conditions from the Shantung peninsula,
and this he had to balance against the danger of getting no
results at all.

Another bitterly contested point was the size of the indemnity or reparations to be demanded of the loser.   English and
French leaders had encouraged their people to expect impossible sums,—Lloyd George going so far as to name $120,-
000,000,000 as the amount.   American experts estimated Germany's capacity to pay at a quarter of that figure.   For Lloyd
George and Clemenceau (the leader of the French delegation)
to accept so small an indemnity for all that England and
France had suffered seemed likely to mean their dismissal
from office.   Wilson, on the other hand, desired to fix a definite sum so that Germany and the rest of the world might
know what was to be expected.   So complete was this *impasse*
that the Reparation Commission was established, composed of
representatives of the United States, Great Britain, France
and Italy, together with other nations when their interests
were involved.   To it was delegated the task of determining
the amount of Germany's damages, and of drawing up a schedule of payments extending over a period of thirty years beginning May 1, 1921.   In the meanwhile Germany was to pay
the equivalent of five billion dollars.

Most important of all, in the mind of President Wilson was
the establishment of an association of the nations of the world
to act as a clearing house for the study and settlement of international disputes.   Lacking such an organization, the world
would forthwith divide into new alliances and ententes, thus

preparing the way for another world war. In this opinion he was backed by Americans of all parties, including eminent Republicans like ex-President Taft and Elihu Root, and by publicists in many of the allied countries like Lord Robert Cecil and General Smuts. The compromises which Wilson agreed to—like that concerning Shantung—were based on the belief that small evils might be tolerated if necessary to attain the greater good. The principle of a League of Nations was approved without dissent on January 25 (1919), but the details of its organization were the source of almost endless debate. In mid-February a "Covenant" or constitution for the League was completed and President Wilson returned to America to spend a short time in explaining its provisions and discovering and trying to meet the objections of several prominent American public men. It was ominous that opposition was fast growing in the Senate—the very body which would ratify or reject the work of the Conference. Nevertheless, on April 28th the Conference adopted the Covenant, including an amendment, suggested by American objectors, which expressly stated that none of its provisions should be deemed to affect the validity of the Monroe Doctrine. Including the Covenant of the League, the Peace Treaty was at length completed and signed on June 28th.

By its provisions, Germany ceded Alsace-Lorraine to France, and large portions of eastern Germany to Poland; her colonies were relinquished; her army was reduced to 100,000 men; she assumed payment of damages as assessed by the Reparation Commission; and until the treaty was carried out the Allies were to occupy strategic points on the Rhine.

The Covenant of the League of Nations provided for two representative bodies, an Assembly and a Council. The Assembly was to be composed of delegates from all the member nations; the Council was to contain permanent representatives of five leading powers, the United States, Great Britain, France, Italy and Japan, to which were to be added representatives of four other nations, to be chosen by the Assembly "from time to time in its discretion." Of equal importance, perhaps, in actual operation is the Secretariat, which consists of a Secretary General and a staff of assistants. This is the permanent, active working force of the League. The fundamental purpose of the organization is to minimize the likelihood of international conflicts, by drawing up plans for decreasing armament, establishing a Permanent Court of International Justice, registering treaties with the League so as to do away with secret agreements, and severing economic relations with nations which enter upon war in violation of their obligations under the Covenant.[3]

The next step was to refer the treaty, including the Covenant of the League to the Senate, which has the constitutional right of consenting or refusing to consent to such arrangements. Here the situation was confusing, not to say ominous. By a narrow margin, that body was in the control of the Republicans and the Committee on Foreign Relations was headed, as has been seen, by an opponent of the President, while its other members were, on the whole, only less opposed than Senator Lodge. Moreover, Wilson had not taken care to make the Senate feel that it had been closely in touch with the negotiations at Paris from the start. He had not, for example, appointed any member of that body on the Commission; nor had he kept moving to senators who might be spokesmen for him a flow of confidential information concerning the difficulties which the Conference met, and the compromises which

---

[3] Impartial students of the Paris Conference disagree as to the amount of success achieved by President Wilson in infusing a new spirit into international relations. Although written as far back as 1921, Professor Seymour's statement seems to me the most fair-minded: " . . . the future historian will probably hold that the Peace Conference, with all its selfish interests and mistakes, carried into effect an amazingly large part of President Wilson's programme, when all the difficulties of his position are duly weighed." *Woodrow Wilson and the World War*, pp. 323 *ff*.

seemed to be necessary, while negotiations were in progress. In accord with custom, the treaty was referred to the Committee on Foreign Relations, from which it emerged with thirty-eight amendments and four reservations, including a vigorous condemnation of Wilson's treatment of the Senate. Against such changes Wilson stood stiffly and not over-tactfully.

Then ensued eight months of debate and vain attempts at amendment. Most of the Democrats were willing to ratify the treaty as it stood; a small group, mainly of Republicans, were bitterly opposed—"the bitter-enders"; others were willing to vote for ratification if reservations were added to make sure that the United States could not be committed by the League to serious acts—like war, for example,—without a vote by Congress. In other words they feared that adhesion to the League might deprive the United States of part of its sovereignty and restrict its possibilities of independent action. Nor was the debate permeated solely by the question of the virtues or defects of the treaty. The election of 1920 was soon forthcoming. The ratification of the treaty would make Wilson the outstanding figure in the world, enhance the reputation of his party and provide it with accomplishments which would make unexampled campaign material.

And so the debate tailed off into a wrangle not unlike that which Lincoln and Johnson suffered during an earlier reconstruction epoch. In despair Wilson set out in September, 1919, to urge popular support for his treaty, hoping in that way to get favorable action. But the task was too great for a man whose physical resources, none too great at best, had been sapped by more than six anxious years in the presidency and the uncommon strains of the Paris Conference. Late in the month he collapsed and had to be brought back to Washington. He never regained his strength. At the most important time, therefore, the friends of the treaty were left without leadership. When, on March 19, 1920, a vote was taken, ratification lacked seven votes of the necessary two-thirds.[4] The Senate had defeated Wilson's foreign policy as it had defeated the Lincoln-Johnson plan for reconstructing the South.

While the treaty of peace was coming to naught, so far as the United States was concerned, the execution of the Espionage Act and similar laws indicated that the question of freedom of speech was as contentious a problem during the World War as it had been in the Civil War. The espionage law of June 15, 1917, had forbidden attempts to incite disloyalty and to procure military information to be used to the injury of the United States. This was strengthened by the act of May 16, 1918, which forbade the utterance of any scurrilous or abusive language about the American form of government, the Constitution, the military forces or the flag. The penalty was a fine of $10,000 or twenty years in prison or both. Nearly 2,000 cases were prosecuted under these laws, and many persons were given the drastic prison penalty. Unhappily the legislation was so loosely woven as to give over-zealous officials an opportunity to misuse their power and greatly to endanger the traditional American freedom of speech. A woman was tried, for example, for saying "I am for the people, and the government is for the profiteers," and sentenced to ten years in prison (although the decision was reversed in 1920). While the trial was in progress these presumably dangerous words were repeated in the newspaper accounts of the case throughout the country.

Other over-zealous officials feared that the safety of the country was being endangered by radical, alien anarchists.

4 Some observers think that if the President had accepted the suggested reservations early and sympathetically, instead of tardily and reluctantly, he might have obtained the consent of the Senate. This opinion is based on the assumption that the reservationists would generally have accepted the treaty if he had agreed to their conditions. Other observers believe that if he had agreed to the early reservations, still more would have been added, the purpose being to discredit the President before the next election.

Their reliance was an act of October 16, 1918, which allowed the Secretary of Labor to deport aliens who advocated the overthrow of the government or the unlawful destruction of property, or belonged to any organization which upheld such doctrines. There was no jury trial and no appeal from the decision of the Secretary. Since the Secretary could scarcely try the cases in person or even interview the accused, he had to delegate the authority to officials here and there throughout the country. During 1919 many arrests were made, and in December, 249 people were deported in the *Buford*. Vigorous protests resulted from eminent lawyers, including members of the law faculties of Harvard and the University of Chicago. The Secretary of Labor, William B. Wilson, and his assistant, L. F. Post, were reluctant to enforce the law, and action under it promptly slackened.

The same fear that American institutions were unstable was illustrated in the removal of five Socialist members by the legislature of the state of New York. The action was forcefully condemned by the Bar Association of the state, and by a former Republican governor, Charles E. Hughes, as well as by non-Socialists in other states. Mr. Hughes asserted "This is not, in my judgment, American government." The five Socialists were re-elected by their constituents, only to be ousted again. The legislature then desisted from further action against radicals, but it had succeeded in rousing unusual interest in the Socialist party and sympathy with its members.[5]

The effect of the war is also seen in the climax of the prohibition movement in 1919. The use of intoxicating liquors has long been condemned by the religious forces of America, but not until after the Civil War did organization proceed on a national scale. In 1869 the National Prohibition Party was formed; in 1874, the Woman's Christian Temperance Union;

[5] More accurately, three were ousted the second time, and the other two resigned because of the decision.

and in 1893 the Anti-Saloon League. Efforts were made to get towns or states to adopt prohibition laws or constitutional amendments. By 1900, five states had acted; by 1919, thirty-two. The World War came at an opportune time for the prohibition campaign. In the first place, intoxicating liquors in the hands of soldiers and particularly of officers who commanded large military forces would almost certainly do great harm. In the next place, it was illogical to urge the country to restrict its food-consumption and make great efforts to enlarge production, when more than seven billion pounds of food materials were demanded for the distilling and brewing of intoxicants. Accordingly the sale of liquor to men in uniform was forbidden, and on August 1, 1917, the Eighteenth Amendment was sent to the people. Its ratification was announced on January 16, 1919, to go into effect a year later.[6]

The law providing for the enforcement of the amendment, popularly known as the Volstead Act, was passed (over President Wilson's veto), on October 28, 1919. The degree to which the law has since been broken has given rise to an acute political question: the opponents of the act declare that the statute should be weakened or the amendment repealed; while its friends assert that the people have amended their Constitution in the legal manner and that obedience to the law is the only safety in a democracy.[7]

Neither the facts which have just been mentioned, nor the economic tendencies which will presently be recounted had

[6] The Eighteenth Amendment is as follows:
Section 1. After one year from the ratification of this article the manufacture, sale, or transportation of intoxicating liquors within, the importation thereof into, or the exportation thereof from the United States and all territory subject to the jurisdiction thereof for beverage purposes is hereby prohibited.
Section 2. The Congress and the several states shall have concurrent power to enforce this article by appropriate legislation.
Section 3. This article shall be inoperative unless it shall have been ratified as an amendment to the Constitution by the legislatures of the several states, as provided in the Constitution, within seven years from the date of the submission hereof to the states by the Congress.
[7] For the Nineteenth Amendment, see above p. 520.

much relation to the political campaign which took place in 1920. The Republicans met in Chicago on June 8. Several leaders, notably General Leonard Wood, Governor F. O. Lowden and Senator Hiram Johnson had large followings who favored them for the presidency. When it became evident that no one of them could obtain the nomination quickly, some of the party chiefs met and determined to urge Senator W. G. Harding, who was subsequently chosen. Calvin Coolidge was the vice-presidential candidate. The Democrats met in San Francisco on June 28. W. G. McAdoo and A. Mitchell Palmer of President Wilson's cabinet, together with Governor J. M. Cox of Ohio, were the leading candidates. As no one of them could command the necessary two-thirds vote and as there was no small group of party chiefs who could dominate the convention, forty-four ballots were necessary before Governor Cox was chosen. Franklin D. Roosevelt, Assistant Secretary of the Navy was the vice-presidential nominee.

President Wilson had hoped that the campaign might be a "solemn referendum" on the subject of the treaty and the League. The problem for the Democrats was simple. Their party had led in advocacy of the League and, whether enthusiastically or not, they accepted it as an issue. In the Republican party a critical situation had developed. The old breach between Progressives and Conservatives had been healed, but opinions on the League were antipodal. Taft, Hughes, Hoover and Root were leaders in their advocacy of the League. Borah, Johnson, Knox and others were the bitterest of "bitter-enders." The League plank in the platform reflected the difficulty which the party chieftains experienced in preventing a schism. It condemned Wilson's attitude toward the Senate, declared that the covenant had departed from the principles of Washington, Jefferson and Monroe to an unnecessary degree, and pledged the party to "an international association" which would not involve the "compromise of the national independence." The "bitter-enders" looked upon this as a complete repudiation of the treaty and the League. On the other hand Root, Hughes, Hoover and others of the leaders of the party issued a public statement urging pro-leaguers to vote for Harding. The Republican party, they asserted, was "bound by every consideration of good faith" to bring about American entrance into the League with reservations. Mr. Harding's stand was not quite clear. At first he had favored the Covenant of the League with some clarifying reservations, but as time went on he seemingly shifted toward the position taken by Johnson and Borah and finally stated in the campaign "it is not interpretation but rejection I am seeking."

In the midst of such confusion it is perhaps not surprising that the campaign and election turned less upon the League issue than upon the attitude of the country toward President Wilson. The note of personal antipathy was first struck officially by Senator Lodge, acting as chairman of the Republican nominating convention:

Mr. Wilson stands for a theory of administration and government which is not American. His methods, his constant if indirect assaults, upon the Constitution and upon all the traditions of free governments, strike at the very life of the American principles upon which our Government has always rested. . . . Many vital economic measures and especially protective tariff legislation . . . are impossible with a Democratic Free Trader of Socialistic proclivities in the White House.

In addition to the normal partisan opposition, there was much complaint in regard to President Wilson's administration. The German element disliked him because they believed that he had assisted the Allies in making the peace treaty a severe one. Italian-Americans were angry because he had opposed the cession of Fiume to Italy. Other elements deeply resented the enforcement of the espionage laws and the deportation of aliens. The result was the choice of Harding and Coolidge by a plurality of 7,000,000, the Republicans receiving 16,000,000 and the Democrats 9,000,000 votes, and the election of Republican majorities in both houses of Congress. So interested an observer as Mr. Coolidge asserted soon afterwards "I doubt if any particular mandate was given at the last election on the question of the League of Nations and if that was the preponderant issue."[8]

The accession of Mr. Harding to the presidency[9] brought to an end the deadlock between the executive and legislative branches of the government. Hitherto the official termination of the war had been prevented on the one hand by the refusal of the Senate to ratify the treaty of Versailles, and on the other by the opposition of Wilson to a separate peace between the United States and her late enemies. It was not until July 2, 1921, therefore, that a joint resolution passed Congress and was signed by the President, which declared the war at an end. By this resolution the United States reserved to itself all the rights and advantages which it would have obtained if it had ratified the treaty of Versailles and the treaty of St. Germain (which the Allies had negotiated with Austria). The obligations contained in the treaties and the enforcement of their

---

[8] Some emphasis was also placed during the campaign on the large amounts of money spent by the administration during the war. A congressional committee was appointed to investigate the charges that money had been wasted or mis-spent. The most interesting witness was Gen. Charles G. Dawes, a life-long Republican, and former General Purchasing Agent in Europe for the A. E. F. He testified that the war was "not a Republican or a Democratic war; it was an American war"; that the investigation was a partisan attempt to find fly-specks in the conduct of the war; and that the essential thing was to win the war and not "keep a double-entry system of books." Most important of all, his testimony was so racy that it was widely read and left the impression that the financial conduct of the war had, on the whole, been unimpeachable. *Cf.* N. Y. *Times,* Feb. 4, 1921.

[9] The cabinet from 1921 to 1926 was as follows: Secretary of State, C. E. Hughes, F. B. Kellogg; Secretary of the Treasury, A. W. Mellon; Secretary of War, J. W. Weeks, D. F. Davis; Attorney General, H. M. Daugherty, H. F. Stone, J. G. Sargent; Postmaster General, W. H. Hays, H. S. New; Secretary of the Navy, E. Denby, C. D. Wilbur; Secretary of the Interior, A. B. Fall, H. Work; Secretary of Agriculture, H. C. Wallace, H. M. Gore, W. M. Jardine; Secretary of Commerce, H. C. Hoover; Secretary of Labor, J. J. Davis.

provisions were left to our allies. Separate treaties were then arranged with Germany and Austria, and proclaimed in November, 1921, which more definitely pointed out the exact portions of the treaties of Versailles and St. Germain to which the United States agreed.

Thus far the administration had merely brought the war legally and constitutionally to a close. It could not, however, fail to recognize the wide-spread demand for some action which might make another world war less likely; and, moreover, there was the platform promise about an "association" of nations. A Conference on the Limitation of Armament was accordingly called to meet in Washington on November 12, 1921. The countries represented were the United States, Belgium, the British Empire, China, France, Italy, Japan, the Netherlands and Portugal.

The first day of the Conference, said Mr. A. J. Balfour, the leader of the British delegation, was a "fateful opening," "the inspired moment" on which all the later events turned. On that day Secretary Hughes astounded the delegates by proposing a radical reduction in the world's naval program. For the United States he proposed that thirty war vessels—half of them new ships under construction—be immediately scrapped; that Great Britain similarly destroy nineteen battleships; and Japan seventeen. He also suggested that the nations agree to a construction holiday of ten years and that the chief navies of the world be kept at the following relative strength so far as the larger or "capital" ships are concerned: the United States and Great Britain, 5; Japan, 3; France and Italy, 1.6. This astonishing and radical proposal was agreed to and put into the form of a treaty.

The next accomplishment of the Conference was an attempt to do away with the great dangers to world peace in the Pacific. Neither the United States nor Japan had the remotest idea of initiating a war about their possessions or interests in the Pacific, but large groups in each country were apprehensive of an attack by the other. Japanese troops were still in the Shantung peninsula; the twenty-one demands upon China drawn up by Japan in 1915 were making the former a protectorate of the island kingdom; the Lansing-Ishii agreement of 1917 had recognized the special interests of Japan in China; and Japanese troops were still in Siberia, having remained there since the World War. Moreover, the alliance between Great Britain and Japan, made in 1911, caused no little uneasiness in the United States. As against these disquieting facts there was only the policy of the "open door" in China, a principle which had proven of great value, but which was only a policy, nevertheless, not a binding international obligation.

Three treaties arranged during the Washington Conference were designed to eliminate these dangers. The Four Power Treaty among the United States, the British Empire, France and Japan terminated the Anglo-Japanese agreement of 1911, and bound the four powers to call a joint conference in case controversies arose over their island possessions in the Pacific which could not be settled by diplomacy. A treaty between China and Japan bound the latter to evacuate Shantung.[10]

A third treaty was entered into by the four larger powers, together with Belgium, China, Italy, the Netherlands and Portugal, generally called the Nine Power Treaty. China agreed, on her part, not to exercise any unfair discrimination on the Chinese railways, and the other powers proposed to maintain equal opportunities for the trade of all nations, respect the sovereignty of China, and give her the fullest opportunity to develop a stable government. The Open Door was "nailed open," and China received its Magna Charta.[11]

[10] When this agreement was announced, Mr. Balfour, on behalf of Great Britain, stated the purpose of his country to restore Wei-Hai-Wei to China.

[11] As a result of this treaty the Lansing-Ishii agreement was abrogated in 1923.

In appointing the American delegates to the Conference, President Harding had prepared the way for ratification in the Senate by appointing Senator Lodge, the chairman of the Committee on Foreign Relations, and Senator Underwood, the leader on the Democratic side. (The other delegates were Secretary Hughes and Elihu Root.) The ratification of the treaties to which the United States was a party met with little opposition except in the case of the Four Power agreement, which was accepted with only four votes in excess of the required two-thirds.

The success of the administration in the Washington Conference closed its open and official effort in the direction of greater international concord.[12] President Harding himself shifted from advocacy of the League with reservations to outright opposition. Despite the fact that both Hughes and Hoover were in the cabinet, no project for an "association of nations" was launched, nor was any public attempt made to re-open the question of American entry into the League. Our remaining associates in the World War, however, continued their interest, and the League came officially into being on January 1, 1920. Before the close of 1921, it had fifty-one members, had organized, had begun to hold regular meetings at Geneva, and was attempting the settlement of international difficulties. Its secretariat or permanent working force comprised 300 persons of thirty-six nationalities, who were divided into groups for the intensive study of such problems as mandates, disarmament, and the international opium traffic. In pursuance of President Wilson's advocacy of open diplomacy, the Covenant of the League required all treaties between member nations to be registered with the secretariat, and thereafter made public. More than 300 international agreements were thus recorded before March 1, 1923.

The project for a Permanent Court of International Justice was immediately taken up by the League, and a committee ap-

[12] Except in regard to the World Court. *Cf.* p. 689.

pointed to formulate a plan of organization. Elihu Root was one of its members. As soon as the plan or "statute" was ratified by the member nations, the fifteen judges were selected (of whom an American, John Bassett Moore was one), and sessions began in 1922. The jurisdiction of the Court is confined to cases which nations voluntarily refer to it, or which are referred to it by treaties and conventions. Nations may also bind themselves to the compulsory arbitration before the Court of disputes which arise with other nations. The judges decide cases by the application of treaties, international law and international custom, rather than by compromise,— by law rather than by bargain.

Inasmuch as almost all the remainder of the civilized world soon joined the League and the Court, the United States found itself in an embarrassing position. The separate treaties with Germany and Austria forbid the president to appoint a representative of the United States on any committee created by the Treaty of Versailles unless Congress gives permission. If carried out in letter and spirit, such a prohibition would insulate the United States from much that is going on in world affairs. Secretary Hughes resorted, therefore, to "unofficial observers" who are sent to cooperate with League committees or agencies, but are not official delegates. "So far as our Government is concerned," said Mr. Hughes, "they represent it just as completely as those designated by the President always have represented our government." In addition, private citizens and representatives of philanthropic organizations have greatly assisted the League, serving on committees of many kinds and cooperating in its financial projects.[13]

More striking yet was the connection of the United States with the question of German reparations, which had been left by the Treaty of Versailles in the hands of a Commission. When disagreements between Germany and France over this

[13] See the succinct account of this aspect in Blakeslee, *Recent Foreign Policy*, pp. 39–50.

matter seemed likely to result in a serious conflict, Secretary Hughes urged in 1922 that the governments concerned choose representatives to recommend a plan for making the payments. The suggestion resulted in the appointment of a group of financial experts by the Reparation Commission, of whom three Americans were leading members,—General C. G. Dawes, Owen D. Young and H. M. Robinson. The experts presented the Dawes plan—understood to be largely the work of Mr. Young. A conference was then held in London in 1924 at which the agreements were drawn up which were necessary to put the plan into operation. Mr. Kellogg, the American Ambassador to England attended to look out for the interests of America; Mr. Hughes happened to be in England, and so also did the Secretary of the Treasury, Mr. Mellon, and they took an unofficial part in the negotiations. In the outcome, Americans were placed in several of the important places in carrying the plan into practical operation. As the United States had claims against Germany amounting to $450,000,000 on account of damage done since 1914, and for loans made to that country after the war by our citizens, the success of the new reparations system became very much an American interest. The appointment of unofficial advisors enabled the administration to circumvent the prohibition against cooperation with the League, and it did away with the necessity of obtaining the consent of the Senate to the choice of delegates. For, as the President well knew, the nomination of strictly official participants in the reparations controversy would have aroused a long and bitter debate in the upper house.[14]

[14] Under the Dawes plan, Germany was to pay to the Allies the first year about $250,000,000, obtained from the railroads, loans and industry. A bank was established in Germany which, under joint German and allied control, acts as the depository and fiscal agent of the German government. French troops which had been in the Ruhr were to be withdrawn. On the acceptance of the plan by the German authorities, the Reparation Commission declared the Dawes plan in operation and appointed Mr. Young as Agent General to see to its administration.

On August 2, 1923, President Harding died and was succeeded by Vice-President Calvin Coolidge, who continued his predecessor's cabinet and general policies of administration.

The presidential election of 1924 did little to further reconstruction in the field of international relations. The Republicans nominated President Coolidge and Charles G. Dawes; the Democrats, John W. Davis, former ambassador to Great Britain, and Charles W. Bryan. Dissatisfied members of both organizations united to form the Progressive party, which nominated a Republican, Robert M. La Follette, for president, and a Democrat, Burton K. Wheeler, for the vice-presidency. The Republican position on the League had definitely shifted since 1920. "This Government has definitely refused membership in the League of Nations," ran the platform statement, "and to assume any obligations under the Covenant of the League. On this we stand." It did, however, indorse the Permanent Court of International Justice. The Democrats renewed their "declaration of confidence in the ideals of world peace, the League of Nations and the World Court." The campaign failed to focus clearly on this issue or any other, however, and in the ensuing election Coolidge received over 15,700,000 votes, while Davis received 8,800,000 and La Follette 4,670,000.

As soon as he was inaugurated, President Coolidge again urged that the United States enter the World Court. In doing so, he advised the passage of several explanatory reservations or conditions. The most important were that in entering the Court we would not assume any obligations under the League; that we should have the right to participate in the election of judges; and that the statute establishing the Court should not be amended without our consent. Despite the fact

In order to set Germany financially on its feet, a loan of $200,000,000 was offered her, half of which was subscribed in the United States. The American claims against Germany are for the costs of the Army of Occupation, loans, and damages claimed by American citizens since 1914.

that both the major parties had committed themselves to such a step, the "bitter-enders" in the Senate were able to hold up action until 1926. At that time the United States officially cast in her lot with the rest of the world.

ECONOMIC AND SOCIAL RECONSTRUCTION

Among the emotions which bestirred the people of the United States during the war, an important one was the feeling that the country would somehow be different—and better —as the result of the trial of blood and iron. The people who brought about the adoption of the prohibition amendment, and the groups who hoped for a new international order well represented this hope for a better world. With the close of the war, however, there was a distinct ebb in the flow of idealism, and the normal power of economic interests again asserted itself.

Several questions connected with war incomes were a case in point. The profits made in the United States during the years following 1914 were unprecedented. The receipts of the treasury from income taxes in 1914 were $71,000,000; in 1920, income and excess profits taxes amounted to nearly four billions. The "war profiteers"—to use the term frequently applied to persons who made sudden fortunes during the war— increased in surprising numbers. Sixty persons had million dollar incomes in 1914; twice as many in 1915; and over 206 in 1916.

The huge receipts which went into the treasury were due in part to the high scale of taxation imposed during the war. Not unnaturally the fortunate classes that were enjoying such incomes were insistent in their advocacy of reduced scales of taxation and government expenditure. Not unnaturally, also, the less well-to-do held with equal vigor to the theory that taxes should first be reduced for people of small income, and that the war "profiteers" might properly be forced to part with a large fraction of their war gains.

The farmer, like the manufacturer, had increased production during the war, due in part to the urgent requests of the government for enlarged food supplies. His income, too, had grown rapidly, and the demands of the allied armies abroad had given him a capacious market. With the close of the war, however, he found himself confronted with enlarged activities, high prices for manufactured goods for which he had to pay,—and his foreign market in a state of collapse because of general European bankruptcy. He had a food surplus which Europe needed, but which it was unable to buy. The agricultural classes accordingly demanded federal relief from their plight.

The laborer, like the farmer, faced serious facts during the period of reconstruction. His war wages had been high,—but so had prices; and prices, he feared, were more likely to stay high than wages were. Moreover, so many men were turned back into peace-time industry from the army and from activities connected with the war, that unemployment quickly increased. Having demonstrated his thorough-going loyalty during the war, the working-man felt that his interests should be cared for as well as those of the profiteers. No more important question faced the country, a keen observer declared, than that concerning the wages of the laboring man: "How are the masses of men and women who labor with their hands to be secured out of the products of their toil what they will feel to be and will be in fact a fair return?"

The returning soldiers felt that their claim on the government was greater than that of any of the other groups. Many of them had faced the greatest hardships and dangers, and all of them had received a mere pittance for pay, as compared with the swollen wages of the factory worker. Hence, as we have seen, the insistent demand for compensation in the form of a bonus.

General business conditions showed fluctuations that were scarcely to be predicted. The cost of living continued to rise until the middle of 1920 when its ratio with 1913 was as 217 is to 100. It then receded until, in December, 1925, it was only 59 per cent. greater than in 1913. The combination of present condition and future prospect in business, which is commonly called the condition of business, showed a distinct instability. During 1919 industry was on the top of the wave; during 1920–1921 it was in the trough. Immediately after the election of Mr. Coolidge in 1924 a period of hopefulness set in which many feared might turn out to be a mere inflation. The condition was best indicated in stock market prices which mounted so fast as to give fortunate investors a "paper prosperity."

The response of the federal government to these several demands was far more rapid than it had been after the Civil War when the proper functions of government were looked at in the light of a *laissez faire* philosophy. In his message to Congress on December 7, 1921, President Harding urged a return to "normalcy"—a sort of *status quo ante bellum* in economic and governmental affairs. Reduced taxes, a higher tariff, aid for the farmers, and attention to the needs of labor and the veterans of the war constituted the program for such a return.

The restoration of pre-war conditions had already been started in the transportation act of 1920 (commonly called the Esch-Cummins act), which provided for the termination of government operation of the railroads on March 1. This important law took account of many recent changes which had affected the prosperity of the railroads, as well as modifications of American theory in regard to what constitutes desirable government regulation. In brief, a combination of circumstances had increased the expenses of the railroads, and had prevented their income from growing in equal proportions. The automobile and the motor truck were carrying increasing numbers of passengers and greater quantities of merchandise; from these facts came the demand for better highways, resulting in the provision for federal aid for state highway construction in 1916, and the appropriation by the states of unprecedented amounts of money for trunk roads; and, therefore, the motor vehicle, operating on a road-bed which was constructed and repaired at public expense, was able to drive the electric street railway into bankruptcy in many places, and seriously to cut into the revenue of the steam roads.[15] Thus government operation of the railroads from 1917 to 1920 occurred during a period of mounting costs for labor and equipment, without compensating increase of income. Then came the return to private hands in 1920.

On the financial side, the Esch-Cummins act provided for government aid, by means of loans, during the transition back to private management. The Interstate Commerce Commission was to determine what rates would enable the roads as a whole or in groups to earn a net income equal to five and a half per cent. on their value until 1922, and after that time a ''fair return.'' A railroad earning more than six per cent. has to pay the government one half of the excess, a part of which is used for making loans to roads which need assistance. In complete reversal of our former practice, the new law provides for pooling and for the voluntary consolidation of railroad lines under the supervision of the Commission. It also gives the Commission exclusive jurisdiction over the issuance of new railroad securities, and provides that no new roads or extensions may be constructed or old ones abandoned without the assent of the ''I. C. C.'' An attempt was likewise made to solve the problem of labor disputes by the establishment of a

[15] The number of miles of electric street railway was less in 1922 than in 1917, and only a little more than in 1912. *Statistical Abstract*, 1923, p. 412.

Railroad Labor Board, but this provision was repealed in 1926. By the latter act, the railroads and employees are to establish adjustment boards to settle controversies.

The next response to the demands of industry was the action taken in regard to the tariff. The tariff of 1913 had remained in force for an unusual period of years, but the abnormal conditions of the war had made impossible any accurate judgment as to the degree of its success or failure. The close of the war found the manufacturers demanding higher rates in order to protect industries which had grown up during the struggle and to prevent the importation of a flood of German-made goods. Their contentions were reenforced, as they had been in 1890, by the western farmers. The latter, as we have seen had been hard hit by the depression of 1920–1921, and turned to a higher tariff as a remedy. The first act was an emergency law passed on May 27, 1921, which imposed duties on cereals, meat, wool and sugar. This was followed by the tariff act of 1922, the highest since the Civil War. Its legislative history was not unlike that of earlier times—beginning with the House, it was raised in many particulars in the Senate, and its final provisions fixed in hurried sessions of a conference committee. Aside from its general high level and its attempt to solve the agricultural problem, the chief innovation in the law was the "equalization" feature. Since the purpose of the act, like that of 1909, was to equalize the differences in cost between the costs of production in the United States and in foreign countries, the president was authorized to raise or lower duties to meet changing conditions. His discretion, however, was limited by the proviso that the change should not exceed fifty per cent. and that he should base his action on recommendations of the Tariff Commission.

The Budget Act of June 10, 1921, was designed to provide a solid foundation for a program of economy and retrenchment. Under its provisions the president is to submit a budget to Congress at the opening of each session. It is to contain estimates of expense and appropriation necessary for the ensuing year. The active officer, under the chief executive, is the director of the budget who supervises the preparation of the estimates, and conducts studies into projects for the more economical and efficient conduct of the various departments. In the vigorous hands of General C. G. Dawes and, later, General H. M. Lord, and with the insistent backing of President Coolidge, the entire process of appropriation and expenditure was greatly systematized. By December, 1925, the President was able to say that the minimum cost of running the government had been about reached.

Since the primary motive in the reduction of expenses was the corresponding lowering of taxes, the administration urged upon a willing Congress a succession of measures which put this purpose into practice. A few comparisons between the revenue act of February 24, 1919, and that of June 2, 1924, will exemplify the changes brought about. By the former act, the first $4,000 of income above exemptions was taxed six per cent.; by the latter act, two per cent. Surtaxes under the earlier law, combined with the normal tax, gave a total levy on the highest incomes of seventy-seven per cent.; under the later law, forty-six per cent. Despite these reductions, the personal income tax returns for 1925 were almost half a billion dollars greater than they were in 1919. Because of the large volume of the revenue and the rigid economy insisted upon by the administration, approximately five billion dollars of the public debt were paid off before June 30, 1925.

Taxation, moreover, did not exhaust the income possibilities of the government. During the war the United States had loaned credits with an open hand to the several allied powers. On the cessation of the conflict, no nation was able to begin at once the liquidation of its debt or even to meet interest charges. An act of February 9, 1922, which was amended on February 28, 1923, established a World War Foreign Debt Commission to arrange for the refunding or conversion of the debts. The

first settlement was that with Great Britain which owed $4,-
600,000,000. Under this agreement, made on February 28,
1923, England is to pay off her entire obligations by a schedule
of annual instalments covering a period of sixty-two years.
By May 1, 1926, twelve similar settlements were made involving the eventual payment of over twenty-three billions,—
another American stake in the stability of Europe.

Another result of the war was the increased demand for
the further restriction of immigration. A temporary act of
May 19, 1921, did not shut out as many aliens as was expected,
and accordingly on May 26, 1924, Congress passed a law which
was radically restrictive. In the first place the total number
of immigrants to be admitted annually was placed at 161,-
990, except that native-born citizens of Canada, Mexico and
other countries in the western hemisphere were to be admitted.
In the next place, no more immigrants could come here from
any country than two per cent. of the number of natives of
that country shown to be here by the census of 1890. This
provision, of course, was intended to reduce the number of
aliens coming to these shores from Italy, Austria and Russia,
and to make the stream more predominantly English, German
and Scandinavian. The drastic character of this portion of
the law is indicated in the following comparisons: [16]

Country	Admitted in 1910	Quota under act of 1924
Russia	186,797	758
Austria	258,737	3,854
Italy	215,537	2,248

A third point in the law of 1924 was that concerning the
exclusion of the Japanese, who had hitherto been debarred
by the "Gentleman's Agreement" of 1907-1908.[16a] The new

[16] The number of immigrants admitted as exceptional cases was
greater than the number admitted under the ordinary routine. Thus,
175,865 natives of Canada and other countries in the western hemisphere made entry.
[16a] Cf. p. 553.

act contained a clause refusing admission to aliens who are not allowed to become citizens. In its practical operation, this clause referred only to the Japanese, and not unnaturally offended that sensitive race. In vain President Coolidge and Secretary Hughes urged Congress to accomplish the same results in a more tactful manner. This could apparently be easily done—by continuing the Gentleman's Agreement—but Congress had the bit in its teeth, and would have its way.

The readiness with which American leaders took hold of the problem of labor during the years immediately following the World War was in striking contrast to the inaction in this particular which characterized reconstruction after the Civil War. The first step was taken when President Wilson called a National Industrial Conference for October 6, 1919. Its purpose was the discussion of methods for "bettering the whole relationship of labor and capital and putting the whole question of wages on another footing." Fifty men representing capital, labor and the public wrestled with the problem until a wide divergence of opinion between the capital and labor groups in regard to collective bargaining indicated that agreement was impossible. On November 20, 1920, another conference was held, this time composed of seventeen men. All of them were supposed to represent the interested public, rather than either labor or capital. Among other things the conference urged the extension of the principle of labor representation in industry by means of shop committees and similar expedients, together with regional industrial conferences for voluntary arbitration. On the whole, the conferences seem to have produced slight tangible results.

In the meanwhile, several strikes of large proportions were resulting from the attempts of labor and capital to readjust themselves to the post-war conditions. The steel strike which lasted from September 22, 1919, to January 7, 1920, affected more than 300,000 strikers and threatened the industrial peace of the nation. It involved the whole gamut of the demands of labor in the steel industry—the right of collective bargaining, an eight hour day, a day's rest in seven and the abolition of the twenty-four hour shift. The United States Steel Corporation and Judge E. H. Gary, the chairman of its board of directors, were looked to as the leaders on the employer side. The controversy presented several important features. In the beginning, Judge Gary refused to confer with the labor leaders because such a conference might be interpreted as a recognition of the closed shop, which he opposed. More remarkable was an investigation of the steel industry made by a commission of the Interchurch World Movement, the most striking example in American history of the newly aroused interest of the modern church in the welfare of industrial society. The report of the commission was widely circulated. It deprecated the fact that wages in the steel industry were fixed "arbitrarily," that is, without bargaining or conferring with the labor force. It noted that 69,000 men were employed for a twelve hour day, and half of these for a seven day week. Moreover, it charged the employers with the use of spies in the labor group and with indefensible violations of the rights of free speech. An investigation committee of the Senate came to the conclusion that the strike had been supported by a radical and even revolutionary element, an assertion which the Interchurch commission characterized as hysterical. The opinion, however, whether well or ill founded, was implanted in the country; the strikers were widely looked upon as Bolsheviki, disloyal and un-American. In a short time the strikers began to disintegrate and eventually their attempt failed.

To many, however, some aspects of the steel industry seemed indefensible, especially the twelve hour day. Among these was President Harding, who went so far as to call a conference at the White House of representatives of the iron and steel manufacturers on May 18, 1922. At his request the manufacturers appointed a committee to consider the possibility of a reform. A year later the committee reported favorably, and on August 16, 1923, the Carnegie Steel Company inaugurated the eight hour day. Other concerns followed,—and one of the last remnants of the dark ages in American labor history became a thing of the past.

In the anthracite coal fields there had been industrial peace since 1903, with the single exception of a disturbance in 1920. On March 31, 1922, however, the existing agreements between the employers and the miners came to an end, and the former refused to enter a conference for the establishment of a new agreement. The workmen desired a continuation of the wage scales of 1920; the operators sought a reduction, and also opposed the ''check-off'' system, by which the employer collects the dues of members of the union by deducting the amount from their pay. On April 1st, accordingly, the workmen in both the soft and the hard coal fields went out—610,000 of them. It was the first time that the two groups had struck simultaneously. In July, 1922, President Harding called a conference and proposed a plan of settlement, but the results were negative. On August 30th the bituminous miners resumed work as the result of agreements between the union and the operators. Within a few days the anthracite controversy was closed under an arrangement continuing the existing wage scale to August 31, 1923. It was also agreed to request Congress to create a commission to investigate the entire coal industry. A commission was appointed and reported with extensive recommendations on July 8, 1923. Nothing came of this, however, despite another strike in 1925, more suffering and another temporary settlement.

The railway strike of 1922–1923 likewise involved the question of wage reduction, but it was complicated by the desire of the roads to deal with their employees through organizations of their own, rather than as part of the American Federation of Labor. 300,000 shopmen struck in all parts of the country. The question then arose as to whether the men would be taken back and given their seniority rights if the disagreement was settled. On this point the employers differed, and the strike gradually came to an end as the result of individual agreements rather than of a general settlement. The cost to the railroads, says Professor Muzzey, was almost twenty per cent. of their income for 1923.

In spite of the great size of the post-war strikes and their cost in money and hardship, several improvements are observable over the conditions which surrounded the railroad strike of 1877 and the Pullman strike of 1894. (1) The attitude of the government was more sympathetic toward labor, more intelligent and more nearly impartial. Federal troops were not called out quite so blithely as had earlier been the case. (2) The interest of the public was more clearly recognized and cared for. (3) A body of facts had been gathered and experts trained. More of an effort was made to settle controversies on the solid basis of facts rather than on the insecure foundation of class prejudice. And finally, (4) although violence had by no means disappeared, there was less of it in proportion to the size of the quarrels than in previous times.

The plight of the American farmer during post-war reconstruction was perhaps more serious than the condition of any other member of society. The situation is clearly seen in the contrast between the agricultural situation in 1919 and that in 1920–1921. In the former year, the crops were huge and sold at an unusually high figure. The wheat crop was the second largest ever known. The value of the entire product of the farms was estimated at nearly sixteen billions of dollars, as compared with an average of about six billions during the five years 1910 to 1914. The volume of cereal exports was prodigious, having reached $448,000,000 in 1919—between two and a half, and three times the $162,000,000 of the pre-war years. Although not organized as compactly as the industrial workers, the farmer nevertheless had his representative in the American Farm Bureau Federation, with its million members, the Grange, the National Board of Farm Organizations and other similar associations. Comfortable as this situation was as compared with what followed, it should not be assumed that American agriculture gave a rich return as contrasted with the profits to be accumulated in other forms of activity. Despite the "boom" times, relatively speaking, the farmer was making only about 6.1 per cent. on his investment in 1919.

In acreage planted and in the size of the crop, 1920 promised to be and was a "bumper" year. But between seed-time and harvest came an unprecedented decline in prices. The farmer had planted, and had borne the cost of production when prices for labor and machinery were high; he harvested when prices were so low that his return was smaller than his outlay. His loss in 1920 was 3.6 per cent. on his investment, and in 1921, 1.7 per cent. Throughout the country the proportion of farmer bankruptcies tripled, and in some states nearly a third of all such catastrophes were among the agricultural classes.

The causes of the distress varied, of course, from place to place, but it cannot be doubted that in the main they arose from the World War. The wages which the farmer paid for help had risen to unprecedented heights because wages everywhere were increasing. Freight rates and taxes had risen during the war to such a degree that they frequently consumed or nearly consumed the farmer's profits. Due to the war, Europe was living on low rations, was unable to purchase as much as she needed from America, and accordingly the export trade in several agricultural products suffered severely. When the farmer's income dropped—and it must be remembered that the agricultural classes comprise a large fraction of the population—he lost his purchasing power, other industries felt the shock, and thus the downward tendency was continued. Hence the huge crops of 1920 seemed like a calamity. With a surplus here, and the foreign demand in many products distinctly lessened, prices naturally suffered a sharp decline. Corn was said to be lower than it had been for twenty-five years. Unrest and complaint among the farmers were rife. Morale ran low, while discouragement and indignation ran high. Everybody seemed to have come through the war better off than the man who grew the food. The only person who appeared to make a fortune on the products of the farm was the Wall Street speculator, who seemed to be able to manipulate the market to suit himself. And so to the remedies.

The influence of the several farmer organizations was quick to make itself felt. In 1919 it was seen in the repeal of the Daylight Saving Act, which the man on the soil everywhere feels to be contrary to his interests. In 1920 the War Finance Corporation was revived. Its most important function was to increase credit facilities, especially in order to assist in exportation to foreign markets. In 1921, in the special session which President Harding called, an "agricultural bloc" appeared. It was an informal, bi-partisan group composed of senators and representatives from the agricultural states, and its purpose was the formulation of a program of relief, and insistence upon its adoption. In some quarters the bloc was decried as being interested only in class legislation and as tending to reduce partisan loyalties. Undeterred, however, the bloc pushed its program. The Future Trading Act of 1921 was an attempt to curb the speculator's control of prices by putting a tax on his operations. The emergency tariff measure of 1921 and the later act of 1922 showed, as has been seen, the influence of agriculture. A Commission of Inquiry in 1921 was established by Congress to study the situation, and in 1922 President Harding called a National Agricultural Conference—the first in American history. Three hundred and thirty-six delegates from thirty-seven states divided into committees for the study of the rural problem. The Capper-

Volstead Act of the latter year enabled farmers to form organizations for disposing of goods in domestic and foreign markets without danger of prosecution under the anti-trust laws. And in 1922, again, as already has appeared, a law adding another member to the Federal Reserve Board was passed with the expectation that the new man would be a farmer,—the farmers believing that the policies of the Board had been formulated without sufficient knowledge of their effects on agriculture. In a word, then, every possible legislative expedient was attempted, the chief impediments being doubt as to whether laws could remedy the situation, and the great number of remedies proposed.

Whether the remedies were efficacious, or whether agriculture was destined to recover with or without legislation, the farmer seems to have turned the corner late in 1922. The improvement in 1923, said the Secretary of Agriculture, was little short of remarkable. By 1924 the value of the harvest was three billion dollars more than in 1921, although the return then was only 3.8 per cent. on the investment. The place of the tiller of the soil remains one of America's unsolved problems.

Reconstruction and the Federal Government

In the field of government, the period of reconstruction bears resemblance in some particulars to the decade following the Civil War. The attempt of Congress to regain the ascendancy which it loses in time of war seems to be the normal reaction. The convention which nominated Grant in 1868 in Chicago declared that Johnson had "usurped high legislative and judicial functions"; the convention which nominated Harding in 1920 (likewise in Chicago), declared that the "President [Wilson] clings tenaciously to his autocratic wartime powers," and that his "usurpation is intolerable." As in the earlier case, it was the Senate that seized leadership

after the World War. In part the revival of the power of
the Senate was due to its constitutional authority to consent
or refuse to consent to treaties made by the president. Without doubt the *esprit de corps* of the Senate had some effect in
bringing about its failure to approve the treaty of Versailles.
Moreover, Mr. Wilson's successor, President Harding, was not
of the aggressive type, and had no desire to enter a contest
with the Senate for leadership in public affairs. Once gained,
the ascendancy of the Senate has been reasserted in numerous
ways, despite the fact that the executive and the Senate have
been of the same party. The Senate was, in all probability,
the chief obstacle in the way of any attempt to carry out the
Republican platform promise of 1920 regarding an association
of nations. It delayed the fulfillment of the World Court
program, it opposed and overcame the President on the matter
of Japanese immigration, and, like the Senate in the administration of Hayes, has frequently refused to ratify nominations
made by the executive.

A striking change in the spirit of government is the degree
to which the progressive movement has lost its *élan*. After
the adoption of the amendments providing for the popular
election of senators and the granting of suffrage for women,
the progressive elements seemed to have spent their force.
The extension of the initiative and referendum became almost
dead issues. Even the constitutional amendment prohibiting
child labor was ratified by only three states, when in January,
1925, it became clear that the proposal was overwhelmingly
defeated. Perhaps more states have considered doing away
with the direct primary than have desired its extension.
President Harding urged more business in government and
less government in business; and President Coolidge resolutely
followed a "hands-off" policy, at least in his public official
utterances, during the coal strike of 1925, and left the controversy to be settled between employers and employees. The

magic of conservation, even, as a political wonder-worker distinctly waned.[17]

The Federal Water Power Act of 1920 was the last great piece of legislation in the series which began with the Reclamation Act of 1902. The elements of the Water Power Act appear in several of the conservation policies so energetically pressed forward by Roosevelt, but the passage of the law with its final details was part of Wilson's progressive domestic program. The act established a Federal Water Power Commission composed of the Secretaries of War, the Interior and Agriculture. The chief task of the Commission was to license private companies to construct and operate water power projects on public lands. In doing so it was bound to adhere to the paramount importance of the public interest. Accordingly the ownership of the land on which development was to take place must remain with the United States, but the sites might be leased to the corporations for periods of not more than fifty years. Any projects must be such as in the judgment of the Commission are "adapted to a comprehensive scheme of improvement and utilization for the purposes of navigation, of water-power development, and of other beneficial public uses." The licensee must pay a fixed annual charge for his lease, and at its expiration the government may renew the lease, lease the site to another company, or take over the property itself by reimbursing the corporation for its investment. While the interest of the public is conserved in these several ways, the advantages of private initiative and management are retained.

As soon as President Harding was in power, there occurred a series of incidents connected with the public lands which would have rivaled the Pinchot-Ballinger controversy in its political effects if it had happened a decade earlier. Since oil

---

[17] The death of the four leading progressives undoubtedly helped bring about this result. Roosevelt died in 1919, Wilson in 1924, and both Bryan and La Follette in 1925.

was coming increasingly to be used for fuel and for motor propulsion, the United States government recognized the necessity of conserving the remaining sources of supply on the public lands. In particular, it seemed essential to retain public ownership of adequate petroleum for the use of the navy. Accordingly the administration of the oil bearing public lands was placed with the Secretary of the Navy. Shortly after his accession, President Harding transferred control from the Secretary of the Navy, Mr. Denby, to the Secretary of the Interior, Mr. Fall. Mr. Fall then leased the so-called "Tea Pot Dome" oil fields in Wyoming to Mr. H. F. Sinclair who turned them over to the Mammoth Oil Company for $106,000,000 of stock. Similar lands in California he leased to E. M. Doheny, the head of another large oil concern. In the meanwhile the Committee on Public Lands of the Senate was engaged in an inquiry about the leasing of government oil reserves, and it investigated the activities of Mr. Fall. The testimony seems to have been conflicting, and in some cases not reliable, but it indicated that Mr. Fall had shown signs of unusual wealth about the time of the oil transfers. Mr. Doheny admitted that on November 30, 1921, he had loaned his friend Mr. Fall $100,000 in cash without interest or security. These facts aroused such a storm of disapproval that Mr. Fall retired from the cabinet March 4, 1923, and Mr. Denby a year later.[18] Mr. Harding died before the election of 1924, and the political effects of the scandal were negligible.

Suits were at once started on behalf of the government to have the courts declare the Doheny and Sinclair leases void on the ground of fraud and conspiracy. The California court declared the Doheny lease invalid and also denied the legality of President Harding's executive order transferring the naval oil lands to the Secretary of the Interior. The Wyoming court upheld the President's order and the validity

[18] In March, 1924, Mr. Daugherty, the Attorney-General, retired under fire because of allegations of corruption in the Department of Justice.

of the Sinclair lease, although admitting that "suspicious circumstances" surrounded the transaction. In both cases, appeals were made to higher courts, and on September 28, 1926,
the Federal Circuit Court of Appeals reversed the decision
of the Wyoming court.

Since the Civil War

So far as the past affects the future, five tendencies since the
Civil War seem to merit particular attention. The first is the
increasing *economic well-being* of the average citizen. Comparative statistics of per capita wealth and savings bank deposits in 1865 and 1926 would only confuse and complicate
the statement of the fact without adding to its validity.[19]
Moreover, personal accumulations of wealth do not tell the
whole story. Public services like fire-protection, hospitals, museums, good roads and a host of other things add to the economic well-being of the individual even if his private holdings
are slight. The second fact is the *decrease in the length of
the working day* with its greater opportunity for recreation
and for well or ill-spent leisure. The third is the *industrialization and the urbanization of America,* bringing in their
wake the numerous questions which have already been discussed at length. The fourth is the *decreasing imperative of
religion,*—the older, puritanical but steadying force of the
"thou shalt" and "thou shalt not." The fifth is the *increase
in the general level of culture and education* as seen in the
attention paid to reading, schools, museums, music, philanthropic enterprises and the like.

It is often mistakenly assumed that a nation is progressing
because it is becoming rich; that leisure is *per se,* under all
circumstances, an advantage; that a city should take pride because the census indicates a growing population and enlarging factories; that more "liberal" religious creeds are

[19] They may be found in *Statistical Abstract,* 1924, pp. 242, 258,
271–274.

necessarily better; and that the spread of general educational facilities are a panacea for all ills. The truth is that all these important changes bring balanced good and evil. Wealth may make for selfishness and moral softness; leisure, for the mischievous waste of time; the growth of cities and factories, for slums, poverty and economic peonage; liberal creeds, for no creeds at all; and education, for the snobbish superiority of the recluse. The history of the United States *Since the Civil War* is, at the foundation, the gigantic contest between progress and decay, and the next generation will add its contribution to one side or the other of the great book of account.

> He speaks not well who doth his time deplore,
> Naming it new and little and obscure,
> Ignoble and unfit for lofty deeds.
> All times were modern in the time of them,
> And this no more than others.
> Do thy part
> Here in the living day, as did the great
> Who made old days immortal!

BIBLIOGRAPHICAL NOTE

Accounts of the most important events of recent years may be found in the *New International Year Book;* the *American Year Book* (except for 1920–1924 inclusive); and *Current History.* The *World Almanac* contains a mass of statistical material. The magazines already mentioned are frequently useful, as well as newspapers, such as the New York *Times.*

On demobilization, consult Crowell and Wilson, *Demobilization* (1921); the reports of the Secretary of War for 1919, 1920; and the final report of General Pershing.

A voluminous literature has already grown up around the Versailles Conference: C. Seymour, *Woodrow Wilson and the World War* (1921), is particularly good in small compass; E. M. House and C. Seymour, eds., *What Really Happened at Paris* (1921), is a series of lectures by men who actually took part in the settlement.

On special aspects: B. M. Baruch, *The Making of the Reparation and Economic Sections of the Treaty* (1920); R. T. Baker, *Woodrow Wilson and World Settlement* (3 vols., 1922); A. Tardieu, *The Truth about the Treaty* (1921); "The Versailles Treaty and After" by R. S. Baker, in *Current History*, Jan., 1924.

On the espionage and similar acts, Z. Chafee Jr., *Freedom of Speech* (1920), is by a professor of law in Harvard University.

On the League and the Court there are excellent historical summaries in the *Handbook of the League of Nations* prepared for the League of Nations Non-Partisan Association; *The Permanent Court of International Justice* by M. O. Hudson. See also S. P. H. Duggan, *The League of Nations* (1919); H. C. Lodge, *The Senate and the League of Nations* (1925) is a defense of the course followed by the Chairman of the Senate Committee on Foreign Relations, and an attack on Wilson. Material opposing the treaty may also be found in the files of the *New Republic*, the *Nation* and the *North American Review*; on the other side, the editorial page of the New York *Times* whenever League or Court were being discussed.

The Dawes plan is explained and its text reprinted in R. McElroy, "America's Share in the Dawes Plan" in *Current History*, Mar., 1925. On most aspects of recent diplomatic history, G. H. Blakeslee, already mentioned.

The financial side of reconstruction may be followed in the annual reports of the Secretary of the Treasury: the cost of living in the *Monthly Labor Review*, published by the Department of Labor; transportation in S. L. Miller, *Railway Transportation* (1924), and R. MacVeagh, *The Transportation Act 1920* (1923); see also E. J. Rich, "The Transportation Act of 1920" in the *American Economic Review* Sept., 1920. On the tariff, in addition to the periodicals, F. W. Taussig, *Tariff History of the United States* (7th. ed., 1923).

The history of relations with Japan over immigration is excellently recounted in Blakeslee, Chap. V; the immigration acts of 1921, 1924, are in *Statutes at Large*, vol. 42, part 1, p. 5, and vol. 43, pt. 1, p. 153; R. L. Buell, *Japanese Immigration* in World Peace Foundation Pamphlets (1924).

"Two Years of President Harding" by W. B. Munro in *Atlantic Monthly*, Mar., 1923 gives a critical contemporary view. The *Yearbook* of the Department of Agriculture presents the Agricultural situation, which is well summarized in the *New International Year Book;* B. H. Hibbard, *Effects of the Great War on Agriculture in the United States and Great Britain* (1919); *Annals of the American Academy of Political and Social Science,* January, 1925.

"The Trend of the Direct Primary" in *American Political Science Review* XVI (1922), 412–421, by R. S. Boots discusses the wane of one phase of progressivism; W. A. White, "The End of an Epoch" in *Scribner's Magazine,* June, 1926.

Details concerning La Follette's progressive party of 1924 may be found in "The New Progressive Party," *Current History,* Aug., 1924, with the platform; and in *Atlantic Monthly,* Oct., 1924, F. E. Haynes, "La Follette and La Folletteism."

APPENDIX

Political Control in the presidency and in Congress, 1865–1927

	President	Senate	House
1865–1867 1867–1869	Johnson R.	Unionist Rep. R	Unionist Rep. R
1869–1871 1871–1873 1873–1875 1875–1877	Grant R.	R R R R	R R R D
1877–1879 1879–1881	Hayes R.	R D	D D
1881–1883 1883–1885	Garfield Arthur } R.	{ 37D–37R R	{ 1 Independent 1 Readjuster } R D
1885–1887 1887–1889	Cleveland D.	R R	D D
1889–1891 1891–1893	Harrison R.	R R	R D
1893–1895 1895–1897	Cleveland D.	D R	D R
1897–1899 1899–1901	McKinley R.	R R	R R
1901–1903 1903–1905	McKinley Roosevelt } R.	R R	R R
1905–1907 1907–1909	Roosevelt R.	R R	R R
1909–1911 1911–1913	Taft R.	R R	R D
1913–1915 1915–1917 1917–1919 1919–1921	Wilson D.	D D D R	D D D R
1921–1923 1923–1925	Harding Coolidge } R.	R R	R R
1925–1927	Coolidge R.	R	R

INDEX

Abbey, Edwin A., 462
A B C powers, 568
Accidents, compensation for, 509
Adams, Charles Francis, 44
Adams, Charles Francis, Jr.: cited on Cleveland, 195; on railroad abuses, 212, 215; on railroad pooling, 220
Adams, John Quincy: comparison of Hayes and, 138; and Latin-American relations, 367
Adamson law, 514, 615
Adee, A. A., 354
Agriculture: development of, in United States, 64 *et seq.;* 438 *et seq.;* conditions at close World War, 691, 700
Aguinaldo, 415
Airplane, 451
Alabama claims, 39
Alaska: negotiations in relation to, 21; seal fisheries dispute, 357 *et seq.;* resources, 497, note; and Canada boundary question, 555
Aldrich, Senator Nelson W.: and Great Tariff Debate, 246; in relation to currency, 591
Algeciras conference, 573
Alger, Russell A., as Secretary of War, 398
Allen, Senator W. V., 322
Alliance, Farmers', 272
Allies: loans to, 648; barring seas to Germany, 641; situation of, when United States entered World War, 649 *et seq.;* Wilson as mouthpiece of, 662
Allison, William B.: and tariff, 121; purchase of bullion, 151; Great Tariff Debate, 246
Allowance and allotment during World War, 636
Alsace-Lorraine, 663

Altgeld, Governor John P.: 301; and Chicago anarchists, 299; protest of, 302
Alverstone, Lord Chief Justice, 556
Amendments to the Constitution: XIII, 7, 95; XIV, 12, 95 *et seq.;* XV, 17, 95; XVI, 589; XVII, 517, 518; XVIII, 680; XIX, 520
American Expeditionary Force: 645 *et seq.;* losses, 662, note
American Federation of Labor: 291 *et seq.;* effect of, upon economic conditions, 503 *et seq.*
American Free Trade League, 121
American Iron and Steel Association, and tariff, 120
American Railway Union, 302
American Sugar Refining Company, frauds, 490
American Tobacco Company, 541
Ames, Oakes, and Credit Mobilier, 40
Amnesty Act, 23
Anarchists, in Chicago, 299 *et seq.*
Ancient Order of Hibernians, 290
Andrews, Samuel, 227
Angell, James B., 156
Anti-Monopolists, 181, 234, 304
Anti-trust Law. *See* Sherman Anti-trust Law
Apia, 360
Arabic incident, 608
Archbold, J. D., on Standard Oil contribution, 522, note
Architecture, 463
Arrears Act of 1879, 314
Arthur, Chester A.: in relation to Hayes and port of New York, 144; vice-presidential nominee, 164; first message of, to Congress, 173; quoted on Indiana for Garfield, 168; eleva-

713